REVISED & EXPANDED

Speaker's Lifetime Library

PRENTICE HALL
Paramus, New Jersey 07652

Leonard & Thelma Spinrad
Revised by Anistatia R Miller & Jared M. Brown

Library of Congress Cataloging in Publication Data

Spinrad, Leonard.
    Speaker's lifetime library / Leonard Spinrad & Thelma Spinrad..
—Rev. and expanded / revised by Jared Brown, Anistatia Miller.
        p.   cm.
    Includes bibliographical references and index.
    ISBN 0-13-496530-2
    1. Public speaking—Handbooks, manuals, etc. I. Spinrad, Thelma.
II. Brown, Jared. III. Miller, Anistatia. IV. Title.
PN4193.I5S64 1997
808.5'1—dc21   97-474
                                                                              CIP

Printed in the United States of America

10 9 8 7 6 5 4 3 2 1

ISBN 0-13-496530-2

PRENTICE HALL
Career & Personal Development
Paramus, NJ 07652
A Simon & Schuster Company

On the World Wide Web at http://www.phdirect.com

Prentice Hall International (UK) Limited, *London*
Prentice Hall of Australia Pty. Limited, *Sydney*
Prentice Hall Canada, Inc., *Toronto*
Prentice Hall Hispanoamericana, S.A., *Mexico*
Prentice Hall of India Private Limited, *New Delhi*
Prentice Hall of Japan, Inc., *Tokyo*
Simon & Schuster Asia Pte. Ltd., *Singapore*
Editora Prentice Hall do Brasil, Ltda., *Rio de Janeiro*

A RESOURCE FOR ALL THE DAYS OF YOUR LIFE

"The difference between the right word and a word," said author Samuel Clemens, "is the difference between lightning and a lightning bug." Words are timeless, they are simple, and they are here in these pages for the taking. You do not have to be an accomplished orator to make a memorable speech. You do need to have good tools.

This second edition of the *Speaker's Lifetime Library* continues the tried-and-true tradition of the first, containing even more anecdotes, wise comments of the ages, historical events and birthdays, figures of speech, "jumping-off" or introductory gambits for speeches on a variety of subjects—all updated and conveniently arranged for easy reference.

Anyone can make a speech, but a delivering good speech—now, that's another story. Speeches that seem to flow spontaneously—orations that appear to roll off the cuff—usually aren't quite that simple. They come from careful research and preparation. They come from knowing what you want to say; understanding how to create a graceful transition from your introduction to the point of your remarks; having relevant facts to support your statements; and making your whole delivery memorable with an appropriate anecdote or wise quotation.

Designed to make speech preparation easier, these critical aspects to artful public speaking are incorporated into the four volumes that make up the *Speaker's Lifetime Library, Second Edition.*

A speech has the same initial problem as an automobile. There has to be a spark, or else it goes nowhere. Even if you know exactly what message you wish to convey to your audience, you've got to grab its attention at the outset. Audiences are generally eager to be your friends; they don't want to be bored or antagonized any more than you do. Whether they expect to enjoy your speech or not, they do *hope.*

And even if they know you well, they still have to be led attractively and dynamically into the nitty-gritty of your remarks. It is sometimes helpful to be introduced by someone else who, so to speak, warms the audience up for you. Even gifted television entertainers like to have somebody warm up the studio audience before they make their entrance. When you step up to speak, you are jumping into a challenging situation: you venture to establish your own quick and clear claim to being heard. Like the farmer who hits a stubborn mule over the head simply "to get the critter's attention," you have to use your opening words—since you can't hit the audience over the head—to get attention.

But an audience's attention span—even after it's initially won—is rather short, and has to be held. Even the audience that greets a speaker with tremendous enthusiasm at the outset won't hold on to that enthusiasm if it is bored to tears.

Few speeches are remembered for their lengthy oratory. Most long-winded deliveries are remembered for a sentence, a paragraph, a turn of phrase here or there.

William Jennings Bryan's great "Cross of Gold" oration—which captured the 1896 Democratic Presidential nomination for him—is generally remembered for the same three quotable quotes, because those relatively few words say so much so well.

Every great speaker in modern times has used notable piths from speakers of earlier vintage. Sometimes quotations are employed directly. Sometimes their wisdom is studied to suggest new approaches or new directions for developing a particular point. In preparing a speech, the wise speaker hunts down everything from quips and epigrams to scholarly citations. Accordingly, Volume 1 of *Speaker's Lifetime Library, Second Edition is* a Speaker's Reference Guide which contains more than 150 different subject headings, several thousand memorable quotations, definitions, anecdotes, witticisms, and epigrams for use in creating, enlivening, and elucidating points the speaker wishes to make. In this same volume are encapsulated overviews of basic facts about most subjects as well as suggested additional information sources. For the conscientious speaker, this volume combines research and preparatory functions which, until now, have required any number of research volumes to obtain.

Most great speeches depend to a large extent upon metaphorical allusions such as Bryan's cross of gold, Churchill's iron curtain, or FDR's forgotten man. Volume 2 of *Speaker's Lifetime Library, Second Edition* is a collection of Apt Comparisons. This is meant to be a quick and convenient guide to similes, metaphors, symbols, and opposites that can be used to make a speaker's word pictures more effective. Some of these comparisons are drawn from literature, some from mythology, and some from comedy routines. All are there to help the speaker say what is to be said in enlivening graphic terms.

When two people are introduced by a mutual friend, their first words are usually small talk as they try to find a common interest or simply feel each other out. This getting to know one another has its parallel at the outset of a speech. Once the speaker has been introduced to the audience, there is still that initial tentativeness; that need to find a way to get started toward the business at hand. The world's best speech still needs some kind of opening tailored to the particular audience. Simply having the speaker express delight at being present in this town on this occasion is not enough. A good speech can get off to a better start than that. Taking note of a timely anniversary, or of some reason why this day or this location happens to be appropriate for the speaker's appearance is always effective as part of the opening "small talk." It helps to let the audience know that the speaker has taken the trouble to find a special bond between them.

Volume 3 of *Speaker's Lifetime Library, Second Edition* is The Day and Date Book, which lists past historical occurrences, notable birthdays, holidays and other observances, eloquent quotes, and unique events that took place on each day of the year. The Day and Date Book also includes, suggested "lead-ins" for speeches appropriate to that day or for that month, based on these events. Some occurrences share a common bond or theme, and have been linked together into a single introduction. Other events took place over the course a few non-consecutive days, and have been cross-referenced throughout this volume so you can take advantage of supporting material found on another day. The lead-ins can be used as ways to introduce the speaker of the day, or as opening gambits for the principal speaker.

Very often, of course, there is a specific reason for a speaking engagement to which the speaker must refer at the outset. If you are asked to speak at a golden wedding anniversary dinner, certainly recognition of that occasion should be offered early in your remarks. Volume 4 of *Speaker's Lifetime Library, Second Edition* is The Special Occasion Book, which is a compilation of special speech material for various occasions, ranging—in alphabetical order—from acceptance of a nomination to welcoming a distinguished visitor. The entries for each occasion are arranged in sequential paragraphs. Every paragraph contains a separate speech angle; they can be used independently or in combination if desired.

What we offer in the following pages, then, is a series of reference books for all the vital elements of a good speech. The various elements can be applied in an infinite array of uses —in terms of the number of different combinations; and in terms of the speaker's brilliance at developing thoughts that might arise from this assembled wisdom.

Above all, every single entry can and should be used to lead into the speaker's own thoughts and words. What is contained in this library is a collection of the precious bricks of a speech's outer walls—the furniture and the warmth of heart must be the speaker's own. If a good speech is a house, this book offers the finest foundations available.

Anistatia R Miller and Jared M. Brown
revisors of the Second Edition

Contents

VOLUME I

THE SPEAKER'S REFERENCE GUIDE

LIST OF SUBJECTS

Accounting

Achievement

Adolescence (*See also* Teenagers, Youth)

Advertising

Age (*See also* Longevity, Youth)

Agriculture

Alibis

Alumni (*See also* College)

Ambition

America

Ancestry

Aristocracy

Armed Forces

Art

Automobiles

Aviation

Babies (*See also* Children, Parents)

Baseball

Basketball

Books (*See also* Literature)

Boxing

Building

Business

Candidates (*See also* Elections, Political Parties, Voting)

Censorship (*See also* Books, Journalism, Liberty, Motion Pictures, Radio, Television)

Charity

Children (*See also* Babies, Parents)

Citizenship

City Life

Civilization (*See also* Society)

Clubs (*See also* Fraternities)

College (*See also* Alumni, Education, School)

Communication (*See also* Computers, Internet, Radio, Television)

Computers (*See also* Communication, Internet, Radio, Television)

Constitution (*See also* Government)

Conventions

Cooking (*See also* Dieting, Food)

Courage

Courts (*See also* Justice, Law)

Creativity

Crime (*See also* Law and Order, Violence)

Criticism

Death

Democracy (*See also* Constitution, Government, Voting)

Dieting (*See also* Food, Health)

Drama (*See also* Theater)

Dreams

Drink

Drugs (*See also* Medicine)

Economics

Education (*See also* College, School)

Elections (*See also* Candidates, Voting)

Energy

Environment (*See also* Nature, Wilderness)

Ethics

Ethnicity (*See also* Immigration, Minorities, Race)

Experience

Political Parties (*See also* Candidates, Elections, Government, Voting)

Population(*See also* Children, Family)

Poverty

Prejudice (*See also* Ethnicity, Minorities, Race)

Presidency (*See also* Lincoln, Washington)

Privacy

Psychology

Public Opinion

Public Relations

Public Speaking

Race (*See also* Ethnicity, Prejudice)

Radio (*See also* Journalism, Television)

Religion

School (*See also* College, Education)

Science

Seasons

Sex (*See also* Love, Marriage)

Society (*See also* Civilization)

South

Space (*See also* Exploration)

Sports (*See also* various individual sports)

Taxes

Teenagers (*See also* Adolescence, Youth)

Television (*See also* Journalism, Radio)

Tennis

Theater (*See also* Drama)

Time

Violence (*See also* Crime, Justice, Law and Order)

Voting (*See also* Candidates, Elections, Political Parties)

War (*See also* Armed Forces, Peace)

Washington, D.C.

Washington, George

Wealth

West

Wilderness (*See also* Environment, Nature)

Women

Worry

Youth (*See also* Adolescence, Teenagers)

ACCOUNTING

DEFINITIONS   Method or system of keeping records; the language of business; the world's greatest balancing act; giving credits where credits are due.

QUOTATIONS

Facts and Figures! Put 'em down! Charles Dickens, *The Chimes,* 1844.

Figures won't lie, but liars will figure. Attributed notably to Ohio's Charles H. Grosvenor, c. late 19th century.

Statistics are like alienists—they will testify for either side. New York Representative Fiorello H. LaGuardia, 1933.

…give an account of thy stewardship. Luke, 16:2.

Don't tell me of facts, I never believe facts; you know Canning said nothing was as fallacious as facts, except figures. Rev. Sydney Smith, quoted by his daughter, Lady Holland, 1855.

…keep your accounts on your thumb-nail. Henry D. Thoreau, *Walden,* 1854.

ANONYMOUS APHORISMS

The difference between an accountant and a bookkeeper is a sizable figure.

There are three kinds of lies—lies, damned lies, and statistics. (Attributed by Mark Twain to Benjamin Disraeli.)

Accounting is ledger de main.

When things look black to an accountant, it means the account is in the red.

CPA stands for Constantly Proposing Audits.

Julius Caesar's motto as a soldier was veni, vidi, vici. If he had been an accountant it would have been aught, ought to, audit.

ANECDOTES

A journalist and an accountant were riding together and passed a flock of sheep. "Look," said the journalist, "the sheep have all been shorn." "On this side, at least," said the accountant.

For thirty years Mr. Peterson had followed the same workday morning ritual: He unlocked his desk drawer, looked in for a moment, then locked it again before beginning his ledger entries. When he passed away, his curious co-workers peered into the mysterious drawer. Inside, there was a single piece of paper taped to the bottom. On it was written: "Credits by the window, debits by the door."

FACTS

The keeping of financial records has been traced back to the 23rd century BC, but it took a long time for accountants to gain full professional recognition. Accounting was recognized officially as a profession in England in 1854, and in the United States in the 1890s—not long after the formation of the American Association of Public Accountants. In 1896, the first certified public accountants were accredited by New York State. As business taxes and methods of financing have become more complicated, accounting education, certification, and professional standards have grown more rigorous.

The American Institute of Certified Public Accountants is located at 1211 Avenue of the Americas, New York, N.Y. 10036-8775, (800) TO-AICPA. 1995 membership of the Institute was 323,000 members. Their official publication, the *Journal of Accountancy,* is published monthly.

ACHIEVEMENT

DEFINITIONS   The result of effort or toil when successful; feat; deed; accomplishment; being able to look back and see how far you've come; reaching or exceeding goals.

QUOTATIONS

The personal equation is the important factor which fixes the gulf between striking success and hopeless fashion. President Theodore Roosevelt, message to the U.S. Congress, December 3, 1901.

You ask me kind of broadly what was [my] greatest accomplishment [in 11 years as Governor]. It was resisting the temptation to put my ego before the agenda and say: "I will do something to let them remember me for all time. I will build myself a pyramid of accomplishment." New York Governor Mario M. Cuomo, in the *The New York Times,* January 5, 1994.

The toughest thing about success is that you've got to keep on being a success. Irving Berlin, 1958.

We succeed only as we identify in life, or in war, or in anything else, a single overriding objective, and make all other considerations bend to that one objective. President Dwight D. Eisenhower, speech, April 2, 1957.

The reward of a thing well done is to have done it. Ralph Waldo Emerson, *Essays, Second Series: New England Reformers, 1844.*

What we call results are beginnings. Ralph Waldo Emerson, *The Conduct of Life: Fate,* 1860.

Death comes to all / But great achievements raise a monument / Which shall endure until the sun grows cold. George Fabricius, "In Praise of Georgius Agricola," c. 16th century.

Well done is better than well said. Benjamin Franklin, *Poor Richard's Almanac,* 1737.

My object all sublime / I shall achieve in time… W.S. Gilbert, *The Mikado,* 1885.

The heights by great men reached and kept / Were not attained by sudden flight, / But they, while their companions slept, / Were toiling upward in the night. Henry Wadsworth Longfellow, "The Ladder of Saint Augustine," 1858.

The difficult we do immediately; the impossible takes a little longer. Attributed variously to George Santayana, Fridtjof Nansen, and the U.S. Army Corps of Engineers.

ANONYMOUS APHORISMS

Getting something done is an accomplishment; getting something done right is an achievement.

They said it couldn't be done, but we did it.

Those who dare, do; those who dare not, do not.

ANECDOTES

At the end of a year out in the world, a young man came home and told his father he was worth $100. His father simply smiled. The following year he reported he was worth $1,000; his father still merely smiled. Year after year, as he came home and reported how much more he was worth, his father merely smiled. Then one year the son came home and said, "Father, this year, in order to keep the business going, I borrowed a million dollars." His father slapped him on the back and said, "Now *that* is an achievement."

"So all the fame and glory of your great achievements, it hasn't gone to your head?" the young director asked the aging screen star whom he'd just hired. "No, not at all," replied the star. "Thank god!" the young director sighed with relief. "You're welcome," replied the star.

FACTS

Achievement is one of the desires that divides humanity from the beasts. It is one of the needs that humanity publicly recognizes: we have Halls of Fame, Grammys, Emmys, Oscars, Nobel and Pulitzer Prizes, and thousands of other formal honors for outstanding achievement. *Who's Who in America* grows larger with every edition. The number of new products available and the new inventions which make life easier from generation to generation all testify to mankind's thirst for more achievement. No matter what kind of society or political system a country may have, it seeks to provide recognition for what it regards as achievement.

For a current assessment of outstanding achievement see lists of awards in various almanacs.

Adolescence

(See also Teenagers, Youth)

DEFINITIONS The process of going from childhood to maturity; the age between childhood and adulthood; a way of passing the time; the time between no responsibility and too much responsibility; the age of raging hormones; "a kind of emotional seasickness" (Arthur Koestler).

QUOTATIONS

Until they become conscious, they will never rebel, and until after they have rebelled they cannot become conscious. George Orwell, *1984*, 1948.

Young people are in a condition like permanent intoxication, because youth is sweet and they are growing. Aristotle, *Nicomachean Ethics*, c. 4th century BC.

A boy becomes an adult three years before his parents think he does, and about two years after he thinks he does. Major General Lewis B. Hershey, director of the Selective Service, December 30, 1951.

Young people are usually thoughtless. Homer, *The Odyssey*, c. 9th century BC.

The imagination of a boy is healthy, and the mature imagination of a man is healthy, but there is a space of life between, in which the soul is in a ferment, the character undecided, the way of life uncertain, the ambition thicksighted. John Keats, preface to *Endymion*, 1818.

ANONYMOUS APHORISMS

Adolescence does not accentuate the last syllable.

They're either too young or too old depending on what you want them to do.

You can always tell an adolescent, but you can't tell her much.

Adolescents like to rebel against conformity by all dressing exactly the same.

Addle essence.

An adolescent is like a new dog learning old tricks.

The question is not how you tell an adolescent but what you tell.

Adolescence is when young people finally break the umbilical cord. They trade it for a telephone cord.

An adolescent is a person whose vice is changing.

First adolescent, then obsolescent.

ANECDOTES

A civic leader brought a group of adolescent boys together and asked them what particularly interested them. "Girls," they all said as one.

After the adolescent party, the young host was seen raiding the refrigerator. His father asked, "How can you do that after you've spent the whole afternoon eating hamburgers and popcorn and drinking soda pop?" "Well," said the adolescent, "eating gives me an appetite."

A short-tempered man was offended by the giggling of a group of adolescent girls who passed him. "What's so funny?" he demanded. "Nothing," said one of the girls, "we were just laughing."

A biologist was excitedly presenting the discovery of a new life form—a tiny animal that lives among the mouth hairs of Norwegian lobsters. "It's born with a brain, but the brain disappears during adolescence and reappears at the onset of adulthood. There's nothing else on earth remotely like it," he said. An elderly woman called out from the back of the room, "I take it that you don't have children."

FACTS

Adolescence is part of the teenage years (which is a separate section in this volume), at the younger half of the teens; but adolescence has its own separate status. Adolescent offenders are treated differently by the legal system than older teenagers. The American awkward age or adolescent population is declining: In 1970, there were 52.5 million Americans between 5 and 17 years of age; but, in 1990, there were only 45.25 million; by the year 2000, most estimates say the proportion of adolescents in the population will be even lower, although the overall population will increase because of better health conditions.

For informed analysis of adolescent behavior patterns, contact the Center for Adolescent Studies, located in the School of Education, Indiana University, Bloomington, IN 47405, (812) 856-8113.

ADVERTISING

DEFINITIONS   A public notice intended to call attention to something; the art of making something more attractive by saying it is; convincing people to buy things they hadn't previously known they wanted; promises, promises; selling by suggestion; "the public face of business" (Neal W. O'Connor); "the only form of graphic design that gets home to everybody" (W.A. Dwiggins); "selective purchase mindset" (George Fertitta).

QUOTATIONS

[Branding is] identifying the exact psychological, physical, and emotional attributes of a product or service and locking that imagery into the minds of the consumers. George Fertitta, president and co-founder of Margeotes Fertitta & Partners, in *adobe.mag,* July 15, 1996.

Advertise, or the sheriff may do it for you. Attributed to P.T. Barnum, c. late 19th century.

The advertisements in a newspaper are more full of knowledge in respect to what is going on in a state or community than the editorial columns are. Rev. Henry Ward Beecher, *Proverbs from Plymouth Pulpit,* 1887.

...we've got to know what we've got a choice of. This is the function of advertising. Tom Dillon, chairman, BBD&O, July 1, 1976.

You can tell the ideals of a nation by its advertisements. (George) Norman Douglas, *South Wind,* 1917.

Advertisements contain the only truths to be relied on in a newspaper. Thomas Jefferson, letter to Senator Nathaniel Macon, 1819.

Advertisements are now so numerous that they are very negligently perused, and it is therefore become necessary to gain attention by magnificence of promises, and by eloquences sometimes sublime and sometimes pathetic. Promise—large promise—is the soul of advertising. Samuel Johnson, *The Idler,* No. 40, 1759.

Half the money I spend on advertising is wasted; the trouble is I don't know which half. Attributed to John Wanamaker, c. mid-20th century.

ANONYMOUS APHORISMS

Advertising is the art form that introduces itself by saying buy, buy.

You always buy familiar names, the ones you recognize; that's why the adman always claims it pays to advertise.

Advertising is sell service.

When business is good, it pays to advertise. When business isn't good, you've got to advertise.

Advertising moves the goods—if it's good advertising. Bad advertising doesn't move the goods because it doesn't move the buyers.

Events being what they are these days, advertising is the good news amid the bad news.

Advertisers are merchants of dreams.

Admen are the true trendsetters.

ANECDOTES

A friend said to a man who had a hot dog stand by the side of the road, "If you put up a sign advertising your stand a mile up the road so people see it before they get here, they might be influenced to stop." He put up the sign and it worked. So as time went on he put up more signs further and further away on the road; and more and more people bought the hot dogs; and the owner was able to send his son to the finest university. When the son returned he said, "You're spending too much money on your advertising. You don't need all those signs." So the father took down some of the signs. The business went down a little, but so did the expense for advertising. With less business, they decided to cut down a little more on the advertising, and the business went down a little more, until finally they were back to a little hot dog stand without any signs on the road at all. The moral of this story is that if you don't advertise your product—if you are quiet about your business—your business is apt to be quiet, too.

"Anybody can advertise," said the skeptic to the ad man, "and get the same results." They agreed to test this by both advertising the same offer in the same paper on the same day. The skeptic's ad read, "Free trip to Disneyland. Driver needed to deliver new car from New York." He got three responses. But the advertising man got 103 answers to his ad, which consisted of the same number of words: "Drive free from New York to Disneyland delivering new air-conditioned Cadillac." It isn't always what you advertise, it's how you advertise.

FACTS

Many people think advertising is purely a capitalistic enterprise, but it is not. Even in state-owned economies without a profit system, there is advertising directed at consumers and potential customers, which may include various forms of political propaganda. In profit-oriented societies, advertising is a competitive business and marketing tool. Political and public service organizations also rely on strategic media placement of their messages. Since 1960, advertising expenditures in the U.S.

have more than tripled in dollar totals. American advertising alone is a multi-billion dollar industry. And the globalization of market economies have stimulated the growth of many U.S. advertising agencies. McCann-Erikson, Leo Burnett, J. Walter Thompson, and Chiat-Day are just a few of the agencies that have a worldwide network of offices. The economic downturn of the early 1990s forced many advertisers to cut their advertising budgets. Yet in 1995, the advertising industry itself had a recordbreaking profit which was due in part to the introduction of new, alternative media resources such as cable networks, infomercials, and the World Wide Web. In the past half-century, advertising has been included in university curricula. Advertising has financed the American radio and television broadcast industries as well as most newspapers, magazines, and a portion of the Internet. It has been estimated that the average adult is the target of at least 1600 broadcast, print, billboard, and specialty ads per day.

The American Association of Advertising Agencies is at 405 Lexington Avenue, New York, NY 10174-1801, (212) 682-2500.

A G E

(See also Longevity, Youth)

DEFINITIONS   The length of time a person or thing has existed; the time of your life; a woman's secret and a man's fear; the opposite of youth; the inevitable aftermath of youth.

QUOTATIONS

There's always a hunger, when you're young, to go from peak to peak, and avoid the valleys. I had a pretty hilariously gloomy few years in the '70s. But today I'm quite at home wandering those valleys and occasionally climbing a peak. Peter O'Toole, actor, in *Time,* February 6, 1989.

To me, old age is always 15 years older than I am. Bernard M. Baruch, c. 1940s.

Behold, thou has made my days as an handbreadth; and mine age is as nothing before thee: Verily every man at his best state is altogether vanity. Psalms 39.

Grow old along with me! / The best is yet to be, / The last of life, for which the first was made... Robert Browning, Dramatis Personae in *Rabbi Ben Ezra,* 1864.

When a man fell into his anecdotage, it was a sign for him to retire. Benjamin Disraeli, *Lothair,* 1870.

At twenty years of age, the will reigns; at thirty the wit; at forty the judgment. Benjamin Franklin, *Poor Richard's Almanac,* 1741.

Gather ye rosebuds while ye may / Old Time is still a-flying: / And this same flower that smiles today / Tomorrow will be dying. Robert Herrick, "To Virgins, To Make Much of Time," 1648.

…there's nothing that keeps its youth, / So far as I know, but a tree and truth. Oliver Wendell Holmes, "The Deacon's Masterpiece," 1858.

Youth longs and manhood strives, but age remembers… Oliver Wendell Holmes, "The Iron Gate," 1880.

The riders in a race do not stop short when they reach the goal. There is a little finishing canter before coming to a standstill. There is time to hear the kind voices of friends and to say to one's self, "the work is done." Oliver Wendell Holmes, Jr., speech on his 91st birthday, March 8, 1932.

My only fear is that I may live too long. Thomas Jefferson, letter to Philip Mazzei, 1801.

It makes me shudder to think that I graduated from college thirty years ago and how doddering and venerable the thirtieth reunion class looked to me then. Adlai E. Stevenson, Jr., speech in Madison, WI, October 8, 1952.

It is better to be a young June bug than an old bird of paradise. Mark Twain, *The Tragedy of Puddinhead Wilson,* 1894.

ANONYMOUS APHORISMS

Old age is no bar to men chasing women; they just have trouble remembering why.

We grow too soon old and too late smart. (Pennsylvania Dutch saying.)

A man is as old as he feels, a woman is as old as she looks.

In life, it's always later than you think.

Age is a relative thing; you're young as long as you have a relative who's older.

Human beings are like steak: a little aging helps, but it can go too far.

ANECDOTES

An actress told Bob Hope she was "approaching thirty." Hope asked, "From which direction?"

U.S. Supreme Court Justice Oliver Wendell Holmes, Jr., was out for a stroll with a friend when a pretty young girl walked by. "Oh," said the ninetyish Justice to his friend, "what I'd give to be seventy again!"

Half a dozen years after he had been her cameraman, a Hollywood cinematographer worked on another film with a glamorous Hollywood beauty, and she was very upset with the results. "When you filmed me before, I looked much more beautiful," she complained. "Well," said the diplomatic cameraman, "I was six years younger then."

FACTS

Of all the privileges and restrictions applied to human beings, more have been based on age than on anything else. There are age qualifications for various public offices (35 for the Presidency, 30 for the Senate, 25 for the House, for example), for marriage, for retirement, for enlistment in the armed forces, and for voting. Some of these age requirements have changed over the years; some have remained constant. The vote for 18-year-olds came after the draft of 18-year-olds. Retirement at 65 was mandated during the depression of the 1930s to produce more jobs for younger people; it was raised to 70 in 1978. In earlier times, retirement was less of a problem because not as many people lived long enough to retire. American male life expectancy in 1900 was 46.3 years; in 1940, it was 60.8 years; in 1974, it was 68.2 years; and, in 1994, it was 72.3 years. For women, life expectancy has extended from 48.3 years in 1900, to an age of 79.0 years in 1994. The median age in 1860 was 20 years; in 1996, it was 34.6 years; and more than three-quarters of the U.S. population is now 18 or older. There were 31 million Americans over age 65, and twice as many under 18 years of age.

Information: *U.S. Health Report.*

For more information, contact the AARP, 601 E Street, NW, Washington, D.C. 20049, (800) 424-3410.

AGRICULTURE

DEFINITIONS   Farming; tilling the soil; working the land; raising crops or livestock; the original growth business; down-to-earth America.

QUOTATIONS

Burn down your cities and leave our farms, and your cities will spring up again as if by magic; but destroy our farms and the grass will grow in the streets of every city in the country. William Jennings Bryan, speech to the Democratic National Convention, July 8, 1896.

Farming looks mighty easy when your plow is a pencil, and you're a thousand miles from the corn field. President Dwight D. Eisenhower, September 11, 1956.

The first farmer was the first man, and all historic nobility rests on possession and use of land. Ralph Waldo Emerson, *Society and Solitude, Farming,* 1870.

A Plowman on his legs is higher than a Gentleman on his Knees. Benjamin Franklin, *Poor Richard's Almanac,* 1746.

Those who labor in the earth are the chosen people of God, if ever He had a chosen people, whose breasts He has made His peculiar deposit for substantial and genuine virtue. Thomas Jefferson, *Notes on Virginia,* 1781.

Farmers are farmers in the first place because they have the deep-seated instinct to raise crops, not to cut them back, not to leave the land unproductive. President Lyndon B. Johnson, October 7, 1964.

I know of no pursuit in which more real and important services can be rendered to any country, than by improving its agriculture—its breed of useful animals—and other branches of a husbandman's cares. President George Washington, July 20, 1794.

It will not be doubted that with reference either to individual or national welfare agriculture is of primary importance. In proportion as nations advance in population and other circumstances of maturity this truth becomes more apparent, and renders the cultivation of the soil more and more an object of public patronage. Institutions for promoting it grow up, supported by the public purse; and to what object can it be dedicated with greater propriety. President George Washington, address to the U.S. Congress, December 7, 1796.

Let us never forget that the cultivation of the earth is the most important labor of man. Daniel Webster, January 13, 1840.

ANONYMOUS APHORISMS

Agriculture is what happens when people go to seed.

Forty acres can be ruined by one wise acre.

Agriculture is a good field to work in.

Agriculture is people waiting to see what comes up.

A successful farmer is one who is outstanding in his field.

The farmer and the manufacturer agree that prosperity comes from thriving plants.

ANECDOTES

The farmer's son said, "Goodbye, Dad, I'm off to the big city so my talents can flower." "Same reason the corn stays here," said the farmer.

Farmer Brown was being paid not to plant crops on several of his fields one year, and he thought he had figured out a way to make more money. He asked the government how much they would pay him not to dig for oil.

FACTS

People think of agriculture as America's first preoccupation. But the first European colonists came here as traders and trappers; or to escape religious persecution.

They began growing food simply for subsistence, and then to sell their crops to others. At one time, a majority of Americans were farmers. In 1935, there were 6.8 million American farms. The proportion of farmland is still higher in the U.S. than in the world as a whole, even though the number of American farmers has shrunk tremendously. In 1992 there were only 1.9 million farms—dipping for the first time in this century to fewer farms than before the Civil War. In the United States, 40 percent of the total land area is farmland. The average farm size in the 1970s was 385 acres. By 1992, it was 491 acres; with the largest 17 percent of farms accounting for 83 percent of U.S. agricultural production.

For detailed statistics on agriculture in the United States contact: Customer Services, Bureau of the Census, Washington, D.C. 20233, (301) 457-4100.

ALIBIS

DEFINITIONS   Excuses; evidence to disprove allegations; slip covers; provable absence from the scene at the time of the crime.

QUOTATIONS

Bad excuses are worse than none. Thomas Fuller, *Gnomologia,* 1732.

The absent are always in the wrong. George Herbert, *Jacula Prudentum,* 1640.

"Alibi Ike": Title of a Ring Lardner story about a ball player who had an excuse for everything, 1924.

Hence with denial vain, and coy excuse. John Milton, *Lycidas,* 1637.

It is better to offer no excuse than a bad one. George Washington, letter to his niece Harriet, Washington, October 30, 1791.

ANONYMOUS APHORISMS

There may be a bible in every hotel room, but the register can be an alibible.

Too often a successful alibi depends on finding someone else who will do what the word says—a lie buy.

Absence is usually easier to explain than presence.

If at first you don't succeed, lie, lie, again.

The purpose of an alibi is to get away with something by getting away from it.

The accused protests innocence by saying, "Who, me?" and tries to prove it by saying "Me, where?"

An alibi is something else again.

An alibi is like a good shot in tennis—a matter of placement.

An alibi is like a submarine; if it isn't airtight it doesn't work.

A bad alibi is a poor excuse for an answer.

The perfect alibi is not a claim of innocence; it is a proof.

ANECDOTES

A man claiming not to have been at the scene of the crime was nevertheless accused because his car had been seen the night of the crime parked for hours outside the home of the victim. While he was out on bail he parked his car overnight outside a monastery. "If you believe I committed the crime," he said the next day, "then you have equal proof that I have repented."

FACTS

The word alibi comes from the Latin, meaning "elsewhere." In legal terms, an alibi is a defense that proves the accused was someplace else when the crime was committed. In modern times, alibi's meaning has been broadened to cover all sorts of excuses. Author Ring Lardner's title character in his novel, *Alibi Ike,* was a baseball player who had an excuse for everything. The word excuse—like the term alibi—comes from the Latin and originally had a legal meaning, namely to take out of or remove from a lawsuit.

ALUMNI

(See also College)

DEFINITIONS Graduates or former attendees of a particular school, college or institution; members of a permanent class; the Monday morning quarterbacks of the groves of academe; refugees from the good old days.

QUOTATIONS

I find that the three major administrative problems on a campus are sex for the students, athletics for the alumni and parking for the faculty. Clark Kerr, president, University of California, 1958.

ANONYMOUS APHORISMS

The alumni of an educational institution are like the wake of a ship; they spread out and ultimately disappear, but not before they have made a few waves.

Alumni graduate from the university, but the university never graduates from its alumni.

Everybody belongs to an alumni group, even if it is the School of Hard Knocks.

The students ask why; the faculty asks how; and the alumni ask how much.

An alumni reunion is living history in the process of being rewritten.

A student becomes an alumnus when he stops thinking of class as a side in a revolution and starts thinking of class as something that has a reunion.

Students and alumni are like acorns and oaks; there's a lot more bark to the oak and a lot more nuttiness to the acorn.

A student keeps trying to win a letter at college; an alumnus keeps getting letters from the college.

An alumni homecoming brings out the youth in all the old alumni.

Many alumni believe there should be more recognition of the most important of all conspicuous alumni achievements—survival.

ANECDOTES

"The old school isn't what it used to be," sighed the alumnus to the college president. "No," said the president tactfully, "but then, neither are we."

Trying to find words of comfort for the pitifully few members of the class at its fiftieth reunion, the class president said, "As we look at our ranks today and compare them to the long roster of classmates when we were at school and the grades that were posted, let us remember that by now a lot more of us have passed."

FACTS

More than 40 million living Americans have spent time in college and thus constitute alumni. In terms of high school alumni, the figures of course are considerably higher. College and university alumni are not a cohesive or class group in the U.S., and their role is different from one institution to another. In some cases, they elect trustees to help govern the institution; in some places they have an automatic voice in the university family; while in others they have to pay dues to qualify. Except for the American Association of University Women—which reported having 150,000 members and 1,600 branches nationwide in 1996—alumni associations and organizations are generally separate for individual schools, colleges, and universities. A number of large alumni groups maintain clubs in larger cities such as The Yale Club in Manhattan, and in some cities there are also university clubs serving alumni of different institutions in one facility.

Ambition

(See also Opportunity)

DEFINITIONS   Desire and enthusiastic effort for advancement, power or success; high hopes combined with goal tending; "avarice on stilts and masked" (Walter Savage Landor, *Imaginary Conversations: Brooke and Sydney*); "the glorious fault of angels and of gods" (Alexander Pope, "Elegy to the Memory of an Unfortunate Lady").

QUOTATIONS

Don't be content with things as they are. Attributed to Winston Churchill.

If we do not succeed, then we run the risk of failure. Vice President Dan Quayle, speech to the Phoenix Republican Forum, March 23, 1990.

If you're going to be thinking anyway, you might as well think big. Donald Trump, real estate developer, in *Time,* January 16, 1989.

Hitch your wagon to a star. Ralph Waldo Emerson, *Society and Solitude: Civilization, 1870.*

Nothing is so commonplace as to wish to be remarkable. Oliver Wendell Holmes, *The Autocrat of the Breakfast-Table,* 1858.

I would sooner fail than not be among the greatest. John Keats, letter to James Hessey, 1818.

One often goes from love to ambition, but one rarely returns from ambition to love. Francois Duc de La Rochefoucauld, *Maxims,* c. 17th century.

Most people would succeed in small things if they were not troubled with great ambitions. Henry Wadsworth Longfellow, *Driftwood:* "Table Talk," 1857.

Not failure, but low aim, is crime. James Russell Lowell, *Under the Willows and Other Poems:* "For an Autograph," 1868.

Ambition should be made of sterner stuff. William Shakespeare, *Julius Caesar,* 1599.

I charge thee, fling away ambition. / By that sin fell the angels; how can man then, / The image of his Maker, hope to win by it? William Shakespeare, *Henry VIII,* 1613.

Ambition often puts men upon doing the meanest offices; so climbing is performed in the same posture with creeping. Jonathan Swift, *Miscellanies,* 1711.

Ambition is like the sea wave, which the more you drink / The more you thirst— yea—drink too much, as men / Have done on rafts of wreck—it drives you mad. Alfred Tennyson, *The Cup,* 1880.

If you think you're a second-class citizen, you are. Ted Turner, 1977.

ANONYMOUS APHORISMS

Ambition is hard work.

Ambition lubricates the mind.

Onward and upward.

There's always room at the top.

Keep your sights high—and your powder dry.

Most people want to improve themselves, but not too many work at it.

Where there's a will there's a way.

Where there's a will, there's a beneficiary.

The way to go from rags to riches is to start by getting a decent set of rags.

Ambition looks up; failure looks down.

ANECDOTES

The brash young man barged into the boss's office and declared, "Ambition makes its own opportunities." "Yes," replied the boss, "but opportunity knocks."

Then there's the story of the man who was so busy climbing the ladder of success he forgot to watch his step.

In high school and college everybody knew how anxious Johnny Brown was for success. The college yearbook labeled him as the class's most ambitious member. But 20 years later, he hadn't gotten anywhere. He had a ready explanation. "Everybody thought I would be a success because I talked about it. So I was a success already. I was a successful talker. I had realized my ambition before I understood that it was my ambition. Ambition, in the last analysis, is to do well what you like doing best. And I like to talk."

FACTS

In rigid class-based societies, there are not as many outlets for ambition. In open societies, there is more room for inventiveness, new business ideas, and new arts. America was settled by generations of immigrants who came here with a burning ambition to make something of themselves and something better of their children. They are the men and women who built America. With the highest salary levels, the greatest variety of creature comforts, and the broadest range of opportunity in the world, it is logical that ambition should flourish in America. Ambition, essentially, is the desire to fulfill what the Declaration of Independence described as "the pursuit of happiness."

AMERICA

DEFINITIONS   Name generally given to the North American continent and usually to the United States portion; "a country where anything can happen" (George and Helen Papashvily, *Anything Can Happen*); "the land of the free and the home of the brave" (Francis Scott Key, "The Star Spangled Banner"); "a nation of many nationalities, many races, many religions—bound together by a single unity, the unity of freedom and equality" (President Franklin D. Roosevelt, 1940); "the melting pot of the world" (Israel Zangwill, *The Melting Pot,* 1908); melting pot turned pressure cooker; "Columbia, the gem of the ocean, / The home of the brave and the free" (adapted from "Brittania Pride of the Ocean" Thomas Becket and/or David T. Shaw, 1843); "sweet land of liberty" (Rev. Samuel F. Smith, "America," 1831, adapted from "God Saves the Nation's King"); the States.

QUOTATIONS

Whether we like it or not, we are one nation, one family, indivisible. And for us divorce or separation are not options. President Bill Clinton, speech, October 16, 1995.

The American is a new man, who acts upon new principles; he must therefore entertain new ideas, and form new opinions.... It is in consequence of that change, that he becomes an American. Michel-Guillaqhme de Crevecoeur, *Letters from an American Farmer,* 1782.

We [the U.S.] are the last great superpower—we should be walking gently in the world. Ronald V. Dellums, U.S. Representative, in *The Washington Post,* September 19, 1994.

Whatever America hopes to bring to pass in the world must first come to pass in the hearts of America. President Dwight D. Eisenhower, inaugural address, January 20, 1953.

Here in America we are descended in blood and in spirit from revolutionists and rebels—men and women who dared to dissent from accepted doctrine. President Dwight D. Eisenhower, May 31, 1954.

Now, we Americans understand freedom. We have earned it, we have lived for it, and we have died for it. This nation and its people are freedom's models in a searching world. We can be freedom's missionaries in a doubting world. Senator Barry M. Goldwater of Arizona, acceptance speech for the Republican Presidential nomination, July 16, 1964.

...not merely a nation but a nation of nations. President Lyndon B. Johnson, 1965.

Give me your tired, your poor, / Your huddled masses yearning to breathe free, / The wretched refuse of your teeming shore. / Send these, the homeless, tempest-tost to me, / I lift my lamp beside the golden door! Emma Lazarus. "The New Colossus," inscribed upon the base of the Statue of Liberty, 1883.

I believe in the United States of America as a government of the people, by the people, for the people, whose just powers are derived from the consent of the governed; a democracy in a republic; a sovereign nation of many sovereign states; a perfect union, one and inseparable; established upon those principles of freedom, equality, justice and humanity for which Americans sacrificed their lives and their fortunes. I therefore believe it is my duty to my country to love it, to support its Constitution, to obey its laws, to respect its flag and to defend it against all enemies. William Tyler Page, "The American's Creed," adopted by the U.S. House of Representatives April 3, 1918.

The American idea...a democracy—that is, a government of all the people, by all the people, for all the people...Rev. Theodore Parker, speech in Boston, MA, May 29, 1850.

Since the days when the fleet of Columbus sailed into the waters of the New World, America has been another name for opportunity... Frederick Jackson Turner, "The Significance of the Frontier in American History," 1893.

In America the President reigns for four years, and Journalism governs for ever and ever. Oscar Wilde, *The Soul of Man Under Socialism,* 1891.

The youth of America is their oldest tradition. Oscar Wilde, *A Woman of No Importance,* 1893.

Just what is it that America stands for? If she stands for one thing more than another, it is for the sovereignty of self-governing people. President Woodrow Wilson, January 20, 1916.

ANONYMOUS APHORISMS

Baseball, hot dogs, and apple pie.

America is the land of opportunity.

America is fast foods, fast cars, and fast friends.

An American believes more than anything else in the last four letters of that title— I can.

America is still the New World.

America is a mobile civilization that some day will rediscover walking.

America is wide open spaces and traffic jams, sometimes in the same place.

The colossus of the north.

America is still the promised land.

America is a nation on the move.

When the going gets tough in America, the tough get going.

ANECDOTES

A Frenchman, an Austrian, and an American were discussing national traits of character. "We French are quick to see others' faults," said the Frenchman, "while you Austrians always sit and wonder what's behind a remark and you Americans think you know it all." "I know," said the American.

The pessimist said gloomily, "America just isn't what it used to be." The optimist answered, "It never was. We always have room here for improvement."

Q: What's the difference between the American Dream and everybody else's dream? A: Everybody else's dream is to come to America.

FACTS

What is unique about America is not its wealth, its size, its natural resources, its democratic government, its ethnic diversity, the achievements of its athletes, or the popularity of its arts. What is unique is to have all these in a single country. No nation has ever contributed more inventions to the world or accepted more immigrants from the rest of the world. No nation has descendants from such a wide variety of ethnic, religious, and economic backgrounds. No nation has freedom of movement throughout its 3.67 million acres of territory with the exception of its northern neighbor—Canada—which has 3.85 million acres of free-range territory. In fact, no two nations in the world have a longer, peaceful, and unarmed border between them. Few nations have political parties older than the U.S. and its cousin, Great Britain. No nation's scientists have probed more of the universe thanks to the contributions of its immigrant scientists. No nation has more psychiatrists and psychoanalysts. No nation has more good food, more junk food, or more overweight citizens. Some countries, it has been said, are punctuated by a question mark. For America, the best punctuation is an exclamation point.

ANCESTRY

DEFINITIONS   Line of descent; parents, grandparents and on back into history; the bloodlines you were born with; family tree; pedigree; genealogy.

QUOTATIONS

People will not look forward to posterity who never look backward to their ancestors. Edmund Burke, Reflections on the Revolution in France, 1790.

The pride of ancestry increases in the ratio of distance. George W. Curtis, *Prue and I,* 1856.

Men resemble their contemporaries even more than their progenitors. Ralph Waldo Emerson, *Representative Men:* "On the Uses of Great Men," 1850.

I can trace my ancestry back to a protoplasmal primordial atomic globule. Consequently my family pride is something inconceivable. I can't help it. I was born sneering. W.S. Gilbert, *The Mikado,* 1885.

A child's education should begin at least one hundred years before he was born. Oliver Wendell Holmes, *The Autocrat of the Breakfast-Table,* 1858.

We are all omnibuses in which our ancestors ride, and every now and then one of them sticks his head out and embarrasses us. Oliver Wendell Holmes, *The Guardian Angel,* 1867.

Men have their intellectual ancestry, and the likeness of some one of them is forever unexpectedly flashing out in the features of a descendant; it may be after a gap of several generations. In the parliament of the present every man represents a constituency of the past. James Russell Lowell, "Keats," 1854.

It is certainly desirable to be well descended, but the glory belongs to our ancestors. Plutarch, "Morals," c. 1st century.

He who boasts of his ancestry is praising the deeds of another. Seneca, "Hercules Furens," c. 1st century.

Our ancestors are very good kind of folks; but they are the last people I should choose to have a visiting acquaintance with. Richard Brinsley Sheridan, *The Rivals,* 1775.

Whoever serves his country well has no need of ancestors. Voltaire, *Mérope,* 1743.

Anonymous Aphorisms

Good birth in your lineage is apt to lead to a good berth in life.

Nobody got here without ancestors.

Lineage is a gift we inherit from our ancestors and pass on to our descendants.

Ancestry is a hereditary condition.

You can't choose your ancestors, and neither can your descendants.

People are generally prouder of their ancestors or pretend to be prouder than their ancestors would be of them.

Ancestry tells us where we come from, and posterity is apt to tell us where to get off.

Anecdotes

A snob and an egalitarian were arguing. "My people," said the snob, "go back to the Mayflower." "I wish they would," said the egalitarian.

Asked about his family's coat of arms, the mechanic said, "We never had a coat of arms. We were lucky to have a coat of grease."

He was always describing himself as coming from one of "the first families." He explained that his was one of the first families to come to the New Land. The trouble with that, someone observed, was that you never knew whether it was a spirit of adventure that was responsible or whether the family had been thrown out of the old world they came from.

"I can trace my ancestors back 23 generations," proclaimed the haughty dowager. "I never felt the need," her friend retorted.

FACTS

Ancestor worship—though not formally practiced in the U.S. as it still is in Japan and China—is one of humanity's oldest devotions. The practice is almost as old as the tendency to scoff at other people's ancestry. We have upwards of one hundred generations of ancestors, which offers plenty of latitude and longitude. Associations based on ancestry are numerous: for example, the Society of Mayflower Descendants, the Daughters of the American Revolution, the Sons of Union Veterans of the Civil War, the Ancient Order of Hibernians. General family groups can be large. There are well over two million Americans named Smith, which is the nation's most common surname, followed by Johnson, Williams, Jones, Brown, and Miller. The genealogy business is a thriving commercial enterprise, as is the sale of family crests. In a relatively classless or fluid society, ancestry still has importance beyond pride of antecedents, in establishing claims to legal inheritances and in tracing genes and physical characteristics.

The National Genealogical Society is located at 4527 17th Street, North Arlington, VA 22207-2399, fax (703) 525-0052.

ARISTOCRACY

(See also Society)

DEFINITIONS   A privileged class; government by a select elite; a state with a privileged class; upper-class; the better people; "masters of the universe" (Tom Wolfe).

QUOTATIONS

Some animals are more equal than others. George Orwell, *Animal Farm,* 1945.

What is Aristocracy? A corporation of the best, of the bravest. Thomas Carlyle, *Chartism,* 1839.

I was told that the Privileged and the People formed two nations. Benjamin Disraeli, *Sybil,* 1845.

The aristocrat is the democrat ripe and gone to seed. Ralph Waldo Emerson, *Representative Men:* "Napoleon," 1850.

All communities divide themselves into the few and the many. Alexander Hamilton, speech at the Constitutional Convention in Philadelphia, PA, 1787.

He comes of the Brahmin caste of New England. This is the harmless, inoffensive, untitled aristocracy. Oliver Wendell Holmes in *The Atlantic Monthly,* 1860.

…I agree with you that there is a natural aristocracy among men. The grounds of this are virtue and talents…. There is also an artificial aristocracy, founded on wealth and birth, without either virtue or talents; for with these it would belong to the first class. Thomas Jefferson, letter to John Adams, October 28, 1813.

Thus our democracy was, from an early period, the most aristocratic, and our aristocracy the most democratic in the world. Thomas Babington Macaulay, *History of England,* 1849.

Aristocracy is always cruel. Wendell Phillips, "Toussaint L'Ouverture," 1861.

It is an interesting question how far men would retain their relative rank if they were divested of their clothes. Henry D. Thoreau, *Walden,* 1854.

ANONYMOUS APHORISMS

Some aristocrats are born and others simply cannot be borne.

In a democracy it can be said that when it comes to aristocrats many are culled and few are chosen.

The best people always know who they are, or always think they know.

The true aristocrat is not merely a descendant of previous generations, but more particularly an improvement.

In a free country, the aristocracy are the people who are more free than the rest .

FACTS

There is no country without a privileged class, and no country where such privilege does not "rub off" on the children of its aristocracy. The American aristocracy has various components—first families, elected officials, the intelligentsia, the wealthy—but ancestry is less important than wealth or power. Throughout the world, the hereditary nature of aristocracy is in decline, except where hereditary wealth accompanies it. The collateral descendants of George Washington cover the full spectrum of American life without any hereditary aristocratic overtones. The pace of modern life has so quickened that not even the inheritance of wealth can last as long as it once did.

Armed forces

(See also Peace, War)

DEFINITIONS   Army, Navy, Air Force, and Marine Corps; the military, naval, and aviation uniformed organizations and installations of the nation; the military; the GIs; the dogfaces; the peacekeepers; defenders of freedom; our national defense; the defense establishment; our boys.

QUOTATIONS

The difference between a good officer and an excellent one is about ten seconds. Admiral Arleigh Burke, Former Chief of Naval Operations, in *The Washington Post,* September 15, 1989.

...the best way of telling offensive from defensive weapons is to ask the other side what weapons of yours they perceive as offensive. Paul Walker, co-director, Institute for Peace and International Security, in *The Atlantic Monthly,* June, 1989.

I am convinced that the best service a retired general can perform is to turn in his tongue along with his suit, and to mothball his opinions. General of the Army Omar N. Bradley, Armed Forces Day address, May 16, 1959.

Our country has long been remarkable for utilizing officers of the army and the navy in works of peace. Andrew Carnegie, March 5, 1914.

Before we cast away the solid assurances of national armaments for self-preservation, we must be certain that our temple is built, not upon shifting sands or quagmires, but upon the rock. Winston Churchill, speech in Fulton, MO, March 5, 1946.

No nation ever had an army large enough to guarantee it against attack in time of peace or insure it victory in time of war. President Calvin Coolidge, October 6, 1925.

In the councils of government, we must guard against the acquisition of unwarranted influence, whether sought or unsought, by the military-industrial complex. President Dwight D. Eisenhower, farewell address, January 17, 1961.

Praise the Lord and pass the ammunition. Chaplain Howell M. Forgy, U.S.S. *New Orleans* at Pearl Harbor, HI, December 7, 1941.

There is a kind of valorous spleen which, like wind, is apt to grow unruly in the stomachs of newly made soldiers, compelling them to box-lobby brawls and broken-headed quarrels, unless there can be found some more harmless way to give it vent. Washington Irving, *A History of New York by Diedrich Knickerbocker,* 1809.

Then it's Tommy this, an' Tommy that, an' "Tommy, 'ow's yer soul?" / But it's "Thin red line of 'eroes" when the drums begin to roll . . . For it's Tommy this, an' Tommy that, an' "Chuck him out, the brute!" / But it's "Saviour of 'is country," when the guns begin to shoot... Rudyard Kipling, "Tommy," 1892.

Old soldiers never die; they just fade away. General of the Army Douglas MacArthur, attributed to an "old barracks ballad," speech to joint session of Congress, April 19, 1951.

...the soldier above all other people prays for peace, for he must suffer and bear the deepest wounds, and scars of war...General of the Army Douglas MacArthur, speech at West Point, May 12, 1962.

...we've got the enemy on our right flank, our left flank, in front of us and behind us. They won't get away this time. General Lewis (Chesty) Puller, U.S. Marines, 1950.

The Army and Navy forever / Three cheers for the red, white and blue. "Columbia, the Gem of the Ocean" adapted from David T. Shaw and/or Thomas Becket, "Britannia, the Pride of the Ocean," 1848.

Retreat Hell! We're just advancing in another direction. Marine General O.P. Smith, U.S. Marines, 1950.

When we assumed the soldier, we did not lay aside the citizen. George Washington, speech in New York, NY, June 26, 1775.

To be prepared for war is one of the most effectual means of preserving peace. President George Washington, message to the U.S. Congress, January 8, 1790.

Anonymous Aphorisms

Join the Navy and see the world.

He isn't old enough to be a sergeant. He must be an officer. (Second World War joke about Air Force personnel.)

Uncle Sam wants you. (First World War recruiting motto.)

Military procurement and streetwalking have many things in common—the business is interestingly solicited; it does its best when your defenses are down; and one side or the other is always at the disadvantage.

There are three ways of doing it—the right way, the wrong way and the Army way.

They used to say all officers were gentlemen, but that wasn't even true before women joined the services.

Rank has its privileges, and privileges have their rank.

ANECDOTES

During an uprising in a primitive land, a single U.S. Marine was sent in, only to be greeted by a furious local leader. "Why did they just send one man?" the leader roared. "Well," said the Marine, "they figured there was only one uprising."

After completing all but one day of his enlistment, Tim was bawled out furiously by the same familiar noncommissioned officer for the 1000th time for failing to fall in line. "When I'm out of service tomorrow with the rest of the guys," Tim said, "I'm going to bust him in the nose." "Well," said his friend, "you'll have to stand in line to do it."

"Tomorrow's wars will be fought by push-button," said the young scientist to the wounded veteran. "By the way, where were you wounded?" "On the button," said the veteran.

Q: Why do you salute officers? A: To make them salute back.

FACTS

Throughout our nation's history, Americans have distinguished themselves in military service, in times of war and peace. Service with the U.S. armed forces has been on a voluntary basis, except during major wars. But all Americans are required, through taxes, to do their part to pay for the national defense. During the heat of the "cold war," this cost rose from $53.5 billion in 1960, to $136 billion in 1970. From 1980 to 1989, the defense budget more than doubled again as the U.S. competed with the Soviet Union during the final days of the "arms race." The military budget rose not only because of the increasing outlays for more armament, but also because of higher pay for the armed forces, including retired military personnel. But with the breakup of the Soviet Union in the early 1990s, the sole perceived threat was removed from the world map and Washington began looking for ways to reign in defense spending without weakening national security.

The National Security Council, in Washington, D.C., publishes a series of fact sheets on current military planning and proposed expenditures. The Department of State has facts on current military threats around the world.

ART

DEFINITIONS   Skill used in the production or performance of an aesthetic object or impression; skillful graphic presentation; "silent poetry and speaking painting"

(Ralph Waldo Emerson, *Society and Solitude:* "Art," 1870); "surface and symbol" (Oscar Wilde, *The Picture of Dorian Gray,* 1891).

QUOTATIONS

Nothing is truly beautiful except that which can serve for nothing…Whatever is useful is ugly. Theophile Gautier, preface to *Mademoiselle Maupin,* 1835.

Art isn't art because someone uses a paintbrush. Photography is either good or bad, and when it's good it's like any other art that's good. It becomes Art. Richard Avedon, photographer, in *Vogue,* February, 1994.

Art like this will never die. Nina Ananiashvili, in *Dance Magazine,* July, 1992.

Certainly riding a rocket to the moon is the biggest kick you can have. But when I paint, I get the same feeling that I got when I flew in space. Well, certainly the view isn't as good, but the best part of life is internal. Alan L. Bean, astronaut, in the *The New York Times,* July 20, 1994.

Every artist dips his brush in his own soul, and paints his own nature into his pictures. Rev. Henry Ward Beecher, *Proverbs from Plymouth Pulpit,* 1887.

New arts destroy the old. Ralph Waldo Emerson, *Essays,* "First Series: Circles," 1841.

Art is a jealous mistress. Ralph Waldo Emerson, *The Conduct of Life:* "Wealth," 1860.

Every artist was first an amateur. Ralph Waldo Emerson, *Letters and Social Aims:* "Progress of Culture," 1876.

In art, as in life, instinct is enough. Anatole France, *The Garden of Epicurus,* 1894.

Art is not a tender or fragile thing. It has kept alive in the habitations of cruelty and oppressions. It has struggled toward light from the manifold darkness of war and conflict and persecution. Yet it flourishes most abundantly when the artist can speak as he wishes and describe the world as he sees it without any official direction. President Lyndon B. Johnson, June 14, 1965.

We must never forget that art is not a form of propaganda; it is a form of truth. President John F. Kennedy, speech in Amherst, MA, October 26, 1963.

In free society art is not a weapon. President John F. Kennedy, speech in Amherst, MA, October 26, 1963.

The arts cannot thrive except where men are free to be themselves…. President Franklin D. Roosevelt, speech in New York, NY, May 10, 1939.

Great art is precisely that which never was nor will be taught; it is preeminently and finally the expression of the spirits of great men. John Ruskin, *Modern Painters, Vol. III,* 1856.

Art should never try to be popular; the public should try to make itself artistic. Oscar Wilde, *The Soul of Man Under Socialism*, 1891.

…the moment that an artist takes notice of what other people want, and tries to supply the demand, he ceases to be an artist, and becomes a dull or an amusing craftsman, an honest or dishonest tradesman. Oscar Wilde, *The Soul of Man Under Socialism*, 1891.

ANONYMOUS APHORISMS

Great art is regarded as a luxury, but for the great artist, it is a necessity.

Even the greatest of art, if copied unduly, becomes less than great. Greatness is Titian; dullness is repetition.

Art is what separates man from beast.

Chimpanzees have painted interesting pictures; but they were interesting only to human beings, not to other chimpanzees.

ANECDOTES

Abraham Lincoln was once asked to look at a painting. His comment was that the artist was clearly a gifted and devout man—devout because he followed the commandment of the Good Book not to make "any likeness of any thing in heaven above, the earth beneath or the water under the earth."

"How will I ever get into the Metropolitan Museum of Art?" the aspiring young artist asked a great teacher. "You can either take the Fifth Avenue bus to 81st Street," said the teacher, "or work hard, be inspired, wait 20 years, and have them come to you."

"I know great art when I see it," said the critic. "And I know great art when I feel it," said the artist.

FACTS

Ancient Greece divided the arts into three families: the fine arts for beauty; the liberal arts for useful knowledge; and the arts of conduct or behavior for the goodness in humanity. Today when we speak of art we think principally of the fine arts, but beauty is no longer the constant aim. Art today is often challenging and intellectual rather than beautiful; it is sometimes deliberately controversial and shocking. These modern values brought federal funding of the arts under fire during the 1980s. The fine arts today can be highly rewarding; it has proven to be a good—though highly speculative—investment to buy artwork; and the market prices for fine works of art such as drawings, paintings, sculpture, and graphic prints; applied arts; books; dramatic works; and music is rising, along with the number of people who either work or play at the arts.

National Arts Policy Clearinghouse, American Council for the Arts, 1 East 53rd Street, New York, NY 10022-4210, (212) 223-2787, ext. 225, is a national organization whose purpose is to promote public policies that advance and document the contributions of the arts and artists to American life.

The Art Information Center at 189 Lexington Avenue, New York, NY 10016, serves as a clearing house for information on contemporary fine arts.

Automobiles

DEFINITIONS   Self-propelled, dual-axled, wheeled vehicle; horseless carriage; highway horsepower; "The Insolent Chariots" (John Keats, 1958); wreckcreation; a traffic cop's moving target; the extension of the male ego; motor car.

QUOTATIONS

My greatest achievement was in imitating American cars…American and Japanese cars are like humans. Some are good in some aspects and some are bad in some aspects. Soichiro Honda, founder of Honda Motor Company, in the *Los Angeles Times,* October 10, 1989.

Except the American woman, nothing interests the eye of the American man more than the automobile…. Alfred H. Barr, Jr., 1963.

…For much too long, the man who owns and drives an automobile has been treated like a stepchild. We require him to pay for the highways he uses and we require him to pay in advance. We divert his taxes to other uses but we delay the building of the roads he deserves. We denounce him for getting snarled in traffic jams not of his making. We complain about what he costs us but we never thank him for what he adds to the worth and wealth of our economy. We could not get along without him, but we often talk as though we can't live with him. President Lyndon B. Johnson, August 13, 1964.

More than any country, ours is an automobile society. President Lyndon B. Johnson, message to U.S. Congress, February 8, 1965.

The automobile…created suburbia in America. President Lyndon B. Johnson, October 15, 1966.

This is the only country that ever went to the poorhouse in an automobile. Will Rogers, c. early 1930s.

The one who drives/when he's been drinking/depends on you/to do his thinking. Burma Shave highway sign, c. 1940s.

ANONYMOUS APHORISMS

Drivers careless may wind up carless.

Money makes the wheels go round.

The American automobile salesman waits to see who walks in; the American automobile customer waits to see what's thrown in.

America's favorite step is a step on the gas.

Drive carefully; the life you save may be your own.

Drive carefully; we love our children. (U.S. highway sign during 1930s and 1940s.)

The easiest way to determine a person's innermost character is to put that person behind the wheel of a high-powered car on a U.S. highway.

You can drive a car for less money a day in some cities than it costs to park it.

The most dangerous animal in the U.S.A. is the road hog.

Too many used car buyers drive a hard bargain.

Would you buy a used car from this man?

American automobile driving is highway roulette.

The only foolproof car is one without a driver.

ANECDOTES

Then there's the used car salesman who described his profession as autosuggestion.

Mr. Jones watched his 17-year-old son labor over an old jalopy: keeping it in perfect mechanical condition; polishing its chrome; washing it down; and fussing over it hour after hour. "Maybe," said Mr. Jones, "if we put his room on wheels he'd clean that, too."

He had been hard put to keep up the payments on his nice, shiny new sports car, and finally he went to his boss for advice. "Well" said his boss, "you'll either have to stop eating or stop driving." The sports car owner didn't say a word. "I said you'll either have to stop eating or stop driving," the boss repeated. "Why don't you say something?" "It's a hard choice," said the sports car owner, "I'm thinking."

FACTS

The automobile is responsible for more employment, more movement, more pleasure, and more business than any other American product. It sparked the expansion of suburban life; the worldwide appetite for oil; the air pollution problem; and installment purchasing. The automobile mobilized America. It is a democratizing factor: used cars put transportation within easy reach for millions who in previous generations would have been confined to their own home areas. In 1994, 3.9 million passenger cars were imported into the U.S.; American automotive plants manufactured 12.3 million motor vehicles—more than any other country. The worldwide manufacturing total for that same year was 49.7 million vehicles. There are more than 175 million licensed American drivers; and the average licensed driver covers 14,000 miles behind the wheel annually.

The American Automobile Association, 1000 AAA Drive, Heathrow, FL 32779, has over 37 million members. There are affiliated organizations throughout the world.

Aviation

DEFINITIONS   The field and science and/or components of airplane transportation; flying; cloud hopping; riding on air.

QUOTATIONS

Oh, I have slipped the surly bonds of earth / And danced the skies on laughter-silvered wings; / Sunward I've climbed, and joined the tumbling mirth / Of sun-split clouds—and done a hundred things / You have not dreamed of—wheeled and soared and swung / High in the sunlit silence. Hov'ring there, / I've chased the shouting wind along, and flung / My eager craft through footless halls of air / Up, up the long, delirious, burning blue / I've topped the windswept heights with easy grace / Where never lark, or even eagle flew. / And, while with silent, lifting mind I've trod / The high untrespassed sanctity of space, / Put out my hand, and touched the face of God. John Gillespie Magee, "High Flight," 1941.

Soon shall thy arm, unconquer'd steam! afar / Drag the slow barge, or drive the rapid car; / Or on wide-waving wings expanded bear / The flying chariot through the field of air. Erasmus Darwin, *The Botanic Garden,* 1795.

In the space age, man will be able to go around the world in two hours—one hour for flying and the other to get to the airport. Neil H. McElroy, Secretary of Defense, 1958.

For I dipt into the future far as human eyes could see— / Saw the vision of the world, and all the wonders that would be— / Saw the heavens fill with commerce, argosies of magic sails, / Pilots of the purple twilight, dropping down with costly bales; / Heard the heavens fill with shouting, and there rain'd a ghastly dew / From the nations' airy navies grappling in the central blue. Alfred Tennyson, *Locksley Hall,* 1842.

Off we go into the wild blue yonder / Flying high into the sun. The Air Force Song.

Souls of men dreaming of skies to conquer / Gave us wings ever to soar. The Air Force Song.

ANONYMOUS APHORISMS

A white-knuckle flier is one whose fears are groundless.

First-class air travel is a flight of fancy; cheap economy travel is fly-by-night.

Today's airport is three big parking lots—one for the planes, one for the autos and one for the passengers, waiting to get to the planes or the autos.

ANECDOTES

Mrs. Harris thought she could pick any plane she wanted because she heard they were stacked up at the airport.

Mr. Brown arrived at the airport one minute before the flight was due to leave. The check-in clerk asked him, "Do you have a reservation?" "Well," he said, "I'm a little skeptical about flying."

The little old lady wanted to buy a ticket for a cross-country flight, and the clerk said, "I'm sorry; we're full, but I can have you waitlisted." "My goodness," she said, "I didn't know you were that careful. My weight is 102 pounds."

FACTS

Aviation is perhaps our most truly international business. Every nation seems to insist on having its own airline; and air transportation has ended the isolation of the most remote countries on the face of the earth. Aviation in most countries is far more heavily subsidized by the government than in the U.S. as a matter of both national pride and national defense. But that hasn't stunted the growth of the American commercial airline industry, nor have rising fuel prices, deregulation, and air traffic controllers' strikes. In 1979, there were 5.4 million recorded departures from U.S. airports; in 1994, that figure had risen to 7.5 million. Chicago's O'Hare airport was the busiest in the world, with 66 million passengers passing through that year. Jet-setting was the term coined in the 1960s to describe the growing number of affluent, international travelers who hopped onto jet plane flights for business and pleasure as frequently as the average person got into the family car. Bi-coastal was a 1980s term—born of an increased number of flights and carriers—that aptly describes a person who lives on both the east and west coasts, and commutes regularly on a weekly or monthly basis.

The Air Transport Association of America, 1301 Pennsylvania Avenue, NW, Suite 1100, Washington, D.C. 20004-1707, founded in 1936, is the trade organization for the principal American airlines.

Babies

(See also Children, Parents)

DEFINITIONS Newborn humans; young children; small fry; small change; the next generation; toothless tyrants; rug rats; munchkins; the true junior league.

QUOTATIONS

There is no finer investment for any community than putting milk into babies. Winston Churchill, British Prime Minister, broadcast, March 21, 1943.

Every baby born into the world is a finer one than the last. Charles Dickens, *Nicholas Nickleby,* 1838-1839.

Infancy conforms to nobody; all conform to it. Ralph Waldo Emerson, *Essays, First Series:* "Self-Reliance," 1841.

Who can tell what a baby thinks? Josiah Gilbert Holland, "Cradle Song," c. 1860.

O child! O new-born denizen / Of life's great city! on thy head / The glory of the morn is shed, / Like a celestial benison. Henry Wadsworth Longfellow, "To a Child," 1846.

Who would not tremble and rather choose to die than to be a baby again, if given such a choice? St. Augustine, *The City of God,* c.5th century.

Sweetes' li'l feller— / Everybody knows; / Dunno what ter call 'im, / But he's mighty lak' a rose! Frank L. Stanton, "Mighty Lak' A Rose," 1901.

Thrice happy state again to be / The trustful infant on the knee, / Who lets his rosy fingers play / About his mother's neck and knows / Nothing beyond his mother's eyes! Alfred Tennyson, "Supposed Confessions," 1830.

But what am I? / An infant crying in the night; / An infant crying for the light: / And with no language but a cry. Alfred Tennyson, *In Memoriam,* 1850.

Heaven lies about us in our infancy! William Wordsworth, "Ode on Intimations of Immortality," 1807.

ANONYMOUS APHORISMS

A baby is the world's longest suspense story; you have to wait for a generation to see how it turns out.

A mother bears a baby for nine months; then the family has to bear the child for years.

Every adult lives in dread of his own old baby pictures.

Politicians woo adult votes by kissing babies; they'd get more parents' votes if they changed a few diapers.

ANECDOTES

"Now that you've got a baby, you have to plan ahead," said the proud father's boss. "That's how we got the baby," said the proud father.

"When the baby cries," said the pediatrician to the new parents," you have two alternatives—one at each end."

FACTS

Babies remain the focal points of two of the twentieth century's most bitter issues: population limitation and abortion. An increasing number of industrialized nations, including the U.S., are moving downward or leveling off in their birthrate, but increases in the quality of obstetrical and pediatric care are giving more babies the chance to survive. In the past, those same infants would have been doomed. In underdeveloped countries, improved health care is creating an explosion. In 1994, the American infant mortality rate reached an all-time low. Science has helped to equip babies better for the rigors of life, and governments throughout the world are assuming greater responsibility for early childhood care. Since human babies are just about the most helpless living creatures, and the slowest to become self-sufficient, they still are principal victims of both man's and nature's wars and cruelties.

The Child Welfare League of America, 440 First Street, NW, Suite 310, Washington, DC 20001-2085, is an organization of child-care agencies.

B ASEBALL

(See also Sports)

DEFINITIONS   A game played by two teams, usually of nine players each, with bat and ball; the ball used in the game; the national pastime; hardball; sandlot, little league, minor league, and major leagues (American and National leagues).

QUOTATIONS

A baseball club is part of the chemistry of the city. A game isn't just an athletic contest. It's a picnic, a kind of town meeting. Michael Burke, president, New York Yankees, testifying before the New York City Council, 1971.

You've got to be a man to play baseball for a living, but you've got to have a lot of little boy in you, too. Roy Campanella, 1957.

Why do I like baseball? The pay is good, it keeps you out in the fresh air and sunshine and you can't beat them hours. Attributed to umpire Tim Hurst.

Hit 'em where they ain't. Willie Keeler, c. early 1920s.

"Take Me Out to the Ball Game," Jack Norworth, song title, 1908.

"Casey at the Bat," Ernest L. Thayer, poem title, 1888.

But there is no joy in Mudville—Mighty Casey has struck out. Ernest L. Thayer, "Casey at the Bat," 1888.

ANONYMOUS APHORISMS

If at first you don't succeed, try short stop.

Step up to the plate.

Kill the umpire!

Slide, Kelly, slide!

Three strikes, you're out.

The hit and run is on.

No hits, no runs, no errors.

Don't give him anything he can hit.

ANECDOTES

An American took a British friend to a baseball game. In the bottom of the ninth inning, with two out, the home team loaded the bases, and the fans began to cheer. The Britisher, puzzled, asked why the fans were so excited. "There's a man on every base," said the American, "our team has a man on every base." "But," said the Brit, "so does the other side."

Mr. and Mrs. Jones finally got into the ballpark an hour after the baseball game had started. It was a tight pitcher's battle, sixth inning, 0-0. "Good," said Mrs. Jones, "we haven't missed a thing."

FACTS

America's first successful professional team sport and amateur team pastime was dubbed the national pastime many years ago, but it is played around the world. Latin America and Japan adopted their own versions of the game; and Little League champions have come from as far away as Taiwan; many Americans now play for foreign teams such as the Tokyo Carp and the Hanshin Tigers. American professional baseball was racism's Maginot Line until Branch Rickey broke the "color barrier" by bringing Jackie Robinson to the Brooklyn Dodgers after the Second World War. Baseball was the first professional sport to be given exemption from various government regulations governing other businesses. Major league baseball lost some of its innocence during the 234 days of the 1994 players' strike; fans gained their first glimpse of the business behind the game and attendance declined; but America is forgiving of its sports heroes.

The National Baseball Hall of Fame is located in Cooperstown, NY. Main number: (607) 547-7200, library & archive appointments: (607) 547-2101.

B ASKETBALL

(See also Sports)

DEFINITIONS   Game between two teams in which points are scored by throwing a large inflated ball through a basket hoop on the wall; a tall story; dribble, pass and shoot; shooting hoops; one on one; the "Dream Team" (American Olympic team); the Big Ten (Midwestern collegiate conference); the ACC (Southern collegiate conference); "Dean Smith Country" (Billy Packer referring to the University of North Carolina at Chapel Hill NC).

QUOTATION:

The word "retire" means that you can do anything you want from this day on. So if I desire to come back and play again, maybe that's what I want to do. Maybe that's the challenge that I may need someday down the road. I'm not going to close that door. I don't believe in "never." Michael Jordan, interview, October, 1994.

ANONYMOUS APHORISMS:

When it comes to starting a basketball game, a lot of people jump at the chance.

Basketball is America's—and maybe the world's—second favorite indoor sport.

The play-by-play report of a basketball game is a running commentary, a passing phenomenon and a shooting sensation.

Basketball is a game in which nobody tries to hide his light under a basket.

Most professional sports in this country are on the up and up, but basketball is on the up and up and up and up and . . .

In basketball dribbling isn't a mess, it's a talent.

A highboy is either a traditional piece of furniture or a bright new basketball prospect.

Basketball players go back and forth a great deal, but the rules say you can't travel with the ball.

ANECDOTES

They asked the coach why Bill had left the basketball team. "Well," said the coach, "as a forward he was backward, as a center he was always out of position, and he thought the guards should be armed."

Q: Where can you keep shooting and never be shot?

A: On a basketball court.

FACTS

Basketball may well be the most universal of sports. Other sports are as international, but basketball can be played practically anyplace. It was invented by Dr. James Naismith at the YMCA in Springfield, MA, which is also home to the Basketball Hall of Fame. But Naismith's game had one flaw. Someone had to get up on a ladder and retrieve the ball from the elevated basket when points were scored. A Canadian gym coach came up with the idea of cutting a hole in the basket, and from that day forward, the game's popularity soared. As an amateur sport, it is within the economic and geographic reach of even the poorest young people, and is especially popular in urban areas where pavement predominates. Professional basketball was largely confined to the U.S. until the 1980s; now there are professional leagues around the world; but the NBA is the aspiration for any young player. The U.S. "Dream Team" swept up the gold at both the 1992 and 1996 Olympics; the silver and bronze went to Yugoslavia and Lithuania. Another "Dream Team" of sorts, took the gold in the 1936 Berlin Olympics: the American team towered over the rival Canadian team—from an American 6' 6" average to Canada's 6' 1" average height per player; the game was played on a converted clay tennis court, which had recently been rained on, making it extremely slippery. The final score of that game was 19-8.

B OOKS

(See also Literature)

DEFINITIONS Bound volumes of printed sheets of prose, poetry or visual reproductions; "sepulchers of thought" (Henry Wadsworth Longfellow); "the legacies that genius leaves to mankind, to be delivered down from generation to generation" (Joseph Addison); knowledge bound and shelved; "silent conversation" (Walter Savage Landor).

QUOTATIONS

This book has pores. It has features. This book can go under the microscope. You'd find life under the glass, streaming past in infinite profusion. The good writers touch life often. The mediocre ones run a quick hand over her…So now do you see why books are hated and feared? They show the pores in the face of life. Ray Bradbury, *Fahrenheit 451,* 1953.

Some books are to be tasted, others to be swallowed, and some few to be chewed and digested: that is, some books are to be read only in parts, others to be read, but not curiously, and some few to be read wholly, and with diligence and attention. Francis Bacon, Essays: "Of Studies," 1625.

Many books require no thought from those who read them, and for a very simple reason; they made no such demand upon those who wrote them. Charles Caleb Colton, *Lacon,* c.1820s.

Books are the quietest and most constant of friends; they are the most accessible and wisest of counselors, and the most patient of teachers, Charles W. Eliot, *The Happy Life,* 1896.

In the highest civilization, the book is still the highest delight. He who has once known its satisfactions is provided with a resource against calamity. Ralph Waldo Emerson, Letters and Social Aims: "Quotation and Originality," 1876.

Who knows whether in retirement I shall be tempted to the last infirmity of mundane minds, which is to write a book. Attributed to Geoffrey Fisher, Archbishop of Canterbury, 1961.

Books give not wisdom where was none before,/ But where some is, there reading makes it more. Sir John Harington, *Epigrams,* 1613.

Old books, as you well know, are books of the world's youth, and new books are fruits of its age. Oliver Wendell Holmes, *The Professor at the Breakfast-Table,* 1860.

I cannot live without books. Thomas Jefferson, letter to John Adams, 1815.

The love of learning, the sequestered nooks, / And all the sweet serenity of books. Henry Wadsworth Longfellow, "Morituri Salutamus," 1875.

As good almost kill a man as kill a good book: who kills a man kills a reasonable creature, God's image; but he who destroys a good book, kills reason itself, kills the image of God, as it were, in the eye. John Milton, *Areopagitica,* 1644.

All books are divisible into two classes: the books of the hour, and the books of all time. John Ruskin, *Sesame and Lilies,* 1865.

Books are good enough in their way, but they are a mighty bloodless substitute for life. Robert Louis Stevenson, *Virginibus Puerisque,* 1881.

How many a man has dated a new era in his life from the reading of a book. Henry D. Thoreau, *Walden:* "Reading," 1854.

With books, as with men, a very small number play great parts, while the rest are lost in the crowd. Voltaire, *Philosophical Dictionary,* 1764.

There is no such thing as a moral or an immoral book. Books are well written, or badly written. That is all. Oscar Wilde, preface to *The Picture of Dorian Gray,* 1891.

ANONYMOUS APHORISMS

You can't tell a book by its cover.

It's what's between the covers that counts.

Books produce more royalty than kings do.

A book is a constant friend.

A book is new until you have read it.

ANECDOTES

"The book will soon be completely replaced by the Internet," the whiz-kid remarked smugly to his professor. "Really? Then where will you get a book on how to fix your computer?"

The book was a novel, preceded by a statement that declared any resemblance to any real person, living or dead, was purely coincidental. The reviewer wrote that the book fully lived up to that statement.

"Enough about me," said the author to the interviewer. "Have you read my new book?"

FACTS

Although there were handwritten, bound manuscripts and scrolls before there were printing presses, books were very scarce and very expensive, and very few people knew how to read them. Gutenberg's printing press made books available to the masses, and Thomas Edison's electric light gave them the light to read them by after the workday was done. Television, computers, the Internet, and even radio were proclaimed to be the final replacement for conventional books when each first became popular. But more books than ever are being published; and more copies are being sold. The size of the book trade is due largely to several comparatively recent phenomena: the book club—which came into its own during the Second World War—and the inexpensive, mass-market paperback reprint. Book publishing is an international industry. The Frankfurt Book Fair, London Book Fair, and the American Booksellers Association's annual convention are just a few of the conventions that develop the huge market of available titles found on the world's shelves.

The American Booksellers Association is located at 828 South Broadway, Tarrytown, NY 10591; and the Association of American Publishers is at 220 E.23rd Street, New York, NY 10010.

Boxing

(See also Sports)

DEFINITIONS   The pastime of fighting with the fists; the manly art of self-defense; prizefighting; the fights; pugilism; throwing fists; stepping into the ring.

QUOTATIONS

The bigger they come, the harder they fall. Bob Fitzsimmons, comment before his bout with champion Jim Jeffries who won, 1902.

A boxing match is like a cowboy movie. There's got to be good guys and there's got to be bad guys. And that's what people pay for—to see the bad guys get beat. Attributed to Sonny Liston in his obituary in the *The New York Times,* 1971.

He can run but he can't hide. Joe Louis, before his bout with Billy Conn, 1946.

Don't bet on fights. Sports page slogan in *The New York Sun,* c. 1920s.

Fly like a butterfly, sting like a bee. Muhammed Ali, 1965.

ANONYMOUS APHORISMS

When a Sunday punch lands, it gives its target a day of rest.

Here lies a fighter who ran out of gas; / His fists were steel but his jaw was glass.

Boxing is an art with overtones of nobility—you put up your dukes, worry about taking the count and observe the Marquess of Queensberry rules.

Boxing is dueling with gloves on.

Boxing is a case of fist things first.

Prizefighting is a Punch and Judy show without Judy.

Years ago a fighter sometimes telegraphed a punch; now they televise the whole fight.

ANECDOTES

Mr. Jones claims that mugging is a direct descendant of prizefighting, because in both you find men fighting over purses.

"I am opposed to prizefighting," said the reformer, "because it involves brutal conflict." "What do you plan to do about it," asked the reporter. "I will fight it with every weapon at my command," said the reformer.

FACTS

Though it has evolved considerably since its bareknuckle origins, boxing could be considered the oldest sport known to man. Fights were a part of the original Olympic games in ancient Greece—long before the Marquess of Queensberry rules established strict guidelines in the late 1800s. John L. Sullivan was the last and best-known of the great bareknuckle boxers. The sport became more civilized when "Gentleman Jim" Corbett introduced the world to strategic boxing techniques and knocked out Sullivan's brute fighting force in the "fight of the century." Besides introducing the Marquess of Queensberry rules to the American boxing ring, Corbett also ushered in the era of the eloquent boxer—a crown that wasn't duly filled again until Olympic gold-medalist Cassius Clay won the heavyweight title in the mid-1960s. Other boxing greats like Sonny Liston, Joe Louis, Floyd Patterson, George Foreman, and Olympic-medalist Sugar Ray Leonard also contributed to the elevation of the American boxing profession. There are now many governing bodies at the amateur and professional levels; the best known are the WBC, WBA, and IBF. Attempts to ban boxing have failed—though each high-profile injury brings new cries for regulation. With title purses in the tens of millions, and fans in the hundreds of millions, it is unlikely that the sport will fade in the near future.

BUILDING

DEFINITIONS   The act of constructing or erecting a structure; construction; carpentry; the edifice complex; a structure with walls and a roof; architecture; the monuments of civilization.

QUOTATIONS

God is in the details. Attributed to architect Mies van der Rohe, c. mid-20th century.

An architect's most useful tools are an eraser at the drafting board, and a wrecking bar at the site. Attributed to Frank Lloyd Wright, c. mid-20th century.

Form follows function—that has been misunderstood. Form and function should be one, joined in a spiritual union. Attributed to Frank Lloyd Wright, c. mid-20th century.

Houses are built to live in, not to look on; therefore, let use be preferred before uniformity, except where both may be had. Francis Bacon, *Essays:* "Of Building," 1623.

He builded better than he knew... Ralph Waldo Emerson, "The Problem," 1840.

A man builds a fine house; and now he has a master, and a task for life: he is to furnish, watch, show it, and keep it in repair, the rest of his days. Ralph Waldo Emerson, *Society and Solitude:* "Works and Days," 1870.

In Building, rather believe any man than an Artificer for matter of charges. Should they tell thee all the cost at the first, it would blast a young Builder in the budding. Thomas Fuller, *The Holy State and the Profane State,* 1642.

Light, God's eldest daughter, is a principal beauty in a building. Thomas Fuller, *The Holy State and the Profane State,* 1642.

Build thee more stately mansions, O my soul… Oliver Wendell Holmes, "The Chambered Nautilus," 1858.

To build is to be robbed. Samuel Johnson, *The Idler,* June 23, 1759.

Ah, to build, to build! / That is the noblest of all the arts. Henry Wadsworth Longfellow, *Michael Angelo,* 1882.

When we build, let us think that we build for ever. John Ruskin, *Modern Painters,* 1843.

We require from buildings, as from men, two kinds of goodness: first, doing their practical duty well; then that they be graceful and pleasing in doing it. John Ruskin, *The Stones of Venice,* 1851.

ANONYMOUS APHORISMS

A big city building is one story on top of another.

It isn't so much what you build as how well you build it.

A building is what you make of it.

They call it a high rise because that's what happens to its taxes.

ANECDOTES

Mr. Brown: I hear that you are planning to park a trailer here instead of putting up a building. Mr. Jones: That is without foundation.

A builder who was known for the shabby quality of his structures invited the city planning commission to inspect a plot of land that he had bought in a crowded area. He asked them what kind of building they felt would serve the community best in that location. Their answer was unanimous. They all suggested he build a park.

FACTS

Architecture—the art of building buildings—is many businesses rolled into one: designed by architects as lasting monuments to their civilized functions; financed by dollars from savings institutions and commercial banks; built with building materials whose manufacture, storage, and transportation are basic industries in themselves; engineered by masons and steelworkers; and permitted by local governments. The value of buildings is directly related to the revenues of government, since so much of our local tax system is based on real estate and building taxes. Construction rates are also a leading measure of national prosperity. The U.S. Census Bureau issues regular reports on national and regional housing starts and building permits under the heading of U.S. Economic Indicators.

The U.S. Census Bureau can provide more information concerning the housing starts data through the Housing Starts Branch at (301) 457-4666; and on building permits through the Building Permits Branch at (301) 457-1321.

Business

DEFINITIONS   Commercial, industrial or mercantile enterprise; trade; commerce; manufacture, distribution, buying or selling of goods or services; the seeking of profit in other than professional capacities; the working day, as opposed to time devoted to leisure or pleasure; capitalism; that which, when you don't have any, you go out of; enterprise and the entrepreneurs who run it.

QUOTATIONS

There is a sense in which the businessmen of America represent America, because America has devoted herself time out of mind to the arts and achievements of peace, and business is the organization of the energies of peace. President Woodrow Wilson, speech at Shadow Lawn, NJ, September 23, 1916.

I think business is very simple. Profit. Loss. Take the sales, subtract the costs, you get this big positive number. The math is really quite simple. Bill Gates, in *U.S. News & World Report,* February 15, 1993.

Few people do business well who do nothing else. Lord Chesterfield, letter to his son, August 7, 1749.

Civilization and profits go hand in hand. Vice President-elect Calvin Coolidge, November 27, 1920.

The business of America is business. President Calvin Coolidge, January 17, 1925.

Keep thy shop and thy shop will keep thee. Benjamin Franklin, *Poor Richard's Almanac,* 1735.

If you would have your business done, go; if not, send. Benjamin Franklin, *Poor Richard's Almanac,* 1758.

The most sensible people to be met within society are men of business and of the world, who argue from what they see and know, instead of spinning cobweb distinctions of what things ought to be. William Hazlitt, "On the Ignorance of the Learned," 1821.

It is just as important that business keep out of government as that government keep out of business. Herbert Hoover, presidential candidate, October 22, 1928.

I hold it to be our duty to see that the wage-worker, the small producer, the ordinary consumer, shall get their fair share of the benefit of business prosperity. But it either is or ought to be evident to everyone that business has to prosper before anybody can get any benefit from it. Theodore Roosevelt, February 1, 1912.

To business that we love we rise betime. / And go to't with delight. William Shakespeare, *Antony and Cleopatra*, 1607.

This world is a place of business. Henry D. Thoreau, published after his death.

In democracies, nothing is more great or brilliant than commerce; it attracts the attention of the public, and fills the imagination of the multitude; all passions of energy are directed towards it. Alexis de Tocqueville, *Democracy in America, Vol. II*, 1840.

Put all your eggs in the one basket and—WATCH THAT BASKET. Mark Twain, *The Tragedy of Puddinhead Wilson*, 1894; also attributed to Andrew Carnegie, 1885.

ANONYMOUS APHORISMS

Business is a two-way street.

The secret of business is simple: buy low and sell high.

Business before pleasure.

There's no room for sentiment in business.

The customer is always right.

The difference between a bad investor and a good investor is how quickly they panic.

ANECDOTES

Business is a matter of perspective, and I can illustrate it. A maker of backup lights is happy to meet reverses.

Then there was the man whose life was so tied up in his business that his family organized a union so he'd have to meet them around the table.

"If business is hard work," asked the skeptic, "then how come when businessmen relax what they do is sometimes described as monkey business?"

FACTS

Business is an ancient human occupation, but it deals more and more with new products and new services. In our own time, these have included television, jet airplanes, cellular phones, fax machines, and computers. The number of American corporations tripled from 2.8 million in 1980, to nearly 9 million in 1993. The number of employee-owned and -operated corporations—through various employee stock ownership plans (ESOPs)—has had a similarly dramatic increase, rising from 1,601 companies in 1975, to over 9,700 participating firms in 1992, involving over 11.1 million employees.

In the 1967 movie *The Graduate,* a suburban businessman summed up the future in a single word: plastics. Today, that word might be: the Internet, hi-tech, geriatrics, or service.

For current information see the U.S. Department of Commerce periodical, *Survey of Current Business;* or consult the latest *Statistical Abstract of the U.S.*

CANDIDATES

(See also Elections, Political Parties, Voting)

DEFINITIONS   Those who seek or are proposed for a particular office or honor; incumbents and challengers; those whose hats are in the ring; lame ducks, white knights and dark horses; running targets; those who ask not what they can do for their country, but what their country can do for them.

QUOTATIONS

In war there are rules. Even mud wrestling has rules. Only politics has no rules. Ross Perot, in *U.S. News & World Report,* May 17, 1993.

Politics makes strange bedfellows rich. Wayne G. Haisley, *New Teeth in Old Saws,* 1928.

You can't beat somebody with nobody. Attributed to Joseph Cannon, Speaker of the House of Representatives, c. early 20th century.

I do not choose to run. President Calvin Coolidge, August 2, 1927.

Offices are acceptable here as elsewhere, and whenever a man has cast a longing eye on them, a rottenness begins in his conduct. Vice President Thomas Jefferson, letter to Tench Coxe, May 21, 1799.

For many are called but few are chosen. *Matthew,* 22:14.

If nominated, I will not accept; if elected, I will not serve. General William T. Sherman, telegram to Republican National Convention in Chicago, June 5, 1884.

The idea that you can merchandise candidates for high office like breakfast cereal…is, I think, the ultimate indignity for the democratic process. Illinois Governor Adlai E. Stevenson, accepting Democratic Presidential nomination in Chicago, IL. August 18, 1956.

ANONYMOUS APHORISMS

Before the people raise their voice, how many are called "the people's choice."

Very few candidates are actually drafted; most are swept along by a lot of wind, but it's a wind, not a draft.

Running for office is often a primary consideration.

Nobody ever ran for office against his or her will. It takes only one word to say no to a nomination.

In this country they run for office and in England they stand for office. It doesn't matter as long as they don't lie for office.

A favorite son candidacy is more of a courtesy than a candidacy.

ANECDOTES

Early in the primary stages of the 1960 Presidential election, Senator John F. Kennedy told another senator he had dreamed that the Lord above had told him he would be the nominee. The other senator said it was strange because he'd had the same dream and the Lord had told him he would be the nominee. The two senators told their story of the matching dreams to senatorial colleague, Lyndon Johnson. And Senator Johnson—according to Senator Kennedy—remarked, "I can't remember tapping either of you for the job."

FACTS

One of America's favorite exercises is running for office. In the 1976 Presidential campaign, there were 125 candidates before the summer conventions. While there are less than 600 elective posts in the federal government, there are some 80,000 state and local governments and governmental units. And the 50 largest U.S. cities have elected city boards or councils with more than 650 elected members in just that one particular category. An individual voter is called upon to choose among candidates for the Presidency (through choice of electors), the House, the Senate, the governor's chair, the state legislature, the city or town council, judges in various courts, school boards, district attorneys etc. And if that roster does not provide enough candidacies, there are also races for offices in associations, unions and all kinds of institutional governing boards.

Censorship

(See also Books, Journalism, Liberty,
Motion Pictures, Radio, Television)

DEFINITIONS Prohibition of the publication or utterance of material; excision of passages from what is permitted to be published or uttered; suppress agentry; "Big Brother" (George Orwell).

QUOTATIONS

Don't join the book burners. Don't think you are going to conceal thoughts by concealing evidence that they ever existed. President Dwight D. Eisenhower, speech at Dartmouth College, June 14, 1953.

...every burned book or house enlightens the world... Ralph Waldo Emerson, *Essays, First Series:* "Compensation," 1841.

Every society has a right to preserve public peace and order, and therefore has a good right to prohibit the propagation of opinions which have a dangerous tendency. Samuel Johnson, according to James Boswell in *Life of Samuel Johnson,* May 7, 1773.

If all mankind, minus one, were of one opinion, and only one person were of the contrary opinion, mankind would be no more justified in silencing that one person, than he, if he had the power, would be justified in silencing mankind. John Stuart Mill, *On Liberty,* 1859.

We can never be sure that the opinion we are endeavoring to stifle is a false opinion; and if we were sure, stifling it would be an evil still. John Stuart Mill, *On Liberty,* 1859.

And though all the winds of doctrine were let loose to play upon the earth, so truth be in the field, we do injuriously by licensing and prohibiting to misdoubt her strength. Let her and falsehood grapple; whoever knew truth put to the worse, in a free and open encounter? John Milton, *Areopagitica,* 1644.

When indecent books no longer find a market, when pornographic films can no longer draw an audience, when obscene plays open to empty houses, then the tide will turn. Government can maintain the dikes against obscenity, but only people can turn back the tide. President Richard M. Nixon, message to the U.S. Congress, May 2, 1969.

Tell it not in Gath, publish it not in the streets of Askelon; lest the daughters of the Philistines rejoice... *Samuel II,* 1:20.

The moment we begin to fear the opinions of others and hesitate to tell the truth that is in us, and from motives of policy are silent when we should speak, the divine floods of light and life no longer flow into our souls. Elizabeth Cady Stanton, 1890.

Once a government is committed to the principle of silencing the voice of opposition, it has only one way to go, and that is down the path of increasingly repressive measures, until it becomes a source of terror to all its citizens and creates a country where everyone lives in fear. President Harry S. Truman, August 8, 1950.

ANONYMOUS APHORISMS

The noncontroversial dies, but the banned plays on.

Blessed are the censors, for they shall inhibit the earth.

What you don't know can hurt you.

Given his choice, the censor will choose asterisks over other risks every time.

The almighty censor, good old Julius Scissor . . .

What the public is not permitted to see or hear or read, it generally imagines much more vividly. Why else would show business for so many years have been advertising happily that this or that presentation was banned in Boston or given an X rating? Forbidden fruit, as the story of Adam and Eve bears witness, is most inviting.

ANECDOTES

NBC-TV's "The Tonight Show" host Johnny Carson used to demonstrate the way censorship can make things seem even more objectionable. He would take a familiar passage and remove words here and there. If you read or heard these lines and were told that the words removed were objectionable ones, what would you believe the original really said? Little Miss Muffet [blank] on a [blank], eating her [blank] and [blank]; along came a [blank] and [blank] down [blank] her and [blank] Miss Muffet away.

Censorship in modern times has not merely included banning material; it has also included the forced inclusion of material or messages. This in turn has led to some really creative writing, such as the letter from an American who had gone to explore conditions in a total dictatorship and wrote back from there: "What you have been reading about terror and fear here is absolutely untrue. Please be sure to tell what I have said to the editors and the broadcasters, and above all tell it to the Marines."

FACTS

Official statistics on censorship are hard to come by, impossible to believe, and rarely even issued. Many countries, while denying that they have official censorship, impose heavy penalties on those who speak or write against the official party line. Even in free countries there are ongoing censorship problems such as the so-called gag rules limiting news reports in connection with a trial; the imposition of secrecy classifications on government documents; and the selection or refusal of shelf space for books in libraries. Many American journalistic and civil liberties groups maintain current dossiers of pending censorship cases. There are also a number of international organizations monitoring censorship around the world.

Among key advocacy organizations are the American Society of Newspaper Editors, the Reporters Committee for Freedom of the Press, and the American Library Association.

Charity

DEFINITIONS Giving assistance to those in need; alms; a helping hand; poor comfort; "the sterilized milk of human kindness" (Oliver Herford).

QUOTATIONS

We are destroying human spirits when we create a [welfare] system which is focused totally on the elimination of deprivation, instead of a system which encourages autonomy, encourages people to develop their skills, encourages people to live lives of disciplined virtue… [Under the current system,] we're mandating virtue, but paying for vice. Bret Schundler, in *Christianity Today,* June 20, 1994.

A man who dies rich, dies in disgrace. Attributed to Andrew Carnegie, 1902.

In charity to all mankind, bearing no malice or ill-will to any human being….John Quincy Adams, letter to A. Bronson Alcott, July 30, 1838.

He that defers his charity until he is dead is, if a man weighs it rightly, rather liberal of another man's than of his own. Francis Bacon, c. 17th century.

Charity suffereth long, and is kind; charity envieth not; charity vaunteth not itself, is not puffed up. *Corinthians I,* 8:1.

And now abideth faith, hope, charity, these three; but the greatest of these is charity. *Corinthians I,* 13:13.

We do not quite forgive a giver. The hand that feeds us is in some danger of being bitten. Ralph Waldo Emerson, *Essays, Second Series:* "Gifts," 1844.

He gives twice that gives soon; i.e., he will soon be called to give again. Benjamin Franklin, *Poor Richard's Almanac,* 1752.

…charity must be built upon justice. Henry George, *The Condition of Labor,* 1891.

It has been said that we feed the hungry, clothe the naked, bind up the wounds of the man beaten by thieves, pour oil and wine into them, set him on our own beast and bring him to the inn, because we receive ourselves pleasure from these acts. Thomas Jefferson, letter to Thomas Law, June 13, 1814.

With malice toward none; with charity for all; with firmness in the right, as God gives us to see the right... President Abraham Lincoln, second inaugural address, March 4, 1865.

...when thou doest alms, let not thy left hand know what thy right hand doeth. *Matthew,* 4:3.

As for charity, it is a matter in which the immediate effect on the persons directly concerned, and the ultimate consequence to the general good, are apt to be at complete war with one another. John Stuart Mill, *The Subjection of Women,* 1869.

...charity shall cover the multitude of sins. *Peter I,* 4:8.

He that hath pity upon the poor lendeth unto the Lord; and that which he hath given will he pay him again. *Proverbs,* 19:17.

Blessed is he that considereth the poor... *Psalms,* 41:1.

ANONYMOUS APHORISMS

Charity begins at home.

He that has no charity deserves none.

He gives twice who gives quickly.

Giving honors the giver.

Thank the Lord that you can give, instead of depending on others to give to you.

ANECDOTES

The 12th-century Jewish sage Moses Maimonides outlined eight grades of charity: The first is to give reluctantly; the second is to give cheerfully but not sufficiently; the third is to give cheerfully and sufficiently, but only after being asked; the fourth is to give cheerfully and sufficiently and without being asked, but to put it in the recipient's hand in such a way as to make him feel ashamed; the fifth grade of charity is to let the recipient know who the donor is but not let the donor know the identity of those receiving the charity; the sixth grade of charity is to know who is getting your charity but to be unknown to them; the seventh is to have neither the donor nor the recipient aware of the other's identity; but the eighth—and highest— grade of charity is to forestall it by enabling your fellow humans to have the where- withal to earn a livelihood.

The tightwad decided that instead of giving money to charity he would give of him- self in good deeds. That morning, as he was headed for the office, he saw an old bent-over lady, standing on a corner. The traffic was racing by; so he came up to her;

took her by the arm; and gently yet firmly guided her across the street. "That," the tightwad proudly announced, "was part of my pledge to give of myself by helping others." "Helping others!" cried the old lady, "I was waiting for a bus!"

FACTS

In addition to the long-standing efforts of religious organizations in the U.S., there has been great growth in number of nonreligious charitable organizations. Limitations on tax deductibility of contributions to charities and the economic slump of 1987 marked a sweeping downturn in the amount of corporate donations received by many charities and other nonprofit organizations. However, increased giving by foundations, bequests, and individuals has increased steadily—almost making up for the lost corporate funds. The majority of private philanthropic contributions by far goes to religious institutions—and religiously based organizations like the Salvation Army—with education second and health third.

The Foundation Center, an information center, is at 79 Fifth Avenue, New York, NY 10003-3076.

CHILDREN

(See also Babies, Parents)

DEFINITIONS
Young human beings, who are older than babies and younger than adults; small fry; the tomorrow generation; youngsters; pre-adolescents; creatures that are always halfway between their parents and the television set; kids; the lunchbox set; our future.

QUOTATIONS

Grown-ups never understand anything for themselves, and it is tiresome for children to be always and forever explaining things to them. Antoine de Saint-Exupéry, *The Little Prince,* 1943.

Backward, turn backward, O Time, in your flight, / Make me a child again, just for tonight. Elizabeth Chase Akers, "Rock Me to Sleep, Mother," 1860.

Late children, early orphans. Benjamin Franklin, *Poor Richard's Almanac,* 1742.

Children are without pity. Jean de La Fontaine, *Fables,* c. 17th century.

Between the dark and the daylight, / When the night is beginning to lower, / Comes a pause in the day's occupations, / That is known as the children's hour. Henry Wadsworth Longfellow, "The Children's Hour," 1860.

Suffer the little children to come unto me, and forbid them not: for of such is the kingdom of God. *Mark,* 10:14.

The childhood shows the man, / As morning shows the day. John Milton, *Paradise Regained,* 1671.

Train up a child in the way he should go: and when he is old, he will not depart from it. *Proverbs,* 23: 6.

Give a little love to a child, and you get a great deal back. John Ruskin, *The Crown of Wild Olive,* 1866.

A child should always say what's true, / And speak when he is spoken to, / And behave mannerly at table: / At least as far as he is able. Robert Louis Stevenson, "Whole Duty of Children," 188s.

I have found the best way to give advice to your children is to find out what they want and then advise them to do it. Harry S. Truman, May 27, 1955.

Children begin by loving their parents. After a time, they judge them. Rarely, if ever, do they forgive them. Oscar Wilde, *A Woman of No Importance,* 1893.

ANONYMOUS APHORISMS

The two things children wear out are clothes and parents.

The worst children are always somebody else's.

The universal language of children is called "gimme," otherwise known as "I wanna."

Children should be seen and not heard.

Children are poor people's riches.

The child is father to the man.

ANECDOTES

"Where do I come from?" the little girl asked her mother. The mother launched a long explanation about the birds and the bees. "No," said the child impatiently. "My friend Susie comes from Boston. Where do I come from?"

The garrulous child kept pestering the distinguished houseguest and finally told the distracted adult, "Gee, you certainly know a lot." The adult said, "What am I supposed to say to that?" "You're supposed to say thank you," said the child.

FACTS

In 1860, about half the American population was less than 20 years old; in the 1970s, 35 percent were teenaged or younger; in 1994, that segment of the population represented less than 25 percent of the national total. People are living longer and children are not quite as dominant in the composition of the total population. Today's child is part of a generally smaller family than heretofore, with fewer siblings, better nutrition, and better medical care, as well as more years of education. But all is not bright. More children today—than at any time in the past—are confronted by marriages ending up in divorce courts. But fortunately, being the child of divorced parents or being born out of wedlock are no longer the bar sinister that they were in the past; and one out of four families is headed by a single parent. Thus, the stigma traditionally attached to these households has generally faded.

Statistics are available from U.S. Public Health Service and U.S. Census Bureau, as well as annual almanacs.

CITIZENSHIP

DEFINITIONS   The condition of owing allegiance to and/or being a participant in a governmental jurisdiction such as a city or nation; the attributes of participation in community activities; allegiance to a nation; the only ship where everyone is expected to be a part of the crew; what everyone expects his neighbors to demonstrate.

QUOTATIONS

Amongst the virtues of the good citizen are those of fortitude and patience. William Cobbett, *Advice to Young Men,* 1829.

Presidents learn—perhaps sooner than others—that our destiny is fashioned by what all of us do, by the deeds and desires of each citizen, as one tiny drop of water after another ultimately makes a big river. President Lyndon B. Johnson, September 5, 1966.

Political activity is the highest responsibility of a citizen. Senator John F. Kennedy of Massachusetts, presidential candidate, October 20, 1960 .

The first requisite of a good citizen in this republic of ours is that he shall be able and willing to pull his weight. President Theodore Roosevelt, November 11, 1902.

No man can be a good citizen unless he has a wage more than sufficient to cover the bare cost of living, and hours of labor short enough so that after his day's work is done he will have time and energy to bear his share in the management of the community, to help in carrying the general load. We keep countless men from being good citizens by the conditions of life with which we surround them. Theodore Roosevelt, August 31, 1910.

I am a citizen not of Athens or Greece, but of the world. Socrates, as reported by later chroniclers.

Who is the Forgotten Man? He is the clean, quiet, virtuous, domestic citizen who pays his debts and his taxes and is never heard of out of his little circle. William Graham Sumner, "The Forgotten Man," 1883.

Citizenship is man's basic right, for it is nothing less than the right to have rights. U.S. Supreme Court Chief Justice Earl Warren, commenting on *Perez v. Brownell,* 1958.

Citizens by birth or choice of a common country, that country has a right to concentrate your affections. President George Washington, farewell address, 1796.

ANONYMOUS APHORISMS

A good citizen doesn't rely on government. Government relies on him.

A good citizen is her own best friend.

Citizenship is a right for the native born and a goal for the foreign born.

Citizenship is apt to be more appreciated by those who earn it than by those born to it.

A good citizen is one who doesn't always keep his mouth shut.

The more you take part in government, the less government will take part of you.

Oppressed foreigners seek American citizenship for shelter, while wealthy Americans apply to the Bahamas seeking shelters.

ANECDOTES

When Mrs. Schultz got her citizenship papers, she had them framed and placed on the living room wall where previously she had kept a picture of her home town in the Old Country. "I know where I came from," she explained, "but now I want to see what I stand for."

Mr. Brown was active in many different organizations, and he kept ringing his neighbors' doorbells trying to get them to take part in the various community activities. "He's a very good citizen," said one neighbor to another. "No," said the second neighbor, "he's just a guy looking for good citizens."

FACTS

Citizenship began as the privilege of participating in the affairs of the community. In ancient Greece, citizens were those property owners entitled to vote. In feudal England, there were gradations of citizenship ranging from the serfs—who had no rights—to the barons—who asserted for the normal rights of citizenship by writing the Magna Carta and forcing their king to sign it. In the United States and other nations, noncitizens are fully protected, but nevertheless subjected to entry and residency requirements which do not apply to natural citizens of that nation. In some other nations, noncitizens face discrimination in traveling rights, location of residence, and the right to conduct business. Naturalization is a relatively simple process in the U. S., but in some other nations it is difficult or virtually impossible. Citizenship entitles the citizen to the protection of the home government when traveling abroad; although refugees can often travel as stateless persons under the protection of international agreements.

CITY LIFE

DEFINITIONS   Living in a modern, high-population-density metropolitan community; urban multiple dwelling, mass-transportation existence; the big apple (New York City), the windy city (Chicago), The City (San Francisco); metropolitanism; cosmopolitanism.

QUOTATIONS

...a city of many people can rarely, if ever, be well governed... Aristotle, *Politics,* c. 4th century BC.

If you would be known, and not know, vegetate in a village; if you would know, and not be known, live in a city. Charles Caleb Colton, *Lacon,* c. 1820s.

Cities degrade us by magnifying trifles. Ralph Waldo Emerson, *The Conduct of Life:* "Culture," 1860.

The city is recruited from the country. Ralph Waldo Emerson, *Essays, Second Series:* "Manners," 1844.

Great cities seldom rest; if there be none / T'invade from far, they'll find worse foes at home. Robert Herrick, *Hesperides,* 1648.

When we get piled upon one another in large cities, as in Europe, we shall become as corrupt as Europe... Thomas Jefferson, letter to James Madison, December 20, 1787.

To say the least, a town life makes one more tolerant and liberal in one's judgment of others. Henry Wadsworth Longfellow, *Hyperion,* 1839.

We need help, and we need it yesterday. Cleveland Mayor Carl Stokes, at U.S. Senate hearing, June 3, 1971.

I love to see the other mayors; misery loves company. Seattle Mayor Wesley C. Uhlman, April 21, 1971.

A great city is that which has the greatest men and women... Walt Whitman, "Song of the Broad-Axe," 1856.

ANONYMOUS APHORISMS

City people think they are the smartest, but that's where the population is the most dense.

A city is a large town made up of people being lonely together.

The modern city has skyscrapers reaching for the heavens because it has run out of room on earth.

In the country you live longer than in the city—or does it just seem longer?

In the cities these days they worry more about parking than about parks.

America is becoming one large urban community, in which the components are separated from each other by traffic jams.

ANECDOTES

One recent exile from big-city life told his friend, "I prefer the country to the city, because you don't have to rush." But his city-loving friend scoffed, "Maybe that's because there's nothing to rush to or from."

When people are young, they leave the country to come to the city. When they are old, they leave the city to go to the country. But what do you think makes them old?

"I love the big city because I can do whatever I want to without anybody bothering me," said Mr. Smith. "Funny," said Mr. Jones, "that's precisely why I moved out of the city."

FACTS

In the U.S.—as in most of the world—the percentage of the total population living in urban as opposed to rural places rose steadily during the first 75 years of the twentieth century. In 1975, about 75 percent of the American population was urban; and by 1992, cities housed 80 percent of the population. However, our cities and suburbs are spreading out, with slightly less density. Business as well as residency is shifting from central cities to suburban rings, prompted by rise in urban crime rates, mid-city transportation difficulties, population increases, and new building. Suburbs, however, mature into urban centers as they grow.

The National League of Cities is at 1301 Pennsylvania Ave. NW, Washington, D.C. 20004-1701.

CIVILIZATION

(See also Society)

DEFINITIONS   A developed culture and mode of life; man's "improvements" on nature; man's advance from pushing a plow to pushing a button; the triumph of the bathtub over the outdoor shower.

QUOTATIONS

Every advance in civilization has been denounced as unnatural while it was recent. Bertrand Russell, *A History of Western Philosophy*, 1945.

The beginning of civilization is marked by an intense legality; that legality is the very condition of its existence, the bond which ties it together; but that legality—that tendency to impose a settled customary yoke upon all men and all actions—if it goes on, kills out the variability implanted by nature, and makes different man and different ages facsimiles of other men and other ages, as we see them so often. Walter Bagehot, *Physics and Politics*, 1869.

For the first time in history it is now possible to take care of everybody at a higher standard of living than any have ever known. Only ten years ago the 'more with less' technology reached the point where this could be done. All humanity now has the option of becoming enduringly successful. Buckminster Fuller, 1980.

The whole history of civilization is strewn with creeds and institutions which were invaluable at first, and deadly afterwards. Buckminster Fuller, 1980.

Civilization and profits go hand in hand. Vice President Calvin Coolidge, November 27, 1920.

Increased means and increased leisure are the two civilizers of man. Benjamin Disraeli, April 8, 1872.

The civilized man has built a coach, but has lost the use of his feet. He is supported on crutches, but lacks so much support of muscle. He has a fine Geneva watch, but he fails of the skill to tell the hour by the sun. Ralph Waldo Emerson, *Essays, First Series:* "Self-Reliance," 1841.

The true test of civilization is, not the census, nor the size of cities, nor the crops—no, but the kind of man the country turns out. Ralph Waldo Emerson, *Society and Solitude:* "Civilization," 1870.

A sufficient measure of civilization is the influence of good women. Ralph Waldo Emerson, *Society and Solitude:* "Civilization," 1870.

A decent provision for the poor is the true test of civilization. Samuel Johnson, 1770.

A civilization without culture and art is no civilization. New York Governor Nelson A. Rockefeller, August 1970.

Civilization is the making of civil persons. John Ruskin, *The Crown of Wild Olive*, 1866.

ANONYMOUS APHORISMS

Civilization is what took the country away from the native people.

Civilization, like beauty, is in the eye of the beholder.

Civilization is a process whereby those who have already experienced it impose it on others.

Civilization is always our way of doing things, compared to theirs.

Civilization is what separates human beings from the beasts.

ANECDOTES

The man wandered, alone in the trackless waste and past the towering mountainside gleaming with wildflowers, walking on and on, desperate. At last he came to a change in the landscape, a desolate little valley in which he saw an automobile junkyard. "Thank the Lord," he said, "I've finally reached civilization."

The upperclassman separated the two freshmen who were fighting each other. "Civilized people settle their differences across the table," he said. "Or under it," said a passing professor.

FACTS

Most social groups regard themselves as civilized, and see the ways of the rest of the world as uncivilized. Westerners thought they were bringing civilization to the Far East, while Orientals felt they were being invaded by barbarians. Indigenous peoples in the Americas had what they regarded as civilized ways of life, with their own array of complex cultures and subcultures; standards of conduct and morality; and decorative art; but the European colonists thought that what they imposed on the Americas—and the way they imposed their form of civilization—was civilized. The entire course of human history has been marked by clashes between different civilizations and their rise and fall.

See the writings of such historians as Arnold Toynbee, H.G. Wells, and Oswald Spengler, as well as the works of anthropologist Joseph Campbell.

C LUBS

(See also Fraternities)

DEFINITIONS   Groups of people associated for a common purpose; membership organizations which establish their own criteria for admission; places where members of an organization meet; home away from home; "an assembly of good fellows, meeting under certain conditions" (Samuel Johnson).

QUOTATIONS

I don't want to belong to any club that will accept me as a member. Attributed to Groucho Marx, c. 1930s.

No place in England where everyone can go is considered respectable. This is the genesis of the club—out of the Housewife by Respectability. George Moore, *Confessions of a Young Man,* 1888.

Good company and good discourse are the very sinews of virtue. Izaak Walton, *The Compleat Angler,* 1653.

Every boy needs a good club. New York Boy's Clubs slogan, c. 1980.

ANONYMOUS APHORISMS

A club is a mutual association of people who like each other's society.

A country club is part park and part parking lot.

If you want to be a member of the club, you have to pay your dues.

A club has to have more than one person and it also has to exclude more than one person. If everybody's a member, it is no longer a club.

The more exclusive a club is, the more people want to get in.

Clubs used to be meeting places for like-minded people; now they are ways of getting chartered airline rates.

A club may be judged by its choice of members, and an individual by choice of clubs.

ANECDOTES

Q:Do you have any problems with dues at the club? A: No, just with the don'ts.

This particular club—which shall be nameless—was notorious for the single-minded fervor with which it espoused the status quo. "Indeed," said one observer, "it wasn't just a club, it was a blunt instrument."

FACTS

The modern club is a lineal descendant of the British coffeehouse clubs where people met to dine and talk during the 17th and 18th centuries. Membership organizations also have a tradition which goes back to fraternal orders of rather ancient vintage as well as to the medieval crafts and trade guilds. The Gale Research Company's Encyclopaedia of Associations—which is confined to national organizations—lists thousands of such groups and that number is far exceeded by local groups. However, the heyday of the professional organization suffered a severe setback in the 1980s when a restructuring of federal and state tax codes curtailed the deductibility of membership dues for professional and trade associations. Some failed, but many survived on the strength of their active membership.

COLLEGE

(See also Alumni, Education, School)

DEFINITIONS   An institution of higher education, granting either a degree or a certificate of accomplishment beyond the secondary or high school level; the groves of academe; sheepskin alley; the alma mater; the hallowed halls and ivy walls; "places where pebbles are polished and diamonds are dimmed" (Robert Ingersoll); the ivory tower.

QUOTATIONS

We must always uphold the idea of our colleges as incubators of ideas and havens for free thought. Hillary Rodham Clinton, First Lady, speech at University of Pennsylvania commencement, May 17, 1993.

America short-changes half its youth, the half that doesn't go to college. Harold Howe II, U.S. Commissioner of Education, in *The Washington Post,* November 18, 1988.

A university should be a place of light, of liberty, and of learning. Benjamin Disraeli, speech in House of Commons, 1873.

Colleges, in like manner, have their indispensable office—to teach elements. But they can only highly serve us, when they aim not to drill, but to create; when they gather from far every ray of various genius to their hospitable halls, and, by the concentrated fires, set the hearts of their youth on flame. Ralph Waldo Emerson, "The American Scholar," 1837.

One of the benefits of a college education is to show the boy its little avail. Ralph Waldo Emerson, *The Conduct of Life:* "Culture," 1860.

Learn to give / Money to colleges while you live. / Don't be silly and think you'll try / To bother the colleges, when you die, / with codicil this, and codicil that, / That Knowledge may starve while Law grows fat... Oliver Wendell Holmes, "Parson Turell's Legacy," 1857.

The idea of a college education for all young people of capacity, provided at nominal cost by their own states, is very peculiarly American. We in America invented the idea. We in America have developed it with remarkable speed. President Lyndon B. Johnson, August 13, 1964.

It might be said that I have the best of both worlds: a Harvard education and a Yale degree. President John F. Kennedy, a Harvard alumnus accepting an honorary degree at Yale, June 11, 1962.

The most conservative persons I ever met are college undergraduates. Woodrow Wilson, president, Princeton University, November 19, 1905.

The use of a university is to make young gentlemen as unlike their fathers as possible. President Woodrow Wilson, October 24, 1914.

ANONYMOUS APHORISMS

A college diploma used to be a license to look for a job. Now it is a license to look for a higher degree.

There are two classes in every college—passers and failures.

College is a storehouse of learning because so little is taken away.

It says something about the popular attitude toward college that adults speak of their children having a choice: Go to college or go to work. When did they become opposites?

For lots of students their college letter is X: the unknown quantity.

ANECDOTES

College professors are apt to be more subtle than secondary and primary school teachers in rebuking their students. A college professor was in the middle of an important point when the bell rang to end the period. The students began leaving immediately, without waiting for the teacher's point among his words of wisdom. "One moment," said the dismayed professor, "I have a few more pearls."

When Clark Kerr was President of the University of California he said that "the three major administrative problems on a campus are sex for the students, athletics for the alumni and parking for the faculty." But that was a college generation ago. Now, with the financial crisis for higher education, the problems are fees from the students, contributions from the alumni and berths for the faculty.

FACTS

In 1963, there were 3.28 million undergraduate students in degree-granting U.S. colleges. Enrollment peaked in 1984 at 6.43 million, and slipped to 5.92 million in 1994 as the U.S. population aged. The U.S. National Center for Education Statistics found that the percentage of persons aged 18 to 21 attending college had risen from 33.2 percent in 1960, to 48.4 percent in 1974, and was expected to go a bit higher—at least until 1984. In 1970, there were 50 public college students for every 18 private college students; and for 1984, the forecast was 76 public college students to 17 private school students. In public and private colleges, tuition and required fees have more than doubled since 1980. Public institutions, of course, are still charging less than private colleges.

Communication

(See also Journalism, Radio, Television)

DEFINITIONS   Transmitting and receiving facts or information; dissemination of knowledge; getting the message across.

QUOTATIONS

The difference between the right word and a word is the difference between lightning and a lightning bug. Attributed to Mark Twain.

...have the courage to speak honestly and frankly, and then ... have the discipline to listen quietly with an open mind and an open heart as others do the same. President Bill Clinton, speech, October 16, 1995.

I stand by all the misstatements that I've made. Vice President Dan Quayle to commentator Sam Donaldson, August 17, 1989.

...it's always a possibility to get a few words tangled here and there. Senator Dan Quayle of Indiana, in the *The Los Angeles Herald Examiner,* October 3, 1988.

ANONYMOUS APHORISMS

Talk is cheap, but misunderstandings can be costly.

If you're talking, you're not listening.

Communication is hit or miss.

Eschew obfuscation.

FACTS

Communication can be as basic and innate as a baby's cry, or as profound as the Bible. No other species we know of has languages as complex as the 6,500 variations which make up the world's dialects. And clearly, at no time in history were there as many important advances in communication technology as in the 20th century. The communication age dawned when Gugliemo Marconi broadcast the first transatlantic radio message in 1901. Since then, television, teletype, facsimile, beepers, cellular phones, and the Internet have joined the telephone, the telegraph, and the radio in transforming the face of civilization; nearly 160 countries can now be contacted by e-mail on the Internet. From banking transactions to late-breaking news to marriage proposals, there are more ways of getting words moved from speaker to listener than ever before.

Computers

(See also Internet/World Wide Web)

DEFINITIONS A programmable electronic device capable of receiving, processing, storing and retrieving data; artificial intelligence.

QUOTATIONS

Computers are an inescapable facet of modern life. Ivars Petersen, *Fatal Defect,* 1995.

There's more computers around, and more scientists are bowing and scraping before them and believing what comes out of them as if they were some kind of oracle. You have to remember that 90 percent of what comes out of a supercomputer is junk...it's a tricky business. You have to be careful. Art Winfree, biologist, University of Arizona, in *The Washington Post,* September 11, 1989.

...the computer has become the most fundamental economic force. George Gilder, author/economist, in the *The Los Angeles Times,* September 10, 1989.

A computer lets you make more mistakes faster than any invention in human history with the possible exceptions of handguns and tequila. Mitch Ratliffe, in MIT's *Technology Review,* April, 1992.

I believe that the silicon chip is not the evolution of conventional industrial technology. The chip is a radical new machine, and it teaches us radically new truths. For a long time, people imagined that the first computers were just other machines. But there's no relation between the early computers and the assembly of hundreds of transistors on something the size of the head of a pin. George Gilder, author/economist, in the *The Los Angeles Times,* September 19, 1989.

The day may come when we will replace politicians with computers. Judging from some of the reasoning of politicians I've seen over the years, I would sooner take the logic of a computer. The machine may suffer the same lack of intelligence as some politicians, but at least there is a consistency to its idiocy. Senator Samuel J. Ervin, Jr., in *The Washington Post,* August 14, 1973.

We cannot be Neanderthal in a high-tech world. U.S. Representative Douglas E. Applegate, speech at a debate in the House of Representatives, June 6, 1991.

Our technology has already outstripped our ability to control it. General Omar N. Bradley, quoted on "The World Tomorrow," April 9, 1989.

It would appear that we have reached the limits of what it is possible to achieve with computer technology, although one should be careful with such statements, as they tend to sound pretty silly in five years. Attributed to John Von Neumann, c. 1949.

ANONYMOUS APHORISMS

Computer is as user does.

Garbage in. Garbage out.

If at first you don't succeed—reboot.

To err is still human.

The first computer users needed a Ph.D. Now they've got PHD computers: push here dummy.

ANECDOTES

Mr. Perkins spent weeks struggling with a particularly complex piece of software. Then one Monday morning, he arrived and immediately showed everyone else how to use it—including a few advanced tricks that weren't in the manuals. "How'd you figure it out?" his assistant asked once they were alone. "Well, every time I called the software company they said it was so simple a ten-year-old could figure it out. So this past weekend, I hired a ten-year-old to come over and explain it to me."

Then there's the story of the woman who lost her assembly line job to a robot. She went back to school to learn computer programming, and after a year she got a job at the same factory running the robot that had replaced her.

Robert X. Cringely, the online magazine *InfoWorld* summed up the evolution of the computer as follows: "If the automobile had followed the same development cycle as the computer, a Rolls-Royce would today cost $100, get a million miles per gallon, and explode once a year, killing everyone inside."

FACTS

It's not surprising that Thomas Watson, former head of IBM, reputedly said in 1947, "I see a world market for about five computers." At the time, a computer capable of executing the most basic instructions could fill an entire room, or two. That was before transistors replaced vacuum bulbs, and before silicon chips were invented. Computers are now used in everything from children's toys to pacemakers to airplane navigational controls. And America is at the forefront of computerization. According to the *World Almanac* there are 288 computers in use per 1000 people in the U.S.; Japan has the next highest per capita at 98 units per 1000 people, while worldwide the figure is only 31 units per 1000 people. Just as machines can perform superhuman physical tasks, computers can outperform their human counterparts in many specialized tasks. This doesn't mean we're in danger of being replaced, however, because computers are incapable of true intelligence—they can't reason beyond the information given or apply creative solutions.

CONSTITUTION

(See also Government)

DEFINITIONS   The basic law or statute of a governed community; "the soul of a state" (Socrates); "the fundamental and paramount law of the nation" (Chief Justice John Marshall); "the night watchman of democratic representative government" (Alfred E. Smith).

QUOTATIONS

The Constitution of the United States was made not merely for the generation that then existed, but for posterity—unlimited, undefined, endless, perpetual posterity. Senator Henry Clay of Kentucky, February 6, 1850.

The Constitution of the United States is a law for rulers and people, equally in war and in peace, and covers with the shield of its protection all classes of men, at all times, and under all circumstances. U.S. Supreme Court Associate Justice David Davis, commenting on Ex Parte Milligan, December 1866.

Our Constitution works. Our great republic is a government of laws and not of men. Here, the people rule. President Gerald R. Ford, Inaugural address, August 8, 1974.

We are under a Constitution, but the Constitution is what the judges say it is. New York Governor Charles Evans Hughes, May 3, 1907.

Our peculiar security is in the possession of a written Constitution. Let us not make it a blank paper by construction. President Thomas Jefferson, in a letter to Wilson C. Nicholas, September 7, 1803.

The government of the United States, then, though limited in its powers, is supreme; and its laws, when made in pursuance of the Constitution, form the supreme law of the land, "anything in the constitution or laws of any State to the contrary notwithstanding." U.S. Supreme Court Chief Justice John Marshall, commenting on *McCulloch v. Maryland,* March 6, 1819.

A constitution is a thing antecedent to a government, and a government is only the creature of a constitution. The constitution of a country is not the act of its government, but of the people constituting a government. Thomas Paine, *The Rights of Man,* 1791.

The United States Constitution has proven itself the most marvelously elastic compilation of rules of government ever written. New York Governor Franklin D. Roosevelt, March 2, 1930.

Keep your eye on the Constitution. This is the guarantee, that is the safeguard, that is the night watchman of democratic representative government… Alfred E. Smith, speech at Harvard University, June 22, 1933.

Constitutions are checks upon the hasty action of a majority. They are the self-imposed restraints of a whole people upon a majority of them to secure sober action and a respect for the rights of the minority, and of the individual… President William Howard Taft, veto message, August 22, 1911.

The basis of our political systems is the right of the people to make and alter their constitutions of government. But the constitution which at any time exists, until changed by an explicit and authentic act of the whole people, is sacredly obligatory upon all. President George Washington, farewell address, September 1796.

ANONYMOUS APHORISMS

A nation—like its citizens—needs a strong Constitution.

For some people the Constitution guarantees life, liberty, and the pursuit of loopholes.

The Constitution is the Supreme Court law of the land.

The Constitution is the yardstick of the law.

What's the Constitution among friends?

FACTS

The idea of a written constitution formulated by the designated representatives of the people, is an American original derived from the philosophy of British thinkers. Constitutions existed long before the one adopted by the rebellious British colonies in America—even though they were wrung from monarchs like England's King John I by privileged groups like his enraged barons who forced him to sign the Magna Carta. The uniqueness of the United States Constitution—which became a model for the modern democratic world—was that it was the supreme law of the land as interpreted by the Supreme Court, which the same constitution had also established. Although it has been amended numerous times, the Constitution is the basic law, the provisions of which all further laws must satisfy.

Conventions

DEFINITIONS   Groups of delegates or representatives meeting for a common purpose; gatherings of people of common interests; meetings of minds who don't mind meeting; billet and ballot.

QUOTATIONS

A convention is a splendid place to study human nature. Man in a crowd is quite a different creature than man acting alone. William Jennings Bryan, 1912.

Of representative assemblies may not this good be said: That contending parties in a country do thereby ascertain one another's strength? They fight there, since fight they must, by petition, parliamentary eloquence, not by sword, bayonet and bursts of military cannon. Thomas Carlyle, *Chartism,* 1839.

Observe any meeting of people, and you will always find that their eagerness and impetuosity rise or fall in proportion to their numbers: When the numbers are very great, all sense and reason seem to subside, and one sudden frenzy to seize on all, even the coolest of them. Lord Chesterfield, September 1748.

More than a generation ago, there existed widespread disapproval of the kind of national convention which became merely a trading post for a handful of powerful leaders, and where the nomination itself had nothing to do with the popular choice of the rank and file of the party itself... The rank and file should be heard. New York Governor Franklin D. Roosevelt, comment some months before 1932 Democratic National Convention.

ANONYMOUS APHORISMS

Running a convention is the art of the passable.

A convention—particularly a presidential nominating convention—is a rostrum for nostrums.

It is only natural that visiting firemen should look for a hot time in the old town tonight.

An individual starts off by facing his problem with resolution, but a convention saves the resolution for the end.

At a convention some delegates reach for the stars and others keep reaching for the floor.

ANECDOTES

William Jennings Bryan compared the way a convention feels about demonstrations to the feeling of a big man whose wife "was in the habit of beating him. When asked why he permitted it, he replied that it seemed to please her and did not hurt him."

"Since you regard conventions as a waste of time," the reporter asked the old convention delegate, "why do you keep going to them?" "If I didn't," answered the old convention delegate, "how could I be sure?"

FACTS

Political decisions in the U.S. have been made by selecting delegates to meet and vote since well before the American Revolution. The U.S. Constitution was created by the Constitutional Convention which had been called for that purpose, and then submitted for ratification to the states. The first modern, national political party conventions were called for the purpose of nominating presidential candidates for the 1832 election. The Democrats nominated Andrew Jackson; (the national Republicans nominated Henry Clay, and the Anti-Masonic Party named William Wirt at their assemblies). In our own time, the convention has also become popular among trade and labor groups, learned societies, sales staffs, and all kinds of social organizations.

For information, many major cities have Convention and Visitors' Bureaus.

COOKING

(See also Dieting, Food)

DEFINITIONS   Preparation of food for eating through processes such as grilling, roasting, baking, boiling, frying, broiling, stewing, etc.; the art of formulating recipes and processes for the preparation of tasty dishes; burnt offerings; kitchen mechanics; the culinary art; the kitchen sciences.

QUOTATIONS

You cannot know a dish until you have made it one thousand times. Attributed to Antheline Brillat-Savarin, c. early 19th century.

The discovery of a new dish does more for human happiness than the discovery of a new star. Antheline Brillat-Savarin, Physiologie du Gout, 1825.

We may live without friends; we may live without books;/ But civilized man cannot live without cooks. E. R. Bulwer-Lytton (Lord Lytton; Owen Meredith), *Lucile*, 1860.

Cookery is become an art, a noble science; cooks are gentlemen. Robert Burton, *The Anatomy of Melancholy,* 1621.

Meat so dressed and sauced and seasoned that you didn't know whether it was beef or mutton—flesh, fowl, or good red herring. George du Maurier, *Trilby,* 1894.

What is food to one may be bitter poison to others. Lucretius, *De Rerum Natura,* c. 2nd century BC.

Kissing don't last; cookery do! George Meredith, *The Ordeal of Richard Feverel,* 1859. (Also attributed to a Pennsylvania Dutch saying.)

ANONYMOUS APHORISMS

Too many broths spoil the cook.

A good cook makes a delicacy out of what an ordinary cook makes hash.

Very few state secrets are guarded as fiercely as a great recipe.

The motto of most short-order cooks is "come fry with me."

There is basically one season in the kitchen—a long hot simmer.

American cooking is 4F—fast, frozen, and fat-free.

There are two kinds of food at the average American banquet—warmed over and wondered over.

She calls him her recipe, because he tells her what she can do with the food.

ANECDOTES

"I always feel like a god when I come home," said the dyspeptic diner, "because for dinner there is always a burnt offering."

Mrs. Brown was a fabulous cook, but her recipes—when she was asked for them—were always a little vague. Finally, someone asked her, "What do you mean by a pinch of this or a touch of that? Can't you give us exact quantities?" "Well," replied Mrs. Brown, "it depends on what you're pinching or how touched you are."

FACTS

The preparation of food was probably humanity's first skill—or art. Cookbooks are among the most widely published and read books of all time. In the U.S. Census Bureau's tabulation of various types of retail trade, the "eateries" category has the largest number of establishments. The American concept of fast-food cooking and merchandising—from the hamburger to frozen foods—has captured the world's imagination and the world market. Fast-food restaurants cropped up during the 1980s and 1990s in some unlikely places such as Paris' Rive Gauche, Moscow's Red Square, and even mainland China's capitol city of Beijing. American palates also have awakened, setting international culinary trends from bagels to low-fat menus to Tex-Mex fajitas to Southern ribs and Cajun blackened fish. Chefs from around the globe now travel to America to learn the finer points of American-style cooking.

Courage

DEFINITIONS   The opposite of fear or the ability to conquer it; bravery; valor; standing up to danger; guts; nerve; chutzpah.

QUOTATIONS

It is a brave act of valor to condemn death; but where life is more terrible than death, it is then the truest valor to dare to live. Sir Thomas Browne, *Religio Medici,* 1642.

The Red Badge of Courage, Stephen Crane, book title, 1895.

None but the brave deserves the fair. John Dryden, *Alexander's Feast,* 1697.

Damn the torpedoes, full speed ahead! Rear Admiral David G. Farragut, August 5, 1864.

Some have been thought brave because they were afraid to run away. Thomas Fuller, *Gnomologia,* 1732.

It is better to die on your feet than to live on your knees. Dolores Ibarruri, September 3, 1936.

…every submission to our fear enlarges its dominion… Samuel Johnson, *The Rambler,* June 29, 1751.

I have not yet begun to fight. Captain John Paul Jones, September 23, 1779.

No one can prove his courage when he has never been in danger. Francois Duc de La Rochefoucauld, *Maxims,* 1665–1672.

Don't give up the ship. Captain James Lawrence , 1813.

What though the field be lost? / All is not lost—th' unconquerable will,/ And study of revenge, immortal hate, / And courage never to submit or yield;/ And what else is not to be overcome. John Milton, *Paradise Lost,* 1667.

But screw your courage to the sticking place, / And you'll not fail. William Shakespeare, *Macbeth,* 1606.

Cannon to right of them, / Cannon to left of them, / Cannon in front of them / Volley'd and thunder'd;/ Storm'd at with shot and shell, / Boldly they rode and well, / Into the jaws of Death, / Into the mouth of Hell, / Rode the six hundred. Alfred Tennyson, "The Charge of the Light Brigade," 1854.

Bravery never goes out of fashion. William M. Thackeray, *The Four Georges,* 1860.

ANONYMOUS APHORISMS

When the going gets tough, the tough get going.

Those who dare not, do not.

If a thing is worth having, it's worth fighting for.

Stand up and fight.

Stand up and be counted.

ANECDOTES

"It took real courage to stand up to that gunman in the cocktail lounge," one lounge lizard complimented another. "Not really—I didn't know I was loaded," the satiated lounger shrugged.

An unlikely hero was being hailed for standing up to an attacker twice his size and asked how he could be so brave. "I was too scared to run," he said, "and too dumb to think of anything else." But his friends said, "No, you didn't have time to think. Courage is a natural instinct if you have it."

FACTS

Courage has always been regarded as one of the major human virtues. Today, modern psychology has sought to make it possible for a greater portion of society to accept without condemnation an individual's admission to a lack of courage. But collectively—on a nation-by-nation basis—courage still must always be proclaimed. Nations fear that giving up without a fight may mean having to give up more again tomorrow. On an individual basis, the most courageous act is often that of finding a peaceful solution. Perhaps the best point to remember is that the courage to accept a difficult and disagreeable fact has often been demonstrated by gallant people.

COURTS

(See also Justice, Law)

DEFINITIONS   Places where judgments and decisions of law are rendered; the machinery of justice, determining guilt or innocence; tribunals; halls of justice; the domain of judges; the bench; where a suit is pressed and a man can be taken to the cleaners.

QUOTATIONS

Judges ought to remember that their office is *Ius dicere* and not *Ius dare;* to interpret law, and not to make law, or give law. Francis Bacon, "Of Judicature," 1625.

Agree, for the law is costly. William Camden, *Remains Concerning Britain,* 1605.

...th' supreme court follows th' iliction returns. Finley Peter Dunne, *Mr. Dooley:* "The Supreme Court's Decisions," 1900.

When a judge puts on his robes he puts off his relations to any, and, like Melchiscdech, becomes without pedigree. Thomas Fuller, *The Holy State and the Profane State,* 1642.

A good and faithful judge prefers what is right to what is expedient. Horace, "Carmina," c. 13 BC.

It is emphatically the province and duty of the judicial department to say what the law is. U.S. Supreme Court Chief Justice John Marshall, commenting on *Marbury v. Madison,* February 24, 1803.

I have always thought, from my earliest youth till now, that the greatest scourge an angry Heaven ever inflicted upon an ungrateful and sinning people was an ignorant, a corrupt, or a dependent judiciary. U.S. Supreme Court Chief Justice John Marshall, recorded in the Debates of the Virginia (Constitutional) Convention of 1829–31.

If one man sin against another, the judge shall judge him... *Samuel I, 2:25.*

ANONYMOUS APHORISMS

Sue now, settle later.

Court is the only place where the bench warmer is the boss.

A court calendar has no pin-ups but lots of put-offs.

In court, you present your briefs and run the risk of losing your shirt.

If at first you don't succeed, sue, sue again.

Everyone is entitled to his day in court—no matter how many days he has to wait.

ANECDOTES

A man asked to be excused from jury duty because he was needed where he worked. "Your business will have to get along without you," said the judge, "you're not indispensable." "That's what I'm afraid they'll find out," said the man with dismay.

Q: When does a judge commit a public nuisance? A: When he sends a peeping Tom to jail.

FACTS

Never have the courts had more laws to interpret and more litigants with whom to deal. The caseload has grown far more than the dimensions of the judicial system. In 1950, U.S. Courts of Appeals had 2,830 cases brought before them; in 1980 there were 23,200. Since then the number has risen to more than 49,700 cases. The greatest increases have taken place in criminal and private civil cases. In 1994, U.S. District Courts commenced 44,900 criminal and 236,000 civil cases. Part of the increase is due to rising crime rates; part is simply due to the fact that there is a larger population; and part is also due to the fact that every legislative session seems to pass new laws defining new crimes or establishing new court remedies. Years ago, courts had far fewer ecological or discrimination cases simply because there were fewer laws pertaining these subjects. As precedents are set on the parameters of crimes such as spousal abuse and date rape, the courts face additional cases. It is estimated that the U.S. population will double in the next fifty years. Unless crime rates decrease by half, the court system will need to be equipped to manage double the number of court cases.

CREATIVITY

DEFINITIONS Originality; the talent or inspiration to conceive and express new ideas; inspiration; inventiveness combined with artfulness; making something out of nothing.

QUOTATIONS

Men are like trees: each one must put forth the leaf that is created in him. Rev. Henry Ward Beecher, *Proverbs from Plymouth Pulpit*, 1887.

No great thing is created suddenly, any more than a bunch of grapes or a fig. If you tell me that you desire a fig, I answer that there must be time. Let it first blossom, then bear fruit, then ripen. Epictetus, *Discourses*, c. 1st–2nd centuries.

Thine was the prophet's vision, thine / The exaltation, the divine / Insanity of noble minds, / That never falters nor abates, / But labors and endures and waits, / Till all that it foresees it finds, / Or what it cannot find creates! Henry Wadsworth Longfellow, "Keramos," 1878.

In creating, the only hard thing's to begin; / A grass blade's no easier to make than an oak. James Russell Lowell, *A Fable for Critics*, 1848.

Nothing can be created out of nothing. Lucretius, *De Rerum Natura*, c. 1st century BC.

All good things which exist are the fruits of originality. John Stuart Mill, *On Liberty*, 1859.

We want the creative faculty to imagine that which we know. Percy Bysshe Shelley, *A Defence of Poetry*, 1821.

He or she is greatest who contributes the greatest original practical example. Walt Whitman, "By Blue Ontario's Shores," 1856.

Every great and original writer, in proportion as he is great and original, must himself create the taste by which he is to be relished. William Wordsworth, May 21, 1807.

ANONYMOUS APHORISMS

Creativity has no precedents.

Creativity, not necessity, is the true mother of invention.

It is better to create than to cremate.

New ideas are rare; good new ideas are even rarer.

Too many people think they are being creative when they are just being different.

Creativity has no script; it is inspired ad libbing.

Originality is not necessarily better than imitation, but it makes imitation possible.

ANECDOTES

Billy wasn't doing well at school, so his mother went to see his teacher. "I've asked Billy why he did so poorly in mathematics and reading and history," she said to the teacher, "and he seemed to have lots of excuses." Searching for soothing words of comfort, the teacher replied, "Well, ma'am, he doesn't work very hard but he certainly shows a lot of creativity."

An art class was assigned to copy Michelangelo's *Creation of Adam*. One student produced a confusing pattern of straight lines that bore no more resemblance to the master's painting than to a blank wall. "I felt I had to express my own instinctive spirit of creativity," said the student. "What you have created," said the teacher, "is a void."

FACTS

Historically, human creativity has had its high and low eras in history. The Renaissance was one of the high points because greater creative freedom and increased support for creative people came together. Amid all the problems of the modern world, the combination of these same conditions encourages creativity today. Though tax exemptions and positive government subsidies have been in jeopardy since the 1970s, places where creative talents can be nurtured and creativity displayed continue to thrive. These include publishing houses, theaters for the dramatic and concert arts, museums and galleries, professional groups and schools. The climate for creativity can be attested to by one admittedly incomplete statistic. Not all creative ideas can be copyrighted, but the number of copyrights can be considered at least partial evidence of creativity.

The U.S. Copyright Office, located in the Library of Congress, handles over 500,000 registrations annually for original and derived written, visual, and audio creative works.

Crime

(See also Law and Order, Violence)

DEFINITIONS   Violation of the law; offenses against legal standards of conduct; wrongdoing; a story told in sentences; the underworld; the mob; white-collar, petty, and organized; wrongdoers.

QUOTATIONS

The greatest incitement to crime is the hope of escaping punishment. Cicero, *Pro Milone,* c. 52 BC.

I hear much of people's calling out to punish the guilty, but very few are concerned to clear the innocent. Daniel Defoe, *An Appeal to Honor and Justice,* 1715.

You cannot do wrong without suffering wrong. Ralph Waldo Emerson, *Essays, First Series:* "Compensation," 1841.

The greater the man the greater the crime. Thomas Fuller, *Gnomologia,* 1732.

My object all sublime, / I shall achieve in time— / To let the punishment fit the crime / The punishment fit the crime... W.S. Gilbert, *The Mikado,* 1885.

...where legitimate opportunities are closed, illegitimate opportunities are seized. Whatever opens opportunity and hope will help to prevent crime and foster responsibility. President Lyndon B. Johnson, March 9, 1966.

All go free when many offend. Lucan, *Pharsalia,* c. 1st century.

Whoso diggeth a pit shall fall therein: and he that rolleth a stone, it will return upon him. *Proverbs,* 26:27.

He who does not prevent a crime when he can, encourages it. Seneca, *Troades,* c. 1st century.

ANONYMOUS APHORISMS

Crime doesn't pay.

No crime is victimless.

Wrong never comes right.

Whoever profits from crime is part of it.

Temptation makes thieves, but some thieves make their own temptations.

There are black sheep in every flock.

Murder will out.

It takes a thief to catch a thief.

Give a thief enough rope to hang himself.

Straight trees can have crooked roots.

ANECDOTES

They say Diogenes came to the big city to look for an honest man, but he didn't stay long. Someone stole his lantern.

A practical joker sent the same anonymous wire to ten leading citizens of the town, saying "Everything has been found out, but you still have time to leave town." Seven of the ten left.

FACTS

Crime is an international growth industry. Its growth stems from various causes. More things are characterized as crimes today. It is increasingly difficult to control individuals through the family and other established institutions; and yet popular "direct action" has grown against governmental restraint in various parts of the world. Although crime statistics vary by each nation's unique reporting system, the U.S. appears to lead the world's modern nations in crimes involving a firearm. In the U.S., the perception that crime is rising is largely a result of increased media coverage. Televised documentaries of police making arrests have become prime-time television programming. In truth, murder, rape, auto theft, and assault rates have recently fallen.

CRITICISM

DEFINITIONS Expressions of judgment of a work of art; reviews; comments and observations; grandstand quarterbacking; first nighters and second guessers.

QUOTATIONS

As soon Seek roses in December—ice in June; / Hope constancy in wind, or corn in chaff, / Believe a woman or an epitaph, / Or any other thing that's false, before / You trust in Critics. George Gordon, Lord Byron, *English Bards and Scotch Reviewers,* 1809.

It is much easier to be critical than to be correct. Benjamin Disraeli, January 24, 1860.

You know who critics are?—the men who have failed in literature and art. Benjamin Disraeli, *Lothair,* 1870.

Blame-all and praise-all are two blockheads. Benjamin Franklin, *Poor Richard's Almanac,* 1734.

What a blessed thing it is, that Nature, when she invented, manufactured and patented her authors, contrived to make critics out of the chips that were left! Oliver Wendell Holmes, *The Professor at the Breakfast-Table,* 1860.

Criticism is a study by which men grow important and formidable at very small expense. Samuel Johnson, *The Idler,* June 9, 1759.

Nature fits all her children with something to do, / He who would write and can't write can surely review. James Russell Lowell, *A Fable for Critics,* 1848.

A wise skepticism is the first attribute of a good critic. James Russell Lowell, *Among My Books,* 1870.

Judge not, that ye be not judged. *Matthew,* 7:1.

You do not get a man's most effective criticism until you provoke him. Severe truth is expressed with some bitterness. Henry D. Thoreau, *Journal,* March 15, 1854.

If you can't stand the heat you better get out of the kitchen. Attributed by President Harry S. Truman to an "old friend and colleague on the Jackson County Court," in speech, December 17, 1952.

ANONYMOUS APHORISMS

One man's work is another man's target.

Those who can, do; those who can't, review.

Those who do well like criticism; those who do not do well resent it.

ANECDOTES

It was Eugene Field who reviewed a performance of "King Lear" by saying that the role of the King was played as though someone else was about to play the Ace.

It was said of one of the great Broadway theater critics that "he left no turn unstoned."

An art critic who got tired of being asked what he thought of this painting and that one now offers the same answer to all: "What a picture!"

FACTS

The Encyclopaedia Britannica names Plato as the first theater critic. Thus, criticism of the arts is consequently almost as old as the arts themselves. Criticism is a staple of most American newspapers, magazines, and broadcasting stations, but even with the multitude of reviews available today, a handful of Broadway critics can often make a significant difference in a play's box office success or failure. Until the emergence of television, the public depended on reviews, choosing what they would go to see or pick up to read. But, despite pre-reviewing by newspaper critics, most television broadcasts are seen by the public before detailed reviews of them are read. Through the television medium, critics like Gene Siskel, Roger Ebert, and Michael Medved have gained world stature alongside those whose work they review. Excerpts from favorable reviews are still considered among the best ways of promoting interest in a book, movie, or theatrical presentation. Indeed, some critics, who do not like to be quoted in advertising, go to considerable lengths to couch their reviews in language that cannot be easily excerpted.

DEATH

DEFINITIONS   The end of life; passing on; the opposite of life; the ultimate equality; the end; the way of all flesh; the final reward; the peace of the grave; the next step; the unknown and unknowable; the big sleep.

QUOTATIONS

It's not death I fear, it's reality—which means for me that I will never accomplish or learn to be all that I wish I could be before the final curtain. Joanne Woodward, in *Lear's,* September, 1989.

O death; where is thy sting? O grave, where is thy victory? *Corinthians I,* 15:55.

Death, be not proud, though some have called thee / Mighty and dreadful, for thou art not so, / For those whom thou think'st thou dost overthrow / Die not, poor Death, nor yet canst thou kill me. John Donne, *Holy Sonnets, X,* c. early 17th century.

…in this world nothing is certain but death and taxes. Benjamin Franklin, letter to Jean-Baptiste Leroy, November 13, 1789.

Why fear death? It is the most beautiful adventure in life. Attributed to Charles Frohman, passenger on the *S.S. Lusitania,* May 7, 1915.

…dust thou art, and unto dust shalt thou return. *Genesis,* 3:19.

The paths of glory lead but to the grave. Thomas Gray, "Elegy Written in a Country Churchyard," 1751.

Dust thou art, to dust returnest, / Was not spoken of the soul. Henry Wadsworth Longfellow, "A Psalm of Life," 1839.

I have a rendezvous with Death at some disputed barricade. Alan Seeger, "I Have a Rendezvous with Death," 1916.

...death— / The undiscover'd country, from whose bourne / No traveller returns. William Shakespeare, *Hamlet,* 1601.

...I hope to see my Pilot face to face / When I have crost the bar. Alfred Lord Tennyson, "Crossing the Bar," 1889.

...Adam, the first great benefactor of our race. He brought death into the world. Mark Twain, *The Tragedy of Puddinhead Wilson,* 1894.

Nothing can happen more beautiful than death. Walt Whitman, "Starting from Paumanok," 1860.

ANONYMOUS APHORISMS

Say nothing but good about the dead.

Life ends, but memory lives.

Death is the last great accomplishment of life.

Living is temporary; death is recorded in stone.

Death is another stage in the life of the soul.

Death, like life, is a gift of God.

There is no arguing with death.

ANECDOTES

When an uncle died and left him a substantial inheritance, the French writer Henri du Balzac commented that now both he and his uncle had passed on to a better life.

The fable is told of the man who lived in Baghdad and one day came rushing in to see the Grand Vizier to ask permission to go immediately to Samarra. When the Vizier asked him why he was in such a rush, he explained that in a dream he had seen the face of Death, who said they would meet that night. "But," said the man, "if I ride swiftly, I will not be here tonight. I will be safely far away in Samarra." And so he fled. That night the Grand Vizier dreamt that he saw the face of Death, and Death said to him, "Do not be afraid, for I am not concerned with you. Tonight I have an appointment in Samarra."

When the French author Voltaire was asked to comment about the death of a famous man, he said, "He was a man of character, of whom nothing but good should now be said—provided he's really dead."

FACTS

Probably humanity's oldest aspiration is to defeat death in the ultimate personal battle for life. Because we are mortal, we never conquer death; but we have slowed it down. In 1995, the U. S. government was able to report that the nation's infant mortality rate was at the a record low, and longevity set a record high. For the first time, infant deaths had dropped to 8.4 deaths for every 1,000 births, while our average life span has increased beyond 75.5 years. Humanity's attitude toward death has also showed signs of change. Euthanasia—the idea of letting doomed people die with dignity rather than keeping them painfully alive, still creates the most bitter arguments. But the concept of death as release—long a mark of all the major religions—is becoming a sociological concept as well. Death has always provided a rallying point for families and friends, not merely to help the bereaved but to come together and reassert the eternal continuum of human life. In some primitive cultures, the old would go off to die when they ceased to be active. They do not think of this as a cruel practice, but rather as a sensible and inevitable one. In our society, however, the idea of a person determining voluntarily the time of his own death remains contrary to our heritage of both law and custom.

D EMOCRACY

DEFINITIONS   A majority rule, where the ultimate power rests in the hands of and is exercised directly by an informed citizenry; "a government of all the people, by all the people, for all the people" (Rev. Theodore Parker, speech in Boston, MA, May 29 , 1850); the will of the masses; free-market government; the original political free-for-all.

QUOTATIONS

Democracy requires change to function well, because ideas of government need to be refreshed every so often. Andre Glucksmann, French philosopher, in *The Washington Post,* April 14, 1992.

It would be a profound mistake to take the survival and success of democracy for granted. Its durability will depend on the ability of governments to translate the promise of democracy into a better life for their people. U.S. Representative Steven J. Solarz, in *U.S. News & World Report,* May 22, 1989.

Ours was the first revolution in the history of mankind that truly reversed the course of government, and with three little words: "We the people." "We the people" tell the government what to do; it doesn't tell us. "We the people" are the driver; the government is the car. And we decide where it should go and by what route and how fast. President Ronald Reagan, in *The Washington Post,* January 12, 1989.

I believe we are on an irreversible trend toward more freedom and democracy— but that could change. Vice President Dan Quayle, May 22, 1989 (reported in *Esquire,* August, 1992).

Democracy is the worst form of government except—all the others that have been tried. Attributed to Winston Churchill.

ANONYMOUS APHORISMS

Democracy gives everyone an equal chance to shout.

Democracy is just one party after another.

Ambivalence is the thief of democracy.

There is no democracy without the people.

Education is the line between democracy and anarchy.

ANECDOTES

"Young man," the matronly election volunteer scolded, "placing your ballot is your right as this is a democracy. But sticking your gum over the opposition's voting lever is not."

Democracy, as described by playwright George Bernard Shaw, is "a form of government that substitutes election by the incompetent many for appointment by the corrupt few." Author H.L. Mencken, defined it as "the theory that the common people know what they want and deserve to get it good and hard."

FACTS

At the time of the American revolution, democracy was ridiculed as being a short step from anarchy. But a few centuries later, many of the forms of government those naysayers touted as the best alternatives have been discredited. In the final years of the 20th century there was a worldwide trend toward installing democratic regimes. Though the roots of democracy stretch back thousands of years—Athens, Greece, during the Periclesian Age is generally acknowledged as the birthplace of democracy—in its modern form it has never been more popular. Many countries are now claiming to be democratic nations. While this is true of some, such as Switzerland, France, Costa Rica, and Panama, other countries seem more interested in the title than in actually practicing democracy. For example, China—while claiming to be a democratic nation—regularly imprisoned protesters demanding freedom of speech and freedom of the press throughout the 1990s, both of which are essential for informing the public. George Santayana, author and modern critic of democracy said, around the turn of the 20th century, that "Knowledge, and knowledge alone, gives divine right to rule. Santayana protested that the downfall of democracy was that the majority of citizens were too uneducated or self-interested to be capable of the responsibility of self-government. His suggested solution was to take the government out of the hands of the people. In the United States, a different solution has proven highly successful: Educate the people.

DIETING

(See also Food, Health)

DEFINITIONS   Eating less or eating selected foods with an cyc toward losing or controlling weight, improving health or increasing vitality; reducing; counting calories; slimming; weight watching; thinking thin.

QUOTATIONS

To lengthen thy life, lessen thy meals. Benjamin Franklin, *Poor Richard's Almanac*, 1737.

Kill no more pigeons than you can eat. Benjamin Franklin, letter to Catherine Ray, October 16, 1755.

A little with quiet is the only diet. George Herbert, *Outlandish Proverbs*, 1640.

Who ever hears of fat men heading a riot, or herding together in turbulent mobs? Washington Irving, *History of New York, by Diedrich Knickerbocker*, 1809.

One must eat to live, not live to eat. Moliere, *The Miser*, 1668.

What some people call health, if purchased by perpetual anxiety about diet, isn't much better than tedious disease. George Dennison Prentice, *Prenticeana*, 1860.

The appetite grows by eating. Francois Rabelais, *Gargantua*, 1534.

O, that this too too solid flesh would melt... William Shakespeare, *Hamlet*, 1601.

Everything I like is either illegal, immoral, or fattening. Attributed to Alexander Woollcott, c. 1920s or 1930s.

ANONYMOUS APHORISMS

Taste makes waistline.

Dieting is a losing battle.

Inside every fat person there's a thin person hoping to get out.

One exercise that is guaranteed to help you lose weight is pushing away from the table.

Dieting is a weighty problem.

Too much food on the table goes to waste or it goes to waist.

Rich food is usually poor eating.

ANECDOTES

"I have the perfect diet," said Mr. Hopkins. "I eat my head off one day and starve the next." "And how do you feel?" he was asked. "Great," he said, "every other day."

An author approached a publisher with a manuscript entitled *The 100-Year Diet.* The publisher said it was a crazy idea, because the kind of book that sells is one telling how to lose a lot of pounds quickly. "Maybe so," said the author, "but my book tells you how long you have to stay on the diet to avoid getting the pounds back."

The robust gourmand begged his doctor to devise a diet which would allow him to eat anything he wanted. His doctor thought about it for a moment and replied, "Try this. You can eat anything you want, and as much as you want. Just don't swallow."

FACTS

There are almost as many weight-control diets extant as there are cookbooks. Indeed, more and more of the cookbooks today are low-fat, low-cholesterol, or spa-cuisine cookbooks. That is one reason for the tremendous boom in sugar substitutes and health foods. "Miracle" diets have been readily available for decades. Diet fads have included: chocolate, champagne, grapefruit, steak and egg, liquid protein, powdered supplements, and numerous weight-loss pills. But no magic formulae are needed to explain the diet crazes. One reason is the extent to which physical exercise through hard labor has disappeared in the age of electric power and automation. We ride where we used to walk; we push a button where we used to turn a hand-powered tool. Food is almost always readily available, and with the current American culinary renaissance, the temptations are greater than ever . But there has been another change in our ways. A couple of generations ago, the fatter a baby was the healthier we thought he was. In those years there was no thought that butterfat might be harmful or that eggs or milk were allergenic. The discovery that fat was not a harbinger of health caused sweeping changes in our culture. Even our ideas of beauty changed. The heartbreakers of the 1950s look rather ample and unfit to aesthetic eyes of the health-conscious observers in the 1990s. The sleek creatures of the 1960s appear emaciated and malnourished in those same eyes. Diet and health foods—whether for weight reduction or other health reasons—have become a multibillion dollar industry in the United States.

DRAMA

(See also Theater)

DEFINITIONS Theatrical presentation involving the enactment of a narrative; by-play between conflicting forces; what is usually more fun to watch than to be part of; an offering in acts and scenes, in return for an offering at the box office.

QUOTATIONS

The business of plays is to recommend virtue, and discountenance vice; to show the uncertainty of human greatness, the sudden turns of fate, and the unhappy conclusions of violence and injustice; 'tis to expose the singularities of pride and fancy, to make folly and falsehood contemptible, and to bring everything that is ill under infamy and neglect. Jeremy Collier, "A Short View of the Immorality and Profaneness of the English Stage," 1698.

A play ought to be a just and lively image of human nature, representing its passions and humors, and the changes of fortune to which it is subject, for the delight and instruction of mankind. John Dryden, "An Essay of Dramatic Poesy," 1668.

The anomalous fact is that the theater, so called, can flourish in barbarism, but that any drama worth speaking of can develop but in the air of civilization. Henry James, letter to C. E. Wheeler, April 9, 1911.

The drama's laws, the drama's patrons give, / For we that live to please, must please to live. Samuel Johnson, prologue at opening of Drury Lane Theater, 1747.

The business of the dramatist is to keep out of sight and let nothing appear but his characters. Thomas B. Macaulay, "Essay on Milton," 1825.

The play's the thing / Wherein I'll catch the conscience of the king. William Shakespeare, *Hamlet*, 1601.

Through all the drama—whether damned or not— / Love gilds the scene, and women guide the plot. Richard Brinsley Sheridan, *The Rivals*, 1775.

ANONYMOUS APHORISMS

Too many dramas these days are in the hands of people who don't have any dramatic license.

Life is like a drama—they're both likely to have third act trouble.

The central idea of the drama is that you can escape from your own problems by watching somebody else's.

There is no play on the stage that isn't hard work.

ANECDOTES

Actor Danny Kaye once noted that there was a clear difference in Russian drama between comedy and tragedy. In both, everybody dies; but in a comedy, they die happy.

It was Oscar Wilde who commented after a disastrous opening night that the play was a great success but the audience was a failure.

FACTS

The novel had not yet been invented, when drama was first entertaining the multitudes. Of all the great forms of human creativity, the drama has the longest history of effectiveness. Ancient Greek drama is as great in theatrical presentation today as it was three thousand years ago. Shakespearean plays have been translated and played in every corner of the world. Kabuki and Noh theatrical productions are still performed to critical audiences throughout Japan. And Chinese operatic productions are still used as an educational medium in rural areas. Over the centuries, those connected with drama have been alternately sneered at and idolized, but "play acting" has always been a part of community life. Today the drama is more widespread an art form than ever, and in a greater variety of formats than ever before, thanks to the miracles of motion pictures, radio, and television.

D REAMS

DEFINITIONS   Thoughts, experiences or emotions seen in the mind's eye during sleep; imagined things; optimistic visions; idealistic hopes; what you see clearly with your eyes closed; out of Morpheus by indigestion; wishing while you work.

QUOTATIONS

…your young men shall see visions, and your old men shall dream dreams. *Acts of the Apostles,* 2:17.

I walked beside the evening sea / And dreamed a dream that could not he; / The waves that plunged along the shore / Said only: "Dreamer, dream no more!" George William Curtis, "Ebb and Flow," c. late 19th century.

We need men who can dream of things that never were. President John F. Kennedy, speech in Dublin, Ireland, June 28, 1963.

…a dreamer lives forever, / And a toiler dies in a day. John Boyle O'Reilly, "The Cry of the Dreamer," 1873.

All that we see or seem / Is but a dream within a dream. Edgar Allan Poe, "A Dream Within a Dream," 1827.

Those who dream by day are cognizant of many things which escape those who dream by night. Edgar Allan Poe, "Eleanora," 1842.

I talk of dreams; / Which are the children of an idle brain, / Begot of nothing but vain fantasy. William Shakespeare, *Romeo and Juliet,* 1595.

Men never cling to their dreams with such tenacity as at the moment when they are losing faith in them, and know it, but do not dare yet to confess it to themselves. William Graham Sumner, "The Banquet of Life," 1887.

…if one advances confidently in the direction of his dreams, and endeavors to live the life which he has imagined, he will meet with a success unexpected in common hours. Henry D. Thoreau, *Walden,* 1854.

ANONYMOUS APHORISMS

Unimaginative people dream in black and white, but poets dream in glorious color.

One man's dream is another man's Dramamine.

Those who dream the night away wonder why throughout the day.

Young people dream dreams; old people dream memories.

A dream is a very exclusive production, played for an audience of one.

A dream is the subconscious at work; a daydreamer is the unconscious at work.

Dreams are the stuff of progress.

ANECDOTES

"I keep having this dream," said the patient, "that I am a real-estate mogul with a gorgeous girlfriend, a yacht, a marvelous physique, and I just won the lottery." "So what's your problem?" asked the doctor. "I keep waking up," said the patient.

"Every time I eat scallops," said Mr. Jones, "I dream I have struck oil. I suppose I should stop eating scallops, but then I wouldn't know any more what it's like to strike oil."

FACTS

Dreams have fascinated human beings since virtually the dawn of time. In ancient times, they were regarded as paranormal prophecies, and even to this day, dream interpreters offer to predict a customer's future by the portents of his dreams. But modern science prefers to regard dreams as mirrors of the subconscious, echoes of what has been thought, experienced or feared in the past. Published in 1900, Sigmund Freud's book, *The Interpretation of Dreams*, gave great impetus to this view, with particular emphasis on the idea that dreams were expressions of secret desires. Many leading modern psychiatrists and psychologists disagree, but all are to some degree the heirs of what might be termed Freud's own dreams.

DRINK

DEFINITIONS   Beverage; liquid refreshment; alcoholic beverages in particular; over-consumption of spirituous beverages; brew; the demon rum; hard stuff; potent potables; wino (wine); Irish courage (whiskey); "mother's milk" (gin according to George Bernard Shaw).

QUOTATIONS

With about two-thirds of Americans calling themselves drinkers, the U.S. is unlikely to ever again ban alcohol, and it shouldn't. But most Americans are like me and drink relatively little, yet we all pay for alcohol-related [car] crashes. C. Everett Koop, Surgeon General of the United States, in *The Washington Post,* June 1, 1989.

A man will be eloquent if you give him good wine. Ralph Waldo Emerson, *Representative Men:* "Montaigne," 1850.

He that drinks fast, pays slow. Benjamin Franklin, *Poor Richard's Almanac,* 1733.

Bacchus hath drowned more men than Neptune. Thomas Fuller, *Gnomologia,* 1732.

What doesn't drunkenness do? It unlocks secrets, confirms our hopes, pushes the lazy into battle, relieves the burdens of tense brains, teaches new wiles. Horace, *Epistles, Book I,* 5:16, c. 16 BC.

Claret is the liquor for boys; port for men; but he who aspires to be a hero must drink brandy. Samuel Johnson, according to James Boswell in *Life of Samuel Johnson,* April 7, 1779.

I don't drink any more—just the same amount. Joe E. Lewis, c. 1940s.

Whether or not the world would be vastly benefited by a total banishment from it of all intoxicating drinks seems not now an open question. Three-fourths of mankind confess the affirmative with their tongues, and I believe all the rest acknowledge it in their hearts. Abraham Lincoln, speech in Springfield, IL, February 22, 1842.

The Elixir of Perpetual Youth, / Called Alcohol... Henry Wadsworth Longfellow, "The Golden Legend," 1851.

All experience shows that temperance, like other virtues, is not produced by lawmakers, but by the influences of education, morality and religion. Men may be persuaded—they cannot be compelled to adopt habits of temperance. New York Governor Horatio Seymour, statement on vetoing state Prohibition Act, 1854.

A bumper of good liquor / Will end a contest quicker / Than justice, judge or vicar. Richard Brinsley Sheridan, *The Duenna,* 1775.

ANONYMOUS APHORISMS

There are more old drunkards than old doctors.

Too much of here's mud in your eye can mean a face in the dirt.

Drink loosens a man up until he gets tight.

Work is the curse of the drinking classes.

He shot off his mouth because he didn't know he was loaded.

I would rather forget to drink than drink to forget.

The drunks are on the house.

ANECDOTES

During the Civil War, when someone complained to him that General Grant was a heavy drinker, President Lincoln supposedly replied, "Find out what brand he drinks, so I can send some to my other generals."

Not all drunks recognize their weakness. In one crowd of drinkers, Jones started to go wild, removing his clothes until, as he was down to his underwear, he collapsed and passed out. "Good old Jones," said one of his drinking buddies approvingly, "he always knows when to stop."

FACTS

Drink has been a problem for humankind as long as the processes of fermentation and distillation have existed. In this country, the Prohibition Amendment that was in effect during the 1920s failed, and the results since its repeal have not been much better. Alcohol is still regarded by crime and health authorities as creating more victims than drugs. At the same time, the values and pleasures of alcoholic beverages in moderation—whether as refreshment or as cooking ingredients—have long been recognized. Even the medical establishment has conceded that a glass of wine every day may significantly reduce a person's risk of heart attack. The idea of drunkenness as a crime in itself seems to be declining, although there is greater recognition of its health costs to society, the dangers of drunk drivers, and the need to treat alcoholism as a disease. But with police making over 1 million arrests for driving under the influence in 1993 alone, alcohol abuse is still very much a problem in the United States.

The National Council on Alcoholism and Drug Abuse, Inc., at 12 West 21st Street, New York, NY 10010, (212) 206-6770, is one of several active national groups working in this field.

D RUGS

(See also Medicine)

DEFINITIONS   Medicines, stimulants, depressants, or mood elevators that affect living creatures' moods, attitudes or conditions; habit-forming substances that are ingested, injected or inhaled; narcotics; mother's little helpers (barbiturates and sedatives); an inclusive term for hash, grass, pot, speed, cocaine, crack, heroin, acid, etc.; addictives.

QUOTATIONS

...every time drugs course through the veins of another child, it clouds the future of all our American children. President Bill Clinton, speech, October 16, 1995.

Opiate: An unlocked door in the prison of Identity. It leads into the jail yard. Ambrose Bierce, *The Devil's Dictionary,* 1906.

There is no dirtier or deadlier bullet than the illegal drug capsule. George Bush, U.S. delegate to the United Nations, 1971.

The spirit of the world, the great calm presence of the Creator, comes not forth to the sorceries of opium or of wine. Ralph Waldo Emerson, *Essays, Second Series:* "The Poet," 1844.

The young physician starts life with 20 drugs for each disease, and the old physician ends life with one drug for 20 diseases. Dr. William Osler, c. early 20th century.

ANONYMOUS APHORISMS

Drugs are escapes from which there is no escape.

People who peddle drugs are called pushers, but they should be called clutchers.

A shot in the arm can indicate a hole in the head.

For every high the lows get lower.

Nobody ever solved a problem by giving it the needle.

Better a party-pooper than a pill-popper.

People who will try anything once may not get a second chance.

Heroin is not the stuff of dreams; it is the stuff of nightmares.

ANECDOTES

"Once a person is addicted," said Dr. Jones, "it is better to switch him to something like methadone than to try to cure him, because the odds against cure are so great." "That," said Dr. Smith, "is like saying if you can't beat them join them." "No," said Dr. Jones, "it's more like taking rat poison away from a baby and substituting a teething ring."

FACTS

Primative cultures have used mind-altering substances as part of spiritual rituals throughout history, and drug abuse has existed for nearly as long. Addiction to drugs and narcotics is an ancient and universal vice. In the era of easy global transportation, it has become a more pressing problem because the younger Western nations provide such a lucrative market. Government efforts to control drug traffic began largely in this century, and no one would say they have been notably successful. Indeed, the milder of the drugs—such as marijuana—have gained increasing societal tolerance despite American legislation. The U.S. Department of Justice found that, as of 1993, an estimated 77 million Americans over age 12 had used an illicit drug at least once in their lives. In American high schools, unlawful use of alcohol and tobacco far exceeds all other illicit substances. The debate continues as to whether stricter laws or legalization and regulation would more effectively reduce drug abuse in America, though neither seem to guarantee positive results.

The National Council on Alcoholism and Drug Abuse, Inc., at 12 West 21st Street, New York, NY 10010, (212) 206-6770, is one of several active national groups working in this field.

Economics

DEFINITIONS The function and relationship of the creation, production, distribution, and consumption of resources, goods and services; supply and demand; the science of the cost of living; "the dismal science" (Thomas Carlyle).

QUOTATIONS

Our economy is no more unsinkable than the *Titanic*. It needs to be managed carefully. Robert Hormats, vice-chairman, Goldman, Sachs International, in *U.S. News & World Report,* December 25, 1989.

I tell you that capitalism has no future. Capitalism has destroyed in 100 years almost all the oil that it took millions of years to create. What would happen if every Indian, every Eskimo had a car to drive? Fidel Castro, to visiting Americans, Havana, Cuba, *Vanity Fair,* March, 1994.

Capitalism is on a roll right now that's just extraordinary. Susan Sontag, in *Mother Jones,* May 1989.

...the age of chivalry is gone. That of sophisters, economists, and calculators, has succeeded; and the glory of Europe is extinguished forever. Edmund Burke, "Reflections on the Revolution in France," 1790.

Annual income twenty pounds, annual expenditure nineteen six, result happiness. Annual income twenty pounds, annual expenditure twenty pound ought and six, result misery. Charles Dickens, *David Copperfield,* 1849.

Our economy is the result of millions of decisions we all make every day about producing, earning, saving, investing, and spending. President Dwight D. Eisenhower, May 20, 1958.

If you would know the Value of Money, go and try to borrow some. Benjamin Franklin, *The Way to Wealth,* 1757.

From an economic standpoint, I like to think of society as having two functions. First, it must direct its attention to the age-old problem of converting the earth's resources into goods and commodities. Second, it must direct its attention to placing those goods and commodities into the hands of the men, women, and children who use them. President Lyndon B. Johnson, December 13, 1963.

We have always known that heedless self-interest was bad morals; we know now that it is bad economics. President Franklin D. Roosevelt, second inaugural address, January 20, 1937.

The number of useful and productive laborers is everywhere in proportion to the quantity of capital stock which is employed in setting them to work, and to the particular way in which it is so employed. Adam Smith, *The Wealth of Nations,* 1776.

ANONYMOUS APHORISMS

Bad money drives good money out of circulation. (Known as Gresham's Law because it was mistakenly attributed to Sir Thomas Gresham.)

Competition is the life of trade.

Everyone, in the final analysis, is in business for himself.

Nobody has ever repealed the law of supply and demand.

Economics is nothing more nor less than keeping your head as far above water as you can.

ANECDOTES

When presidential candidate John F. Kennedy was campaigning in Grand View, Missouri, he told the story of a farmer who planted some corn. He met his neighbor on his way home from the fields, and said to him with some concern, "I hope I break even this year. I really need the money."

FACTS

Economics is a comparatively new science—and many contend it isn't a science at all. Unlike anthropology or history, the economist operates in a field with fewer and fewer—rather than more and more—established truths. Perhaps more than other fields of learning, economics depends on the ingenuity of science: the efficiency with which advances in technology are created, or ways are devised to extract the wealth of the earth. The opposite poles of economic theory are laissez-faire—which critics find less than fair to the poorer multitudes—and the totally managed economy— which has yet to prove its ability to provide just and acceptable long-term functionality. One unmistakable truth is that in modern times, for good or bad, the world of economics, the world of politics, and the world of government have become more and more intertwined, and the world's economies are following suit. The 1995 World

Bank report on Global Economic Prospects and Developing Countries highlighted globalization as transforming the world economy.

EDUCATION

(See also College, School)

DEFINITIONS The field or process of teaching or learning; the teaching establishment; academia; preparation for life; "that which discloses to the wise and disguises from the foolish their lack of understanding" (Ambrose Bierce); organized but sometimes synthetic experience; learning by note and by rote.

QUOTATIONS

"The reality is that we have not taught until students have learned. And if students are not learning, the performance of teachers and administrators is not satisfactory." Franklin L. Smith, District of Columbia superintendent of schools, in *The Washington Post,* August 28, 1995.

A teacher affects eternity; he can never tell where his influence stops. Henry Adams, *The Education of Henry Adams,* 1907.

We're going to have the best-educated American people in the world. Senator Dan Quayle of Indiana, September 21, 1988.

Only the educated are free. Epictetus, *Discourses,* c. 1st century.

Next in importance to freedom and justice is popular education, without which neither freedom nor justice can be permanently maintained. U.S. Representative James A. Garfield, letter accepting Republican Presidential nomination, July 12, 1880.

To the strongest and quickest mind it is far easier to learn than to invent. Samuel Johnson, *The Rambler,* September 7, 1751.

A child miseducated is a child lost. President John F. Kennedy, message to the U.S. Congress, January 11, 1962.

…it was in making education not only common to all, but in some sense compulsory on all, that the destiny of the free republics of America was practically settled. James Russell Lowell, *Among My Books: New England Two Centuries Ago,* 1870.

'Tis education forms the common mind: / Just as the twig is bent the tree's inclined. Alexander Pope, *Moral Essays,* 1731.

Learn to live, and live to learn. Bayard Taylor, "To My Daughter," c. mid-19th century.

Training is everything. The peach was once a bitter almond; cauliflower is nothing but cabbage with a college education. Mark Twain, *The Tragedy of Puddinhead Wilson,* 1894.

Today, education is perhaps the most important function of state and local government. U.S. Supreme Court Chief Justice Earl Warren, commenting on *Brown v. Board of Education of Topeka,* May 17, 1954.

ANONYMOUS APHORISMS

School ends, but education doesn't.

Unlearning is harder than learning.

Education has moved from three R's to six: remedial reading, remedial 'riting and remedial 'rithmetic.

He was highly educated—his classroom was on the top floor.

It is hard to teach an old dog new tricks and easy to teach a new dog old tricks.

The only thing more expensive than education is ignorance.

It is more important to use an education than to show it.

ANECDOTES

According to James Boswell, when Samuel Johnson was asked what he thought should be taught to children first, the great writer replied that "It is no matter what you teach them first, any more than what leg you shall put into your breeches first. Sir, you may stand disputing which is best to put in first, but in the mean time your breech is bare. Sir, while you are considering which of two things you should teach your child first, another boy has learnt them both."

"Before you get to the three R's," said Grandpa, "you've got to master the three L's—look, listen, and learn."

FACTS

The gross domestic expenditure on education for the 1994-95 school year is estimated at $509 billion. Approximately 65.1 million students were enrolled in U.S. schools and colleges in 1995, while another 8.1 million were involved in teaching or administration. The total number of college degrees of all kinds has increased from 1.2 million in the mid-1970s to more than 2.241 million. At the turn of the 19th century, U.S. colleges presented under 400 graduates with doctorates; in 1994, over 40,000 doctorates were awarded. The recent trend is to devote more time and more money to education. This is not simply a matter of spontaneous enthusiasm for the learning process. It is largely a result of the increasingly complicated world in which we live; the development of new science and technology and the instinct of most parents to want more education for their children than they had themselves. The baby boom after the Second World War sparked an explosion of educational needs, but even though that baby boom is over, the expansion of educational facilities has continued. Sophisticated teaching machines combined with the use of television and computers have all been part of the onward march of organized education, even while the costs pose increasing problems for both government and individuals. One notable aspect of the modern educational challenge is the growth of nursery schools and preschool facilities that enable both parents to work. The result has been to extend the educational experience by adding on both preprimary and postsecondary years. Though school takes time out of a person's life, statistics indicate that educated people live longer. According to the U.S. Department of Health and Human Services' *1995 U.S. Health Report,* the mortality rate of Americans aged 25 to 64 who had not completed their high school education was twice as high as those who had; and the mortality rate of those who continued their education after high school was 79 percent less than those who earned only a high school diploma.

An excellent source for further information on the dimensions and growth of education is the *Digest of Educational Statistics,* available through the U.S. Government Printing Office Superintendent of Documents, Mail Stop: SSOP, Washington, D.C. 20402-9328.

E LECTIONS

(See also Candidates, Voting)

DEFINITIONS   Acts or processes involved in electing, or casting ballots; going to the polls; where you decide what basket to put your X in; where we learn the public will and the public won't; the candidates' moment of reckoning; the public's voice.

QUOTATIONS

Politics is not a profession that rewards purity or perfection. U.S. Representative Dan Rostenkowski, victory statement, Chicago, IL, March 15, 1994.

When annual elections end, there slavery begins. John Adams, "Thoughts on Government," 1776.

To govern according to the sense and agreeably to the interests of the people is a great and glorious object to government. This object cannot be obtained but through the medium of popular election, and popular election is a mighty evil. Edmund Burke, speech on the Duration of Parliaments, May 8, 1780.

Turn the rascals out! Charles A. Dana, in *The New York Sun,* c. 1870s.

Public confidence in the elective process is the foundation of public confidence in government. President Lyndon B. Johnson, letter to U.S. Congressional leaders, May 26, 1966.

...ballots are the rightful and peaceful successors of bullets... President Abraham Lincoln, message to the U.S. Congress, July 4, 1861.

Democracy substitutes election by the incompetent many for appointment by the corrupt few. George Bernard Shaw, *Man and Superman,* 1903.

You know how it is in an election year. They pick a President and then for four years they pick on him. Adlai E. Stevenson, Jr. August 28, 1952.

After the election's over I bear no malice or feel badly toward anyone because the fellow who lost feels badly enough without eating crow. President Harry S. Truman, November 4, 1948.

ANONYMOUS APHORISMS

If you want your vote to register, be sure to register to vote.

The reason they have no electioneering at the polls is that you never find enough voters there.

For every X on a ballot there is a why.

I care not who writes the nation's songs, as long as I can count the votes.

Elections are the way we find chosen people.

ANECDOTES

It was a crucial election. And Mr. Jones had to stand on line for almost an hour to cast his vote. "I've heard the expression 'Stand up and be counted,' " he said, "but I didn't expect it to be taken literally."

Mr. Brown disliked both candidates but, like a good citizen, he voted anyway. He refused to say which candidate he had voted for, but when asked, he said, "I cast my pearls."

"I vote by proportional representation," said Mr. Green. "How can you do that when you have to choose between two candidates?" he was asked. "It's simple," he replied. "If I'm only 30 percent for one candidate, and 20 percent for the other, I vote for the top percentage."

FACTS

Twentieth-century history has been marked by the steady expansion of the franchise: woman suffrage, lowering of the voting age, abolition of the poll tax, and passage of voting rights laws. Voter turnout has been fairly consistent over the last few decades, ranging from 47 to 69 percent on presidential election years, and slipping as low as 44 percent during the interim-year elections. Older Americans (aged 45+ years) have traditionally turned out for the polls in higher percentages. One possible explanation for voter apathy is the misconception that a single vote is unimportant. But as evidenced by the number of major elections won by a narrow margin, this couldn't be further from the truth; for example, President John F. Kennedy beat Richard Nixon by less than 2 percent. The American electorate is now called upon to vote on more issues than ever before—ecological proposals, housing policies, new taxes and many others as well as the selection of government officials.

The *Statistical Abstract of the United States* also has a section devoted to elections. The Federal Election Commission, located at 999 E. Street, NW, Washington, D.C. 20463, was established in 1975 to enforce and administer the Federal Elections Campaign Act.

Energy

DEFINITIONS   The power output derived from fossil and other fuels, and other sources such as nuclear, water, wind, and solar used to run civilization's machines; fuel.

QUOTATIONS

And God said, let there be light. *Genesis* 1:3.

We are all facing a common problem, which is, how are we going to keep this single resource we have, namely the world, viable? Peter Raven, director, Missouri Botanical Garden, in *Time,* January 2, 1989.

Nuclear power is really too costly to continue in its present form. As other energy options become more cost-effective, the financial risks...associated with nuclear power are going to make it a less attractive option. Many utilities have already identified that. Stephen Smith, executive director, Tennessee Valley Energy Reform Coalition, in *The Christian Science Monitor,* December 14, 1994.

We are here to make a choice between the quick and the dead. Bernard M. Baruch, speech at United Nations Atomic Energy Commission, June 14, 1946.

We are now facing a problem more of ethics than physics. Bernard M. Baruch, speech at United Nations Atomic Energy Commission, June 14, 1946.

We have grasped the mystery of the atom and rejected the Sermon on the Mount. General Omar N. Bradley, Armistice Day speech, 1948.

...the element uranium may be turned into a new and important source of energy in the immediate future. Certain aspects of the situation which has arisen seem to call for watchfulness and, if necessary, quick action on the part of the Administration. Albert Einstein, letter to President Franklin D. Roosevelt, August 2, 1939.

It is not enough just to take this weapon out of the hands of the soldiers. It must be put into the hands of those who will know how to strip its military casing and adapt it to the arts of peace. President Dwight D. Eisenhower, speech to United Nations General Assembly, December 8, 1953.

Today at last we really have good reason for believing that the atom can be made the servant and not the scourge of mankind. President Lyndon B. Johnson, message to International Conference on Peaceful Uses of Atomic Energy, August 30, 1964.

This energy is to propel the machines of progress; to light our cities and our towns; to fire our factories; to provide new sources of fresh water; and to really help us solve the mysteries of outer space as it brightens our life on this planet. We have moved far to tame for peaceful uses the mighty forces unloosed when the atom was split. And we have only just begun. President Lyndon B. Johnson, August 26, 1966.

There is no evil in the atom; only in men's souls. Adlai E. Stevenson, Jr., September 18, 1952.

Never in history has society been confronted with a power so full of promise for the future of man and for the peace of the world. President Harry S. Truman, message to the U.S. Congress, October 3, 1945.

ANONYMOUS APHORISMS

Energy may not make the world go round, but that's about the only thing it doesn't power.

The world has atomic ache.

The question of nuclear energy has created more heat than nuclear energy itself has produced.

Nuclear energy provides endless fuel for discussion.

The idea of self-sustaining nuclear energy is that there is no fuel like an old fuel.

The problem of nuclear energy is a fission expedition.

ANECDOTES

Johnny Brown wanted a career in atomic energy but he found it was too dangerous. It was not because of radiation; it was because everybody wanted to argue with him.

"I don't believe in nuclear energy," said Mr. Jones. "I think we would be better off trying to get energy from sunlight." "What exactly do you think the source of sunlight is?" asked Mr. Smith.

FACTS

From 1970 to 1993, domestic energy production has remained fairly steady, rising from 62 million to 66 million BTUs (British thermal units); consumption, on the other hand, has risen steadily from 66.4 million to nearly 84 million BTUs. Thus, America relies heavily on imports of energy. Until the oil embargo in the mid 1970s resulted in a gas crisis, Americans took energy for granted. Houses, cars, even whole industries are now more energy efficient than ever, but as the population grows, its needs outstrip these conservation measures. Renewable and alternative sources such as wind, water, solar, and wood are now supplementing our energy production, though even these have their impacts. But few contemporary issues have generated as much heat as nuclear energy. In the wake of the atom bomb, the peaceful use of atomic energy was envisioned as the hope of mankind, and despite a sustained effort to block the development of nuclear energy plants on the basis of danger from leakage and problems of waste disposal, the U.S. has grown to rely on nuclear energy for more than 20 percent of domestic electricity. Crude oil, natural gas, liquid natural gas, coal, hydroelectric, and nuclear power are the primary sources of energy for the U.S.

ENVIRONMENT

(See also Leisure, Nature, Population, Wilderness)

DEFINITIONS   The balance of nature which supports human and other life; the external forces which act upon living organisms and determine their survival; the surrounding conditions; Mother Nature's embrace; "Spaceship Earth" (R. Buckminster Fuller).

QUOTATIONS

Clean water is not an expenditure of Federal funds; clean water is an investment in the future of our country. U.S. Representative Bud Schuster, in *The Washington Post,* January 9, 1987.

It isn't pollution that's harming the environment. It's the impurities in our air and water that are doing it. Attributed to Dan Quayle.

For a long time, the protection of the environment was a subject of concern to a few public figures, acting more or less in isolation, and a number of associations or movements. What we are seeing now is a more acute awareness of this requirement among political leaders. Michel Rocard, Prime Minister of France, in the *Los Angeles Times,* October 10, 1989.

We're finally going to get the bill for the Industrial Age. If the projections are right, it's going to be a big one: the ecological collapse of the planet. Jeremy Rifkin, president, Foundation on Economic Trends, in the *Toronto Star* reprinted from *World Press Review,* December 30, 1989.

ANONYMOUS APHORISMS

Man against the environment is like a canary against a mirror—in a coal mine.

In the future, landfills may hold the world's greatest concentrations of natural resources.

If we want to sweep any more environmental destruction under the rug, we're going to need to raise the ceiling.

If we don't care for the environment it will, undoubtedly, take care of us.

ANECDOTES

A hermit came down from the mountains for the first time in a decade to buy some provisions in a little town in the middle of a forest. Though the half dozen buildings were completely unchanged, down to the wildflowers pushing up through every crevice in the sidewalk, much to his surprise, Main Street was paved. "It's a shame," he muttered, "what they're doing to the environment these days."

FACTS

The environment has supported human life since man moved from four legs to two, but man's knowledge of it keeps expanding. And the more knowledge we have, the more miraculous nature seems, with its constant balancing of forces, its mathematical preciseness and its inexorable workings. Man's use of the resources of nature constantly grows, although in our time we have come to learn that these resources are not infinite. According to a report by the Environmental Protection Agency, releases of pollutants have fallen in recent years, while recycling has increased significantly. Many industries are discovering that going green saves them green; reducing waste of resources and waste output reduces costs of production in most cases. But considerable damage has already been done, and continues to be done to the environment. There are hazardous waste sites in every state; from 1 in Nevada to 108 in New Jersey as of 1995. And for every finding by environmental organizations there are industry lawyers prepared to dispute the findings; whether this system leads to a cleaner planet, or the demise of civilization only our children and their children will know.

For current statistics on pollution, and other information relating to the condition of the environment, contact the Environmental Protection Agency, 401 M St., S.W., Washington, D.C. 20460, which was established in 1970.

ETHICS

DEFINITIONS   Principles of right or justice; morals; a science or set of moral principles; standards of conduct; societal dictates of proper behavior for all individuals toward others.

QUOTATIONS

No one spends another person's money as wisely as he spends his own. U.S. Representative Richard K. Armey, in the *The New York Times,* December 6, 1994.

The moral education of our children is the first priority of a nation. We're not just talking about learning subjects here, about history or calculus—whatever. In the education of our children, we're involved in nothing less than the architecture of souls. William J. Bennett, former U.S. Secretary of Education, speech at Oregon State University, August, 1994.

Expedients are for the hour, but principles are for the ages. Rev. Henry Ward Beecher, *Proverbs from Plymouth Pulpit,* 1887.

A people that values its privileges above its principles soon loses both. President Dwight D. Eisenhower, inaugural address, January 20, 1953.

The shield against the stingings of conscience is the universal practice of our contemporaries. Ralph Waldo Emerson, *Representative Men:* "On the Uses of Great Men," 1860.

Everybody has a little bit of Watergate in him. Rev. Billy Graham, February 3, 1974.

The moral sense, or conscience, is as much a part of man as his leg or arm. Thomas Jefferson, letter to his nephew Peter Carr, August 10, 1787.

We cannot divide ourselves between right and expedience. Policy must yield to morality. Immanuel Kant, *Critique of Pure Reason,* 1781.

This above all: to thine own self be true, / And it must follow, as the night the day, / Thou canst not then be false to any man. William Shakespeare, *Hamlet,* 1600.

Goodness is the only investment that never fails. Henry D. Thoreau, *Walden:* "Higher Laws," 1854.

There is only one morality, as there is only one geometry. *Voltaire,* Philosophical Dictionary, 1764.

ANONYMOUS APHORISMS

All's fair in love and war.

We live in a society where the sin is getting caught.

Honesty is the best policy, but sometimes it has a high premium.

Knowing what's right doesn't mean much unless you do what's right.

Do right or get left.

ANECDOTES

"The worst thing that can happen to a youngster starting school," said the lawyer, "is to be caught cheating." "Not at all," said the clergyman, "the worst thing at the start of a person's life is to cheat and not get caught."

FACTS

On the heels of recurrent tales of corruption in every aspect of modern life, it is a commonly accepted fact that ethics are what each of us thinks other people should apply. But the fact is that in many respects, life today is infinitely more ethical than any previous era. We have simply created more and higher ethical standards than in the past. For example, we no longer permit rich people to buy their way out of compulsory service or to hire a surrogate in time of war, although this was once considered perfectly ethical and proper. Once considered a marital right, domestic violence is now recognized as a crime. Indeed, there is room to believe that what seems to be a decline in ethics is actually a considerable rise in acceptable standards.

ETHNICITY

(See also Immigration, Minorities, Race)

DEFINITIONS   The subject of race, nationality, cultural heritage or customs maintained in common by a recognizable group of people; background; origins; ancestral derivation; the club you were born in; ingredients in the melting pot.

QUOTATIONS

We conceive distinctly enough the French, the Spanish, the German genius, and it is not the less real, that perhaps we should not meet in either of those nations a single individual who corresponded with the type. Ralph Waldo Emerson, *Essays, Second Series:* "Nominalist and Realist," 1844.

We are a nation of many nationalities, many races, many religions—bound together by a single unity, the unity of freedom and equality. President Franklin D. Roosevelt, November 1, 1940.

ANONYMOUS APHORISMS

Many people who speak fondly of the old country were either born here or only began to think of it fondly after they got out of it.

America is its own league of nations.

You can take a man out of a country, but you can't take that country out of the man.

We are all ethnics; some of us just work at it harder than others.

Some people are more concerned with where they sprung from than with where they are going.

ANECDOTES

When New York politicians used to refer to the Three-I League, they were not referring to Dartmouth, Yale, and Harvard Universities. They were referring to the political trip that any aspiring mayoral candidate of the New York melting pot felt he had to make to kick off his campaign: a visit to Ireland, Italy, and Israel.

"You can't tell anything by people's names anymore," lamented Mr. Jones, "because all the foreigners take new ones." "On the contrary," said Mr. Smith, "you can tell the most important thing about them. They don't want to be treated like foreigners."

FACTS

There are more than 140 nations holding membership in the United Nations. There are at least ten separate major religions, with innumerable sects and cultural or national divisions among them: in the same way so many nations have different racial groups within their borders. There are roughly 6,500 languages spoken in the world. The *World Almanac* lists some 220 languages, each spoken by over 1 million people. The variety of ethnicity is almost infinite; and the richest and healthiest life is in those countries which have managed to blend and absorb a number of different ethnic heritages. It's a multiethnic world, and the U.S. is that world in miniature.

Ethnologue: Languages of the World, 12th edition, edited by Barbara F. Grimes (Summer Institute of Linguistics), contains extensive information on the world's languages and is illustrated with maps indicating ethno-linguistic divisions.

EXPERIENCE

DEFINITIONS   Knowledge gained from having performed or been part of a specific event or function; an event or function that is remembered by those who participated; the school of hard knocks; "the name everyone gives to their mistakes" (Oscar Wilde); what's left after everything else is gone.

QUOTATIONS

Whatever I was going to be able to do had to be by virtue of my dealing with the only asset I had, and that was my experience. Attributed to R. Buckminster Fuller.

I'm utterly convinced that we are all here for one another and that every experience that everyone is having is relevant. It all counts. The Universe is so extraordinarily well designed that it needs all those experiences. Attributed to R. Buckminster Fuller.

Men are wise in proportion, not to their experience, but to their capacity for experience. James Boswell, *Life of Samuel Johnson,* 1791.

The knowledge of the world is only to be acquired in the world, and not in a closet. Lord Chesterfield, Letters to His Son, 1774.

Experience keeps a dear school, yet fools will learn in no other. Benjamin Franklin, *Poor Richard's Almanac,* 1743.

Measurement of life should be proportioned rather to the intensity of its experience than to its actual length. Thomas Hardy, "A Pair of Blue Eyes," 1873.

I have but one lamp by which my feet are guided, and that is the lamp of experience. I know of no way of judging the future but by the past. Patrick Henry, March 23, 1775.

Nothing ever becomes real till it is experienced. John Keats, letter to George and Georgiana Keats, February 14 through May 3, 1818.

One thorn of experience is worth a whole wilderness of warning. James Russell Lowell, *Among My Books:* "Shakespeare Once More," 1870.

A strong and secure man digests his experiences (deeds and misdeeds alike) just as he digests his meat, even when he has some bits to swallow. Friedrich Wilhelm Nietsche, *Genealogy of Morals,* 1887.

I had rather have a fool to make me merry than experience to make me sad. William Shakespeare, *As You Like It,* 1600.

ANONYMOUS APHORISMS

Experience is largely nontransferable.

The trouble with experience is that it sometimes teaches you too late.

Experience is the dividend you get from your mistakes.

Experience is good if not bought too dear.

ANECDOTES

According to James Boswell, his friend Samuel Johnson once commented, in 1791, about a gentleman who had been very unhappy in marriage, and had married again immediately after his wife died. He said that it was "the triumph of hope over experience."

The matchmaker for the local boxing champion arranged a match with an opponent he had never seen. He had simply asked for an experienced fighter. On the day of the fight, a middle-aged man with a crooked nose, a punch-drunk manner, and two huge cauliflower ears arrived in the dressing room. The matchmaker was aghast. "I asked for an experienced fighter," he complained, "but not a damaged one."

Exploration

(See also Space)

DEFINITIONS   Traveling to or through unknown areas to determine their nature; going places and seeing things; getting to know the unknown; "to boldly go where no man has gone before" (Gene Rodenberry).

QUOTATIONS

Knowledge begets knowledge. The more I see, the more impressed I am—not with what we know—but with how tremendous the areas are that are as yet unexplored. Lt. Col. John H. Glenn, Jr., speech to a joint session of the U..S. Congress, February 26, 1962.

The future leaves no option. Responsible men must push forward in the exploration of space, near and far. Their voyages must be made in peace for purposes of peace on earth. President Lyndon B. Johnson, message to the U.S. Senate, February 7, 1967.

Together let us explore the stars, conquer the deserts, eradicate disease, tap the ocean depths and encourage the arts and commerce. President John F. Kennedy, inaugural address, January 20, 1961.

Behind him lay the gray Azores, / Behind, the Gates of Hercules; / Before him not the ghost of shores; / Before him only shoreless seas. / The good mate said: "Now must we pray, / For lo! the very stars are gone. / Brave Admiral, speak; what shall I say." / "Why, say 'Sail on! Sail on! and on!'" Joaquin Miller, "Columbus," 1896.

The learn'd is happy Nature to explore, / The fool is happy that he knows no more... Alexander Pope, *Essay on Man*, 1734.

ANONYMOUS APHORISMS

One man's exploration is another man's home ground.

There is always someone who wants to see what's on the other side of the mountain, and there's always another mountain.

The more you explore, the more you find that needs exploring.

The Atlantic was outer space to Christopher Columbus' generation.

Exploration means going where the hand of man has never before set foot.

ANECDOTES

Explorers often prefer wild territory to the sophisticated civilization they called home. This has given rise to a new version of the dialogue between reporter Henry

Stanley who finally found Dr. Livingstone and uttered the words, "Dr. Livingstone, I presume?" "You certainly do," the good doctor should have said. After all, he liked being where he had hoped to remain undiscovered.

Columbus set out to find a passage to the Indies and failed; he found North America instead. Ponce de Leon looked for the fountain of youth and found Florida. The greatest explorers seem to find something other than what they seek.

FACTS

Terrestrial exploration—as opposed to space exploration—is far from over. Indeed, there is more exploration today than at any time in humanity's history. Centuries ago, people hunted for gold; new routes to Asia; and new lands. Today we continue to seek gold and other minerals, fossil fuels, and the secrets of the ocean depths. Remote and hidden portions of our planet remain undiscovered or unexplored: awaiting the next generation to add their names to a roster which includes people like Captain James Cook, Ferdinand Magellan, Margaret Mead, and Sir Richard Burton.

The Society of Exploration Geophysicists, 8801 South Yale, Tulsa, OK 74137; the Explorers Club, Northern California Chapter, c/o U.S. Geological Survey, MS-901, 345 Middlefield Road, Menlo Park, CA 94025; and the National Geographic Society, 1145 17th St. NW, Washington, D.C. 20036, span the range of modern exploration.

FAMILY

DEFINITIONS A household composed of parents and children; a group of persons closely related by blood, marriage or similar commitment; a creation of nature which is never what it used to be; the original mom and pop enterprise; "the nucleus of civilization" (Will and Ariel Durant).

QUOTATIONS

Building a family is the hardest job a man can do, but it's also the most important. President Bill Clinton, speech, October 16, 1995.

We can only build strong families when men and women respect each other, when they have partnerships, when men are as involved in the homeplace as women are in the workplace. President Bill Clinton, speech, October 16, 1995.

We [Democrats would] rather preserve a family than build an orphanage. We believe that we're too good as a people to seek solutions by hurting the weakest among us—especially our children. And at our wisest, we believe that we [Americans] are all in this together. New York Governor Mario M. Cuomo, in the *The New York Times,* December 17, 1994.

It is not observed in history that families improve with time. George William Curtis, *Prue and I,* 1856.

Men are what their mothers made them. Ralph Waldo Emerson, *The Conduct of Life:* "Fate," 1860.

Late children, early orphans. Benjamin Franklin, *Poor Richard's Almanac,* 1742.

In back of every achievement is a proud wife and a surprised mother-in-law. Brooks Hays, sworn in as aide to President Kennedy, December 1, 1961.

...how convenient it would be to many of our great men and great families of doubtful origin, could they have the privilege of the heroes of yore, who, whenever their origin was involved in obscurity, modestly announced themselves descended from a god... Washington Irving, *A History of New York by Diedrich Knickerbocker,* 1809.

...a family...is a little kingdom, torn with factions and exposed to revolutions. Samuel Johnson, *Rasselas,* 1759.

The family is one of nature's masterpieces. George Santayana, *The Life of Reason, Vol. 2:* "Reason in Society," 1905.

...I do not condemn nepotism, provided the relatives really work. U.S. Senator Margaret Chase Smith of Maine, speech to National Women's Republican Conference, April 16, 1962.

The family—that great conservator of national virtue and strength—how can you hope to build it up in the midst of violence, debauchery and excess? Mrs. Elizabeth Cady Stanton, testimony to New York State Senate Judiciary Committee, 1861.

ANONYMOUS APHORISMS

An ounce of blood is worth a pound of friendship.

Large family, quick help.

Blood is thicker than water.

You pick your friends, you accept your family.

ANECDOTES

The salesman knocked at the front door, and a young woman with two toddlers clinging to her answered the door. "Hello," said the salesman, "I'm looking for the head of the house." "How about talking to its heart and soul," replied the young woman.

It has been said that some families look after each other, but others merely look like each other. When this was told to Mr. Brown, he disagreed. "What makes a family," he said, "isn't whether they look alike or look after each other; it's that they share a common will—waiting for probate."

FACTS

According to U.S. Census information, the average family size has been shrinking slowly but steadily since the 1940s. The concept of family has been thoroughly redefined by modern times. Past generations declared the death of the family when young people emigrated from their families' farms to seek their fortunes elsewhere. The concept of family has been reshaped from an extended unit that included up to three generations living together to a nuclear unit consisting of parents and children; to a broader scope which now recognizes nontraditional groupings such as single-parent homes and unmarried couples with children. It is apparently the habit of every generation to worry about the decline of the family. Currently, the doomsayers point to the tremendous rise in the number of households in which both parents work, leaving children and teenagers to raise themselves. They also point to the increased mobility of young people, even before they go off to college and careers. And they discern in the trend toward smaller families a decline in the number of uncles, aunts, cousins, sisters, and brothers who comprise the larger family edifice. But there are some good prospects for the family of the future. For example, longer life expectancy gives hope that more young people will know their grandparents and great grandparents longer, and that older people will have more older relatives around, too. The nature of family life continues to change, of course. In the 1940s, 20 percent of wives worked outside of their homes. Fifty years later, both spouses work among the majority of married couples. In 1975, there were 56.7 million American families. In 1994, there were 97 million households according to the *World Almanac*.

The publications of the U.S. Census Bureau provide basic information about various statistical aspects of American family life.

FASHION

DEFINITIONS
The established style of the time; that which is considered the height of contemporary taste in clothing, homes, automobiles and lifestyles; keeping up with the Joneses; the look-of-the-month club.

QUOTATIONS
If you are not in fashion, you are nobody. Lord Chesterfield, Letters to His Son, 1774.

Eat to please thyself, but dress to please others. Benjamin Franklin, *Poor Richard's Almanac,* 1738.

Be not the first by whom the new are tried, / Nor yet the last to lay the old aside. Alexander Pope, *An Essay on Criticism,* 1711.

On the whole, I think that it cannot be maintained that dressing has in this or any country risen to the dignity of an art. Henry D. Thoreau, *Walden:* "Economy," 1854.

Every generation laughs at the old fashions, but follows religiously the new. Henry D. Thoreau, *Walden:* "Economy," 1854.

When seen in the perspective of half-a-dozen years or more, the best of our fashions strike us as grotesque, if not unsightly. Thorstein Veblen, *The Theory of the Leisure Class,* 1899.

Fashion is that by which the fantastic becomes for a moment universal. Oscar Wilde, *The Picture of Dorian Gray,* 1891.

ANONYMOUS APHORISMS

Fashion is just a more polite name for forced obsolescence.

There is no tyrant stronger than fashion.

Yesterday's fashion will probably be tomorrow's; but it isn't today's.

Those who follow the fashion never create it.

Fashion is one human being's unconquerable will to look just like all the others.

ANECDOTES

"This," said the salesman as he trotted out a new suit for Mr. Jones, "is what they are wearing." "In that case," came the reply, "I think I'd like to see something newer."

"I can't keep up with the hemlines," said Mrs. Jones. "The way they go up and down, with the fashions, they should call them hem and haw lines."

FACTS

The fashion industry is a major economic factor when there is sufficient prosperity to afford discretionary spending. That is because the fashion business depends so much on the look of a product becoming out of date, rather than on products wearing out. Fashions are not all dependent on forced obsolescence, however. Some fashion trends arise from the desire of people to be accepted by those who adhere to a particular style. In the view of some observers, it's no accident that adolescent fashions in dress and speech are adapted from what they have observed contemporary celebrities and television characters publicly flaunting. Satellite television has brought the same American programming to a worldwide audience, creating a heterogeneous global style no matter what the social or political system of the particular place.

FLAG

DEFINITIONS   Usually a piece of cloth, apt to be oblong or square, bearing the distinctive arrangement of uniquely identifiable symbols and colors of a nation, or state, or having a meaning as a signal; in the U.S., "Old Glory" or "The Stars and Stripes" or "The Star Spangled Banner;" the colors; our national trademark; banner.

QUOTATIONS

I pledge allegiance to the flag of the United States of America and to the Republic for which it stands, One Nation under God, indivisible, with liberty and justice for all. *Pledge of Allegiance,* initiated by the Reverend Francis Bellamy, 1892.

The Republic never retreats. Its flag is the only flag that has never known defeat. Where that flag leads we follow, for we know that the hand that bears it onward is the unseen hand of God. Albert J. Beveridge, speech in Philadelphia, February 15, 1899.

"You're a Grand Old Flag," George M. Cohan, song title from *George Washington, Jr.,* 1906.

Oh, say, does that star-spangled banner yet wave / O'er the land of the free, and the home of the brave? Francis Scott Key, "The Star-Spangled Banner," September 14, 1814.

Yes, we'll rally 'round the flag, boys, we'll rally once again / Shouting the battle cry of Freedom... George F. Root, "The Battle Cry of Freedom," 1863.

"Shoot, if you must, this old gray head, / But spare your country's flag," she said. John Greenleaf Whittier, "Barbara Frietchie," 1868.

The flag is the embodiment, not of sentiment but of history. It represents the experiences made by men and women, the experiences of those who do and live under that flag. President Woodrow Wilson, speech in New York, NY, June 14, 1915.

ANONYMOUS APHORISMS

Folding the flag is like taking care of the nation.

Under whose colors do you march?

Three cheers for the red white and blue.

Show your colors.

As long as your flag is flying, your cause is still alive.

ANECDOTES

Nobody knows who devised the first flag, but there is a story about how it happened. Seems that one warrior got hurt in a fight between two tribes, and held up his bloody garment to show that he needed help, and everybody followed him. That's why so many flags use the color red.

Q: Why do you have such respect for the flag? A: Because it's so easy to follow.

FACTS

The American flag has grown with the nation, both in its international stature and the number of stars it bears. The first official American flag, recognized by an Act of Congress, was raised on June 14, 1777. Its 13 stars were in a pattern similar to the contemporary 50-star flag. It's appropriate to fly the flag from sunrise to sunset when the weather permits. Holidays when the flag should be displayed are as follows: New Year's Day, Inauguration Day, Rev. Dr. Martin Luther King, Jr.'s Birthday, Presidents' Day, Patriots Day (April 19), Armed Forces Day, Memorial Day (half-staff until noon), Flag Day (June 14), Independence Day (July 4th), Labor Day, Constitution Day, Columbus Day, Navy Day, Veterans Day, and all election days. There is no reliable estimate of the number of flags flown every day in the United States, but the Elks as well as various military and veterans groups have material about the American flag's history, and protocols for its care, use, and display that can be helpful.

FOOD

(See also Cooking, Dieting)

DEFINITIONS   That which is ingested by living organisms in solid form to sustain life (although food can also be in liquid form and drunk rather than eaten); nutrients; victuals; provisions; grub; comestibles.

QUOTATIONS

An army marches on its stomach. Attributed to Napoleon Bonaparte, c. late 18th century.

Tell me what you eat, and I will tell you what you are. Anthelme Brillat Savarin, *The Physiology of Taste,* 1825.

A Book of Verses underneath the Bough, / A Jug of Wine, a Loaf of Bread— / and Thou Beside me singing in the Wilderness— / Oh, Wilderness were Paradise enow. Edward Fitzgerald, *Rubaiyat of Omar Khayyam* (translation of 11th century Persian philosopher-poet), 1859–1872.

Life, within doors, has few pleasanter prospects than a neatly arranged and well-provisioned breakfast table. Nathaniel Hawthorne, *The House of the Seven Gables,* 1851.

Other circumstances being the same, it may be affirmed that countries are populous according to the quantity of human food which they produce or can acquire, and happy according to the liberality with which this food is divided, or the quantity which a day's labor will purchase. Thomas R. Malthus, *Essay on the Principle of Population,* 1798.

Avoid fried meats, which angry the blood. Leroy (Satchel) Paige, in *Collier's,* June 13, 1953.

Upon what meat doth this our Caesar feed, / That he is grown so great. William Shakespeare, *Julius Caesar,* 1599.

There is no love sincerer than the love of food. George Bernard Shaw, *Man and Superman,* 1903.

ANONYMOUS APHORISMS

Man cannot live by bread alone, he must have peanut butter. (Attributed to Bill Cosby, c. 1960s.)

One man's meat is another man's poison.

Eat to live, not live to eat. (Attributed to Benjamin Franklin, but going back to an ancient Roman saying.)

America is the home of fast food and slow burns.

Destiny may shape our ends, but it gets a lot of help from the food we eat.

The way to a man's heart is through his stomach. (Attributed to author Fanny Fern.)

ANECDOTES

A man was dying in the endless desert when suddenly he came across a bottle in the sand. It was empty but he rubbed it against his chest and as he did so there was a cloud of vapor and a huge genie popped out of the bottle, saying, "For three wishes, I am yours to command." The man did not make a wish immediately, because he realized that he had only three, so he thought carefully and commanded, "My first wish is to have the greatest riches of every kind in the world: food, drink, women, and power." "It is done," replied the genie, and with a snap of fingers the man was transported to a magnificent mansion, elegantly dressed, surrounded by adoring beauties who fed him and fondled him. "Now what is your second wish?" the genie asked. "To be once more in the absolute prime of life," mused the man. Once again the genie snapped his fingers and there, in the same magnificent mansion, surrounded by the same beauties, the man became a magnificent physical specimen of young manhood. "You have one wish left," the genie advised. The man thought to himself, "I have everything I have always wanted, but as long as I know there is one thing more—" and he said to the genie, "Make me a malted." And in another snap of the finger there was the mansion, there were the beautiful women, and there, on the couch where the man had been, there rested a soda fountain glass containing a chocolate malted. The moral of this story is that what you eat is always food for thought.

FACTS

The 20th century saw the burgeoning of the so-called green revolution: the development of hybrid and mutant forms of major foods like rice and wheat that resist the familiar ravages of nature better than ever before. As a result, the world's supply of food has generally risen; but the big problem is that the world's population has risen much more quickly. Food and population conferences in the 1990s agreed that with about 86 million people a year being added to the world's population, the collective appetite was growing faster than the crops to feed it. The U.S. Department of Agriculture issues quarterly reports on the National Food Situation, as well as annual crop estimates; and the Food and Agriculture Organization of the United Nations, founded in 1945, concentrates on increasing global nutrition, improving standards of living, monitoring world food supply, assisting nations in agricultural development, and acting as an international food and agricultural data resource.

F OOTBALL

(See also Sports)

DEFINITIONS   The name for several related games played on a rectangular field with a ball, the American game using an oval ball, and involving considerable physical contact; tackle, run, pass and punt; gridiron mayhem; week-end war.

QUOTATIONS

Some people say if you're scared, you should take off your uniform. But I feel there's nothing wrong with being a little bit scared. I think you play your best football when you're scared. Jerry Rice, in the *Los Angeles Times,* January 20, 1989.

Pro football is like nuclear warfare. There are no winners, only survivors. Frank Gifford, in *Sports Illustrated,* July 4, 1960.

Football is really and truly an American institution. It embodies our highest ideals of character and courage. President Lyndon B. Johnson, January 13, 1966.

Football today is far too much a sport for the few who can play it well; the rest of us, and too many of our children, get our exercise from climbing up the seats in stadiums, or from walking across the room to turn on our television sets. President John F. Kennedy, speech in New York, NY, December 5, 1961.

In short, in life, as in a football game, the principle to follow is: Hit the line hard; don't foul and don't shirk, but hit the line hard. Theodore Roosevelt, *The Strenuous Life,* 1910.

…you base foot-ball player. William Shakespeare, *King Lear,* 1605.

As concerning football, I protest unto you that it may rather be called a friendly kind of fight than a play or recreation… Philip Stubbes, *The Anatomie of Abuses,* 1588.

ANONYMOUS APHORISMS

Football is sport's battlefield, where they speak of quarterbacks throwing bombs, penalties, kicks, hits, blitzing and defense.

For every quarterback on the field, there are a thousand in the stands.

It's quite a game when you risk a foot to gain a yard.

Making the team is hard enough for a single player, but hardest for the coach.

The most wide open position in football is that of Monday morning quarterback.

ANECDOTES

When Mr. Brown went to the stadium to see his son play quarterback for the local team in the big game, he found himself surrounded by fans for the other team. Throughout the game, they yelled, "Offense!" He screamed, "Defense!" When his son was on the field, he yelled, "Pass!" They yelled, "Intercept!" It was a close game, and the clamor grew and grew. Finally, time came for the last play. Quarterback Brown threw a long pass. Just as time ran out his teammate caught it and scored the winning touchdown. When the Browns got home, young Brown said, "I've got to go lie down. It's been a hard afternoon." "You had a hard afternoon," said his father. "It was nothing compared to what I went through in the stands."

FACTS

The modern American game of football is only a bit more than 100 years old, but its ancestors go back to the early tribal cultures. Today, American football is a major professional sport with many international cousins. Canadian football is played on a longer field; rugby and soccer are played worldwide on almost every continent; and Australian football has an interesting array of passing and tackling rules. Like all American spectator sports, football has become big business. But the game has also helped support educational institutions; provided television entertainment; and built commercial sports enterprises in dozens of cities. Football's advocates regard it as the ultimate team sport, requiring a degree of coordination more demanding than in any other team competition. The game's critics say it is unnecessarily rough and risky to the players. These are points of view. The indisputable fact is that more than 50 million spectators attend college and professional games each year, and football is running neck and neck with horseracing as the most popular American spectator sport.

Unlike some other sports, football has no single rule-making authority. The professional and college games are governed by their constituent associations—the principal ones being the National Football League, 410 Park Avenue, New York, NY 10022, and the National Collegiate Athletic Association, 6201 College Blvd., Overland Park, KS 66211-2422.

Foreign Affairs

DEFINITIONS A government's conduct of its dealings with other nations; the whole subject of relations among nations; statesmanship; the function of diplomats; the striped-pants set; diplomacy; us and them.

QUOTATIONS

The trick of statesmanship is to turn the inevitable to one's own advantage. Christopher Layne, in *The Atlantic Monthly,* June, 1989.

Allies trust each other in all matters. That is what an alliance is… Raising a club to conduct negotiations is simply not permissible. Sosuke Uno, Foreign Minister of Japan, in *The Los Angeles Times,* June 2, 1989.

What [today's] balance of power says is that we are trying to arrange an international order in which disagreements… do not threaten the overall system… You do this by making it difficult for any nation or group of nations to achieve preponderant power. Henry A. Kissinger, former U.S. Secretary of State, in *The Washington Post,* April 11, 1994.

…the Constitution follows the flag… We warn the American people that imperialism abroad will lead quickly and inevitably to despotism at home… Democratic Party platform, 1900.

We live…in a sea of semantic disorder in which old labels no longer faithfully describe. Police states are called "people's democracies." Armed conquest of free people is called "liberation." President Dwight D. Eisenhower, State of the Union message, January 7, 1960.

Millions for defense but not a cent for tribute. Robert Goodloe Harper, June 18, 1798.

…peace, commerce and honest friendship, with all nations—entangling alliances with none. President Thomas Jefferson, first inaugural address, March 4, 1801.

Let us never negotiate out of fear. But let us never fear to negotiate. President John F. Kennedy, inaugural address, January 20, 1961.

The country is as strong abroad only as it's strong at home. President John F. Kennedy, speech in St. Paul, MN, October 6, 1962.

Our policy is directed not against any country or doctrine but against hunger, poverty, desperation, and chaos. George C. Marshall, U.S. Secretary of State, introducing the Marshall Plan at Harvard University, June 5, 1947.

We seek friendly relations with all nations. Any nation can be our friend without being any other nation's enemy. President Richard M. Nixon, July 15, 1971.

We must be the great arsenal of democracy. President Franklin D. Roosevelt, December 29, 1940.

There is a homely adage which runs, "Speak softly and carry a big stick; you will go far." If the American nation will speak softly and yet build and keep at a pitch of the highest training a thoroughly efficient navy, the Monroe Doctrine will go far. Vice President Theodore Roosevelt, September 2, 1901.

I believe that it must be the policy of the United States to support free peoples who are resisting attempted subjugation by armed minorities or by outside pressures. President Harry S. Truman, speech to a joint session of the U.S. Congress, March 12, 1947.

It is our true policy to steer clear of permanent alliances with any portion of the foreign world. President George Washington, farewell address, September 1796.

ANONYMOUS APHORISMS

International relations are as difficult as any other in-laws.

The United States always seems to lose when it wears a diplomat's striped pants.

In international diplomacy, it isn't as important being right as not getting left.

The language of international diplomacy, when you get down to it, is a language of signs, smoke signals, and ultimatums; its actions speak louder than its words.

Diplomacy is the language of international relations, which can say one thing that has two absolutely opposite meanings for the two parties involved.

International diplomacy requires the ability to commit to saying absolutely nothing definitively that can be understood in many different languages.

ANECDOTES

One veteran foreign emissary asked a new recruit, "How did you like your trip abroad?" The recruit replied, "Well, it was all right, but all the people there are foreigners."

Q: Who was the first person to settle in America? A: I don't know; undoubtedly some damned foreigner.

"The trouble with international relations," said the expert, "is that we have a whole new group of powers involved." "Not at all," said the other expert, "they're the same powers as before—the power of persuasion and the power of superior force."

FACTS

Even as George Washington and Thomas Jefferson were counseling our infant nation against foreign alliances, America's ships were building international commerce and an array of visitors were landing on America's shores. In the old days, the U.S. thought of itself as self-sufficient. Today its own natural resources are not sufficient; it is both customer and supplier to the world. Consequently, America plays host to the world. This is where the United Nations has its headquarters. New York City hosts the U.N. assembly, which is already the longest-lived attempt at any kind of international Parliament. The United Nations began with 51 nations; by the mid-1970s, it was approaching a membership of 150 nations; and in 1996, there were 185 member nations. Some are very tiny, and some are huge, but in the U.N. General Assembly each nation is a member unto itself.

For a list of the currently operating international organizations and their particular subjects, see the latest *World Almanac*.

FRATERNITIES

(See also Clubs)

DEFINITIONS   Collegiate or sometimes high school social clubs which were originally restricted to male membership, but the term is now used collectively to embrace sororities as well, with Greek letters as their names; "the Greeks;" frats.

QUOTATIONS

Man seeketh in society comfort, use, and protection. Francis Bacon, *The Advancement of Learning,* 1605.

All men seek the society of those who think and act somewhat like themselves. William Cobbett, *Advice to Young Men,* 1829.

Brothers all in honor, as in one community, / Scholars and gentlemen. William Wordsworth, *The Prelude,* 1850.

ANONYMOUS APHORISMS

His college fraternity was Gotta Getta Gal.

College today is like a batch of French Revolutions—the students take liberties, the parents worry about fraternities and the government insists on equalities.

The basis of the fraternity system is that not all men are brothers.

ANECDOTES

After Johnny was invited to join a college fraternity, he had to undergo a rather arduous initiation. When it was over, he said to the fraternity head, "If this is what happens when you get tapped, what happens when they don't like you?"

"Remember," said the fraternity man to a prospective member, "when you join a fraternity you become part of a carefully selected group." "But," said the student, "that's what I was told my whole college class was—part of a carefully selected group." "Yes," said the fraternity man, "but our group is smaller and even more selective." "So am I," said the student.

FACTS

After a generation of decline, college fraternities seem to be holding their own. One reason is that they have broadened their base of potential membership. This is due to the abandonment of certain traditional racial and religious restrictions. Another reason is that fraternity houses offer an interesting alternative to dormitory residence. The honorary scholastic fraternities such as Phi Beta Kappa have not had the problems that have faced the social clubs. During the long membership drought, a number of the social fraternities and sororities lost chapters to an unprecedented extent, and for a while the colleges themselves did nothing to help "The Greeks" because it was generally believed that modern egalitarianism frowned on exclusive clubs. But this has also become moderated with time. With the passage of amended by-laws that banned the traditional hazing rituals, "The Greeks," it appears, are here to stay on most modern campuses.

FREEDOM

(See also America, Liberty)

DEFINITIONS   The right or privilege to make one's choices for oneself, unimpeded by another's will; the condition of unfettered self-determination; that which no one cares too much about until it's gone.

QUOTATIONS

It is true that you cannot eat freedom and you cannot power machinery with democracy. But then neither can political prisoners turn on the light in the cells of a dictatorship. Corazon C. Aquino, in *The Washington Post,* June 29, 1992.

We know what works: Freedom works. We know what's right: Freedom is right. We know how to secure a more just and prosperous life for man on earth—through free markets, free speech, free elections and the exercise of free will unhampered by the state. President George Bush, in *The Washington Post,* January 21, 1989.

Democracy, human rights, the rule of law, these are the building blocks of peace and freedom. President George Bush, in the *The New York Times,* February 1, 1992.

Now, we Americans understand freedom. We have earned it; we have lived for it, and we have died for it. This nation and its people are freedom's models in a searching world. We can be freedom's missionaries in a doubting world. Senator Barry M. Goldwater of Arizona, accepting Republican Presidential nomination in San Francisco, July 16, 1964.

The most stringent protection of free speech would not protect a man in falsely shouting fire in a theater and causing a panic. U.S. Supreme Court Associate Justice Oliver Wendell Holmes, Jr., commenting on *Schenck v. U.S.,* March 3, 1919.

If there is any principle of the Constitution that more imperatively calls for attachment than any other it is the principle of free thought—not free thought for those who agree with us but freedom for the thought we hate... U.S. Supreme Court Associate Justice Oliver Wendell Holmes, Jr., commenting on *U.S. v. Schwimmer,* May 27, 1929.

Where the press is free and every man able to read, all is safe. Thomas Jefferson, letter to Charles Yancey, 1816.

Since the general civilization of mankind, I believe that there are more instances of the abridgment of the freedom of the people by gradual and silent encroachments of those in power than by violent and sudden usurpations. James Madison, speech to the Virginia Convention, June 16, 1788.

We look forward to a world founded upon four essential human freedoms. The first is freedom of speech and expression everywhere in the world. The second is freedom of every person to worship God in his own way—everywhere in the world. The third is freedom from want...everywhere in the world. The fourth is freedom from fear...everywhere in the world. President Franklin D. Roosevelt, message to the U.S. Congress, January 6, 1941.

A free press stands as one of the great interpreters between the government and the people. To allow it to be fettered is to fetter ourselves. U.S. Supreme Court Associate Justice George Sutherland, commenting on *Grosjean v. American Press Co.,* February 10, 1936.

ANONYMOUS APHORISMS:

Nothing is more precious than freedom.

It may be free, but it doesn't come cheap.

Freedom is a matter of choice.

Better to be a free bird than a lion in chains.

For freedom of speech to work, we must be willing to let others speak their views. But then, with that same right, we are free to object to what they say.

ANECDOTES

There's a story about two convicts who, after 6 months in solitary confinement, were allowed to rejoin the other prisoners. As they strolled out into the prison yard, one said to the other, "Ain't freedom grand?"

"I can't wait until I'm old enough to have my freedom!" the spoiled teen fumed, "I'll be able to go where I want, when I want, and wear what I want." "And I'll be free from paying for it," replied her weary father.

FRIENDSHIP

DEFINITIONS   The bond of affection which exists between two individuals, or among more than two individuals; the state of being emotionally close with another or others; the sharing of common interests with another or others; "a union of spirits" (William Penn); "a plant of slow growth" (George Washington); "a ship big enough to carry two in fair weather, but only one in foul" (Ambrose Bierce).

QUOTATIONS

Ultimately what makes your life worthwhile are the other people you've cared about. Sherry Lansing, in *Cosmopolitan,* August 1989.

Friendship makes prosperity more shining and lessens adversity by dividing and sharing it. Cicero, *On Friendship,* c. 44 BC.

The only way to have a friend is to be one. Ralph Waldo Emerson, *Essays, First Series:* "Friendship," 1841.

The ornament of a house is the friends who frequent it. Ralph Waldo Emerson, *Society and Solitude:* "Domestic Life," 1870.

There are three faithful friends—an old wife, an old dog, and ready money. Benjamin Franklin, *Poor Richard's Almanac,* 1738.

Friendship is seldom lasting but between equals, or where the superiority on one side is reduced by some equivalent advantage on the other. Samuel Johnson, *The Rambler,* 1750.

Friendship is constant in all other things, / Save in the office and affairs of love. William Shakespeare, *Much Ado About Nothing,* 1599.

A man cannot be said to succeed in this life who does not satisfy one friend. Henry D. Thoreau, *Journal,* February 19, 1857.

The holy passion of Friendship is of so sweet and steady and loyal and enduring a nature that it will last through a whole lifetime, if not asked to lend money. Mark Twain, *The Tragedy of Puddinhead Wilson,* 1894.

You cannot be friends upon any other terms than upon the terms of equality. President Woodrow Wilson, speech in Mobile, AL, October 27, 1913.

ANONYMOUS APHORISMS

A friend to everyone is a friend to none.

You are born with your relatives, but you pick your friends.

A friend in need is a friend indeed.

Friendship is not a one-way street.

The surest bond of friendship is having enemies in common.

ANECDOTES

Half of Mr. Jones' friends stopped calling him after he lost his money. Most of the others simply disappeared when they found out.

Someone once asked a great philosopher which he would rather have—a gift of money or a gift of friendship. "Friendship," replied the philosopher, "because money is spent but friendship can last forever." "I shall think of that advice forever," the questioner responded, "as a mark of your friendship." "Sorry," the philosopher apologized, "my friendship is free, but my advice isn't. Pay up."

GAMBLING

DEFINITIONS   Taking a chance; wagering, betting; playing a game with stakes of money; man's passion for getting nothing for something; everybody's ante; a chance encounter; seeing gold in the cards.

QUOTATIONS

If you take no risks, you suffer no defeats. But if you take no risks, you win no victories. Richard M. Nixon, in *U.S. News & World Report,* March 30, 1987.

The gambling known as business looks with austere disfavor on the business known as gambling. Ambrose Bierce, attributed to *The Devil's Dictionary,* 1881–1906.

Most men (till by losing rendered sager) / Will back their own opinions by a wager. George Gordon, Lord Byron, *Beppo,* 1818.

Whoever plays deep must necessarily lose his money or his character. Lord Chesterfield, Letters to His Godson, 1776.

No gambler was ever yet a happy man. William Cobbett, *Advice to Young Men,* 1829.

Man is a gaming animal. Charles Lamb, "Mrs. Battle's Opinions on Whist," 1820.

The roulette table pays nobody except him who keeps it. George Bernard Shaw, *Man and Superman,* 1903.

If there were two birds sitting on a fence, he would bet you which one would fly first. Mark Twain, "The Celebrated Jumping Frog of Calaveras County," 1865.

October. This is one of the peculiarly dangerous months to speculate in stocks. The others are July, January, September, April, November, May, March June, December, August and February. Mark Twain, *The Tragedy of Puddinhead Wilson,* 1894.

…the child of avarice, the brother of iniquity, and the father of mischief. General George Washington, in a letter to his nephew Bushrod Washington, January 15, 1783.

ANONYMOUS APHORISMS

Giving up gambling is a four-to-one shot. Winner take all, but not all are winners.

Bet me no bets.

A man who always plays the odds rarely ends up even.

When it comes to gambling, every country is a nation of losers.

Most of the time that you are asked to take a chance, chance ends up taking you.

ANECDOTES

The horse was a 1000-to-1 shot. Never in the history of racing had there been so dismal a prospect. But Mr. Jones bet $10 on him and when asked why said, "At those odds, how could I resist?"

The devout young man went to his pastor to ask whether it was all right to take part in the office football pool. "Don't you know," said the pastor, "that such gambling is contrary to the views of the church, with our own bingo night coming up tomorrow?"

FACTS

Gambling is nearly as old as the concept of money itself. Records of and references to gambling have been discovered in the remains of ancient Greek, Roman, and

Egyptian cultures. When the U.S. Committee on the Review of the National Policy Toward Gambling, reported on a three-year study in 1976, it was decided that gambling was here to stay—and that the government might as well be in the business. Indeed, the American government raised public funds in its early days through lotteries. Today, more than 80 percent of Americans approve of some form of gambling. Various daily, weekly, and monthly lotteries are as close as the nearest newsstand. But that clearly doesn't satisfy some people's needs. In 1993, there were approximately 17,300 arrests in the U.S. for illegal gambling. How profitable is gambling? The state of Nevada collects over 40 percent of its general-fund revenues from gambling taxes. Casinos are proliferating on Indian reservations, which are less controlled by U.S. laws. When it comes to gambling, it seems virtually everybody wants a piece of the action.

GEOGRAPHY

(See also Exploration)

DEFINITIONS   The science that deals with the natural appearance or climate of the earth, area by area; the nature of a region; faraway places with strange sounding names; what's on earth; the terrain and its contents.

QUOTATIONS

Seas and oceans do not only separate continents, they also unite peoples living on those continents. Vice Admiral Igor V. Kasatonov, Soviet Navy, in *The Los Angeles Times,* July 22, 1989.

Mountains interposed / Make enemies of nations, who had else / Like kindred drops been mingled into one. William Cowper, *The Task,* 1785.

In the world today, with air the means of communication, with time and space almost annihilated, geography still remains a fact. Secretary of State John Foster Dulles, April 11, 1955.

The difference between landscape and landscape is small, but there is a great difference in the beholders. Ralph Waldo Emerson, *Essays, Second Series:* "Nature," 1844.

In America, the geography is sublime, but the men are not... Ralph Waldo Emerson, *The Conduct of Life:* "Considerations by the Way," 1860.

All rivers do what they can for the sea. Thomas Fuller, *Gnomologia,* 1782.

A mountain and a river are good neighbors. George Herbert, Jacula Prudentum, 1651.

Oh, East is East, and West is West, and never the twain shall meet... Rudyard Kipling, "The Ballad of East and West," 1889.

There Are No Islands Any More, Edna St. Vincent Millay, book title, 1940.

ANONYMOUS APHORISMS

Geography is what's where in the world.

Where we live is environment; where everybody else lives is geography.

Geography is where they make history.

Geography always sets the scene.

ANECDOTES

What's the difference between history and geography?" a child was asked. "Well," she said, "geography tells me where I am and history tells me how I got here."

"Geography," said the philosopher, "is the most important study of man, because it ends up telling him where he can go."

FACTS

Geography not only concerns explorers and environmentalists, it is also a major consideration for governments and businesses. An entire section of the U.S. Statistical Abstract is devoted to the subject; and at least three separate national survey units work at geographical tasks—the Geological Survey, the National Ocean Survey, and the U.S. National Oceanic and Atmospheric Administration. The search for everything from oil and minerals to endangered plant and animal species pushes the world into ever more intensive examination, exploration and charting of its geography.

The National Geographic Society, 1145 17th Street NW, Washington, D.C. 20036, testifies to humankind's insatiable curiosity about the world around us.

G O L F

(See also Sports)

DEFINITIONS   Game played with variety of clubs and small hard ball on specially prepared grounds with nine or 18 holes; "cow pasture pool" (O.K. Bovard); "an expensive way of playing marbles" (G. K. Chesterton); a game in which the balls lie on the ground and the players lie in the clubhouse.

QUOTATIONS

The golf links lie so near the mill / That almost every day / The laboring children can look out / And see the men at play. Sarah Cleghorn, "The Golf Links," 1915.

Auld Pawkie. It holed many a guid putt! inscribed on a silver plaque attached to the shaft of the long-nosed putter which helped Willie Park, Sr. win the first Open Championship match, 1860.

The dirty little pill…rolling down the hill… Frank Crumit, novelty song broadcast, c. 1930s.

Houston, you might recognize what I have in my hand is the handle for the contingency sample return. It just so happens to have a genuine 6 iron on the bottom of it. In my left hand I have a little white pellet that's familiar to millions of Americans. I'll drop it down. Unfortunately, the suit is so stiff I can't do this with two hands but I'm going to try a little sand trap shot here. Captain Alan B. Shepard, Jr., U.S. Navy, message broadcast while on the moon, February 6, 1971.

ANONYMOUS APHORISMS

As a game golf is full of holes.

Golf is for swingers.

A golfer never feels better than when he's below par.

At one time a very exclusive sport, golf now gives every player a choice of clubs.

When a golf ball lies poorly, the guy who hit it usually does too.

ANECDOTES

A golfer was being distracted by his noisy and contemptuous partner and finally said, "You are driving me out of my mind." "That," said his partner, "is not a drive; it's a putt."

A duffer was ruining the course with his bad strokes, digging up the turf with every shot. Finally, as he approached the ball, he said to his caddy, "What club do you think I should use?" "Why don't you try the one in the next county?" asked the caddy.

FACTS

Golf was invented in Scotland, and enthusiastically embraced by England after King James I imported the Highlanders' favorite game. But even those early hearty souls could never imagine how much the number of American golfers has skyrocketed since the 1960s. And the number of North American golf courses has also almost tripled since that time. The costs of golfing, and the prizes for the professional, have gone much the same route. Much of the increase is based on the fact that land near population centers is much less available for golf courses than it was in the past and therefore, more expensive to purchase and develop. In 1949, the leading money maker of the Professional Golfers Association was Sam Snead who made $31,593 per year; by contrast, in 1994, Nick Price won nearly $1.5 million in prize money. Part of the upsurge is, of course, a reflection of inflation; but the balance seems to be the result of increased leisure time and more mobility for both men and women alike. Golf as a spectator sport has also boomed in recent years.

The U.S. Golf Association is at Golf House, Far Hills, NJ 07931.

Government

(See also Constitution)

DEFINITIONS   The organization which exercises regulatory and civil authority over the population; the act of governing; the administration in office; the administration of public office; Uncle Sam; Washington; city hall; the establishment; "Big Brother" (George Orwell).

QUOTATIONS

As the happiness of the people is the sole end of government, so the consent of the people is the only foundation of it. John Adams, *Thoughts on Government,* 1776.

The worst thing in this world, next to anarchy, is government. Rev. Henry Ward Beecher, *Proverbs from Plymouth Pulpit,* 1887.

…government is not an exact science… U.S. Supreme Court Associate Justice Louis D. Brandeis, commenting on *Truax v. Corrigan,* 1921.

Government is a contrivance of human wisdom to provide for human wants. Edmund Burke, *Reflections on the Revolution in France,* 1790.

In the long run every Government is the exact symbol of its people, with their wisdom and unwisdom. Thomas Carlyle, *Past and Present,* 1843.

Government is a trust, and the officers of the government are trustees; and both are created for the benefit of the people. Henry Clay, 1829.

While the people should patriotically and cheerfully support their government, its functions do not include the support of the people. President Grover Cleveland, veto message, February 16, 1887.

Our best protection against bigger government in Washington is better government in the states. Dwight D. Eisenhower, speech to the National Governors Conference in Cleveland, OH, June 8, 1964.

A government that is big enough to give you all you want is big enough to take it all away. Senator Barry M. Goldwater of Arizona, October 21, 1964.

The natural progress of things is for liberty to yield and government to gain ground. Thomas Jefferson, letter to Col. Edward Carrington, May 27, 1788.

…the republican is the only form of government which is not eternally at open or secret war with the rights of mankind. Thomas Jefferson, letter to Mayor William Hunter of Alexandria,VA, March 11, 1790.

A President's hardest task is not to *do* what is right, but to *know* what is right. President Lyndon B. Johnson, State of the Union Message, January 4, 1965.

The general story of mankind will evince, that lawful and settled authority is very seldom resisted when it is well employed. Samuel Johnson, *The Rambler,* September 8, 1750.

The basis of effective government is public confidence. President John F. Kennedy, message to the U.S. Congress, April 27, 1961.

No man is good enough to govern another man without that other's consent. Abraham Lincoln, October 16, 1854.

…and that government of the people, by the people, for the people, shall not perish from the earth. President Abraham Lincoln, Gettysburg Address, November 19, 1865.

… a government of all the people, by all the people, for all the people. Rev. Theodore Parker, speech in Boston, MA, May 29, 1850.

If men be good, government cannot he bad. William Penn, "Fruits of Solitude," 1693.

…government should do only those things the people cannot do for themselves. California Governor Ronald Reagan, June 23, 1971.

The government is us; we are the government you and I. President Theodore Roosevelt, September 9, 1902.

No government is perfect. One of the chief virtues of a democracy, however, is that its defects are always visible and under democratic processes can be pointed out and corrected. President Harry S. Truman, address to the U.S. Congress, March 12, 1947.

The basis of our political systems is the right of the people to make and to alter the constitutions of government. But the constitution, which at any time exists, until changed by an explicit and authentic act of the whole people, is sacredly obligatory upon all. President George Washington, farewell address, September 1796.

I think every nation has a right to establish that form of government under which it conceives it shall live most happy; provided it infarcts no right, or is not dangerous to others; and that no governments ought to interfere with the internal concerns of another, except for the security of what is due to themselves. George Washington, letter to Lafayette, December 25, 1798.

It is, Sir, the people's Constitution, the people's government, made by the people, and answerable to the people. Senator Daniel Webster of Massachusetts, reply to Hayne, January 26, 1830.

ANONYMOUS APHORISMS

Government never shrinks.

The people's government is always run by government people.

In business, money makes the wheels go 'round. In government, the wheels make the money go 'round.

Before you can govern people you've got to learn to govern your tongue.

Government gets the best people—one way or another.

Popular government is a collective enterprise for the common good.

American government is a system of checks and balances, as long as the checks don't bounce.

ANECDOTES

"Government," said the scholar, "is double taxation." "How do you mean?" asked the student. "It not only taxes your income," the scholar replied, "it taxes your patience."

The Chaplain of the Senate was asked whether he prayed for the Senators. "No," he said, "I pray for the country."

"The American system of government," said the professor, "is a system of checks and balances. How would you say it is working?" One student quickly responded: "The checks don't balance."

Q: Why do they call our government Uncle Sam? A: Because it's always fiddling around with our ante.

FACTS

The two biggest facts about government—both here and abroad—is the way it has grown; and that, in the U.S., it is not growing. Much of the growth has come from the assumption of new functions in many different fields: regulation, welfare, exploration, and defense. Much has also come from the fact that people work shorter hours today than they did a century ago, so more people are needed to do the same amount work. But another element of growth that is sometimes overlooked is the simple fact that there are more people to be served by government. During the

Second World War, there were 3.4 million American civilian federal government employees. From 1968 to 1984, the number of employees ranged between 2.8 and 3 million people, before rising to a high of 3.1 million in 1987. From 1990 to 1995, the number of federal employees has steadily declined. The *Statistical Abstract of the United States* and the budgets of local governments provide details.

Graduation

DEFINITIONS   The bestowal of a degree or diploma in recognition of completion of a course of study; commencement; completion of school; the end of the beginning; ceremonies attendant on bestowal of a degree or diploma for completion of a particular educational level.

QUOTATIONS

I am not unmindful of the fact that countless middle-aged moralists like me are rising these days on countless platforms all over the world to tell thousands of helpless young captives the score—and I suspect that all of those commencement orators are almost as uncomfortable as I am. Adlai E. Stevenson, Jr., Smith College commencement, June 6, 1955.

I don't see this meeting as some sort of entertainment. You are getting ready to go out into the game of life, to graduate into reality. I don't see this as some sort of side exercise, but as part of the absolute frontier—the frontier of whether we are going to survive on our planet or not. Every minute is counting now. Attributed to R. Buckminster Fuller.

…it's not at all hard for me to remember that vivid day of my own graduation. Strangely enough, the one thing about that day that I cannot remember is what the commencement speaker had to say. My thoughts, like yours, were targeted upon my family and my friends and my plans for the summer. But of one thing I'm sure: If the speaker made a short speech, I know I blessed him. Thomas J. Watson, Jr., Brown University commencement, 1964.

ANONYMOUS APHORISMS

When they are supposed to be receiving their sheepskins, too many new graduates are wool-gathering.

Graduation is an academic ritual to the nth degree.

Graduation is the intermission between school and real life.

Too many graduates are really getting honorary degrees.

When you graduate, it's one for the books.

For a great many people, graduation is like jumping from the frying pan onto the job pyre.

The greatest achievement of graduation is sitting through the commencement exercises.

ANECDOTES

"I'm building a new wall to show off the most expensive thing in the house," said Mr. Jones. "Come see it." It was his son's diploma.

"Are you going to the graduation exercises?" "No, it took enough exercise to qualify for them."

On graduation day, a proud father presented to his son his treasured "ruptured duck"—the symbol of his own honorable discharge from the service. "I'm giving you this," he beamed, "because you too have finished something you won't have to go through again."

FACTS

Graduation ceremonies have probably changed less than any other customary rituals in recent centuries—although what is worn under the cap and gown has changed considerably. Some people think the same is true of commencement speeches. But one change is notable. Instead of being reserved for higher education, graduation ceremonies are now held by schools at all levels. The average American today has gone through at least three formal graduation ceremonies not including college. Even the supplying of "graduation props" has become a viable business enterprise. Cap and gown rentals are readily available in most cities.

GRATITUDE

DEFINITIONS   Thankfulness; appreciation; the memorial to good deeds; what some people consider payment in full.

QUOTATIONS

Next to ingratitude, the most painful thing to bear is gratitude. Rev. Henry Ward Beecher, *Proverbs from Plymouth Pulpit*, 1887.

Gratitude is not only the greatest of virtues, but the parent of all others. Cicero, "Pro Plancio," c. 54 BC.

Revenge is profitable, gratitude is expensive. Edward Gibbon, *The Decline and Fall of the Roman Empire, Vol. II,* 1781.

Every acknowledgment of gratitude is a circumstance of humiliation; and some are found to submit to frequent mortifications of this kind, proclaiming what obligations they owe, merely because they think it in some measure cancels the debt. Oliver Goldsmith, *The Citizen of the World,* 1762.

I sincerely wish ingratitude was not so natural to the human heart as it is. The public has neither shame nor gratitude. William Hazlitt, *Characteristics,* 1823.

We seldom find people ungrateful as long as we are in a position to be helpful. Francois Duc de La Rochefoucauld, *Maxims,* 1665.

Evermore thanks, the exchequer of the poor. William Shakespeare, *Richard II,* 1596.

How sharper than a serpent's tooth it is / To have a thankless child! William Shakespeare, *King Lear,* 1605.

ANONYMOUS APHORISMS

Gratefulness is the poor man's payment.

Thanksgiving is the only kind of giving some people know.

Gratitude can only be given. It cannot be taken.

Thanks is a memory.

Gratitude begets more kindness.

Gratitude is sometimes more easily given than received.

Thanks is sometimes a mask for ingratitude. True gratitude is expressed in deeds rather than words.

Gratitude is an attitude.

ANECDOTES

When a group of Cambridge University students read that Rudyard Kipling was being paid a shilling a word (an enormous salary for an author in those days), they sent him a shilling with a note asking for one word. Much to their surprise, he responded. His reply read: "Thanks."

A four-year-old actress was appearing in a movie with an aging, crotchety star. One day, the star came on the set made up to the nines, and the little girl said to her, "Gee, you look so nice." The actress made a pouty face and replied: "What am I supposed to say to that?" The little girl politely remarked, "You could say thank you."

An old Wild West prospector came upon a little house in a clearing. It was surrounded by neat rows of vegetables; chickens in the yard; cows in the nearby pasture; and from the house itself came the wonderful scent of home-cooked food. Upon seeing the old sourdough, the farmer invited him in to dine with him, his wife, and their lovely children. When dinner was done, the old prospector smiled and said, "You must be very grateful for all this." "Grateful!" the whole family echoed. "How'd you like to live all alone with no neighbors?"

Happiness

DEFINITIONS   State of contentment, joy and well-being; bliss; euphoria; good cheer, ecstasy; elation.

QUOTATIONS

True happiness is of a retired nature, and an enemy to pomp and noise; it arises, in the first place, from the enjoyment of one's self, and in the next, from the friendship and conversation of a few select companions. Joseph Addison, *The Spectator,* March 17, 1911.

Happiness is speechless. George William Curtis, *Prue and I,* 1856.

To fill the hour—that is happiness… Ralph Waldo Emerson, *Essays, Second Series:* "Experience," 1844.

He is happy that knoweth not himself to be otherwise. Thomas Fuller, *Gnomologia,* 1732.

Happiness is the only good. / The time to be happy is now. / The place to be happy is here. / The way to be happy is to make others so. Robert G. Ingersoll, "Creed," c. late 19th century.

…the pursuit of happiness… Thomas Jefferson, The Declaration of Independence, July 4, 1776.

A merry heart doeth good like a medicine… *Proverbs,* 17:22.

The happiest is the person who suffers the least pain; the most miserable who enjoys the least pleasure. Jean-Jacques Rousseau, *Émile,* 1762.

It is the inalienable right of all to be happy. Elizabeth Cady Stanton, February 1861.

Man is the artificer of his own happiness. Henry D. Thoreau, *Journal,* January 21, 1838.

"Happy days are here again." Jack Yellen, song title, 1929. (Also used as Democratic Party motto in the 1932 election.)

ANONYMOUS APHORISMS

Be happy. (Motto used by eastern spiritual elder Meher Baba.)

The pursuit of happiness is humankind's favorite sport.

People cannot be ordered to be happy.

It is better to enjoy happiness than to analyze it.

One man's happiness may be another man's hell.

Happiness sometimes comes from ignorance—not knowing how much better your life might be.

Some people are happy remembering the past, and some happy forgetting it.

Happiness can be contagious.

ANECDOTES

There was a poor family that was overrun with children. A gracious lady came to visit their careworn mother, who kept complaining about all the work the children gave her, and about how hard it was to keep going. "My dear," said the gracious lady, "they now have all kinds of birth control methods. Let me give you the money to go to an expert for guidance." "What," exclaimed the horrified mother, "are you trying to take away my only happiness?"

HEALTH

(See also Dieting, Fitness, Food, Medicine)

DEFINITIONS   Soundness of bodily functions; freedom from disease; physical and mental well-being; "the first wealth" (Ralph Waldo Emerson).

QUOTATIONS

The old thinking was: once you find the virus, the next step will be easy. But this [HIV] virus is proving to be a formidable adversary. It is fighting for its survival, just as we are. Jay A. Levy, professor of medicine, University of California at San Francisco, in the *The Los Angeles Times,* June 20, 1990.

People have told me they are more fearful of social isolation than they are of death from AIDS. Alan Brownstein, executive director, National Hemophilia Foundation, in *The Los Angeles Times,* January 2, 1989.

You can't use the word 'enough' in science. Enough is when the problem is solved. Anthony S. Fauci, chief of AIDS research, National Institutes of Health, in *The Los Angeles Times,* June 20, 1990.

Discrimination against people affected [by AIDS] or thought to be so is dangerous, because it slows the effectiveness of measures intended to prevent the spread of the disease. Hiroshi Nakajima, in *Le Monde,* reprinted from *World Press Review,* March, 1989.

Health is not a condition of matter, but of Mind... Mary Baker Eddy, *Science and Health,* 1908.

Early to bed, and early to rise, makes a man healthy, wealthy and wise. Benjamin Franklin, *The Way to Wealth,* 1757.

Health is not valued till sickness comes. Thomas Fuller, *Gnomologia,* 1732.

If you mean to keep as well as possible, the less you think about your health the better. Oliver Wendell Holmes, *Over the Teacups,* 1891.

...health is worth more than learning... Thomas Jefferson, letter to his cousin John Garland Jefferson, June 11, 1790.

...the world's "wealthiest nation" can never be satisfied until we are the world's healthiest. President Lyndon B. Johnson, March 31, 1966.

We should pray for a sound mind in a sound body. Juvenal, *Satires* (10:356), c. 115 AD.

The first medical right of all Americans is care within their means. Senator Edmund S. Muskie of Maine, May 27, 1971.

Look to your health; and if you have it, praise God, and value it next to a good conscience; for health is the second blessing that we mortals are capable of; a blessing that money cannot buy. Izaak Walton, *The Compleat Angler,* 1653.

Health that mocks the doctor's rules. / Knowledge never learned of schools. John Greenleaf Whittier, "The Barefoot Boy," 1855.

ANONYMOUS APHORISMS

Health doesn't insure happiness; but there's not much happiness without it.

People who enjoy good health should think of the doctor's bill as an amusement tax.

While there's health there's hope, and while there's hope at least there's healthy thinking.

You have to heal to have health.

Having a good constitution is as important for an individual as for a nation.

Health is better than wealth.

Money can't buy health, but can certainly make it easier to stay healthy.

ANECDOTES

"If you want to enjoy good health," advised the doctor, "you must get eight hours sleep every day; don't burn the candle at both ends; and practice moderation in all things." "In that case," said his patient, "what am I being healthy for?"

"My bones ache," said Mr. Jones as he left the gym, "My feet hurt. I can't seem to get out of bed in the morning. And the muscles in my neck are in permanent knots." "Well," said his friend, "as long as you're healthy."

Old man Jones worried his children because he ate junk food regularly; partied enthusiastically; and gambled frenziedly. "You're killing yourself," they warned him. "Then it must be a slow death," he replied, "because I've been doing it already for so many years."

"I'm as strong as an ox," said eager Harry as he went out without a coat to shovel the snow off his walkway. "And just about as bright," muttered his wife.

FACTS

Health is primarily a scientific challenge, because it depends on how much we know or can find out about preventing disease, improving nutrition, and curing ailments. But the major problem of public health is the problem of rising costs. With previously incurable heart, liver, and kidney ailments, and other terminal diseases such as leukemia, the question is no longer the hope of finding a cure; now, it's all too often a question of being able to afford treatment. As it is impossible to place a value on a human life, it is difficult to say when treatment costs have gone too high. According to the U.S. Census, Americans spent $74 billion on health care in 1970; and in 1994, health care cost Americans $752 billion. It is estimated that in 1994, 39.7 million people—15.2 percent of the population—were living without health insurance. There has been a resurgence of tuberculosis and other chronic diseases once thought to be eradicated. But many parents no longer immunize their children; and neglect to complete a full course of antibiotic treatment, allowing diseases to mutate into medication-resistant forms. Previously unrecognized diseases like AIDS, E-bola, and Hanta virus have brought new challenges to the medical community. But despite these modern plagues, infant mortality is at an all time low; and Americans are living longer and healthier lives than ever before. Figures from the World Health Organization indicate great worldwide success in limiting—and in some instances eradicating—the threat of infectious and contagious diseases such as smallpox, typhoid, and cholera.

The U.S. Social Security Administration publishes helpful Social Security Bulletins on related statistics; and the United Nations' World Health Organization publishes regular reports and bulletins on international health watches and related statistics.

HISTORY

DEFINITIONS   The record or study of events of the past; "clarified experience" (James Russell Lowell); "the propaganda of the victors" (Ernst Toller), what happened when, where and why; today's view of yesterday's actions.

QUOTATIONS

History is not always just to those who make it. Vladimir A. Kitaev, professor of history, Volgograd University, in *The Los Angeles Times,* May 1, 1995.

…history is the drama, for heaven's sake, of human existence. And history is the story of people, and how they coped, how they met problems, and of the competition between them, the rivalries between them. With all the emotions—jealousy, hate, love. And it's never taught this way. It's taught in this dull rote—dates and places. People never come alive. All these people lived dramatic lives. Every history lesson, every hour in history class, ought to be a terribly exciting lecture on the lives and loves of these peoples, and their personalities. Because the personalities of these leaders, and of those who sought to be, is what affected history. But we don't learn it that way, and as a consequence history is a course that most people hate in school. It' just a shame. Walter Cronkite, in *American Heritage,* December, 1994.

Histories make men wise; poets witty; the mathematics subtle; natural philosophy deep; moral grave; logic and rhetoric able to contend. Sir Francis Bacon, *Essays:* "Of Studies," 1625.

Peoples and governments have never learned anything from history…George Wilhelm Friedrich Hegel, *Philosophy of History,* (posthumously) 1832.

…a page of history is worth a volume of logic. U.S. Supreme Court Associate Justice Oliver Wendell Holmes, Jr., commenting on *New York Trust Co. v. Eisner,* 1921.

History fades into fable… Washington Irving, *The Sketch Book,* Westminster Abbey, 1820.

We can draw lessons from the past, but we cannot live in it. President Lyndon B. Johnson, December 13, 1963.

Thrice happy is the nation that has a glorious history. New York Governor Theodore Roosevelt, speech in Chicago, IL, April 10, 1899.

Those who cannot remember the past are condemned to repeat it. George Santayana, *The Life of Reason, Vol. I,* 1905.

…the frontier has gone, and with its going has closed the first period of American history. Frederick Jackson Turner, "The Significance of the Frontier in American History," 1893.

It has been said that the only thing we learn from history is that we do not learn. U.S. Supreme Court Chief Justice Earl Warren, eulogy for President John F. Kennedy, November 24, 1963.

ANONYMOUS APHORISMS

Some people make history and some make it up.

History doesn't repeat itself; humankind repeat history.

History is the rear view mirror on the road of life.

History is the past imperfect.

History is not simply what happened; it is the way what happened is remembered.

History is the way the present views the past.

Your life is your grandchildren's history.

ANECDOTES

During the Second World War, Great Britain's Prime Minister, Winston Churchill once suggested that history would deal gently with him. "Because," as Mr. Churchill admitted, "I intend to write it."

"I don't want to discuss the mark I got in history," said Johnny to his father, "because that's all in the past."

FACTS

The recording and analysis of history is one of man's oldest preoccupations. Unlike reading, writing and arithmetic, history did not require formal instruction to be handed down from generation to generation. History has been taught through the ages in the form of written legends; as an elemental subject of oral traditions, as a part of the narrative of religious scripture, and as the subject of epic songs that tell adventures of a key heroic figure or event. More degrees are granted, books written, and tales told in history that in any other social science. A world that prides itself on looking toward the future, in fact, is often equally preoccupied with discovering its past. As the work of so-called revisionist historians and government committees alike bears witness, commonly accepted historical facts are constantly being re-examined, such as the authenticity of the Dead Sea Scrolls, the location of Noah's Ark, the details concerning the Tienenmen Square massacre and the Iran/Contra affair, and the eagerness to open classified documents to public scrutiny. These recurring activities illustrate man's constant appetite for the study of, control over, and traffic in history.

The National Council for the Social Studies, though not an organization restricted to teachers of history, provides in its journals a continuing review of the latest historical thinking. The Council is located at 3501 Newark Street, NW, Washington, DC 20016.

Hobbies

(See also Leisure)

DEFINITIONS   A field of endeavor or interest engaged in for relaxation and enjoyment rather than for a living; avocations; hard work you wouldn't do for a living; what you do to avoid doing nothing.

QUOTATIONS

And now each man bestride his hobby, and dust away his bells to what tune he pleases. Charles Lamb, *Essays of Elia:* "All Fools' Day," 1823.

Nothing is as certain as that the vices of leisure are gotten rid of by being busy. Seneca, *Moral Letters to Lucilius,* c. 64 AD.

So long as a man rides his hobby-horse peaceably and quietly along the king's highway, and neither compels you or me to get up behind him—pray, Sir, what have either you or I to do with it? Laurence Sterne, *Tristram Shandy,* 1759.

ANONYMOUS APHORISMS

Time is the factor in all hobbies: Some are practiced to kill time, some have time set aside for them and all are intended to provide a good time for the hobbyist.

One man's work is another man's hobby.

Those who can, do; those who can't, think they can.

If you spend money on it, it's a hobby; if you make money on it, it's a business.

Your hobby is none of your business.

A hobby is what you love to do, rather than what you live to do.

Hobbies are fire escapes in the conflagration of life.

ANECDOTES

"My work is my hobby," the businessman said. "He only says that," remarked his wife, "because he doesn't make a living at it."

John Jones went to see the doctor because he was nervous, unable to relax. "You ought to take up a hobby," the doctor said. "I have a hobby," said Mr. Jones; "I make miniature furniture carved by hand to exact scale, and I love doing it." "And you don't find it relaxes you?" asked the doctor. "Not when my wife throws out a year's work by mistake," said Mr. Jones. "Her hobby is redecorating."

FACTS

In past generations, men and women had to work at the very things that have now gained the status of hobbies—needlecraft, carpentry, tinkering, and metalwork—to put bread on the table. Do-it-yourself in those days was a necessity, not a desire born of increased leisure time. In previous centuries, leisure time was equated with seasonal work. For example, farmers' ornate winter carvings gave birth to the expression "whittling away the time." In our age, shorter work weeks, convenience tools, electric power, and prefabricated supplies have made it possible for millions upon millions to devote countless hours to doing things for no reward other than the fun of doing. As a result, hobby industries today are big business. Many, indeed, are not hobby industries essentially, but rather enterprises and sources that are principally suppliers to business. Stained glass, for example, comes from the same manufacturers who turn out materials for church windows. So the dimensions of hobbies in the United States can't be measured simply by the number of hobby businesses. One good illustration of the industry's growth can be found in the field of photography. At first, all nonprofessional photographs were taken to the drug store to be developed and printed, but now home equipment for the amateur photographer's darkroom can be found in camera stores around the world. Undoubtedly, the most popular segment of the hobby industry is collectibles. Whether it's antiques, wines, comic books, or cars, we are truly a nation of collectors. Your local library, under the heading of "hobbies" in the card catalogue, can probably tell you a good deal about the extent of interest in hobbies in your own community.

Horseracing

(See also Sports)

DEFINITIONS Competitions at fixed distances and over specified courses among horses ridden by humans or driven as in trotting carts; the sport of kings; the horses; the flats and the trotters; the ponies; the track.

QUOTATIONS

A horse! A horse! My kingdom for a horse!… William Shakespeare, *Richard II*, 1595.

Gwine to run all night! / Gwine to run all day! / I'll bet my money on de bob-tail nag— / Somebody bet on de bay. Stephen Foster, "Camptown Races," c. 1850.

Hast thou given the horse strength? Hast thou clothed his neck with thunder? *Job*, 39:19.

Spur a free horse, he'll run himself to death. Ben Jonson, *The Tale of a Tub*, 1633.

The ways of a man with a maid be strange, yet simple and tame / To the ways of a man with a horse, when selling or racing that same. Rudyard Kipling, "Certain Maxims of Hafiz," 1886.

Competition makes a horserace. Ovid, *The Art of Love,* c. 1 BC.

The spirited horse, which will try to win the race of its own accord, will run even faster if encouraged. Ovid, *Epistolae ex Ponto,* c. 9 AD.

I wish your horses swift and sure of foot… William Shakespeare, *Macbeth,* 1606.

O for a horse with wings! William Shakespeare, "*Cymbeline*," 1609.

It is a good horse that never stumbles. C.H. Spurgeon, *John Ploughman's Talk,* 1869.

ANONYMOUS APHORISMS

Horseracing is the sport of kings and the trap of fools.

Can you ever imagine horses betting on people?

I got it right from the horse's mouth.

A racetrack is a place where the human race is secondary.

A horserace is where a horse performs for his bettors.

The race is to the swiftest.

ANECDOTES

"Never bet on a polite horse," my friend said. "What's a polite horse?" I asked. "A horse that lets the others in first," he simply replied.

A visitor sat next to a veteran gambler at the racetrack. "Do you follow the horses?" the observer casually inquired. "Yes," replied the gambler, "with about the same results as the street cleaners after a mounted parade."

"Today was my best day at the track," the inveterate loser sighed. "Did you win?" his friend asked. "No," he replied, "my horse was scratched before I could get to the window."

FACTS

In the United States there are more than 13,000 racing days per year. That is to say, the total number of days various race tracks are open during the year adds up to over 13,000. More than 60 million people go to the track every year. And, from the pari-mutuel turnover, approximately $600 million in revenue goes to the state coffers. In New York and other cities, the government itself is also in the off-track betting business. Horseracing is not only one of America's favorite spectator sports, it is also, to a considerable extent, the world's favorite spectator sport. Hong Kong's Happy Valley and England's Ascot tracks attest to the "sport of kings'" international appeal.

You can update the statistics above in the latest Statistical Abstract of the U.S., or contact the Association of Racing Commissioners International, Inc., in Lexington, KY, for further information.

HOSPITALITY

DEFINITIONS   Cordial treatment as a guest in a home or hotel; the hotel industry; enthusiastic welcome and courtesy from a host; "a little fire, a little food, and an immense quiet" (Ralph Waldo Emerson); the red-carpet treatment; making people feel at home in your home even when you don't.

QUOTATIONS

It came seventeen years ago—and to this day It shows no intention of going away. Edward Gorey, *Amphigorey:* "The Doubtful Guest," 1972.

The ornament of a house is the friends who frequent it. Ralph Waldo Emerson, *Society and Solitude:* "Domestic Life," 1870.

Fish and visitors smell in three days. Benjamin Franklin, *Poor Richard's Almanac,* 1736.

True friendship's laws are by this rule express'd, / Welcome the coming, speed the parting guest. Homer, *The Odyssey,* 800 BC, translated by Alexander Pope, c. 18th century.

If your house be like an inn, nobody cares for you. Samuel Johnson, according to James Boswell in *Life of Samuel Johnson,* May 15, 1783.

I was hungered, and ye gave me meat: I was thirsty, and ye gave me drink: I was a stranger, and ye took me in. *Matthew,* 25:35.

...you are very welcome to our house: / It must appear in ways other than words... William Shakespeare, *The Merchant of Venice,* 1597.

ANONYMOUS APHORISMS

When there is room in the heart there is room in the house.

A good host puts the first stain on the tablecloth.

The master of the house is the servant of the guest.

Hospitality is homemade.

My house is your house. (Translation of the Spanish greeting "Mi casa es su casa.")

The acid test of hospitality is the uninvited guest.

Hospitality is tested by the quality of the guest.

The drinks are on the house.

Hospitality begins with the invitation.

ANECDOTES

Mrs. Brown always managed to come up with a delicious meal for unexpected guests. When asked how she did it, she said, "I simply add tomorrow's dinner to yesterday's leftovers."

"The secret of always seeming happy when you have guests," says the wise host, "is to go around smiling at the thought of how nice it will be when they leave."

HOUSING

(See also Building, Population)

DEFINITIONS   Places of abode; dwelling places; dwellings; cover, protection or shelter; a roof over one's head; residences; habitation; where you hang your hat.

QUOTATIONS

Homelessness affects a small proportion of Americans but concerns us all…it's a national shame. President George Bush, speech March 14, 1989.

He that builds a fair house upon an ill seat committeth himself to prison. Sir Francis Bacon, "Of Building," 1625.

A man's house is his castle. Sir Edward Coke, *Institutes, Vol. III,* 1644.

A man builds a fine house; and now he has a master, and a task for life; he is to furnish, watch, show it, and keep it in repair the rest of his days. Ralph Waldo Emerson, *Society and Solitude:* "Works and Days," 1870.

Let me live in my house by the side of the road / And be a friend of man. Sam Walter Foss, "The House by the Side of the Road," 1897.

The house shows the owner. George Herbert, *Jacula Prudentum,* 1651.

From Plymouth Rock to Puget Sound, the first priority of the men and women who settled this vast and this blessed continent was to put a roof over the heads of their family. And that priority has never, and can never, change. President Lyndon B. Johnson, signing the Housing and Urban Development Act, August 10, 1965.

I suppose I've passed it a hundred times, / but I always stop for a minute / And look at the house, the tragic house, / the house with nobody in it. Joyce Kilmer, "The House with Nobody in It," c. 1917.

I see one-third of a nation ill-housed, ill-clad, and ill-nourished. President Franklin D. Roosevelt, second inaugural address, January 20, 1937.

Our houses are such unwieldy property that we are often imprisoned rather than housed in them. Henry D. Thoreau, *Walden:* "Economy," 1854.

ANONYMOUS APHORISMS

A house divided is a multiple dwelling.

It takes a heap to make a house a home.

In housing there is always room for improvements.

America is a land of opportunity where anybody can owe his own home.

Fools build houses and wise men buy them.

High-rise apartments don't get their name from their rental prices—or do they?

ANECDOTES

"If a man's home is his castle," said the tax assessor, looking at Mr. Jones' badly neglected abode, "this one should have a moat around it."

Q: How many stories does your house have? A: As many as there are people who have lived in it.

"My house is your house," said the tenant to the visitor at the door. "You're darned right," said the stranger, "I just bought the building."

FACTS

There has never been a time in American history when there was enough housing. Originally, the cause was the growth of population and the expansion into new territory. But then, as now, cost was also a factor. In the 1930s, President Franklin D. Roosevelt asserted that one-third of the nation was ill-housed. In the years since then, there has been steady growth in low-rent public housing units and in subsidized housing construction. By way of example, in 1950, there were 302,100 housing units already in existence, in the planning stage, or in the final phases of construction, according to the Statistical Yearbook of the U.S. of the Department of Housing and Urban Development (HUD). This particular federal department was founded in 1965 to improve housing standards for low-income families. As of 1993, 3361 local H.U.D. agencies recorded 1.31 million occupied low-income housing units. The ambition to own one's own home is common in every sector of the nation and among every ethnic group. Housing is, by every measure, our most popular necessary expenditure. The 1994 U.S. Census indicated that out of a total of 105 million housing units in America; 60 percent of those were single family detached homes. But housing must keep pace with population growth; the number of housing units started each year is one of the measures of basic prosperity for the nation.

Humanity

DEFINITIONS   The state of being human; people in general; the study or learning related to general human culture; compassion; human understanding.

QUOTATIONS

Humanity transcends nationality. We're human beings before anything else. John Hume, Member of British Parliament representing Northern Ireland, in the *The New York Times,* April 1, 1992.

The conscious act of remembering is crucial to our survival as civilized human beings. Charles Windsor, Prince of Wales, in *U.S. News & World Report,* May 22, 1995.

Love, hope, fear, faith—these make humanity; / These are its sign and note and character. Robert Browning, "Paracelsus," 1835.

I come to speak to you in defense of a cause as holy as the cause of liberty—the cause of humanity. William Jennings Bryan, speech to the Democratic convention in Chicago, IL, July 8, 1896.

There is but one law for all, namely, that law which governs all law, the law of our Creator, the law of humanity, justice, equity—the law of nature, and of nations. Edmund Burke, May 28, 1794.

No human ideal is ever perfectly attained, since humanity itself is not perfect. Herbert Hoover, presidential campaign speech in New York, NY, October 22, 1928.

We will be remembered not for the power of our weapons but for the power of our compassion, our dedication to human welfare. Vice President Hubert H. Humphrey, September 15, 1966.

...our similarities and our differences have been like separate rivers, flowing from a common lake of humanity. President Lyndon B. Johnson, remarks in Bangkok, Thailand, October 29, 1966.

Be ashamed to die until you have won some victory for humanity. Horace Mann, address at Antioch College, 1859.

Know then thyself, presume not God to scan; / The proper study of mankind is man. Alexander Pope, *An Essay on Man,* 1733.

Rejoice with them that do rejoice, and weep with them that weep. *Romans,* 12:15.

The still, sad music of humanity. William Wordsworth, "Tintern Abbey," 1798.

ANONYMOUS APHORISMS

It's not the heat, it's the humanity.

Some people show their humanity by their mistakes; some by their accomplishments.

Humanity is the difference between being human and being humane.

Why is it we hear so little about man's humanity to man, when there is so much more of it than of man's inhumanity?

Humanity separates us from the beasts—which may be lucky for the beasts.

ANECDOTES

"When you study the humanities," said the professor to his college class, "what you are really studying is the stories of people. Or is it the people of stories?"

"Show a little humanity," the defense attorney pleaded with the jury. So they cried when they found the defendant guilty.

There was a tremendous fire, and the animals were fleeing before it; but when they came to the outskirts of the city, the king of the beasts let out a roar and said, "Go no further." "But the fire may come closer," said the animals. "First enemies first," said the lion. "And the first enemy is not the heat, it's the humanity."

HUMOR

DEFINITIONS   That which is designed to arouse laughter; wit; comedy; jokes; laughing matters.

QUOTATIONS

Comic ideas have an analogy to architecture. You set someone up here, and then the punchline is over there. Joseph Esherik, architect, in *Connoisseur,* August, 1989.

Fun is a good thing but only when it spoils nothing better. George Santayana, *The Sense of Beauty,* 1896.

Man is distinguished from all other creatures by the faculty of laughter. Joseph Addison, *The Spectator,* September 26, 1712.

What a waste it is to lose one's mind. Or not to have a mind is being very wasteful. How true that is. Vice President Dan Quayle, speech at a meeting of the United Negro College Fund, May 9, 1989.

Men will let you abuse them if only you will make them laugh. Rev. Henry Ward Beecher, *Proverbs from Plymouth Pulpit,* 1887.

Wit is so shining a quality that everybody admires it; most people aim at it, all people fear it, and few love it unless in themselves. Lord Chesterfield, letter to his godson, December 18, 1765.

A difference of taste in jokes is a great strain on the affections. George Eliot, Daniel Deronda, 1876.

Wit makes its own welcome, and levels all distinctions. No dignity, no learning, no force of character, can make any stand against good wit. Ralph Waldo Emerson, *Letters and Social Aims:* "The Comic," 1876.

Thou canst not joke an enemy into a friend, but thou may'st a friend into an enemy. Benjamin Franklin, *Poor Richard's Almanac,* 1739.

Men show their characters in nothing more clearly than in what they think laughable. Johann Wolfgang von Goethe, c. early 19th century.

That frolic which shakes one man with laughter will convulse another with indignation. Samuel Johnson, *The Rambler,* September 28, 1751.

Laugh at yourself first, before anyone else can. Elsa Maxwell, September 28, 1958.

All Human Race would fain be Wits, / And Millions miss, for one that hits. Jonathan Swift, "On Poetry: A Rhapsody," 1733.

Laugh and the world laughs with you; / Weep and you weep alone... Ella Wheeler Wilcox, "Solitude," 1883.

Laugh and the world laughs with you, snore and you sleep alone. Attributed to Bob Hope, c. 1950s.

ANONYMOUS APHORISMS

A punchline analyzed is as a attractive as a daisy after you've found that "she loves me not."

Being funny is no laughing matter.

A joke that has to be explained is at its wit's end.

Whether something is funny often depends on whom it is happening to.

Laughter is more contagious than tears.

He who laughs lasts.

People who can agree on what's funny can usually agree on other things.

Many friends have been lost by jest, but few have been gained.

ANECDOTES

It was his sixth sense that made him successful—his sense of humor.

"Laughter is God's gift to mankind," said the preacher. "And mankind," said the cynic, "is the proof that God has a sense of humor."

How would you define the situation when a group of 100 people were locked in with you in an abandoned theater? "A potential lawsuit," said the attorney. "An emergency for the fire department or the police," said the building inspector. "A great opportunity," said the comedian.

Every time Mr. Jones told a joke and joined in the laughter, Mrs. Jones would say disapprovingly, "I don't think that's funny." One day Mr. Jones told what he thought was an uproarious joke and—as he burst into a laugh at the punchline—he found he was laughing alone. Everybody else had a puzzled look. "Now that," said Mrs. Jones, "is funny."

FACTS

Humor is a most salable commodity. Popular comedians make more money than the President of the United States (but then of course so do business executives and professional athletes), and situation comedies are the nation's favorite television viewing. Comedy clubs can be found in most major cities. Humorous books have found their way onto best-seller lists for as long as such lists have been kept. On college campuses, a humor magazine is as much a staple as the pretentious literary periodical. Slapstick comedy was the keystone of Hollywood's movie success. And over the years, Americans have laughed at many of the same things time after time: a pie in the face; irreverence toward government; the silliness that can be found in daily life. It's been reported that laughter often improves the recovery odds of patients with serious illnesses. So, it seems reasonable to say that a sense of humor often seems to be the best sense of all.

IMMIGRATION

(See also Ethnicity, Minorities, Race)

DEFINITIONS   The act or state of entering a strange or foreign land and settling there; entering a country for the purpose of establishing permanent residence there; the food for the melting pot; choosing your country rather than being born in it.

QUOTATIONS

We are the Romans of the modern world—the great assimilating people. Oliver Wendell Holmes, *The Autocrat of the Breakfast-Table,* 1858.

I think it fortunate for the United States to have become the asylum for so many virtuous patriots of different denominations. Thomas Jefferson, letter to M. de Meusnier, April 29, 1795.

The fundamental, longtime American attitude has been to ask not where a person comes from but what are his personal qualities. On this basis men and women migrated from every quarter of the globe. By their hard work and their enormously varied talents they hewed a great nation out of a wilderness. By their dedication to liberty and equality, they created a society reflecting man's most cherished ideas. President Lyndon B. Johnson, message to the U.S. Congress, January 13, 1965.

A Nation of Immigrants. John F. Kennedy, book title, (posthumously) 1964.

"Keep, ancient lands, your storied pomp!" cries she / With silent lips. "Give me your tired, your poor, / Your huddled masses yearning to breathe free, / The wretched refuse of your teeming shore. / Send these, the homeless, tempest-tost to me, / I lift my lamp beside the golden door!" Emma Lazarus, "The New Colossus," also inscribed on the base of the Statue of Liberty, 1883.

My folks didn't come over on the Mayflower, but they were there to meet the boat. Will Rogers, commenting on his Native American origins, c. 1920s.

Remember, remember always that all of us, and you and I especially, are descended from immigrants and revolutionists. President Franklin D. Roosevelt, speech to the Daughters of the American Revolution, April 21, 1938.

Some Americans need hyphens in their names because only part of them has come over. President Woodrow Wilson, May 16, 1914.

We may have come over on different ships, but we're all in the same boat now. Whitney Young, Jr., speech in New York, NY, May 7, 1970.

America is God's Crucible, the great Melting Pot where all the races of Europe are melting and reforming! Israel Zangwill, The Melting-Pot, 1908.

ANONYMOUS APHORISMS

When the white man, the black man, the brown man, and the yellow man came to the land of the red man, they were all greenhorns.

In the history of the world, people have more often struggled to get out of a country than to get in it. But everyone struggles to get into the United States.

America is interested in the rest of the world because that's where most of us came from.

The most important ship for the immigrants who come here is citizenship.

An immigrant is here by choice, a native by chance.

ANECDOTES

The newly-arrived immigrant drove his host crazy by talking about how much better food was back in the Old Country; about how much better the weather was there; and how much better everything was back in the homeland. Finally, his frustrated host remarked, "If everything was so much better there, why did you come here?" With an ear-to-ear smile, the immigrant replied, "Because if I said over there that something was better elsewhere they would have shot me. The one thing that's better here is that now I can complain."

People like to think that I and millions of others came here because we thought the streets were paved with gold. Many of us were happy enough to find that the streets were paved at all.

"America," the native son proudly proclaimed, " is the best place in the world to come from." "I don't know about that," remarked the immigrant, "but I do know it's the best place in the world to come to."

FACTS

Over the centuries, immigration has been America's greatest asset. Immigrants opened this vast territory to civilization, planted and grew the crops, swelled the population, and supported the ideals of independence. We may see immigration as a past page of American history, flourishing in the late 19th and early 20th centuries when millions of Europeans went through the portals at New York's Ellis Island; and Asians streamed through the doors of San Francisco's Angel Island. But immigrants are part of today's mainstream as well. In 1994, nearly 800,000 immigrants were admitted into the U.S.—a figure many times larger than the annual average in the 1890s. About 25 million people—or 9 percent—of the population in this country are foreign-born. Like earlier arrivals, they tend to settle on the coasts. California has 7.7 million of these new arrivals in residence; New York is home to 2.9 million; and Miami houses 2.1 million. To people all over the world, the United States is still the peerless sanctuary of freedom and opportunity. As President John F. Kennedy once remarked, "We are a nation of immigrants."

The Immigration and Naturalization Service, part of the Department of Justice, was established in 1891. To update the above statistics, contact the INS Office of Information at 425 I Street NW, Washington, D.C. 20536.

INDIVIDUALISM

DEFINITIONS   The act or philosophy of asserting the individual as the most important element of society; that which is self-centered rather than group-centered; egoism; independent individual action or thought; the personal element; maverick; one who conforms to personal taste rather than accepted trends.

QUOTATIONS

What is a rebel? A man who says no. Albert Camus, *The Rebel,* 1951.

It is in vain to talk of the interest of the community, without understanding what is the interest of the individual. Jeremy Bentham, *An Introduction to the Principles of Morals and Legislation,* 1789.

Nature never rhymes her children, nor makes two men alike. Ralph Waldo Emerson, *Essays, Second Series:* "Character," 1844.

God helps them that help themselves. Benjamin Franklin, *Poor Richard's Almanac,* (drawn from an ancient Greek maxim), 1733.

When the war closed…we were challenged with a peacetime choice between the American system of rugged individualism and a European philosophy of diametrically opposed doctrines—doctrines of paternalism and state socialism. Herbert Hoover, presidential campaign speech in New York, NY, October 22, 1928.

The strongest man in the world is he who stands alone. Henrik Ibsen, *An Enemy of the People,* 1882.

Down to Gehenna or up to the throne, / He travels the fastest who travels alone. Rudyard Kipling, "The Winners," 1888.

Let me emphasize that serious as have been the errors of unrestrained individualism, I do not believe in abandoning the system of individual enterprise. President Franklin D. Roosevelt, radio address, August 24, 1935.

If a man does not keep pace with his companions, perhaps it is because he hears a different drummer. Let him step to the music which he hears, however measured or far away. Henry D. Thoreau, *Walden,* "Conclusion," 1854.

…the frontier is productive of individualism. Frederick Jackson Turner, "The Significance of the Frontier in American History," 1893.

ANONYMOUS APHORISMS

No one ever became renowned for being a normal person.

True leaders are a maverick breed.

One of a kind isn't much of a poker hand, but it's a pretty good description of a real leader.

It's fine to stand out from the crowd, unless they're shooting at you.

Everyone to his own taste.

One man's meat is another man's poison.

He stands the tallest who stands alone.

ANECDOTES

"I don't want to suggest that he is an egotist," said an opponent of a notoriously independent candidate, "but after that egotist was born, they definitely threw away the mold."

Because people insist on doing things their own way doesn't mean they will do things individually. Consider what happens when the kids at school are told they can dress as each one pleases. They all come in looking exactly the same.

FACTS

Conformism is a social pressure, common to most societies. The person who looks or acts outside of the social norms is somehow set apart. That which is individual is regarded as eccentric, at best, if not downright heretical. Yet the world's history has been created primarily by people who were highly individualistic; and did not behave according to the standard for their class, or their people, or their time. This, of course, has been the story behind many of the world's great scientists, philosophers, soldiers, political leaders, and business people, who started with the courage of their convictions and ended up by leading the world into new frontiers of knowledge or accomplishment. In the United States, the first written guarantee of individual rights was written into the U.S. Constitution, derived in part from the tradition of mother England; but every attempt to guarantee individualism in the world today traces back to the seminal American document, The Declaration of Independence, and its lineal descendant, the Constitution. Perhaps the most dedicated American advocate of individualism was Henry David Thoreau, who chose to live outside of social convention and wrote about his naturalist views in works like "Civil Disobedience" and *Walden.*

INSPIRATION

DEFINITIONS   An infusion of light or spirit that provides a solution for a challenge; a flash of revelation for the solution of a problem; a subconscious message that impels a course of conduct; a moment of genius; a revelation of wisdom; accomplishment that doesn't come through perspiration.

QUOTATIONS

Genius is one percent inspiration and 99 percent perspiration. Thomas A. Edison, c. 1890s.

Any new formula which suddenly emerges in our consciousness has its roots in long trains of thought; it is virtually old when it first makes its appearance among the recognized growths of our intellect. Oliver Wendell Holmes, *The Autocrat of the Breakfast-Table,* 1858.

An idea, to be suggestive, must come to the individual with the force of a revelation. William James, *The Varieties of Religious Experience,* 1902.

No man ever became great by imitation. Samuel Johnson, *The Rambler,* September 7, 1751.

A god dwells within our breast; when he awakens us, we are inspired with a holy rapture that grows from the seed of divine thought planted in man. Ovid, *Fasti,* c. 5 AD.

ANONYMOUS APHORISMS

Inspiration is sometimes another name for desperation.

Inspiration starts with aspiration.

It's only an inspiration when somebody makes it work.

Inspiration is sometimes used to explain what cannot be explained.

Inspiration and imagination go hand in hand.

ANECDOTES

A maker of pornographic movies was asked how he came to his line of work and said it was pure inspiration. "Yes," said a critic, "he was inspired by a hunger for money."

Ambitious young Joe Smith never missed a day of submitting a new idea to his boss; and his boss never missed a day rejecting Joe's idea. One day, Joe submitted a suggestion and his boss said, "That's sheer inspiration!" "No," said Joe, "99 percent aspiration, 1 percent inspiration."

Q: Why do most people seem to get their inspirations overnight? A:. Because inspiration comes from dreams.

INTERNET/WORLD WIDE WEB

(See also Computers, Science)

DEFINITIONS   A global computer network allowing computers to exchange information via telephone lines; the 'net; the information highway; the Web; "Cyberspace" (William Gibson, *Neuromancer,* 1984).

QUOTATIONS

The Internet is the first medium that allows anyone with reasonably inexpensive equipment to publish to a wide audience. It is the first medium that distributes information globally at almost no marginal cost. Bill Gates, CEO of Microsoft Corporation, February 22, 1996.

The Internet's potential is enormous, and the stakes high. The Internet can raise the quality of political debate, the quality of education, the quality of life. It is precious and important, and we must not take it for granted. Bill Gates, CEO of Microsoft Corporation, February 22, 1996.

[The Internet] is the one of the most profound communications events in the history of man. James L. Barksdale, CEO of Netscape Corporation, in speech delivered at the Commonwealth Club of California, September 13, 1995.

Let us reach for a goal in the 21st century of every home connected to the Internet and let us be brought closer together as a community through that connection. President Bill Clinton, in speech delivered in Knoxville, TN, October 10, 1996.

ANONYMOUS APHORISMS

The Internet is a mirror of humanity—unfortunately.

Remember the good old days, when kids just sat around watching television, and talking on the phone for hours?

It may only be a superhighway of information, but a crash brings traffic to a halt just as quickly.

ANECDOTES

Two old friends were discussing their lives at a high school reunion. "My girlfriend just left me," moaned the first one, "she was having an affair over the Internet." "Well, I'm sorry to hear that," replied the other, "I don't pay too much attention to technology myself." "What?" remarked a third friend, who'd just walked up, "I thought you just told me that you met your wife on the 'net."

FACTS

The Internet is not new, only its popularity is. It was originally developed in 1969 to allow the U.S. Defense Department to network incompatible computers to exchange information. Over the years the Internet grew steadily as research institutes and other academic, technical and governmental organizations joined in. The main reason for the Internet's success is that it allows any computer to connect with any other, no matter what type of computer it is. In 1991, Senator Al Gore introduced a bill which would allow businesses to purchase access to the network for commercial purposes. Businesses linked in and independent service providers began offering Internet access to individuals; by September 1995, it was estimated that over 50 million people worldwide were using the Internet. The World Wide Web exists on the Internet. It is a graphically enhanced environment, and allows users to move from site to site via direct links. At roughly 340,000 percent growth, the Web is the fastest growing segment of the Internet. Only a small percentage of

Americans have home computers connected to the 'net, but this could be compared to the 1920s, when only a few people had home telephones.

INVENTION

DEFINITIONS   A device, mechanism or procedure that did not previously exist; a new way of doing something; the secret of progress; the act of devising new machines or processes; what necessity is the mother of; "The Mother of Necessity" (Thorstein Veblen); a new or original paradigm.

QUOTATIONS

…God hath made man upright: but they have sought out many inventions. *Ecclesiastes,* 7:29.

'Tis frivolous to fix pedantically the date of particular inventions. They have all been invented over and over fifty times. Ralph Waldo Emerson, *The Conduct of Life:* "Fate," 1860.

Invention breeds invention. Ralph Waldo Emerson, *Society and Solitude:* "Works and Days," 1870.

What good is a newborn baby? Benjamin Franklin, August 27, 1783.

What hath God wrought!… Samuel F. B. Morse, first telegraph message, May 24, 1844.

ANONYMOUS APHORISMS

Did you ever think how much labor went into inventing a labor-saving device?

One civilization after another has reinvented the wheel.

It takes one invention to replace another.

Mother is the necessity of invention.

Invention is the son of need and the father of prosperity.

These days invention requires subvention, defies convention and often calls for divine intervention.

The inventor's motto is: If you don't see what you want, make it.

ANECDOTES

An American and an Englishman were arguing the virtues of their countries. "In England," said the American "when we said we had a new way to process cotton, you said it was 'impossible.' When we came up with the airplane, you said it was 'an interesting invention.' When we produced the computer, you said it was promising. Apart from the steam engine and some looms, what have you invented?" "Your language," replied the Englishman.

An inventor and an explorer compared their callings. "I go out looking for new things," said the explorer. "I stay home making new things," said the inventor.

"Surely you don't classify any inventor as more important to the world than Christopher Columbus," a reporter commented during an interview with a well-known inventor. "How about the guy who invented the boat?" replied the inventor.

FACTS

Invention constantly changes the face of existence. From the wheel to the computer, invention has made it possible for humankind to be more productive; to expand his horizons; to make life easier and more fruitful. The U.S. Constitution took pains to protect the rights of inventors by providing in Article 1, Section 8 (8) that Congress shall have the power "To promote the Progress of Science and useful Arts, by securing for limited Times to Authors and Inventors the exclusive Right to their respective Writings and Discoveries." Since its establishment in 1790, the U.S. Patent Office has issued patents for inventions at a rate of more than 100,000 a year. Not every invention, of course, is an earth-shaking one; but one need only recall those in the fields of medicine, transportation, communication, and computerization to realize how much of modern life is the product of inventive genius.

An annual report is published by the U.S. Commissioner of Patents. *The New York Times* began publishing a Saturday news column about patents many years ago.

JOBS

(See also Labor, Opportunity)

DEFINITIONS   Work; occupations; gainful employment; tasks; assigned functions; what people do for a living; bread and butter; the 9-to-5 grind.

QUOTATIONS

In an age in which change is the only constant, competitive success now requires constant, sustained innovation. That means for governments and businesses and workers, we must constantly be reinterpreting and reinventing how we work. U.S. Secretary of Commerce Ronald H. Brown, speech, July 26, 1993.

Success is feeling good about yourself. If you're low on self-esteem, no job or amount of money in the world is going to make you feel good. John J. Curley, chairman and president of Gannett Company, in *USA Today,* May 24, 1989.

Work is not the curse, but drudgery is. Rev. Henry Ward Beecher, *Proverbs from Plymouth Pulpit,* 1887.

Blessed is he who has found his work; let him ask no other blessedness. Thomas Carlyle, *Past and Present,* 1843.

He that hath a trade hath an estate; he that hath a calling hath an office of profit and honor. Benjamin Franklin, *The Way to Wealth,* 1757.

Too many young men and women face long and bitter months of job hunting or marginal work after leaving school. Our society has not yet established satisfactory ways to bridge the gap between school and work. President Lyndon B. Johnson, message to the U.S. Congress, May 1, 1967.

People who are hungry and out of a job are the stuff of which dictatorships are made. President Franklin D. Roosevelt, message to the U.S. Congress, January 11, 1944.

Far and away the best prize that life offers is the chance to work hard at work worth doing. President Theodore Roosevelt, September 7, 1903.

In order that people may be happy in their work, these three things are needed: They must be fit for it; They must not do too much of it; And they must have a sense of success in it. John Ruskin, *Pre-Raphaelitism,* 1850.

…work saves us from three great evils: boredom, vice and need. Voltaire, *Candide,* 1759.

…there is as much dignity in tilling a field as in writing a poem. Booker T. Washington, *Up from Slavery,* 1901.

ANONYMOUS APHORISMS

First get the job, then get the job done.

Don't send a boy to do a man's job these days; send a woman.

A job is regular work you get paid for before you find a position.

Finding a job is sometimes harder work than doing a job.

All work and no play makes Jack a dull boy.

All work and no play makes jack.

Make the best of a bad job.

ANECDOTES

"If you can't find employment," said Mr. Jones to his son, "at least go down and collect your unemployment insurance." "No," said the son, "it's too much of a job."

When Willie was caught robbing the poorbox at the church, he pleaded for mercy. "I've been looking day and night for a job," he said. "This is a funny place to look," said the sexton.

"Young man," said Mr. Brown, "I have selected you for this job over scores of other applicants. You should regard that as a clear vote of confidence in your ability and your training. Work hard and this could be the start of a fine career." The young man fidgeted for a moment and then answered, "Thanks, Dad."

FACTS

Jobs are one of the measures of the success of any society. When there is not enough work for everybody who wants to work, there are problems; and there are also problems when there is work enough but not reward enough. In earlier generations, jobs were guaranteed for a lifetime. Today, because of the mortality rate of business enterprises and the desire for upward mobility on the part of jobholders, one person is apt to hold many, or at least several, jobs in a lifetime. The technological revolution is phasing out many jobs and creating new ones. In 1996, the U.S. Department of Labor reported that there were over 1.3 million Americans in the workplace, clocking an average of 34.5 hours per week, for an average of just over $11 per hour.

For the latest figures on unemployment, consult the Bureau of Labor Statistics, whose monthly reports on Employment and Earnings are widely covered in the press. The Bureau is a unit of the U.S. Department of Labor, at 200 Constitution Avenue NW, Washington, D.C. 20210.

JOURNALISM

(See also Radio, Television)

DEFINITIONS   Writing, editing, and publishing material on contemporary news and trends; reporting current events; "literature in a hurry" (Matthew Arnold); the news; the media; the press.

QUOTATIONS

To be a journalist, you need a strong cultural base and a lot of practice. You also need a good deal of ethics. There are so many bad journalists who, when they have no news, invent it. Gabriel Garcia Marquez, in *El Pais* reprinted from *World Press Review,* July, 1994.

The one thing a good journalist wants is to blend into the background. We should never be the story. Peter Jennings, in *Good Housekeeping,* April, 1991.

In a democracy, the public has a right to know not only what the government decides, but why and by what process. President Gerald Ford, September 13, 1976.

How beautiful upon the mountains are the feet of him that bringeth good tidings... *Isaiah,* 52:7.

...were it left to me to decide whether we should have a government without newspapers or newspapers without a government, I should not hesitate a moment to prefer the latter. Thomas Jefferson, letter to Colonel Edward Carrington, January 16, 1787.

In a world of daily—nay, almost hourly—journalism, every clever man, every man who thinks himself clever, or whom anybody else thinks clever, is called upon to deliver his judgment point-blank and at the word of command on every conceivable subject of human thought. James Russell Lowell, "Democracy," 1884.

All the news that's fit to print. Adolph S. Ochs, slogan on the editorial page of the *The New York Times,* October 25, 1896.

...in recent years, both print and broadcast journalism have been the subject of a growing if irrational suspicion—sometimes expressed in high places that the press is somehow to blame for unhappy events and trends, merely because it performs its duty of reporting them. William S. Paley, chairman, CBS, December 7, i976.

We live under a government of men and morning newspapers. Wendell Phillips, January 28, 1852.

As cold waters to a thirsty soul, so is good news from a far country. *Proverbs,* 25:25.

The men with the muckrakes are often indispensable to the well-being of society; but only if they know when to stop raking the muck... President Theodore Roosevelt, April 14, 1906.

Nobody likes the bearer of bad news. Sophocles, *Antigone,* c. 440 BC.

It is a newspaper's duty to print the news, and raise hell. Wilbur F. Storey, editor, *The Chicago Times,* statement of editorial purpose, 1861.

When we hear news we should always wait for the sacrament of confirmation. Voltaire, letter to Le Comte d'Argental, August 28, 1760.

ANONYMOUS APHORISMS

Dog bites man. That's not news. Man bites dog. Now, that's news.

Freedom of the press is a right; freedom from the press is an illusion.

News is where you find it.

Bad news travels fast.

No news is good news.

Journalism consists of producing headlines against deadlines.

It isn't news until it's reported.

News is instant history.

ANECDOTES

"Where's your story on the big game today?" the editor asked the cub reporter. "I didn't write it," replied the reporter, "because the game was called off when the stadium collapsed." "Then where is the story on the stadium collapse?" the editor queried. "That wasn't my assignment," the reporter shrugged.

To illustrate how the daily news is reported, journalism professors like to tell the tale of how successive days' headlines in a Parisian gazette related the news about Napoleon's escape from Elba. When the story first broke, the headline spoke of the "Corsican Monster." Two days later, the headline called him the "Pretender." The next day, he was simply "Bonaparte." And finally, the headline announced "His Imperial Majesty Will Be in Paris Tomorrow."

"My father," one boy proudly declared, "has been in the newspaper business for thirty years." "What does he do?" his friend asked. "Oh, he sells them at his stand on the corner," the boy replied.

FACTS

Journalism is considered a relatively modern innovation, which flowered during the American Revolution. Freedom of the press was largely an American product; and journalism has been more varied and more free in this country than anyplace else on earth. Although the number of daily newspapers has declined since the introduction of television, there are still more daily newspapers in this country than in any other. With nearly 7700 daily, weekly and specialized newspapers listed in the 1996 edition of the *Working Press of the Nation Newspaper Directory,* and 14,000 broadcasting stations, the multiplicity of journalistic voices in the U.S. far surpasses the rest of the world. The newspapers with the largest circulation in the world, however, are not based in America. They are nationally circulated newspapers in other countries such as Russia, Japan and the United Kingdom. Journalism used to be a profession that one learned only from experience, but today there are hundreds of schools and departments of journalism in colleges and universities such as the University of North Carolina at Chapel Hill and Northwestern University; a number of them award advanced degrees.

The annual *Editor & Publisher Yearbook* offers interesting statistics on the newspaper as an American institution.

JUSTICE

(See also Courts, Law)

DEFINITIONS   The administration of law; that which is just and right; "the crowning glory of the virtues" (Cicero); "the great standing policy of civil society" (Edmund Burke); "truth in action" (Joseph Joubert).

QUOTATIONS

In baseball it's three strikes and you're out. Here [in the law], it's three strikes and you're in, for life. New York Governor Mario M. Cuomo, State of the State Address, January 24, 1994.

Peace and justice are two sides of the same coin. President Dwight D. Eisenhower, February 6, 1957.

One man's justice is another's injustice. Ralph Waldo Emerson, *Essays, First Series:* "Circles," 1841.

Eye for eye, tooth for tooth, hand for hand, foot for foot. *Exodus,* 21:24.

...moderation in the pursuit of justice is no virtue. Senator Barry M. Goldwater of Arizona, acceptance speech for the Republican Presidential nomination in San Francisco, CA, July 16, 1964.

Justice delayed is democracy denied. Robert F. Kennedy, "To Secure These Rights," 1964.

The love of justice in most men is only the fear of suffering injustice. Francois Duc de La Rochefoucauld, *Maxims,* c. 17th century.

Why should there not be a patient confidence in the ultimate justice of the people? Is there any better or equal hope in the world? President Abraham Lincoln, first inaugural address, March 4, 1861.

Yet shall I temper so / Justice with mercy. John Milton, *Paradise Lost,* 1667.

...this even-handed justice... William Shakespeare, *Macbeth,* 1606.

Expedience and justice frequently are not even on speaking terms. Senator Arthur H. Vandenberg of Michigan, March 8, 1945.

Justice, sir, is the great interest of man on earth. It is the ligament which holds civilized beings and civilized nations together. Daniel Webster, September 12, 1845.

Judging from the main portions of the history of the world, so far, justice is always in jeopardy. Walt Whitman, *Democratic Vistas,* 1870.

Justice has nothing do with expediency. President Woodrow Wilson, February 26, 1916.

ANONYMOUS APHORISMS

Justice wears different faces for different people.

Justice is blind.

He couldn't get justice so he went to court.

Everyone sees his own cause as just.

Justice often satisfies neither side.

Justice can always be found in court, even if sometimes it is only the title of the official on the bench.

Justice always needs a friend at court.

ANECDOTES

"We all define justice the same way in the abstract," said a scholarly judge to a colleague, "but we are bound to differ in the concrete. For example, ask the two parties in the case I just decided what they thought of the verdict, and I think you'll find that they have different concepts." So the two parties were asked about the verdict. "That's justice," said the plaintiff. And the defendant retorted, "That's justice?"

"Justice," said a lawyer of our acquaintance, "is like meat. Everybody comes into court to see justice done, but some want it rare, some medium and some well done."

"Excuse me," said the jury foreman to the judge, "but we have a question of law. What is justice?" "That's not a question of law," replied the judge, "it's a question of judgment."

FACTS

Justice is one of the first functions of any society, whether it is dispensed on the basis of free and fair trial or by dictatorial fiat, and whether it is in fact just or not. The administration of justice calls for a vast machinery: in the U.S. there are well over 800,000 lawyers and thousands of courts, as well as correctional institutions and law enforcement agencies. It involves guarantees not only of basic rights, fairness of evidence, and the machinery for appeals to higher jurisdictions; but also a system of checks and balances in the selection of judges, a requirement for jury trials in various kinds of cases and, above all, constant reaffirmation of the basic principles of justice embodied in the U.S. Constitution.

There are numerous organizations dedicated to ensuring justice through adequate legal representation (the Legal Aid Society, for example), through seeking protection of the interests of particular groups (such as the American Association of Retired Persons or the National Association for the Advancement of Colored People) and through the normal voicings of conscience by religious groups.

KNOWLEDGE

DEFINITIONS   Direct perception; understanding or cognition; a body of information; that which has been learned and retained; "the only elegance" (Ralph Waldo Emerson); "the great sum in the firmament" (Daniel Webster); "the amassed thought and experience of innumerable minds" (Ralph Waldo Emerson); "a species of money" (Jean-Jacques Rousseau).

QUOTATIONS

Knowledge is power. Sir Francis Bacon, *Religious Meditations:* "Of Heresies," 1597.

Knowledge is the only good, and ignorance the only evil. Diogenes Laertes, *Lives of the Philosophers:* "Socrates," c. 200 AD.

To be conscious that you are ignorant is a great step to knowledge. Benjamin Disraeli, *Sybil,* 1845.

We are wiser than we know. Ralph Waldo Emerson, *Essays, First Series:* "The Over-Soul," 1841.

Knowledge is the antidote to fear… Ralph Waldo Emerson, *Society and Solitude:* "Courage," 1870.

To be proud of knowledge is to be blind with light. Benjamin Franklin, *Poor Richard's Almanac,* 1766.

Knowledge and timber shouldn't be much used till they are seasoned. Oliver Wendell Holmes, *The Autocrat of the Breakfast-Table,* 1858.

It is the province of knowledge to speak and it is the privilege of wisdom to listen. Oliver Wendell Holmes, *The Poet at the Breakfast-Table,* 1872.

I think by far the most important bill in our whole code, is that for the diffusion of knowledge among the people. No other sure foundation can be devised, for the preservation of freedom and happiness. Thomas Jefferson, letter to George Wythe, August 13, 1786.

The gathering of knowledge is the supreme achievement of man. President Lyndon B. Johnson, January 22, 1964.

Promote then as an object of primary importance, institutions for the general diffusion of knowledge. In proportion as the structure of a government gives force to public opinion, it is essential that public opinion be enlightened. President George Washington, farewell address, September 1796.

ANONYMOUS APHORISMS

What you don't know can hurt you.

He that knows little soon repeats it.

The most important thing to know is what you don't know.

If you don't know, ask.

We know so many things that aren't so.

The more you know, the more you want to know more.

The person who thinks he knows everything has a lot to learn.

ANECDOTES

In 1962, a dinner was held for the American Nobel Prize recipients. At that dinner, President John F. Kennedy remarked: "I think this is the most extraordinary collection of talent, of human knowledge, that has ever been gathered together at the White House—with the possible exception of when Thomas Jefferson dined alone."

Popular legend has it that once, when a colleague asked Albert Einstein for his telephone number, Einstein reached for a phone directory and looked it up. The startled man asked, "You don't remember your own number?" The great genius shrugged and replied, "Why should I memorize something I can so easily get from a book?"

Every time somebody asked Mr. Jones a question he couldn't answer he would say something like, "I think you'll have to find that out for yourself" or "look it up yourself" or "ask somebody with more time to explain it to you." His problem, of course, was that he didn't know how to say he didn't know.

FACTS

The world's store of knowledge is growing at an ever-increasing rate of speed, partly because more people are working to find more answers than ever before, and partly because they have better means for learning than ever before, such as the computer. But the most important factor is the advent of means to rapidly disseminate new information. Television, newspapers, and the Internet instantly carry new discoveries to hundreds of millions of people worldwide. In astronomy, for example, we have seen stars born—an event which has been a mystery to scientists throughout history. Through genetic engineering, we have the ability to create new species of plants and animals. We can store more on a silicon chip than the entire contents of the famed library of Alexandria, and scan it quicker. In the 1970s, it was estimated that in the space of a single generation, the world would have four times as much knowledge as it did at that time. There are few people who would doubt that we have exceeded that figure many times over. Knowledge is considered to be such a valuable asset in today's society that its importance in creating a future has been summed up in the motto of the United Negro College Fund: "A mind is a terrible thing to waste."

There is a simple way to illustrate the march of knowledge. Take an old edition of your favorite encyclopedia and compare it to a new one. Pick a sample volume from each and see how many more entries there are in the newer one. And then try to imagine what additional knowledge we will have a generation from now.

LABOR

(See also Jobs)

DEFINITIONS Work; collective word for those who are organized employees; wage earners; blue-collar workers; skilled workers; unions; the working class; "horny-handed sons of toil" (Denis Kearney).

QUOTATIONS

There can be no distress, there can be no hard times, when labor is well paid. The man who raises his hand against the progress of the working man raises his hand against prosperity. W. Bourke Cockran, speech in New York, NY, August 18, 1896.

There is no right to strike against the public safety by anybody, anywhere, any time. Massachusetts Governor Calvin Coolidge, telegram on Boston police strike, September 14, 1919.

Honest labor bears a lovely face. Thomas Dekker, Patient Grissell, 1603.

The right to work, I had assumed, was the most precious liberty that man possesses. U.S. Supreme Court Associate Justice William O. Douglas, commenting on *Barsky v. Regents,* April 26, 1954.

Take not from the mouth of labor the bread it has earned. President Thomas Jefferson, inaugural address, March 4, 1801.

I like work: it fascinates me. I can sit and look at it for hours. Jerome K. Jerome, *Three Men in a Boat,* 1889.

American labor, whenever it gathers, does so with love for its flag and country and loyalty to its government. New York Mayor Fiorello H. LaGuardia, Labor Day speech at Chicago World's Fair, September 3, 1934.

No man is born into the world whose work is not born with him… James Russell Lowell, "A Glance Behind the Curtain," 1843.

Far and away the best prize that life offers is the chance to work hard at work worth doing. President Theodore Roosevelt, September 7, 1903.

…work saves us from three great evils: boredom, vice and need. Voltaire, *Candide,* 1759.

ANONYMOUS APHORISMS

Labor is a working combination.

One man's labor is another man's capital.

The real secret power of labor is that it works.

Labor is a striking phenomenon.

Organized labor is a big business.

Labor is the ultimate power of the people.

ANECDOTES

Q: Why are members of unions supposed to refer to their fellow members as brothers and sisters? A: Because they're all waiting for the same cry of "uncle."

Years ago a middle-aged man in working clothes used to come religiously to every free evening lecture at Cooper Union in New York, no matter what the subject. No matter who the lecturer was, this same man would always rise to ask the same question, and it always elicited an answer. The question was: "Now, all this that you've been telling us, is it good or bad for the working man?"

Labor and capital have opposing views of collective bargaining. Labor puts the accent on the first part of the phrase: collect. Capital is more interested in the second part, the word whose first two syllables say, "bar gain."

FACTS

Between 1940 and 1968, union membership in the U.S. more than doubled, reaching nearly 20 million. In the early 80s membership slipped below 17 million, but it eventually stabilized, and has remained near that figure until the present. The early growth surge was due, in large measure, to successful organization of the previously unorganized; and in the gaining of labor contracts in fields such as public education where there had not previously been union agreements. The growth of labor unionism in this country has been promoted by a variety of factors, ranging from management's insensibility to the demands of workers to favorable laws enacted by political bodies responsive to their labor constituencies. In addition to the growth of labor unions, labor has won a steadily greater degree of government protection for minimum wage scales, basic working conditions, and fair employment practices. At times, however, organized labor has found itself part of the establishment, confronted with demands from working people. As the custodian of various pension and welfare plans, labor has found itself somewhat a part of capital management and the investment group. Not all labor unions are "horny handed sons of toil." The talent unions—actors', musicians', and dramatists' unions, for example—have salary scales far beyond those of some of their brethren in the labor movement.

For a helpful list of unions, see the material provided by the U.S. Bureau of Labor Statistics or the AFL-CIO in the leading annual almanacs.

L ANGUAGE

(See also Ethnicity)

DEFINITIONS Oral or printed combinations of words that convey messages from one being to another; the vehicle of communication between people; tongue; the way human beings express thoughts to each other; a distinctive vocabulary understood by a definable group of people; "the archives of history" (Ralph Waldo Emerson).

QUOTATIONS

All words are pegs to hang ideas on. Rev. Henry Ward Beecher, *Proverbs from Plymouth Pulpit,* 1887.

It is with language as with manners: They are both established by the usage of people of fashion… Lord Chesterfield, letter to his son, April 5, 1754.

Language gradually varies, and with it fade away the writings of authors who have flourished their allotted time… Washington Irving, *The Sketch Book:* "The Mutability of Literature," 1820.

I am sorry when any language is lost, because languages are the pedigree of nations. Samuel Johnson, according to James Boswell in *Journal of a Tour to the Hebrides with Samuel Johnson, LL.D.,* September 18, 1775.

Man does not live by words alone, despite the fact that sometimes he has to eat them. Adlai E. Stevenson, Jr., presidential candidate, speech in Denver, CO, September 5, 1952.

It is the man who determines what is said, not the words. Henry D. Thoreau, *Journal,* July 11, 1840.

Language, as well as the faculty of speech, was the immediate gift of God. Noah Webster, preface to *American Dictionary of the English Language,* 1828.

Wondrous the English language, language of live men… Walt Whitman, "As I Sat Alone," 1856.

ANONYMOUS APHORISMS

The test of your command of language is whether you can describe a spiral staircase or a screen goddess without using your hands.

More people have been hurt by words than by guns.

Language sometimes interferes with communication.

Talk is cheap and silence is golden.

Harsh words are hard to heal.

Choose your words or your words will keep you from being chosen.

Anecdotes

Three cows were grazing in a pasture. The first one said, "Moo!" The second one said, "Moooo!.." The third one said, "Argh!" "See," said the proud farmer to his friend, "she speaks another language."

An American college student was assigned a dormitory room with a young Englishman. The American's father asked his son how he liked rooming with the Englishman. "Except for the one standing argument," said the student, "it's fine." "What's the argument?" his father inquired. "Each of us accuses the other of having an accent," he replied.

Two men were having a very heated discussion. Both were very voluble and neither was having much success with convincing the other. Finally one clenched his fist and hit the other on the jaw, knocking him down. The fallen gentleman looked up and said, "Why didn't you say that in the first place?"

Facts

Language is a fluid and changing art form. Most modern languages are derived from earlier versions which we would find hard to understand today; and it is hard enough to understand accents and dialects that are not our own. All told, the world today has approximately 6,500 languages, with more than 200 of them characterized as major. And we can't even agree on the alphabets we use to record them. In terms of shear numbers of people who speak them, the top five languages are Mandarin, Hindi, Spanish, English, and Bengali; which are followed by Arabic, Russian, Portuguese, and Japanese. Surprisingly, Portuguese is the mother tongue of more people than French—although French has historically been considered the official language of diplomacy. One of the marks of a vigorous language is that it frequently adds new words and new shades of meaning. Slang is the spice in any language's vocabulary stew. That is why, for example, different generations sometimes have trouble understanding each other even when they think they are both speaking the same language. The colloquialisms used by one generation or group can be virtually unintelligible to their language compatriots. In your local library or book store, you will find specialized dictionaries of ethnic English, business and hobby group English (such as computer and Citizen's Band language), as well as updated colloquial English.

For a list of the world's current languages, see the principal annual almanacs, such as the *World Almanac*.

L A W

(See also Courts, Justice, Law and Order)

DEFINITIONS   Rule of conduct established and enforced by government; the body of such rules; the process and practice of administering such rules; the professional practice of the law; "the last result of human wisdom acting upon human experience for the benefit of the public" (Samuel Johnson).

QUOTATIONS

Most of the great trial lawyers I know are very, very scared. Fear, for an actor, stirs you to a greater performance. Arthur Liman, lawyer, in *Esquire,* January, 1989.

...you cannot live without the lawyers, and certainly you cannot die without them. Joseph H. Choate, speech in New York, NY, May 13, 1879.

Laws must be justified by something more than the will of the majority. They must rest on the eternal foundation of righteousness. Calvin Coolidge, January 7, 1914.

Anyone who takes it on himself, on his own authority, to break a bad law, thereby authorizes everybody else to break the good ones. Denis Diderot, *Supplement to the Voyage of Bougainville,* 1796.

Law is not self-executing. Unfortunately, at times its execution rests in the hands of those who are faithless to it. And even when its enforcement is committed to those who revere it, law merely deters some human beings from offending, and punishes other human beings for offending. This does not make men good. This task can be performed only by ethics or religion or morality. Senator Sam J. Ervin, Jr., of North Carolina, statement as Chairman of Senate Watergate Committee with its final report, July 12, 1974.

Laws too gentle are seldom obeyed; too severe, seldom executed. Benjamin Franklin, *Poor Richard's Almanac,* 1756.

There are not enough jails, not enough policemen, not enough courts to enforce a law not supported by the people. Vice President Hubert H. Humphrey, May 1, 1965.

...a strict observance of the written laws is doubtless one of the high duties of a good citizen, but it is not the highest. The laws of necessity, of self-preservation, of saving our country when in danger, are of higher obligation. Thomas Jefferson, letter to John B. Colvin, September 20, 1810.

Our nation is founded on the principal that observance of the law is the eternal safeguard of liberty and defiance of the law is the surest road to tyranny. President John F. Kennedy, September 20, 1962.

Ye shall have one manner of law, as well for the stranger, as for one of your own country. *Leviticus* 24:22.

Wherever Law ends, Tyranny begins. John Locke, *Two Treatises of Government,* 1690.

Ignorance of the law excuses no man; not that all men know the law, but because 'tis an excuse every man will plead, and no man can tell how to confute him. John Selden, *Table Talk:* "Equity," (posthumously published) 1689.

To make laws that man cannot, and will not obey, serves to bring all law into contempt. Elizabeth Cady Stanton, testimony before New York State Senate Judiciary Committee, 1861.

ANONYMOUS APHORISMS

A lawyer's briefs aren't.

A government of law is a government of lawyers.

Necessity hath no law.

A lawsuit helps keep the lawyers clothed.

The more laws the more offenders.

Law is a bottomless pit.

God save us from a lawyer's et ceteras.

ANECDOTES

Two angels had a furious argument and decided to settle their differences before a higher authority; they asked St. Peter where they could get lawyers to plead their case. "You'll have to ask for a change of venue," St. Peter shook his head, "we don't get the lawyers up here."

A doctor and a lawyer were discussing the merits of their respective professions. "In my profession," said the doctor, "we cure people." "And in mine," said the lawyer, "we probate your failures."

In a faraway land, a king issued a law that ordered the sun to stand still. The sun, of course, continued to rise and set in its accustomed way. The king was furious, but when his advisers tried to explain to him that it was his law, not the sun, that was at fault, he refused to accept this fact. "Ignorance of the law," he decalred, "is no excuse."

FACTS

Even primitive societies have established institutions such as medicine and religion, but law—in its modern sense—comes with alleged civilization. In that case, the United States is becoming more civilized all the time, not only because we have more laws but because we are steadily acquiring more lawyers. Some people say that we inherited our litigious nature from our British forefathers. But, at the turn of the century, the proportion of the American population in the legal profession was less than .09 percent: less than one lawyer per 1,000 people. Today, it is about one attorney for every 320 people. The total number of lawyers in the U.S. has risen from 285,933 in 1960, to 542,205 in 1980, to 805,872 in 1991. The same trend has been evident in most of the principal occidental nations. Some of this is due to the fact that the government keeps adding more laws to the books, providing more reasons for litigation. Part of the reason for the increased number of lawyers is that the opportunities to go to law school have been broadened, particularly for minorities and women. And part of the reason is that the profession of the law has become, more than ever before, a good means of entry into both government and business management.

Your local bar association library can provide pertinent statistics on the growth of the profession both in your area and throughout the nation. The American Bar Association is located at 750 North Lake Shore Drive, Chicago, IL 60611.

L AW AND ORDER

(See also Crime, Justice, Law, Violence)

DEFINITIONS   The absence of crime in an orderly society; the protection of the rights of law-abiding citizens and of their safety; safe streets and safe homes.

QUOTATIONS

Law and order is the first responsibility of government. President Bill Clinton, speech, October 16, 1995.

Law is order, and good law is good order. Aristotle, *Politics,* c. 330 BC.

Of all the tasks of government, the most basic is to protect its citizens against violence. Secretary of State John Foster Dulles, April 22, 1957.

History shows us, demonstrates that nothing, nothing prepares the way for tyranny more than the failure of public officials to keep the streets safe from bullies and marauders. Senator Barry M. Goldwater of Arizona, accepting Republican Presidential nomination in San Francisco, CA, July 16, 1964.

Law enforcement cannot succeed without the sustained—and informed— interest of all citizens. It is not enough to reflect our concern over the rise in crime by seeking out single answers or simple answers. The people will get observance of the law and enforcement of the law if they want it, insist on it, and participate in it. President Lyndon B. Johnson, message to the U.S. Congress, March 8, 1965.

There is no greater wrong in our democracy than violent, willful disregard of law. President Lyndon B. Johnson, August 15, 1965.

There is no grievance that is a fit object of redress by mob law. Abraham Lincoln, speech in Springfield, IL, January 27, 1838.

The age of the social conscience, social justice and concern seems to have coincided with the age of crime, pornography, mugging and international terrorism. What started out as a liberalization of restrictive social conventions seems to have developed into a dictatorship of license. Prince Philip of Great Britain, October 17, 1977.

ANONYMOUS APHORISMS

Law and order are not necessarily partners.

The best protection for people on the street is a lot of other people on the street.

Many of those who call for law and order mean the old order.

Law and order are far surer when they reflect the popular will than when imposed upon a dissident public.

The value of law and order depends on whose law it is, and who gives the order.

When you read the riot act, be prepared to enforce it.

A vigilante is the product of not keeping a sharp enough vigil and having to raise the ante.

ANECDOTES

The leader of a mob attacking the town jail to get hold of a hated prisoner told the sheriff, "We're taking the law into our own hands." "If it's in your own hands," said the sheriff, "it isn't the law. Nobody owns the law." "Oh, yeah," yelled the defiant mob leader, "you seem to think you own it." "No," said the sheriff, quietly, "the law owns me."

"How can you have law and order and still have a democracy?" a foreign dictator asked an American visitor. "Democracy," replied the American, "depends on who orders the law."

FACTS

Throughout American history there have been challenges to law and order, ranging from Shays' Rebellion to the excesses of San Francisco's; from lynch mobs to the student rebellions and anti-war demonstrations of the 1960s and the race riots of the early 1990s. It becomes clear that our society has succeeded more in defusing the violence and intimidation of mob action than in solving the problems of criminal attacks on the individual citizen. The great dilemma in safeguarding law and order is to maintain decent order without offending the law. We are still fighting the battle of keeping people from taking the law into their own hands. To that end, governments have steadily expanded the ways the individual citizen can have recourse to public help in protecting his rights and safety.

The problem is that in expanding individual freedom we have had, of necessity, to limit the freedom of government. In an earlier era, it was commonplace to say that law and order was enforced by the policeman's nightstick; but today the use of the nightstick has been circumscribed to protect individual citizens' rights.

At different positions in the law and order spectrum can be found such organizations as the American Civil Liberties Union, 132 West 43rd Street, New York, NY 10036-6599; and the National Council on Crime and Delinquency, 685 Market Street, Suite 620, San Francisco, CA 94105.

LEADERSHIP

DEFINITIONS   The ability, duties or act of leading; the art of directing and guiding others; the ability to motivate others toward a common goal; the ship that leads the way; the guiding light.

QUOTATIONS

Leaders need to be primarily in service to the people and values of the organization that they lead. Leaders almost never need to exercise power. They need to lead in ways that create a vision that motivates people. Claire L. Gaudiani, president, Connecticut College, in the *The Christian Science Monitor,* February 28, 1992.

There's two things in coaching. One, is winning and two, is misery. Chuck Knox, football coach, Seattle Seahawks, in *The Los Angeles Times,* January 14, 1991.

There are men, who, by their sympathetic attractions, carry nations with them, and lead the activity of the human race. Ralph Waldo Emerson, *The Conduct of Life:* "Power," 1860.

The American people want leadership which believes in them, not leadership which berates them. President Lyndon B. Johnson, October 14, 1964.

In time of peril, like the needle to the lodestone, obedience, irrespective of rank, generally flies to him who is best fitted to command. Herman Melville, *White Jacket,* 1850.

Experts should be on tap, but never on top. Attributed to Winston Churchill, c. mid-20th century.

No man is fit to command another that cannot command himself. William Penn, *No Cross, No Crown,* 1669.

People ask the difference between a leader and a boss…The leader works in the open, and the boss in covert. The leader leads, and the boss drives. Theodore Roosevelt, October 24, 1910.

Reason and judgment are the qualities of a leader. Tacitus, *Histories,* c. 116 AD.

ANONYMOUS APHORISMS

If the people lead, the leaders will follow.

You can always tell a leader, but you can't tell him much.

Before a leader can come first, he has to come forth.

Judge a leader by the followers.

Take me to your leader.

In any group of people, a small fraction will be leaders, a larger fraction will be followers and a substantial proportion just won't get involved.

Leadership is the only ship that doesn't pull into a safe port in a storm.

Leadership casts a long shadow.

ANECDOTES

President John F. Kennedy told the story of one French Revolutionary leader who said, "There go my people. I must find out where they are going so I can lead them."

President Harry S. Truman provided a down-to-earth definition of political leadership while lecturing at Columbia University. He said, "When a leader is in the Democratic Party he's a boss; when he's in the Republican Party he's a leader." Mr. Truman, of course, had his tongue in his cheek because he also once commented on the tactics of Republican leadership as being, "If you can't convince them, confuse them."

LEISURE

(See also Hobbies and various sports)

DEFINITIONS   Time free from work; activities pursued for entertainment or relaxation: spare time; rest and relaxation (also known as R&R).

QUOTATIONS

There can be no high civilization where there is not ample leisure. Rev. Henry Ward Beecher, *Proverbs from Plymouth Pulpit,* 1887.

Increased means and increased leisure are the two civilizers of man. Benjamin Disraeli, April 3, 1872.

A life of leisure and a life of laziness are two different things. Benjamin Franklin, *Poor Richard's Almanac,* 1746.

No man is so methodical as a complete idler, and none so scrupulous in measuring out his time as he whose time is worth nothing. Washington Irving, *Wolfert's Roost:* "My French Neighbor," 1855.

All intellectual improvement arises from leisure… Samuel Johnson, according to James Boswell , April 13, 1773.

Idle folks have the least leisure. John Ray, *English Proverbs,* 1670.

He enjoys true leisure who has time to improve his soul's estate. Henry D. Thoreau, *Journal,* February 11, 1840.

In itself and in its consequences the life of leisure is beautiful and ennobling in all civilized men's eyes. Thorstein Veblen, *The Theory of the Leisure Class,* 1899.

ANONYMOUS APHORISMS

Half a loaf is better than not loafing at all.

Some people merely spend their leisure time; others enjoy it.

The busiest people have the most leisure or get the most out of it.

The best way to appreciate leisure is to work hard for it.

Time to spare spares the soul.

All work and no play isn't much better than all play and no work.

ANECDOTES

Q: Would you care to define your leisure activities? A: Nothing doing.

There was once a man whose daily job entailed carpentry. A friend called on him at home one day and found him busy in his workshop, doing more carpentry. "What kind of leisure activity is that?" the friend asked, "it's the same thing you do to earn a living." "Yes," said the carpenter, "but here I am able to hang around my own joints."

FACTS

There are two principal reasons for the proliferation of leisure activities. The first and most important is that the average American has more leisure time. In production, labor-saving devices have cut the required number of work hours; in American industry the average work week was 39.8 hours in 1950; 35.7 hours in 1975; and 34.5 hours in 1995. But leisure is also good business; from resorts and casinos, to professional sports, to film and television, there is a wide array of industries that depend on the dollars we spend on the pursuit of leisurely activities. Improvements in transportation—more ownership of cars, better roads, speedier air travel—have increased the availability of leisure-time activities too. Finally, the wisdom of medicine is spreading the gospel that relaxation and the pursuit of a hobby can be good for your health.

L I B E R T Y

(See also Democracy, Freedom)

DEFINITIONS   Freedom; "the right to do what the laws allow" (Charles de Secondat Montesquieu); absence of restraint; the original free-for-all; without sanction; release from restriction; rescue from imprisonment.

QUOTATIONS

The greatest dangers to liberty lurk in insidious encroachment by men of zeal, well-meaning but without understanding. U.S. Supreme Court Associate Justice Louis D. Brandeis , commenting on *Olmstead v. U.S.,* June 4, 1928.

Give me liberty or give me death! Patrick Henry, speech to the Virginia Assembly, March 25, 1775.

The very aim and end of our institutions is just this: that we may think what we like and say what we think. Oliver Wendell Holmes, *The Professor at the Breakfast-Table,* 1860.

It behooves every man who values liberty of conscience for himself, to resist invasions of it in the case of others… President Thomas Jefferson, letter to Dr. Benjamin Rush, April 21, 1803.

It has been observed that they who most loudly clamor for liberty do not most liberally grant it. Samuel Johnson, *Lives of the English Poets,* "Milton," 1779.

Our reliance is in the love of liberty which God has planted in us. Our defense is in the spirit which prized liberty as the heritage of all men, in all lands everywhere. Destroy this spirit and you have planted the seeds of despotism at your own doors. Abraham Lincoln, speech in Edwardsville, IL, September 11, 1858.

Four score and seven years ago our fathers brought forth on this continent a new nation, conceived in liberty and dedicated to the proposition that all men are created equal. President Abraham Lincoln, address at Gettysburg, PA, November 19, 1863.

…that this nation, under God, shall have a new birth of freedom… President Abraham Lincoln, address at Gettysburg, PA, November 19, 1863.

...the freedom of the press is one of the great bulwarks of liberty, and can never be restrained but by despotic governments. George Mason, Virginia Bill of Rights, adopted June 12, 1776.

My country, 'tis of thee, / Sweet land of liberty, / Of thee I sing: / Land where my father died, / Land of the pilgrims' pride, / From every mountainside / Let freedom ring. Rev. Dr. Samuel F. Smith, "America" adapted from "God Save Our Nation's King," 1831.

God grants liberty only to those who love it, and are always ready to guard and defend it. Senator Daniel Webster of Massachusetts, June 3, 1834.

The history of liberty is a history of limitation of government power, not the increase of it. New Jersey Governor Woodrow Wilson, 1912.

ANONYMOUS APHORISMS

Too often, liberty is not appreciated until it is taken away.

To protect your liberty, respect the liberty of others.

Liberty is the freedom of people you agree with; license is for those of other views.

Liberty is not free; it is paid for with good citizenship.

ANECDOTES

Q: Why do they describe an actor who isn't working as being at liberty? A: Because his time is free.

At a town meeting, a couple of obstreperous citizens kept monopolizing the floor. Finally, one outraged townsman demanded to know whether they were on the town's tax rolls. He was asked why and replied, "Because I don't think people should get liberty free."

Q: Why is liberty symbolized by a statue of a lady with a torch? A: Because it is a thing of beauty that can only be seen when its light shines.

FACTS

Liberty is a perishable commodity. In the 1990s, freedom gained in nations such as Panama and the republics that made up the former Soviet Union; and declined in such places as Hong Kong and Bosnia-Herzegovina. Governments do not hold complete power over liberty; the greatest threat to liberty is fast becoming domestic and international terrorism, which strips us of our freedom to travel safely, and even our "freedom from fear . . . everywhere in the world."

Freedom House, 120 Wall Street, 26th floor, New York, NY 10005-3904, does an annual survey of the state of freedom in the world. The Reporters Committee for Freedom of the Press at 1101 Wilson Blvd., Suite 1910, Arlington, VA 22209;

Amnesty International; and the national, state, and municipal units of the American Civil Liberties Union also maintain current dossiers on the subject.

L I F E

(See also Nature)

DEFINITIONS   The condition or experience of existence; the way a being lives; the original one-way street; the first thing we receive and the last we give up; the eternal road.

QUOTATIONS

We are not the sum of our possessions. They are not the measure of our lives. President George Bush, in *The Washington Post,* January 21, 1989.

Life is an incurable disease. Abraham Cowley, "To Dr. Scarborough," 1656.

…for a living dog is better than a dead lion. *Ecclesiastes,* 9:4.

Life is a series of surprises. Ralph Waldo Emerson, *Essays, First Series:* "Circles," 1841.

Life is too short to waste / In critic peep or cynic bark, / Quarrel or reprimand; / 'Twill soon be dark; / Up! mind thine own aim, and / God save the mark! Ralph Waldo Emerson, Poems: "To J.W.," 1847.

Tell me not in mournful numbers, / Life is but an empty dream! / For the soul is dead that slumbers, / And things are not what they seem. / Life is real! Life is earnest! / And the grave is not its goal; / Dust thou art, to dust returnest, / Was not spoken of the soul. Henry Wadsworth Longfellow, "A Psalm of Life," 1839.

We breathe today the same air that Julius Caesar breathed. Thanks, however, to the recycling labors of chlorophyll-bearing plants on land and plankton in the sea, we can safely inhale the air that has already served a thousand emperors. Russell W. Peterson, chairman, U.S. Council on Environmental Quality, September 29, 1976.

As for man, his days are as grass: as a flower of the field, so he flourisheth. For the wind passeth over it, and it is gone; and the place thereof shall know it no more. *Psalms,* 103:15-16.

Life's but a walking shadow, a poor player / That struts and frets his hour upon the stage / And then is heard no more: it is a tale / Told by an idiot, full of sound and fury, / Signifying nothing. William Shakespeare, *Macbeth,* 1606.

Let us endeavor so to live that when we come to die even the undertaker will be sorry. Mark Twain, *The Tragedy of Puddinhead Wilson,* 1894.

Why is it that we rejoice at a birth and grieve at a funeral? It is because we are not the person involved. Mark Twain, *The Tragedy of Puddinhead Wilson,* 1894.

…this world is a comedy to those who think, a tragedy to those who feel… Horace Walpole, December 31, 1769.

ANONYMOUS APHORISMS

Life is what you make it.

Nobody gets out of life alive.

While there's life there's hope—and while there's hope there's life.

To everyone, life in the first person is a mystery.

Life is the same old story, but every individual reaches his own ending.

Life is the only thing worth living.

Life doesn't seem so bad when you consider the alternative.

ANECDOTES

The scientist who discovered over a hundred uses for the peanut was credited with the story that best defines life. When George Washington Carver was contemplating life's mysteries, he asked the Lord to explain the mystery of the universe and the secret of life. The Lord told him such knowledge was not within the scope of human existence. "Well, then," Mr. Carver asked, "what about the mystery of the peanut?" "That," replied the Lord, "is closer to your size."

A young philosophy student traveled high into the Himalayan Mountains to speak to a venerable seer. When he arrived, he asked the sage, "Master, what is life?" The sage closed his eyes in thought for a few moments, then replied, "Life is simply the scent of a rose." "But, master," said the young student, "in the Andes an elderly Inca told me that life was a sharp stone." "That's his life," said the Himalayan sage.

LINCOLN, ABRAHAM

DEFINITIONS   Abraham Lincoln; 16th U.S. President; "The Great Emancipator"; "Honest Abe."

QUOTATIONS

In him was vindicated the greatness of real goodness and the goodness of real greatness. Rev. Phillips Brooks, sermon at Independence Hall, Philadelphia, PA, April 1865.

His heart was as great as the world, but there was no room in it to hold the memory of a wrong. Ralph Waldo Emerson, *Letters and Social Aims:* "Greatness," 1876.

There is a singular quality about Abraham Lincoln which sets him apart from all our other Presidents…a dimension of brooding compassion, of love for humanity: a love which was, if anything, strengthened and deepened by the agony that drove lesser men to the protective shelter of callous indifference. President Lyndon B. Johnson, February 12, 1967.

That nation has not lived in vain which has given the world Washington and Lincoln, the best great men and the greatest good men whom history can show. Senator Henry Cabot Lodge of Massachusetts, February 12, 1909.

Here was a man to hold against the world, / A man to match the mountains and the sea. Edwin Markham, "Lincoln, the Man of the People," 1901.

…the well-assured and most enduring memorial to Lincoln is invisibly there, today, tomorrow and for a long time yet to come in the hearts of lovers of liberty, men and women who understand that wherever there is freedom there have been those who fought, toiled and sacrificed for it. Carl Sandburg, speech to a joint session of the U.S. Congress on Lincoln's 150th birthday, February 12, 1959.

Now he belongs to the ages. U.S. Secretary of War Edwin M. Stanton, eulogy, April 15, 1865.

Oh Captain! My Captain! Walt Whitman, "Oh Captain! My Captain!" 1865.

Anonymous Aphorisms

Lincoln was a rail splitter; he was followed by hair splitters.

Only a man with the common touch would get his picture on the penny.

If Lincoln were alive today, he'd ride around in a Ford.

They called him Father Abraham because he kept the American family together.

Anecdotes

(Editor's Note: Although the anecdotes told by and about Abraham Lincoln are endless, these two particular stories capture Lincoln's essential attitude toward life.)

Adlai Stevenson, Jr., once recalled one of Lincoln's remarks after losing an election. Lincoln commented that he felt like a youngster who had stubbed his toe, and was too old to cry, but it hurt too much to laugh.

Lincoln himself, when asked in the White House how it felt to be the President of the United States, told the story of the man who was tarred and feathered and ridden out of town on a rail. The man was asked how he felt about being treated that way and replied, "If it wasn't for the honor of the thing, I'd just as soon walk."

FACTS

Abraham Lincoln was the first martyred President, the last of the frontier Presidents (his successor, Andrew Johnson, was the only Commander in Chief since Lincoln to be virtually entirely self-educated) and indubitably the most eloquent. If sainthood could be bestowed upon a secular leader, Lincoln would be canonized. He is undoubtedly the President most depicted in drama; most often cited as an advocate of reconciliation and tolerance. In this context, the personal tragedies of his life—the family losses and difficulties which, along with the Civil War, etched those great lines on his familiar face—have become part of the drama which keeps Lincoln so familiar a figure to the American people and to the world. One place and several dates have always been particularly associated with him. The place, of course, is the Lincoln Memorial in Washington, D.C., which was dedicated in 1922. One date is February 12, Lincoln's birthday. Born in Kentucky on that date in 1809, his birth is now celebrated in collaboration with George Washington's birthday on the third Monday in February as Presidents' Day. Another date which is closely tied to Lincoln's life is November 19, 1863. On that date, he dedicated the National Cemetery at Gettysburg, Virginia, and delivered the immortal Gettysburg Address. Lincoln was shot by John Wilkes Booth at Ford's Theater in Washington at a performance of *Our American Cousin* on the evening of April 14, 1865. He died shortly after seven the following morning.

LITERATURE

(See also Books)

DEFINITIONS   Written compositions in prose or verse; the field of endeavor concerned with the writing, publication, preservation and study of such work; prose or verse collectively; the magic of words; "an investment of genius which pays dividends to all subsequent times" (John Burroughs).

QUOTATIONS

I learned a very valuable thing as a writer: to maintain my anxieties in the face of all good fortune. E.L. Doctorow, in *Book World* (*Washington Post*) reprinted from *The Writer,* November, 1989.

I don't believe the notion that out of suffering comes a story, and I find it an offensive idea. The suffering isn't worth the book—life is more important than art. Susanna Moore, in *The New York Times Book Review* reprinted from *The Writer,* August, 1989.

To me, the act of creating is the most exciting thing in the world. In a sense, every writer is God. What else could be more exciting than that? Sidney Sheldon, in *Esquire,* July, 1989.

Payoff? Who needs payoff? You write because you're a writer and it's your responsibility to communicate. And if you're a responsible citizen, you do it. Edward Albee, first quoted in *Dramatics*, reprinted from *The Writer,* June, 1994.

Literary reputation is everything. I want to be read. I want to be valued. That is perhaps the only shot at immortality a human being can have. Anne Rice, in *Esquire,* July, 1989.

Life comes before literature, as the material always comes before the work. The hills are full of marble before the world blooms with statues. Rev. Phillips Brooks, "Literature and Life," c. late 19th century.

Autobiography is both history and fiction. It is not just a mirror; it is a painting. Robert Sayre, in *U.S. News & World Report,* October 23, 1989.

All literature is yet to be written. Ralph Waldo Emerson, "Literary Ethics," 1838.

An old author is constantly rediscovering himself in the more or less fossilized productions of his earlier years. Oliver Wendell Holmes, *Over the Teacups,* 1891.

The literary world is made up of little confederacies, each looking upon its own members as the lights of the universe; and considering all others as mere transient meteors, doomed soon to fall and be forgotten, while its own luminaries are to shine steadily on to immortality. Washington Irving, *Tales of a Traveler:* "Literary Life," 1824.

It takes a great deal of history to produce a little literature. Henry James, *Hawthorne,* 1879.

The chief glory of every people arises from its authors... Samuel Johnson, preface to *A Dictionary of the English Language,* 1755.

Our American professors like their literature clear and cold and pure and very dead. Sinclair Lewis, acceptance speech for Nobel Prize for Literature in Stockholm, Sweden, December 12, 1930.

...poetry...says more, and in fewer words, than prose. Voltaire, *Philosophical Dictionary,* 1764.

ANONYMOUS APHORISMS

Literature is the art of words and the wordiest of the arts.

Write makes might.

Great books are the voices of their times; the greatest literature is timeless.

Literature bridges the centuries.

One man's letter is another man's literature.

Literature to be popular usually combines the shock of recognition and the recognition of shock.

ANECDOTES

A college student asked his adviser whether he could obtain permission to skip the compulsory course in English literature. "After all," he shrugged, "it's nothing but dead books." "No," the professor contested, "they aren't dead. Books are the living thoughts that dead people leave behind." "Well," the student retorted, "if books aren't dead, they are still too old—at least the ones in the literature course." "No," his adviser sagely concluded, "they're not old. They're vintage."

The first person to write down a particular composition of words is an originator; then somebody else polishes his words, as an editor; then three or four more people do their own variations, switching names of characters, or settings; and finally, somebody writes a learned treatise about all this. When you put all this work together, it is what we call literature.

Q: What's the difference between today's best-sellers and great literature? A: One or more generations.

FACTS

As the world becomes more populated and more literate; and as the frontiers of human experience and imagination expand, literature grows. The body of written works which we call literature don't wither with time; some items may be outdated and become archaic, but great literature has lasting value. The opportunities and reward for literary effort in all its forms, playwrighting, documentation, the novel, are greater than ever; but so is the competition. A best seller today sells more copies and at a higher price than ever before. But the study of literature's history, and of classic literature, is not high on the list of priorities for today's students. What has happened is that formal study has become less attractive than the kind of self-study reflected in the tremendous surge in the purchase of reading materials. Literature began as a transcript of tales, oral traditions, and comments heard around an evening campfire. Literature today is once again relating to the continuity of experience from one generation to the next. The riches of literature past and present are more readily available today than ever before, in the age of the mass-market paperback reprint, the library, the Internet and the used-book exchange.

LONGEVITY

(See also Age)

DEFINITIONS   Long duration of life; the condition of living a long time; the extent of one's lifespan; life expectancy; biology's Holy Grail.

QUOTATIONS

'Tis very certain the desire of life / Prolongs it. George Gordon, Lord Byron, *Don Juan,* 1819.

I have been asked, "How do you grow old so easily?" I reply, "Very easily. I give all my time to it." U.S. Representative Emanuel Celler of New York, commenting as Dean of the House of Representatives on his 83rd birthday, May 6, 1971.

Few envy the consideration enjoyed by the oldest inhabitant. Ralph Waldo Emerson, *Society and Solitude:* Old Age, 1870.

Wish not so much to live long as to live well. Benjamin Franklin, *Poor Richard's Almanac,* 1738.

All would live long, but none would be old. Benjamin Franklin, *Poor Richard's Almanac,* 1749.

The longer thread of life we spin, / The more occasion still to sin. Robert Herrick, *Noble Numbers,* 1647.

…whoever lives long must outlive those whom he loves and honors. Such is the condition of our present existence, that life must one time lose its associations, and every inhabitant of the earth must walk downward to the grave alone and unregarded, without any partner of his joy or grief, without any interested witness of his misfortunes or success. Samuel Johnson, *The Idler,* January 27, 1759.

…Age is opportunity no less / Than Youth itself, though in another dress. Henry Wadsworth Longfellow, "Morituri Salutamus," 1874.

Nobody loves life like an old man. Sophocles, *Acrisius,* c. 5th century BC.

Every man desires to live long; but no man would be old. Jonathan Swift, *Thoughts on Various Subjects,* 1711.

ANONYMOUS APHORISMS

Life is habit forming.

Life has a certain ending and uncertain timing.

Long life is a gift that nobody gets to keep.

The people who live long are those who long to live.

The years in your life are less important than the life in your years.

Life should be measured by its breadth, not its length.

ANECDOTES

On Mr. Smith's 100th birthday, a reporter came to interview the centarian on the front porch of Smith's farm house. "Tell me, to what do you attribute your long life?" the reporter asked. "Well, I never drink, smoke or swear," Mr. Smith began.

Just then, there was a tremendous crash inside the house, followed by a fusillade of expletives. "What's that?" asked the startled reporter. "Oh, that's just my dad. Drunk again."

"How come the ancient fathers in the Bible and even the dinosaurs lived so much longer than we do?" the professor was asked. "Because they didn't know they weren't supposed to," he replied.

The average elephant lives longer than the average human being, which proves that there may be something to working for peanuts; but some people think that it proves the secret of long life is a thick skin.

FACTS

The highest life-expectancy rate in American history up to that time was recorded in 1994, when the average male baby could look forward to living 72.3 years; and the average newborn girl could expect to live 79.0 years. Compared to those reported in 1920, these rates were 19 years longer for men and 25 years longer for women. The longer life expectancy for females is worldwide—except in some parts of Asia where life expectancy is generally quite low. The explanation used to be that the males faced more pressures to their health from trying to support their families. Now, with an equal number of women working outside the home, and presumably the pressures of earning a living are greater upon them, the difference in life expectancy has grown, instead of shrinking as expected. Nevertheless, statistics at best are generalizations. Some American nonagenarians and centarians have attributed their long lifespans to eating yams and to drinking a glass of wine every day. But the fact is longevity is somewhat a matter of heredity, somewhat a matter of circumstance—and somewhat a matter of fate.

The Statistical Yearbook of the United Nations, the Statistical Abstract of the U.S. and state and local health department reports can provide further details.

LOVE

(See also Marriage, Sex)

DEFINITIONS Strong affection; an emotional bond of mutual attraction; "the will to extend one's self for purpose of nurturing one's own or another's spiritual growth" (M. Scott Peck, M.D., *The Road Less Travelled,* 1978); emotional attachment involving sexual desire; intimate concern for some person or thing; "the river of life in this world" (Henry Ward Beecher); what we keep by giving.

QUOTATIONS

The hunger for love is much more difficult to remove than the hunger for bread. Mother Teresa, in *Time,* December 4, 1989.

Love is not just looking at each other, it's looking in the same direction. Antoine de Saint-Exupéry, *Wind, Sand, and Stars,* 1939.

He loves not who does not see the faults of the beloved as virtues. Johann Wolfgang von Goethe, c. early 19th century.

Whoso loves / Believes the impossible. Elizabeth Barrett Browning, "Aurora Leigh," 1856.

All mankind love a lover. Ralph Waldo Emerson, *Essays, First Series:* "Love," 1841.

Life's greatest happiness is to be convinced we are loved. Victor Hugo, *Les Miserables,* 1862.

There is no fear in love; but perfect love casteth out fear... *John I* 4:18.

There's nothing in this world so sweet as love, / And next to love the sweetest thing is hate. Henry Wadsworth Longfellow, "The Spanish Student," 1842.

The course of true love never did run smooth. William Shakespeare, *A Midsummer Night's Dream,* 1595.

'Tis better to have loved and lost / Than never to have loved at all. Alfred Tennyson, *In Memoriam,* 1850.

There is no remedy for love but to love more. Henry D. Thoreau, *Journal,* July 25, 1839.

Love conquers all. Virgil, *Eclogues: 10,* c. 37 BC.

...love has never known a law / Beyond its own sweet will. John Greenleaf Whittier, "Amy Wentworth," 1862.

Men always want to be a woman's first love—women like to be a man's last romance. Oscar Wilde, *A Woman of No Importance,* 1893.

ANONYMOUS APHORISMS

All's fair in love and war.

Love makes the world go square.

The love that lasts is the love that's last.

Love will find a way.

Love and a cough cannot be concealed.

The difference between love and lust is what makes the world go round in circles.

Love is blind.

ANECDOTES

A young man staggered into a small bakery just as it was opening at the crack of dawn on a miserable, stormy day. "Thank goodness you're open," he said, "I've been walking all over town looking for a place where I can get her the fresh blueberry buns she wants. I must have walked miles. And at last I find them—right here. She'll love them. Give me three." The clerk wrapped them and asked, "Are these for your mother?" "Come on," said the young man, "would my mother send me out on a night like this? And would I go?"

"Love," said the romantic, "is the last word." "Only in a telegram," the cynic scoffed.

After their son came home and announced he had fallen in love at first sight with a girl he had just met, his mother commented to his father, "What do you think of that?" "Well," said the father, "it's a great time-saver."

LOYALTY

DEFINITIONS   Fidelity; commitment; faithfulness, consistent adherence to and support of a cause, principle or person; something that arouses oaths; the original high fidelity system.

QUOTATIONS

Trust men and they will be true to you; treat them greatly, and they will show themselves great. Ralph Waldo Emerson, *Essays, First Series:* "Prudence," 1841.

Enlightened loyalty requires that each citizen take the trouble to learn about, to discuss, to think through, the crucial issues of our time. President Lyndon B. Johnson, Loyalty Day Proclamation, April 6, 1967.

Since this country was founded, each generation of Americans has been summoned to give testimony to its national loyalty. President John F. Kennedy, inaugural address, January 20, 1961.

Statesman, yet friend to truth! of soul sincere, / In action faithful, and in honor clear; / Who broke no promise, serv'd no private end, / Who gain'd no title, and who lost no friend. Alexander Pope, *Moral Essays VII:* "To Mr. Addison," 1720.

…be thou faithful unto death, and I will give thee a crown of life. *The Revelation of St. John the Divine,* 2:10.

…go on, and I will follow thee, / To the last gasp, with truth and loyalty. William Shakespeare, *As You Like It,* 1600.

My kind of loyalty was loyalty to one's country, not to its institutions or its office-holders. Mark Twain, *A Connecticut Yankee in King Arthur's Court,* 1889.

Loyalty to petrified opinion never yet broke a chain or freed a human soul. Mark Twain, inscription in the Hall of Fame.

I do solemnly swear (or affirm) that I will support and defend the Constitution of the United States against all enemies, foreign and domestic; that I will bear true faith and allegiance to the same; that I take this obligation freely, without any mental reservation or purpose of evasion, and that I will well and truthfully discharge the duties of the office on which I am about to enter. So help me God. U.S. Oath of Office, adopted July 11, 1868.

ANONYMOUS APHORISMS

Loyalty is an animal instinct; we can take lessons in it from dogs.

Loyalty oaths are words, not deeds.

Loyalty can be blind, but it can't be lame.

The best way to get loyalty is to give it.

Any loyalty that is bought can be bought away.

ANECDOTES

During one of those sedition scares, an investigator arrived at Mr. and Mrs. Smith's home. When Mrs. Smith answered the door, the investigator politely said, "I'm here to find out what party Mr. Smith belongs to." "I'm the party he belongs to," Mrs. Smith replied as she slammed the door.

Mr. Brown always described himself as a loyal supporter of the local college football team, but a friend ran into him on the street when the team was playing a game. "I thought you were a loyal rooter," said the friend. "Oh," said Mr. Brown, "I root for them all the time, but I only go to see them when they're likely to win."

"My loyalty," said Mr. Jones, "is a matter of principle. I can change it, of course, when the interest is raised."

FACTS

Few societies are immune to the idea that loyalty can be brought about by coercion. The Chinese government is notorious for its intolerance of citizens who attempt to speak out against the ruling party; but in the age of security-consciousness, western democracies periodically worry about how to determine and insure the loyalty of their own key people. This is not a human characteristic of modern vintage. It existed among the ancient Greeks and in every other civilization. Different philosophies, of course, have different ideas of loyalty. In a dictatorship, loyalty is nondeviationism; no straying from the absolute party line. In a democracy, loyalty involves less absolute criteria. The U.S. Oath of Office—which is in essence a loyalty oath—was adopted after the Civil War. The U.S. Constitution to which it refers has freedom of conscience guaranteed in it; hence, loyalty in this country has become a catchword referring more to reliability than to beliefs. In an age of complicated defense and industrial secrets involving thousands of people, the question of loyalty is a euphemism for the basic question of trustworthiness.

L U C K

DEFINITIONS   Chance; fortune; the way the cookie crumbles; the roll of the dice; a failure's explanation for someone else's success; opening the door when opportunity knocks; the cut of the cards; the fortunate side of Fate.

QUOTATIONS

Luck is the result of a mixture of many things. We all get chances in life, but probably a lot of us don't notice them—don't notice they've happened, don't notice we've missed them. Jeremy Irons, actor, in *The Los Angeles Times,* December 1, 1991.

A hundred million miracles are happening every day. Oscar Hammerstein III, song lyric from *The Flower Drum Song,* 1953.

Better be born lucky than rich. John Clarke, *Paroemiologia Anglo-Latina,* 1639.

Shallow men believe in luck. Ralph Waldo Emerson, *The Conduct of Life:* "Worship," 1860.

Diligence is the mother of good luck. Benjamin Franklin, *Poor Richard's Almanac,* 1735.

Luck is a mighty queer thing. All you know about it for certain is that it's bound to change. Bret Harte, "The Outcasts of Poker Flat," 1869.

True luck consists not in holding the best of the cards at the table: / Luckiest he who knows just when to rise and go home. John Hay, "Distichs," c. late 19th century.

Fortune never seems blinder than to those she doesn't favor. Francois Duc de La Rochefoucauld, *Maxims,* 1665.

Fortune gives too much to many, but enough to none. Martial, *Epigrams,* c. 1st century.

Luck never made a man wise. Seneca, *Moral Letters to Lucilius,* c. 65 AD.

Times go by turns, and chances change by course, From foul to fair, from better hap to worse. Robert Southwell, "Times Go By Turns," c. 1595.

ANONYMOUS APHORISMS

Luck isn't always a lady.

Luck means being at the right place, at the right time; and recognizing it when it bites you on the nose.

Luck is how the other guy made it.

He who puts his trust in luck is apt to end up putting himself in hock.

If you can't change your luck, change your game.

Not all luck is good, and not all good is luck.

Lucky at cards, unlucky at love.

The people who believe most in luck are those who lack it.

Luck often masquerades as wisdom.

ANECDOTES

No matter what happened to Tommy Brown, he always described it as pure luck. He decided to prospect for gold and went into the mountains through a bitter winter. Nearly freezing to death, he kept looking for a golden vein in the rugged ground. Finally, as the spring thaw began—when Brown was down to his last meager food ration and his mule was gasping its last—he broke into the earth in a likely looking spot and dug and dug until, at last, he hit a box. A million miles from nowhere, with no food left and his strength ebbing fast, Tommy Brown managed to lift the box out and open it while his mule watched. Inside was a carton of Army C rations. "Boy am I lucky," he sighed to his faithful companion, "it could have been gold."

When Jane Jones, a beautiful, hard-working girl, married an ugly, shiftless man, her mother had a simple explanation: "Jane's bad luck was his good luck."

FACTS

Luck is one of humanity's names for unexplainable turns of good or bad fortune. Other names are fate, chance, and destiny. Throughout history we have sought to explain people's coincidental changes of circumstances. Religion, superstition, dream interpretation, astrological consultation, mathematical odds formulae, all are used to try to explain and to ensure the smile of Lady Luck. We pray and we do things which we hope will "make things turn out better" for us. In both ancient and modern Chinese culture, office and household objects are arranged in a precise pattern to draw luck into that space. In the west, we base businesses on mankind's indomitable belief in luck—not merely gambling businesses and gaming tables and lotteries. We enter into speculative ventures and invest in high-risk stocks, bonds, and futures. The selling of good luck charms and tokens is itself a steady business, and perhaps the best commentary is that a lucky rabbit's foot never does much for the rabbit.

Mail

Definitions   The postal system; letters and other material sent and delivered through the postal system; correspondence; snail-mail (as opposed to e-mail on the Internet).

Quotations

A Committee on the Post office, too, have found, a thousand difficulties. The Post is now very regular, from the North and South, altho it comes but once a Week. It is not easy to get faithfull Riders, to go oftener. The Expence is very high, and the Profits (so dear is every Thing, and so little Correspondence is carried on, except in franked Letters), will not Support the office. John Adams, letter to Thomas Jefferson, May 26, 1797.

The United States may give up the post office when it sees fit, but while it carries it on, the use of the mails is almost as much a part of free speech as the right to use our tongues. U.S. Supreme Court Associate Justice Oliver Wendell Holmes, Jr., commenting on *Milwaukee Social Democratic Publishing Company v. Burleson,* 1921.

A short letter to a distant friend is, in my opinion, an insult like that of a slight bow or cursory salutation—a proof of unwillingness to do much, even where there is a necessity of doing something. Samuel Johnson, letter to Joseph Baretti, June 10, 1761.

The mailman is the agent of impolite surprises. Friedrich Wilhelm Nietzsche, *Human, All Too Human,* 1878.

The postal service touches the lives of all Americans. Many of our citizens feel that today's service does not meet today's needs, much less the needs of tomorrow. I share this view. President Richard M. Nixon, message to the U.S. Congress, February 25, 1969.

There is no Democratic or Republican way of delivering the mail. There is only the right way. President Richard M. Nixon, message to the U.S. Congress, May 27, 1969.

Correspondences are like small-clothes before the invention of suspenders; it is impossible to keep them up. Sydney Smith, letter to Mrs. Crowe, January 31, 1841.

I never received more than one or two letters in my life—I wrote this some years ago—that were worth the postage. Henry D. Thoreau, *Walden:* "Where I Lived and What I Lived For," 1854.

Neither snow, nor rain, nor heat, nor gloom of night stays these couriers from the swift completion of their appointed rounds. Inscription on the facade of the central Manhattan Post Office, adapted from "The Histories" of Herodotus.

ANONYMOUS APHORISMS

The way it comes through, they ought to call it partial post.

Some mail goes out under a frank and some ends up in a john.

The postal system has two sexes—mail and miss.

The mails must go through.

As welcome as a letter from home.

ANECDOTES

A goodwill ambassador for the Postmaster General was addressing a school class about the U.S. mail system. "What's the fastest thing in the Postal Service?" he asked. A boy in the back raised his hand and replied, "The fastest thing in the Postal Service is the way the rates go up."

A linguistics student wondered why the words for postal service and for a masculine human being sound so much alike. His professor told him it was because both kinds of mail (male) have a lot of room for improvement.

A foreign visitor asked a mail clerk why the Post Office called its sorting system the Zip Code. The clerk replied, "Without the numbers you're apt to get zip."

Q: What's the difference between a postage stamp and the postal system? A: You can lick a stamp but you can't lick the system.

FACTS

Back in 1966, President Lyndon B. Johnson reported that America was "generating mail at the rate of 76 billion pieces a year. That is more than all of the rest of the mail generated in the entire world combined." In 1995, the U.S. Postal Service's 753,000 employees processed 181 billion pieces—or 40 percent—of the world's mail; Japan's postal service was second largest, handling 8 percent. The Postmaster General is elected by the Board of Governors of the U.S. Postal Service. It has operated on its own revenues since 1982, not on taxpayers' dollars. And it posted a record net income of $1.8 billion in 1995. But the Postal Service still has all the obligations and privileges which go with its governmental relationship. The privileges are principally related to the fact that the Postal Service is a chosen instrument. It monopolizes access to mailboxes; it is the instrument of international postal operations. The obligations are those which come from being a chosen instrument—including the necessity of maintaining full postal service to communities where such business incurs a substantial loss. Competition from private carriers and couriers is much smaller than it appears. The Postal Service carries as much mail in a day as Federal Express does in a year.

Manners

DEFINITIONS   Deportment; social conduct; the style and custom of social intercourse; civility with polish; etiquette.

QUOTATIONS

If a man be gracious, and courteous to strangers, it shows he is a citizen of the world… Sir Francis Bacon, *Essays:* "Of Goodness," c. 1597.

In the days of old / Men made the manners; / manners now make men. George Gordon, Lord Byron, *Don Juan,* 1824.

Good manners are, to particular societies, what good morals are to society in general: their cement and their security. Lord Chesterfield, letter to his son, November 3, 1749.

Fine manners need the support of fine manners in others. Ralph Waldo Emerson, *The Conduct of Life:* "Behavior," 1860.

Civility costs nothing, and buys everything. Lady Mary Wortley Montagu, letter to the Countess of Bute, May 30, 1756.

We cannot learn from one another until we stop shouting at one another—until we speak quietly enough so that our words can be heard as well as our voices. President Richard M. Nixon, inaugural address, January 20, 1969.

We meet at meals three times a day, and give each other a new taste of that old musty cheese that we are. We have had to agree on a certain set of rules, called etiquette and politeness, to make this frequent meeting tolerable and that we need not come to open war. Henry D. Thoreau, *Walden:* "Solitude," 1854.

There are few things that so touch us with instinctive revulsion as a breach of decorum. Thorstein Veblen, *The Theory of the Leisure Class,* 1899.

ANONYMOUS APHORISMS

Other times, other manners.

You can learn good manners from the bad manners of others.

It takes good manners to put up with bad ones.

Knowing good manners depends on practicing them.

Man is judged by his manners more than by his looks.

ANECDOTES

The little boy at family dinner was asked whether he'd like some French fries, and he said, "Yes." His mother said, "Yes, what?" "Yes, before the meat," he politely answered.

An old grouch, about to enter a building, found that the door was being held open for him, with considerable effort, by a little boy. "Never mind that," said the old grouch, "I don't need your help." The little boy smiled up at him and said, "You're welcome."

Marriage

(See also Family, Love, Sex)

Definitions   The state of wedlock; the condition of having a spouse; the consensual and legal union of a man and woman; "the state or condition of a community consisting of a master, a mistress and two selves, making in all, two" (Ambrose Bierce); altar ego; a labor of love; a union of better halves.

Quotations

Can two walk together, except they be agreed? Amos, 3:3.

…to have and to hold from this day forward, for better, for worse, for richer, for poorer, in sickness and in health, to love and to cherish, till death do us part. *Book of Common Prayer,* Solemnization of Matrimony.

One was never married, and that's his hell; another is, and that's his plague. Robert Burton, *The Anatomy of Melancholy,* 1621.

Marriage is a feast where the grace is sometimes better than the dinner. Charles Caleb Colton, *Lacon,* c. 1820s.

Every woman should marry—and no man. Benjamin Disraeli, *Lothair,* 1870.

Is not marriage an open question, when it is alleged, from the beginning of the world, that such as are in the institution wish to get out, and such as are out wish to get in? Ralph Waldo Emerson, *Representative Men:* "Montaigne," 1850.

Where there's marriage without love, there will be love without marriage. Benjamin Franklin, *Poor Richard's Almanac,* 1734.

Keep your eyes wide open before marriage, half shut afterwards. Benjamin Franklin, *Poor Richard's Almanac,* 1738.

More belongs to marriage than four legs in a bed. Thomas Fuller, *Gnomologia,* 1732.

I believe it will be found that those who marry late are best pleased with their children, and those who marry early with their partners. Samuel Johnson, *Rasselas,* 1759.

What therefore God hath joined together, let not man put asunder. *Mark,* 10:9.

Marriage may be compared to a cage: the birds outside frantic to get in and those inside frantic to get out. Michel Eyquem de Montaigne, *Essays:* "III," 1588.

Marriage is popular because it combines the maximum of temptation with the maximum of opportunity. George Bernard Shaw, *Man and Superman,* 1903.

Remember, it's as easy to marry a rich woman as a poor woman. William Makepeace Thackeray, *Pendennis,* 1850.

ANONYMOUS APHORISMS

In the ideal marriage one partner is blind and the other is deaf.

If a wife always laughs at her husband's jokes, is he funny or she smart?

Marriage is a mutual assistance pact.

Marriage may be made in heaven, but sometimes it can be hell on earth.

Marriage is an institution run by the inmates.

Marriage runs the risk of going from bed to worse.

Marriage is a union with a limited membership.

Marry in haste, repent at leisure.

ANECDOTES

On their 75th wedding anniversary, Mr. and Mrs. Jones were asked what they felt their marriage had taught them. "Patience," replied Mr. Jones; "Fortitude," said Mrs. Jones.

You never can tell about a marriage from the outside, said the old philosopher. Some couples hold hands because they're afraid that if they let go they'd kill each other.

At a London dinner party, Lady Nancy Astor listened to Winston Churchill converse on a heated topic and grew more and more angry over the views he was expressing. Finally, she blurted, "If you were my husband I'd put poison in your coffee." Churchill calmly replied, "If I were your husband, I'd drink it."

FACTS

After a more than a decade of increase, from 2.5 per 1,000 people in 1966, to a high of 5.3 per 1,000 people in 1979, the divorce rate fell and leveled off at 4.7 per 1,000 people, from 1988 to 1993. In an age when more and more young men and women are living together without the possession of a marriage certificate, divorce rates have been highest among women in their late teens and men in their early twenties. If anything, marriage in recent years has become somewhat more difficult in the U.S. and divorce has become easier. Further, with the growth of community property laws and the acceptance of open nonmarried partnerships, as well as unmarried parenthood, the institution of marriage has become less attractive to some men and women. In the early-1990s, Nevada led the country in divorces, renewing its reputation as America's divorce capital. But despite the possibility of divorce, nearly 2.4 million Americans married in 1992.

The *World Almanac* and *Statistical Abstract of the United States* contain comparative figures for the nation and states, and historical figures as well.

Medicine

(See also Drugs, Health)

DEFINITIONS   The science, art or materials used in the diagnosis, treatment, and prevention of illness and disease; the profession of providing medical treatment; health care; the healers.

QUOTATIONS

Medicine is not just black and white. It's a matter of judgments... Marianna Bauder, president, St. Joseph Hospital, Denver, CO, in the *Los Angeles Times,* August 24, 1995.

The constitution says that if you are charged with a crime you have a right to a lawyer. But it's even more fundamental that if you're sick, you should have the right to a doctor. Senator Harris Wofford, in *Time* magazine, November 11, 1991.

In the 1940s and 1950s, medicine was too much an art and not enough of a science. Now we have more science than we know what to do with. Louis J. Kettel, Association of American Medical Colleges, in *U.S. News & World Report,* April 29, 1991.

There are no such things as incurables, there are only things for which man has not found a cure. Bernard Baruch, April 1954.

...the only profession that labors incessantly to destroy the reason for its own existence. James Bryce, March 23, 1914.

God heals, and the doctor takes the fees. Benjamin Franklin, *Poor Richard's Almanac,* 1736.

Into whatever houses I may enter I will go for the benefit of the sick and will abstain from every voluntary act of mischief and corruption, and further from the seduction of females or males, bond or free. Whatever in connection with my professional practice or not in connection with it I may see or hear I will not divulge, for I hold that all such things should be kept secret. Hippocrates, the Hippocratic oath for doctors, c. 400 BC.

...if the whole materia medica, as now used, could be sunk to the bottom of the sea, it would be all the better for mankind—and all the worse for the physicians. Dr. Oliver Wendell Holmes, address to the Massachusetts Medical Society, Boston, MA, May 30, 1860.

The patient, treated on the fashionable theory, sometimes gets well in spite of the medicine. President Thomas Jefferson, letter to Dr. Casper Wistar, June 21, 1807.

Diseases desperate grown / By desperate appliances are relieved... William Shakespeare, *Hamlet,* 1600.

The miserable have no other medicine / But only hope. William Shakespeare, *Measure for Measure,* 1604.

ANONYMOUS APHORISMS

In medicine, the more practice a doctor has, the less practice he needs.

Only a fool would make his doctor his heir.

Why do the best doctors have the sickest patients?

The family physician is disappearing faster than a healthy man's symptoms.

The doctors cure all kinds of ills, except the shock of doctors' bills.

Call the doctor early and you won't be late.

Good doctors are usually bad patients.

Nobody cares about the doctors till we need them.

ANECDOTES

The doctor tried in vain to impress on his patient the seriousness of his illness. "There's no point in hiding from you the fact that you are very, very, very sick. Do you have any last requests?" the doctor said. "Yes," replied the patient, "get me another doctor."

A man telephoned his doctor and said, "I have this shooting pain in my throat when I swallow and I'm very hoarse. What should I do?" The doctor replied, "Until you can see me at the office tomorrow, just keep your neck swathed in hot compresses." "My maid told me to use cold compresses," protested the man. "Nonsense," said the doctor. "My maid says hot compresses."

"Doctor," the patient complained, "every morning when I get up I'm nauseous for an hour." "What you should do," said the doctor, "is to get up an hour later."

FACTS

Medicine is an ancient science, but professional medical education and licensing in America only date back to the founding of the American Medical Association in 1847. When one reflects that only in the 19th century was modern anesthesia developed, and that surgeons routinely perform countless operations today that would have been impossible in our grandparents' time, the incredible speed with which the professional practice of medicine has developed can be better appreciated. During the 1920s, medical schools graduated an average of 5,700 new American doctors each year. During the 1930s, there were only some 4,500 new medical graduates and fewer medical schools because state legislations made licensing requirements tougher. During the 1940s and 1950s, the AMA and state licensing boards tightened the requirements even further, especially on immigrating physicians, in an attempt to guarantee the quality of American health care. According to the U.S. Census Bureau's *The Statistical Abstract of the United States*, 86 medical schools graduated 8,314 new physicians in 1960. By 1986, the figure rose to 16,041 new graduates; and in 1990, 124 schools graduated 15,075 new physicians. The down side of this increased availability of care is that patients' medical costs have also risen in that time.

The American Medical Association, 515 North State St., Chicago, IL 60610, has a membership roster of 300,000 health care professionals. Since it was founded in 1899, the American Hospital Association, 1 North Franklin St., Chicago, IL 60606, has grown to represent over 5100 hospitals nationwide. Both organizations are an excellent source for the latest health care statistics.

M EMORY

DEFINITIONS   The process or faculty of remembering; that which is recalled or remembered; "the diary we all carry about with us" (Oscar Wilde).

QUOTATIONS

Memory is the mother of all wisdom. Aeschylus, *Prometheus Bound,* c. 5th century BC.

...let us remember that the times which future generations delight to recall are not those of ease and prosperity, but those of adversity bravely borne. Charles W. Eliot, president, Harvard University, December 22, 1877.

That which is bitter to endure may be sweet to remember. Thomas Fuller, *Gnomologia,* 1732.

'Tis sweet to thinke on what was hard t'endure. Robert Herrick, "Satisfaction for Suffering," c. 17th century.

Memory is a net; one finds it full of fish when he takes it from the brook; but a dozen miles of water have run through it without sticking. Oliver Wendell Holmes, *The Autocrat of the Breakfast-Table,* 1858.

The tumult and the shouting dies; / The captains and the kings depart: / Still stands Thine ancient sacrifice, / An humble and a contrite heart. / Lord God of Hosts, be with us yet, / Lest we forget—lest we forget! Rudyard Kipling, "Recessional," 1897.

Everyone complains of his lack of memory, but nobody of his want of judgment. Francois Duc de La Rochefoucauld, *Maxims,* c. 17th century.

If I do not remember thee, let my tongue cleave to the roof of my mouth... *Psalms,* 167:6.

Better by far that you should forget and smile / Than that you should remember and be sad. Christina Rossetti, "Remember," 1862.

When to the sessions of sweet silent thought / I summon up remembrance of things past, / I sigh the lack of many a thing I sought, / And with old woes new wail my dear time's waste. William Shakespeare, *Sonnets: 30,* 1609.

It is not so easy to forget. Richard Brinsley Sheridan, *The Rivals,* 1775.

ANONYMOUS APHORISMS

Things that live in memory have no visible means of support.

I'll never forget what's-his-name.

Some of our most vivid memories are of things that never happened, for we remember the images and the imagination of our childhood dreams.

We are apt to remember most vividly what we are most anxious to forget.

Memory plays strange tricks.

ANECDOTES

"I am trying desperately to remember why I came here," one disgruntled foreign legionnaire said to his colleague. Consolingly, his companion him patted on the back and said, "Forget it." Upon hearing this, the legionnaire stood up and in a delighted tone said, "That's it! That's what I came here for—to forget."

"People attach much too much importance to memory," said the absentminded professor. "I disagree," said his colleague. "Disagree with what?" asked the professor.

The classic story of memory is about the man who had gone to the circus as a small boy and returned years later. He was sitting in a cheap seat when an elephant came along; reached up into the stand; wrapped his trunk gently about the man; and carried him over to deposit him gently in the best seat in the circus tent. The man turned to his neighbor and said, "The elephant remembered that the last time I was here, years ago, I fed him peanuts." Just then the elephant came back, lifted his trunk, pointed it straight at the man and blew a stream of water in his face. "I forgot I gave them to him in the bag," the man added.

FACTS

Memory is a mental faculty which occurs naturally, but which can also be developed. There is a constant stream of books and courses in how to develop a better memory. As the world has developed, humans have had to remember more with each passing generation. But students of physiology insist that the capacity of the human brain to retain information is far greater than what we currently use. Some people are blessed with so-called photographic memories; while other people suffer from physical deficits that affect the mind's ability to remember, such as poor nutrition, dehydration, lack of sleep, and cellular degeneration caused by illness or birth defects. Remembering is easier when what we are trying to memorize or store away in our minds is related to something we already know; hence many memory methods urge that we try to associate something new with something we know very well. Memory is not always a conscious process. We all have memories that come to mind seemingly by themselves, sometimes even unwelcome ones.

M E N

DEFINITIONS   Human adult males; humans of the gender God made first, before he worked out improvements; former boys; the guys.

QUOTATIONS

Remember, all men would be tyrants if they could. Abigail Adams, letter to her husband, John Adams, March 31, 1776.

The best works, and of greatest merit for the public have proceeded from the unmarried or childless men. Sir Francis Bacon, *Essays:* "Of Marriage and Single Life," c. 1600s.

Men are but children of a larger growth. John Dryden, *All for Love,* 1678.

Men are what their mothers made them. Ralph Waldo Emerson, *The Conduct of Life:* "Fate," 1860.

Our self-made men are the glory of our institutions. Wendell Phillips, December 21, 1860.

I wonder men dare trust themselves with men. William Shakespeare, *Timon of Athens,* 1605-9.

We do not ask man to represent us; it is hard enough in times like these for man to carry backbone enough to represent himself. Elizabeth Cady Stanton, March 19, 1860.

There is no escape—man drags man down, or man lifts man up. Booker T. Washington, address to Howard University alumni, 1896.

Men become old, but they never become good. Oscar Wilde, *Lady Windermere's Fan,* 1892.

At thirty man suspects himself a fool; / Knows it at forty, and reforms his plan; / At fifty chides his infamous delay, / Pushes his prudent purpose to resolve: / In all the magnanimity of thought / Resolves; and re-resolves; then dies the same. Edward Young, *Night Thoughts,* c. 1740s.

ANONYMOUS APHORISMS

A good man isn't only hard to find—he's hard to keep good.

A real man's man is no man's man.

Man's chief pursuit is neither fame nor fortune; man's chief pursuit is woman.

Men like to make the wheels go round, which is why so many men go around in circles.

A man is like a plank of wood—soft until seasoned.

A self-made man is judged by his product.

ANECDOTES

The angry father objected to his son's lighthearted approach to adult life. "When I was a boy your age," he blurted out, "I was a man."

Q: Why did the Lord make man first and woman thereafter? A: Because after He saw Adam, He realized man needed some help.

Q: What is the message of civilized man? A: If you don't wear a beard, life is one close shave after another.

MIDWEST

DEFINITIONS   The central section of the United States between the East and the Continental Divide, above the South and Southwest; the corn belt; the hinterland; America's heartland; the breadbasket of the nation.

QUOTATIONS

Ohio is the farthest west of the east and the farthest north of the South. Louis Bromfield, *Pleasant Valley,* 1945.

These are the gardens of the Desert; these / The unshorn fields, boundless and beautiful, / For which the speech of England has no name— / The Prairies. William Cullen Bryant, "The Prairies," 1832.

Minnesotans are used to their people running for President. We usually have two or three in there. Senator Walter F. Mondale of Minnesota, 1972.

…covered partly with majestic trees, partly with flowery prairies, immeasurable to the eye, and intersected with large rivers and broad lakes—a land where everybody could do what he thought best, and nobody need be poor, because everybody was free. Carl Schurz, c. 1850s.

I come from a state that raises corn and cotton and cockleburs and Democrats, and frothy eloquence neither convinces nor satisfies me. I'm from Missouri. You have got to show me. U.S. Congressman Willard D. Vandiver of Missouri, 1899.

When anything is going to happen in this country, it happens first in Kansas. William Allen White, quoted by John Gunther.

ANONYMOUS APHORISMS

Iowa, where the tall corn grows.

A Missouri mule isn't stubborn. He's just hard to convince.

The Midwest isn't one region; it's several that you can't really tell apart.

Great Lakes make great states.

Illinois calls itself the land of Lincoln, but Lincoln is a city in Nebraska.

The Midwest is what you have to cross to get to there from here.

ANECDOTES

Perhaps the oldest intercity rivalry is that of Minnesota's Twin Cities which can be illustrated by the story that a Minneapolis bookstore refused to stock a popular book entitled, *In the Steps of Saint Paul.*

Midwesterners are often accused of pronouncing the words merry, marry, and Mary in exactly the same way; but Midwesterners say the rest of the country thinks everything is the same throughout the Midwest.

Then there's the man from Kansas who objects to New York City because it isn't centrally located.

Q: Where are the old people in Iowa? A: In California.

FACTS

Although there is a tendency to think of the Midwest as a single entity, it is much more aptly described as an inland empire, with terrain ranging from forests to prairies, climate that ranges from very cold to stiflingly hot and a combination of vast farm acreage and great cities. Its eastern states—like Ohio, Indiana, and Illinois—have five times the population per square mile of land of its western states—including North and South Dakota, Nebraska, and Minnesota. Much of its metropolitan growth has been a direct result of its raising of food—wheat and corn processing, stockyards and meat processing, and transportation of foodstuffs.

Minorities

(See also Ethnicity, Immigration, Prejudice, Race)

Definitions Those groups of the population not of the same race, ethnic origins or religion as the majority; also applied in some senses to people classified by age, gender, sexual preference, ethnicity, religious orientation, political affiliation, social and economic level; those with fewer votes.

Quotations

There is compelling evidence that in the years just ahead, the fulfillment of the aspirations of black and other minority Americans will be fundamental to the continued success of the American dream itself. William H. Gray III, president, United Negro College Fund, in the *The New York Times,* May 18, 1992.

I believe the life of the Negro race has been a life of tragedy, of injustice, of oppression. The law has made him equal, but man has not. Clarence Darrow, plea to a jury, 1926.

Though the colored man is no longer subject to be bought and sold, he is still surrounded by an adverse sentiment which fetters all his movements. In his downward course he meets with no resistance, but his course upward is resisted at every stop of his progress. Frederick Douglass, September 24, 1883.

My hope for the Negro is largely based on his enduring qualities. No persecutions, no proscriptions, no hardships are able to extinguish him. He neither dies out, nor goes out. He is here to stay, and while here he will partake of the blessings of your education, your progress, your civilization and your Christian religion. His appeal to you today is for an equal chance in the race of life, and, dark and stormy as the present appears, his appeal will not go unanswered. Frederick Douglass, 1894.

The real hero of this struggle is the American Negro. His actions and protests, his courage to risk safety and even to risk his life, have awakened the conscience of this nation. President Lyndon B. Johnson, March 15, 1965.

I have a dream that one day in the red hills of Georgia, sons of former slaves and the sons of former slave-owners will be able to sit down together at the table of brotherhood. Rev. Dr. Martin Luther King, Jr., address at the Lincoln Memorial in Washington, D.C., August 28, 1963.

I want to be the white man's brother, not his brother-in-law. Attributed to Rev. Dr. Martin Luther King, Jr. after his death.

What a happy country this will be, if the whites will listen. David Walker, abolitionist, September 28, 1829.

The history of most countries has been that of majorities—mounted majorities, clad in iron, armed with death, treading down the tenfold more numerous minorities. Oliver Wendell Holmes, May 30, 1860.

Though the will of the majority is in all cases to prevail, that will, to be rightful, must be reasonable; the minority possess their equal right, which equal laws must protect, and to violate would be oppression. President Thomas Jefferson, inaugural address, March 4, 1801.

If by the mere force of numbers a majority should deprive a minority of any clearly written constitutional right, it might in a moral point of view justify revolution; certainly would, if such a right were a vital one. President Abraham Lincoln, inaugural address, March 4, 1861.

Governments exist to protect the rights of minorities. The loved and the rich need no protection—they have many friends and few enemies. Wendell Phillips, December 21, 1860.

One, with God, is always a majority, but many a martyr has been burned at the stake while the votes were being counted. U.S. Representative Thomas B. Reed of Maine, 1885.

No democracy can long survive which does not accept as fundamental to its very existence the recognition of the rights of minorities. President Franklin D. Roosevelt, letter to National Association for Advancement of Colored People, June 25, 1938.

ANONYMOUS APHORISMS

Every majority is a gathering of minorities.

Each of us is a minority of one.

This country was settled by people who found themselves to be minorities, for one reason or another, in the lands they came from.

There are two kinds of minorities—those that the majority sets apart, and those that set themselves apart.

In every minority there are two groups—those who take pride in being different and those who differ with that pride.

The real measure of minority progress will be when everyone can spurn professional sports careers with equal candor.

A nation that doesn't have minorities manufactures them.

ANECDOTES

Two members of distinguished First Families were discussing the way members of minorities had poured into their city. "Do you know the worst thing about them?" one asked the other. "It isn't their clothes, or their looks. It is their obvious determination to outnumber us."

"If you look at American history," said the professor to his class, "you will see very clearly what the greatest weapon of the minorities has been." "Bombs? Riots? Arson? Welfare?" asked the student. "No," said the professor, "the conscience of the majority."

FACTS

Minorities are the inevitable consequences of two primitive human instincts—tribal and territorial. The first possessors of a piece of land become a tribe, with a feeling of kinship. They find themselves fearing, fighting or perhaps merely resenting other neighboring tribes, and when different tribes are part of the same geographic or political unit, some find themselves to be minorities. The history of Western democracy has shown a growing attempt to expand the idea of the greatest good for the greatest number, to bring more minorities into the mainstream. At times, however, this well-intentioned effort ignores the fact that there are some respects in which minorities may not want to be brought into the mainstream. They may value some of the uniqueness which set them apart. The great difficulty is to guarantee both equality and respect for diversity. The laws of the United States bar discrimination in employment and housing. But the line between desegregation and homogenization is one over which surprisingly many words continue to be spilled, and the extent to which a majority culture destroys minority cultures is not purely a matter of law. Ethnic tensions are inevitable, but in the U.S. there is considerably more tolerance than in countries such as Bosnia-Herzegovina, Rwanda and Sri Lanka where recent wars between minorities have resulted in the needless deaths of hundreds of thousands.

Local, state, federal, and international human rights advocacy agencies and organizations generally have annual reports available to the public which give some idea of current problems and accomplishments.

Motion pictures

(See also Censorship)

DEFINITIONS   A series of images projected on a screen which give the effect of continuous motion, often accompanied by sound; theatrical presentations photographically reproduced and projected on screens in theaters or on privately owned videotape players; the flicks; pix; the cinema; the movies; the film industry; also known by nicknames for specialized categories such as comedies, musicals, art films, foreign films, etc.

QUOTATIONS

Writing a novel I've always thought of as writing a letter to somebody. Movies are like sending a postcard. Lucian K. Truscott, quoted in a program sponsored by the Folio Society, London, reprinted in *The Writer,* June, 1989.

If we paid serious attention to one tenth of one percent of what looks like legitimate protest, it would be utterly impossible for us to make any pictures at all, or have any kind of villain unless he were a native born, white American citizen, without a job and without any political, social, religious or fraternal affiliations of any kind. Joseph I. Breen, Production Code Administrator, 1938.

It cannot be doubted that motion pictures are a significant medium for the communication of ideas. They may affect public attitudes and behavior in a variety of ways, ranging from direct espousal of a political or social doctrine to the shaping of thought which characterizes all artistic expression. The importance of motion pictures as an organ of public opinion is not lessened by the fact that they are designed to entertain as well as to inform... U.S. Supreme Court Associate Justice Tom Clark, commenting on *Burstyn v. Wilson,* 1962.

A wide screen just makes a bad film twice as bad. Samuel Goldwyn, 1956.

Everybody has two businesses—his own and the movies. Will Hays, "czar" of the U.S. motion picture industry, 1923.

Most arts appeal to the mature. This art appeals at once to every class, mature, immature, developed, undeveloped, law abiding, criminal... Production Code of the Motion Picture Association of America, c. early 1960s.

ANONYMOUS APHORISMS

Read the book, see the picture.

Veni, vidi, video: I came, I saw, I bought the video.

The movies are larger than life, and any resemblance is sometimes entirely coincidental.

The big question in the movie-rating system is this: when a movie is rated PG, indicating parental guidance required, who is supposed to guide the parents?

Basically there are three kinds of movies—skin flicks, sin flicks and kin flicks.

ANECDOTES

A long time ago, the American movie industry decided to conduct a mammoth promotional campaign to bring people back to the movie theater. They adopted as a motto "Movies Are Your Best Entertainment" and prepared to go to town. Then somebody noticed that the initials of their slogan spelled MAYBE .

A.H. Weiler of *The New York Times* was one of the film reviewers who, in the early days of color movies, found himself inundated with adjectival descriptions of the chromatic values of upcoming films—to the point where he announced happily in one review that he had just seen a picture "in glorious black and white."

Sam Goldwyn was credited with devising the all-purpose answer when someone closely connected with a new film comes up to you after the preview to ask what you thought of it. Say "What a picture!" and leave fast.

FACTS

Motion pictures were the first mass medium that incorporated sight and eventually sound aimed at bringing drama and entertainment to millions of people around the world at the same time. Until the advent of television, the cinema was unchallenged for the attention of the world's largest audiences. Because it served so universal a public, it was also the first of the mass-entertainment media to adopt a uniform code of standards. For many years, the film industry has enforced that code with varying degrees of rigidity. When the Motion Picture Production Code was formalized into the current rating system—in the early 1970s—pictures rated X, or "for adults only," became box office attractions, as U.S. Supreme Court decisions greatly restricted the scope of any possible censorship. But as productions pushed the bounds of the law, audiences trickled away leaving the X-rating to become a mark, not of adult content, but of pornography. The invention of the VCR—or videotape player—and the emergence of cable television have provided two lucrative secondary markets for motion pictures in addition to national and local television broadcasts. More and more high-budget films which, in the new tradition, would have premiered in the theaters, then on cable television, then as videos for rent and for sale, are being released directly on video. This caused a brief fear that movie theaters would go the way of drive-in movies, but no form of home entertainment can replicate the spectacle of a good movie on a huge theater screen.

For information on the top-grossing films of all time, most popular videos or industry trends, consult the *World Almanac* or a copy of one of the more popular entertainment weeklies such as *Premiere, Entertainment Weekly,* or *People.*

Motivation

(See also Ambition, Opportunity, Luck)

DEFINITIONS   The will to strive to achieve a desired goal; drive; swimming at the top of the food chain; moving and shaking.

QUOTATIONS

Everybody looks at the world through his own glasses, and those glasses mean more than the facts you are looking at. Milton Friedman, economist, in *Time,* January 30, 1989.

After 20 years and 12 books, all of them still in print, I really don't have to write anymore. I do it because I genuinely love it. And that's the secret to success. Jackie Collins, author, in *Esquire,* July 1989.

...fear is what stops us in life. Tommy Tune, dancer/choreographer, in *Dance Magazine,* November, 1991.

ANONYMOUS APHORISMS

Success comes from knowing what you want, not wanting what you know.

The only failures are the ones who never try.

ANECDOTES

A young actress, having trouble grasping a scene, reputedly asked director Alfred Hitchcock, "What's my motivation?" "My dear," he replied, "I'm paying you."

A famous New York divorce lawyer demonstrated where motivation can lead when he was told that the fate of a multi-million dollar art collection, and a large part of his fee, would be decided with a coin toss. He had a batch of quarters analyzed, and determined that there is more metal on one side of a quarter than the other, had his assistants toss hundreds of coins, and determined that quarters land face down slightly more often than face up, yet most people call "heads" in a coin toss. He graciously allowed the opposition to choose; they chose heads, and he gained his fee.

Music

DEFINITIONS   The art or profession of creating combinations of tones and rhythms to produce vocal or instrumental melody or emotional effects; "the universal language of mankind" (Henry Wadsworth Longfellow); "the food of love" (William Shakespeare); "the only cheap and unpunished rapture on earth" (Sydney Smith).

QUOTATIONS

Music is well said to be the speech of angels; in fact, nothing among the utterances allowed to man is felt to be so divine. It brings us near to the Infinite. Thomas Carlyle, *On Heroes, Hero-Worship and the Heroic in History,* 1841.

Music has charms to soothe a savage breast... William Congreve, *The Mourning Bride,* 1697.

My favorite music is the music I haven't heard yet...I don't write music that I hear; I write music to hear what it sounds like. John Cage, composer, in *The Washington Post,* May 8, 1989.

Take a music-bath once or twice a week for a few seasons, and you will find that it is to the soul what the water-bath is to the body. Oliver Wendell Holmes, *Over the Teacups,* 1891.

Music is invaluable where a person has an ear. Where they have not, it should not be attempted. Thomas Jefferson, letter to Nathaniel Burwell, March 14, 1818.

And the night shall be filled with music, / And the cares that infest the day, / Shall fold their tents, like the Arabs, / And as silently steal away. Henry Wadsworth Longfellow, "The Day Is Done," 1845.

Hell is full of musical amateurs. Music is the brandy of the damned. George Bernard Shaw, *Man and Superman,* 1903.

Let music swell the breeze, / And ring from all the trees / Sweet Freedom's song... Rev. Samuel F. Smith, "America," 1832.

Of all the arts I think Music has the most mighty, universal, and immediate effect. Sir Arthur Sullivan, May 2, 1891.

...music is perpetual, and only hearing is intermittent. Henry D. Thoreau, *Journal,* February 8, 1857.

I hear America singing, the varied carols I hear...Walt Whitman, "I Hear America Singing," 1855.

ANONYMOUS APHORISMS

Dance to the music.

I care not who writes the nation's laws, if I can write its songs.

Music is the international language because everybody responds to its notes.

The song is ended but the melody lingers on.

Face the music.

Some of the strongest people in the world can't carry a tune.

ANECDOTES

An ardent music lover came to New York especially to attend a concert by a great European pianist who had never before performed live in this country. The music lover got lost walking to the concert, so he stopped at a doorway where an old man was playing the violin and said, "Excuse me, but this is something you would know. How do I get to Carnegie Hall?" "Practice," replied the old man, "practice."

The orchestra played Tschaikovsky's *Romeo and Juliet* overture, and the long-haired elderly man in the audience wept and wept. "You must be an incurable romantic," commented the lady sitting next to him. "No," he sobbed, "I'm a musician."

FACTS

In the arts explosion that has occurred in the United States in recent years, music has led the march. Sales of phonograph records trickled off with the advent of compact discs; but compact discs allowed the industry to reissue past hits and misses, frequently exceeding original LP sales, and contributing to sales levels which nearly tripled between 1985 and 1994, from $4.3 billion to $12 billion. Music videos are recognized as another significant factor in the rise of music. This generation of listeners—known as the MTV (music television) generation—is the first to be named after a medium rather than a musical genre. MTV has over 60 million subscribers. Rock is the most popular music form, followed by country, which surged from relative obscurity in the mid-1980s. But those who find this joyful noise too noisy will be happy to know that classical music is showing a rise in sales, roughly in proportion to rap's decline. But in the field of creativity, one cannot point to statistics as easily. Music is more present than ever in our everyday world. Your ears will tell you.

The American Society of Composers, Authors, and Publishers (ASCAP) is located at 1 Lincoln Plaza, New York, NY 10023.

NATURE

(See also Life)

DEFINITIONS   The physical world; that which exists in the world independent of humankind; the forces of life, vegetable, animal, mineral and kinetic; "but a name for an effect/Whose cause is God" (William Cowper); "the art of God" (Sir Thomas Browne); the iron law of life; the environment; the earth, land, water and air in which we live; a place that some people want to go back to.

QUOTATIONS

You can't just let nature run wild. Alaska Governor Walter J. Hickel, in *The Los Angeles Times,* January 13, 1993.

To him who in the love of Nature / Holds Communion with her visible forms, she speaks / A various language... William Cullen Bryant, "Thanatopsis," 1817.

We must realize that we can no longer throw our wastes away because there is no "away." New Jersey Governor William T. Cahill, 1971.

Nature works on a method of all for each and each for all. Ralph Waldo Emerson, *Society and Solitude:* "Farming," 1870.

We have met the enemy and he is us. Walt Kelly, Pogo comic strip, 1970.

It were happy if we studied nature more in natural things, and acted according to nature, whose rules are few, plain and most reasonable. William Penn, *Fruits of Solitude,* 1693.

Men and Nature must work hand in hand. The throwing out of balance of the resources of Nature throws out of balance also the lives of men. President Franklin D. Roosevelt, message to the U.S. Congress, January 24, 1935.

The conservation of our natural resources and their proper use constitute the fundamental problem which underlies almost every other problem of our national life. President Theodore Roosevelt, message to the U.S. Congress, December 3, 1907.

Everything is good when it leaves the hands of the Creator; everything degenerates in the hands of man. Jean-Jacques Rousseau, *Émile,* 1762.

...the laws of nature are the same everywhere. Whoever violates them anywhere must always pay the penalty. Carl Schurz, 1889.

One touch of nature makes the whole world kin. William Shakespeare, *Troilus and Cressida,* 1602.

Nature never did betray the heart that loved her. William Wordsworth, "Lines Composed a Few Miles Above Tintern Abbey," 1798.

ANONYMOUS APHORISMS

It's not nice to fool Mother Nature.

Nature does nothing without a purpose.

Nature is the greatest show on earth.

Mother Nature and Father Time's lives revolve around their only sun.

Nature is a revolving door: what goes out in one form comes back in another.

Nature's laws are the real wisdom of the ages.

Nobody fools nature over the long run.

Nature always wins in the end.

ANECDOTES

A resort developer bought a large plot of land including a beautiful mountain. He flattened the top of the mountain to build a lodge; removed all the trees on one side of the hill to put in a terraced swimming pool; and built a sculpture garden on the other side. Then he advertised his creation in the travel journals using the slogan: "Ain't nature grand!"

"The first law of nature," said the professor, "is survival." "No," said a second scholar, "the first law is that nothing lasts forever." "Prove it," said the professor. "That's easy," said the scholar. "If the first law of nature were survival, how come no plant, animal or human being lives forever?"

"Nature isn't perfect," said the old philosopher, "which is why cosmetics were invented." "Long before cosmetics," said his wife, "nature came up with another invention—the darkness of night."

FACTS

The world and laws of nature are constant, capricious, and sometimes fierce. And humans have spent millennia constructing walls, houses and cities as shields against it. Nature was a great treasure trove of raw materials from which to scratch a living. But more and more Americans are discovering, enjoying, and respecting the great outdoors as never before for the unique beauty, tranquillity, and adventures it has to offer. The number of visitors to the more than 80 million acres of national parks has skyrocketed over the past few decades; in 1990 alone, there were 258 million national parks visits according to the *Statistical Abstract* of the U.S. Census. In 1994, the National Park Service reported an increase to 268.64 million visitors. Another 11.2 million visits were recorded at the nation's state parks. In about the same period, according to the U.S. Fish and Wildlife Service—though even they acknowledge that these numbers are likely to be a little inaccurate—the number of people who went fishing and hunting was 35 million and 14 million respectively.

The Department of the Interior can provide more information concerning the National Parks Service and individual national parks. The Nature Conservancy, 1815 North Lynn St., Arlington, VA 22209, can provide further information on the preservation and conservation of our national environment.

NEIGHBORS

DEFINITIONS People living adjacent to each other, with a common boundary or meeting place; residents of the same or adjacent areas; those who share a common spirit or interest in a given geographical area; one's human environment; the folks next door.

QUOTATIONS

No man is an island, entire of itself; every man is a piece of the continent, a part of the main;…any man's death diminishes me, because I am involved in mankind; and therefore never send to know for whom the bell tolls; it tolls for thee. John Donne, *Devotions: XVII,* 1624.

Nor knowest thou what argument / Thy life to thy neighbor's creed has lent. / All are needed by each one / Nothing is fair or good alone. Ralph Waldo Emerson, "Each and All," 1839.

Good fences make good neighbors. Robert Frost, "Mending Wall," 1914.

Your own safety is at stake when your neighbor's house is burning. Horace, Epistles I, c. 10 BC.

The impersonal hand of government can never replace the helping hand of a neighbor. Vice President Hubert H. Humphrey, February 10, 1965.

Thou shalt love thy neighbor as thyself. *Leviticus,* 19:18.

…better is a neighbor that is near than a brother far off. *Proverbs,* 21:10.

In the field of world policy, I would dedicate this nation to the policy of the good neighbor. President Franklin D. Roosevelt, first inaugural address, March 4, 1933.

As we have recaptured and rekindled our pioneering spirit, we have insisted that it shall always be a spirit of justice, a spirit of teamwork, a spirit of sacrifice, and, above all, a spirit of neighborliness. President Franklin D. Roosevelt, October 4, 1933.

…I am as desirous of being a good neighbor as I am of being a bad subject… Henry D. Thoreau, *Civil Disobedience,* 1849.

ANONYMOUS APHORISMS

We can live without our friends, but not without our neighbors.

When you have a plot of land, the best thing to cultivate is your neighbors.

Two's company, three's a neighborhood.

Check the neighbors before you buy the house.

A good neighbor is the next best thing.

The best next-door neighbor is the one who overlooks things.

The greatest luxury in life is to be able to pick your neighbors.

ANECDOTES

Two Native Americans watched the Pilgrims landing at Plymouth Rock, and one sighed with dismay to the other, "There goes the neighborhood!"

Then there's the man who puts a sign on his front door when he goes off on vacation, reading: "Attention thieves! Do not bother to enter. Everything of value has already been borrowed by my neighbors."

A young couple planning to buy a new home was interested in a particular housing development, so they rang a few doorbells to see what kind of neighbors they potentially would have. They decided not to buy because every neighbor tried to sell them his house, saying he was getting too old to worry about the neighborhood.

FACTS

The concept of neighborhood is at the root of much of contemporary life in the United States and elsewhere. For example, the question of how much neighborhood control of schools there should be, and how many neighborhoods should be in a single school district, has been a burning issue with regard to questions of funding and taxation. Many metropolitan and suburban areas are still trying to determine where the neighborhood community prerogative in government lies and where it must be overridden. The right to regulate residential construction and the size of building lots is bitterly defended by communities determined to maintain the existing character of their neighborhood and just as bitterly opposed by those who think that such neighborhoods are un-neighborly. Out of fear for personal security, or a desire for close community, an increasing number of Americans are moving into gated communities. This is hardly a new concept. During the middle ages and earlier, villages, even whole towns, existed within walls constructed to keep out wild animals or invading forces. But as both of these threats are long past, the question arises as to the necessity of contemporary gated communities, and whether they foster or divide neighborhoods. As the poet Robert Frost said, "Before I built a wall I'd ask to know / What I was walling in or walling out, / And to whom I was like to give offense."

NEW ENGLAND

DEFINITIONS The northeast section of the United States; "Down East"; baked bean country; Yankee country; the land of "yup" and "nope" answers to every question; the place the Devil would go if hell ever froze over.

QUOTATIONS

And this is good old Boston, / The home of the bean and the cod, / Where the Lowells talk only to Cabots / And the Cabots talk only to God. John C. Bossidy, "On the Aristocracy of Harvard," 1910.

The courage of New England was the "courage of conscience." Rufus Choate, speech at bicentennial of Ipswich, MA, 1834.

...a sup of New England's air is better than a whole draft of old England's ale. Rev. Francis Higginson, New England's Plantation, 1630.

O, Eleazar Wheelock was a very pious man; / He went into the wilderness to teach the Indian, / With a Gradus ad Parnassum, a Bible, and a drum, / And five hundred gallons of New England rum... Richard Hovey, "Eleazar Wheelock," the Dartmouth College song, c. late 19th century.

New England has a harsh climate, a barren soil, a rough and stormy coast, and yet we love it, even with a love passing that of dwellers in more favored regions. Henry Cabot Lodge, Forefathers' Day speech in New York, NY, December 22, 1884.

The New Englanders are a people of God, settled in those which were once the Devil's territories. Rev. Cotton Mather, *Wonders of the Invisible World*, 1693.

...New England, where the clergy long held a monopoly of what passed for learning. Francis Parkman, article in *The Nation*, 1869.

There is a sumptuous variety about the New England weather that compels the stranger's admiration—and regret...In the spring I have counted one hundred and thirty-six different kinds of weather inside four-and-twenty hours. Mark Twain, speech in New York, NY, December 22, 1876.

ANONYMOUS APHORISMS

If you don't like the New England weather, just wait a moment and it'll change for you.

New England is neither new nor England; it is its own tradition.

New England, where ever since Myles Standish people have spoken for themselves.

Living through a New England winter develops Yankee ingenuity.

You can always tell a Yankee but you can't tell him much.

If New England did not exist it would never have been invented.

ANECDOTES

New Englanders' lack of loquaciousness is legendary, as perhaps is this story of a New England-born U.S. President named Calvin Coolidge, who was asked what had been the subject of the pastor's sermon in church that Sunday. Coolidge replied, "Sin." "What did the preacher say?" the questioner further inquired. "He's agin it," Mr. Coolidge elaborated.

Mrs. Jenkins bought a house in Maine. As the years past, she found that her neighbors, though friendly, still considered her to be an out-of-towner. When she discovered she was pregnant with twins she excitedly told the owner of the general store, "Well, I may never be a Mainer, but my kids will." "Now, Mrs. Jenkins," he cautioned, "Just because a cat has kittens in the oven, it don't make 'em muffins."

"The trouble with New Englanders," said Mr. Jones, "is that they refuse to argue. No matter how stupid you accuse them of being, they refuse to argue." "You don't say," said his New England friend.

FACTS

The six New England states are Maine, New Hampshire, Vermont, Massachusetts, Rhode Island, and Connecticut. New England is geographically the smallest American region, but it wasn't always. In the days of the American Revolution, the U.S. was largely confined to the Eastern seaboard states, and New England was one of the larger sections. Today, New England's influence remains larger than its area. The measure of any presidential candidate's success is his performance in the New Hampshire primaries, and on election night New Hampshire's polls are watched closely as a barometer for the returns across the nation. The names of cities as far west as Oregon (Portland and Salem, for example) bear witness to the extent of the nation's New England heritage, and among America's great colleges, Harvard, Yale, Dartmouth, Brown, Williams, Amherst, and others retain Down East's claim to historic intellectual leadership. There are great colleges all over the country today, but the chances are that more of them have grown from seeds sown in New England than from any other region.

OPPORTUNITY

(See also Jobs, Luck)

DEFINITIONS   A chance to advance oneself or profit; the occasion of being in the right place at the right time with the right qualifications; the knock that's a boost; that which comes disguised as hard work.

QUOTATIONS

A wise man will make more opportunities than he finds. Sir Francis Bacon, *Essays*, "Of Ceremonies and Respect," 1625.

God helps them that help themselves. Benjamin Franklin, *The Way to Wealth*, 1757.

Our country has become the land of opportunity to those born without inheritance… Herbert Hoover, presidential candidate, October 22, 1928.

We have set out in this country to improve the quality of American life. We are concerned with each man's opportunity to develop his talents. President Lyndon B. Johnson, July 12, 1966.

All of us do not have equal talent, but all of us should have an equal opportunity to develop our talents. President John F. Kennedy, June 6, 1963.

…Age is opportunity no less Than Youth itself, though in another dress. Henry Wadsworth Longfellow, "Morituri Salutamus," 1874.

I seen my opportunity and I took it. George Washington Plunkitt, quoted by William L. Riordon in *Plunkitt of Tammany Hall,* 1905.

When the iron is hot, strike. John Heywood, *Proverbs,* 1546.

There is a tide in the affairs of men, / which, taken at the flood, leads on to fortune; / Omitted, all the voyage of their life / Is bound in shallows and in miseries. William Shakespeare, *Julius Caesar,* 1599.

Since the days when the great fleet of Columbus sailed into the waters of the New World, America has been another name for opportunity… Frederick Jackson Turner, "The Significance of the Frontier in American History," 1893.

ANONYMOUS APHORISMS

Some people get the breaks; some people make their own.

Opportunity makes the man.

Today's opportunity is yesterday's dream and tomorrow's memory.

Opportunity doesn't necessarily knock on the door; it may be leaning against the wall waiting to be noticed.

Opportunity comes to those who go looking for it.

Not every opportunity is a good one; some are invitations to disaster.

Opportunity makes the thief.

ANECDOTES

Mr. Smith ran a piano school. One day, a piano needed tuning. Every tuner he called was busy for at least a month, except one individual named Johann Sebastian Oppornockety, who arrived that same afternoon, tuned the instrument in half an hour, and charged half the normal price. After he left, Mr. Smith decided Oppornockety had done such an outstanding job, he would have him return to tune the rest of his pianos. He called Oppornockety, but the tuner refused his offer. "Mr. Smith," he said, "Oppornockety only tunes once."

The saleswoman at the door was very persistent. When Mr. Jones slammed the door in her face, she yelled through it about what a wonderful opportunity she was offering—a once in a lifetime opportunity at a special sale price. "I've heard of opportunity knocking," yelled back Mr. Jones, "but when it starts pounding on the door there's got to be a catch to it."

PARENTS

(See also Adolescence, Babies, Children, Family, Marriage)

DEFINITIONS Those who beget offspring; mothers and fathers; heir conditioners; immediate progenitors; line of descent.

QUOTATIONS

All the [education] reforms in Washington will not matter a great deal unless parents are parents and give their children the love of learning. U.S. Secretary of Education Richard W. Riley, in the *The Christian Science Monitor,* June 10, 1994.

I'll have to check with my dad. Dan Quayle, responding when an Indiana GOP county chairman asked him to run for Congress, 1976.

We never know the love of our parents for us till we have become parents. Rev. Henry Ward Beecher, *Proverbs from Plymouth Pulpit,* 1887.

Honor thy father and thy mother... *Exodus,* 20:12.

The longer we live, and the more we think, the higher value we learn to put on the friendship and tenderness of parents and of friends. Parents we can have but once; and he promises himself too much, who enters life with the expectation of finding many friends. Samuel Johnson, according to James Boswell's *The Life of Samuel Johnson,* 1791.

Men are generally more careful of the breed of their horses and dogs than of their children. William Penn, *Some Fruits of Solitude,* 1693.

It is a wise father that knows his own child. William Shakespeare, *The Merchant of Venice,* 1597.

All women become like their mothers. That is their tragedy. No man does. That's his. Oscar Wilde, *The Importance of Being Earnest,* 1895.

ANONYMOUS APHORISMS

Parenthood is the sin—or the virtue—of repetition.

There are two stages for parents—when your children ask all the questions and when they think they know all the answers.

In loco parentis—Latin for "Children can drive parents crazy."

"Why" is the question children ask their parents and parents sometimes ask each other.

Life is richer when one gives it to another.

A parent's training starts when that future parent is still a child.

Parents should be their children's parents first, their children's friends later.

ANECDOTES

The classic story is of the man who murdered both his parents and then called for the court's mercy as he was recently orphaned.

The ambitions of Old World parents have been the subject of many jokes, as for example, the one about Mrs. Smith, who was asked about her two children in elementary school and answered: "The doctor is in the third grade and the lawyer is in the first!"

How many times, as the kids were growing up, has a harried mother or father said to them, "I hope you have a child just like you, so you'll go through what I'm going through now!"

Q: What do a prince, the child of a thief, and a gorilla have in common at birth? A: The prince is his parents' heir apparent; the thief's child is born to an erring parent; and the gorilla is born to a hairy parent.

FACTS

Though many aspects of parenthood are as timeless and universal as a child's smile, parenthood's status in our modern era has changed considerably from that in past generations. The development of contraceptive methods has given couples much greater control over when and whether they will have children, resulted in more childless families or smaller households with only one or two children. Single parenthood has become much more prevalent; and women are often waiting until they are older to have children. It has suddenly become more common for couples in their thirties and forties to start a family. In our aging society, the image evoked by the term "parents" less often refers to a young couple with a child, and more often to an elderly couple.

PEACE

(See also Armed Forces, War)

DEFINITIONS   Condition of amity or concord among parties who might otherwise be engaged in strife or combat; the opposite of war; the time between wars; "in international affairs, a period of cheating between two periods of fighting" (Ambrose Bierce); something humankind persists in fighting over; something each person wishes for in mind and on earth.

QUOTATIONS

I am convinced that although war and violence are, alas, contagious, peace is equally so. Let us give it every chance. Pope John Paul II, in *The Los Angeles Times,* January 9, 1995.

The source of peace is within us; so also is the source of war. And the real enemy is within us, and not outside. Dalai Lama, in *The Wall Street Journal,* July 17, 1989.

Peace upon any other basis than national independence, peace purchased at the cost of any part of our national integrity, is fit only for slaves, and even when purchased at such a price it is a delusion, for it cannot last. Senator William E. Borah of Idaho, speech in the U.S. Senate, November 19, 1919.

There never was a good war or a bad peace. Benjamin Franklin, letter to Josiah Quincy, September 11, 1783.

They shall beat their swords into plowshares, and their spears into pruning-hooks; nation shall not lift up sword against nation, neither shall they learn war any more. *Isaiah,* 2:4.

In this age when there can be no losers in peace and no victors in war, we must recognize the obligation to match national strength with national restraint. President Lyndon B. Johnson, speech to a joint session of the U.S. Congress, November 27, 1963.

The mere absence of war is not peace. President John F. Kennedy, State of the Union address to the U.S. Congress, January 14, 1963.

Blessed are the peacemakers: for they shall be called the children of God. *Matthew,* 5:9.

Peace hath her victories No less renown'd than war. John Milton, "To the Lord General Cromwell," 1652.

Peace, like charity, begins at home. President Franklin D. Roosevelt, August 14, 1936.

We desire the peace which comes as of right to the just man armed; not the peace granted on terms of ignominy to the craven and the weakling. President Theodore Roosevelt, December 3, 1901.

No nation ever yet enjoyed a protracted and triumphant peace without receiving in its own bosom ineradicable seeds of future decline. John Ruskin, *Modern Painters, Vol. IV,* 1856.

When the bells of peace ring there will be no hands to beat the drums of war .Even if they existed, they would be stilled .Egyptian President Anwar el-Sadat, address to the Knesset Parliament of Israel, November 20, 1977.

Where they make a desert, they call it peace. Tacitus, *Life of Agricola,* c. 100 AD.

Peace hath higher tests of manhood Than battle ever knew. John Greenleaf Whittier, "The Hero," 1853.

Only a peace between equals can last... President Woodrow Wilson, speech to the U.S. Senate, January 22, 1917.

ANONYMOUS APHORISMS

Peace makes plenty.

Better to keep peace than to have to make peace.

If peace is to last it must come first.

War breaks out, peace settles in.

It isn't real peace if it includes a piece of somebody else's property.

Better an uneasy peace than an easy war.

Peace is for the strong, subjugation for the weak.

ANECDOTES

It is a measure of the normal state of things that some years ago the *New York Daily News,* noting that there was no war going on in the world, headlined its story: "Peace Breaks Out."

Two pacifists were arguing about who was more idealistic. "I love peace so much," said one, "that I am willing to fight for it." "And I love peace so much," said the other, "that I am willing not to fight for it."

POLITICAL PARTIES

(See also Candidates, Elections, Government, Voting)

DEFINITIONS   Organizations dedicated to a particular political philosophy and/or espousing the candidacy of groups of candidates under a common banner; organizations of voters seeking to elect their group's choices to public office; the ins and the outs; the government and the opposition.

QUOTATIONS

Any man who can carry a Republican primary is a Republican. Senator William E. Borah of Idaho, 1923.

I think probably politicians are about half ego and half humility. President Jimmy Carter, April 11, 1975.

Turn the rascals out. Attributed to Charles A. Dana, and slogan of Liberal Republican Party, 1872.

The Democratic party is like a mule. It has neither pride of ancestry nor hope of posterity. Ignatius Donnelly, speech in the Minnesota legislature, September 13. 1860.

Of the two great parties, which at this hour almost share the nation between them, I should say that one has the best cause, and the other contains the best men. Ralph Waldo Emerson, *Essays, Second Series:* "Politics," 1844.

...the conservative is an old democrat. Ralph Waldo Emerson, *Representative Men:* "Napoleon," 1850.

You cannot adopt politics as a profession and remain honest. Louis McHenry Howe, January 17, 1933.

They see nothing wrong in the rule that to the victor belong the spoils of the enemy. Senator William L. Marcy of New York, speech in the U.S. Senate, January 21, 1832.

Any party which takes credit for the rain must not be surprised if its opponents blame it for the drought. Dwight W. Morrow, October 10, 1930.

The fact is that a reformer can't last in politics. He can make a show for a while, but he always comes down like a rocket. Politics is as much a regular business as the grocery or the drygoods or the drug business. George Washington Plunkitt, quoted by William L. Riordon in *Plunkitt of Tammany Hall,* 1905.

The best system is to have one party govern and the other party watch. U.S. Representative Thomas B. Reed of Maine, speech in the U.S. House of Representatives, April 22, 1880.

I am not a member of any organized political party. I am a Democrat. Attributed to Will Rogers, c. 1920s.

When a leader is in the Democratic Party he's a boss; when he's in the Republican Party he's a leader. Harry S. Truman, speech at Columbia University, April 28, 1959.

ANONYMOUS APHORISMS

Promise them anything but get out the vote.

Politicians don't like to talk turkey because they hate to eat crow.

A mugwump is a political animal with his mug on one side of the fence and his wump on the other.

Conservative means small change and radical means large bills.

A political club is better than a policeman's club.

A political party always tries to take the cake.

Politics is the art of the passable.

ANECDOTES

The story is told that Theodore Roosevelt was once heckled by a man who kept interrupting to proclaim, "I'm a Democrat. My father was a Democrat. My grandfather was a Democrat!" Roosevelt finally turned to him and stormed, "If your father had been a jackass, and your grandfather a jackass, what would you be?" The heckler replied, "A Republican."

A candidate had spent the evening at the home of a local opinion leader, trying to woo her and her family to his candidacy. The evening went very pleasantly and when he was leaving the lady commented, "You have made a great impression here. We are delighted that you're running, and there's only one person in the whole world that I would rather vote for." "That's very complimentary," the candidate politely replied, "but I'd like to know who that one person is." The lady smiled sweetly and said, "Your opponent."

FACTS

Political parties vary in different countries. In the United States and Great Britain, there have generally been two major parties contending, although not always the same two. (Labor replaced the Liberals as the British opponents of the Tories who later became the Conservatives; and in the U.S., the Republicans came on the scene after the Whigs faded.) There have been a number of notable attempts to introduce a third major party to both political scenes; but American campaign funds are allocated by a government composed of Democrats and Republicans only to the major parties in an election, so it has been nearly impossible. Billionaire businessman H. Ross Perot's "United We Stand Movement" and the Independence Party became the 1990s challenge to the two-party system. In both Europe and Canada, democratic nations are apt to have more parties competing more equally in the political arena, and more coalition governments as a result.

POPULATION

(See also Children, Family)

DEFINITIONS   The people or total number of people of a given area or governmental entity; humanity; those who inhabit the earth.

QUOTATIONS

If you have to single out the one biggest threat facing humanity, it's population control. We didn't have to face it before. Politically, it's very difficult. The pressure of population converts forests into fields. Russell Train, former EPA administrator, in *The Washington Post,* September 12, 1994.

If government knew how, I should like to see it check, not multiply the population. Ralph Waldo Emerson, *The Conduct of Life:* "Considerations by the Way," 1860.

I was ever of the opinion that the honest man who married and brought up a large family, did more service than he who continued single and only talked of population. Oliver Goldsmith, *The Vicar of Wakefield,* 1766.

A reliable estimate shows that, at present rates of growth, the world population could double by the end of the century. The growing gap—between food to eat and mouths to feed—poses one of mankind's greatest challenges. It threatens the dignity of the individual and the sanctity of the family. President Lyndon B. Johnson, message to the U.S. Congress, February 2, 1966.

Population, when unchecked, increases in a geometrical ratio. Subsistence only increases in an arithmetical ratio. Thomas R. Malthus, *An Essay on the Principle of Population,* 1798.

The people are a many-headed beast. Alexander Pope, *First Epistle of First Book of Horace,* 1735.

Men, like all other animals, naturally multiply in proportion to the means of their subsistence. Adam Smith, *The Wealth of Nations,* 1776.

We have been God-like in our planned breeding of our domesticated plants and animals, but we have been rabbit-like in our unplanned breeding of ourselves. Arnold Toynbee, June 1963.

ANONYMOUS APHORISMS

People are people's number-one problem.

The world is full of people getting closer all the time.

People try to get away from it all, but it all comes along with them.

The rich get richer and the poor get children.

People speak of the problem of growing population, but even when population is standing still it is growing—growing older.

It isn't the heat, it's the humanity.

ANECDOTES

A young woman asked to express her views of the population problem said "It is better to be gotten than to beget; it is better to beget than to be gone."

A young student was asked to summarize the state of the population of the world. "The population of the world," she answered, "shows that you don't have to go to school to learn how to multiply."

Then there's the character who thinks that Zero Population Growth means we're breeding more people who amount to nothing.

FACTS

Population growth has helped to spark both the advance of civilization and the crisis of modern times. It has been one of the forces that made possible the development of new worlds in the Americas—and the growth of old tensions elsewhere. It has created a vast appetite for the world's natural resources and outstripped those natural resources. According to United Nations' statistics, as of 1996, the world population was 5.8 billion, and increases by over 86 million annually. This means that the world population is likely to exceed 6 billion by 1998. To get an idea of how rapidly it is increasing, consider that it took over 100 years for the population to rise from 1 billion to 2 billion; it took only 33 years to reach 3 billion; 14 years to reach 4 billion; and 13 years to reach 5 billion. It is estimated that the world population will level off in the year 2050 at 11 billion. In the past, starvation and fatal diseases—such as cholera, bubonic plague, and influenza—limited population growth; but man's ingenuity has grown with man's numbers. In the meantime, the ability to limit population growth—and even the understanding of why this is a serious matter—is lagging far behind. The biggest part of the population challenge is that, in general, those segments of population least able to take care of themselves are the segments that most prolifically reproduce. The population of third world countries is growing far more rapidly than that of industrialized nations.

The United Nations Department for Economic and Social Information and Policy Analysis regularly monitors and reports on world-population statistics.

Poverty

DEFINITIONS   The condition of being poor; lack of possessions or resources; "life near the bone" (Henry D. Thoreau); the world's most chronic social disease.

QUOTATIONS

Poverty for us is freedom. It is not a mortification, a penance. It is joyful freedom... Mother Teresa, in *Time,* December 4, 1989.

Over the hill to the poor-house I'm trudgin' my weary way... Will Carleton, "Over the Hill to the Poor-House," 1871.

Thousands upon thousands are yearly brought into a state of real poverty by their great anxiety not to be thought poor. William Cobbett, *Advice to Young Men,* 1829.

Poverty is the open-mouthed, relentless hell which yawns beneath civilized society. Henry George, *Progress and Poverty,* 1878.

Poverty has many roots, but the tap root is ignorance. President Lyndon B. Johnson, message to the U.S. Congress, January 12, 1865.

A decent provision for the poor is the true test of civilization. Samuel Johnson, according to James Boswell in *The Life of Samuel Johnson,* 1770.

If a free society cannot help the many who are poor, it cannot save the few who are rich. President John F. Kennedy, inaugural address, January 20, 1961.

No men living are more worthy to be trusted than those who toil up from poverty... President Abraham Lincoln, message to the U.S. Congress, December 3, 1861.

For ye have the poor always with you… *Matthew,* 26:11.

How the Other Half Lives. Jacob A. Riis, book title on the subject of slum conditions on Manhattan's Lower East Side, 1890.

I see one-third of a nation ill-housed, ill-clad, ill-nourished. President Franklin D. Roosevelt, second inaugural address, January 20, 1937.

There is only one class in the community that thinks more about money than the rich, and that is the poor. The poor can think of nothing else. That is the misery of being poor. Oscar Wilde, *The Soul of Man Under Socialism,* 1891.

I remember, before we were married, I was working at University Settlement in New York and Franklin called for me there late one afternoon. I wasn't ready because there was a sick child and I had to see that she was taken home. Franklin said he would go with me. We took the child to an area not far away and Franklin went with me up the three flights to the tenement rooms in which the family lived. It was not a pleasant place and Franklin looked around in surprise and horror. It was the first time, I think, that he had ever really seen a slum and when he got back to the street he drew a deep breath of fresh air. "My God," he whispered, "I didn't know people lived like that!". Eleanor Roosevelt, speech at the opening of the Golden Age Center in Sara Delano Roosevelt Park, New York, NY, 1942.

ANONYMOUS APHORISMS

Poverty is rich in all the wrong things.

Being poor provides plenty of room for improvement.

There is none so poor as he who knows not the joy of what he has.

Poverty is only evident when there is wealth alongside it.

The rich get richer and the poor get children.

It is possible to be poor in purse but rich in blessings.

ANECDOTES

Writer Sam Levenson often described the funny and warm incidents of growing up in a family that was hard pressed for a decent income, and as he explained it, "We didn't know we were poor."

The impoverished son of an impoverished family was asked how he could have managed to live so pennilessly for so long. "You must remember," he said, "I had a head start."

FACTS

It is a sad but immutable fact that in many parts of the world poverty is rampant. A lesser known, and infinitely more shocking statistic is that nearly 40 million of the world's poor are American citizens. Who are they? According to the U.S. Census

Bureau, in 1994, 50 percent were between the ages of 18 and 64; 40 percent of those people living below the poverty level worked (earning less than $7,547 per year for an individual, or $11,821 per year for a family of 4); and a record 10.5 percent worked full time. Poverty has decreased significantly for senior citizens: dropping from 19.8 percent in 1969, to 9.6 percent in 1994. The poverty rate decreased in 1994 to 14.5 percent from 15.1 percent the year before; this small decrease meant 1.2 million Americans rose above the poverty level. Poverty has been an issue since the U.S. early colonial days. During the late 1890s, social workers like Jane Addams of Hull House, Stanton Coit of University Settlement House and authors like Charles Dickens, Upton Sinclair, and Jacob A. Riis brought the plight of the urban-dwelling poor to the public's attention. But it wasn't until the presidential terms of Franklin Delano Roosevelt and Lyndon Baynes Johnson that light was shed on the agonies of rural Americans living below the poverty level. How to eradicate poverty has always been a topic for debate in Washington. The outcome of calls for welfare reforms as well as adjustments to the Medicaid, Medicare, and Social Security systems will determine the future well-being of the majority of the U.S. population, as those who are not impoverished bear the costs of these services through taxes, and diversion of government funds.

P REJUDICE

(See also Ethnicity, Minorities, Race)

DEFINITIONS   A preformed bias; an attitude or opinion based on prejudgment; "a vagrant opinion without visible means of support" (Ambrose Bierce); "an opinion without judgment" (Voltaire); a closed mind, often combined with an open mouth.

QUOTATIONS

He prided himself on being a man without prejudices; and this itself is a very great prejudice. Anatole France, *The Crime of Sylvestre Bonnard,* 1881.

For, when you assemble a number of men to have the advantage of their joint wisdom, you inevitably assemble with those men all their prejudices, their passions, their errors of opinion, their local interests, and their selfish views. Benjamin Franklin at the Constitutional Convention, Philadelphia, PA, September 17, 1787.

Prejudice is the child of ignorance. William Hazlitt, *Sketches and Essays,* "On Prejudice," 1839.

Our nation's long neglect of minorities whose skin is dark is perhaps only a little worse than our neglect of another minority whose hair is white. President Lyndon B. Johnson, September 5, 1966.

Irrational barriers and ancient prejudices fall quickly when the question of survival itself is at stake. Senator John F. Kennedy of Massachusetts, April 12, 1959.

There is nothing stronger than human prejudice. Wendell Phillips, January 28, 1852.

Ignorance is stubborn and prejudice dies hard. Adlai E. Stevenson, Jr., U.S. Ambassador to the U.N., October 1, 1963.

It is never too late to give up our prejudices. Henry D. Thoreau, *Walden:* "Economy," 1854.

ANONYMOUS APHORISMS

Prejudice isn't just a closed mind; it's an open wound.

Prejudice begins at home.

Hate does as much harm to the one who hates as to the target.

Prejudice is blanket judgment without looking under the blanket.

To be tolerant of prejudice is to be part of it.

Prejudice has an insatiable appetite for believing the worst.

ANECDOTES

A notorious bigot was attempting to show how broadminded he was by talking about his daily habits. "Every day," he told an African-American woman, "I walk through your neighborhood and pass your house." "Thanks for not stopping," she promptly replied.

"There isn't a single Jew or nonwhite or Catholic in my little village," a tourist remarked to a city official. "Maybe that's why it's still a village," the official replied.

FACTS

Prejudice has more forms than a cat has lives, but in all its forms the backbone of prejudice is ignorance: It is easier to prejudge a stereotype than to judge an individual. In this country, and internationally, there are many organizations fighting prejudice. Unfortunately, even minor prejudicial incidents easily overshadow the great progress these organizations have made in the last few decades. Society's increased mobility has been a tremendous factor in the integration of communities. Hate groups, though highly visible in the media, have surprisingly small core memberships in limited sectors of the nation.

The ACLU, NAACP, the Anti-Defamation League as well as local, state, and federal equal or civil-rights governmental offices can provide information about particular aspects of prejudice and the names of organizations active in those areas.

PRESIDENCY

DEFINITIONS   The period during which a president holds office; duration of elected leadership; the highest office in the land.

QUOTATIONS

Being President is like running a cemetery: you've got a lot of people under you and nobody's listening. President Bill Clinton, in *U.S. News & World Report,* January 23, 1995.

Political exposure is like exposure to the sun: half an hour can be good, but if you expose yourself too much, you can get burned. Diego Fernandez (de Cevallos), President of Mexico, in the *The New York Times,* July 27, 1994.

ANONYMOUS APHORISMS

Hail to the chief!

Presidency is a term of endearment. The term lasts as long as the endearment.

ANECDOTES

Mrs. Jenkins was asking her fourth-grade students what they wanted to be when they grew up. After hearing the usual fireman, policewoman, doctor, and pilot, Bobby answered, "President." Another child chimed in, "I hope so, because if he gets elected, I'm going to be rich." "Why is that?" Asked Mrs. Jenkins. "Because I saw him stealing cookies yesterday."

Asked about life after the White House, former President Bush replied, "Well, for one thing, I find that I no longer win every golf game I play."

FACTS

Had George Washington accepted the offer to be crowned King of the United States, the political scene might be quite different today. But, as the historical record shows, he declined, ran for office, and took the oath of office on April 30, 1789. The scope and limits of the office were formed first by the founding fathers who, in lieu of an extant political model drew from the position of the Governor of New York, which had been described in the New York Constitution in 1777. The Founding Fathers were also influenced by the political writings of John Locke, Montesquieu, and Sir William Blackstone. From that time up to the present, the exact role of the President has continually shifted and evolved. Much of that evolution has taken place because of political wrestling matches between the President and Congress—each seeking to shift the balance of power in their favor. Fortunately, inherent in our government is a system of checks and balances, held in place by a division of power between the Legislative, Judicial, and Executive branches preventing any single person from seizing a preponderance of power. Since the day George Washington left office, the following men have been elected President: John Adams, Thomas Jefferson, James Madison, James Monroe, John Quincy Adams, Andrew Jackson, Martin Van Buren, William Henry Harrison, John Tyler, James Knox Polk, Zachary Taylor, Millard Fillmore, Franklin Pierce, James Buchanan, Abraham Lincoln, Andrew Johnson, Ulysses S. Grant, Rutherford Birchard Hayes, James Abram Garfield, Chester Alan Arthur, Grover Cleveland, Benjamin Harrison, William McKinley, Theodore Roosevelt, William Howard Taft, Woodrow Wilson, Warren G. Harding, Calvin Coolidge, Herbert C. Hoover, Franklin D. Roosevelt, Harry S. Truman, Dwight D. Eisenhower, John F. Kennedy, Lyndon B. Johnson, Richard M. Nixon, Gerald R. Ford, James Earl (Jimmy) Carter, Ronald Reagan, George Bush, William Jefferson (Bill) Clinton. To be eligible for the presidency, a person must be a "natural born citizen" at least 35 years old, who has never been convicted of a felony. Though perhaps the greatest obstacles for any prospective candidate to overcome in our times are the inevitable airing of any dirty laundry secreted in the family closet, and the necessity of consistent on-camera performance. Still, the presidency will no doubt be the first aspiration of many youths for generations to come.

P RIVACY

DEFINITIONS   The condition of or right to be secure from other people's presence or knowledge of one's affairs; the right to be left alone; that which is nobody else's business.

QUOTATIONS

...the right to be let alone—the most comprehensive of rights, and the right most valued by civilized men. U.S. Supreme Court Associate Justice Louis D. Brandeis, commenting on *Olmstead v. U.S.,* June 4, 1928.

The right of every person "to be let alone" must be placed in the scales with the right of others to communicate. U.S. Supreme Court Chief Justice Warren E. Burger, May 4, 1970.

There has been too much Government secrecy and not enough respect for the personal privacy of American citizens. Jimmy Carter, presidential candidate in debate with President Gerald R. Ford, September 23, 1976.

...a man's house is his castle... Sir Edward Coke, Third Institute, 1644.

A man must ride alternately on the horses of his private and his public nature. Ralph Waldo Emerson, *The Conduct of Life:* "Fate," 1860.

I never said I want to be left alone. I said I want to be let alone. Attributed to Greta Garbo by a close friend, c. 1960s.

Some persons who were intended by nature to adorn an inviolable privacy are thrust upon us by paragraphers and interviewers whose existence is a dubious blessing... Sir Henry Irving, February 14, 1898.

Every man should know that his conversations, his correspondence, and his personal life are private. President Lyndon B. Johnson, March 10, 1967.

A man has a right to pass through this world, if he wills, without having his picture published, his business enterprises discussed, his successful experiments written for the benefit of others, or his eccentricities commented upon, whether in handbills, circulars, catalogues, newspapers or periodicals. Chief Judge Alton B. Parker, New York State Court of Appeals, commenting on *Roberson v. Rochester Folding Box Co.,* 1901.

I feel the necessity of deepening the stream of life; I must cultivate privacy. It is very dissipating to be with people too much. Henry D. Thoreau, *Journal,* August 2, 1854.

ANONYMOUS APHORISMS

In the computer age it is disturbing to realize that machines have your number, and can converse with one another.

There are always casualties in the invasion of privacy.

People who live in glass houses are still entitled to window shades.

The government has no more right than anybody else to be a Peeping Tom.

Not everybody wants to be on America's Funniest Home Videos.

Goldfish, not men, are supposed to live in transparent bowls.

Nobody's life is expected to be a totally open book.

ANECDOTES

"My daughter," said Mrs. Brown, "is only 13, and already she has her own apartment." "Where?" asked Mrs. Smith. "In ours," said Mrs. Brown.

A certain college professor liked to stress that privacy is defined differently, depending on one's perspective. "The government," he said, "isn't usually interested in finding out who lost money gambling; but they are forever trying to identify the winners."

Beverly Hills is known as a community with a passion for privacy, even to the fact that there are practically no sidewalks. As comedians point out, in what is by now a piece of faulty folklore, it's such a private community that even the police have an unlisted phone number.

FACTS

Privacy is a rare privilege in this world, and a civil right in the United States. To protect the individual's right to privacy, the federal government faces many challenges. We are required to file details of our income annually with the Internal Revenue Service; our credit history is stored in business companies' computer databases; our purchasing habits are detailed in our computerized credit card receipts; our telephone calls—though private, unless we use cellular phones—leave a trail of phone numbers on phone company computers; our reading habits are recorded in magazine subscription lists; and both private and government computers follow us virtually from birth to death. This information can also be vital to law enforcement to protect us from terrorists, extremist groups and other dangers to society. But as George Orwell warned in his book 1984, which was published in 1948: "Big Brother is watching you." There is always a danger connected to data collection and retrieval. These sophisticated tracking systems can also be used to learn intimate details of the lives of good citizens. It is the government's task to balance the need for information and the right to privacy as dictated in federal and state laws. The courts and the legislatures have attempted to codify and define the limits of governmental invasions of privacy such as wire-tapping and interception; or reading of standard and electronic mail. Efforts are being made to strengthen provisions against self-incrimination, and to protect the confidentiality of various types of messages and notes, such as those between patient and doctor, or a news reporter's unpublished notes or tapes. Part of the difficulty in some cases arises from the fact that the federal government very legitimately acquires more information about more people all the time—through the workings of the Social Security System, for example.

PSYCHOLOGY

DEFINITIONS   The science of mental processes and behavior; mind matter; the couch trip; head shrinking, civilized style.

QUOTATIONS

Happiness, or misery, is in the mind. It is the mind that lives. William Cobbett, *Grammar of the English Language,* 1819.

Neurosis seems to be a human privilege. Sigmund Freud, *Moses and Monotheism,* 1958.

Castles in the air—they are so easy to take refuge in. And so easy to build as well. Henrik Ibsen, *The Master Builder,* 1892.

Depend upon it, Sir, when a man knows he is to be hanged in a fortnight, it concentrates his mind wonderfully. Samuel Johnson, according to James Boswell in *Life of Samuel Johnson,* 1777.

Every man values himself more than all other men, but he always values others' opinions of him more than his own. Marcus Aurelius, *Meditations,* c. 2nd century.

The mind is its own place, and in itself, / Can make a Heaven of Hell, a Hell of Heaven. John Milton, *Paradise Lost: Book 1,* 1667.

Suspicion always haunts the guilty mind... William Shakespeare, *King Henry VI: Part III,* 1592.

Among all the diseases of the mind there is not one more epidemical or more pernicious than the love of flattery. Richard Steele, *The Spectator,* December 3, 1711.

ANONYMOUS APHORISMS

Psychology sometimes determines what's in your head by getting under your skin.

Anyone who goes to a psychologist should have his head examined.

Psychologists say a lot of people lie on the couch, but some tell the truth.

Was the world happier before psychology, or was that a delusion?

Psychology is only a state of mind.

Psychology is the science of predicting how people behave—and explaining why they don't.

ANECDOTES

Probably the most familiar of all psychologist stories is that of the two who met at an elevator. The first one smiled at the second and said, "Hello. How are you?" And the second one said to himself, "Now why did he say that?"

Q: What's the difference between neurotic and psychotic? A: Neurotics build castles in the sky, psychotics live in them.

A psychologist was administering a test to a job applicant, and asked the individual to say the first word that popped into her head after every word the psychologist gave her. "Food," said the psychologist. "Dirty," said the applicant. "Vacation," said the psychologist. "Dirty," said the applicant. "Love," said the psychologist. "Dirty," said the applicant. "Excuse me," said the psychologist, "but no matter what I say, you keep replying 'dirty.' Why are you doing that?" "Because," said the applicant, "you keep using dirty words." "Well, then," said the psychologist, "suppose you give me a few words that aren't dirty." "What," said the applicant, "and let you dirty them?"

FACTS

Psychology is a comparatively modern science. In 1960, there were 772 doctorates in psychology conferred in the U.S.; in 1974, there were more than 2,500 doctorates awarded. As with other sciences, general practitioners are being displaced by specialists as the bodies of knowledge which are the foundation of psychology grow larger and more complex. Despite the remarkable advancements that have been made in this century, it has been said that as much remains to discover about the mind as there was for internal medicine to learn about the body in the Middle Ages. Few fields are still as wide open to further discovery.

The American Psychiatric Association, 1400 K St. NW, Washington, D.C. 20005; and the American Psychological Association, 750 1st St. NE, Washington, D.C. 20002-4242, are two professional organizations that have further information on professions in the field of psychology.

PUBLIC OPINION

DEFINITIONS   Attitude or opinion held generally or collectively by the public; popular consensus; the voice of the people; the views of two cab drivers and a bartender as transmuted in the telling.

QUOTATIONS

Public opinion is no more than this. / What people think that other people think. Alfred Austin, *Prince Lucifer,* 1887.

When the people have no other tyrant, their own public opinion becomes one. E.G. Bulwer-Lytton, Ernest Maltravers, 1837.

The constant appeals to public opinion in a democracy, though excellent as a corrective of public vices, induce private hypocrisy, causing men to conceal their own convictions when opposed to those of the mass, the latter being seldom wholly right, or wholly wrong. J. Fenimore Cooper, *The American Democrat,* 1838.

...what we call public opinion is generally public sentiment. Benjamin Disraeli, August 3, 1880.

With public sentiment, nothing can fail; without it, nothing can succeed. Abraham Lincoln, August 21, 1858.

There is no group in America that can withstand the force of an aroused public opinion. President Franklin D. Roosevelt, June 16, 1933.

Public opinion is a weak tyrant compared with our own private opinion. Henry D. Thoreau, *Walden:* "Economy," 1854.

Public opinion is stronger than the legislature, and nearly as strong as the ten commandments. Charles Dudley Warner, *My Summer in a Garden,* 1870.

In proportion as the structure of a government gives force to public opinion, it is essential that public opinion should be enlightened. President George Washington, farewell address, September 1796.

ANONYMOUS APHORISMS

Everybody knows better than anybody.

A great leader molds public opinion; a wise leader listens to it.

What the public thinks depends on what the public hears.

Public opinion is itself a matter of opinion.

The voice of the people sometimes depends on which people you hear.

Public opinion and the weather are equally hard to predict, and equally changeable.

Public opinion is sometimes shown by public silence.

ANECDOTES

A U.S. Congressman was asked how he determined public opinion on pending issues in his district. "On most questions," he replied, "the first thing I have to try to find out is whether there is a public opinion."

A journalist who has traveled all over the world has gotten used to being asked about public opinion in this country on various issues, and he has found what he describes as the absolutely safe and accurate answer, no matter what the subject. When asked to describe public opinion on anything, anyplace, he always says, "It's divided."

FACTS

Public opinion—or, more exactly, the reporting of it—has become a big business, in the United States and around the world. It is a tool of market research, through readership and viewing surveys to determine what the public watches and likes. It is used by every major potential candidate planning an election campaign. Canvassing public opinion aids in uncovering which issues and which points of view interest the targeted constituency. The biggest problem is that while surveys can be quite accurate, the time between the field interviews and the computation of results leaves just long enough for people to change their minds.

Public relations

DEFINITIONS   The business or profession of branding an image of a person or enterprise in the public eye; "the engineering of consent" (Edward L. Bernays); "the hidden persuaders" (Vance Packard); putting your best foot forward; the strategy of dealing with the media and the public; the imagemakers; creating public mindset; hype; propaganda; what "they" want you to believe.

QUOTATIONS

...you have to watch every single word you utter. Every once in a while, you let a word or phrase out and you want to catch it and bring it back. You can't do that. It's gone, gone forever. Vice President Dan Quayle, in *U.S. News & World Report,* May 29, 1989.

All propaganda has to be popular and has to accommodate itself to the comprehension of the least intelligent of those whom it seeks to reach. Adolf Hitler, *Mein Kampf,* 1925.

Be it true or false, what is said about men often has as much influence upon their lives, and especially upon their destinies, as what they do. Victor Hugo, *Les Miserables,* 1862.

Perhaps the most direct way to attain fame is to insist, confidently and consistently, that we already have it. Count Giacomo Leopardi, c. 19th century.

What rage for fame attends both great and small! / Better be damn'd than mentioned not at all. John Wolcot (Peter Pindar), "To the Royal Academicians," c. late 18th century.

ANONYMOUS APHORISMS

The public-relations motto: if you lead a horse to water, even if you can't make him drink, maybe you can make him swim.

A bistro is a saloon with a public-relations person.

Public relations is the art of putting your best foot forward and keeping the boot behind you from kicking you in the pants.

Public relations is sometimes like the practice of medicine: occasionally you can improve a condition, but often your major success is to keep a bad condition from getting worse.

The difference between press agentry and public relations is that a press agent gets your name into the paper, and a public-relations person knows when to get your name out of the paper.

Some public-relations people are suppress agents.

Getting the press to mention you is press agentry; getting them to mention you kindly is public relations.

ANECDOTES

Public relations is like the story of the farmer and his stubborn old mule. The farmer hit the mule over the head with a bat. Why? Because the first thing you have to do is to make sure you have your target's attention. But it doesn't end there. Next the farmer produced a carrot from up his sleeve, led the mule out to plow, and let him enjoy that carrot. Sometimes it takes a carrot to convince your audience to follow your lead.

A New York publicist insisted that his profession was mentioned in the Bible; and that Aaron was the first public-relations person. If you look in the Book of Exodus, Chapter IV, Verse 16, it becomes clear; for the Bible tells us that the Lord said to Moses, that Aaron "shall be thy spokesman unto the people."

PUBLIC SPEAKING

DEFINITIONS Addressing gatherings of people; the art or process of oration or declaration; platform appearance; oratory; standing on a soapbox; grandstanding.

QUOTATIONS

Public speaking is very easy. Senator Dan Quayle of Indiana, October, 1988.

Discretion of speech is more than eloquence. Sir Francis Bacon, *Of Discourse,* 1625.

That which we are capable of feeling, we are capable of saying. Miguel de Cervantes Saavedra, *Novelas Ejemplares, El Amante Liberal,* 1613.

Let your speech be always with grace, seasoned with salt, that ye may know how ye ought to answer every man. *Colossians,* 4:6.

All the great speakers were bad speakers at first. Ralph Waldo Emerson, *The Conduct of Life:* "Power," 1860.

Every man is eloquent once in his life. Ralph Waldo Emerson, *Society and Solitude: Eloquence,* 1870.

A soft tongue may strike hard. Benjamin Franklin, *Poor Richard's Almanac,* 1744.

Amplification is the vice of modern oratory... Speeches measured by the hour die by the hour. Thomas Jefferson, letter to David Harding, April 20, 1824.

True eloquence does not consist in speech. Words and phrases may be marshaled in every way, but they cannot compass it. It must consist in the man, in the subject, and in the occasion. U.S. Representative Daniel Webster of Massachusetts, August 2, 1826.

ANONYMOUS APHORISMS

Public speaking is an audience participation event; if it weren't, it would be private speaking.

A good speech is like a sharpened pencil; it has a point.

Great public speakers listen to the audience with their eyes.

Exhaust neither the topic nor the audience.

No good speech ever came to a bad end.

Do not open the mouth until the brain is in gear.

When a speaker is on too long, his audience may get short with him.

ANECDOTES

The story is told of the way Secretary of State William M. Evarts began a Thanksgiving dinner speech. He said, "You have been giving your attention to a turkey stuffed with sage; you are now about to consider a sage stuffed with turkey."

"Why is it," a famous lecturer was asked, "that the speeches always come after the dinner?" "Because," the esteemed lecturer explained, "it's hard for the speaker to talk when empty stomachs are growling."

A newly elected congressman, nervous about making his first presentation before the House, asked an ancient colleague how he always managed to look so composed when he stepped up to the podium. "I remember the words of my sixth-grade teacher, one of the greatest orators I ever heard. He said, just before you have to speak, go into a room where no one can see you—and make sure your zipper is up."

The story is told of a public speaker whose problem was that he couldn't cope with hecklers. This was discovered one evening in a college town, when his prepared remarks were interrupted, rather mildly, and he said, "Why is it every time I open my mouth, some jackass speaks?"

RA C E

(See also Ethnicity, Minorities, Prejudice)

DEFINITIONS A distinctive group within a biological species, in the case of humankind involving physical characteristics such as color of skin; broadly categorized among humans as Caucasian, African, Asian, Native American, Hispanic, and Aboriginal; differences that are more apparent than real; tribal differentiation.

QUOTATIONS

We must be one, as neighbors, as fellow citizens, not separate camps but family—white, black, Latino, all of us, no matter how different—who share basic American values and are willing to live by them. President Bill Clinton, speech, October 16, 1995.

I think there are many more voices [and diversity in the black community] in 1993 than we had in 1963, and the question is, is there a uniting theme among these voices. I would suggest that the uniting theme focuses around economic justice. In other words, racial justice and racial equality are seen now in the context of achieving...economic power. Benjamin F. Chavis, executive director, NAACP, in *The Washington Post,* August 28, 1993.

The difference of race is one of the reasons why I fear war may always exist; because race implies difference, difference implies superiority, and superiority leads to predominance. Benjamin Disraeli, February 1, 1849.

Every man has pride of race, and under appropriate circumstances when the rights of others, his equals before the law, are not to be affected, it is his privilege to express such pride and to take such action based upon it as to him seems proper.... Our Constitution is color-blind, and neither knows nor tolerates classes among citizens. U.S. Supreme Court Associate Justice John Marshall Harlan, commenting on *Plessy v. Ferguson,* May 18, 1896.

Men are not superior by reason of the accidents of race or color. They are superior who have the best heart—the best brain. Robert G. Ingersoll, lecture on liberty, c. late 19th century.

Men of different ancestries, men of different tongues, men of different colors, men of different environments, men of different geographies do not see everything alike. Even in our own country we do not see everything alike. President Lyndon B. Johnson, February 11, 1964.

We must learn to live together as brothers or perish together as fools. Rev. Dr. Martin Luther King, Jr., March 23, 1964.

After all, there is but one race—humanity. George Moore, *The Bending of the Bough,* 1900.

Morality knows nothing of geographical boundaries or distinctions of race. Herbert Spencer, *Social Statics,* 1850.

I believe in the brotherhood of man, not merely the brotherhood of white men but the brotherhood of all men before the law. Senator Harry S. Truman of Missouri, June 15, 1940.

We conclude that in the field of public education the doctrine of "separate but equal" has no place. Separate educational facilities are inherently unequal. U.S. Supreme Court Chief Justice Earl Warren, commenting on *Brown v. Board of Education of Topeka,* May 17, 1954.

Our nation is moving toward two societies, one black, one white—separate and unequal. Report of National Advisory Commission on Civil Disorders, February, 29, 1968.

ANONYMOUS APHORISMS

Things might be simpler if we were all born polka-dotted.

The stock they come from is some people's stock in trade.

When some people see black, they see red.

The real colors of the United States are red, white, black, yellow and brown.

The surest way to go broke is to put all your money on a single race.

Mankind consists of five races and an infinite number of heats.

We are all brothers and sisters under the skin, but some people only look at the color of the skin.

ANECDOTES

An African-American business man who had tried for years, in vain, to become a member of an exclusive club, died and went to heaven, where he had no trouble gaining entry because of his upright life. As he entered the pearly gates, he commented to St. Peter, "Isn't it strange that I can get into heaven, but I couldn't get into the club I wanted, because they would not accept African-Americans, Asians, or Jews as members?" "We knew that before you came," said St. Peter; "the Boss's son ran into the same thing."

A Korean millionaire went to the optometrist for a pair of glasses and was shown a thick tortoise shell frame. He tried it on, looked doubtful, and said to the optometrist, "You don't think it makes me look too Japanese?"

FACTS

The U.S. Census groups citizens into the following racial classifications: "white; black; American Indian, Eskimo and Aleut; Asian and Pacific islander; and of Hispanic origin." The anthropological races are: australoid, negroid, mongoloid, and caucusoid. However, there is still no recognition given to people of mixed-race origin such as mulattos, mestizos, Creoles, Eurasians, Amerasians, Afrasians, and "half-breeds" anywhere in the world, even though it is a segment of the world population that has grown since the last half of the 20th century. Race is a fact of life; its impact through the years has been the cause of extensive strife, though the differences between people of varied ancestry have historically had more to do with socio-economic disparities and stereotyping than physiological or even cultural differences. In the U.S. the application of the equal rights guaranteed in the constitution has led to policies of granting citizenship to all Americans, segregation, integration, affirmative action and enforced "color-blindness" in education, business, housing, clubs and associations, and every other facet of Americans' lives. Each of these approaches has had its measure of success, but racial tensions and biases are still very real.

Radio

(See also Journalism, Television)

DEFINITIONS The transmission of electric signals through the air that carry sound from a transmitting antenna to receivers tuned to the proper frequency; wireless; boom box; Walkman; where talk is cheap; the chatterbox.

QUOTATIONS

[Radio] is the most intimate and the most powerful medium in broadcasting. Tom Snyder, television talk-show host, in *The Los Angeles Times,* January 1, 1995.

There have been few developments in industrial history to equal the speed and efficiency with which genius and capital have joined to meet radio needs. U.S. Secretary of Commerce Herbert Hoover, c. 1925.

The radio is doing a great job in our country in extending the real spirit of democracy.... The radio has changed and elevated the technique of political campaigns. And what is more important, it has done a great deal to debunk, and to compel political parties to state the facts and stick to the issues. New York Mayor Fiorello H. LaGuardia, November 6, 1936.

Broadcasting gets broader all the time. William S. Paley, chairman, CBS, May 25, 1954.

...we had to learn what our new broadcasting medium was for. Some people thought broadcasting would be for education. Some thought merely that it would replace the phonograph. Some thought it would remake the world, which it hasn't. Some thought it would revolutionize politics, which it has.... But, of course, broadcasting did not limit itself to any one of these. Instead it became almost all the things that were imagined for it. William S. Paley, chairman, CBS, May 25, 1954.

The broadcasting industry has, indeed, a very great opportunity to serve the public, but along with this opportunity goes an important responsibility to see that this means of communication is made to serve the high purposes of a democracy. President Franklin D. Roosevelt, message to the National Association of Broadcasters, February 1938.

ANONYMOUS APHORISMS

Radio is the talk of the town.

The miracle of radio is that you can always tune in on another voice.

Radio made the whole world an echo chamber.

Radio reaches everywhere; it's the world you take with you.

From the crystal set to the transistor, radio has had the last word.

ANECDOTES

Being afraid of a microphone is rare today because it's such a familiar gadget, but mike fright has afflicted some prominent people. Several generations ago, the eminent Republican statesman, Elihu Root, found someone putting a microphone in front of him. "Take that away," Mr. Root demanded. "I can talk to a Democrat but I cannot speak into a dead thing." Perhaps that was how they came to refer to a switched-on microphone as being "live."

Radio preceded television, of course, but a child of the television age, asked to describe radio, said it was "television without pictures."

FACTS

The prominence of television in the nation's attention has a tendency to overshadow public awareness of the dimensions of radio broadcasting. The fact is that, in the U.S., there are more coast-to-coast radio networks than television channels, and about nine times as many radio as television stations. There were over 10,000 American radio stations in 1995—nearly a thousand more than in 1989. There are so many thriving radio stations that they can specialize to a degree unheard of in all but cable television—all-news stations, all-classical music, all-sports, and so forth. In some services, such as up-to-the-minute rush-hour traffic and road-condition reports, radio has developed unique capabilities unmatched by any other media. Radio still has the smallest, most portable receivers; the longest reach in terms of mileage; and the most instantaneous immediacy of any communications medium today. And because it is simpler to transmit voice than video, radio stations have begun to appear on the Internet giving them instant global reach, whereas television will have to wait for the next generation of technology.

For more information about radio, contact the International Radio and Television Society Foundation, 420 Lexington Ave., Suite 1714, New York, NY 10170.

RELIGION

DEFINITIONS   Belief in a system of faith, a divinity or supernatural force; an organized ritual and/or hierarchy of worship and faith; a set of beliefs and tenets; "a daughter of Hope and Fear, explaining to Ignorance the nature of the Unknowable" (Ambrose Bierce); "the opiate of the masses" (Karl Marx); the explanation of the unexplainable; the Church.

QUOTATIONS

We tend to turn the Christian religion into a religion of virtues, but it is a religion of grace. You become a good person because you are loved. You are not loved because you are good. Desmond M. Tutu, South African Anglican Archbishop, in the *The Christian Science Monitor,* October 26, 1994.

There is no greater peace than that which comes from prayer, and no greater fellowship than to join in prayer with others...All of us should not try to fulfill the responsibilities we now have without prayer and a strong faith in God. President George Bush, in *The Los Angeles Times,* February 3, 1989.

We all have the right to wear religion on our sleeves. But we should also hold it in our hearts and live it in our lives. And if we are truly to practice what we preach, then Americans of every faith and viewpoint should come together to promote the common good. President Bill Clinton, in *The New York Times,* September 12, 1992.

The First Amendment has erected a wall between Church and State which must be kept high and impregnable. U.S. Supreme Court Associate Justice Hugo L. Black, commenting on *McCollum v. Board of Education of Champaign County District 71,* March 8, 1948.

In God We Trust. Authorized by Secretary of the Treasury Salmon P. Chase to be imprinted on U.S. currency, 1864.

All religions united with government are more or less inimical to liberty. All separated from government are compatible with liberty. Henry Clay, Speaker of the House, speech in House of Representatives, March 24, 1818.

...the most acceptable service of God is the doing of good to man ... Benjamin Franklin, *Autobiography,* 1784.

Mine eyes have seen the glory of the coming of the Lord; / He is trampling out the vintage where the grapes of wrath are stored; / He hath loosed the fateful lightning of his terrible, swift sword; / His truth is marching on. Julia Ward Howe, "Battle Hymn of the Republic," February 1862.

An honest God is the noblest work of man. Robert G. Ingersoll, *The Gods,* 1872.

...religion is a matter which lies solely between man and his God, that he owes account to none other for his faith or his worship... President Thomas Jefferson, letter to Danbury Baptist Association of Connecticut, January 1, 1802.

To be of no church is dangerous. Religion, of which the rewards are distant and which is animated only by Faith and Hope, will glide by degrees out of the mind unless it be invigorated and reimpressed by external ordinances, by stated calls to worship, and the salutary influence of example. Samuel Johnson, *Life of Milton,* 1799.

I believe in an America where the separation of church and state is absolute....where religious intolerance will someday end—where all men and all churches are treated as equal—where every man has the same right to attend or not attend the church of his choice.... I do not speak for my church on public matters— and the church does not speak for me. Senator John F. Kennedy of Massachusetts, speaking as a presidential candidate in Houston, TX, September 12, 1960.

Every religion is good that teaches man to be good. Thomas Paine, *The Rights of Man,* 1792.

Going to church doesn't make a man a Christian any more than going to a garage makes him an automobile. Billy Sunday, evangelist, c. 1920s.

We have just religion enough to make us hate, but not enough to make us love one another. Jonathan Swift, *Miscellanies,* 1711.

No people can be bound to acknowledge and adore the invisible hand, which conducts the affairs of men, more than the People of the United States. President George Washington, first inaugural address, April 30, 1789.

God requireth not any uniformity of religion to be enacted and enforced in any civil state; which enforced unanimity (sooner or later) is the greatest occasion of civil war, ravishment of conscience, persecution of Jesus Christ in his servants, and of the hypocrisy and destruction of millions of souls. Rev. Roger Williams, The Bloody Tenent of Persecution for the Cause of Conscience, 1644.

...we are bounde by the law of God and men to doe goode unto all men and evil to noe one. The Flushing Remonstrance, addressed by citizens of Flushing, NY to Governor Peter Stuyvesant of New Amsterdam, December 27, 1657.

Congress shall make no law respecting an establishment of religion, or prohibiting the free exercise thereof... Constitution of the United States, First Amendment, adopted December 15, 1791.

ANONYMOUS APHORISMS

A man's faith, more than his house, is his castle.

I'd rather deal with a God-loving person than with a God-fearing one.

Religion's greatest miracle is the survival of faith.

Religion is a combination of the hereafter and the heretofore.

Belief in God is part of religion; acting like God's children is the rest.

There are no atheists in foxholes.

Faith is stronger than steel.

ANECDOTES

President John F. Kennedy once remarked that he had asked the U.S. Supreme Court Chief Justice whether a proposed new education bill was constitutional, and the Chief Justice had told him, with no further amplification, that "It was clearly constitutional—it hasn't got a prayer."

Then there's the story of the devoted worker in the congregation who couldn't believe she was in heaven because they didn't have a Las Vegas Night.

A group of congregants were asked by their pastor whether they prayed regularly to God, and if so, what did they always pray would be granted. One said he prayed for health, another for happiness, another for salvation in the world to come. But one congregant kept shaking his head. And when it came his turn, he said, "It's very simple. I believe in God and what I pray for is that He believe in me."

FACTS

In the mid-1990s, the U.S. had more than 250,000 religious congregations, with a membership of over 130 million, plus innumerable smaller religious groups for a total of over 288 million North American congregants. The most substantial recent increases in church membership have taken place outside of the mainstream, in evangelical and nondenominational churches (many of which trace their origins back only a few decades); but in truth, this is nothing new. Christianity was a radical concept when it began, as was virtually every religious body that has branched off from it; and the same can be said for the other major religions of the world. In terms of worldwide followers, the most populist belief systems are: Christian (1.9 billion), Muslim (1 billion), Hindu (764 million), Buddhists (338 million), Chinese Folk Religions (149 million), and new religions (128 million).

The annual *Yearbook of American and Canadian Churches* contains much information about the numerical position and trends in the religions of America. The *World Almanac* lists the leading denominations and their headquarters.

S C H O O L

(See also College, Education)

DEFINITIONS   An educational institution, particularly below college level; a place where subjects are taught to students; class warfare; the learning experience; the world of the classroom; life's dress rehearsal; the blackboard jungle.

QUOTATIONS

I believe that the school is primarily a social institution. Education being a social process, the school is simply that form of community life in which all those agencies are concentrated that will be most effective in bringing the child to share in the inherited resources of the race, and to use his own powers for social ends. John Dewey, article in *School Journal,* January 16, 1897.

The public school is in most respects the cradle of our democracy. U.S. Supreme Court Associate Justice William O. Douglas, commenting on *Adler v. Board of Education,* 1952.

You send your child to the schoolmaster, but 'tis the schoolboys who educate him. Ralph Waldo Emerson, *The Conduct of Life:* "Culture," 1860.

No greater nor more affectionate honor can be conferred on an American than to have a public school named after him. Herbert Hoover, June 5, 1966.

Tomorrow's school will be the center of community life, for the grownups as well as the children: "a shopping center of human services."...It will employ its buildings round the clock and its teachers round the year. We just cannot afford to have an $85 billion plant in this country open, less than 30 percent of the time. President Lyndon B. Johnson, February 16, 1966.

...the common school, improved and energized as it can easily be, may become the most effective and benignant of all the forces of civilization. Horace Mann, 1848.

A teacher works in a sensitive area in a schoolroom. There he shapes the attitude of young minds towards the society in which they live. In this, the state has a vital concern. It must preserve the integrity of the schools. U.S. Supreme Court Associate Justice Sherman Minton, commenting on *Adler v. Board of Education,* 1952.

In the first place God made idiots. This was for practice. Then he made school boards. Mark Twain, *Following the Equator,* 1897.

ANONYMOUS APHORISMS

For too many of today's school population, there aren't three Rs, there are six— remedial 'ritin', remedial readin' and remedial 'rithmetic.

Too many people stop caring about the schools when their own kids are grown.

The first thing to learn in school is how to learn.

Too many schoolteachers these days seem to be setting a striking example.

Some kids learn more about life going to and from school than in the schoolroom.

ANECDOTES

At Open School Day, the teacher told Johnny's parents that he didn't take part in classroom discussion, so when they got home they instructed Johnny to mend his ways. The next day when he came back from school his mother asked him, "Johnny, did you raise your hand today?" "Yes," said Johnny. "And what did you talk about?" his mother asked. "Nothing," said Johnny; "By the time I got back to the room it was time for recess."

Children in school are not exactly putty in the hands of their teachers. Sometimes they can teach precision to their elders. For example, a teacher once instructed her students to write a composition on the subject of "My Ideal Room." One youngster turned in a one-sentence paper and received a zero mark. Her father promptly came to school to find out why, and when the teacher showed him the composition he pointed out that instead of a zero it deserved 100 percent, because it was a fair response to the teacher's topic. The student had carefully entitled her composition "My Ideal Room," and then had written, "I like my room just as it is."

They call the custodian of this particular school Daniel, because he's always reading the writing on the walls.

FACTS

Public education in America has roots that date back far earlier than the formation of the United States. The first public school on American soil, Boston Latin School, opened its doors in 1635. Throughout its history the U.S. public school system has rarely made headlines, except as the backdrop for landmark U.S. Supreme Court cases such as *Brown vs. Board of Education of Topeka,* and sensitive issues such as school prayer and sex education. But at the same time, public schools have quietly provided quality education to hundreds of millions of Americans. In 1994, nearly 47 million children and adolescents were enrolled in public nursery, primary, and secondary schools; while an additional 7.3 million attended private schools. And if college entrance examination scores are any indication, the naysayers who claim that the quality of education in American schools is in decline haven't been doing their homework. The real trouble is that to keep up with the advances which are taking place in every field of study—for students and teachers alike, there's a lot more to learn than there was a few decades ago.

The National Education Association, sometimes described as the largest professional association in the world, is headquartered at 1201 16th Street NW, Washington, D.C. 20036.

SCIENCE

DEFINITIONS   Study or knowledge of laws and products of nature; particularly and collectively, physics, chemistry, biology, astronomy, geology and related subjects; subjects based on the workings of natural laws of action, reaction, persistence of matter etc.; "organized knowledge" (Herbert Spencer); "nothing but developed perception, interpreted intent, common sense rounded out and minutely articulated" (George Santayana); "the knowledge of consequences and dependence of one fact upon another" (Thomas Hobbes); "the slaying of a beautiful hypothesis by an ugly fact" (Thomas H. Huxley).

QUOTATIONS

In science, as in everything else, people should treat every pronouncement as fallible in the first place, and tentative in the second place. Alex Michalos, in *The Los Angeles Times,* April 24, 1993.

It is far more important for us economically to be exploring the innermost corners of matter than to be visiting the far reaches of space. U.S. Representative Vic Fazio, speech before the House of Representatives, June, 1993.

Science is the great antidote to the poison of enthusiasm and superstition. Adam Smith, *The Wealth of Nations,* 1776.

Math and science are unlike almost any other subject in that they must build one on the other. You can read Madame Bovary without having to read Shakespeare. But you can't do algebra without first knowing how to multiply and divide...Either the whole system works, or the whole system fails. Fred Easter, executive director, California MESA program, in *The Los Angeles Times,* October 10, 1990.

Science and math are the substance of this age, just as exploration and warfare were the substance of other ages. Science is the way to prepare Americans for the 21st century. William Baker, former chairman of AT&T Bell Telephone Laboratories, in *Time,* September 11, 1989.

Science is my passion, my politics, my duty. Attributed to Thomas Jefferson, c. 18th century.

Science has not yet mastered prophecy. We predict too much for the next year and yet far too little for the next ten. Neil A. Armstrong, astronaut, address to a joint session of the U.S. Congress, September 16, 1969.

When you look back in history you'll see that new technologies build new civilizations. Technology determines the quality and quantity of the human economy. The medieval age gave way to the modern age because of the art of navigation, the invention of gun powder and Gutenberg's art of printing. Now the modern age has come to a close because of nuclear power and electronics. Shintaro Ishihara, Japanese politician, in *Time,* October 20, 1989.

Nine-tenths of modern science is in this respect the same: It is the product of men whom their contemporaries thought dreamers—who were laughed at for caring for what did not concern them—who, as the proverb went, "walked into a well from looking at the stars"—who were believed to be useless, if anyone could be such. Walter Bagehot, *The English Constitution,* 1867.

Men love to wonder, and that is the seed of our science. Ralph Waldo Emerson, *Society and Solitude:* "Works and Days," 1870.

Today, our enormous investment in science and research is our evidence of our faith that science can not only make man richer—but science can make man better. President Lyndon B. Johnson, February 6, 1967.

Let both sides seek to invoke the wonders of science instead of its terrors. Together let us explore the stars, conquer the deserts, eradicate disease, tap the ocean depths... President John F. Kennedy, inaugural address, January, 20, 1961.

...man is still the most extraordinary computer of all. President John F. Kennedy, May 21, 1963.

The language of science is universal, and perhaps scientists have been the most international of all professions in their outlook. President John F. Kennedy, October 22, 1963.

The simplest schoolboy is now aware of truths for which Archimedes would have given his life. Ernest Renan, *Souvenirs d'Enfance et de Jeunesse,* 1883.

Our science and industry owe their strength to the spirit of free inquiry and the spirit of free enterprise that characterize our country. President Harry S. Truman, letter to Senator Brien McMahon, February 1, 1946.

The Congress shall have Power...to promote the Progress of Science and useful Arts, by securing for limited Times to Authors and Inventors the exclusive Right to their respective Writings and Discoveries .... Constitution of the United States, Article 1, Section 8, March 4, 1789.

ANONYMOUS APHORISMS

Science is the ascertainment of facts and the refusal to regard facts as permanent.

To err is human; to try to prevent recurrence of error is science.

Every science thinks it is the science.

Yesterday's dreams are today's science.

Great science is an art.

Science is forever rewriting itself.

The banker asks, "How much?" The scientist asks, "How come?"

ANECDOTES

A science professor attended a party with a group of university colleagues from the drama department. During an impromptu entertainment one comic dropped his pants; everybody laughed uproariously except the science professor. "Why weren't you laughing?" he was asked. "Because," he said, "it reminded me that my next lecture was on the law of gravity."

"One of the great quests of science," the teacher said to her class, "has been to design a perpetual motion machine. What do you think has been the biggest problem?" "Easy," replied one student; "getting it to stop."

Three scientists were in a travel group that visited the Grand Canyon. The geologist mused, "I wonder how old it is." The mathematician pondered, "I wonder how many inches it erodes each year." The meteorologist asked, "How hot is it down there?"

"For every action," said the science teacher to the class, "there is a reaction. For example, what happens when you step into a bathtub?" "The telephone rings," replied a student.

FACTS

Science—which in the broadest sense is the accumulation of knowledge—has been growing at an ever increasing rate throughout history. That is because every gain in scientific knowledge or in the sophistication of scientific techniques and equipment opens up new areas for study. According to the U.S. Census Bureau, in 1992 there were 1.7 million people employed as engineers, 531,000 natural scientists, and 1 million mathematical and computer scientists. Mathematical and computer sciences reflected the largest employment increase among the sciences—more than tripling between 1989 and 1992. The annual report on Research and Development in Industry by the U.S. National Science Foundation estimated that, in 1994, more than 172 billion dollars went toward research and development in all industries, up from 13.5 billion in 1960. In between those years, of course, we saw the "science explosion" produced by man's success in space exploration, the step-up in the search for more efficient ways to use our finite natural resources, and developments in medicine.

S E A S O N S

DEFINITIONS   The four divisions of the year, based on the changing positions of regions of the earth in relation to the sun; four distinctively different climate transitions which occur at regular intervals throughout a calendar year; particular periods of the year distinguished by special characteristics, as the football season; summer, autumn, winter and spring.

QUOTATIONS

The melancholy days are come, the saddest of the year / Of wailing winds, and naked wood, and meadows brown and sere. William Cullen Bryant, "The Death of the Flowers," 1825.

To every thing there is a season, and a time to every purpose under the heaven… *Ecclesiastes,* 3.1.

Hot midsummer's petted crone, / Sweet to me thy drowsy tone / Tells of countless sunny hours, / Long days, and solid banks of flowers… Ralph Waldo Emerson, "The Humblebee," 1839.

Oh, the long and dreary Winter! / Oh, the cold and cruel Winter! Henry Wadsworth Longfellow, "The Song of Hiawatha," 1855.

Came the Spring with all its splendor, / All its birds and all its blossoms, / All its flowers and leaves and grasses. Henry Wadsworth Longfellow, "The Song of Hiawatha," 1855.

What is so rare as a day in June? James Russell Lowell, *The Vision of Sir Launfal,* 1848.

No price is set on the lavish summer; / June may be had by the poorest comer. James Russell Lowell, *The Vision of Sir Launfal,* 1848.

When the frost is on the punkin…. James Whitcomb Riley, "When the Frost Is on the Punkin," 1883.

In the Spring a young man's fancy lightly turns to thoughts of love. Alfred Tennyson, "Locksley Hall," 1842.

We remember autumn to best advantage in the spring; the finest aroma of it reaches us then. Henry D. Thoreau, *Journal,* May 10, 1852.

ANONYMOUS APHORISMS

Summer heals winter's scars and winter cools summer's passions.

Spring is what separates the snow from the heat waves.

Spring hopes eternal.

Every summer is headed for a fall.

If there were no natural seasons, people would invent them.

In some parts of the world, there are two seasons—rainy and rainier, in others, dry and drier.

Nature saves her biggest shocks for solstice and for equinox.

There are five seasons—winter, spring, summer, fall and slack.

Spring ahead, fall behind. (A reference to the seasonal time change.)

ANECDOTES

A South American was explaining to a New Yorker that when it is summer in New York, it is winter in Brazil. "I prefer," said the New Yorker, "to think that one of us has cold summers and warm winters, so that it's the same season at the same time with just a few changes." "Fine," said the South American. "Have a good winter this July."

FACTS

Man is a creature of the seasons—in his leisure habits, in his clothing, his shelter, his occupations. The farmer's year is governed by the season, because the products of nature are governed by the seasons. Even in an age where we build domed, heated, air-conditioned structures to defy normal seasonal climate, there is a seasonal cycle. We follow it with the school year, or the crop cycle. But if nature has created the climate and the natural conditions that identify each season, man has provided artificial characteristics. Christmas in the Northern hemisphere is a winter holiday, Easter a spring one. Thanksgiving is an autumn highlight in the U.S. January is the time of department store white sales, September or thereabouts the time for the new model cars—and so forth. For every single thing, there is a season.

S E X

(See also Love, Marriage)

DEFINITIONS   The physical qualities which differentiate between male and female; the act of coition by male and female; gender; the method of reproduction of species; where surrender is often victory.

QUOTATIONS

The Creeks Had a Word for It. Zoe Akins, title of a play, 1929.

The threat of AIDS should be sufficient to permit a sex-education curriculum. U.S. Surgeon General C. Everett Koop, speech, October, 1986.

Sex and obscenity are not synonymous. U.S. Supreme Court Associate Justice William J. Brennan, Jr., commenting on *Roth v. U.S.,* June 24, 1957.

Sex, a great and mysterious motive force in human life, has indisputably been a subject of absorbing interest to mankind through the ages. U.S. Supreme Court Associate Justice William J. Brennan, Jr., commenting on *Roth v. U.S.,* June 24, 1957.

Men and women do not always love in accordance with the prayer… Sinclair Lewis, acceptance speech for the Nobel Prize for Literature, Stockholm, Sweden, December 10, 1930.

... is there any greater or keener pleasure than physical love? No, nor any which is more unreasonable. Plato, *The Republic,* c. 6th century BC.

Give me chastity and continence, but not just now. Saint Augustine, *Confessions,* c. 5th century.

Is it not strange that desire should so many years outlive performance? William Shakespeare, *Henry IV: Part II,* 1598.

Whatever may befall me, I trust that I may never lose my respect for purity in others.... Can I walk with one who by his jests and by his habitual tone reduces the life of men and women to a level with that of cats and dogs? Henry D. Thoreau, *Journal,* April 12, 1852.

Is Sex Necessary? James Thurber and E.B. White, book title, 1929.

ANONYMOUS APHORISMS

The battle of the sexes has more surrenders than casualties, and a great many hand-to-hand encounters.

The difference between men and women doesn't come between them; it's what brings them together.

A sexpot is sometimes self-heating.

It isn't important that we be able to tell the boys from the girls. It's important that they be able to tell.

Only in the so-called civilized world is sex an over-the-counter—or under-the-counter—commodity.

ANECDOTES

The dignified doctor was caught in lovers' lane with his pretty nurse and tried to explain it away to the police by telling them he was conducting an exploratory operation.

The little boy looked very upset as he came in to talk to his parents. "What's the matter?" they asked him. "Tommy Jones just told me how I got here, and I can't believe it. It sounds terrible." "Oh no," cried his mother. "It isn't terrible at all. I guess I should tell you about it." "I don't want to hear any more about it," said the little boy. "Everybody else came here in a car; why did I come in a baby carriage?"

Q: Why isn't there more sex in nudist camps? A: Because a near miss is apt to have no mystery.

Myron Cohen's most famous story is probably about the suspicious husband who came home sure that his wife was entertaining a lover, threw open the closet door, and found a little man cowering there. What the little man said is as good an explanation of sexual dalliance as any. "Everybody," said the little man, "got to be someplace."

FACTS

Probably every generation since the dawn of time has contemplated the sexual mores of its offspring and decided that the world was going to pot. Attitudes toward the relations between the sexes, and toward what used to be regarded as obscenities and perversions, have changed; but unless all the lessons of history are to go for naught, it is part of an inevitable cycle that goes from permissiveness to Puritanism to prurience and back. In some areas of subject matter, however, the march of events has not been cyclical. Sex education—once regarded as the work of the devil—is now an acceptable concept, even though the degree of explicitness and the age at which such education should be begun are still subjects of considerable argument. Planned families, methods of birth control—some not involving religious problems—and even marital blood tests all reflect a modern expansion of the permissible and socially acceptable contemporary approaches to the subject of sex. At the same time, attitudes toward sex are among the great controversies in various religions and between differing sects. Nothing has had greater impact on contemporary views of sex and sex education than the AIDS epidemic. In the past, sexually-transmitted diseases (STDs) meant embarrassment, and a visit to the doctor. Herpes—a common STD—was feared because there was no cure; but in the case of AIDS, a single irresponsible sexual act suddenly carried a potential death sentence for heterosexuals and homosexuals alike.

S O C I E T Y

(See also Civilization)

DEFINITIONS The community as a whole; the upper caste or exclusive portion of the population; everybody else; the club to which everybody who is somebody belongs; the 400.

QUOTATIONS

There never has yet existed a wealthy and civilized society in which one portion of the community did not, in point of fact, live on the labor of the other. Senator John C. Calhoun of South Carolina, speech in the U.S. Senate defending slavery, 1837

All men plume themselves on the improvement of society, and no man improves. Society never advances. It recedes as fast on one side as it gains on the other. It undergoes continued changes; it is barbarous, it is civilized, it is christianized, it is rich, it is scientific; but this change is not amelioration. For every thing that is given something is taken. Society acquires new arts and loses old instincts. Ralph Waldo Emerson, *Essays, First Series:* "Self-Reliance," 1841.

It is not from top to bottom that societies die; it is from bottom to top. Henry George, *Progress and Poverty,* 1879.

The original of all great and lasting societies consisted not in the mutual good will men had towards each other, but in the mutual fear they had of each other. Thomas Hobbes, *Philosophical Rudiments Concerning Government and Society,* 1650.

[The great society] is a place where men are more concerned with the quality of their goals than the quantity of their goods. President Lyndon B. Johnson, May 22, 1964.

In civilized society we all depend upon each other, and our happiness is very much owing to the good opinion of mankind. Samuel Johnson, according to James Boswell in the *Life of Samuel Johnson,* 1763.

Man is a social animal. Seneca, *On Benefits,* c. 55 AD.

To get into the best society nowadays, one has either to feed people, amuse people, or shock people. Oscar Wilde, *A Woman of No Importance,* 1893.

The society of excess profits for some and small returns for others, the society in which a few prey upon the many, the society in which a few took great advantage and many took great disadvantage, must pass. Wendell L. Willkie, presidential candidate, October 18, 1940.

High society is for those who have stopped working and no longer have anything important to do. President Woodrow Wilson, February 24, 1915.

ANONYMOUS APHORISMS

High society sometimes favors low dives.

The great society found it still needed dues-paying members.

When people talk about what society needs, they are apt to be talking about what they need; but when they talk about what society should do, they are talking about other people.

Society always seems to thrive by keeping somebody out.

Society is based on the fact that misery loves company.

Society is what some people yearn to break into and others yearn to get away from.

Society is composed of the classes, the masses, the full cups, and the demitasses.

ANECDOTES

Mr. Brown was very impressed with his new neighbors when he heard from Mrs. Jones that Mr. Jones moved in society circles—till he found out that Mr. Jones was a moving man.

The college graduating class was being addressed by a commencement speaker whose theme was their debt to society. Finally, one graduate's father could stand it no longer; he muttered to the new graduate's mother, "Maybe these others have a debt to society, but I paid for his tuition in cash."

A lawyer was pleading for her slum-born client, who was on trial for a mugging. "You should not blame him," proclaimed the attorney, "because he is, after all, simply a product of his society." When the prosecutor's turn came to address the jury, she declared, "My worthy opponent has described the defendant as the product of society. It might have been more accurate to describe him as the byproduct."

FACTS

One of the notable characteristics of American society is not that it is classless, though it often likes to think of itself as such, but that it is open to upward class mobility. Unlike some older European societies—particularly where the heritage of an established nobility and a landed aristocracy persists—America has lived the Horatio Alger rags-to-riches story time and again: Men of the humblest origins have become society's stars and family position conversely has been no guarantee of success.

SOUTH

DEFINITIONS   That portion of the United states below the Mason-Dixon line; the states which formed the Confederate States of America during the Civil War; the grits, chitlins, and cotton country; the solid South; "way down upon the Swanee River" (Stephen Foster); Dixie; the plantation belt; the Bible belt.

QUOTATIONS

The whole country is South. It's down South. up South, over South and out South. Joseph E. Lowery, president, Southern Christian Leadership Conference, in the *The New York Times,* November 10, 1992.

"Carry Me Back to Old Virginny." James A. Bland, song title, 1875.

The North excels in business, but the South leads in romance. Irvin S. Cobb, speech in New York, NY, January 6, 1917.

The North has put her heroes on a pension, but the South has put hers on a pedestal. Irvin S. Cobb, speech in New York, NY, January 6, 1917.

Then I wish I was in Dixie! Hooray! Hooray! / In Dixie's land we'll take our stand, / To live and die in Dixie! / Away, away, away down South in Dixie. Daniel Decatur Emmett, "Dixie," 1859.

The sun shines bright on my old Kentucky home. Stephen C. Foster, song lyrics "My Old Kentucky Home," 1853.

There is a New South, not through protest against the old, but because of new conditions, new adjustments and, if you please, new ideas and aspirations. Henry W. Grady, December 22, 1886.

ANONYMOUS APHORISMS

Very few people speak of Northern charm, or Northern hospitality—or Northern fried chicken.

The girls in the South are pretty because the weather gives them more time to bloom.

From corn pone to Cape Kennedy in one generation.

The South shall rise again.

Go North for your living; go South for your health.

The people in the South are warmer.

Y'all come back now, y'hear?

ANECDOTES

When Jimmy Carter of Georgia was elected President, a common comment in the South was that he was the first President in more than a hundred years who "spoke English without an accent."

The story is told of a student in the South who was asked to describe the Atlantic Ocean and said it was a large body of water extending from Virginia to Florida.

A New York forger, who heard Southerners were rather dimwitted, figured he couldn't be arrested if he printed a batch of eighteen dollar bills and headed south. When he arrived, he asked for change of one in the first store he came to. Without looking up, the shopkeeper replied, "Would you like that in threes or sixes?"

FACTS

The "New South" that Henry W. Grady talked about in 1886, has grown a lot newer since those days. Today it is a section where agriculture and manufacturing share with tourism the credit for a great economic step forward. Tobacco and cotton, while still great staples, are no longer the only bellwether crops. Peanuts, peaches, pecans, as well as Florida's orange and grapefruit groves, vegetable farms and livestock, are part of the Southern agricultural landscape. Textiles and other manufactures which use the South's relatively plentiful hydroelectric power, and timber and mineral resources make Southern views of the future blossom with enthusiasm.

S PACE

(See also Exploration)

DEFINITIONS   The universe beyond earth; out of this world; physical infinity; where there is always room for exploration; "the final frontier" (Gene Rodenberry).

QUOTATIONS

The belief that space is the next frontier and that America will follow its manifest destiny and lead mankind into space is over. We are still the leader because it just so happens our competitors are in worse shape than we are... No space-faring country seems able to do what it takes to keep people in space in a value-enhancing way. Laurel L. Wilkening, provost, University of Washington, in *The Los Angeles Times,* April 15, 1993.

The cold war is over, and NASA cannot survive as a relic of bygone days. I personally am tired of Apollo [spacecraft] stories... It's time we started writing history and not reading it. Daniel S. Goldin, administrator, NASA, speech before the American Astronautical Society, March 10, 1993.

If there is a key to eternity, it's probably in space. Jean-Loup Cretien, French astronaut, in the *The Christian Science Monitor,* September 23, 1992.

The Universe is but one vast Symbol of God. Thomas Carlyle, *Sartor Resartus,* 1834.

Think of our world as it looks from that rocket that's heading toward Mars. It is like a child's globe, hanging in space, the continents stuck to its side like colored maps. We are all fellow passengers on a dot of earth. President Lyndon B. Johnson, inaugural address, January 20, 1965.

Space is the stature of God. Joseph Joubert, *Pensees,* 1842.

[The universe] is an infinite sphere whose center is everywhere and boundary nowhere. Blaise Pascal, *Pensees,* 1670.

From a wild weird clime that lieth, sublime, / Out of Space—out of Time. Edgar Allan Poe, "Dreamland," 1845.

The poet's eye, in a fine frenzy rolling, / Doth glance from heaven to earth, from earth to heaven; / And as imagination bodies forth / The forms of things unknown, the poet's pen / Turns them to shapes, and gives to airy nothing / A local habitation and a name. William Shakespeare, *A Midsummer Night's Dream,* 1596.

It is easier to suppose that the universe has existed from all eternity than to conceive a Being beyond its limits capable of creating it. Percy Bysshe Shelley, notes from *Queen Mab,* 1813.

ANONYMOUS APHORISMS

Space exploration is a weighty problem without any gravity.

We're back where Alexander the Great was thousands of years ago, looking for new worlds to conquer.

The further out in space we go, the more space we find to go in.

They don't sing about racing for the moon any more, because that boat has landed.

The bigger our discoveries about space, the smaller we become.

There may be other creatures in space, but we see no air apparent.

ANECDOTES

Q: Did you hear about the crooked astronaut? A: He ran a rocket racket.

Apollo 8 astronauts Anders, Borman and Lovell, broadcasting from outer space back to the earth, provided a commentary that truly seemed amazing. They simply read the words of the Book of Genesis, and they were incredibly accurate as captions for pictures:"…and the earth was without form, and void; and darkness was upon the face of the deep….And God said, Let there be light and there was light…."

FACTS

On April 12, 1961, cosmonaut Yuri Gagarin won the race to space for the Soviet Union, becoming the first person to orbit the earth in outer space; less than a month later, Alan Shepard became the first American to travel into space. The two countries' space programs would continue to alternately compete and cooperate for two decades, but the American invention of the space shuttle tipped the balance toward the U.S., as the Soviet economy began to crumble after they developed the *Salyut* and *Soyuz* space stations. As of 1994, 322 people—including 204 Americans—had traveled into space. Though we have yet to attempt a trip to another planet, unmanned probes such as *Viking, Voyager,* and *Magellan,* and the Hubble Space Telescope, have opened up outer space to scientific study as never before,

The National Aeronautics and Space Administration is headquartered at 300 E Street SW, Washington, D.C., 20546.

PORTS

(See also the various individual sports)

DEFINITIONS   The organized and often competitive exercise of physical skills; athletics; America's weekend madness; a lot of hit and run.

QUOTATIONS

Sports mirror society. In our achievement-oriented society there is an urge to be number one. And competitive sports mirror this, including the violence that can result from that urge. Until society resolves its underlying problems... There is trickle-down in sports. The highest level in sports sets the example for all the other levels. When former heavyweight fighter Mike Tyson talks about driving a guy's nose into his brain, that type of mentality is sure to trickle down to the next level. It happens in all sports. Fighting is now commonplace in baseball, and it wasn't 20 years ago. The epitome of violence today is hockey... The irony is that sports were introduced in the late 1800s to help juvenile delinquents because they had been alienated by the industrial revolution... Now it seems sports pushes [sic] some young people toward violence." Albert Applin, vice chancellor, United States Sports Academy, in the *The Christian Science Monitor,* January 6, 1994.

Exercise ferments the humors, casts them into their proper channels, throws off redundancies, and helps nature in those secret distributions, without which the body cannot subsist in its vigor, nor the soul act with cheerfulness. Joseph Addison, *The Spectator,* July 12, 1711.

Sport is 90 percent mental and the other half is physical. Attributed to Yogi Berra, c. mid-20th century.

The wise, for cure, on exercise depend; / God never made his work for man to mend. John Dryden, "Epistle to John Driden of Chesterton," c. 17th century.

Winning isn't everything. It's the only thing. Attributed to Vincent Lombardi, football coach, Green Bay Packers, c. 1960s.

I wish to preach, not the doctrine of ignoble ease, but the doctrine of the strenuous life. Vice President Theodore Roosevelt, April 10, 1899.

...I do not in the least object to a sport because it is rough. President Theodore Roosevelt, February 23, 1907.

The battle of Waterloo was won on the playing fields of Eton. Attributed to Arthur Wellesley, Duke of Wellington, c. early 19th century.

ANONYMOUS APHORISMS

You don't have to be athletic to have a case of athlete's foot.

Isn't it strange that a man can spend all week racing for his commuter train, walk up and down the station stairs and yearn for the weekend when he can get some exercise?

Athletics is America's favorite exercise—to sit and watch.

They keep saying that what really matters is not whether you win or lose, but how you played the game. The trouble is that the best way to determine how you played the game is by whether you won or lost.

Amateur athletics is part training, part physical ability, part will to win, and part time.

The difference between amateur and professional athletics is what exercises a lot of people.

Running for your college team is athletics; running for a train is exercise; running for office is work

ANECDOTES

The team had lost seventeen games in a row, so they tried both alternatives; first they tried to find some new players and when that failed, they fired the coach.

After examining the postures of all the customers in the health club, the visiting professor reached his diagnosis: "Americans are prone to exercise."

FACTS

Never in history have more people participated in athletics than now; and never have as many types of athletics been popular. Each new edition of the Olympic games includes more events, and this athletic explosion has been heightened by the great surge of women's participation in sports. Since 1963, the number of sporting goods stores and bicycle shops in the U.S. has doubled. The development of year-round, climate-proof facilities helped encourage booms in such sports as tennis; basketball proved to be a sport for which room could be found in the most crowded quarters; indoor pools proliferated and made participation in swimming and diving more easily available. The number of golf courses in the U.S. has doubled since 1950 and the number of golfers more than tripled.

Information: Amateur Athletic Union, 3400 West 86th Street, Indianapolis, IN 46268; or American Alliance for Health, Physical Education and Recreation, 1201 16th Street NW, Washington, D.C. 20036.

TAXES

DEFINITIONS Fees or levies imposed by government on property or income or transactions; duties, tariffs, or assessments; "what we pay for civilized society" (Justice Oliver Wendell Holmes, Jr.); the eternal revenue service.

QUOTATIONS

[Republicans] talk about tax-and-spend Democrats. [But] the nature of government is taxing and spending. What is at issue is what it's spent on. William J. Althaus, Mayor of York, PA, in *The Washington Post*, May 26, 1993.

I am in favor of an income tax. When I find a man who is not willing to bear his share of the burdens of the government which protects him, I find a man who is unworthy to enjoy the blessings of a government like ours. William Jennings Bryan, July 8, 1896.

The present tax structure is a disgrace to this country. It's just a welfare program for the rich. Jimmy Carter, presidential candidate, debate with. President Gerald R. Ford, September 23, 1976,

...in this world nothing is certain but death and taxes. Benjamin Franklin, letter to Jean-Baptiste Leroy, November 13, 1789.

...as certain as death and taxes. Daniel Defoe, *Political History of the Devil,* 1726.

The wisdom of man never yet contrived a system of taxation that would operate with perfect equality. President Andrew Jackson, Proclamation to the People of South Carolina, December 10, 1832.

Taxation is, in fact, the most difficult function of government—and that against which their citizens are most apt to be refractory. Thomas Jefferson, letter to bookdealer Joseph Milligan, April 6, 1816.

The power to tax is the power to live, at least as far as local government is concerned. New York Mayor John V. Lindsay, April 26, 1971.

...the power to tax involves the power to destroy... U.S. Supreme Court Chief Justice John Marshall, commenting on *McCulloch v. Maryland,* March 6, 1819.

Nothing brings home to a man the feeling that he personally has an interest in seeing that Government revenues are not squandered, but intelligently expended, as the fact that he contributes individually a direct tax, no matter how small, to his Government. Secretary of the Treasury Andrew Mellon, *Annual Report,* 1925.

In constitutional states liberty is compensation for heavy taxes; in dictatorships the substitute for liberty is light taxes. Charles de Montesquieu, *The Spirit of the Laws,* 1748.

We shall never make taxation popular, but we can make taxation fair. President Richard M. Nixon, message to the U.S. Congress, April 21, 1969.

Taxation without representation is tyranny. Attributed years later to James Otis, February 1761.

Taxes, after all, are the dues that we pay for the privilege of membership in an organized society. President Franklin D. Roosevelt, October 21, 1936.

ANONYMOUS APHORISMS

Government is an endless pursuit of creative taxation.

Internal Revenue Service even taxes your patience.

Carpet tacks—the only tax that doesn't keep going up.

Taxes are the price we pay for a government that guarantees us the freedom to earn just enough money to pay our taxes.

I don't know why they couple death and taxes. Death only comes once.

They used to say that the only thing the government didn't tax was taxes. Then they invented the surtax.

ANECDOTES

Oscar Wilde is said to have protested about the taxes on his house. When told that it was taxed because, by living there, he used the protection and services of the government, which operated even while he slept, Wilde is supposed to have answered, "But I sleep so badly."

"What bracket are you in?" Mrs. Gotrocks asked Mr. Loaded. "I'm not in a bracket," he replied, "I'm in a pincer."

The history teacher asked the class, "What caused the American Revolution?" Immediately a little girl raised her hand and said, "Taxation." A little boy raised his hand at that and the teacher said, "Tommy, do you have anything to add?" "Yes," said Tommy, "why do they teach that we won?"

FACTS

Our modern American system of income taxation began in 1862, when taxes were imposed to defray the costs of the Civil War. Like the modern tax structure, it was progressive; but it began at 3 percent. We all know that government has grown more expensive, not only because the cost of goods and services has risen, but also because government is doing so many more things than it used to, from space exploration to relief and welfare, to attempting to grapple with soaring national debt. According to the Internal Revenue Service, the tax per individual taxpayer was $4,878 in 1994, with 204 million returns filed. Tax Freedom Day, the day on which taxpayers have earned enough to cover their federal, state, and local taxes for the year usually comes in early May. In 1995, Tax Freedom Day was May 6; though if timeless campaign promises come true, that day will fall earlier and earlier each year.

TEENAGERS

(See also Adolescence, Youth)

DEFINITIONS   People in their teens, that is age 13 through 19; the age when you feel complimented to be told you look older.

QUOTATIONS

We can no longer be surprised by the outcomes experienced by young people who grow up in environments where violence and teenage pregnancies are more prevalent than high-school diplomas and good jobs. Douglas Nelson, executive director, Annie E. Casey Foundation, in the *The Christian Science Monitor,* April 25, 1994.

…your budding Miss is very charming, / But shy and awkward at first coming out, / So much alarmed, that she is quite alarming, / All Giggle, Blush; half Pertness and half Pout. George Gordon, Lord Byron, *Beppo,* 1818.

The imagination of a boy is healthy, and the mature imagination of a man is healthy; but there is a space of life between, in which the soul is in a ferment, the character undecided, the way of life uncertain, the ambition thick-sighted: thence proceeds mawkishness. John Keats, preface to *Endymion,* 1818.

When the brisk minor pants for twenty-one. Alexander Pope, Imitations of Horace, *Epistles: Book l,* c. 1733.

Just at the age 'twixt boy and youth, / When thought is speech, and speech is truth. Sir Walter Scott, Marmion, 1808.

Eighty odd years of sorrow have I seen, / And each hour's joy wreck'd with a week of teen. William Shakespeare, *Richard III,* 1593.

He has quit the awkward stage; he is out of his teens. Terence, *Andria,* c. 166 BC.

ANONYMOUS APHORISMS

Teenage is a moment that seems like an eternity.

Teenage means perpetual emotion.

Teenage is cured by time, which brought it on in the first place.

Teenage is life viewed through a magnifying glass.

Teenage is a rest and relaxation stop in the march of time.

ANECDOTES

Comedienne Jean Carroll used to like to describe her teenage daughter's lifestyle this way: "She has her own apartment, in mine."

Psychologists define teenage as the time when an individual exchanges the silver cord for the telephone cord.

Mr. Jones was asked to describe his son's desperate attempt to look older than his actual teen age. "He's growing a beard on the installment plan," said Mr. Jones. "You know, just a little down, and more when he can manage it."

FACTS

The teen years mark the difficult transition from childhood to adulthood, but in the eyes of the law, exactly what people are capable of being responsible for at what age is continually shifting. Teens used to be minors, they are now eligible to vote at 18. In most states, they used to be able to purchase and consume alcoholic beverages at 18, now it's 21. They used to be prosecuted for serious crimes as minors, now frequently they are tried in criminal court. Where they used to be more or less at the mercy of parents, they are now recognized as having individual rights. And they are also targeted by the business community as probably the most impressionable and lucrative market for many different types of goods and services. But the idea that teenagers conform to a single pattern is one of the great myths of our time. They may tend to dress alike; so, in the aggregate, do their parents. They are the age group with generally the most difficult employment problems. Because of their liability record, their automobile insurance rates, particularly for males, are the highest in many areas. But if these and other problems lump them together as a class of our population, they are also separated into many different types and categories. They differ in race, in educational interests and attainments, regional attitudes. But they all face the same future; that world which they will soon inherit from the generation preceding them, and which—improved or ravaged—they will pass along to the generation that follows.

Television

(See also Journalism, Radio)

DEFINITIONS   Transmission and reception over long distances of both sight and sound; the home screen; the tube; the magic box: TV; the entertaining babysitter.

QUOTATIONS

Anyone who has intimations of fame or immortality chose the wrong career in TV news. This business is so fast and fleeting, I don't think anything lasts for very long. Charles Kuralt, in the *The Christian Science Monitor,* April 11, 1994.

Television newscasters are role models for our students. It says something about the centrality of the media in our time. Dale Rogers Marshall, president, Wheaton College, in the *The New York Times,* May 21, 1994.

The most powerful social force in the world's most powerful nation—this is what broadcasting, and television broadcasting in particular, has been called with increasing frequency during the past two decades. DuPont-Columbia Survey and Awards Jurors, 1969.

Like most basic national institutions, television operates at the center of American life. As a result, it is always under pressure from the left and the right. Julian Goodman, president, NBC, June 23, 1970.

When television is good, nothing—not the theater, not the magazines or newspapers—nothing is better. But when television is bad, nothing is worse… a vast wasteland. Newton H. Minow, chairman, Federal Communications Commission, May 9, 1961.

This instrument can teach, it can illuminate, it can even inspire, but only if human beings are willing to use it to those ends. Otherwise it is only wires and lights in a box. Edward R. Murrow, broadcaster, January 1, 1952.

The revenues from advertising support the free, competitive American system of telecasting, and make available to the eyes and ears of the American people the finest programs of information, education, culture and entertainment. National Association of Broadcasters, *Preamble to the Television Code,* 1952.

...broadcasting has consistently demonstrated a remarkable and ever-expanding capacity to serve the needs of both commerce and society. William S. Paley, chairman, CBS, April 18, 1973.

ANONYMOUS APHORISMS

Everybody is an authority on television.

Veni, video, vici: I came, I appeared on television, I conquered.

In the age of television, they still describe secret proceedings as being in camera when what they really mean is that they aren't on camera.

Television is everybody's window on the world.

Television bears watching.

Television is the great democratizer; it gives everybody the same front row seat.

FACTS

In 1995, it was estimated that 98 percent of all U.S. households had television sets, which probably means that there are more households with televisions than with telephones. Television has long since established itself as the nation's leading medium for information, entertainment, and advertising. Cable television, which reached less than 17 percent of households in 1977, reached over 63 percent—or 60 million viewers—in 1994. Merely recalling such events as the O.J. Simpson trial, the Olympics, the final episodes of M*A*S*H or Cheers testifies to the impact of the most complete communications medium yet devised.

TENNIS

DEFINITIONS   A game played across a net by two or four players, using rackets and a felt-covered, rubber, air-filled ball; the bouncing ball set.

QUOTATIONS

My whole career, people have been talking about how tough I am. Now that I'm losing some, I can see how tough I was—the killer instinct, the single-mindedness, playing like a machine. Boy, that's what made me a champion. Chris Evert, tennis player, in *Time,* September 11, 1989.

When we have match'd our rackets to these balls, / We will, in France, by God's grace play a set / Shall strike his father's crown into the hazard. William Shakespeare, *King Henry V,* 1598.

They must either...leave those remnants / Of fool and feather that they got in France ... / ... renouncing clean / The faith they have in tennis.... William Shakespeare, *King Henry VIII,* 1612.

My advice to young players is to see as much good tennis as possible and then attempt to copy the outstanding strokes of the former stars. William T. Tilden, July 1926.

ANONYMOUS APHORISMS

In tennis even a grudge game can be a love match.

His tennis game is a net loss.

Some people play tennis as if they are relying on a higher court.

In mixed doubles the mix is very important.

Tennis is like a lawsuit; you can always be surprised by what happens on the other side of the court.

There are would-be bullies on a tennis court whose net game can be described as gross.

Tennis is a sport in which an unseeded player can still flower.

ANECDOTES

Supreme Court Justice Hugo Black was one of the more famous elderly tennis players. He liked to joke about being advised by his doctor that a man in his forties shouldn't play tennis. Justice Black said he couldn't wait to reach 50 so he could play the game again.

FACTS

In the 1970s, tennis was considered the fastest growing sport in the U.S. both for participants and for spectators. Its growth was greatly stimulated by allowing professionals and amateurs to play in the same tournaments—and indeed by recognizing that it was a profession for professional players. Today, top players can gross over $1 million annually in prize money, and sign endorsements worth at least as much. There is no question of tennis' professional standing. The millions of amateur and recreational players attest to tennis' true popularity. The proliferation of indoor courts has allowed tennis to become a year-round sport.

The U.S. Tennis Association, founded in 1881 as the U.S. Lawn Tennis Association (the name changed when other surfaces replaced the previously dominant lawn courts) is the oldest governing body for any sport in the United States. It is located at 70 West Red Oak Lane, White Plains, NY 10604.

THEATER

(See also Drama)

DEFINITIONS   Presentation of drama or other entertainment on a stage before an audience; performances before the public; the stage; the legitimate theater; performances in the setting of an auditorium designed for this purpose; the limelights.

QUOTATIONS

As long as people seek the mysteries of life, they will want to come together in the theater. Marc Scorca, chief executive officer, OPERA America, in *Opera News,* February 4, 1995.

[To become a great actor] you need talent, luck, stamina and sex... Of these, the most important is luck. By far. Sir Laurence Olivier, in *Ladies' Home Journal,* December, 1989.

A play ought to be a just and lively image of human nature, representing its passions and humors, and the changes of fortune to which it is subject, for the delight and instruction of mankind. John Dryden, *An Essay of Dramatic Poesy,* 1668.

On the stage he was natural, simple, affecting; / 'Twas only that when he was off he was acting. Oliver Goldsmith, *Retaliation,* 1774.

The Fabulous Invalid. George S. Kaufman and Moss Hart, title of play, 1938.

To wake the soul by tender strokes of art, / To raise the genius, and to mend the heart; / To make mankind, in conscious virtue bold, / Live o'er each scene, and be what they behold: / For this the Tragic Muse first trod the stage. Alexander Pope, "Prologue to Mr. Addison's Cato," 1713.

Judge not the play before the play is done: / Her plot hath many changes.... Francis Quarles, "Epigram, Respice Finem," c. early 1600s.

All the world's a stage, / And all the men and women merely players: / They have their exits and their entrances; / And one man in his time plays many parts.... William Shakespeare, *As You Like It,* c. 1599.

It is an extremely difficult thing to put on the stage anything which runs contrary to the opinions of a large body of people. George Bernard Shaw, testimony before a committee, July 30, 1909.

Whoever condemns the theater is an enemy of his country. Voltaire, June 20, 1733.

ANONYMOUS APHORISMS

There's a broken heart for every light on Broadway.

Real life is not necessarily good theater.

The show must go on.

Comedy on the stage is very serious business.

The stars may be on stage, but the audience is king.

Theater is whatever people will buy tickets to see.

Theater is like baseball; it depends on hits and runs.

ANECDOTES

Then there's the actor who describes himself as "the off Broadway type." He doesn't mean he specializes in little theater. He means he can't get a job on Broadway.

A showman was asked to define theater. "When a man falls down in the street and a crowd gathers round him," he explained, "that's an event. But when a crowd pays money at a box office to go into a building to see a man fall down, that's theater."

It was Oscar Wilde who commented after the opening of a play which he enjoyed that "the play was a great success but the audience was a failure."

FACTS

The theater has been called the fabulous invalid because for most of the twentieth century it has been described as dying. Broadway—the legendary "great white way" of the stage—was labeled as doomed when motion pictures came upon the scene, and every movie theater could present the sight and sound of stage triumphs in living color. When television developed into the nation's most popular theatrical form, the legitimate theater's doomsday prophets renewed their predictions. But a mutually beneficial relationship has emerged between theater, television, and motion pictures. Successful actors regularly shift between screen and stage; the current trend of making classic plays, such as *Much Ado About Nothing*, into hit movies has drawn people to live theater as well. When ticket prices soared to as much as $100 on Broadway, the vitality of living theater went up. Off Broadway and Off Off Broadway bloomed; and regional theater became a thriving reality.

TIME

DEFINITIONS   The period during which a condition exists, a process occurs, or an action continues; the duration of a condition, process, or action; a fixed moment during a given period; "that which man is always trying to kill, but which ends up killing him" (Herbert Spencer); the one thing that never stands still; "a very shadow that passeth away" (Solomon).

QUOTATIONS

The past is not dead; it is not even past...Timeless feelings are common to all of us. Martha Graham, in *Dance Magazine,* May, 1989.

Backward, turn backward, / O Time, in your flight, / Make me a child again, just for tonight. Elizabeth Chase Akers, "Rock Me to Sleep, Mother," 1860.

Take care of the minutes, for the hours will take care of themselves. Lord Chesterfield, letter to his son, October 4, 1746.

This time, like all times, is a very good one, if we but know what to do with it. Ralph Waldo Emerson, "The American Scholar," 1837.

...time is money. Benjamin Franklin, *Advice to a Young Tradesman,* 1748.

If Time be of all Things the most precious, wasting Time must be, as Poor Richard says, the greatest Prodigality; since, as he elsewhere tells us, Lost Time is never found again. Benjamin Franklin, *The Way to Wealth,* 1757.

Art is long, and Time is fleeting.... Henry Wadsworth Longfellow, "A Psalm of Life," 1839.

Lives of great men all remind us / We can make our lives sublime, / And, departing, leave behind us / Footprints on the sands of time. Henry Wadsworth Longfellow, "A Psalm of Life," 1839.

Time makes more converts than reason. Thomas Paine, "Common Sense," 1776.

For a thousand years in thy sight are but as yesterday when it is past, and as a watch in the night. *Psalms,* 90:4.

Never before have we had so little time in which to do so much. President Franklin D. Roosevelt, February 27, 1942.

Time is but the stream I go a-fishing in. Henry D. Thoreau, *Walden,* 1854.

ANONYMOUS APHORISMS

One today is worth two tomorrows.

Time is on my side.

Time heals all wounds, and wounds all heels.

When you're out of time, you're out.

You can save time but you can't bank it.

It is always later than you think.

When it's high time there's no time to spare.

Time and tide wait for no one.

ANECDOTES

"Time," said the sage," is a great healer." "But," asked his pupil, "what if you're feeling fine in the first place?"

"How do you explain the relativity of time?" the professor was asked. "Well," he replied, "if I am rushing to catch a plane, and the check-in clerk is so slow that I miss it, the extra two minutes don't mean much to him but they sure make a difference to me. That's relativity."

A husband-and-wife exploration team had returned from spending several years on a lonely expedition. "Did you get tired of just being with each other," they were asked by a friend. "Well," said the woman explorer, "he was away for one night." "Then you were together virtually all the time?" the friend inquired. "No," she replied, "you see we were in the Arctic; the night was three months long."

VIOLENCE

(See also Crime, Law and Order)

DEFINITIONS   Use of physical force to destroy or coerce; conflict; brawn over brain; disorder; lashing out; brute force.

QUOTATIONS

When a child is gunned down in the street in the Bronx, no matter what our race, he is our American child. When a woman dies from a beating, no matter what race ours or hers, she is our American sister. President Bill Clinton, speech, October 16, 1995.

We know what causes violence in our society: poverty, discrimination, the failure of our educational system. It's not the genes that cause violence in our society. It's our social system. Paul Billings, clinical geneticist, Stanford University, in the *Los Angeles Times,* December 30, 1993.

It is organized violence on top which creates individual violence at the bottom. Emma Goldman, June 15, 1917.

When a fact can be demonstrated, force is unnecessary; when it cannot be demonstrated, force is infamous. Robert G. Ingersoll, Prose-Poems and Selections, 1884.

...violence is the sign of temporary weakness. Jean Jaures, Studies in Socialism, 1902.

It is easier today to buy a destructive weapon, a gun, in a hardware store, than it is to vote. President Lyndon B. Johnson, December 20, 1963.

Democracy will never solve its problems at the end of a billy club. President Lyndon B. Johnson, July 28, 1964.

...for all they that take the sword shall perish with the sword. *Matthew, 26.52.*

Perseverance is more prevailing than violence; and many things which cannot be overcome when they are together, yield themselves up when taken little by little. Plutarch, *Parallel Lives*, c. 100 AD. (Sertorius)

These violent delights have violent ends. William Shakespeare, *Romeo and Juliet*, 1596.

ANONYMOUS APHORISMS

Violence is self-destructive.

I like violence because they're purple and they smell so good.

Don't start a fight if you're not prepared to finish it.

Violence on behalf of the right side can make it the wrong side.

People who live in glass houses shouldn't throw stones.

When there is an epidemic of violence, nobody can consider himself immune.

Some people think the only way to shut 'em up is to shoot 'em up.

ANECDOTES

An urban youth-gang leader visited a Quaker community. He watched everyone settle their differences by quietly talking to their opponents. One Quaker asked the gang leader, "Don't you think this is better than fighting?" "No," he sadly replied, "it takes all the fun out of life."

Every time a controversial issue came up at the town meeting, the local dissenter yelled out, "We'll stage a demonstration." Finally one of the elders lost his temper. "You don't accomplish anything by your demonstrations," he exclaimed, "They always end up in a riot, and what good is that?" "Well," retorted the dissenter, "it gets a lot more attention than when I talk in the town meeting."

There was a violence-prone young man who got into a fight by smashing a merchant's window; starting a fire; and battling with the firemen. When the police came, he lunged after them with a knife and they in turn beat him to a pulp while defending themselves. As he lay moaning on the sidewalk, he raised his head and snarled, "Have you had enough?"

FACTS

Violence has existed in every civilization. Today there is great concern over the graphic depictions of violence in television, movies and music. The concern is a reaction—not exclusively to what is reported or depicted in the media—but also as the result of recent events. Real crime has replaced much of the dramatized television violence; video footage from various police departments is shown on prime time and late evening television daily. The bombing of an Oklahoma City federal building was initially blamed on international terrorists; when suspicion fell on an American, it was a public loss of innocence for the nation. Like the problem of international violence, however, these acts depend on one fact: violence continues to exist as long as the practice of violence goes unpunished, and the causes go unsolved. Metal detectors are now as commonplace in inner city schools as they are in prison visitors' areas. It should be remembered, too, that not all the increase in real-life violence is created by crime or war. Contact sports have become more violent. The professional hockey and basketball leagues both tolerate a level of contact and roughness which would have led to the permanent dismissal of players in previous decades. The development of high-speed automobiles has led to an increase in violent accidents. Violence is a fact of life; its control is a problem of life.

VOTING

(See also Candidates, Elections, Political Parties)

DEFINITIONS   The expression of choices and preferences among candidates and issues by casting ballots; suffrage; the exercise of the franchise; the voice of the people; the poll that counts.

QUOTATIONS

At the bottom of all the tributes paid to democracy is the little man, walking into the little booth, with a little pencil, making a little cross on a little bit of paper—no amount of rhetoric or voluminous discussion can possibly diminish the overwhelming importance of the point. Winston Churchill, Prime Minister of Great Britain, speech. in the House of Commons, October 31, 1944.

Your every voter, as surely as your chief magistrate, under the same high sanction, though in a different sphere, exercises a public trust. President Grover Cleveland, inaugural address, March 4, 1885.

A straw vote only shows which way the hot air blows. O. Henry, *Rolling Stones:* "A Ruler of Men," 1913.

Voting is the first duty of democracy. President Lyndon B. Johnson, August 11, 1964.

The ignorance of one voter in a democracy impairs the security of all. President John F. Kennedy, May 18, 1963.

The ballot is stronger than the bullet. Abraham Lincoln, c. 1856.

Inside the polling booth every American man and woman stands as the equal of every other American man and woman. There they have no superiors. There they have no masters save their own minds and consciences. President Franklin D. Roosevelt, October 21, 1936.

Nobody will ever deprive the American people of the right to vote except the American people themselves. President Franklin D. Roosevelt, October 5, 1944.

Even voting for the right is doing nothing for it. Henry D. Thoreau, "Civil Disobedience," 1849.

By their votes ye shall know them. President Harry S Truman, September 23, 1948.

Act as if the whole election depended on your single vote... John Wesley, "A Word to a Freeholder," 1748.

ANONYMOUS APHORISMS

If you walk past the polling place without casting your vote, you're voting with your feet.

The most important single exercise for Americans is the exercise of the franchise.

A write-in vote is often designed to keep some candidates right out.

The votes that count are the votes you can count.

ANECDOTES

During his 1948 whistle-stop presidential campaign, candidate Harry Truman supposedly asked one man in the crowd how he planned to vote. The man replied, "I wouldn't vote for you if you were the only man on the ballot." "Put that man down as doubtful," Truman commented to one of his aides.

A defeated candidate went back to a little community of ten voters that he had visited during the campaign. "I'm disappointed in you," he said. "When I was here before the election, all ten of you said you would vote for me; and when the votes were counted not one of you had done what you promised. Now, if only one of you had been smart enough to vote for me, I wouldn't know which one of you had told the truth. Instead, I know that you all lied."

FACTS

The most important single fact about voting in the United States is that, although we are the oldest major democratic, popularly elected representative government in the world, we have proportionately fewer people participating in our elections than in the rest of the self-governing world. In the 1992 Presidential election, 61.2 percent of the eligible voters cast ballots. According to the American Voter Coalition, more than 6 million voters did not exercise their rights in the 1992 elections because of negative campaign advertising. America, of course, has greatly increased the number of eligible voters by abolishing poll taxes, enfranchising 18-year-olds, and enforcing voters' rights legislation.

The *Statistical Abstract of the United States* contains comparative information through the years on the number of eligible voters and the extent of their election participation.

War

(See also Armed Forces, Peace)

DEFINITIONS   A state or period of armed conflict between regions or peoples; the clash in battle of opposing military, naval, and air forces; "a byproduct of the arts of peace" (Ambrose Bierce); that which determines not who is right, but who is left.

QUOTATIONS

The source of war is not the existence of nuclear weapons or other arms. It is the minds of human beings who decide to push the button and to use those arms out of hatred, anger or greed. Dalai Lama, in *The Wall Street Journal,* July 17, 1989.

In peace the sons bury their fathers and in war the fathers bury their sons. Sir Francis Bacon, *Apothegms,* 1624.

It takes twenty years or more of peace to make a man; it takes only twenty seconds of war to destroy him. King Baudouin I of Belgium, address to a joint session of the U.S. Congress, May 12, 1959.

There is no greater pacifist than the regular officer. Any man who is forced to turn his attention to the horrors of the battlefield, to the grotesque shapes that are left there for the burying squads he doesn't want war! General of the Army Dwight D. Eisenhower, June 19, 1945.

By the rude bridge that arched the flood, / Their flag to April's breeze unfurled, / Here once the embattled farmers stood, / And fired the shot heard round the world. Ralph Waldo Emerson, "Concord Hymn," April 19, 1837.

Older men declare war. But it is youth that must fight and die. Herbert Hoover, June 27, 1944.

It is well that war is so terrible—we would grow too fond of it. Confederate General Robert E. Lee, December 13, 1862.

I know war as few other men now living know it, and nothing to me is more revolting. I have long advocated its complete abolition, as its very destructiveness on both friend and foe has rendered it useless as a means of settling international disputes.... In war there is no substitute for victory. General of the Army Douglas MacArthur, speech to a joint session of the U.S. Congress, April 19, 1951.

It is always easy to begin a war, but very difficult to stop one, since its beginning and end are not under the control of the same man. Sallust, *Bellum Jugurthinum,* c. 1st century BC.

There is many a boy here today who looks on war as all glory, but boys, it is all hell. General William T. Sherman, August 11, 1880.

For it is all too obvious that if we do not abolish war on this earth, then surely, one day, war will abolish us from the earth. Harry S Truman, January 25, 1966.

ANONYMOUS APHORISMS

War is blind.

Young men fight wars, but it's up to old men to make the peace.

People used to go off to war, but modern science can now bring it to your doorstep.

Those who yearn for war have already started it in their hearts.

In the next war, there will be no rear echelon.

War creates more evils than it cures, and yet war against evil cannot always be avoided.

Many a victorious war turned to ashes in peace.

ANECDOTES

An elderly cannibal and a missionary were comparing their philosophies. The sage cannibal reminisced about the tribal wars he had fought, and how he had eaten his foes. And the missionary commented, "We fight wars for higher reasons—for truth, for defense of democracy, for freedom." "You must eat many, many people," exclaimed the cannibal. "Oh, no," the missionary responded, "we don't eat human beings." "Then," said the cannibal sage, "you have no reason to kill each other."

'We will bomb your cities, set fire to your crops, defoliate your forests, kill your people by the millions," the belligerent dictator roared across the conference table at the visiting ambassador. "We will reduce your country to nothing. We will fight—and we will win the war." "Given your description," the ambassador remarked, "just what do you expect to win?"

FACTS

War is mankind's oldest weakness. No civilization has been able to abolish it. In the twentieth century alone, the United States has been involved in four major wars—the First World War, Second World War, Korean War, and Vietnam War—plus various minor military confrontations. In that same period, the world has tried to abolish war through nonaggression compacts, United Nations sessions, disarmament and arms limitation agreements, peaceful sanctions against aggressors, and peace accords. But military preparedness continues to be reflected around the world in mounting armament sales and the increased sophistication of equipment. Recent incidents in Kuwait, Somalia, and Bosnia-Herzegovina, to name just a few, are clear indications that this generation is no more immune to war than those that preceded us. And while the U.S. has entered each of these conflicts as a peacekeeper, the war against war is being waged at great cost.

WASHINGTON, D.C.

DEFINITIONS The capital city of the United States; "a city of southern efficiency and northern charm" (John F. Kennedy).

QUOTATIONS

What rules this town is power and access to power. Alex Benes, managing director, Center for Public Integrity, in *The Los Angeles Times,* January 5, 1995.

Washington is no place for a civilized man to spend the summer. Attributed to President James Buchanan, c. 1857–1861.

There are a number of things wrong with Washington. One of them is that everyone has been too long away from home. President Dwight D. Eisenhower, May 11, 1955.

Washington is not a place to live in. The rents are high, the food is bad, the dust is disgusting and the morals are deplorable. Horace Greeley, July 13, 1865.

Washington is full of famous men and the women they married when they were young. Mrs. Oliver Wendell Holmes, Jr., January 8, 190S.

The condition of our capital city is a sign of the condition of our nation—and is certainly taken as such by visitors, from all the states of the Union, and from around the globe. President Richard M. Nixon, message to the U.S. Congress, April 28, 1969.

Every man who takes office in Washington either grows or swells, and when I give a man an office, I watch him carefully to see whether he is swelling or growing. President Woodrow Wilson, May 15, 1916.

ANONYMOUS APHORISMS

When Congress is in session, the city is so crowded that the D.C. stands for Don't Come.

When you work in Washington a few years you are apt to stay.

Washington: Where the buck starts.

Washington: Where the lame ducks are on the pond.

Washington: Named for the only President who didn't have to live there.

The only reason Washington is the nation's capital is that Boston was too far North, Philadelphia didn't want New York, New York didn't want Philadelphia, and nobody yet had heard of Las Vegas.

ANECDOTES

A springtime visitor to Washington said to her guide, "The cherry blossoms are absolutely lovely, but is it always this windy?" "Madam," replied the guide, "you must remember this is the nation's capital. Where the government meets it's always windy."

During a Washington rainstorm, the lawn sprinklers in front of the White House suddenly turned on and began operating full force. A passerby turned to his companion and said, "Why do you suppose those sprinklers went on now?" "It's an old rule," said his companion. "Whatever nature does, Washington thinks it can do better."

FACTS

Washington, D.C. is an anomaly, it was always represented in Congress; it's where the President lives; but its residents could not vote in the presidential elections until 1964. Washington D.C. has more people paid by the same employer—the Federal government—than any other city of comparable size. Washington has one of the largest African-American urban populations in the nation. And despite the flow of wealth and power through the capital, the city itself faces all the problems of poverty, drugs, and crime that plague other metropolitan areas. But it is also a city where almost everybody has some roots elsewhere. Because it is the place where the nation's elected representatives meet, it has something of every state of the Union.

WASHINGTON, GEORGE

DEFINITIONS   The first President of the United States under the Constitution; "the Father of the Country."

QUOTATIONS

Surely Washington was the greatest man that ever lived in this world uninspired by divine wisdom and unsustained by supernatural virtue. Henry P. Brougham (Lord Brougham and Vaux), *Historical Sketches of Statesmen Who Flourished in the Time of George III,* 1839–1843.

...I know that it is impossible for me to bestow anything like adequate praise on a character which gave us, more than any other human being, the example of a perfect man; yet, good, great, and unexampled as General Washington was, I can remember the time when he was not better spoken of in this House than Bonaparte is now. Charles James Fox, speech in the House of Commons, February 3, 1800.

To contemplate his unselfish devotion to duty, his courage, his patience, his genius, his statesmanship and his accomplishments for his country and the world, refreshes the spirit, the wisdom and the patriotism of our people. President Herbert Hoover, proclamation for Washington's 200th birthday, issued February 2, 1932.

...never did nature and fortune combine more perfectly to make a man great... Thomas Jefferson, January 2, 1814.

...first in war, first in peace, first in the hearts of his countrymen. Henry ("Light Horse Harry") Lee, text of resolution introduced in the U.S. Congress on his behalf by John Marshall December 19, 1799.

Washington is the mightiest name on earth—long since mightiest in the cause of civil liberty; still mightiest in moral reformation. Abraham Lincoln, February 22, 1842.

That nation has not lived in vain which has given the world Washington and Lincoln, the best great men and the greatest good men whom history can show. Senator Henry Cabot Lodge of Massachusetts, February 12, 1909.

ANONYMOUS APHORISMS

When George Washington beat King George III's armies, many of his fellow Americans wanted to make him King George I; but he didn't like the idea, which two centuries later saved us from having King Richard I.

George Washington couldn't tell a lie because it would have had a harmful effect on American mythology.

If George Washington slept every place they say he did, he must have won the war in his sleep.

Washington was a man of great accomplishments, but there was one thing he couldn't do; he couldn't tell a lie.

ANECDOTES

Q: Why was Washington a great man? A: Because he was born on a national holiday.

Q: Why was Washington, D.C. named after George Washington? A: Because he was born first.

Wealth

DEFINITIONS   Abundant supply of property or resources; riches; affluence; prosperity; "a conventional basis of reputability" (Thorstein Veblen); "the holiest of our gods" (Juvenal).

QUOTATIONS

Wealth belongs to him who creates it. Populist Party slogan, 1892.

I don't waste too much time philosophizing about wealth. I just recommend it to everyone. Malcolm S. Forbes, in *The Los Angeles Times,* July 21, 1989.

The men who have earned five million dollars have been so busy earning it that they have not had time to collect it; and the men who have collected five million dollars have been so busy collecting it that they have not had time to earn it. William Jennings Bryan, "The Price of A Soul," c. early 20th century.

The problem of our age is the proper administration of wealth, so that the ties of brotherhood may still bind together the rich and poor in harmonious relationship. Andrew Carnegie, "Wealth," 1889.

It requires a great deal of boldness and a great deal of caution to make a great fortune, and when you have got it, it requires ten times as much wit to keep it. Ralph Waldo Emerson, *The Conduct of Life:* "Power," 1860.

The Affluent Society, John K Galbraith, book title, 1958.

Ill fares the land, to hastening ills a prey, / Where wealth accumulates and men decay. Oliver Goldsmith, *The Deserted Village,* 1770.

Put not your trust in money, but put your money in trust. Oliver Wendell Holmes, *The Autocrat of the Breakfast-Table,* 1858.

Few rich men own their own property. The property owns them. Robert G. Ingersoll, October 29, 1896.

It is easier for a camel to go through the eye of a needle, than for a rich man to enter into the kingdom of God. *Mark,* 10:25.

The loved and the rich need no protection—they have many friends and few enemies. Wendell Phillips, December 21, 1860.

...a man is rich in proportion to the number of things he can afford to let alone. Henry D. Thoreau, *Walden,* 1854.

ANONYMOUS APHORISMS

You can always love a poor man, but you can love a rich one better. (Attributed to Mae West)

The rich get richer and the poor get children.

There are as many millionaires from humble beginnings as there are inheritances lost.

One man's wealth is another man's pocket money.

He is a poor man if he has to watch his wealth.

A fat purse never lacks friends.

Money can't buy happiness, but it certainly doesn't discourage it.

A little among neighbors is better than riches in a wilderness.

ANECDOTES

The story is told of a multimillionaire who insisted on doing business in a genteel but very shabby office. His lawyer once said to him, "A man of your position and resources should really have a better furnished office." "Why?" asked the multimillionaire. "Everybody will charge me more for what I buy."

A feeble old millionaire, confined to his bed with the infirmities of age, pointed out the window at a husky teenager who was having an obviously enjoyable conversation with a pretty girl. "I wish I was as rich as he," remarked the old man. "But he has no job, his family has ten mouths to feed, and he doesn't even know whether he'll be able to go to college," the rich man's nurse commented. "Yes," said the rich man, "but he has health and youth and hope—he's rich in all the things that money can't buy."

Humphrey, who loved to spout statistics, was an advocate of increased taxation to pay for more social programs until somebody gave him a little pocket calculator. Then he announced that he had changed his political philosophy. When asked why, he said, "Well, I did a little figuring and discovered that if they shared the wealth I wouldn't be getting any, I'd have to give some up."

FACTS

In the final analysis, wealth is not an absolute, but a comparative asset. A wealthy family is usually given that distinction because it has more assets than other families, rather than because it has everything. This is illustrated by a few simple statistics. In 1994, half of the American population earned a median household income of $32,265 per year. In the mid-1990s, to be in the top fifth percentile of American income, a family had to bring in $114,000 a year. According to a U.S. Census Bureau Statistical Abstract, there were 3.3 million people, in 1989, whose assets exceeded $600,000; their average holdings were $3.8 million dollars. These are truly America's well-to-do.

The U.S. Internal Revenue Service publishes annual Statistics of Income which can also provide helpful information.

W EST

DEFINITIONS That portion of the United States adjacent to or west of the Continental Divide; generally speaking, the states of Montana, Wyoming, Colorado, New Mexico, Arizona, Nevada, Utah, Idaho, Oregon, Washington, and California; where men are men; the wide open spaces; the Wild West.

QUOTATIONS

Westward the course of empire takes its way... Bishop George Berkeley, "On the Prospect of Planting Arts and Learning in America," 1752.

Out where the handclasp's a little stronger, / Out where the smile dwells a little longer, / That's where the West begins. Arthur Chapman, "Out Where the West Begins," 1917.

...westward, look, the land is bright. Arthur H. Clough, "Say Not the Struggle Naught Availeth," 1862.

Go West, young man, go West and grow up with the country. Credited to Horace Greeley, who indeed said it, but attributed the initial thought to John L. Soule, c. 1850s.

East is East and West is San Francisco, according to Californians. Californians are a race of people; they are not merely inhabitants of a State. They are the Southerners of the West. O. Henry, "A Municipal Report," 1910.

Westward, Ho! Charles Kingsley, book title, 1855.

I come...from the West, where we have always seen the backs of our enemies. Major General John Pope, July 14, 1862.

We go eastward to realize history and study the works of art and literature, retracing the steps of the race; we go westward as into the future, with a spirit of enterprise and adventure. Henry D. Thoreau, "Walking," 1862,

ANONYMOUS APHORISMS

The West is yet to come.

Every Western state seems to regard itself as all that's left of the old West.

There is no more enthusiastic Westerner than a transplanted Easterner.

They used to say when someone died, that he "went West." When they say someone went West these days, it usually means he got a new lease on life.

The greatest mineral riches of the West are found in the gold mine known as Las Vegas.

California is a state, but southern California is a state of mind.

The sun rises in the East, and smiles on the West.

ANECDOTES

I suppose you've heard about the prospector who was looking for gold in the desert and struck it rich. He hit water.

Recently settled residents of the West have always been the region's biggest boosters. One new Nevada resident named Mr. Jones dressed up in his cowboy clothes and went to the local bar. When this native New Yorker started monopolizing the conversation—talking about how weak and helpless he felt when he first saw the West—an Eastern visitor asked him, "What part of the East did you come from?" Mr. Jones immediately responded, "I didn't come from the East. I was weak and helpless because I was so young. I was born here."

A Westerner died and found himself in the next world, which was comfortable, sunny, and had a number of delightful ways to pass the time. After a few days, another heavenly resident asked, "How do you like it here?" "Well," the Westerner replied, "for Hell it isn't too bad." "What do you mean Hell?" his companion asked, "This isn't Hell. It's Heaven." "You must be from the East," the Westerner remarked, "Anything you come to after living in the East seems like Heaven. But I'm from the West, and believe me, anything else seems like Hell to me."

FACTS

The American West is by far the largest of the nation's traditional regions, and potentially the richest. It already contains the nation's most populated state, California, and its neighbors continue to grow. Western agriculture and livestock feed a large portion of the nation, and the national economy. Its climate is generally salubrious, particularly with the growth of air conditioning and solar energy. Its coastline is picturesque; its mountains the nation's largest except for those in Alaska (which in spirit is an extension of the West); and it continues its pioneering traditions while the rest of nation becomes more sophisticated. With the development of the Pacific Rim, the American West has become as important for its ports and international atmosphere as for its inland empires.

WILDERNESS

(See also Environment, Nature)

DEFINITIONS   A tract of uninhabited, uncultivated land; an area unaltered by human activity; the woods; "... area[s] where humans are only visitors who do not remain. . . generally greater than 5,000 acres which have retained their primeval character" The National Park Service.

QUOTATIONS

We cannot create wilderness. We can only protect what we have, or it's lost forever. Fran Hunt, environmentalist, Wilderness Society, in *U.S. News & World Report,* September 18, 1995.

The Earth does not belong to man, man belongs to the Earth. All things are connected like blood which unites us all. Man did not weave the web of life, he is merely a strand in it. Whatever he does to the web, he does to himself. Attributed to Chief Seattle (Sealth), Chief of the Duwamish Tribe, c. 19th century.

ANONYMOUS APHORISMS

Man created civilization, with its skyscrapers and cities. The wilderness is God's creation.

Take only pictures, leave only footprints.

The wilderness shrinks in proportion with population growth.

If items gain value as they become increasingly rare, our wilderness areas will soon be worth far more than our gold reserves.

ANECDOTES

Bill Smith was showing his neighbor his brand new recreational vehicle. "It's got a color TV, VCR, satellite dish, CD player, cellular phone, Jacuzzi, full kitchen, wet bar, a roll-out awning, even a pair of mopeds. Everything you need to really enjoy the wilderness."

On a sunny summer afternoon, a city-born bookkeeper headed out to Central Park. After strolling for a while, he got daring and headed off the path. Passing a few couples picnicking he reached a spot where there wasn't a single other person to be seen. "Ah, wilderness," he sighed. At that same moment, halfway around the world, a man crawling across the Australian outback, nearly dead from dehydration, spotted a tiny shack on the horizon. "Ah, finally, civilization," he sighed.

FACTS

On September 3rd, 1964, Congress passed the Wilderness Act. The stated goal was, "To establish a National Wilderness Preservation System for the permanent good of the whole people. . ." More specifically, it was enacted "to assure that an increasing population, accompanied by expanding settlement and growing mechanization, does not occupy and modify all areas within the United States and its possessions, leaving no lands designated for preservation and protection in their natural condition." Unfortunately, this has been a nearly impossible struggle. Considerable damage was done before 1964, and with each shift in the political wind—and each million added to the population—the devastation continues. Aside from the aesthetic loss, the world stands to lose one of its greatest and least explored resources. If there are cures for the diseases we have been unable to conquer, chances are they're hidden in the rapidly dwindling forests. "From the forest and wilderness" Henry David Thoreau said, "come the tonics and barks which brace mankind." There are approximately 104 million acres of national wilderness in the U.S., though over half of that wilderness is in Alaska. Management of these lands is largely the responsibility of the Forest Service, and three branches of the Department of the Interior: the National Park Service, the Fish and Wildlife Service, and the Bureau of Land Management.

For more information contact The National Park Service, Department of the Interior, 1849 C St., NW, Washington, D.C. 20240; or the Sierra Club, 85 Second St., Second Floor, San Francisco, CA 94105-3441.

W O M E N

DEFINITIONS   Adult female humans; the female of the species; the first improvement on man; "the last thing civilized by man" (George Meredith); the better half; the fairer half.

QUOTATIONS

Pro-choice with limitations; pro-life with exceptions. Senator John W. Warner, in *The Wall Street Journal,* February 13, 1990.

…can't live with them, or without them. Aristophanes, *Lysistrata,* c. 411 BC.

A sufficient measure of civilization is the influence of good women. Ralph Waldo Emerson, *Society and Solitude:* "Civilization," 1870.

Man has his will—but woman has her way. Oliver Wendell Holmes, *The Autocrat of the Breakfast-Table,* 1858.

You have to make more noise than anybody else, you have to make yourself more obtrusive than anybody else, you have to fill all the papers more than anybody else, in fact you have to be there all the time and see that they do not snow you under, if you are really going to get your reform realized. That is what we women have been doing, and in the course of our desperate struggle we have had to make a great many people very uncomfortable. Emmeline Pankhurst, speech in Hartford, CT, November 13, 1913.

Too often the great decisions are originated and given form in bodies made up wholly of men, or so completely dominated by them that whatever of special value women have to offer is shunted aside without expression. Mrs. Eleanor Roosevelt,

U.S. Delegate to the United Nations, speech at the United Nations, December 1952.

We hold these truths to be self-evident: that all men and women are created equal… Seneca Falls Declaration of Sentiments and Resolutions at Women's Rights Convention, Seneca Falls, NY, July 19, 1848.

The history of mankind is a history of repeated injuries and usurpations on the part of man toward woman, having in direct object the establishment of an absolute tyranny over her. Seneca Falls Declaration of Sentiments and Resolutions at Women's Rights Convention, Seneca Falls, NY, July 19, 1848.

Resolved, that woman is man's equal—was intended to be so by the Creator, and the highest good of the race demands that she should be recognized as such. Seneca Falls Declaration of Sentiments and Resolutions at Women's Rights Convention, Seneca Falls, NY, July 19, 1848.

The world cannot afford the loss of the talents of half its people if we are to solve the many problems that beset us. Dr. Rosalyn S. Yalow, at Nobel Prize dinner in Stockholm, Sweden, December 10, 1977.

There is in every true woman's heart a spark of heavenly fire, which lies dormant in the broad daylight of prosperity, but which kindles up and beams and blazes in the dark hour of adversity. Washington Irving, *The Sketch Book:* "The Wife," 1820.

It is a good time to be a woman because your country, now more than at any time in its history, is utilizing your abilities and intelligence. Claudia Taylor (Mrs. Lyndon B.) Johnson, March .31, 1964.

…the colonel's lady an' Judy O'Grady / Are sisters under their skins. Rudyard Kipling, "The Ladies," 1895.

The female of the species is more deadly than the male. Rudyard Kipling, "The Female of the Species," 1911.

Women are not entirely wrong when they reject the rules of life prescribed for the world, for these were established by men only, without their consent. Michel Eyquem de Montaigne, *Essays, Book III,* 1588.

Too often the great decisions are originated and given form in bodies made up wholly of men, or so completely dominated by them that whatever of special value women have to offer is shunted aside without expression. Mrs. Eleanor Roosevelt, U.S. Delegate to the United Nations, speech at United Nations, December 1952.

ANONYMOUS APHORISMS

Woman's intuition is man's tuition.

It is an incontrovertible fact that women bear watching and men watch their bearing.

When a woman has no answer, the sea has no salt.

It is easier for a woman to be famous for her genius than to be forgiven for it.

God took one look at Adam and brought out a new design called Eve.

ANECDOTES

Corporate executive who had been dealing with a women's rights group was warned that they were outspoken. "By whom?" he asked.

A pretty woman got on a crowded bus. There were no seats available, but as she began to pass by an elderly man, he arose and offered her his seat. Instead of accepting and sitting down, she smiled at him and said, "Sir, it's nice that you are so old-fashioned, but this is a new era and men don't have to get up to offer seats to women any more." "They do if they want to get off at the next stop," said the old gentleman, as he moved to the exit.

FACTS

The changing status of women can be noted in many ways. They are working more often outside the home; they are increasingly independent of men; and they have more recourse to the protection of the law in their search for equal opportunity and equal status. According to the Bureau of Labor Statistics, 33 percent of adult women were in the workforce, while 86 percent of the male population worked during the 1970s; in 1980, 51 percent of women were working outside the house, versus 77 percent of men; in 1996, the figures were 59 percent and 77 percent respectively. In 1994, 18 percent of all households were headed by a single female parent—up from 10 percent in 1970. Though women's liberation and the feminist movement don't make headlines anymore, there is still a battle being waged over inequality in pay scales, promotions and even hiring policies. But no one will deny that these dilemmas represent a small fraction compared to the equalities women have achieved in the last few decades alone. There have been substantial increases in the number of women entering law and medical schools, there are more women business executives, more women-owned and -operated businesses, and more women are going to college.

WORRY

DEFINITIONS   Anxiety; nervous concern; sleepless nights; fear of what is to come; that which is almost always premature.

QUOTATIONS

A crust eaten in peace is better than a banquet attended by anxiety. Aesop, "The Town Mouse and the Country Mouse," c. 6th century BC.

There are two days in the week about which and upon which I never worry. ...One ... is Yesterday. ...And the other day I do not worry about is Tomorrow. Robert J. Burdette, "The Golden Day," c. late 19th century.

As a rule, men worry more about what they can't see than about what they can. Julius Caesar, *Gallic War,* c. 1st century BC.

When you're laying awake with a dismal headache, and repose is tabooed by anxiety, / I conceive you may use any language you choose to indulge in, without impropriety. W.S. Gilbert, *Iolanthe,* 1882.

How much pain have cost us the evils which have never happened. Thomas Jefferson, letter to Thomas Jefferson Smith, February 21, 1825.

...the misfortunes hardest to bear are those which never come. James Russell Lowell, Democracy and Other Addresses, 1887.

Deep into that darkness peering, long I stood there wondering, fearing, / Doubting, dreaming dreams no mortal ever dared to dream before. Edgar Allan Poe, "The Raven," 1845.

ANONYMOUS APHORISMS

Worry makes the world go round and round and round.

He who never worries never cares.

You can always find something to worry about.

Worry comes before wisdom.

It takes a lot of imagination to worry.

Worry never paid a bill.

Worry tries to cross the bridge before you come to it.

ANECDOTES

"Most of the things you worry about," the psychiatrist advised Mr. Brown, "never happen." "I know that," Mr. Brown admitted, "but then I find myself worrying about why they didn't happen."

One airline passenger was obviously a member of the white-knuckle brigade. The plane hadn't even begun its take-off, and he was clutching his seat with evident anxiety. His seat mate tried to relieve the man's tensions by saying, "You're jumping the gun; we're not even in the air yet." "That's your worry," the anxious passenger responded. "Mine is that I missed the flight. I should have been on an hour ago. And I'm going to miss my connecting flight." It's easy to see when someone is worried, but not so easy to know what he's worried about.

Two men were going to fly to the moon together. One was calm and the other anxious. The calm one mused, "He should be calm." The worried one pondered, "He should be worried."

YOUTH

(See also Adolescence, Teenagers)

DEFINITIONS   The period between childhood and full maturity; young adulthood; "a stuff will not endure" (William Shakespeare); that which is old to children and young to their parents; that which we can't wait to grow out of, then spend the rest of our lives trying to regain; "perpetual intoxication...a fever of the mind" (La Rochefoucauld).

QUOTATIONS

The young are in a state like intoxication; for youth is sweet and they are growing. Aristotle, *Nicomachean Ethics,* c. 4th century BC.

Young men think old men are fools, but old men know young men are fools. George Chapman, *All Fools,* 1605.

America is a country of young men. Ralph Waldo Emerson, *Society and Solitude: Old Age,* 1870.

...the young must fight in the ranks. Homer, *Iliad,* c. 800 BC.

Every old man complains of the growing depravity of the world, of the petulance and insolence of the rising generation. He recounts the decency and regularity of former times, and celebrates the discipline and sobriety of the age in which his youth was passed; a happy age that is now no more to be expected, since confusion has broken in upon the world, and thrown down all the boundaries of civility and reverence. Samuel Johnson, *The Rambler,* September 8, 1750.

The mental disease of the present generation, is impatience of study, contempt of the great masters of ancient wisdom, and a disposition to rely wholly upon unassisted genius and natural sagacity. The wits of these happy days have discovered a way to fame, which the dull caution of our laborious ancestors durst never attempt; they cut the knots of sophistry which it was formerly the business of years to untie, solve difficulties by sudden irradiations of intelligence, and comprehend long processes of argument by immediate intuition. Samuel Johnson, *The Rambler,* September 7, 1851.

How beautiful is youth! How bright it gleams / With its illusions, aspirations, dreams! Henry Wadsworth Longfellow, "Morituri Salutamus," 1875.

If youth be a defect, it is one that we outgrow only too soon. James Russell Lowell, November 8, 1886.

Certainly the time when the young are to be seen and not heard is gone in America—and gone for good. President Richard M. Nixon, December 1, 1971.

We cannot always build the future for our youth, but we can build our youth for the future. President Franklin D. Roosevelt, September 20, 1940.

My salad days, / When I was green in judgment. William Shakespeare, *Anthony and Cleopatra,* 1606.

The youth of America is their oldest tradition. It has been going on now for three hundred years. Oscar Wilde, *A Woman of No Importance,* 1893.

ANONYMOUS APHORISMS

You are as young as you feel.

There are two choices in life: you can age gracefully, or you can fight it at every turn.

The younger generation is always displaced by a younger generation.

Instead of chips off the old block some people think we now have saps out of old trees.

We are so concerned with making a good world for our heirs that it can be said we are heir conditioned.

You're only young once. How long that once lasts is the question.

Youth will have its fling, even if it means flinging away its youth.

Youth is wasted on the young.

ANECDOTES

On his 50th birthday, a man was asked by his friend, "What would you give to be young again?" "That's easy," he replied. "I'd give twenty years off my life."

Q: What is the line between youth and age? A: It's that point in your life when you stop yearning to look older and begin to hope that you look younger than your years. In other words, youth gives way to a new wrinkle.

A patient asked her psychiatrist, "Why do young people always seem to feel they can get away with things?" "It's because they know they have more time to improve," the psychiatrist replied.

At the college commencement, the senior alumni whispered to each other about how young the faculty looked; the faculty said the same thing about the graduating class; and the graduating class said the same thing about the freshmen. Youth is a relatively old story.

FACTS

Since the 1950s, America has had a split personality about its younger generation. On the one hand, the nation has lowered the age for voting eligibility; and broadened the students' rights charters. On the other hand, rates for car insurance still discriminate against men under 25 years of age. There is considerable prejudice against the views expressed by under 25-year-olds. And there is still considerable resentment of that generation's attempts to make themselves separate from the bosom of the family. Part of this scenario has existed throughout time, but it has been heightened by the pace and scope of modern life. As the population grows older, youth has acquired different connotations. Methods of maintaining a youthful appearance are marketed more aggressively than ever before, and the number of options is continually broadening. From health clubs and cosmetics, to collagen treatments and cosmetic surgery, youth is a salable commodity in America and around the world.

VOLUME II

APT COMPARISONS

The next several pages contain a list of the words for which comparisons and symbols are given in this particular volume of the *Speakers' Lifetime Library, Second Edition*. Each listed word has its own section of unique comparative similes, apt symbols and personifications, cross references to other listed words, and words with opposite meanings.

If you can't find the particular word in this list, then scan again for a similar term. For example, you won't find the word "afraid," but you will find the word "frightened."

Finding a suitable metaphor to reinforce a comparison is as easy as referring to a chosen section and picking one of several ways to paint an image in listener's minds.

Symbols and personifications used in place of a particular word have varying degrees of meaning, and in such cases they may be used to signify more than one word. *Midas,* for example, is a personification of the words "acquisitive" and "miserly." These terms are often applied as flexible images that can not only spice up a speech, but conjure up colorful word-pictures in a variety of contexts.

Similar and opposite terms—synonyms and antonyms—are the backbone of this volume. They are a handy reference for you to use to draw your own apt comparisons.

Words listed

A

abandoned
abbreviated
abiding
abrupt
absolute
absorbent
absorbing
abstinent
absurd
abundant
abused

abusive
accidental
accommodating
accomplished
accountable
accurate
acquisitive
active
acute
adaptable
adjustable
admirable
admired
adventurous

affected
affectionate
affirmative
afflicted
aged
aggravated
aggressive
agile
agitated
agreeable
aimless
airy
alien
alike

alone
aloof
amateurish
amazing
ambitious
amiable
ample
ancient
anemic
angelic
angry
anguished
annoying
anonymous
antagonistic
anxious
apathetic
apologetic
apparent
appealing
appreciated
approachable
appropriate
arbitrary
arguable
argumentative
arid
aromatic
arresting
arrogant
artful
artistic
assertive
assorted
athletic
atrocious
attentive
attractive

austere
authentic
authoritative
automatic
available
average
awful
awkward

B

backhanded
backward
bad
baffling
balanced
bald
bankrupt
barbarous
bare
barren
basic
beastly
beautiful
believable
beloved
bent
bewildered
big
bigoted
binding
biting
bitter
black
blank
bleak
blemished

blended
blessed
blind
bloody
blue
boisterous
bold
booming
bored
boring
botched
bothered
bottomless
bountiful
brave
breathless
breezy
brief
bright
brilliant
bristling
brittle
broad
broke
brutal
bulging
bulky
bumpy
bungled
burdensome
buried
busy

C

callous
calm

camouflaged
carefree
careful
carnal
casual
catching
cautious
ceaseless
celebrated
censored
certain
changeable
changed
changeless
chaotic
charitable
charming
chaste
chcap
cheated
cheerful
cherished
childish
choked
chronic
civilized
classic
classified
clean
clear
clever
close
closed
cloudy
coarse
cold
colorful
colorless

colossal
comfortable
comforting
comical
commanding
commendable
commercial
committed
common
commonplace
compelling
competitive
complete
complex
complicated
complimentary
compressed
compulsory
concealed
concentrated
concerned
concise
condensed
condescending
conditional
confident
confidential
confined
conformist
confused
congenial
congested
conscientious
considerate
consistent
constant
contagious
continuous

contrived
convenient
convincing
cool
cooperative
corny
correct
corrupt
cosmetic
cosmopolitan
courageous
courteous
cowardly
cracked
crafty
cranky
crass
craven
crazy
creative
criminal
critical
crooked
crucial
crude
cruel
crumbly
cultured
curious
cutting
cynical

D

dainty
damaged
damaging

dangerous

daring

dark

dashing

dated

dead

deadly

deaf

deafening

dear (affectionate)

dear (costly)

debatable

decadent

decayed

deceitful

deceptive

decisive

dedicated

deep

defensive

defiant

definite

delayed

deliberate

delicate

demonic

dense

dependable

deprived

deserted

deserving

desirable

desolate

desperate

despondent

destructive

detached

detestable

devious

devoted

dictatorial

different

difficult

dignificd

diplomatic

direct

dirty

disagreeable

disastrous

discounted

discouraged

discreet

disguised

dishonest

dismal

disorganized

disposable

dissipated

distant

distinguished

distorted

distracting

divided

dizzy

docile

doctored

dogged

dogmatic

dopey

doubtful

downhearted

dreadful

dreary

drowsy

drunk

dry

dubious

dull

dumb

duplicitous

durable

dutiful

E

eager

early

earthy

easy

economical

edgy

educated

eerie

effective

efficient

egotistical

elastic

electrifying

elegant

elementary

elevated

eligible

eloquent

elusive

embarrassed

eminent

emphatic

empty

enchanting

encouraging

endangered

endless

enduring

energetic
engaging
enigmatic
envious
erratic
erroneous
essential
established
estimable
euphoric
evasive
evil
exaggerated
exalted
excessive
exciting
exclusive
excusable
exemplary
exhausted
expensive
experienced
experimental
explicit
explosive
expressive
extended
extinct
extravagant
extreme

F

faceless
faded
faint
faithful
false
familiar
famous
fancy
far
fascinating
fast
fat
fatal
faulty
favorable
feeble
fertile
festive
feverish
fierce
filthy
final
fine
finished
firm
fishy
fit
flabby
flashy
flat
flattering
flawless
fleeting
flexible
flowery
foggy
foolish
forgetful
forgivable
forgotten
formal
forsaken
fortunate
fragrant
frail
frank
frantic
fraudulent
free
frequent
fresh
friendly
frightened
frightful
frugal
fruitful
fruitless
furious
fussy
futile
fuzzy

G

gallant
gaseous
gaudy
generous
genial
gentle
genuine
ghastly
gifted
glaring
gloomy
glorified
glorious
glossy
good

graceful

gracious

gradual

grand

grasping

grateful

greedy

gripping

gross

grouchy

grudging

guilty

H

habitual

hairy

handicapped

handsome

happy

hard

hard-core

hardy

harmful

harmless

harmonious

harsh

hasty

hateful

haughty

haunted

healing

healthy

hearty

heated

heavenly

heavy

heavy handed

hellish

helpful

helpless

hcretical

hcsitant

hidden

high

holy

honest

hopeful

hopeless

horrible

hospitable

hot

huge

humble

hungry

hurried

hybrid

hypocritical

I

icy

ideal

idealistic

idle

idolatrous

ignorant

ill-advised

illegible

ill-mannered

illogical

ill-tempered

imaginary

imitative

immaculate

immature

immediate

imminent

immodest

immoral

impartial

impatient

impersonal

important

impressive

improper

impudent

impulsive

impure

inaccessible

inaccurate

inadequate

incalculable

incompetent

incongruous

indelible

independent

indifferent

indiscreet

indulgent

ineffective

inefficient

ineligible

inept

inert

inevitable

inexcusable

infinite

inflamed

inflammable

inflated

informal

innocent

innovative

inquisitive

insincere

insistent

inspired

instantaneous

instinctive

instructive

insulting

intangible

intimate

intolerant

intoxicating

intricate

intrusive

intuitive

inventive

inviting

involved

irrational

irregular

irrelevant

isolated

J

jaded

jammed

jarring

jealous

Jewish

juicy

K

keen

kind

knotty

knowledgeable

L

laborious

large

lasting

late

lavish

lawless

lazy

leakproof

leaky

learned

left-handed

left out

legal

legendary

lethal

liberal

light

limited

limp

lingering

little

lonely

lonesome

long

loose

loud

lovable

lovely

low

loyal

lucky

M

mad

magnificent

magnified

majestic

matchless

meager

mean

meddlesome

meek

memorable

menacing

messy

mighty

militant

minimal

miraculous

misplaced

mistaken

misunderstood

mixed

mixed up

modern

modest

momentary

monotonous

monumental

moody

moving

muddled

N

naive
naked
narrow
nasty
natural
near
neat
necessary
needless
needy
negative
neglected
negligent
neighborly
nervous
neurotic
neutral
new
nice
nimble
noble
noisy
nostalgic
noticeable
notorious
nourishing
numerous
nutty

O

obedient
objectionable
oblivious
obscure

obsolete
obvious
odorous
offensive
officious
old
old-fashioned
ominous
open
opinionated
optimistic
original
overlooked
overwhelmed
overwhelming
overworked

P

packed
painful
pale
panic-stricken
paradoxical
parched
parochial
particular
partisan
passionate
patient
patronizing
peaceful
perfect
permanent
permissive
perpetual
personal

persuasive
pessimistic
pestilential
picky
piratical
pitiless
placid
plain
planned
plausible
playful
pleasant
pleased
pliable
pointed
poisonous
polished
polite
political
polluted
pompous
poor
popular
porous
portable
positive
possessive
powerful
precious
precise
predictable
prejudiced
premature
pretty
prevalent
privileged
productive

profitable
promising
prophetic
provocative
prudent
punctual
pure
puzzled

Q

quaint
quarrelsome
queasy
queer
questionable
quick
quiet
quoted

R

rabid
radiant
radical
random
rapid
rare
rash
raw
reactionary
reasonable
rebellious
reckless
red
refined

regular
regulated
rejected
relaxed
relentless
reliable
repentant
repetitious
replaceable
representative
repressed
resented
resolute
respectable
restless
revolutionary
rich
ridiculous
righteous
rigid
rotten
rough
rude
run-down
rushed
rusty

S

sacred
sacrificial
sad
safe
satisfied
savage
scandalous
scanty

scarce
scared
scattered
scornful
secret
seldom
selective
selfish
sensitive
sentimental
shady
shallow
sharp
short
shrewd
shrill
shy
sick
silent
simple
skinny
slim
slippery
slow
sly
small
smelly
smooth
smug
sneaky
sober
soft
solemn
solid
soothing
sore
sought after
soulful

sound
sour
sparse
special
spectacular
speculative
spontaneous
spotless
square
steadfast
sticky
strong
subtle
subversive
superficial
sure
surprised
suspicious
sweet
sympathetic
systematic

T

tactless
talkative
tame
tangled
tarnished
tasteful
tasteless
taxing
temporary
tense
tentative
thick
thin

threatening
tight
timeless
timely
tolerant
tough
transient
transparent
treacherous
tricky
true
trustworthy

U

ugly
uncertain
unclean
uncomfortable
uncompromising
underdeveloped
understandable
unfinished
unlucky
unnecessary
unpopular
unprepared
untruthful
urgent
useful
useless

V

vague
vain

varied
vast
versatile
visionary
volatile
vulgar

W

warm
watered
wayward
weak
wealthy
weary
welcome
wicked
wily
windy
winning
wise
worried
wrong

Y

yellow
young
youthful

Z

zealous

A

Abandoned: as a ghost town; as Salome's veils; as a used Kleenex; as a condemned house
  symbols: wreck of the Hesperus (Henry Wadsworth Longfellow); old mine shaft; an old, unloved toy
  see also: deserted; empty; forgotten
  opposite: crowded; jammed; populated

Abbreviated: as a grouch's smile; as a frost in August; as a classified ad; as a mini skirt
  symbols: Tom Thumb; pocket edition
  see also: condensed; short; small; brief
  opposite: windy; large; big; vast; long; excessive

Abiding: as the U.S. Constitution; as a mother's love; as a family feud; as a permanent house guest
  symbols: Rock of Ages; words written in stone; the Pyramids
  see also: enduring; endless; lasting; permanent
  opposite: temporary; momentary

Abrupt: as a military order; as a slap to an insult
  symbols: bolt from the blue; thunderbolt
  see also: rude; hasty; hurried
  opposite: gradual; smooth; leisurely

Absolute: as the laws of nature; as the state of virginity; as a miser's greed
  symbols: monarch of all he surveys; Tsar; emperor
  see also: arbitrary; rigid
  opposite: flexible; limited

Absorbent: as a child's mind; as a house plant
  symbols: sponge; blotting paper
  see also: imitative; pliable; porous
  opposite: closed; leakproof; impervious

Absorbing: as a good book by a cozy fire; as a fairy tale to a four-year-old; as a new love; as an entertaining discussion with a good friend
  symbols: Diogene's tub
  see also: exciting; fascinating; inviting
  opposite: dull; forgotten; overlooked

Abstinent: as a new nun; as a reformed sinner; as a recovering addict; as a vestal virgin
    symbols: Alcoholics Anonymous; Nazarite; the wagon
    see also: sober; dry; chaste
    opposite: drunk; dissipated

Absurd: as a clown's makeup; as an elephant playing a piccolo; as a monkey in a dinner jacket
    symbols: Alice in Wonderland; Wittgenstein
    see also: queer; strange; ridiculous; foolish
    opposite: wise; reasonable

Abundant: as the salt in the sea; as the corn in Kansas; as excuses in a traffic court; as sand in the Sahara; as the girth of a glutton
    symbols: Cornucopia; horn of plenty; a cup running over
    see also: numerous; fruitful
    opposite: scarce; sparse; rare

Abused: as a betrayed confidence; as a battered child; as the privileges of rank
    symbols: Job; Oliver Twist
    see also: damaged; deprived; excessive
    opposite: privileged; blessed; cherished

Abusive: as a heckler with a foul mouth; as a baseball fan disagreeing with the umpire; as an anonymous letter; as a crank phone call
    symbols: billingsgate; fishwife
    see also: nasty; insulting; impudent
    opposite: courteous; kind; polite

Accidental: as a slip on a banana peel; as an automobile crash; as a chance meeting of old friends; as being hit by lightning; as the whims of the gods
    symbols: spilled milk, Wrong-way Corrigan
    see also: casual; lucky; unlucky
    opposite: planned; deliberate

Accommodating: as a five-star hotel; as a salesman with a closing deal; as a new spouse; as a head waiter whose palm has been greased; as a doting mother
    symbols: Little Dorrit; Mother Hubbard
    see also: hospitable; helpful; welcome; neighborly
    opposite: disagreeable; cold; offensive

Accomplished: as the winner of a national merit scholarship; as an old master; as a finished performance; as a stroke of genius; as a Nobel Prize winner

    symbols: The Renaissance Man; Leonardo da Vinci; Madame Marie Curie

    see also: gifted; finished; complete

    opposite: unfinished; incompetent; inept

Accountable: as a businessman's books; as an income tax return; as the manager of a mint; as a sinner on Judgment Day

    symbols: where the buck stops; an audited taxpayer

    see also: guilty; reliable; responsible

    opposite: innocent; evasive; fraudulent; negligent; slippery

Accurate: as a champion sharpshooter; as a dictionary definition; as a hole in one; as perfect vocal pitch; as a knife thrower

    symbols: Kentucky rifleman; Annie Oakley

    see also: correct; perfect

    opposite: inaccurate; faulty; erroneous

Acquisitive: as a billionaire bond broker; as an empire builder; as the guy with his eye on the pie in the sky

    symbols: gold digger; Midas; Lorelei Lee; Fagan

    see also: greedy; grasping; wealthy; rich

    opposite: generous; poor; kind

Active: as a drop of water on a hot plate; as the toe of a tap dancer's shoe; as an angry volcano; as a tumbler on a trampoline

    symbols: whirling Dervish

    see also: busy; restless; involved

    opposite: inert; lazy; quiet

Acute: as a rupturing appendix; as a wise one's vision; as the pangs of hunger; as a blood hound's sense of smell

    symbols: the razor's edge; eagle's eye

    see also: sharp; keen; quick

    opposite: dull; dumb; slow

Adaptable: as putty; as an army wife; as an ambidextrous athlete

    symbols: chameleon

    see also: adjustable; flexible; pliable; changeable

    opposite: rigid; changeless; reactionary; absolute

Adjustable: as a pair of suspenders; as a tripod; as an insurance claim; as a bargainer's price
> symbols: Proteus
> see also: adaptable; flexible; changeable
> opposite: rigid; final; changeless

Admirable: as other people's courage in the face of adversity; as a young man's respect for an old man's years; as an anonymous charity
> symbols: The Admirable Crichton
> see also: exemplary; respectable; good; attractive
> opposite: hateful; detestable

Admired: as a teen idol; as a fashion model; as an old master; as the other guy's good luck
> symbols: folk hero; household god
> see also: cherished; lovable
> opposite: detestable; hateful

Adventurous: as Huck Finn on a raft; as a foreign correspondent; as a soldier of fortune
> symbols: Lochinvar; Daniel Boone; Davy Crockett; Lewis and Clark
> see also: brave; aggressive; daring
> opposite: hesitant; frightened; scared; shy

Affected: as a debutante actress; as a sophomore trying to look like a senior; as a ham actor; as an egotist trying to act humble
> symbols: Gongora; Gongorism; Restoration comedy
> see also: superficial; shallow
> opposite: plain; simple; humble; natural

Affectionate: as a cat let in from the cold; as newlyweds on their honeymoon
> symbols: lovebirds; Tristan and Isolde; Romeo and Juliet; turtledoves
> see also: dear; warm; devoted
> opposite: distant; disagreeable; cold; threatening

Affirmative: as a standing ovation; as a unanimous vote
> symbols: yes man
> see also: positive; confident; agreeable
> opposite: neutral; negative

Afflicted: as an itch that can't be scratched; as the first born sons of ancient Egypt; as a miser whose money turns out to be counterfeit

>   symbols: Job
>   see also: painful; pitiful; run-down
>   opposite: blessed; healthy; happy

Aged: as an old family heirloom; as choice Scotch whiskey; as ancient history; as the Petrified Forest

>   symbols: Methuselah; senior citizen; Sequoia National Forest
>   see also: old; ancient
>   opposite: young; youthful

Aggravated: as an atrocious assault; as a wound rubbed with salt

>   symbols: The Terrible Tempered Mr. Bang
>   see also: angry; anguished; bothered; furious
>   opposite: soothing; relaxed; calm

Aggressive: as a fighting cock; as a winning prizefighter; as a shopper at a bargain counter

>   symbols: Mars; Aries
>   see also: adventurous; menacing; threatening; assertive
>   opposite: relaxed; friendly; peaceful

Agile: as a circus acrobat; as a mountain goat; as a tightrope walker

>   symbols: Hermes; Mercury
>   see also: nimble; fast; graceful
>   opposite: awkward; confused

Agitated: as a Ping Pong ball in a blender; as troubled waters

>   symbols: Jeremiah; nervous Nellie; the Terrible Tempered Mr. Bang
>   see also: nervous; chaotic; frantic; anxious
>   opposite: relaxed; calm; placid

Agreeable: as an employee seeking a raise; as political candidate; as a cool breeze on a hot night

>   symbols: Elysium; Elysian fields
>   see also: amiable; pleasant; happy; kind
>   opposite: disagreeable; annoying; bristling

Aimless: as a caravan in a sandstorm; as a kite without a string; as a falling leaf; as a shot in the dark
symbols: drifter; a Kerouac character; rebel without a cause
see also: vague; bored; limp
opposite: ambitious; decisive; dedicated; deliberate

Airy: as a balloon ride; as a breeze through a thin dress; as cotton candy
symbols: Olympus; Pegasus
see also: carefree; light; windy; breezy
opposite: heavy; worried; tense

Alien: as corn in a field of rice; as a man on the moon; as a fish out of water; as a basketball player in a pygmy village; as a curmudgeon at a tea social
symbols: a man from Mars; little gray men; visitors from outer space; a greenhorn; a wetback
see also: different; strange
opposite: familiar; conformist; natural

Alike: as two eggs in a nest; as matched candlesticks; as ripples in a river
symbols: Tweedledee and Tweedledum; Chip and Dale; Gemini twins; Romulus and Remus
see also: conformist
opposite: different; matchless

Alone: as a hermit on a desert island; as an astronaut walking in space; as a person without a friend
symbols: Robinson Crusoe; Adam
see also: abandoned; desolate; isolated; lonely; lonesome; aloof
opposite: dense; crowded; jammed

Aloof: as a cat that doesn't want to be bothered; as woman who doesn't want to be wooed
symbols: Howard Hughes; Greta Garbo; the invisible man
see also: alone; cool; distant; icy; indifferent; haughty
opposite: friendly; amiable; charming; warm; approachable

Amateurish: as a Sunday painter; as a first music lesson; as a college athlete
symbols: duffer; home video
see also: inept; awkward
opposite: experienced

Amazing: as the transition from youth to adulthood; as the miracle of sunrise; as a child's imagination
>   symbols: The Twilight Zone; Believe It or Not
>   see also: surprised; miraculous
>   opposite: predictable

Ambitious: as a stage mother; as a young executive; as a politician with his eye on the White House
>   symbols: the new woman; the new guy at the office
>   see also: aggressive; hopeful
>   opposite: aimless; vague; relaxed

Amiable: as a happy drunk; as a class reunion; as a department store Santa; as a well-tipped waiter
>   symbols: life of the party
>   see also: agreeable; friendly; pleasant
>   opposite: disagreeable; nasty

Ample: as a fat man's waistline; as a rich person's assets; as a mother's love
>   symbols: the groaning board; cornucopia; horn of plenty
>   see also: abundant; fat; numerous; large
>   opposite: scarce; limited

Ancient: as the Pyramids; as the age of the dinosaurs; as the tides in the sea
>   symbols: Father Time; Methuselah; Father Abraham
>   see also: aged; old; dated; old-fashioned
>   opposite: modern; new

Anemic: as a pauper's bankroll; as an overdrawn bank account; as a flimsy excuse
>   symbols: tired blood; vampire's victim
>   see also: weak; sick
>   opposite: healthy; rich; strong

Angelic: as an innocent babe; as the heavenly choir; as the backers of a Broadway show
>   symbols: Gabriel; Ezriel; St. Peter; cherubs
>   see also: heavenly; pure; kind; good
>   opposite: disagreeable; bad; evil

Angry: as a mother bear defending her cubs; as a righteous man wrongly accused; as an open wound; as a woman scorned
    symbols: seething volcano; an unworshipped god
    see also: mad; ill-tempered; sore; inflamed
    opposite: calm; peaceful

Anguished: as parent who's lost a child; as a day of mourning; as a deserted lover
    symbols: Elektra
    see also: sad; painful; afflicted; worried; anxious
    opposite: happy; breezy; calm

Annoying: as an itch where you can't scratch; as rain on your best clothes; as an unanswered car alarm
    symbols: pain in the neck; the nasties
    see also: disagreeable; hateful
    opposite: agreeable; pleasant

Anonymous: as an obscene phone call; as a graffiti writer; as a ransom note; as a button in the church collection box
    symbols: John Doe; Jane Doe; Joe Blow
    see also: secret; hidden
    opposite: barefaced; open

Antagonistic: as oil and water; as fighters in a ring; as sin and redemption
    symbols: The Hatfields and the McCoys
    see also: argumentative; defiant; ill-tempered; pugnacious
    opposite: friendly; agreeable; affectionate; pleasant; apathetic

Anxious: as an expectant parent; as a taxpayer about to be audited; as a job applicant
    symbols: Nervous Nellie
    see also: agitated; bothered; worried; concerned
    opposite: calm; placid

Apathetic: as the audience at a dull lecture; as a speaker in a cemetery
    symbols: zombie
    see also: dull; placid
    opposite: anxious; eager

Apologetic: as a defendant trying to appease the judge; as a guest who comes too early; as an errant spouse caught erring
    symbols: Caspar Milquetoast; repentant sinner
    see also: embarrassed; hesitant; humble
    opposite: nasty; cutting; ill-mannered

Apparent: as the nose on your face; as the signature on a contract; as the writing on the wall; as the newness of a honeymoon couple; as the guilt of a man holding a smoking gun

    symbols: first blush

    see also: obvious; clear; certain; sure; noticeable

    opposite: debatable; uncertain; arguable; dubious; questionable

Appealing: as an uncrowded beach; as a free sample; as a child's laughter; as a friendly puppy

    symbols: heartthrob; a charismatic character; a film star

    see also: attractive; sympathetic; charming; nice

    opposite: ugly; hateful; nasty; rotten

Appreciated: as a kind word in a tense moment; as an unexpected compliment; as a paid vacation; as an unexpected bonus

    symbols: best-seller; people's choice; hot property

    see also: popular; welcome; desirable

    opposite: unpopular; objectionable

Approachable: as a prostitute walking the street; as a candidate looking for a hand to shake; as a puppy that wants to be petted

    symbols: open door; outstretched hand

    see also: amiable; friendly; pleasant; agreeable; affectionate

    opposite: aloof; haughty; antagonistic

Appropriate: as a coat in a cold snap; as a bottle in a barroom; as a bowl in a china shop; as a black tie at a formal affair

    symbols: protocol secretary; diplomat

    see also: ideal; correct

    opposite: wrong; unnecessary

Arbitrary: as a two-year-old's decision; as the strike of a lightning bolt

    symbols: Dutch uncle; a tin god

    see also: rigid; uncompromising; dictatorial

    opposite: adjustable; flexible; pliable

Arguable: as an umpire's call; as what came first, the chicken or the egg; as a lawyer's brief; as a case in court

    symbols: the great debate; the question before the house

    see also: questionable; uncertain; debatable; dubious; doubtful

    opposite: certain; sure; clear; obvious

Argumentative: as a session of the United Nations; as a spoiled child; as rival candidates in a hot election
> symbols: Philadelphia lawyer; barracks lawyer; jailhouse lawyer
> see also: quarrelsome; antagonistic; defensive; opinionated
> opposite: peaceful; agreeable; reasonable

Arid: as the Sahara; as a dry spell in the dust bowl
> symbols: Gobi Desert; Death Valley; dry bones
> see also: dry; parched; dull; empty
> opposite: watered; fruitful; deep; memorable

Aromatic: as a perfume counter; as a spice shop; as a pie in the oven
> symbols: the nose knows
> see also: smelly; fragrant; odorous
> opposite: blank; dead; arid

Arresting: as a banner headline; as a growl from a police dog; as a beautiful face; as a nudist on a crowded street
> symbols: John Law; a clock-stopper
> see also: impressive; noticeable; spectacular
> opposite: dull; blank; boring

Arrogant: as a person oversure of his abilities; as a civil servant with seniority; as the Caesars
> symbols: commissar; Dutch uncle
> see also: haughty; rude; offensive; officious
> opposite: humble; kind; courteous

Artful: as contrived simplicity; as a pitchman's presentation; as a master craftsman; as an old master
> symbols: The Artful Dodger; Michelangelo
> see also: wily; sly; tricky; calculating; artistic; devious
> opposite: simple; plain

Artistic: as a Louvre masterpiece; as a sonata by Beethoven; as a master chef's best creation
> symbols: Picasso; Mozart; the Muses
> see also: beautiful; tasteful; gifted
> opposite: coarse; vulgar; tasteless

Assertive: as a convert; as a Washington lobbyist; as a hungry puppy
> symbols: town crier
> see also: loud; positive; argumentative
> opposite: apathetic; neutral; hesitant; quiet

Assorted: as a laundry list; as a fancy antipasto; as the items at a rummage sale
    symbols: hash; a mixed bag
    see also: varied; mixed; blended; different
    opposite: alike

Athletic: as a decathlon champion; as a fitness instructor; as a triathlon athlete
    symbols: the Olympics; Hercules; Charles Atlas; Arnold Schwarzenegger
    see also: healthy; active; strong; fit
    opposite: inert; flabby

Atrocious: as a terrorist bombing; as the crime of the century; as the diary of Vlad the Impaler
    symbols: Ivan the Terrible; Count Dracula
    see also: awful; cruel; horrible; frightful; hellish; evil
    opposite: kind; warm; gentle; good; angelic

Attentive: as someone hoping to be remembered in your will; as a spellbound audience
    symbols: Argus; "His Master's Voice"
    see also: devoted; obedient; considerate; warm
    opposite: indifferent; distant; cool

Attractive: as a beauty to the beast; as a cool drink on a hot day; as metal to a magnet; as young love; as sunlight after a storm
    symbols: Helen of Troy; the Sirens; the Lorelei
    see also: appealing; charming; fascinating; beautiful
    opposite: ugly; crumby; beastly

Austere: as a monastery on a mountain top; as a Puritan's wardrobe; as a hearing in the Supreme Court
    symbols: Spartan; Draco; Amish
    see also: harsh; hard; frugal; minimal
    opposite: extravagant; lavish; soft; rich

Authentic: as a fingerprint; as an Act of Congress; as a certified check; as a coin fresh from the mint
    symbols: the real McCoy; the Holy Grail; the genuine article
    see also: real; true; genuine
    opposite: false; lying; untruthful

Authoritative: as the Ten Commandments; as a Supreme Court decision; as a holy writ; as divine inspiration
    symbols: the horse's mouth; the Oracle at Delphi; the Almanach de Gotha
    see also: reliable; compelling; true; trustworthy; positive
    opposite: untruthful; false; evasive; uncertain

Automatic: as the lunch time whistle; as the stroke of midnight; as a recorded message; as the blink of an eye; as a traffic signal; as a cadet's salute

    symbols: Big Ben; voice mail; e-mail, auto-pilot

    see also: certain; predictable; constant; habitual; planned; sure

    opposite: spontaneous; uncertain; chaotic; disorganized

Available: as a teacher on summer vacation; as an actor at liberty; as a vacant billboard; as the air we breathe

    symbols: Available Jones

    see also: open; abundant; numerous

    opposite: scarce; sparse

Average: as the middle of the road; as the Dow Jones index; as the man on the street

    symbols: John Q. Public; Normal Norman

    see also: normal; regular

    opposite: special; different; extreme

Awful: as sin; as the face of death; as a shriek in the night; as the truth when it hurts

    symbols: the fires of Hell; the Days of Awe; the wrath of the gods

    see also: bad; atrocious; horrible; disastrous; impressive; mighty

    opposite: modest; small; cheerful; good; exemplary; pleasant

Awkward: as an adolescent; as a toddler's dancing class; as a flimsy alibi; as a blind date

    symbols: the awkward age; a penguin on the shore

    see also: inept; heavy-handed

    opposite: graceful; gracious; agile; nimble

B

Backhanded: as damning with faint praise; as a tennis shot at Wimbledon; as praising with faint damns; as a cynic's smile

    symbols: the sly fox

    see also: devious; duplicitous; sly; awkward; hypocritical

    opposite: direct; barefaced; graceful; gracious

Backward: as a horse and buggy on a superhighway; as the glances of a gangster on the lam; as a ten-year-old in kindergarten; as a trip in reverse; as a trip in a time machine

    symbols: Simple Simon; dinosaur; village idiot; bumpkin; yokel

    see also: slow; delayed; ignorant

    opposite: bright; wise; quick

Bad: as a rotten apple; as the wicked witch of the west; as a mob's manners; as an illiterate's spelling; as a Christmas fruitcake in July

    symbols: the big bad wolf; the Devil; Satan; Lucifer; Boris Badinov

    see also: evil; rude; mean; sick

    opposite: good; pleasant; amiable

Baffling: as the mystery of life; as a *New York Times* crossword puzzle; as the birth of the universe

    symbols: the Sphinx

    see also: confused; complex; complicated; difficult

    opposite: understandable; clear; easy

Balanced: as a man on a tightrope; as a banker's checkbook; as the scales of justice; as a report by Price, Waterhouse

    symbols: juggler; unicyclist

    see also: alike; harmonious; honest

    opposite: extravagant; extreme; distorted

Bald: as a billiard ball; as the American eagle; as a newborn baby

    symbols: Mexican Hairless; skinhead

    see also: bare; smooth; naked; obvious

    opposite: hairy; hidden; devious

Bankrupt: as a junk bond trader on Judgment Day; as a buyer of the Brooklyn Bridge; as an inept gambler

    symbols: gone to the cleaners; taking a bath; ten cents on the dollar

    see also: broke; poor; deprived; run down

    opposite: rich; wealthy; affluent; prosperous

Barbarous: as human sacrifice; as the Spanish Inquisition; as the Bataan Death March; as the Holocaust

    symbols: Attila the Hun; frontier justice; the Black Hole of Calcutta

    see also: savage; brutal; cruel

    opposite: civilized; kind; cultured

Bare: as the truth uncovered; as maple tree in February; as an empty cupboard

    symbols: September morn; the Emperor with his new clothes

    see also: bald; naked; simple; barren; open

    opposite: concealed; camouflaged; closed

Barren: as the surface of the moon; as a blank page; as a vacant lot; as a pauper's prospects

    symbols: desert; Death Valley

    see also: arid; fruitless; parched; bare

    opposite: fruitful; productive

Basic: as ABC; as boiling water; as the law of supply and demand; as the Ten Commandments; as food and water
    symbols: First Principles; base one; 1-2-3
    see also: essential; elementary; necessary
    opposite: unnecessary; excessive; fancy

Beastly: as the law of the jungle; as the animals in the Ark; as a desert heat wave; as an Arctic winter; as the occupants of the zoo
    symbols: saber-tooth tiger; tooth and claw; an angry lion
    see also: cruel; fierce
    opposite: civilized; kind; polite

Beautiful: as a happy memory; as a bride; as the sunset that ends a perfect day; as the face of true love; as a spring flower
    symbols: Venus; Helen of Troy
    see also: lovely; attractive; appealing; handsome; pretty
    opposite: ugly; awful; coarse; dirty; frightful

Believable: as seeing for yourself; as being there; as a certified check; as a deathbed confession
    symbols: the real McCoy; eye witness
    see also: trustworthy; convincing
    opposite: transparent; treacherous; lying

Beloved: as a nursery rhyme; as a favorite toy; as Orpheus was to Eurydice
    symbols: Daphne and Chloe; Romeo and Juliet; Tristan and Isolde
    see also: affectionate; dear; lovable; precious
    opposite: detestable; hateful; nasty

Bent: as a sink drain; as an old work horse; as a French horn; as a pretzel; as a ritual contortionist
    symbols: the crooked man who walked a crooked mile; a clover-leaf turn
    see also: crooked; distorted
    opposite: direct; straight

Bewildered: as a navigator in the fog; as a pilot in a cloud; as a baby first seeing itself in a mirror; as one awakened from a dream
    symbols: orphan of the storm; the lost soul; the awakened sleepwalker
    see also: confused; puzzled; mixed up
    opposite: confident; commanding; calm; correct

Big: as a billionaire's bankroll; as a pregnant elephant; as a Kansas cornfield; as the Himalayan mountains
  symbols: Behemoth; Leviathan; Gargantua
  see also: huge; large; colossal
  opposite: small; minimal

Bigoted: as a kangaroo court; as a small-town mob facing a stranger
  symbols: Salem witch trial; a book burning
  see also: narrow; prejudiced; ignorant; intolerant; exclusive
  opposite: tolerant; liberal; friendly; neighborly

Binding: as a ball and chain; as a contract signed in blood; as a sworn oath; as a matrimonial oath
  symbols: Ten Commandments; Bushido; Loyalty Oath
  see also: compulsory; effective
  opposite: ineffective; tentative

Biting: as a bad review; as a swarm of mosquitoes; as a cynic's complaint
  symbols: Mr. Vitriol; Dr. Knock
  see also: sharp; bitter; nasty; cutting
  opposite: kind; sweet; soft

Bitter: as a sour lemon; as a Chicago winter; as Passover herbs
  symbols: Eumenides (the Furies); Xanthippe
  see also: cold; sour; sharp; harsh; bleak
  opposite: happy; soft; sweet; kind

Black: as gallows humor; as the dead of night; as a graveyard smile
  symbols: River Styx; Soul
  see also: dark
  opposite: pale; light

Blank: as a stoic's expression; as a fresh canvas; as a new student's mind
  symbols: clean slate
  see also: empty; clean; clear; desolate; bare; barren
  opposite: crowded; messy; congested

Bleak: as the stock market after a crash; as a dry lake bed; as a forest after a fire
  symbols: Slough of Despond; Wuthering Heights
  see also: dismal; bitter; colorless; alone
  opposite: colorful; warm; hospitable; encouraging

Blemished: as a rake's reputation; as a mobster's record; as a sinner's soul
    symbols: damaged goods; Adam after Eden
    see also: impure; tarnished; damaged; faulty
    opposite: pure; flawless; perfect

Blended: as a frozen daiquiri; as a cake batter; as a fine perfume
    symbols: milkshake; mulligan stew
    see also: mixed; varied
    opposite: divided

Blessed: as a bountiful harvest; as the Good Book; as Sunday's child; as a prodigy
    symbols: God's favorites; Fortunate Isles; the gifted one
    see also: exalted; happy; sacred; holy; lucky; fortunate
    opposite: damned; unlucky

Blind: as one who will not see; as a bat; as the three mice who ran after the farmer's wife
    symbols: Justice; Braille; faith
    see also: oblivious; handicapped
    opposite: sensitive; visionary

Bloody: as an operating room; as a battlefield; as an axe murder; as shaving with a dull razor; as a sacrificial altar
    symbols: slaughterhouse; Aceldama
    see also: red; brutal; savage
    opposite: kind; happy; safe; peaceful

Blue: as the skies above; as a disappointed lover; as the waters of the sea; as a field of cornflowers
    symbols: blue Monday; deep ocean
    see also: colorful; anguished; worried
    opposite: colorless; happy; cheerful; clean

Boisterous: as sailors on liberty fresh from the sea; as the winning team's locker room; as Saturday night in the corner saloon; as kids when school lets out
    symbols: the road of the crowd
    see also: loud; noisy; rough
    opposite: quiet; refined; silent

Bold: as a Times Square billboard; as a seasoned warrior; as polished brass; as an avenging angel
    symbols: Achilles; Sir Galahad; Sir Lancelot; Hector
    see also: daring; brave; courageous
    opposite: cowardly; quiet

Booming: as a summer thunderstorm; as business in a bank on payday; as a 21-gun salute; as a bull market; as a baritone's finale

symbols: Big Bertha

see also: loud; noisy; busy; rushed; prosperous

opposite: quiet; slow; poor

Bored: as a two-year-old at a metaphysical lecture; as the audience when an after-dinner speech becomes a forever-after speech; as an arts major in an accounting class

symbols: Sleeping Beauty; Job's comforter

see also: jaded; apathetic

opposite: active; involved

Boring: as somebody else's snapshots; as yesterday's news

symbols: a bad speaker

see also: dull; empty

opposite: fascinating; gripping; compelling; exciting; charming

Botched: as hard-boiled oatmeal; as burnt bacon; as a bad nose job; as the Titanic's navigation; as the Hindenberg's last landing

symbols: Watergate; Waterloo

see also: bungled; spoiled; mixed up

opposite: perfect; right

Bothered: as a bull seeing red; as a politician who's been misquoted; as three women wearing the same dress at a party

symbols: Old Fortunatas (Thomas Dekker)

see also: aggravated; worried; anxious; downhearted; bewildered; concerned

opposite: calm; cool; relaxed; placid

Bottomless: as an adolescent's stomach; as a philanthropist's pockets; as the pits of despair

symbols: quicksand; Tartarus; the lower depths of the ocean

see also: endless; deep; unfinished

opposite: high; narrow

Bountiful: as an abundant harvest; as flowers after a rain; as a Thanksgiving banquet; as praise to a hero

symbols: cornucopia; the horn of plenty; Lady Bountiful; the last of the big-time spenders

see also: fruitful; rich; fertile

opposite: poor; meager; sparse; arid

Brave: as a professional parachute tester; as a matador in the bull ring; as a bearer of bad tidings
- symbols: lion; David; Sir Galahad
- see also: courageous; bold; daring
- opposite: afraid; frightened; cowardly; scared

Breathless: as a middle-aged marathon runner; as a diver with an empty aqualung
- symbols: a cigar smoker; Marilyn Monroe
- see also: exhausted; excited
- opposite: calm

Breezy: as a beach in Barbados; as a balmy spring day
- symbols: Zephyr; Pollyanna; care of Aeolus
- see also: windy; airy
- opposite: calm; quiet

Brief: as a grouch's smile; as an Arctic summer; as the lifespan of a raindrop
- symbols: abridged edition; nutshell; excerpted version
- see also: abbreviated; abrupt; quick; fast
- opposite: extended; long

Bright: as sunshine; as the lights on Broadway; as the sparkle of a ten-carat diamond
- symbols: the Milky Way; the Great White Way
- see also: light; flashy; glaring; brilliant
- opposite: dull; dark; slow

Brilliant: as a flash of lightning; as the invention of the wheel; as a Fulbright scholar
- symbols: Einstein; Leonardo da Vinci; summer sunshine; ball of fire
- see also: glaring; bright; electrifying; inspired
- opposite: dull; dark; slow; blank

Bristling: as a porcupine; as a hedgehog; as an unfriendly witness; as an untamed shrew
- symbols: wild boar; Xanthippe
- see also: angry; aggressive; nasty; rough
- opposite: amiable; friendly; peaceful; calm

Brittle: as the pages of an old book; as old bones; as an eggshell
- symbols: eggshell; glass windowpane
- see also: frail; weak
- opposite: strong; firm; solid

Broad: as the passage to Hell; as the ocean; as an angel's wingspan
    symbols: Dan to Beersheba; the Milky Way; the Big Dipper
    see also: ample; large; big
    opposite: narrow; small

Broke: as an undiscovered artist
    symbols: poorhouse; poverty row
    see also: bankrupt; poor
    opposite: rich; affluent

Brutal: as the deaths of Lizzie Borden's parents; as a hostile takeover
    symbols: Yahoo; Roman holiday
    see also: cruel; savage; barbarous; fierce; harsh
    opposite: civilized; cultured; kind

Bulging: as a greedy squire's cheeks; as Santa's sack; as a magician's sleeves
    symbols: overstuffed chair; Falstaff
    see also: fat; excessive; bulky
    opposite: thin; anemic; skinny

Bulky: as a wet sweater; as a bear in autumn
    symbols: Goliath; Falstaff; Gargantua
    see also: large; big; fat
    opposite: small; thin

Bumpy: as a dirt road in a dog cart; as a toad with measles; as a ride down the rapids
    symbols: air pocket; rocky road; logging trail
    see also: rough; uncomfortable
    opposite: smooth; calm; comfortable

Bungled: as the introduction to the Edsel; as the headline "Dewey beats Truman"; and the charge of the Light Brigade
    symbols: Gallipoli; butterfingers
    see also: botched; spoiled; mixed up
    opposite: perfect; accomplished; brilliant

Burdensome: as a fur coat in July; as a piano salesman's sample bag; as the trials of Job
    symbols: labors of Hercules; Sisyphus; lodestone
    see also: heavy; uncomfortable
    opposite: light; carefree; comfortable; comforting

Buried: as Bluebeard's treasure; as King Tut's tomb; as a nudist's modesty
  symbols: R.I.P.; Lethe
  see also: concealed; secret; hidden; repressed
  opposite: open; apparent; noticeable; obvious

Busy: as a bee in a daisy field; as a bumblebee in a blossom; as a beaver building a dam; as an ant at a picnic; as a sales clerk during a one-day sale
  symbols: beehive; bargain basement sale
  see also: ceaseless; crowded; feverish; overworked; rushed
  opposite: idle; carefree; quiet

C

Calculating: as a fortune teller; as the finance committee at an accountant's convention; as a taxpayer in search of a refund; as an adding machine running amok
  symbols: Delilah; Caesar's Cassius; Iago
  see also: wily; sly; artful; tricky
  opposite: simple; plain; honest

Callous: as the heel of a barefoot boy; as a career criminal; as a dictator's conscience; as a senior clerk in the complaint department
  symbols: Hardhearted Hanna; heart of stone; cold shoulder
  see also: hard; indifferent; cruel
  opposite: soft; considerate; sympathetic; kind

Calm: as still waters; as the quiet after the storm; as sleeping dogs
  symbols: Sunday vespers; deserted village; ghost town; Nirvana
  see also: placid; quiet; relaxed
  opposite: agitated; frantic; chaotic; worried; edgy

Camouflaged: as a wheat shaft in an oat field; as a wolf in sheep's clothing; as laundered money
  symbols: chameleon; Trojan horse; jungle patrol
  see also: concealed; hidden; secret
  opposite: apparent; obvious; noticeable

Carefree: as a kid on vacation; as a prepaid holiday; as a happy ending; as a man at peace with the world;
  symbols: the lotus eaters; the man who broke the bank at Monte Carlo
  see also: happy; relaxed; airy
  opposite: anxious; worried

Careful: as a barefoot boy in a field of broken glass; as a cat on a tightrope; as a parachute inspector

    symbols: by the numbers; by the book

    see also: cautious; conscientious

    opposite: negligent; careless

Carnal: as a satyr's stare; as sex in the barnyard; as an X-rated movie; as Saturday night in a bordello

    symbols: Circean cup; Messalina; Casanova

    see also: earthy; sexy

    opposite: innocent; pure

Casual: as a greeting from an old friend; as an adolescent's attitude; as a beachcomber's attire

    symbols: pot luck; blue jeans; que sera sera

    see also: carefree; relaxed; informal

    opposite: formal; regular; frantic

Catching: as a cold; as a crowd's enthusiasm; as a sprinter chasing a crawler; as a fisherman's net

    symbols: hit parade; epidemic

    see also: contagious; attractive

    opposite: elusive; isolated; ugly

Cautious: as a new keeper with an old gorilla; as a doctor without malpractice insurance; as a taxidermist's cat; as a candidate's speech writer; as a statement from the State Department

    symbols: Fabian

    see also: careful; discreet

    opposite: careless; negligent

Ceaseless: as the stars in the heavens; as the battle of the sexes; as the cycle of life

    symbols: perpetual motion

    see also: endless; constant; perpetual; permanent

    opposite: temporary; momentary

Celebrated: as the Savior's birth; as the cure for polio; as the wages of sin; as children's birthdays

    symbols: hero of the hour; the talk of the town

    see also: famous; important

    opposite: quiet; obscure

Censored: as a prisoner's mail; as a copy of *Playboy* at the Vatican; as a mouth washed out with soap; as a Chinese newscast
  symbols: Mrs. Gundy; Bowdler; book burning
  see also: classified; repressed; concealed; hidden; secret
  opposite: public; permissive; open

Certain: as death and taxes (Benjamin Franklin); as water flowing downhill; as the probability of change; as fate
  symbols: sure thing; money in the bank
  see also: sure; constant; definite
  opposite: uncertain; arguable; changeable

Changeable: as a teenager's taste; as a baby's diaper; as the mood of a mob; as the latest fashions; as the weather
  symbols: Proteus; chameleon
  see also: moody; volatile; elastic
  opposite: constant; steadfast; definite

Changed: as autumn leaves; as a dollar in an origami master's hand; as yesterday's innocence; as a convert's faith
  symbols: new look; metamorphosis
  see also: different; varied; dated
  opposite: alike; conformist

Changeless: as the expression of the Sphinx; as the Ten Commandments
  symbols: rock of ages; words carved in stone
  see also: steadfast; true; constant
  opposite: changeable; uncertain; different

Chaotic: as the construction of the Tower of Babel; as the post office on tax day; as rush hour downtown; as a kindergarten class on rollerblades
  symbols: bedlam; Tower of Babel
  see also: agitated; busy; frantic; panic-stricken; disorganized
  opposite: calm; quiet; peaceful; relaxed

Charitable: as the person who helps those too poor to ever repay; as a helping hand; as forgiving a sinner; as giving people faith and hope
  symbols: the good Samaritan; Lady Bountiful
  see also: generous; kind; helpful; considerate
  opposite: cruel; harsh; mean

Charming: as a person persuading a snake to do tricks; as a performer making a pitch for a part; as innocent young love; as a candidate at a fundraising party; as a finishing school teacher
    symbols: Prince Charming; the three Graces
    see also: appealing; attractive; beautiful; enchanting
    opposite: hateful; objectionable; ugly

Chaste: as a vestal virgin; as ice (Shakespeare); as a suitor who's still chasing; as the mind of a newborn baby
    symbols: an innocent; Artemis; Sir Galahad
    see also: pure; clean; innocent
    opposite: blemished; tarnished; impure

Cheap: as dirt; as a penny stock option; as unsolicited advice; as a rummage sale; as a day old newspaper; as a secondhand toupee
    symbols: Scrooge; Jack Benny; Mickey Mouse
    see also: stingy; crumbly
    opposite: dear; generous

Cheated: as a customer who buys the Brooklyn Bridge; as the person who plans to con the con man; as the victim of a stacked deck; as a junk bond investor
    symbols: sucker; bag holder
    see also: damaged; forsaken; left out; overlooked; unlucky
    opposite: prosperous; rich; wealthy; winning

Cheerful: as school kids on a snow day; as an infectious laugh; as a good meal; in pleasant company; as an incurable optimist
    symbols: Pollyanna; Thalia
    see also: pleasant; agreeable; amiable; happy
    opposite: sad; moody; downhearted; dreary; gloomy

Cherished: as the family heirlooms; as a fond memory; as a good reputation; as a lifelong friend
    symbols: Queen of Hearts; America's sweetheart
    see also: beloved; dear; precious; appreciated
    opposite: forsaken; rejected; forgotten

Childish: as skipping down the sidewalk; as chewing a pacifier; as a security blanket; as a rubber duck in the bathtub; as a spontaneous tantrum
    symbols: the children's hour; kindergarten
    see also: young; youthful; immature; foolish
    opposite: old; mature; wise

Choked: as a nonsmoker at a cigar convention; as a bunter's baseball bat; as an engine coming up for air; as a clogged chimney
    symbols: garrote
    see also: jammed; brief; dead; short
    opposite: clear; strong; long; loose

Chronic: as complaints from critics; as crabgrass; as hay fever; as wondering about the weather; as a compulsive gambler's habit
    symbols: four-time loser; unreformed alcoholic
    see also: regular; constant; lasting; continuous; permanent
    opposite: temporary; uncertain; acute

Civilized: as linen dinner napkins; as a symphony in the park; as an Edwardian drawing room; as a hearing in the U.S. Supreme Court
    symbols: tea social
    see also: educated; cultured; refined
    opposite: coarse; vulgar; rude

Classic: as the Bible; as a Strauss waltz; as a martini; as a '57 Chevy; as a black evening dress
    symbols: Augustan
    see also: lasting; enduring
    opposite: transient; momentary

Classified: as a Pentagon secret; as the ranks of the Army and Navy; as the genuses of Nature; as the Kennedy assassination files; as a sealed bid
    symbols: official secrets; caste system
    see also: assorted; censored; varied
    opposite: open; public; disorganized

Clean: as a pastor's parable; as bones bleached by the sun; as new sneakers
    symbols: new broom; Simon Pure
    see also: pure; flawless; spotless; immaculate
    opposite: dirty; blemished; tarnished; impure; unclean

Clear: as a cloudless sky; as an open road; as an ultimatum; as a fist in the face; as crystal
    symbols: plain English; open book
    see also: obvious; certain; apparent; understandable
    opposite: foggy; fuzzy; cloudy

Clever: as a cautious cat; as a magician
    symbols: old fox
    see also: calculating; intuitive; sly; wise
    opposite: simple; innocent; dumb

Close: as the air in a smoke-filled room; as a tie at a horseshoe toss; as the fingers of your hand; as next year is to New Year's Eve
    symbols: a hair's breadth; Damon and Pythias
    see also: near; stingy; arguable; debatable; questionable; dear
    opposite: distant; certain; sure; obvious; far; antagonistic

Closed: as a bigot's mind; as a deal where the seller has already cashed the check; as a kindergarten at midnight; as a gated community
    symbols: a vaulted door; a tomb
    see also: bigoted; narrow; repressed; isolated; censored
    opposite: open; available; liberal; expressive

Cloudy: as a murky pool; as a New England winter; as November in London; as the dregs of a wine cask
    symbols: nimbus; cumulus
    see also: foggy; fuzzy; dark; dense; uncertain
    opposite: bright; clear; apparent; obvious; certain

Coarse: as burlap; as convict's conversation; as locker room humor
    symbols: Caliban; Goth; Philistine
    see also: vulgar; rude; rough
    opposite: gentle; smooth; refined

Cold: as a hermit's hospitality; as a polar bear's living room; as the dark side of the moon; as Valley Forge
    symbols: North Pole; Arctic; Jack Frost; iceberg; South Pole
    see also: bitter; windy; icy; antagonistic
    opposite: warm; friendly; hospitable

Colorful: as peacock's plumes; as a painter's palette; as the flowers that bloom in the spring
    symbols: rainbow; Joseph's coat
    see also: flashy; bright; brilliant; gaudy
    opposite: colorless; bleak; barren; bare; desolate

Colorless: as the air we breathe; as a deprived chameleon; as a bashful mouse
symbols: Plain Jane
see also: bleak; dull; boring; barren
opposite: colorful; flashy; gaudy; brilliant; spectacular

Colossal: as the national debt; as the expanding universe; as the birth rate of bacteria; as a ham actor's ego
symbols: Colossus of Rhodes; Gargantua
see also: huge; vast; ample; big
opposite: small; little; meager

Comfortable: as a cow in a corncrib; as your own bed; as a friendly conversation; as an old sweater
symbols: Land of Cockaigne; bosom of the family
see also: easy; relaxed; convenient
opposite: restless; uncomfortable

Comforting: as an apology accepted; as a mother's hug; as a vote of confidence; as a hot cup on a cold morning
symbols: Nirvana; purring kitten
see also: encouraging; soothing; sympathetic; warm
opposite: callous; cool; indifferent; cruel

Comical: as clowns; as somebody else slipping on a banana peel; as the Sunday funnies
symbols: slapstick; French farce; the Marx brothers
see also: absurd; nutty; playful
opposite: serious; dull; boring; sad

Commanding: as the tablets from Mount Sinai; as an imperial monarch; as a spoiled child; as the tug of fate; as a date with destiny
symbols: Zeus; brass
see also: dictatorial; compelling; decisive
opposite: weak; shy; uncertain

Commendable: as keeping the faith; as virtue in a sea of temptation; as kindness in a selfish world; as valor on the battlefield
symbols: seal of approval; Congressional Medal of Honor; applause; knighthood
see also: good; desirable; admirable
opposite: bad; inexcusable; objectionable

Commercial: as a sponsor's message; as a shopping mall; as an infomercial; as a pitchman's spiel; as a sale demonstration in a department store
> symbols: the street; over-the-counter
> see also: profitable; speculative; competitive
> opposite: amateurish; speculative; competitive

Committed: as a convict with a life sentence; as a miser is to money; as the folks that signed the contract; as an asylum's inmates
> symbols: dues payer; working member
> see also: dedicated; local; involved
> opposite: indifferent; evasive; cool; casual; left out

Common: as clay; as a crowd; as the lowest denominator; as the ground and the air we breathe; as horse sense
> symbols: run of the mill
> see also: earthy; average
> opposite: rare; special

Commonplace: as the union of consenting adults; as the standard set of sins; as growing old
> symbols: Tom, Dick, and Harry; vanilla
> see also: average; square; frequent
> opposite: rare; affected; special

Compelling: as a court order; as a gun to your head; as the call of the wild; as a good mystery story
> symbols: Hobson's Choice; Fate; the Fates
> see also: binding; persuasive; effective; commanding; convincing; gripping
> opposite: weak; inadequate; debatable; dull

Competitive: as cut-throat capitalism; as baby birds at feeding time; as two prospectors staking out the same claim; as a grudge match; as three horse traders in a one-horse town
> symbols: dog eat dog; price war; survival of the fittest; sharks in the shark pool
> see also: commercial; antagonistic
> opposite: apathetic; indifferent; cooperative

Complete: as a family with 27 children; as Adam's exile from the Garden of Eden; as a total eclipse; as the unabridged dictionary
> symbols: the works; the cosmos
> see also: absolute; final; finished
> opposite: partial; underdeveloped; unfinished

Complex: as a set of unabridged instructions; as filing an income tax form; as French irregular verbs; as the rules of cricket; as explanation of quantum physics
    symbols: Gordian knot; software documentation
    see also: baffling; complicated; difficult
    opposite: understandable; clear; easy; simple

Complicated: as the directions for an assemble-it-yourself computer; as a maze with moving walls; as business between former friends; as a bureaucrat's explanation of the rules
    symbols: labyrinth
    see also: difficult; complex; baffling
    opposite: clear; simple; understandable; easy

Complimentary: as a vote of confidence; as a standing ovation; as a testimonial dinner; as the guest soaps in a hotel room
    symbols: blue ribbon; four stars; the morning meal at a bed-and-breakfast
    see also: gracious; flattering
    opposite: insulting; rude

Compressed: as a three-page summary of the Bible; as the gas in a high-pressure tank; as the Lord's prayer on the head of a pin; as a whale in a sardine can
    symbols: microfilm; CD-ROM
    see also: condensed; concentrated; concise; brief; tight
    opposite: loose; excessive; long

Compulsory: as wearing clothes in public; as going to school; as paying taxes; as plowing is for a farmer
    symbols: a must; the law of the land
    see also: arbitrary; dogmatic; rigid; dictatorial
    opposite: adjustable; pliant; free

Concealed: as a secret love life; as a worm inside an apple; as a hero's fears; as the beauties of poverty; as the identity of an anonymous obscene phone call; as the gloved hand of fate
    symbols: hide and seek; closed doors
    see also: secret; hidden; buried; camouflaged; censored
    opposite: open; obvious; apparent; noticeable

Concentrated: as a hypnotist's stare; as the pain of a hangover; as frozen orange juice
    symbols: Johnny one-note
    see also: compressed; concise; condensed; attentive
    opposite: indifferent; weak; apathetic; loose

Concerned: as an investor watching his stock hit zero; as the bookie when a 100 to 1 shot wins the race; as a new quarterback about to be blitzed
  symbols: Nervous Nellie; worry wart
  see also: anxious; worried; agitated; bothered; tense
  opposite: relaxed; calm; placid; apathetic

Concise: as a headline; as a nice girl's "no"; as the "I do" in a wedding ceremony; as a New Englander's answer
  symbols: Tacitean; nutshell; Spartan brevity
  see also: brief; compressed; concentrated; tight
  opposite: loose; windy; excessive; long

Condensed: as dehydrated soup; as a college cram course; as the milk of human kindness
  symbols: pocket edition; thumbnail; digest
  see also: concise; compressed; concentrated; short; abbreviated; brief
  opposite: long; windy; excessive

Condescending: as a sophomore to a freshman; as a critic trying to make a reputation; as a self-professed connoisseur telling you why you know nothing
  symbols: Lord of the manor; cock of the walk; load of creation; Prima Donna
  see also: haughty; arrogant; officious; patronizing
  opposite: polite; courteous; free; friendly

Conditional: as a politician's ultimatum; as a used car salesman's "last offer"; as a postponed foreclosure; as a doctor's prognosis; as a picnic in April
  symbols: the big if; the "yes" but syndrome
  see also: tentative; uncertain
  opposite: absolute; certain

Confident: as a rooster in a hen house; as the only candidate on the ballot; as a man with lots of money in his pocket and no debts to pay
  symbols: Pollyanna; Pangloss
  see also: sure; bold; certain; positive; resolute
  opposite: hopeless; anxious; worried; concerned

Confidential: as a state secret; as a midnight tryst; as an accountant's audit; as a church confessional
  symbols: sealed lips; closed doors
  see also: classified; secret; censored
  opposite: open; public

Confined: as a goldfish in a teacup; as a dog on a short leash; as a kid in a crib; as a cow in a corset; as an astronaut in a space station

    symbols: caged bird; Devil's Island; Black Hole of Calcutta
    see also: limited; close
    opposite: free

Conformist: as a synchronized swimmer; as a new convert; as a corps of cadets passing in review; as the dancers in a chorus line; as a flock of sheep

    symbols: by the book; the establishment; when in Rome; the Rockettes
    see also: alike
    opposite: different

Confused: as a mouse in a new maze; as quadruplets in a house of mirrors; as a compass in a magnet factory

    symbols: Tower of Babel; Mrs. Malaprop; lost soul
    see also: bewildered; chaotic; disorganized
    opposite: certain; sure; knowledgeable

Congenial: as a cup of cocoa; as peace and quiet; as a happy drunk

    symbols: peaches and cream; sweetness and light; Arcadia
    see also: friendly; harmonious; happy; hospitable
    opposite: angry; annoying; bitter; disagreeable

Congested: as the freeway at rush hour; as a boom town in a gold rush; as steerage; as Times Square on New Year's Eve; as the aisles in the bargain basement the day after Thanksgiving

    symbols: S.R.O. (standing room only); mob scene; the Tokyo subway at rush hour
    see also: crowded; busy; rushed
    opposite: clear; airy; empty

Conscientious: as a religious objector; as a worried watchdog; as a scared patient following the doctor's orders; as a Quaker-style protest

    symbols: Trojan; Trojan service; on the ball
    see also: careful; cautious; honest; devoted
    opposite: indifferent; careless; duplicitous; dishonest

Considerate: as a groom to his new bride; as a good host; as an act of courtesy; as an offer of a second chance

    symbols: Sir Walter Raleigh; Good Samaritan; Mr. Nice Guy
    see also: kind; generous; attentive; charitable
    opposite: callous; indifferent; distant; cruel; cool; harsh

Consistent: as the changing of the seasons; as salmon swimming upstream; as the course of a ferryboat; as a cock's crowing
>   symbols: steady Eddie
>   see also: changeless; uncompromising; certain
>   opposite: changeable; varied

Constant: as the passing minutes; as the northern star (Shakespeare); as the laws of nature; as the cycle of night and day
>   symbols: Penelope; Rock of Gibraltar
>   see also: ceaseless; endless; steadfast; faithful; permanent; changeless
>   opposite: changeable; uncertain; temporary; false

Contagious: as the common cold; as laughter; as a popular tune; as a mob's panic; as a wide-mouthed yawn; as a radio jingle
>   symbols: the hit parade; epidemic
>   see also: catching; attractive
>   opposite: elusive; exclusive

Continuous: as the stars that shine (Wordsworth); as an endless circle; as the earth revolving around the sun
>   symbols: the task of Sisyphus
>   see also: ceaseless; constant; endless; perpetual; chronic; permanent
>   opposite: temporary; final; fleeting

Contrived: as a corny commercial; as a bad plot; as a complicated alibi
>   symbols: a Rube Goldberg invention; bag of tricks; *deus ex machina*
>   see also: false; lying; untruthful; complicated
>   opposite: simple; true; honest; sincere

Convenient: as a timely interruption; as rain after a day of planting; as a 24-hour restaurant that delivers
>   symbols: an all-night Laundromat; an ATM (automated teller machine)
>   see also: helpful; near; appropriate; useful
>   opposite: useless; awkward; jarring

Convincing: as a sign from God; as seeing it for yourself; as a child's testimony
>   symbols: an Academy Award performance; certified check
>   see also: reasonable; reliable; trustworthy
>   opposite: uncertain; untruthful; transparent

Cool: as the proverbial cucumber; as last night's ardor in the morning light; as the morning dew; as a meeting between neighbors who aren't talking

    symbols: Jack Frost; iceberg

    see also: aloof; indifferent; cold; relaxed; icy

    opposite: warm; hot; bothered; worried; anxious; bewildered; tense

Cooperative: as a barn raising; as a grange gathering; as a matched team of horses; as give and take; as a football center and the quarterback

    symbols: helping hand; team play

    see also: helpful; friendly

    opposite: stubborn; balky; quarrelsome

Corny: as the crops in Kansas; as pone in Paducah; as the kernels on the cob; as an opening act in Atlantic City

    symbols: an old vaudeville act; an old familiar story

    see also: dated; old-fashioned; familiar

    opposite: new; original; modern

Correct: as a courtier's conduct; as a curtsey to a queen; as 100% on an exam

    symbols: Emily Post; protocol secretary

    see also: polite; courteous; perfect; accurate

    opposite: rude; ill-mannered; impolite; wrong; erroneous

Corrupt: as a slush fund; as a black market in counterfeit currency; as a stuffed ballot box; as a professional turncoat

    symbols: Teapot Dome; a double agent; a judge with his hand out

    see also: dishonest; crooked; deceitful; evil; treacherous; dirty

    opposite: clean; honest; innocent; good

Cosmetic: as a bobbed nose; as a new coat of paint; as lipstick and powder; as a toupee on a bald man

    symbols: paint job; plastic surgery; a facelift

    see also: beautiful; attractive; lovely; deceitful

    opposite: ugly; raw; harsh

Cosmopolitan: as the proverbial city mouse; as the United Nations; as the crossroads of the world; as a carnival in Cannes; as New York's five boroughs

    symbols: international house; the jet set; bi-coastal marriage

    see also: mixed; tolerant

    opposite: parochial; narrow

Courageous: as the lone defender of a lost cause; as eating a full dinner in a dirty restaurant; as doing something you're scared to death to do

    symbols: Captains Courageous; William Wallace

    see also: brave; bold; daring; gallant

    opposite: cowardly; scared; frightened

Courteous: as the concierge in a five-star hotel; as a courtier to the queen; as a London bus queue; as a waiter working for a big tip; as the salesperson who wants your business

    symbols: Sir Walter Raleigh; Alphonse and Gaston

    see also: considerate; polite; correct

    opposite: ill-mannered; rude; impolite

Cowardly: as a hyena with a food phobia; as a coyote that's afraid of the dark; as a stab in the back; as an anonymous phone call; as a terrorist bombing

    symbols: the Cowardly Lion (*The Wizard of Oz*)

    see also: scared; frightened; yellow

    opposite: bold; brave; daring; gallant

Cracked: as a broken mirror; as the ice in a frozen daiquiri; as the cookies in the asylum; as the iceberg that sank the Titanic

    symbols: a nut; a coot

    see also: crazy; faulty; damaged

    opposite: sane; reasonable; wise; healthy

Crafty: as a conspirator in the cloakroom; as a crow in a cornfield; as a con man on the make; as a kid conning his grandma

    symbols: Cassius of the lean and hungry look (Shakespeare); the sly fox

    see also: artful; deceitful; duplicitous; wily

    opposite: innocent; pure; frank; honest

Cranky: as a colicky kid; as a 1910 tin Lizzie

    symbols: fussbudget

    see also: balky; disagreeable; bristling

    opposite: agreeable; amiable; pleasant; nice

Crass: as profiteering in penicillin; as selling orphaned babies; as a dollop of dolts

    symbols: Elmer Gantry

    see also: gross; vulgar; ignorant; selfish

    opposite: fine; straight; generous; estimable; nice

Craven: as a coward's whimper; as life on one's knees; as voluntary slavery
    symbols: white feather; yellow streak
    see also: cowardly; afraid; scared; frightened
    opposite: bold; daring; brave; courageous

Crazy: as a berserk bedbug; as a cuckoo coot; as a loco loon
    symbols: Mad Hatter; Bedlam
    see also: cracked; mad; irrational
    opposite: responsible; reasonable; normal

Creative: as the gift of life; as a seed sprouting in the earth; as a Picasso painting
    symbols: Michelangelo; Leonardo Da Vinci; William Shakespeare
    see also: artistic; original; inventive; innovative; inspired
    opposite: dull; amateurish; useless; imitative

Criminal: as a killer caught in the act; as everything listed in the penal code; as a mugger in the park
    symbols: Public Enemy No. 1; now starring on a wanted poster; John Dillinger; Jesse James
    see also: evil; lawless; immoral; corrupt; wicked; bad; crooked; hard-core
    opposite: legal; correct; pure

Critical: as a reviewer who hated a play; as the moment of nuclear fission; as confrontation between two killers
    symbols: Devil's advocate; seat on the aisle
    see also: scornful; crucial; serious; attentive
    opposite: safe; secure; friendly; relaxed

Crooked: as a corkscrew; as an inviting finger; as a politician on the take; as a coiled spring
    symbols: the Boss Tweed ring; loaded dice; stacked deck
    see also: bent; distorted; dishonest; criminal; corrupt
    opposite: straight; honest

Crucial: as the last game of the championship; as life and death; as a finger on the trigger
    symbols: moment of truth; the last straw; Judgment Day; the payoff
    see also: important; serious; decisive; urgent
    opposite: useless; needless; unnecessary

Crude: as raw fossil fuel; as country cacti; as rubber dripping from the tree
    symbols: Yahoo; sons of Belial; Goth
    see also: raw; rough; harsh
    opposite: smooth; polished

Cruel: as death by inches; as a creeping cancer; as a cold shoulder in a hot spot; as a kick in the pants
    symbols: Marquis de Sade; Ivan the Terrible; Vlad the Impaler
    see also: awful; atrocious; hellish; horrible; mean
    opposite: kind; amiable; gentle; friendly

Crumbly: as the bottom of the bread box; as cracked biscuits; as the lower crust of life; as a bed after eating crackers
    symbols: Grub Street; Poverty Row
    see also: messy; crass; nasty
    opposite: clean; neat; nice

Cultured: as a college professor; as buttermilk yogurt; as a pearl in a captive oyster; as an Edwardian sophisticate
    symbols: highbrow; intellectual
    see also: knowledgeable; educated
    opposite: ignorant; crass; dopey

Curious: as an inquiring photographer; as a nosy neighbor; as a snowstorm in July; as a young cat
    symbols: The Old Curiosity Shop; Mr. Snoop; paparazzi
    see also: meddlesome; strange; inquisitive
    opposite: indifferent; apathetic; normal; regular

Cutting: as a surgeon's scalpel; as a kitchen knife; as a razor's edge; as a cold shoulder
    symbols: surgery; the axe
    see also: biting; sharp; keen
    opposite: dull; friendly

Cynical: as a sinner scorning salvation; as a psalm by a sadist; as the faith of a sold skeptic
    symbols: Diogenes; doubting Thomas
    see also: biting; bitter; pessimistic; doubtful; dubious
    opposite: optimistic; eager; innocent

D

Dainty: as a dewdrop on a daisy; as a dish to set before the queen; as a dancing doll
    symbols: lifted pinkie; Dresden doll
    see also: delicate; graceful
    opposite: heavy-handed; coarse; gross

Damaged: as a broken wing; as the serpent's reputation in the Garden of Eden; as a car that lost an argument with a train engine
    symbols: the ruins of Pompeii; a fallen woman
    see also: spoiled; faulty; tarnished; blemished; run-down
    opposite: flawless; perfect; pure; fresh

Damaging: as a bite from a black widow; as a fire in an oil refinery; as being caught with a smoking gun at a shooting
    symbols: bull in a china shop; one-man wrecking crew; Vandals
    see also: destructive; harmful; guilty
    opposite: harmless; innocent; helpful

Dangerous: as a pothole on a freeway; as a mail bomb; as a deep sea dive in the dark
    symbols: sword of Damocles; dynamite; psychopathic serial killer
    see also: threatening; ominous; menacing; critical; harmful
    opposite: safe; secure; harmless; trustworthy; reliable

Daring: as a dance in a den of lions; as a duel to the death; as tickling a tiger
    symbols: Evil Knievel; the Flying Wallendas; Lochinvar
    see also: adventurous; defiant; bold; brave; reckless; courageous
    opposite: scared; cowardly; careful; cautious

Dark: as the other side of the moon; as the bottom of the sea; as the doom of the damned; as a moonless night at midnight
    symbols: blackout; Erebus; an uncharted cavern
    see also: black; cloudy; gloomy; sad
    opposite: bright; light; brilliant; cheerful; happy

Dashing: as a cavalier courting a queen; as a sprinter racing to the tape; as a dude with new duds
    symbols: Don Juan
    see also: bold; attractive; adventurous; sexy
    opposite: slow; dreary; dull

Dated: as a dowager; as the dipsy doodle; as the divine right of kings
  symbols: Model T; an antique; a throwback; a dodo
  see also: obsolete; old; ancient; old-fashioned; corny; quaint
  opposite: new; original; fresh; modern

Dead: as a doorknob; as the air in a sealed tomb; as yesterday's headlines; as an abandoned dream
  symbols: a corpse; six feet under; dodo; dinosaur
  see also: finished; dull; quiet; buried; flat; inert
  opposite: fresh; new; hot; innovative; original; young

Deadly: as the seven sins; as a great white shark; as the bubonic plague; as Lucretia Borgia's cooking; as Cleopatra's asp
  symbols: kiss of death; appointment in Samarkand; scorpion's kiss
  see also: lethal; fatal; destructive
  opposite: harmless; safe

Deaf: as a curmudgeon with selective hearing; as justice is blind; as an earless bat
  symbols: tuned out; wearing earmuffs
  see also: indifferent; oblivious; selective
  opposite: involved; concerned

Deafening: as a guitar amplifier turned up to 11; as standing next to a cannon; as the drums of war
  symbols: Big Bertha; thunder; a Kiss concert
  see also: noisy; loud
  opposite: quiet; silent

Dear (affectionate):   as remembered kisses after death (Alfred Tennyson); as days of delight; as the scenes of a happy childhood; as the dawn of love
  symbols: apple of one's eye
  see also: cherished; precious; beloved; lovable
  opposite: rejected; forgotten; forsaken; hateful

Dear (costly):   as the Hope Diamond; as white fish roe masquerading as caviar; as next year's model; as a 2000-year-old rainforest
  symbols: a king's ransom; highway robbery
  see also: high; inflated; rare
  opposite: free; cheap

Debatable: as a campaign issue; as the definition of happiness; as the winner of an argument; as a question of judgment

    symbols: the jury is out; a hung jury; you pays your money and you takes your choice

    see also: questionable; arguable; uncertain; dubious; doubtful

    opposite: established; obvious; certain; sure

Decadent: as Rome during its decline and fall; as the French court before the revolution; as a Beaux Arts Ball

    symbols: Marquis de Sade; Sodom and Gomorrah; Caligula

    see also: decayed; rotten; evil; immoral

    opposite: virtuous; good

Decayed: as garbage gone to seed; as an apple core in the open air; as a cadaver in a haunted house; as a mouthful of cavities

    symbols: rotten apple; city dump; ghost town

    see also: rotten; spoiled; damaged

    opposite: fresh; new; good

Deceitful: as a marked deck of cards; as loaded dice; as a turncoat with a reversible vest

    symbols: double agent; shell game

    see also: lying; tricky; treacherous; dishonest; insincere; false; duplicitous

    opposite: honest; true; sincere; trustworthy; faithful

Deceptive: as a pair of falsies; as a deliberate decoy; as wishful thinking

    symbols: mirage; fool's gold; daydream

    see also: false; lying; duplicitous; deceitful

    opposite: honest; trustworthy; true

Decisive: as death; as Judgment Day; as a knockout; as the battle of Waterloo

    symbols: crossing the Rubicon; the die is cast

    see also: crucial; final; definite; certain; emphatic

    opposite: uncertain; changeable; debatable; uncompromising; compelling

Dedicated: as a missionary on a mission; as a social worker in a slum

    symbols: a saint; a crusader

    see also: devoted; attentive; holy

    opposite: indifferent; aloof; lazy; insincere

Deep: as the ocean; as the Devil's domicile; as first love (Alfred Tennyson)

    symbols: Hades; bottomless pit; the lower depths; the Carlsbad Caverns

    see also: bottomless; endless

    opposite: shallow; superficial

Defensive: as a castle moat; as a middle linebacker; as a criminal caught in the act
  symbols: foxhole; Alibi Ike
  see also: bristling; cautious; defiant; frightened
  opposite: unprepared; hesitant; helpless

Defiant: as a rebel with a cause; as a peasant revolution; as a headstrong teen
  symbols: Boston Tea Party; Sons of Liberty; Robin Hood
  see also: bold; rebellious; fierce; uncompromising
  opposite: yellow; reasonable; cowardly; docile

Definite: as a DNA match; as a fingerprint; as money in the bank; as a signed contract; an oath signed in blood
  symbols: in black and white; Exhibit A
  see also: certain; sure; clear; positive; decisive; emphatic
  opposite: uncertain; questionable; changeable; vague

Delayed: as a double take; as a derailed train; as a limelight lover's entrance
  symbols: Fabian; slow burn
  see also: slow; late; hesitant
  opposite: fast; dashing; instantaneous

Deliberate: as an Act of Congress; as a court order; as aiming a gun; as a five-year plan
  symbols: game plan; outline; blue print
  see also: thoughtful; planned; precise
  opposite: spontaneous; accidental; uncertain

Delicate: as gossamer lace; as fine crystal; as a spider's web; as a surgeon's touch
  symbols: touching a nerve; sensitive area; walking on eggs; a cat's paws
  see also: frail; sensitive; dainty; airy; light; intricate
  opposite: coarse; gross; heavy; crude

Demonic: as the cabinet of Dr. Caligari; as a trip through Hell; as Orpheus' descent; as the eternal underworld
  symbols: Beelzebub; Satan; Lucifer; the Devil
  see also: hellish; bad; evil; mean; disagreeable; hateful
  opposite: angelic; heavenly; good; noble; virtuous

Dense: as the heart of the jungle; as a pea soup fog; as a dummy's brain
  symbols: a rainforest; a log jam; a holly hedge
  see also: foggy; thick; cloudy; crowded; stupid
  opposite: clear; thin; bright; brilliant

Dependable: as clockwork; as the ocean's tides; as sunrise
    symbols: Old Faithful; Big Ben
    see also: steadfast; reliable; trustworthy; faithful
    opposite: changeable; uncertain; dishonest; lying; false

Deprived: as a baseball batter without a bat; as a miser without his money; as a bull left alone in the pasture
    symbols: the tenement dwellers; an abandoned spouse
    see also: poor; broke; needy; neglected; hungry
    opposite: rich; wealthy; prosperous; affluent; privileged

Deserted: as a spent mine shaft; as an uncharted island; as a golf course at midnight
    symbols: haunted house; ghost town; the Flying Dutchman
    see also: empty; blank; desolate
    opposite: crowded; congested; busy

Deserving: as a doer of good deeds; as one good turn; as a hard worker
    symbols: good Samaritan; the Good Guys
    see also: admirable; good
    opposite: objectionable; wayward; wicked

Desirable: as dessert to a dieter; as détente to diplomats; as a date with destiny; as power to a politician
    symbols: *sine qua non*; primary objective; Holy Grail
    see also: sought after; welcome; popular
    opposite: unpopular; objectionable

Desolate: as the depths of despair; as a rejected love; as an unrepentant soul
    symbols: haunted house; ghost town; the Flying Dutchman
    see also: alone; isolated; barren; bare; abandoned; empty; dismal
    opposite: crowded; abundant; fertile; hospitable

Desperate: as a cornered rat; as playing chess with Death; as a last stand
    symbols: forlorn hope; the final appeal
    see also: frantic; mad; extreme; worried
    opposite: calm; hopeful; confident

Despondent: as a spurned suitor; as a bookie paying off a 1000-to-1 shot; as a dying swan; as the beast without his beauty
    symbols: Slough of Despond; sad acres
    see also: sad; gloomy; downhearted; pessimistic; discouraged
    opposite: happy; glad; cheerful; optimistic

Destructive: as moths in the woolen closet; as crows in a cornfield; as an erupting volcano; as a ten-point earthquake
   symbols: the sacking of Rome; the Vandals; hurricanes
   see also: damaging; harmful; disastrous; lethal
   opposite: harmless; safe; helpful

Detached: as a neutral observer; as a caboose without a locomotive; as a cool-hearted lover; as the office daydreamer
   symbols: separate tables; in dreamland
   see also: aloof; apathetic; distant
   opposite: anxious; eager; involved

Detestable: as a heart filled with hate; as a dastardly deed
   symbols: the man you love to hate
   see also: hateful
   opposite: lovable

Devious: as a disguised predator; as a double agent; as a double-dyed deceiver
   symbols: Iago; Uriah Heep
   see also: sneaky; backhanded; sly; hypocritical
   opposite: direct; honest; clear; barefaced

Devoted: as a pet to a good master; as a prophet to his faith; as a mother to her child; as a miser to his money
   symbols: Tristan and Isolde; Penelope; Damon and Pythias; Old Blue
   see also: attentive; dedicated; dear; loyal; committed
   opposite: indifferent; cool; callous; negligent; false

Dictatorial: as a gun to your head; as a master over a slave; as a domineering parent
   symbols: the Generalissimo; the Godfather; der Fuehrer; Stalin
   see also: commanding; arbitrary; rigid; threatening
   opposite: flexible; changeable; free; open

Different: as day and night; as apples and oranges; as men and women
   symbols: one man's meat; the other side of the mountain
   see also: varied; assorted; hybrid
   opposite: alike

Difficult: as making dreams come true; as defying Destiny; as the labors of Hercules; as governing a mob
   symbols: the $64,000 question; Gordian knot
   see also: complicated; baffling; hard
   opposite: easy; understandable; simple

Dignified: as a state funeral; as a diplomat's dinner; as a college commencement
  symbols: a tea social; an embassy ball
  see also: solemn; grand; formal; quiet
  opposite: boisterous; noisy; ill-mannered; loud

Diplomatic: as an artful ambassador; as a public-relations spokesperson; as a discreet word in private; as saying without saying anything at all
  symbols: protocol; treaty conference
  see also: gracious; dignified; artful; tasteful; wily
  opposite: tactless; ill-mannered; rude

Direct: as a straight arrow; as a dentist's drill; as a private-line phone call
  symbols: a bullet's path; blunt instrument
  see also: straight; honest; clear
  opposite: devious; sneaky; sly; crooked

Dirty: as three-day-old socks; as ill-gotten gain; as a double-cross; as a muckraker's shovel
  symbols: ring around the collar; a pigsty; an Augean stable
  see also: unclean; dishonest; tarnished; rusty
  opposite: spotless; clean; honest; straight

Disagreeable: as stormy weather; as sour grapes; as a crotchety curmudgeon
  symbols: pain in the neck; pretty kettle of fish; Pandora's box
  see also: annoying; nasty; rotten; bad
  opposite: agreeable; amiable; kind; friendly; good

Disastrous: as doomsday; as lighting a match to look at a leaky gas line; as the Devil's triumph; as drinking lye
  symbols: Armageddon; Waterloo
  see also: damaging; destructive; harmful; horrible
  opposite: harmless; safe

Discounted: as an unsuccessful rumor; as the clearance prices in the bargain basement; as a convict's testimony
  symbols: markdown; cynic's corner
  see also: cheap; dubious; doubtful
  opposite: dear; believable

Discouraged: as a drunk in a dry county; as an unpublished poet; as a three-time loser
  symbols: in the dumps; listening to Cassandra
  see also: sad; despondent; downhearted; blue; gloomy; pessimistic
  opposite: confident; happy; glad; cheerful; optimistic

Discreet: as a cautious whisper; as a dignified diplomat; as a plain brown wrapper
     symbols: soul of discretion; tiptoe
     see also: cautious; prudent; wise; careful
     opposite: rash; careless; indiscreet

Disguised: as a wolf in sheep's clothing; as the man in the iron mask; as a clown at a masquerade ball
     symbols: chameleon; the man of many faces
     see also: camouflaged; concealed; hidden; doctored
     opposite: obvious; apparent; open; clear; frank

Dishonest: as a meow by a mouse; as cheating your mother; as a forged contract; as a tale-teller telling the truth; as the thief who says "trust me"
     symbols: flim flam man; shell game
     see also: crooked; corrupt; evil; lying; false
     opposite: honest; true; genuine; real; frank

Dismal: as bad news on a nasty day; as a dull speech before dinner; as a dark swamp
     symbols: *Wuthering Heights*; nightmare alley; poverty row
     see also: gloomy; bad; dark; desolate; bleak
     opposite: happy; cheerful; bright

Disorganized: as a daydreamer's world; as a leaderless rebellion; as a construction crew without a blueprint to follow
     symbols: mob scene; Bedlam; the Tower of Babel
     see also: confused; chaotic
     opposite: planned; calculating; neat

Disposable: as extra income; as a spent Kleenex; as a transistor battery
     symbols: a throwaway; orphan of the storm
     see also: obsolete; replaceable
     opposite: permanent

Dissipated: as a departed dollar; as the pleasure of the chase when it's over; as virtue when temptation has won
     symbols: Dorian Gray; Bacchanalia
     see also: wayward; loose; immoral; wicked
     opposite: moral; straight; good

Distant: as from here to eternity; as a dowager's disapproval; as the farthest star
     symbols: the poles; a trillion light years away
     see also: far; cool; indifferent; cold; aloof; haughty
     opposite: near; sympathetic; comforting

Distinguished: as a Nobel prize recipient; as divine inspiration; as a righteous leader
    symbols: top drawer; pillar of the community; cum laude
    see also: eminent; famous; exemplary
    opposite: obscure; overlooked; shady

Distorted: as viewing the world through rose-colored lenses; as an overspent rumor; as a schizophrenic's testimony
    symbols: kaleidoscope; an elephant designed by committee
    see also: crooked; bent; changed; false
    opposite: straight; clear; genuine; true

Distracting: as squeaky shoes in a library; as a coughing fit at a concert; as a nudist in a church; as a heckler during a soliloquy
    symbols: sideshow; second feature; a station break
    see also: arresting; irrelevant; questionable
    opposite: pointed; absorbing; accurate

Divided: as the wheat and the chaff; as oil and water; as the Grand Canyon
    symbols: choosing sides; a house divided; separate tables
    see also: different; partisan; quarrelsome
    opposite: alike; cooperative; harmonious

Dizzy: as a drunk on a dromedary; as a rider on a merry-go-round; as monkeys rolling in a barrel
    symbols: a fruitcake; on spin cycle
    see also: confused; crazy; foolish
    opposite: straight; solid; wise

Docile: as a little lamb; as a devoted dog; as good children on the night before Christmas
    symbols: Caspar Milquetoast; a henpecked spouse
    see also: obedient; meek; gentle
    opposite: stubborn; nasty; rough

Doctored: as loaded dice; as a forged document; as a failed recipe
    symbols: Mickey Finn; a mickey
    see also: changed; distorted; polluted; mixed
    opposite: true; genuine; clean; original

Dogged: as a preacher's patience; as the devil's determination; as a commuter at the end of a long day; as a door-to-door salesperson on commission

      symbols: stick-to-it-tiveness; a bulldog

      see also: stubborn; committed; insistent

      opposite: flexible; easy; lazy

Dogmatic: as a catechism; as a professor's pet theory; as a revolutionary's manifesto

      symbols: written in stone; *ipse dixit*; gospel; Holy Writ

      see also: opinionated; positive; rigid; changeless

      opposite: flexible; pliant; changeable; loose

Dopey: as one of the Seven Dwarfs; as a dimwitted donkey; as a punch-drunk pugilist

      symbols: hophead; Simple Simon; the village idiot

      see also: foolish; ignorant; dumb; doctored; drunk

      opposite: wise; knowledgeable; clever; sober; inspired

Doubtful: as a long-range weather forecast; as a mule's fertility; as full payment for the wages of sin

      symbols: Doubting Thomas; dark horse

      see also: questionable; uncertain; debatable; dubious

      opposite: certain; sure; affirmative; positive

Downhearted: as the devil caught doing a good deed; as a dieter who hasn't lost an ounce

      symbols: blue funk; Slough Despond; depths of despair

      see also: discouraged; despondent; gloomy; sad

      opposite: happy; cheerful; optimistic

Dreadful: as a day of infamy; as the plagues of ancient Egypt; as fooling around with Mother Nature

      symbols: Roman holiday; blood bath; the Devil and his damned

      see also: awful; evil; frightful; atrocious; bad; hellish

      opposite: good; pleasant; heavenly; agile; nice

Dreary: as a dark, damp day; as garbage dump on a dull drab dawn; as the dregs of despair; as an abandoned house

      symbols: *Wuthering Heights;* blue Monday; dullsville

      see also: gloomy; dismal; sad; dark

      opposite: cheerful; bright; happy; pleasant

Drowsy: as a cat in front of a warm fire; as the audience for a long speech after a heavy dinner; as a ten o'clock town at 2 a.m.

    symbols: Sleeping Beauty; Rip van Winkle

    see also: weary; relaxed; bored

    opposite: restless; active; excited

Drunk: as he who prostrate lies, without the power to drink or rise (Thomas Love Peacock); as a one-martini man on a six-martini streak; as a barfly in a barrel of bourbon

    symbols: Bacchus; John Barleycorn; Dutch courage

    see also: dizzy; wet

    opposite: sober; dry

Dry: as the desert sands; as a Death Valley drought; as a Sahara lakebed

    symbols: on the wagon; Pythagorean brotherhood; Dust Bowl

    see also: parched; arid

    opposite: watered

Dubious: as the decision of a kangaroo court; as a forced confession; as a perjurer's testimony; as a bargainer's bargain

    symbols: on the fence; doubting Thomas

    see also: uncertain; questionable; doubtful

    opposite: certain; sure; positive; affirmative

Dull: as the repetition of a bad story; as a butter knife; as a pause between yawns

    symbols: drying paint; a plotless play; dishwater

    see also: boring; colorless; dead; dumb

    opposite: exciting; fascinating; keen; sharp; bright

Dumb: as a dolt in a dunce cap; as the luck of the favored few

    symbols: Simple Simon; the village idiot

    see also: dopey; ignorant; silent

    opposite: wise; clever; smart; ingenious

Duplicitous: as a double double-cross; as a crossed-finger handshake

    symbols: double-dyed deceiver; stacked deck

    see also: hypocritical; sneaky; tricky; doctored; fraudulent

    opposite: true; honest; genuine

Durable: as eternal love; as an honored promise; as a good wool coat; as denim; as a barefoot marathon runner's calluses

    symbols: Rock of Gibraltar; sound investment

    see also: constant; strong; perpetual; permanent; lasting

    opposite: faded; changeable; temporary; weak

Dutiful: as a compliment to a harried host; as a devoted child; as a well-timed thank you letter
- symbols: Sir Galahad
- see also: obedient; devoted; attentive; considerate; courteous; polite
- opposite: indifferent; negligent; careless; antagonistic; nasty

E

Eager: as an eagle eyeing his prey; as two lovers racing to a hideaway; as an early bird catching a worm; as a hungry freeloader at a buffet
- symbols: old up 'n' at 'em; eager beaver; Boy Scout
- see also: hot; zealous; bold; hungry
- opposite: indifferent; slow; cool

Early: as the light of dawn; as an ill-mannered guest; as Neanderthal Man; as a new employee on the first day of work
- symbols: Aurora; the dawn patrol; early bird
- see also: fast; quick; young
- opposite: late; delayed; old

Earthy: as a seaman's advice; as a farmer's figure of speech; as a home in a sod hut
- symbols: Mother Nature; barnyard philosophy
- see also: carnal; crude; vulgar; coarse; natural
- opposite: refined; cultured; delicate; flowery

Easy: as rolling off a log; as drawing a breath in the open air; as relaxing in a rocking chair; as the proverbial pie
- symbols: easy street; piece of cake; cakewalk
- see also: comfortable; understandable; simple
- opposite: complicated; difficult; hard

Economical: as energy taken from the wind; as walking to work; as living off the land
- symbols: Ebenezer Scrooge; pinch purse; close to the vest
- see also: stingy; frugal; close; tight; cheap
- opposite: expensive; generous; dear

Edgy: as a bartender on the brink of a brawl; as a boiler at the breaking point; as a perturbed porcupine; as a prophet of doom
- symbols: Damocles; short fuse; tenterhook time
- see also: nervous; agitated
- opposite: calm; relaxed; placid

Educated: to the nth degree; as a postdoctoral pundit; as a master's touch
    symbols: a Ph.D.; the cap and gown set; the brain trust; the ivory tower
    see also: learned; cultured; civilized
    opposite: ignorant; barbarous; savage; crude

Eerie: as the pit and the pendulum; as a voice from the grave; as the spirits of an abandoned house
    symbols: nightmare alley; the moors at night
    see also: frightful; dismal; bleak; gloomy; threatening
    opposite: warm; colorful; hospitable; friendly; encouraging

Effective: as fuel in the fire; as the eyes of an eagle; as food in the fight against famine; as the offer you can't refuse
    symbols: ball of fire; a lit fuse
    see also: useful; appropriate; accomplished; convincing
    opposite: useless; inefficient; idle; empty

Efficient: as a sharp knife on the Gordian knot; as a wrecking ball on a demolition site; as a ball bearing
    symbols: new broom; a round wheel
    see also: accomplished; systematic; productive
    opposite: inefficient; incompetent; inadequate

Egotistical: as a braggart's boast; as kissing yourself good night; as patting yourself on the back; as awarding yourself the grand prize
    symbols: first person singular; I am, therefore I am
    see also: immodest; vain; selfish
    opposite: humble; meek; modest

Elastic: as a campaign promise; as a criminal conscience; as a tale-teller's story told twice
    symbols: two-way stretch; rubber band
    see also: flexible; changeable; uncertain
    opposite: constant; changeless; certain; tight

Electrifying: as a lightning bolt; as newfound hope; as a high-voltage line; as putting your finger in the plug
    symbols: live wire; dynamo; a charged battery; thunderbolt
    see also: exciting; brilliant; inventive
    opposite: boring; dull; hopeless

Elegant: as a royal coronation; as a peacock's preen; as a black-tie dinner
    symbols: Beau Brummel; fashion plate
    see also: fancy; handsome; beautiful; refined; tasteful
    opposite: coarse; cheap; noisy; dull; gross; frightful

Elementary: as the primary colors; as 2 plus 2; as fire, earth, air, and water
    symbols: bread and butter; the nitty gritty; the basics
    see also: basic; simple
    opposite: complicated; complex; intricate; difficult

Elevated: as the heavens above; as an emperor on his throne; as a penthouse apartment
    symbols: Olympus; highbrow
    see also: high; exalted; special
    opposite: low; common; average; commonplace

Eligible: as a billionaire bachelor; as an experienced employee; as the ticket holder in a sweepstakes
    symbols: the right person for the right job; favorite son
    see also: qualified; fit; deserving
    opposite: ineligible; unprepared

Eloquent: as an orator's finest hour; as the Sermon on the Mount; as action clear and prompt; as the man who talked the devil out of sinning
    symbols: Demosthenes; Daniel Webster
    see also: expressive; authoritative
    opposite: dull; corny

Elusive: as a marauding mosquito; as the charm of a nagging spouse; as a snake slithering in the grass; as the origins of a rumor
    symbols: Scarlet Pimpernel; will-o'-the -wisp
    see also: evasive; slippery; tricky; uncertain
    opposite: catching; definite; certain; straight

Embarrassed: as the chef who flattens the soufflé; as a saint caught sinning; as a nudist caught with clothes on; as a memory expert who forgets his name
    symbols: blushing violet; in the soup
    see also: uncomfortable; confused
    opposite: relaxed; calm; confident

Eminent: as the sun in the sky; as the lion among beasts and the eagle among birds; as the wisdom of the ancients
    symbols: Olympian; Jovian
    see also: distinguished; celebrated; noticeable; admired; important
    opposite: obscure; hidden; overlooked

Emphatic: as a punch in the proboscis; as reading the riot act; as a kick in the pants; as the ultimate ultimatum
    symbols: table-pounding
    see also: loud; positive; dogmatic
    opposite: hesitant; indifferent; soft; apathetic; tentative

Empty: as a bottomless pit; as a pauper's pocket; as a nitwit's noodle
    symbols: the hole in the doughnut; no man's land
    see also: bare; barren; blank; deserted
    opposite: crowded; congested; jammed

Enchanting: as a fairy godmother; as a magic kingdom; as a young love; as a dream of glory
    symbols: Titania; Queen Mab; Cupid's arrow
    see also: charming; attractive; beautiful; lovable
    opposite: awful; hateful; frightful; wicked; ugly

Encouraging: as an encore call; as sweet success; as fuel to a fire
    symbols: cheerleader; Pollyanna
    see also: comforting; sympathetic; helpful; hopeful
    opposite: cool; indifferent; hopeless

Endangered: as a vanishing species; as a lamb lying down in a lion's den; as a sinner's immortal soul
    symbols: Damocles; tigers and cheetahs
    see also: abused; afflicted; damaged
    opposite: safe; enduring

Endless: as the march of time; as eternity itself; as the vastness of the universe; as the line around a perfect circle
    symbols: world without end; continuous performance
    see also: constant; continuous; perpetual; permanent; infinite; ceaseless
    opposite: complete; limited; final; definite; temporary

Enduring: as the sands in the desert; as eternal truth; as a solemn promise
    symbols: Rock of Ages; a fixture
    see also: endless; permanent; perpetual; lasting
    opposite: fleeting; temporary

Energetic: as a daily decathlon; as internal combustion; as perpetual motion; as a rock climber

    symbols: eager beaver; dynamo; Trojan

    see also: active; busy; restless; feverish

    opposite: relaxed; inert; idle; lazy

Engaging: as a siren's smile; as the promise of a profit; as a lover's caressing tone

    symbols: Amoret; Don Juan; Lochinvar

    see also: appealing; fascinating; attractive; charming

    opposite: nasty; detestable; hateful

Enigmatic: as the mystery of life itself; as a riddle without an answer; as a cat's smile

    symbols: Sphinx; Mona Lisa

    see also: uncertain; obscure; hidden

    opposite: clear; certain; understandable

Envious: as a social climber; as a psychopathic sibling; as a rich relative believes a poor relative is

    symbols: green-eyed monster; keeping up with the Joneses

    see also: jealous; greedy

    opposite: indifferent; apathetic; generous; kind; charitable

Erratic: as a compass over a magnet; as a bird flying with one wing; as an egg rolling down hill; as a drunk's doorstep

    symbols: an unguided missile

    see also: queer; strange; absurd

    opposite: sure; steadfast; reasonable

Erroneous: as mistaking a tiger for a tabby cat; as a case of mistaken identity

    symbols: the blunder world; wrong way Corrigan; a Brodie

    see also: wrong; false; mistaken; inaccurate

    opposite: correct; true; accurate

Essential: as food and water; as the breath of life; as the salt in the sea; as a heartbeat

    symbols: meat and potatoes; a must; *sine qua non*

    see also: necessary; basic

    opposite: unnecessary; needless

Established: as the seats of the mighty; as the myths of our time; as the law of supply and demand

    symbols: Rock of Gibraltar; the way the cookie crumbles

    see also: firm; old; constant; certain; permanent

    opposite: uncertain; temporary

Estimable: as a guardian angel; as a good Samaritan in disastrous times; as a good deed in a selfish world; as star who doesn't fall for his own publicity
- symbols: man in the white hat; the White Knight; the good guys
- see also: appreciated; respectable; popular
- opposite: objectionable; disagreeable; unpopular

Euphoric: as a lottery winner; as a pair of newlyweds; as a proud new parent; as an applicant who got the job
- symbols: seventh heaven; Eden; Paradise; Arcadia
- see also: happy; exalted; glad; optimistic
- opposite: sad; unhappy; gloomy; downhearted; pessimistic

Evasive: as an unfriendly witness; as a debtor dodging his debts; as a halfback heading for the goal line; as a forward dribbling toward the basket
- symbols: Reynard the Fox; slippery eel; will-o'-the-wisp
- see also: elusive; wily; tricky; sneaky; untruthful
- opposite: honest; true; real; approachable

Evil: as the devil in his depths; as a bad seed; as the serpent in the Garden of Eden
- symbols: Satan; Lucifer; Beelzebub; snake in the grass
- see also: bad; corrupt; mean; immoral; wicked
- opposite: good; kind; innocent: pure; trustworthy

Exaggerated: as the report of Mark Twain's death; as calling a pond an ocean; as making a mountain out of a molehill; as a braggart's expletives
- symbols: Baron von Munchausen; gilding the lily; laying it on with a trowel; Commander McBragg
- see also: magnified; extravagant; overwhelming
- opposite: modest; small; little; compressed; concise

Exalted: as an emperor on his throne; as the stars in the sky; as the wisdom of All High; as a sinner being born again
- symbols: the king of kings; lord of the manor; the high and the mighty; to the manor born
- see also: high; glorified; elevated; blessed; holy; glorious
- opposite: low; damned; crumbling; heretical

Excessive: as a convert's zeal; as the lust for power; as too much of a good thing
- symbols: Nero; Saturnalia; Falstaff
- see also: extreme; needless; unnecessary; tasteless
- opposite: essential; necessary; basic; modest

Exciting: as passion reciprocated; as the smell of blood to a raging beast; as the prospect of a golden opportunity
    symbols: the thrill of a lifetime; an electric moment
    see also: electrifying; heated; moving
    opposite: dull; boring; placid; quiet

Exclusive: as a key-club key; as a gated community; as a journalistic scoop
    symbols: Nob Hill; snob hill; Fifth Avenue; closed corporation; private club
    see also: selective; closed; narrow; privileged
    opposite: broad; open; hospitable

Excusable: as a child's error; as a dirty diaper; as a slip of the lip
    symbols: a little white lie
    see also: forgivable; understandable; reasonable
    opposite: inexcusable

Exemplary: as a model citizen; as a preacher's parable; as an Olympic athlete
    symbols: perfect specimen; Sir Galahad
    see also: admirable; classic; good; clear
    opposite: bad; poor; wrong; spoiled

Exhausted: as a drained oil well; as a pauper's bank account; as the patience of a short-tempered person after a long wait; as a tot at the end of a hectic day
    symbols: end of the line; totaled; deflated balloon; empty tank
    see also: finished; empty; weary
    opposite: strong; full; energetic

Expensive: as the price of progress; as a bad investment; as a seller's market; as the wages of sin
    symbols: highway robbery; Harry Winston; Tiffany's
    see also: dear; high; inflated
    opposite: cheap; low; economical

Experienced: as a man of the world; as an alumnus of the School of Knocks; as a veteran on the front lines
    symbols: Nestor; old pro; old hand; the pros from Dover
    see also: qualified; educated; wise
    opposite: amateurish; incompetent; unprepared

Experimental: as a laboratory exercise; as a stab in the dark; as an independent film-maker's first work

    symbols: breadboard model; trial and error; run it up the flagpole; the untried and possibly true

    see also: tentative; uncertain

    opposite: certain; sure; absolute; experienced

Explicit: as X marks the spot; as a court injunction; as a gun at your head

    symbols: in black and white

    see also: clear; certain; obvious; definite; precise

    opposite: uncertain; fuzzy; cloudy; inaccurate

Explosive: as the Hiroshima bombing; as the Blitz over London; as a riot waiting to happen; as pepper spray; as an enraged skunk

    symbols: dynamite; TNT; fireworks

    see also: volatile; inflamed

    opposite: calm; mild

Expressive: as a blush; as a bended knee; as falling asleep in the middle of a lecture; as a baby's lower lip

    symbols: a telltale smile; the cat that swallowed the canary

    see also: eloquent; clear

    opposite: flat; faceless; vague

Extended: as the hand of friendship; as a booking that's held over; as a rubber line of credit

    symbols: stretch out; long stretch

    see also: long; delayed

    opposite: brief; short

Extinct: as a dead volcano; as the mastodon and the saber-toothed tiger; as the lost continent of Atlantis

    symbols: the dodo; the dinosaur; the great auk

    see also: dead; finished

    opposite: new modern; timely

Extravagant: as a politician's promises; as a wastrel's wildness; as spendthrift's standards; as a salesperson's high-powered pitch

    symbols: gilding the lily; the last of the big time spenders; good-time Charlie

    see also: exaggerated; flattering; lavish; generous

    opposite: cheap; tight; small; economical

Extreme: as the end of the spectrum; as the lengths desperate people will try; as an opponent's position; as skiing in a kayak

    symbols: the nth degree; all the way

    see also: final; desperate; narrow

    opposite: cautious; moderate; tolerant

F

Faceless: as the phantom's voice; as a headless horseman; as a scream in the night; as a masked marauder

    symbols: masked ball; Phantom of the Opera; the man in the iron mask

    see also: anonymous

    opposite: familiar; obvious

Faded: as vintage denim; as the leaves that fall from the trees; as the light at the end of the day

    symbols: twilight; the invisible man

    see also: colorless; cloudy

    opposite: colorful; brilliant; gaudy; durable

Faint: as the praise that damns; as a distant star; as a glimmer in the black of night; as the heart that ne'er won a fair lady

    symbols: fade away; weak in the knees; a signal from the farthest star

    see also: weak; feeble; frail

    opposite: strong; brilliant; loud; bold

Faithful: as Old Blue; as a good friend; as the words of an honest man

    symbols: fidus Achates; Old Faithful; Penelope

    see also: constant; trustworthy; loyal; true; steadfast

    opposite: false; changeable; lying; uncertain

False: as crocodile's tears; as a fool's illusions; as a phony witness

    symbols: Apples of Sodom; Cressid (Cressida); Achitophel

    see also: dishonest; lying; treacherous; untruthful

    opposite: true; loyal; trustworthy; steadfast; honest; accurate

Familiar: as an old mistake (Edwin Arlington Robinson); as a fond memory; as the old faces back home; as the face in the mirror; as your parent's favorite story

    symbols: Everyman; *déjà vu*; rebroadcast; encore

    see also: normal; natural; common; average

    opposite: rare; strange; different; alien; special

Famous: as the Ten Commandments; as a best-selling author; as the plays of Shakespeare; as professional athletes

    symbols: a household word; Hall of Fame; headliner

    see also: celebrated; eminent; distinguished

    opposite: obscure; forgotten

Fancy: as a fiddler's fingering; as a peacock's plumage; as the costumes at a Beaux Arts Ball; as the flights of imagination; as a fighter's fast footwork

    symbols: French pastry; evening gown

    see also: gaudy; colorful; intricate; elegant; imaginary

    opposite: dull; quiet; incompetent

Far: as angels ken (John Milton); as the farthest star; as a faded memory; as from here to eternity

    symbols: the end of the earth; light years

    see also: distant; infinite; endless

    opposite: close; near; imminent

Fascinating: as a first love; as a fan dancer's fandango; as a rendezvous with destiny; as a siren's song

    symbols: Venus; Diana; Apollo; Adonis

    see also: engaging; attractive; exciting; charming; appealing

    opposite: dull; boring

Fast: as a flash in the pan; as the flight of a rumor; as the speed of light; as the shades of nightfall

    symbols: greased lightning; e-mailed message; an overnight delivery

    see also: quick; rapid; brief; early

    opposite: slow; delayed; hesitant

Fat: as a billionaire's wallet; as a contented cat; as a stuffed goose

    symbols: Big Bertha; Two-Ton Tessie; Falstaff

    see also: flabby; broad; padded; big; large

    opposite: skinny; thin; slim; small

Fatal: as the gift of beauty (Lord Byron); as the passage of time; as two feet in the grave

    symbols: Grim Reaper; angel of death; appointment in Samarra; Thanatos

    see also: lethal; deadly; destructive

    opposite: safe; harmless; secure

Faulty: as a leaking faucet; as a plane with one wing; as a phony alibi; as a television without a picture tube
- symbols: a lemon; a basket case
- see also: cracked; messy; damaged; disastrous
- opposite: flawless; perfect

Favorable: as a vote of confidence; as a friendly breeze; as flattery; as a review from a kind critic
- symbols: the smile of the gods; four stars; thumbs up; good omen
- see also: good; friendly; hopeful; optimistic
- opposite: bad; antagonistic; hopeless; pessimistic

Feeble: as a punctured alibi; as a con-man's conscience; as a coward's courage
- symbols: milksop; tired blood
- see also: weak; anemic; frail
- opposite: strong; powerful; hearty; firm; fierce

Fertile: as the lower forty; as a cornfield in Kansas; as a flowering field; as a forest floor
- symbols: Ceres; Mother Earth; Cybele; Aphrodite; Demeter
- see also: fruitful; bountiful; rich
- opposite: barren; fruitless; poor; meager

Festive: as a golden wedding; as the fourth of July; as a Roman orgy; as a Mardi Gras parade
- symbols: Saturnalia; Roman holiday; red-letter day
- see also: happy; flowery
- opposite: bleak; gloomy; despondent

Feverish: as a hothouse in a heat wave; as panic in the streets; as the activity in an agitated ant hill; as an attack of malaria
- symbols: boiling point; bonfire; beehive
- see also: busy; energetic; active; hot
- opposite: cool; calm; relaxed; inert; quiet; placid

Fierce: as nature in the raw; as the claws of a jungle cat; as the call of the wild; as a rivalry between stallions
- symbols: Mars; Thor; Berserkers; Vikings
- see also: bold: powerful; strong; firm; antagonistic
- opposite: feeble; weak; shy

Filthy: as a fetid garbage dump; as pornographer's daydream; as dishonest dollars
 symbols: Augean stables; flea bag; pigsty
 see also: dirty; messy; unclean; impure
 opposite: clean; spotless; pure

Final: as the grave; as going under for the third time; as three strikes; as the Last Supper
 symbols: Götterdämmerung; Judgment Day; Twilight of the Gods; a wrap; a grand climax
 see also: finished; complete; definite
 opposite: continuous; unfinished; endless; partial

Fine: as rare silk; as the point of a pin; as filigree; as the perfection of paradise
 symbols: gossamer; Augustan
 see also: dainty; delicate; precise; perfect
 opposite: gross; coarse; crude; heavy

Finished: as the fadeout to the closing titles; as a fine performance; as a polished parquet floor
 symbols: closed chapter; end of the masterpiece; epilogue
 see also: complete; perfect; accomplished; final
 opposite: unfinished; partial; coarse; crude; underdeveloped

Firm: as the mountains stand against the sky; as a stone foundation; as the devil with the damned; as the great Wall of China
 symbols: Rock of Gibraltar; Stonewall Jackson
 see also: arbitrary; rigid; strong; commanding; established
 opposite: weak; feeble; brittle; delicate; shy

Fishy: as a salmon run; as a good red herring; as the one that got away; as a phony pedigree
 symbols: whale of a story; old wives' tale; mare's nest
 see also: suspicious; questionable; dubious; false
 opposite: true; correct; established; sure; certain

Fit: as a finely tuned fiddle; as a crown for a king; as a marathon champion
 symbols: Charles Atlas; Mr. Universe; right time, right place
 see also: appropriate; becoming; strong; qualified
 opposite: healthy

Flabby: as the moral fiber in a fleshpot; as a weak handshake; as a limp lump of lard
    symbols: Falstaff; soft stuff
    see also: fat; ample
    opposite: slim; strong; fit

Flashy: as the great White Way; as the lights of Las Vegas; as diamond glinting in the night; as a comet streaming across the sky
    symbols: Roman candle; rhinestone cowboy; fireworks display
    see also: bright; brilliant; colorful; gaudy; loud
    opposite: colorless; dark; quiet

Flat: as the endless prairie; as the ground under a steamroller; as the world before Columbus; as an amateur diva; as a penny on a railroad track
    symbols: pancake; collapsible top hat; stale beer
    see also: thin; skinny; endless; colorless; dreary
    opposite: thick; fat; colorful; gaudy

Flattering: as a testimonial dinner; as an unexpected compliment; as candlelight on a beautiful face
    symbols: Blarney stone; gilding the lily
    see also: complimentary; gracious
    opposite: insulting; rude; nasty

Flawless: as the Hope Diamond; as love's youthful dreams; as a model's complexion
    symbols: Augustan; Attic; Utopia; fine porcelain
    see also: perfect; correct
    opposite: blemished; faulty; tarnished; impure

Fleeting: as a passing memory; as the blink of an eye; as the estate of man (Marcus Aurelius); as an instant in eternity
    symbols: April shower; mayfly; passing fancy
    see also: momentary; brief; temporary; quick
    opposite: enduring; lasting; permanent

Flexible: as a bending knee; as a picture wire; as a murderer's morals; as a bargainer's last offer
    symbols: two-way stretch; a Hindu contortionist
    see also: adjustable; pliable; adaptable; elastic
    opposite: rigid; firm; solid; uncompromising

Flowery: as a spring bouquet; as a gangster's funeral; as a garden in bloom; as Casanova's proposals
>   symbols: Gongorism; Euphuism
>   see also: flattering; complimentary; eloquent; expressive; fancy
>   opposite: dreary; dull, modest

Foggy: as a pair of eyeglasses in a hot shower; as a Turkish bath; as a mountain in the clouds
>   symbols: a London pea souper; a hangover the morning after
>   see also: dense; cloudy; gloomy; dark
>   opposite: bright; clear; brilliant

Foolish: as rushing in where angels fear to tread; as drinking courage from a bottle; as the know-it-all who thinks he knows it all; as each generation thinks the other is
>   symbols: Pickwickian
>   see also: stupid; dopey; dumb; absurd; indiscreet; rash
>   opposite: wise; clever; prudent; careful; cautious

Forgetful: as he who chooses not to remember; as a student who didn't study; as an amnesiac
>   symbols: the absent-minded professor; the waters of Lethe
>   see also: oblivious; negligent; careless
>   opposite: attentive; conscientious; careful

Forgivable: as an honest error; as a wrong step in a righteous cause; as an excess of enthusiasm
>   symbols: a little white lie; on the angel's side
>   see also: excusable; understandable; reasonable
>   opposite: inexcusable; wrong

Forgotten: as a dead man out of mind (Bible; psalms) as unfashionable fanaticism; as old ways in new times; as yesterday's dreams; as an unwanted pet
>   symbols: the forgotten man; watered by Lethe
>   see also: forsaken; deserted; abandoned; neglected
>   opposite: memorable; timely

Formal: as a penguin's coat; as an embassy dinner; as white tie and tails; as an audience with the Pope; as a U.S. Supreme Court hearing
>   symbols: black tie; by the numbers
>   see also: solemn; dignified; grand
>   opposite: boisterous; noisy; ill-mannered; rude

Forsaken: as a wanderer in the desert; as the primrose path of a practicing Puritan; as the way of the wicked; as a lonely grave

  symbols: ghost town; orphan of the storm; deserted ship

  see also: neglected; desolate; forgotten; deserted

  opposite: cherished; sought-after

Fortunate: as a favorite of Fate; as a farmer with a fertile field; as a wise investor; as a lottery winner

  symbols: Midas touch; darling of the gods

  see also: lucky; blessed

  opposite: unlucky; damned

Fragrant: as the flowers that bloom in the spring; as the sweet smell of success; as a vintage wine

  symbols: garden of roses; incense; balsam; balm

  see also: aromatic; flowery; odorous; smelly

  opposite: arid; dead

Frail: as a blade of grass bending in the breeze; as tissue paper; as fleeting fame; as a fading friendship

  symbols: house of cards; eggshell; 90-pound weakling

  see also: brittle; weak; anemic; feeble; delicate

  opposite: strong; powerful; firm; solid; heavy

Frank: as an unrehearsed insult; as a family argument; as puppy's emotions; as a nudist's costume

  symbols: true confession; brass tacks; talking turkey

  see also: open; honest

  opposite: insincere; dishonest; affected

Frantic: as a commuter running for the last train; as a frog in a frying pan; as a photographer without film

  symbols: Bedlam; hoopla; three-ring circus

  see also: agitated; bothered; chaotic; desperate

  opposite: calm; relaxed; quiet; peaceful; casual

Fraudulent: as counterfeit money; as a doctored dissertation; as false piety; as a phony affidavit

  symbols: Cagliostro; confidence game; snake oil salesperson; medicine show

  see also: false; dishonest; lying; untruthful; deceitful; devious; duplicitous

  opposite: genuine; honest; true; correct

Free: as the open road; as the breeze in the trees; as unsolicited advice; as the air we breathe

 symbols: Statue of Liberty; Liberty Bell; on the house
 see also: independent; liberal; generous; permissive
 opposite: limited; confined; rigid

Frequent: as a baby's diaper changes; as a frog's jumps; as the cackles in a hen house

 symbols: epidemic; morning, noon, and night
 see also: numerous; repetitious
 opposite: rare; scarce; seldom

Fresh: as a new coat of paint; as a daisy laden with dew; as an unrepentant sinner sneering at salvation

 symbols: mint condition; sons of Belial; hot off the press
 see also: new; rude; insolent; bold; modern
 opposite: ancient; old; rotten; decayed; old fashioned

Friendly: as a helping hand; as a kind word at a bad moment; as a vote of confidence; as a salesperson trying to make a sale

 symbols: Damon and Pythias; fidu Achates; the Three Musketeers; Welcome Wagon
 see also: amiable; pleasant; agreeable; approachable; warm; affectionate
 opposite: aloof; haughty; nasty; antagonistic

Frightened: as a mouse facing a cat; as a startled fawn; as waking to a spider on your nose

 symbols: seeing a Gorgon; goose flesh
 see also: scared; cowardly
 opposite: brave; daring; bold; courageous

Frightful: as the Devil's dwelling place; as a mob in motion; as the depths of despair; as a holocaust remembered

 symbols: Godzilla; Caliban; Armageddon; the thundering Horde
 see also: atrocious; awful; cruel; horrible; hellish; dreadful
 opposite: good; kind; pleasant; warm; angelic; blessed

Frugal: as a hermit's housewarming; as a bride on a budget; as a miser with his money

 symbols: Spartan; Diogenes; Scotsman
 see also: economical; stingy; close; cheap
 opposite: lavish; generous; extravagant

Fruitful: as a seed that multiplies; as the land of milk and honey; as the lessons of experience; as the parents of a large family

    symbols: Demeter; Pomona; Freya

    see also: bountiful; fertile; rich; productive

    opposite: fruitless; barren; poor; meager; arid

Fruitless: as a forlorn hope; as an overage apple tree; as the search for the Holy Grail

    symbols: wild goose chase; the labor of Sisyphus; Penelope's web

    see also: barren; poor; arid; bare

    opposite: productive; fruitful; bountiful; fertile

Furious: as the courage of a cornered rat; as the frenzy of the damned; as a barroom brawl; as a fight to the death

    symbols: Eumenides (the Furies); Rumpelstiltskin

    see also: angry; mad; ill-tempered

    opposite: placid; calm; peaceful; relaxed

Fussy: as a Persian cat; as a thoroughbred at the starting gate; as a hypochondriac with heartburn

    symbols: fussbudget; Mrs. Prim

    see also: nervous; careful; cautious

    opposite: careless; negligent; reckless; breezy

Futile: as a rain dance in Death Valley; as a spear in a shoot-out; as a conversation with a stone; as forlorn hope

    symbols: Don Quixote; Sisyphus

    see also: useless; vain; hopeless; helpless; inadequate

    opposite: effective; helpful; useful; hopeful

Fuzzy: as a bad connection; as a faulty memory; as a double-knit gone to seed; as a champagne hangover

    symbols: out of focus; smog city; fog bound

    see also: unclear; uncertain; foggy

    opposite: clear; certain

G

Gallant: as a the good fight; as showing one's colors; as a dashing cavalier; as a knight in shining armor

    symbols: Sir Galahad; Robin Hood; Sir Walter Raleigh

    see also: dashing; brave; courageous; bold; courteous

    opposite: sacred; frightened; cowardly; rude; nasty

Gaseous: as the bubble in a glass of soda pop; as a windbag; as a blimp; as a leaking stove
  symbols: gas bag; hot air balloon; lighter than air
  see also: light; volatile; windy; talkative
  opposite: heavy; dense; silent

Gaudy: as all that glitters; as an overly decorated Christmas tree; as the Great White Way; as a psychedelic shirt
  symbols: circus poster; rainbow; flashy dress
  see also: flashy; bright; colorful; vivid
  opposite: colorless; dark; dismal; desolate

Generous: as a doting grandparent; as a forgiving heart; as an act of mercy; as an unsolicited gift; as a helping hand
  symbols: Santa Claus; Saint Nick; Kris Kringle; Lady Bountiful; the Good Samaritan; a fairy godmother
  see also: kind; charitable; considerate; free; helpful
  opposite: grudging; tight; cheap; close

Genial: as a gentle jest; as a gracious host; as the mood of spring; as the look of love
  symbols: glad hander; life of the party
  see also: amiable; friendly; cheerful; agreeable; happy; gracious; congenial
  opposite: quarrelsome; gloomy; disagreeable; biting

Gentle: as a little lamb; as a kitten; as Jesus meek and mild (Charles Wesley); as a mother's touch; as a healing angel
  symbols: timid soul; loving hand; Caspar Milquetoast
  see also: kind; meek; docile
  opposite: biting; nasty; sharp; strong

Genuine: as a baby's burp; as an original masterpiece; as envy unveiled
  symbols: the real McCoy; Simon Pure; 24 carat
  see also: authentic; real; true; original
  opposite: false; imitative; untruthful

Ghastly: as Hamlet's father's fate; as a graveyard ghoul; as the haunts of Hell; as an overnight in a haunted house; as the black hounds on the midnight moors
  symbols: the Flying Dutchman; the mystery of the Mary Celeste
  see also: dismal; bleak; desolate; gloomy
  opposite: bright; happy; cheerful

Gifted: as a favorite of Fate; as a spoiled child on Christmas morning; as the darling of the gods; as a golden voice
    symbols: Renaissance Man; Talent Incorporated; child prodigy
    see also: blessed; fortunate
    opposite: handicapped; deprived

Glaring: as an error in open view; as the brightness of the summer sun; as the glance of a grumpy grouch; as the center of the spotlight
    symbols: front and center; eye stopper; eye opener
    see also: bright; obvious; brilliant; noticeable; apparent; angry
    opposite: overlooked: obscure; hidden

Gloomy: as a friendless funeral; as an untended grave; as a lonely night; as a pessimist's predictions; as the trackless wastes of the dark unknown
    symbols: Hamlet; Erebus; cave of Trophonius; Dracula's castle
    see also: black; dark; sad; pessimistic; dismal; dreary; downhearted; discouraged; eerie
    opposite: happy; cheerful; warm; glad; optimistic

Glorified: as hero worship; as dreams of grandeur; as the Golden Age of Greece; as the grandeur that was Rome; as the Ming Dynasty
    symbols: star billing; matinee idol; a household name
    see also: exalted; elevated; magnified
    opposite: low; common; average

Glorious: as a rainbow after a storm; as the coming of the Lord; as the ascent of man; as the gift of laughter; as the triumph of good over evil; as the flag of truth flying triumphant
    symbols: Paradise; heaven; Eden; Utopia
    see also: spectacular; beautiful; harmonious
    opposite: mean, ugly; low

Glossy: as a dandy's lacquered hair; as a cover girl; as a picture postcard; as a fancy sales brochure
    symbols: tinsel, plastic
    see also: smooth; colorful; polished
    opposite: dull; colorless; unappealing

Good: as gold; as glad tidings; as a nice deed in a naughty world; as the man you can't keep down
    symbols: Mithra; Themis; Sir Galahad
    see also: commendable; admirable; exemplary; pleasant; desirable
    opposite: bad; hellish; horrible; atrocious; mean; awful

Graceful: as a gazelle; as a ballet dancer; as an eagle in flight; as a willow waving in the wind; as the man on the flying trapeze

    symbols: Hebe; Nureyev; Barishnikov; Anna Pavlova

    see also: agile; nimble; dainty; delicate

    opposite: awkward; heavy-handed; heavy

Gracious: as a good loser; as a thoughtful host; as the kingdom of Heaven; as good manners under pressure

    symbols: Sir Walter Raleigh; Emily Post; Miss Manners

    see also: courteous; amiable; polite; kind; pleasant; hospitable

    opposite: ill-mannered; gross; rude; impolite

Gradual: as the passage of time; as the road to hell; as the Chinese water torture; as a tortoise's pace; as the progress of a snail

    symbols: Fabian; pearl

    see also: slow; delayed; hesitant; deliberate

    opposite: fast; instantaneous; dashing

Grand: as the canyons of Colorado; as the great design of life; as the manner of the mighty; as the ultimate illusion

    symbols: Olympian; Jovian

    see also: exalted; solemn; formal; high; dignified

    opposite: low; mean; meek; humble; rotten; relaxed

Grasping: as a stage mother; as a miser for more money; as a gold digger looking for a spouse; as a politician's push for power

    symbols: a gigolo; Silas Marner; Midas; Lorelei Lee

    see also: selfish; vain; cheap; tight; crass

    opposite: idealistic; generous; kind

Grateful: as one who wants another gift; as a puppy for a petting; as those who recognize their debts; as the giver of thanks

    symbols: Thanksgiving; grace

    see also: pleased; appreciated

    opposite: indifferent; arrogant

Greedy: as the lust for lucre; as a hungry dog is for a bone; as one who is searching for sin; as a money grubber in the mint

    symbols: Midas; green-eyed monster; Ebenezer Scrooge

    see also: envious; jealous; cheap; grudging

    opposite: generous; charitable; kind

Gripping: as a bulldog's bite; as a baby's hold on a finger; as the pulse of passion; as a ghost story told by the campfire; as a mysterious noise in the night
    symbols: cliffhanger; crowd-stopper
    see also: fascinating; compelling; exciting; strong
    opposite: dull; boring; weak

Gross: as a belch at a banquet; as picking your nose in public; as an orgy in Sodom and Gomorrah
    symbols: Goth; Caliban
    see also: crass; rude; coarse; vulgar; insulting
    opposite: elegant; educated; refined; cultured

Grouchy: as an overwhelmed complaint clerk; as a bothered bus driver; as a sore loser; as a tired child; as a demon with dyspepsia; as a hermit facing a horde of visitors
    symbols: crab; Tartar
    see also: ill-tempered; angry; mad; nasty; grudging
    opposite: agreeable; genial; friendly; pleasant; amiable

Grudging: as a curmudgeon's compliments; as a gift from a tightwad; as a smile from a sourpuss; as praise from an opponent
    symbols: Ebenezer Scrooge; Fagan
    see also: grouchy; stingy; tight
    opposite: generous; genial; kind; considerate; overwhelming

Guilty: as a killer caught in the act; as a thief with his hand in the till; as the perjurer caught in a lie
    symbols: cop a plea; *mea culpa*
    see also: criminal; wrong
    opposite: innocent; excusable

H

Habitual: as breathing; as brushing your teeth; as hoping for the best
    symbols: daily dozen; house custom
    see also: automatic; regular; constant; changeless
    opposite: irregular; rare; changeable

Hairy: as an orangutan; as an unkempt camel; as a tale of honor; as the floor of a busy barbershop
- symbols: woolly bear; barber bait
- see also: menacing; ominous; fuzzy
- opposite: smooth; bare; clear

Handicapped: as a chef without a kitchen; as a filibusterer with laryngitis; as a one-armed paper hanger; as a student who forgot to study for the exam
- symbols: behind the eight-ball; caught with one's pants down
- see also: limited; underdeveloped
- opposite: privileged; gifted

Handsome: as a Greek god; as a matinee idol; as the bull that kidnapped Europa (Cicero); as the beast when beauty loved him
- symbols: Adonis; Apollo; Ganymede
- see also: attractive; beautiful; fascinating
- opposite: ugly; beastly

Happy: as a lark on the loose; as a fool in love; as the man that hath his quiver full (Bible: Psalms); as the hope of heaven; as a carefree kitten; as those with blessings they can count
- symbols: Arcadia; Elysium; Elysian Fields; Paradise
- see also: euphoric; carefree; cheerful; exalted
- opposite: sad; moody; gloomy; dismal

Hard: as nails of steel; as teaching an old dog new tricks; as the way of transgressors (Bible: *Proverbs*); as the heart of the vilest villain
- symbols: the task of Sisyphus; the labors of Hercules; the trials of Job
- see also: tough; difficult; austere; baffling
- opposite: easy; soft; simple

Hard-core: as a teenaged two-time loser; as a dropout with a habit; as a two-bit hooker
- symbols: street arab; street kid; misfit; unrepentant sinner
- see also: abandoned; forsaken; criminal; immoral; lawless
- opposite: correct; pure; cherished

Hardy: as a healthy hound; as an unpicked weed
- symbols: Hercules; Amazon; Hygeia
- see also: strong; tough; firm; solid; enduring
- opposite: weak; frail; feeble

Harmful: as a cyanide cocktail; as a toadstool tart; as a bull in a china shop
    symbols: Pandora's box; Lucretia Borgia's recipe book
    see also: damaging; destructive; lethal; fatal; deadly; disastrous
    opposite: safe; harmless; helpful; good

Harmless: as a eunuch in a harem; as a moth in a closet full of polyester; as a barking dog without teeth
    symbols: placebo; the good guys
    see also: safe; helpful
    opposite: damaging; harmful; destructive; fatal; lethal; deadly; disastrous

Harmonious: as a pair of lovebirds; as a heavenly choir; as two minds sharing a single thought
    symbols: Orpheus; Entente Cordiale
    see also: alike; agreeable; peaceful; friendly; amiable
    opposite: different; antagonistic; difficult; disagreeable

Harsh: as a drill's sergeant's dressing down; as the school of hard knocks; as nature in the raw; as a naked hate
    symbols: Draco; Eumenides (The Furies)
    see also: austere; sharp; rough; biting; rude; bitter
    opposite: soft; gentle; smooth; kind; gracious

Hasty: as leaping through a window; as a retreat that turns into a rout; as a marriage on the spur of the moment; as a last-minute substitution
    symbols: quickstep; French leave; greased lightning
    see also: fast, quick, hurried, rushed
    opposite: hesitant; slow; delayed; cautious

Hateful: as the gates of Hell (Homer); as the other person's bad habits; as treason at a trying time; as malice aforethought
    symbols: Devil incarnate; Eumenides (The Furies); the harpies; the men in black hats
    see also: detestable; offensive; nasty; annoying
    opposite: admirable; beloved; dear; lovable

Haughty: as the pride that goes before a fall; as a dowager looking down her nose; as a snob among the hoi polloi; as a commoner playing king
    symbols: high horse
    see also: arrogant; rude; distant; cool
    opposite: humble; meek; approachable; warm; friendly

Haunted: as holy ground (Lord Byron); as a ghost's gazebo; as one whose mind is filled with memories; as an old cemetery; as a house of horrors
  symbols: The Flying Dutchman; the Bodmin Moors; the uninvited of the night
  see also: ghastly; damned
  opposite: blessed

Healing: as an angel's touch; as nature's nostrums; as the passage of time
  symbols: *Aesculapius*; *Imhotep*; Hippocrates; Apollo
  see also: helpful; healthy
  opposite: harmful; damaging; fatal; deadly; lethal

Healthy: as a sound mind in a sound body (Juvenal); as a happy horse; as the prime of life; as heaven on earth
  symbols: Hygeia; Salus
  see also: sound; strong
  opposite: sick

Hearty: as a heavenly hosanna; as a rousing welcome; as a friendly handshake; as spontaneous applause
  symbols: Falstaff; the works
  see also: strong; powerful; sincere; warm; zealous
  opposite: feeble; weak; frail; false; insincere

Heated: as a Russian bath; as the peak of passion; as a hundred degrees in the shade; as the halls of Hell
  symbols: volcano; fireworks; thermal fields
  see also: hot; fierce; angry; inflamed; explosive
  opposite: calm; icy; cold; peaceful; amiable

Heavenly: as the abode of angels; as all eternity; as the celestial skies; as the souls of salvation
  symbols: Nirvana; Valhalla; Elysium; pearly gates; the Land of Green Ginger; the home of the Firebird
  see also: angelic; good; pure; high
  opposite: evil; demonic; bad; low; hellish

Heavy: as the hand of fate; as the weight of the world; as a heart of stone; as the burden of guilt
  symbols: Two-Ton Tessie; Big Bertha; the labors of Sisyphus; a millstone; a backbreaker
  see also: burdensome; laborious; big
  opposite: light; dainty; delicate; airy; easy

Heavy handed: as painting with a bush; as a surgeon using a meat cleaver; as cro-
cheting with boxing gloves
>   symbols: Draconian; Prussian; overkill
>   see also: crude; coarse; harsh; severe; cruel
>   opposite: fine; delicate; dainty; graceful; agile; soft; smooth

Hellish: as a housewarming in Hades; as the Devil's disposition; as the fury of a
woman scorned; as a Puritan's private conscience; as unholy wedlock
>   symbols: Satanic; Tartarus; inferno; Gehenna
>   see also: awful; horrible; frightful; dreadful
>   opposite: heavenly; angelic; good; pleasant

Helpful: as a guardian angel; as a fairy godmother; as the gift of hope; as a hand up
when you're down; as a place to hide
>   symbols: Good Samaritan; friend in need; good right arm
>   see also: convenient; encouraging; generous; kind
>   opposite: cool; indifferent; distant; callous

Helpless: as a newborn babe; as an unarmed man in a shoot-out; as an innocent in a
kangaroo court; as a leaf in a hurricane; as a fledgling in the nest
>   symbols: babe in arms; tied to the tracks; Achilles heel
>   see also: inadequate; futile
>   opposite: strong; effective

Heretical: as every orthodoxy when it is first suggested; as the other person's concept
of truth; as the first suggestion that the earth was round
>   symbols: fallen angel; stray lamb; off the reservation
>   see also: different; radical; revolutionary; rebellious
>   opposite: sacred; blessed; holy; regular

Hesitant: as a bashful bride; as a timid toe in the water; as a person caught between
two lovers; as an unconvinced customer
>   symbols: shrinking violet; cold feet; running hot and cold
>   see also: slow; lingering; delayed; tentative
>   opposite: instantaneous; immediate; emphatic; fast; dashing; impulsive; bold

Hidden: as buried treasure; as a secret psyche; as an ulterior motive; as a hermit's
hideaway; as a separate agenda
>   symbols: Trojan horse; star chamber; chameleon
>   see also: buried; concealed; secret; camouflaged; censored; disguised; obscure
>   opposite: obvious; open; apparent; noticeable

High: as a kite on the climb; as the heavens; as the mountain tops; as the price of progress; as a bird on the wing
   symbols: Olympus; Everest; the Andes; the Alps
   see also: elevated; exalted; expensive; heavenly; dear
   opposite: low; cheap; economical; mean

Holy: as the top of Mount Sinai; as the words of the prophets; as the Lord of Creation
   symbols: scripture; Gospel; the anointed
   see also: blessed; exalted; sacred
   opposite: damned; heretical

Honest: as the day is long; as the man Diogenes couldn't find; as a baby's smile
   symbols: Fabricius; a man for Diogenes; true blue
   see also: frank; open
   opposite: lying; dishonest

Hopeful: as a gambler with money to put on the table; as a persistent suitor; as a stage-struck performer; as new salesperson
   symbols: Pollyanna
   see also: confident; promising; optimistic
   opposite: hopeless; desperate; uncertain; pessimistic

Hopeless: as a lost cause; as sucking blood from a stone; as happiness in Hell; as a deal with the Devil; as the dream of eternal youth
   symbols: the den of despair; Cassandra
   see also: desperate; pessimistic
   opposite: hopeful; confident; optimistic

Horrible: as hate on the march; as man's inhumanity to man; as the triumph of terror; as the remembrance of evil; as the depths of Hell
   symbols: Gorgon; Medusa; Pandora's box; the plagues of Egypt
   see also: atrocious; awful; hellish; mean; evil; disastrous
   opposite: good; exemplary; angelic; noble; pleasant

Hospitable: as a friendly host pointing to a banquet; as a warm welcome on a cold night; as an open door and a friendly fireplace; as a place of shelter in a weary world
   symbols: open house; mine host; kill the fatted calf; Boniface
   see also: friendly; gracious; pleasant; warm; welcome
   opposite: antagonistic; aloof; haughty; mean

Hot: as Hades in a heat wave; as a bed of burning coals; as a tin roof in the summer sun; as a full head of steam

    symbols: Turkish bath; sauna; sweat box; bonfire

    see also: heated; inflamed; explosive; volatile

    opposite: cold; icy; calm; gentle; mild

Huge: as an egotist's ego; as the mileage to Mars; as the heavens are high

    symbols: Leviathan; Colossus of Rhodes; Brobdingnagian

    see also: colossal; big; large

    opposite: small; minimal

Humble: as a contrite heart; as ignorance at the feet of wisdom; as he who finds his pride is false; as a petitioner before a prince

    symbols: Caspar Milquetoast; shrinking violet; eating crow; kow tow

    see also: modest; docile; meek; gentle

    opposite: exalted; mighty; haughty; affected; glorified

Hungry: as a starving hyena; as a vulture on a vegetable diet; as a teenager between meals; as a bear by spring

    symbols: torment of Tantalus; tightened belt

    see also: empty; bottomless

    opposite: satisfied

Hurried: as a hasty exit; as a candidate's campaign schedule; as a quick count

    symbols: Hermes; Mercury

    see also: hasty; rushed; fast; quick

    opposite: slow; hesitant; delayed; lingering

Hybrid: as a cross between a worm and a giraffe; as a mule with feathers; as a cat that barks

    symbols: Pan; Minotaur; Centaurs

    see also: mixed; varied; assorted; different

    opposite: pure

Hypocritical: as a humble dictator; as a pious pervert; as a sin calling itself salvation; as hate masquerading as love

    symbols: Pecksniff; Uriah Heep

    see also: duplicitous; false; devious; insincere

    opposite: honest; barefaced; believable; trustworthy

I

Icy: as the northern wilderness; as the hand of death; as a cold shoulder; as the inside of a refrigerator; as a penguin's nest

    symbols: Jack Frost; Siberia; Arctic; South Pole

    see also: cold; bitter; aloof; distant

    opposite: warm; friendly; heated; hot; approachable

Ideal: as Paradise before the fall; as life in an ivory tower; as Heaven come to earth; as a perfect specimen

    symbols: Utopia; New Jerusalem; Erehwon; Shangri-La

    see also: perfect; heavenly; happy

    opposite: wrong; sad; faulty

Idealistic: as the dreams of sophomores; as the hope for heaven on earth; as the view that all men are gods; as the perceptions of young love

    symbols: Don Quixote; castles in the sky

    see also: noble; exalted; optimistic; visionary

    opposite: crass; cynical; pessimistic; bitter

Idle: as a painted ship upon painted ocean (Samuel T. Coleridge); as an unused mind; as empty words; as lost time

    symbols: lotus eater; sloth

    see also: lazy; inert; quiet

    opposite: active; busy; feverish

Idolatrous: as the worship of the Golden Calf; as serving false gods

    symbols: Baal; the Golden Calf; Lares and Penates

    see also: heretical

    opposite: sacred; holy

Ignorant: as those who refuse to learn; as an idle mind; as one who doesn't know he doesn't know

    symbols: Philistine; Yahoo; Jukes

    see also: oblivious; blind; dumb; foolish

    opposite: clever; wise; knowledgeable

Ill-advised: as teasing a tiger; as an atheist in a seminary; as punching a policeman; as sticking your head in a lion's mouth

    symbols: Iago's counsel; Lady Macbeth

    see also: foolish; tactless; dumb; tasteless; wrong

    opposite: wise; appropriate; correct; clever; sound

Illegible: as a doctor's handwriting; as a store receipt
    symbols: hen scratching; Greek
    see also: fuzzy; uncertain; cloudy
    opposite: clear; understandable; obvious

Ill-mannered: as a snob at a soirée; as a weasel in a hen house; as a poltergeist at bedtime
    symbols: bull in a china shop; Goth; Jukes
    see also: rude; nasty
    opposite: polite; refined; courteous

Illogical: as throwing the baby out with the bath water; as biting your nose off to spite your face; as wearing a tie with a turtleneck; as blaming the weatherman for the weather; as chopping off a finger to cure a hangnail
    symbols: pipe dream; Pickwickian; Wittgensteinian
    see also: irrational; incongruous; absurd; strange; mistaken
    opposite: wise; sound; natural

Ill-tempered: as a perturbed porcupine; as a tired taxpayer; as starving infant; as a burrowing badger
    symbols: Xanthippe; Rumpelstiltskin; spitfire
    see also: mad; angry; antagonistic; grouchy; rude; pugnacious; quarrelsome
    opposite: agreeable; charming; calm; peaceful; amiable; pleasant

Imaginary: as a hypochondriac's complaints; as the castles of the mind; as a child's view of life; as what we think right now
    symbols: castles in the air; pipe dreams; Arabian Nights; Chimera
    see also: legendary; false; visionary
    opposite: real; true; accurate

Imitative: as monkey see, monkey do; as a teenager's tastes; as the sincerest form of flattery
    symbols: spitting image; when in Rome (do as the Romans do); like parent, like child
    see also: repetitious
    opposite: original; creative; inventive; innovative; genuine

Immaculate: as a floor you can eat off; as a saint's reputation; as a new page in the book of life
    symbols: Simon Pure; Sir Galahad; Astraea
    see also: clean; pure; spotless
    opposite: dirty; blemished; tarnished; unclean; impure

Immature: as a sapling in the spring; as a babe in arms; as an acorn waiting to be an oak
> symbols: green apple; tadpole; wet behind the ears
> see also: young; youthful; childish; foolish
> opposite: wise; ripe; old; knowledgeable

Immediate: as love at first sight; as the next breath; as right now
> symbols: Johnny on the spot; before you can say Jackie Robinson
> see also: instantaneous; automatic; spontaneous
> opposite: delayed; late; hesitant; slow; tentative

Imminent: as day is to dawn; as the next tick of the clock; as a blink of an eye
> symbols: waiting in the wings; just around the corner
> see also: threatening; close; near
> opposite: uncertain; distant; far

Immodest: as the man who rates himself a genius; as a salvo of self-praise; as a boaster's braggadocio
> symbols: Falstaff; strutting peacock
> see also: egotistical; vain; exaggerated; selfish
> opposite: modest; humble; meek; docile

Immoral: as tearing up the Ten Commandments; as sin on the loose; as selling your soul
> symbols: Jezebel; Paphian; Sodom and Gomorrah; Messalina; Nero; Caligula
> see also: evil; corrupt; bad; wrong
> opposite: angelic; good; exemplary

Impartial: as an honest judge; as the law of nature; as a man who doesn't care; as an outsider should be in a family feud
> symbols: Themis; Rhadamanthus; Switzerland
> see also: neutral; detached
> opposite: prejudiced; opinionated; bigoted; sympathetic; involved; partisan

Impatient: as an anxious lover; as a thoroughbred at the starting gate; as a hurricane waiting to happen; as a glutton looking at a buffet
> symbols: Hotspur; short fuse
> see also: hasty; rushed; hurried; tense
> opposite: calm; relaxed; placid

Impersonal: as junk mail; as an income tax form
> symbols: any Tom, Dick, and Harry; form letter
> see also: anonymous; aloof; cool; detached
> opposite: personal; warm; approachable; involved

Important: as the breath of life; as food to the famished; as prayer for the pious; as the sun in the sky
    symbols: VIP; top of the list; high priority
    see also: crucial; famous; decisive; serious; celebrated; urgent; necessary
    opposite: unnecessary; useless; needless; obscure

Impressive: as the Seven Wonders of the World; as a miracle at your doorstep; as a lion's roar; as thunder and lightning at midnight
    symbols: four stars; the wonders of nature
    see also: arresting; convincing; spectacular; compelling; fascinating
    opposite: dull; boring; colorless; empty

Improper: as thumbing one's nose at the Pope; as putting a button in the poor box; as a peeping Tom
    symbols: Machiavellian; under the table
    see also: indiscreet; wrong; inexcusable; corrupt
    opposite: correct; discreet; wise; prudent

Impudent: as the pot calling the kettle black; as a belligerent child; as an ignorant know-it-all
    symbols: Leo the Lip; sons of Belial
    see also: rude; insulting; arrogant; bold; tactless
    opposite: quiet; courteous; discreet

Impulsive: as hate at first sight; as a last-minute purchase; as a spontaneous sin
    symbols: Hotspur
    see also: daring; bold; reckless; spontaneous
    opposite: hesitant; lingering; delayed; slow

Impure: as a doctored drink; as a half-truth; as rotten food; as a masochist's imagination
    symbols: Sodom; Augean
    see also: blemished; tarnished; doctored; dirty
    opposite: pure; classic; perfect; flawless; innocent

Inaccessible: as an igloo on an iceberg; as a deadbeat ducking a bill collector
    symbols: Ultima Thule; Shangri-La
    see also: far; distant; elusive; isolated
    opposite: near; close

Inaccurate: as calling a spade a club; as a shot in the dark; as a wrong number
    symbols: Mrs. Malaprop; Wrong Way Corrigan; Pickwickian
    see also: wrong; erroneous; faulty
    opposite: correct; true; accurate

Inadequate: as a putter on a driving range; as baling out a boat with a sieve; as hammering nails with a fly swatter

    symbols: 4F; butter knife

    see also: futile; useless; limited; vain; incompetent

    opposite: helpful; ample; effective

Incalculable: as the average hospital bill; as the rewards of whiplash; as an estimate on car repairs

    symbols: pi to the nth degree; counting the stars in the sky

    see also: uncertain; vague; infinite

    opposite: certain; sure; clear; definite; limited

Incompetent: as a glove maker who's all thumbs; as a cashier who can't count; as an exterminator who encourages termites

    symbols: Colonel Blimp; Sad Sack

    see also: inefficient; inept; inadequate; amateurish

    opposite: accomplished; qualified; fit; useful

Incongruous: as a houseboat on the high seas; as steak sauce on ice cream; as a blizzard in a jungle

    symbols: fish out of water; strange bedfellows; apples and oranges

    see also: strange; ridiculous; absurd; illogical

    opposite: normal; natural; appropriate; correct; conformist

Indelible: as a tattoo; as bleaching bones; as a bad impression; as an inherited trait

    symbols: the leopard's spots; mark of Cain; India ink

    see also: permanent; lasting; enduring; perpetual; changeless

    opposite: uncertain; changeable; temporary

Independent: as a candidate without a party; as a runaway teen

    symbols: Statue of Liberty; Liberty Bell; Spirit of '76; the United States of America

    see also: free

    opposite: confined; limited; committed

Indifferent: as a snooty sales clerk; as a car salesperson when cars are selling; as a eunuch in a harem

    symbols: Laodicean; cold shoulder; deaf ear

    see also: aloof; cool; distant; callous; negligent

    opposite: sympathetic; comforting; devoted; attentive; involved

Indiscreet: as a bedroom without a window shade; as salting the chef's signature dish before tasting it
    symbols: bull in a china shop; blabbermouth
    see also: ill-advised; careless; tactless; rude; foolish; hasty
    opposite: prudent; discreet; careful; cautious

Indulgent: as a doting grandparent; as an audience of close friends; as the parent who spares the spanking
    symbols: sugar daddy; Lady Bountiful; guardian angel
    see also: permissive; tolerant; considerate; kind; amiable
    opposite: callous; cool; cruel; rigid

Ineffective: as an umbrella in a hurricane; as eating soup with a fork; as a canoe with a hole in the hull
    symbols: paper tiger; love's labor lost; the labors of Sisyphus
    see also: useless; fruitless; futile; inadequate; helpless; hopeless; weak
    opposite: effective; fruitful; useful; strong; helpful; convincing

Inefficient: as smoke signals in a high wind; as serving soup in a sieve
    symbols: The Poor Soul; Sad Sack; basket case
    see also: incompetent; inadequate; futile
    opposite: effective; smooth; accomplished

Ineligible: as a duffer for the Masters Tournament; as a bigamist at the bridal altar; as an adolescent trying to collect a pension
    symbols: beyond the pale
    see also: left out; picky; inadequate
    opposite: eligible; qualified; deserving

Inept: as a finger painter who's all thumbs; as a juggler with the shakes; as a chef who can't remember a recipe; as a dancer with two left feet
    symbols: Mr. Thumbs; Sad Sack
    see also: incompetent; awkward; amateurish; inefficient
    opposite: accomplished; efficient; effective

Inert: as a cornerstone; as a park statue; as the water in a stagnant pool; as a limp wet rag
    symbols: Sleeping Beauty
    see also: lazy; relaxed; limp; dead
    opposite: active; busy; agitated; energetic

Inevitable: as Judgment Day; as morning, noon, and night; as the march of time
  symbols: The Fates; Kismet
  see also: certain; sure; clear; definite
  opposite: questionable; uncertain; debatable

Inexcusable: as a nudist in a seminary; as graffiti in the Sistine Chapel; as lighting a match to check a gas leak
  symbols: beyond the pale; over the line
  see also: ill-advised; wrong
  opposite: excusable; exemplary; commendable; admirable

Infinite: as the expanding universe; as the duration of eternity; as the power of nature
  symbols: world without end
  see also: endless; perpetual
  opposite: limited; definite; confined

Inflamed: as an angry bull; as a mob in white heat; as a strep throat; as a teenager's first pass at passion
  symbols: Eumenides (The Furies); active volcano
  see also: heated; passionate; angry; sick; painful
  opposite: calm; placid; gentle; peaceful; healthy

Inflammable: as high octane gasoline; as a dry forest; as a demagogue's call to arms
  symbols: tinder box; powder keg
  see also: explosive; dangerous; threatening; ominous
  opposite: safe; harmless

Inflated: as a pneumatic tire; as a braggart's ego; as a pumped-up air mattress; as a hot-air balloon
  symbols: lighter than air; blowfish
  see also: exaggerated; magnified; huge; booming; high
  opposite: small; minimal; low

Informal: as a leisure dress in a nudist colony; as a picnic in the park; as old overalls; as a pajama party
  symbols: homespun; pot luck
  see also: casual; relaxed
  opposite: formal; rigid

Innocent: as a lamb led to the slaughter; as a new-laid egg (W.S. Gilbert); as a passing bystander; as a litter of kittens
  symbols: Arcadian; babes and sucklings; Astraea; babes in the woods
  see also: pure; clean; chaste; harmless
  opposite: blemished; tarnished: crafty; wily; corrupt; deceitful; guilty

Innovative: as an automobile in mule country; as the invention of the wheel; as the first fashion designer
    symbols: new broom; New Deal; latest model
    see also: original; creative; inventive; inspired
    opposite: old fashioned; obsolete; overworked; normal

Inquisitive: as a curious cat; as a grand jury with a scent of sin; as the neighborhood snoop
    symbols: Nosy Parker; Polly Pry; Peeping Tom
    see also: curious; meddlesome
    opposite: indifferent; apathetic; aloof

Insincere: as a flatterer's flowery phrases; as canned laughter; as a diplomat's polished prose
    symbols: Judas' kiss; Punic faith; Machiavellian
    see also: false; contrived; lying; duplicitous; dishonest; hypocritical
    opposite: honest; trustworthy; true

Insistent: as a nagging backache; as a life-insurance salesperson; as a collection agency; as an addiction; as a migraine
    symbols: Hobson's choice; Siren song
    see also: dogged; stubborn; committed
    opposite: hesitant; relaxed; apathetic

Inspired: as a stroke of genius; as a Beethoven sonata; as a Renoir masterpiece; as the menu at a five-star restaurant
    symbols: brainstorm; Moses; prophets' visions
    see also: electrifying; innovative; brilliant; eager
    opposite: bored; dull; apathetic; normal

Instantaneous: as the shock of recognition; as turning on a light; as a bolt of lightning; as the blink of an eye
    symbols: split second; spur of the moment; Johnny on the spot
    see also: immediate; automatic
    opposite: slow; delayed

Instinctive: as ducking for cover; as a tigress protecting her cubs; as the act of breathing; as a cat chasing a mouse
    symbols: nature of the beast; Pavlovian; in the blood; in the genes
    see also: natural; automatic; predictable; intuitive
    opposite: uncertain; contrived

Instructive: as learning from a master; as the school of hard knocks; as seeing is believing
>   symbols: Nestor; Mentor
>   see also: explicit; plain; clear
>   opposite: dumb; obscure

Insulting: as a slap on the face; as an audience that talks through a performance; as a snooty sales clerk; as a snub at a soirée
>   symbols: billingsgate; sons of Belial
>   see also: rude; tactless; impudent
>   opposite: complimentary; polite; diplomatic

Intangible: as human ethics; as memories in the mists of time; as the holes in Swiss cheese
>   symbols: a creature of the mind
>   see also: vague; uncertain
>   opposite: definite; clear

Intimate: as a secret tryst; as bed mates in a boudoir; as an underwear ad
>   symbols: bedroom diplomacy; Venus Genetrix; *tête-à-tête*
>   see also: personal; familiar; close; near; secret
>   opposite: public; distant; far; impersonal

Intolerant: as Carry Nation contemplating a saloon; as a Puritan who sees a sinner; as young success is of old failure; as the sinner is of the saint
>   symbols: the Spanish Inquisition; iron hand
>   see also: bigoted; dogmatic; narrow; prejudiced; closed; parochial
>   opposite: tolerant; liberal; understanding

Intoxicating: as 100 proof whiskey in a ten-ounce glass; as sheer beauty beckoning; as the sense of power
>   symbols: John Barleycorn; Bacchanalian
>   see also: drink; dizzy; euphoric; overwhelming; strong
>   opposite: sober; calm; placid; gloomy

Intricate: as a family tree; as a diplomat's vocabulary; as an income-tax form
>   symbols: Daedalian; Gordian knot; jigsaw puzzle
>   see also: complex; complicated; difficult; baffling
>   opposite: simple; clear; elementary; basic

Intrusive: as the neighbor's gossip; as an unexpected commercial; as a foot in the door; as a peeping Tom
>   symbols: the uninvited guest; buttinsky
>   see also: meddlesome; insistent; ill-mannered; personal
>   opposite: aloof; apathetic

Intuitive: as a woman's hunches; as a good poker player; as a mother's love
>   symbols: feel it in your bones; a little bird's whisper
>   see also: instinctive; automatic
>   opposite: uncertain; bewildered

Inventive: as a gifted liar; as the man who made the wheel; as the design of the universe
>   symbols: Thomas A. Edison; Daedalian
>   see also: imaginative; fertile; creative
>   opposite: dull boring; futile

Inviting: as a lifetime supply of ice cream; as the applause of your peers; as the promise of power; as the come-hither glance of a sexy companion
>   symbols: Siren song; golden apples
>   see also: attractive; provocative; promising; fascinating; appealing
>   opposite: disagreeable; gross; hellish; horrible; insulting; ugly

Involved: as the meatballs are with the pasta; as the electric circuits in a pinball machine; as a network of Swiss bank accounts
>   symbols: partners in crime; Caedalian; Gordian knot
>   see also: committed; dedicated; complex; complicated; intricate; baffling
>   opposite: clear; simple; aloof; cool; casual; left out; indifferent

Irrational: as an hysteric at the height of a fit; as the blindness of hate incarnate; as fear of the unknown
>   symbols: Mad Hatter; Alice in Wonderland; Wittgenstein
>   see also: illogical; angry; mad
>   opposite: normal; reasonable

Irregular: as French verbs; as a shirt with three sleeves; as a rigged election; as a dyspeptic's digestion
>   symbols: cutting corners; throwing out the rule book
>   see also: erratic; wrong; uncertain; changeable
>   opposite: normal; regular; average; constant

Irrelevant: as matzoth balls to clam chowder; as a lawnmower on astro-turf; as water wings in the desert

    symbols: a different kettle of fish; a horse of a different color

    see also: alien; foreign; needless

    opposite: appropriate; essential; necessary

Isolated: as a good example in a bad situation; as a poached egg on toast; as a lonely crouton in a sea of soup

    symbols: Stylites (pillar saints); Robinson Crusoe; sent to a convent

    see also: alone; exclusive; inaccessible; forsaken; left out

    opposite: near; close; crowded; jammed; involved

J

Jaded: as a polygamist on his 25th honeymoon; as the oldest elephant in the circus; as a sinner in Sodom

    symbols: Dorian Gray; the disenchanted; battle fatigue

    see also: bored; weary; apathetic; indifferent; dull; casual

    opposite: eager; zealous; anxious

Jammed: as a commuter bus during rush hour; as the road to the beach on a sunny Sunday in July; as a two-passenger car with a ten-passenger load

    symbols: S.R.O. (standing room only); the Black Hole of Calcutta

    see also: crowded; congested; packed; thick

    opposite: isolated; alone; abandoned; empty

Jarring: as the stop when someone pulls the emergency cord; as a siren in the still of the night; as a no vote in a chorus of ayes; upset the apple-cart

    symbols: apple of discord; upset apple-cart

    see also: harsh; rude; loud; noisy

    opposite: quiet; calm; peaceful; polite

Jealous: as a discarded lover; as a petty officer guarding his privileges; as a suspicious spouse; as sibling rivalry

    symbols: the green-eyed monster; keeping up with the Joneses

    see also: envious; greedy

    opposite: indifferent; generous; charitable; kind

Jewish: as Abraham, Isaac, and Sholen Aleichem; as chicken soup with matzoh balls; as the three B's—bagels, blintzes, and borscht; as Tel Aviv; as John the Baptist
- symbols: the chosen people; the people of the Book
- see also: timeless; legendary
- opposite: transient

Juicy: as a ripe orange; as grapes ready for the pressing; as a chaw of chewing tobacco; as scandalous scuttlebutt
- symbols: Rabelasian; mouth-watering
- see also: fruitful; fascinating
- opposite: fruitless; dry; dull

K

Keen: as a brand new razor blade; as a carving knife; as the pain of a stab in the back
- symbols: Damascus steel; Toledo blade
- see also: cutting; sharp; brilliant; biting
- opposite: dull; slow

Kind: as kings upon their coronation day (John Dryden); as an act of love; as a helping hand in an hour of need; as a friendly kiss
- symbols: Good Samaritan; chivalrous knight; guardian angel; Lady Bountiful; fairy godmother
- see also: generous; charitable; considerate; genial
- opposite: cruel; brutal; harsh; savage; threatening

Knotty: as a pockmarked pine; as tangled twine; as a fouled fishing line
- symbols: Gordian knot; Chinese puzzle; between Scylla and Charybdis
- see also: complex; difficult; complicated; mixed up
- opposite: simple; clear; easy

Knowledgeable: as a scholar from the ivory tower; as the man who wrote the book; as a sage on the mountain top
- symbols: Einstein; walking encyclopedia
- see also: learned; cultured; educated; wise
- opposite: ignorant; immature; dopey; dumb

L

Laborious: as cleaning the Augean stables; as teaching a new dog old tricks; as a hike up Mount Everest; as running a transcontinental marathon
    symbols: Sisyphus; Hercules; the curse of Adam
    see also: hard; difficult; tough
    opposite: easy; simple; clear

Large: as life and twice as natural (Lewis Carroll); as the tail that wags the dog; as an elephant seems to a gnat; as the span of the universe
    symbols: Gargantua; Colossus of Rhodes
    see also: colossal; big; huge; vast; broad
    opposite: small; minimal; little

Lasting: as a wine stain on a Persian carpet; as a happy memory; as a diamond
    symbols: Rock of Ages; laws of the Medes and the Persians; Rock of Gibraltar
    see also: enduring; chronic; endless; perpetual; permanent
    opposite: fleeting; temporary; limited; momentary

Late: as lunch at midnight; as a Christmas card on the Fourth of July; as the horse that finished last; as the dear departed
    symbols: last minute; tail-ender; eleventh hour
    see also: delayed; slow; dead
    opposite: early; new; immediate; punctual

Lavish: as a Roman orgy; as the treasure of the Czars; as the flattery of a man with an axe to grind; as a Hollywood premiere party; as a Ziegfeld production number
    symbols: Lucullus; groaning board
    see also: extravagant; grand; exaggerated; generous
    opposite: stingy; frugal; economical; close; cheap; modest; simple

Lawless: as Jesse James and his gang; as the robber barons; as anarchy on the loose; as the top ten public enemies; as mob rule
    symbols: Judge Lynch; street justice; reign of terror
    see also: corrupt; crooked; wicked; evil; dishonest; immoral
    opposite: legal; innocent; trustworthy; good; correct

Lazy: as Ludlam's dog that leaned his head against a wall to bark (John Ray); as a languid river in the noonday sun; as a hound dog dozing in the heat; as lolling in a hammock; as a cat that's had a bowl of cream
  symbols: Castle of Indolence; lotus-eaters
  see also: idle; relaxed; limp; inert
  opposite: energetic; active; busy; athletic; feverish

Leakproof: as an empty glass; as a plumber's prize pipejoint; as a space capsule
  symbols: Fort Knox; hermetically sealed
  see also: solid; tight; strong
  opposite: loose; leaky

Leaky: as a broken faucet; as a rickety roof in a rainstorm; as a tent with mothholes; as an old tub
  symbols: sieve; blabbermouth
  see also: porous; loose
  opposite: leakproof; tight

Learned: as a doctoral student with a photographic memory; as a wise man in his library; as the proverbial bookworm
  symbols: Socrates; Aristotle; Maimonides
  see also: educated; cultured; knowledgeable; wise
  opposite: ignorant; immature; blank

Left-handed: as a party invitation from a hermit; as damning with faint praise; as British traffic; as a Tokyo freeway
  symbols: portsider; Wrong Way Corrigan
  see also: backhanded; awkward; tactless; heavy-handed
  opposite: artful; gracious; diplomatic

Leftist: as Marx's manifesto; as the sayings of Chairman Mao; as the radicals who believe they're right
  symbols: Marxist; Maoist; Castro
  see also: radical; revolutionary; liberal; heretical; rebellious
  opposite: conformist; reactionary; prudent

Left out: as a dog sent to the doghouse; as a wallflower at a junior prom; as the player neither team wants
  symbols: beyond the pale; sent to Coventry
  see also: forsaken; abandoned; overlooked; isolated; deserted; neglected
  opposite: sought after; involved; popular

Legal: as the Bill of Rights; as a Supreme Court decision; as a document signed before a notary
> symbols: Astraea; Themis; the Bar
> see also: correct; authoritative
> opposite: lawless; corrupt

Legendary: as the knights of the Round Table; as the prowess of Paul Bunyan and his blue ox Babe; as the as the Loch Ness monster; as the abominable snowman; as Bigfoot; as Johnny Appleseed's orchards
> symbols: chimera; household names; folk heroes
> see also: imaginary; uncertain; doubtful; questionable; popular
> opposite: true; accurate; real; boring

Lethal: as a slice of cyanide pie; as a leap off the Golden Gate Bridge; as lead-laced liquor; as the bubonic plague
> symbols: Thanatos; Aceldama; Grim Reaper
> see also: deadly; fatal; destructive
> opposite: harmless; safe; encouraging

Liberal: as a cheerful giver; as a politician with public money; as an indulgent parent; as the New Deal; as a candidate campaigning on the "green" ticket
> symbols: Good Samaritan; left of center; "bleeding heart."
> see also: generous; leftist
> opposite: stingy; tight; reactionary; conformist

Light: as a lamp in a mineshaft; as a load of helium; as a happy heart; as a worry-free spirit; as an illuminated chandelier
> symbols: Apollo; Mithra
> see also: airy; carefree; brilliant; delicate; gaseous; dainty
> opposite: heavy; dark; burdensome

Limited: as liberty in a dictatorship; as a pinch-penny's pocket money; as a pauper's budget; as an illiterate's vocabulary
> symbols: closed company; short tether
> see also: confined; close; inadequate; selective; stingy; endangered
> opposite: free; generous; infinite; overwhelming

Limp: as a wet towel; as a string of licorice; as a serving of well-done spaghetti; as a milksop's handshake
> symbols: dish rag; marshmallow; Caspar Milquetoast
> see also: inert; relaxed
> opposite: rigid; active; busy; agitated; energetic; steadfast

Lingering: as a four-week head cold; as a long liquid lunch; as the scent of perfume in a boudoir; as a favorite memory
>   symbols: slow death; staying power
>   see also: endless; continuous; constant; perpetual; ceaseless
>   opposite: fleeting; momentary; final

Little: as a raindrop of water in the deep blue sea; as a midget in Lilliput; as a grain of sand
>   symbols: Tom Thumb; Munchkin; pocket edition; Lilliputian
>   see also: minimal; meager; small; abbreviated
>   opposite: big; large; huge; colossal; vast

Lonely: as sitting at the top of life's ladder; as solitary senility; as the road to nowhere; as the craters of the moon
>   symbols: pillar saint; Timon of Athens; Diogenes in his tub; Coventry
>   see also: isolated; alone; forsaken; lonesome; abandoned; left out
>   opposite: crowded; involved

Lonesome: as an abandoned house; as the last of the Mohicans; as a wallflower; as a sailor on an endless sea
>   symbols: The Man Without a Country; Robinson Crusoe; Ishmael; Ishi
>   see also: alone; lonely; forsaken; abandoned; left out
>   opposite: sought after; involved

Long: as the Lincoln Highway; as the Trans-Canada Highway; as a speech by Fidel Castro; as the limits of outer space; as life has lived on earth
>   symbols: from here to eternity; slow boat to China; beat around the bush; Silk Road
>   see also: endless; infinite; slow; broad; extended
>   opposite: short; abbreviated; brief; quick; fast

Loose: as a fallen woman; as the wind (George Herbert); as goose grease; as a liar is with the truth; as the tongue of the town gossip; as a lush's lips
>   symbols: rope of sand; long leash; on the town
>   see also: relaxed; immoral; slippery; dishonest; Iying; false
>   opposite: tight; rigid; confined; honest; accurate

Loud: as the howl of a hurricane; as the beat of a kettle drum; as a clap of thunder; as the caw of the crow in a cornfield
>   symbols: fireworks; cymbal crash; car horn
>   see also: noisy; harsh; boisterous
>   opposite: soft; quiet

Lovable: the lily maid of Astelot (Alfred Tennyson); as a little puppy; as a cuddle bunny; as a soft sleepy kitten
>   symbols: Eros; Cupid; Aphrodite
>   see also: beloved; friendly; winning; charming; cherished; enchanting
>   opposite: hateful; nasty; disagreeable; objectionable; rotten; awful

Lovely: as the light of day; as the gift of laughter; as a rose in full bloom; as corn-flowers in a summer meadow; as a debutante at her first ball
>   symbols: The Graces; Helen of Troy; Hebe; Venus
>   see also: beautiful; appealing; charming; enchanting; lovable
>   opposite: frightful; ugly; awful; disagreeable; rotten

Low: as a gnat's knee; as a coward hangs his head; as a basso's bottom note; as the bottom of the barrel
>   symbols: below sea level; bottomed out; down in the dumps
>   see also: deep; bottomless; downhearted; mean; nasty
>   opposite: high; elevated; cheerful

Loyal: as a faithful dog; as mother love; as an old friend; as a loving spouse; as a Boy Scout
>   symbols: fidus Achates; The Three Musketeers; Bushido
>   see also: constant; faithful; true; steadfast; trustworthy; changeless
>   opposite: false; uncertain; treacherous; tricky; changeable

Lucky: as stumbling on a pot of gold at the end of a rainbow; as the man who broke the bank of Monte Carlo; as the man who owns a golden goose
>   symbols: Fortuna; Midas touch; Tyche
>   see also: fortunate; blessed; happy
>   opposite: unlucky; damned

Lying: as a false witness; as a teller of tall tales; as an affidavit by Judas Iscariot
>   symbols: Ananias; Baron von Munchausen
>   see also: dishonest; false; tricky
>   opposite: honest; frank; true; trustworthy

M

Mad: as a March hare (John Heywood); as a rabid dog; as a fool in a full moon
>   symbols: Bedlam; Mad Hatter; the inmates of Charandon
>   see also: crazy; angry; irrational; agitated; feverish; ill-tempered
>   opposite: calm; reasonable; peaceful; relaxed; placid

Magnificent: as the Taj Mahal; as the heavens in their glory; as Wyoming's Grand Teton Mountains

      symbols: Seven Wonders of the World; the Forbidden City

      see also: glorious; beautiful; impressive; majestic

      opposite: ugly; dreadful; frightful; awful; horrible

Magnified: as a molecule viewed through a microscope; as a coward's fears; as a molehill masquerading as a mountain; as a ham actor's ego; as a criminal under investigation; as the farthest star seen at the Palomar Observatory

      symbols: Baron von Munchausen; microscope; camera obscure

      see also: exaggerated; overwhelming; extravagant

      opposite: small; little; minimal; modest

Majestic: as a royal coronation; as the Andes mountain range; as St. Peter's Basilica; as the giant redwoods

      symbols: Olympus; Triton among the minnows; the Himalayas

      see also: magnificent; glorious; impressive; monumental

      opposite: modest; minimal; small

Matchless: as a smoker without a light; as a man without a mate; as the morning sun

      symbols: Kohinoor; the greatest; one in a million

      see also: alone; different

      opposite: alike; conformist

Mature: as Methuselah approaching his millennium; as ripe cheese; as a giant redwood; as vintage wine

      symbols: aged in the wood; prime of life; a good single-malt Scotch

      see also: ripe; experienced; aged

      opposite: naive; raw; immature; childish; young; youthful

Meager: as a know-nothing's knowledge; as a pauper's purse; as a cup of gruel

      symbols: Spartan; Spartan fare; bread and water; slim pickings

      see also: poor; little; minimal; scanty; scarce

      opposite: affluent; rich; wealthy

Mean: as a misanthrope with a migraine; as a bad-tempered bully on a binge; as a man who kicks puppies

      symbols: Scrooge; dog in the manger; injured bear

      see also: cruel; demonic; detestable; objectionable; awful; hellish

      opposite: agreeable; pleasant; charming; angelic; generous; kind

Meddlesome: as too many cooks in the kitchen; as a prying neighbor; as a squirrel eating the birdseed; as a grandstand quarterback
>   symbols: Nosy Parker; buttinsky; Polly Pry
>   see also: intrusive; curious; inquisitive
>   opposite: aloof; indifferent; apathetic; cold

Meek: as a modest mouse; as a little lamb; as a milksop
>   symbols: Caspar Milquetoast; timid soul; Job; a pussycat
>   see also: docile; gentle; quiet; humble; tame; repressed
>   opposite: assertive; aggressive; argumentative; pugnacious; menacing; loud

Memorable: as Moses on the mountain top; as Mohammed on the mount; as man's first steps on the moon
>   symbols: Mnemosyne; big moment; one for the books
>   see also: famous; indelible; enduring; monumental
>   opposite: forgotten; colorless; dull; fuzzy

Menacing: as a thirsty vampire looking for a nightcap; as a Godzilla taking a stroll; as a phantom black dog roaming the moors; as an unknown ailment; as a blackmail letter
>   symbols: sword of Damocles; brinkmanship; Harpies
>   see also: threatening; ominous; dangerous; pugnacious
>   opposite: meek; docile; safe; harmless; trustworthy; kind; gentle

Messy: as a madman's memory; as the town dump; as a beach after a beer bust; as an unmade bed
>   symbols: mare's nest; Bedlam; Babel; Augean stable
>   see also: dirty; disorganized; confused; unclean; muddled; mixed up
>   opposite: clean; neat; planned; efficient

Mighty: as a tidal wave; as the truth on the march; as an erupting volcano
>   symbols: Titan; Hercules; Gargantua; Samson
>   see also: strong; powerful; overwhelming; monumental; colossal
>   opposite: weak; feeble; meager; humble; small; little; underdeveloped

Militant: as an activist with an itch; as a riot looking for a place to happen; as a hungry lioness protecting her cubs; as a mob on the march
>   symbols: Bellona; Mars; Samurai; soldier of fortune
>   see also: aggressive; pugnacious; positive
>   opposite: quiet; peaceful; meek; docile; quiet

Minimal: as a nudist's negligee; as a hermit's hospitality; as a miser's charity; as a zen master's furnishings; as a monastery on a mountain top
- symbols: Lilliputian; drop in the bucket; sub-compact
- see also: small; little
- opposite: big; huge; large

Miraculous: as the spark of life; as blood from a stone; as a walk on the water; as a freshwater spring in the desert
- symbols: act of God; heaven-sent; parting of the waters
- see also: baffling; amazing
- opposite: logical; understandable

Misplaced: as a bull in a china shop; as cash with a con-man; as a saddle on a sea lion; as a saloon in a seminary; as a penguin in white tie and tails
- symbols: fish out of water; square peg in a round hole
- see also: irrelevant; confused; mixed up; wrong; mistaken
- opposite: representative; right

Mistaken: as a miser hoarding three-dollar bills; as a mouse at a cats' convention; as applause at a funeral; as seeds in concrete
- symbols: a Brodie; a blooper
- see also: erroneous; wrong
- opposite: right; correct

Misunderstood: as English in Omsk; as another man's pride; as a wink at the wrong person; as Chile's Nasca lines
- symbols: false impression; wrong end of the stick
- see also: muddled; mixed up; confused; puzzled; uncertain
- opposite: clear; understandable; certain

Mixed: as a malted milkshake; as flea-market fare; as cement waiting to be poured; as boardinghouse hash
- symbols: Tower of Babel; Noah's Ark; crazy quilt
- see also: varied; assorted; blended; hybrid
- opposite: alone; divided; lonely; lonesome

Mixed up: as a scrambled egg; as alphabet soup; as the contents of a cocktail shaker; as a homing pigeon without a home
- symbols: Tower of Babel; Bedlam
- see also: confused; bewildered; puzzled; mistaken
- opposite: clear; right; accurate

Modern: as the day after tomorrow; as an Internet love affair; as a bi-coastal courtship
   symbols: the now generation; the new improved model; the rage
   see also: new
   opposite: old; ancient

Modest: as a maiden's blush; as a poor man's lot luck
   symbols: shrinking violet; Encratite; vestal virgin; Artemis
   see also: humble; frugal; chaste; meek; docile; economical
   opposite: immodest; egotistical; loose; lavish; haughty; affected

Momentary: as the beginning of a blink; as a passing twinge; as a single click of the time clock
   symbols: nine days wonder; flash in the pan
   see also: fleeting; transient; temporary
   opposite: lasting; constant; permanent; enduring; continuous

Monotonous: as breathing; as turnpike driving in heavy traffic; as a thrice-told tale
   symbols: same old story; broken record
   see also: boring; dull; repetitious
   opposite: exciting; fascinating; gripping

Monumental: as Machu Picchu; as a monolith in a sand desert; as Mount McKinley
   symbols: Colossus of Rhodes; Titan; Herculean
   see also: majestic; impressive; memorable; mighty; colossal; overwhelming
   opposite: modest; dull; little; small; forgotten

Moody: as a brooding beatnik; as a paranoid's psyche; as the mists of time; as fickle fortune
   symbols: Hamlet; the cave of Trophonius
   see also: volatile; changeable; gloomy; nervous; neurotic
   opposite: cheerful; steadfast; changeless; happy; constant

Moving: as a mother's love; as the miracle on the mount; as a love letter from a lost love; as the call of the wild
   symbols: Siren song; tear-jerker; hearts and flowers
   see also: warm; appealing
   opposite: cold; cool; ineffective

Muddled: as a message written in molasses; as an indecisive maid deciding between two lovers
   symbols: mare's nest; Gongorism
   see also: mixed up; confused; puzzled; messy; unclean
   opposite: clear; clean; neat; logical

N

Naive: as an innocent falling for a trickster; as students at their first part-time job; as a farmer's daughter moving to the metropolis; as the expectations of first love
  symbols: Arcadian; Simple Simon; wet behind the ears
  see also: idealistic; simple
  opposite: mature; experienced

Naked: as a newborn babe; as a jaybird bathing; as a bald man's scalp; as the unvarnished truth
  symbols: flasher; topless; bottomless; the altogether
  see also: bare; bold; obvious
  opposite: concealed; camouflaged; hidden

Narrow: as a bigot's mind; as a straight arrow's path; as a bureaucrat's vision; as a patrician's condescending nose
  symbols: Mrs. Grundy; bluenose; know-nothing
  see also: bigoted; prejudiced; intolerant
  opposite: tolerant; broad; liberal; open

Nasty: as a nagging spouse; as a nervous hyena; as a batch of paper cuts; as a deliberate doublecross
  symbols: The Furies; goon squad; Xanthippe; snake in the grass
  see also: hateful; detestable; disagreeable; cruel; mean; harsh
  opposite: friendly; agreeable; pleasant; warm; kind

Natural: as Mother Nature herself; as the sunshine and the rain; as the changing seasons; as a mountain stream
  symbols: the real McCoy; primeval forest; the art of God
  see also: true; real; instinctive; spontaneous; innocent
  opposite: false; affected; insincere; fraudulent

Near: as your next-door neighbor; as the end of your nose; as a close shave; as a voice in your ear
  symbols: around the corner; close quarters; hair's breadth
  see also: close; convenient
  opposite: far; distant

Neat: as the proverbial pin; as a straight shot of whiskey; as a Houdini illusion
  symbols: apple-pie order; ship-shape
  see also: clean; precise; spotless; immaculate
  opposite: disorganized; messy; tangled; confused; unclean

Necessary: as eggs in an omelet; as print in a newspaper; as oxygen in the air we breathe
>   symbols: a must; an absolute; will of the gods
>   see also: essential; basic; useful
>   opposite: needless; unnecessary; useless

Needless: as pits in cream cheese; as bones in ice cream; as extra warts; as a hole in the head; as selling ice in the Arctic
>   symbols: coals to Newcastle; gilding the lily; ice cream in Iceland
>   see also: unnecessary; useless
>   opposite: necessary; useful; essential; basic

Needy: as an orphan of the storm; as a waif on welfare; as a deserted family
>   symbols: Poverty Row; over the hill to the poorhouse; wolf at the door
>   see also: poor; deprived
>   opposite: rich; affluent; wealthy; privileged

Negative: as a door slammed in your face; as a Presidential veto; as a rejection slip
>   symbols: downbeat; nihilism; blackball
>   see also: pessimistic; downhearted; uncertain; dubious
>   opposite: positive; affirmative; optimistic; sure; certain

Neglected: as a ghost town gone to seed; as an unwanted child; as a loafer's chores
>   symbols: on the shelf; limbo; out to pasture
>   see also: abandoned; deserted; forgotten; forsaken; overlooked; run-down
>   opposite: cherished; appreciated; welcome; beloved

Negligent: as a drunken driver; as a sleeping watchman; as a teacher playing hookey
>   symbols: Sad Sack; goof-off; grasshopper (compared to the ant)
>   see also: careless; indifferent; improper; lazy
>   opposite: attentive, conscientious; devoted; careful; considerate

Neighborly: as a nearby friend; as a helping hand; as a shared lawnmower
>   symbols: block party; fence; friendship
>   see also: helpful; friendly; pleasant; approachable; amiable; hospitable
>   opposite: aloof; haughty; nasty; antagonistic; indifferent; cold

Nervous: as a cat on a hot tin roof; as a newlywed; as a crapshooter waiting for the roll of the dice; as a caged lion
>   symbols: sword of Damocles; razor's edge; anxious seat
>   see also: edgy; agitated; restless; neurotic; worried; tense; anxious
>   opposite: calm; relaxed; placid

Neurotic: as a psychiatrist's most constant client; as a cat with a complex; as a kid whose id has slid; as a lost libido
    symbols: Freudian; walking wounded; Momus
    see also: nervous; worried; tense; anxious
    opposite: calm; relaxed; healthy; placid

Neutral: as the friend of both sides; as the one who vows to remain uninvolved
    symbols: golden mean; straight down the middle; picket-fence sitting
    see also: impartial; detached; independent; indifferent
    opposite: involved; active; partisan

New: as crisp money fresh from the mint; as today at sunrise; as young wine
    symbols: Genesis; world premiere; hot off the press
    see also: modern; fresh; immediate; young
    opposite: old; obsolete; dated; ancient; aged

Nice: as new clothes; as the guys who finish last (derived from Leo Durocher); as sugar and spice
    symbols: peaches and cream
    see also: appealing; attractive; charming; becoming; friendly; pleasant
    opposite: mean; detestable; nasty; disagreeable

Nimble: as a veteran tap dancer; as a man who lives by his wits; as a macaque swinging from limb to limb; as Jack jumping over the candlestick
    symbols: Hermes; Mercury; twinkle-toes
    see also: agile; fast; active; quick
    opposite: awkward; slow; inept

Noble: as a good cause; as the king's favorite baron; as a wild turkey (Benjamin Franklin)
    symbols: Sir Lancelot; Richard the Lionhearted
    see also: elevated; exalted; high; pure; sacrificial; good; kind; generous
    opposite: nasty; mean; low; selfish; cruel

Noisy: as tea-time at the Tower of Babel; as the sound of angry surf; as baying hounds at midnight; as the cocks crowing at dawn
    symbols: the cave of the winds; an earthquake's roar
    see also: loud; boisterous; jarring
    opposite: soft; calm; quiet

Normal: as 98.6 degrees; as red tape in a bureaucracy; as April showers and May flowers

    symbols: S.O.P. (standard operating procedure); paradigm

    see also: average; familiar; common; representative

    opposite: rare; special; different; high; low

Nostalgic: as a class reunion; as nursery rhyme songs; as the old family album

    symbols: memory book; the good old days; diary

    see also: old-fashioned; sentimental; memorable

    opposite: forgotten; indifferent; cold

Noticeable: as a wart on the end of your nose; as a banner headline; as a star in a spotlight; as a badly fitting toupee

    symbols: exhibit A; front and center

    see also: obvious; glaring; eminent

    opposite: obscure; overlooked; hidden

Notorious: as the nightlife of the gods; as the sins of Sodom and the grossness of Gomorrah; as the habits of a happy hooker

    symbols: talk of the town; hot copy; tabloid feature

    see also: celebrated; famous; scandalous

    opposite: hidden; secret

Nourishing: as three square meals a day; as food for thought; as inspiration for the soul

    symbols: Hygeia; Ceres; Demeter

    see also: healthy; hearty

    opposite: poor; poisonous; rotten

Numerous: as a plague of locusts; as the children of God; as the grains of sand; as the sins of the Devil

    symbols: Briareus; legion

    see also: abundant; fruitful

    opposite: scarce; sparse; scanty

Nutty: as a pecan pie; as a pack of pistachios; as a nougat; as a field of filberts; as moon-bathing during a full moon

    symbols: loony; fruitcake; a midnight golf game

    see also: crazy; mixed up; cracked; mad; irrational

    opposite: reasonable; responsible; normal

O

Obedient: as a trained seal; as a yes-man in a no-win situation; as a faithful hound; as a dutiful child; as a good soldier
   symbols: Myrmidon; Pavlov's dog
   see also: dutiful; faithful; trustworthy; available; agreeable
   opposite: antagonistic; negligent; uncertain; rebellious

Objectionable: as stealing from the poor box; as swearing in a nursery; as cursing in a confessional; as setting fire to your neighbor's house
   symbols: gall and wormwood; public nuisance
   see also: disagreeable; nasty; criminal; evil; hateful; wicked; mean
   opposite: attractive; appealing; lovable; good; beautiful

Oblivious: as a blind man in a blaze of color; as a drunk on a bender; as a sleeping baby in the midst of bedlam
   symbols: Lethe; limbo
   see also: forgetful; apathetic; blind; ignorant; deaf; forgetful
   opposite: attentive; anxious; concerned; worried; careful; tense

Obscure: as the language of diplomacy; as a black crow in a dark field on a moonless midnight; as the mood of the Mona Lisa; as the paths of destiny that lie ahead
   symbols: Cimmerian darkness; Erebus; Gongorism
   see also: concealed; enigmatic; uncertain; dark; secret; hidden
   opposite: obvious; clear; open; certain; understandable

Obsolete: as horse-drawn carriage on an interstate turnpike; as last year's tax form; as the Spanish Inquisition
   symbols: dodo; dinosaur; Colonel Blimp
   see also: ancient; old fashioned; dated
   opposite: new; modern; fresh

Obvious: as a nudist in a store window; as a diamond tiara; as a wolf whistle; as a Rolls Royce in a ghetto
   symbols: landmark; written on one's face
   see also: noticeable; clear; apparent; open
   opposite: obscure; hidden; concealed; camouflaged; overlooked

Odorous: as standing downwind from a slaughterhouse; as sitting in a freshly fertilized field; as a field of flowers in full bloom; as limburger cheese

symbols: the nose knows

see also: smelly; fragrant; aromatic

opposite: blank; faded

Offensive: as an ugly drunk; as an open insult; as a slap in the face

symbols: Belial; gall and wormwood; public nuisance

see also: annoying; insulting; ill-mannered; antagonistic; rude; menacing; threatening

opposite: polite; complimentary; friendly; amiable

Officious: as an uncivil servant; as government prose; as a head waiter with the help; as a bureaucrat hiding his demotion

symbols: Mr. Bumble; bureaucrat; fussbudget; apparatchik

see also: haughty; arrogant; rude; pompous; condescending

opposite: courteous; correct; polite; amiable

Old: as the hills and the heavens; as an over-age century plant; as a sequoia tree in a redwood forest

symbols: Methuselah; Nestor; Father Abraham

see also: aged; ancient; dated; obsolete

opposite: new; modern; young; youthful; fresh

Old fashioned: as hoop skirts and buggy whips; as penny candy; as a nickel cup of coffee

symbols: Mid-Victorian; Model T; stone age; square

see also: ancient; dated; nostalgic; corny; quaint; square

opposite: new; modern; fresh; original

Ominous: as a dark cloud descending; as a burst of gunfire; as a message from the Mafia

symbols: handwriting on the wall; storm cloud; Cassandra

see also: threatening; menacing; dangerous; pessimistic

opposite: favorable; encouraging; cheerful; hopeful; optimistic; safe

Open: as a chatterbox's mouth; as a road with nobody on it; as the trackless seas; as a wastrel's wallet; as the wide spaces of the west

symbols: broad daylight; cards on the table; above board

see also: clear; obvious; talkative; generous

opposite: closed; grudging; concealed; hidden; tight

Opinionated: as a pompous pundit with a permanent pulpit; as a Sunday soapbox speaker; as a market analyst at the end of a fiscal year
>   symbols: Sir Oracle; know-it-all; educated guesser
>   see also: dogmatic; positive; arbitrary; stubborn; partisan; uncompromising
>   opposite: flexible; pliable; changeable; neutral; impartial

Optimistic: as describing a half-empty bottle as half full; as asking a miser for a hand-out; as an unrepentant sinner's plan to get to heaven
>   symbols: Dr. Pangloss; Pollyanna
>   see also: hopeful; cheerful
>   opposite: pessimistic; gloomy; hopeless

Original: as the first sunrise; as Adam and Eve; as spontaneous free verse
>   symbols: new departure; prototype; Genesis
>   see also: creative; inspired; innovative; inventive
>   opposite: imitative; repetitious

Overlooked: as a lost plateau; as a forgotten mistake; as a favorite child's failings; as what we do not wish to see
>   symbols: a sleeper; pigeon-hole; dust-gatherer
>   see also: forgotten; neglected; forsaken; left out
>   opposite: sought after; glaring; obvious; noticeable; clean

Overwhelmed: as a mouse facing a mastodon; as light is by darkness and later the darkness by the light; as a calm sea by a tidal wave; as man in the face of nature's wrath
>   symbols: Waterloo; bite the dust; Custer's last stand; charge of the Light Brigade
>   see also: finished; repressed
>   opposite: overwhelming; strong

Overwhelming: as the odds for a 1000-to-1 shot; as the temptations of envy and the taste of greed; as the unbridled excesses of ambition; as a take-charge hostess
>   symbols: Superman; long shot; desert sandstorm; tornado
>   see also: extravagant; mighty; monumental; exaggerated; magnified; strong
>   opposite: underdeveloped; weak; feeble; indifferent; little; small

Overworked: as the doorbell on Halloween night; as a glutton's epiglottis; as an accountant on April 15th; as a chef at a kids' summer camp
>   symbols: nose to the grindstone; galley slave
>   see also: exhausted; weary; tired; busy
>   opposite: idle; lazy; relaxed

P

Packed: as the Tokyo subway at rush hour; as a souvenir hunter's suitcase; as a crooked election
symbols: S.R.O. (standing room only); can of sardines; Black Hole of Calcutta
see also: crowded; congested; jammed; dishonest; crooked; tight; close
opposite: empty; lonely; lonesome; honest; loose; isolated

Padded: as a psycho's cell; as a false expense account; as a politician's pork barrel; as a mechanic's estimate
symbols: Parkinson's law; falsies
see also: fat; ample; false; contrived; lying; untruthful
opposite: flat; thin; skinny; slim; true; honest

Painful: as paying the piper; as the pangs of conscience; as a soul in torment; as a rude surprise
symbols: the rack; Job's comforter; trial by ordeal
see also: afflicted; anguished; inflamed; raw; uncomfortable; cruel; sore
opposite: soothing; comforting; easy; comfortable

Pale: as a ghost with pernicious anemia; as the fading light of winter sunset; as an inmate in solitary confinement
symbols: Death warmed over; the color of chalk
see also: ghastly; colorless; anemic
opposite: colorful; bright; healthy; dark

Panic-stricken: as a stampeding herd; as a crowd of cowards contemplating a catastrophe; as speculators in a sinking market; as a village in the path of a new volcano
symbols: Deimos; Phobos; gutless wonder; bowl of Jello; trembling aspen
see also: frantic; seared; chaotic
opposite: calm; relaxed

Paradoxical: as feasting during famine; as waging war to produce peace; as the thin line between love and hate; as the wonders and the wastes produced by the same sun in the same sky
symbols: Pickwickian; cross purposes; reductio ad absurdum
see also: illogical; strange
opposite: reasonable; simple

Parched: as a sand dune in the desert; as a dipsomaniac in a dry county; as dirt in the dust bowl; as ancient parchment
    symbols: Sahara; Death Valley; torment to Tantalus
    see also: dry; arid
    opposite: watered; juicy

Parochial: as a parish the Pope forgot; as the local gossip; as a secret society; as a forgotten backwater
    symbols: Lares and Penates; home territory; charmed circle
    see also: narrow; secret; closed; familiar
    opposite: broad; cosmopolitan; open

Particular: as an itemized bill; as a picky eater; as a dude with his duds; as a secret snob; as a personal birthmark
    symbols: Mr. Finicky; tough shopper
    see also: special; selective; exclusive; explicit; intolerant; precise; picky
    opposite: tolerant; open; random; relaxed

Partisan: as a plea by a defense attorney; as a campaign platform; as a cheerleader; as a proud parent
    symbols: fidus Achates; man Friday; cheering section
    see also: sympathetic; political; prejudiced; opinionated; involved
    opposite: impartial; neutral; detached

Passionate: as lovers in an embrace; as the power of lust; as a convert delivering a sermon; as a Salvation Army speaker
    symbols: Aphrodite; Eros; fire in the belly; heavy breathing; Billy Sunday
    see also: inflamed; inspired; rabid; opinionated; fierce; hot
    opposite: cold; cool; icy; indifferent; relaxed

Patient: as those who suffer in silence; as a spider spinning its web; as a cat watching a canary; as the wise man who gives an opponent enough rope to hang himself
    symbols: Job; Fabian; trust in Providence
    see also: tolerant; indulgent; meek; enduring; calm
    opposite: impatient; intolerant; ill-tempered

Patronizing: as a snob in a slum; as a public servant dispensing the public's money; as a salesclerk who confers attention on customers like a Papal blessing; as youth can be to age—and age to youth
    symbols: Snob Hill; lord of the manor; cock of the walk
    see also: haughty; condescending; smug; rude
    opposite: gracious; accommodating; polite; courteous

Peaceful: as a breeze passing through a forest; as an alpine lake; as the house of the Lord; as the sleep of the just; as the lilies of the field; as the dreams of lovers; as the pleasures of home and hearth

    symbols: green pastures; Ferdinand the Bull; alone on a mountain top

    see also: calm; quiet; relaxed; easy

    opposite: aggressive; militant; agitated; chaotic

Perfect: as Paradise before Adam ate the apple; as the peace that passeth all under-standing; as a hole in one; as the place where angels dwell

    symbols: Sir Galahad; paragon; Superman; Minerva; Apollo

    see also: flawless; ideal; chaste; pure

    opposite: blemished; tarnished; faulty; impure

Permanent: as the persistence of matter; as the pyramids; as the inevitability of change; as the pursuit of power; as a grouch's grumbling

    symbols: Rock of Gibraltar; law of the Medes and the Persians; Rock of Ages

    see also: perpetual; endless; enduring; lasting; indelible; timeless; constant

    opposite: momentary; temporary; brief; replaceable

Permissive: as free enterprise in an open society; as a Roman orgy; as the parents that spare the rod and spoil the child; as an asylum run by the inmates

    symbols: laissez-faire; blank check; carte blanche

    see also: indulgent; tolerant

    opposite: intolerant; censored

Perpetual: as the revolution of the earth around the sun; as human emotion; as the pairing of the sexes; as the search for something new

    symbols: Rock of Ages; evergreen; hardy perennial

    see also: permanent; continuous; constant; endless; enduring; timeless; indelible; lasting

    opposite: fleeting; momentary; limited; changeable; replaceable; temporary

Personal: as the inner soul; as a loin cloth; as the pangs of conscience; as a love letter; as a tooth brush

    symbols: first person singular; nobody's business

    see also: intimate; secret

    opposite: public; open

Persuasive: as a super salesperson; as the lure of something for nothing; as a good example; as the power of public opinion; as the promise of power

    symbols: Demosthenes; Grey Eminence

    see also: convincing; winning; compelling; eloquent; powerful

    opposite: dull; inadequate; weak; futile

Pessimistic: as a compulsive crepehanger; as a speculator who sells short; as a candidate who asks for a recount before the vote is in; as a manufacturer of air-raid shelters

symbols: Cassandra; Calamity Jane
see also: gloomy; downhearted; hopeless
opposite: optimistic; hopeful; cheerful

Pestilential: as a plague of locusts; as jungle rot; as tsetse flies

symbols: the plagues of Egypt; the Black Plague
see also: contagious; deadly; fatal; lethal; horrible
opposite: clean; safe; healing; healthy

Picky: as a dentist checking your teeth for cavities; as a horserace bettor; as a critic with an ulcer; as a selective shopper

symbols: Mr. Finicky; bargain hunter; fruit squeezer
see also: particular; selective; precise; explicit
opposite: open; reasonable; adaptable; agreeable

Piratical: as the buccaneers who sailed the Spanish Main; as the bandits of the Barbary Coast; as those who live by the skull and crossbones

symbols: Bluebeard; Captain Kidd; the Jolly Roger; the black flag
see also: lawless; criminal; dishonest; wicked; bad; evil
opposite: honest; generous; correct; trustworthy

Pitiful: as a pauper's pittance; as a beggar's plea; as the plight of a homeless orphan; as the pride that goeth before a fall

symbols: Sad Sack; feeble imitation
see also: sad; incompetent; poor; needy; anguished; hopeless
opposite: happy; accomplished; rich; wealthy; cheerful; hopeful

Pitiless: as a hanging judge; as the law of the jungle; as persistent poverty; as the fury of a scorned woman

symbols: Attila the Hun; Eumenides (The Furies)
see also: cruel; savage; barbarous; callous; indifferent; harsh; hard
opposite: kind; considerate; gentle; charitable; soft

Placid: as the aftermath of rapture; as a miser sitting on a mound of money; as a forest covered in newly fallen snow; as a town that time forgot; as an alpine lake

symbols: Arcadia; Utopia; sea of tranquility
see also: calm; relaxed; quiet; cool
opposite: agitated; feverish; restless; chaotic; frantic; anxious; busy

Plain: as the nose that lies naked upon your face; as a hermit's search for solitude; as the simple pleasures of a little child; as the blunt speech of an honest soul

    symbols: Plain Jane; open book; point-blank; written on one's face

    see also: simple; average; bald; open; commonplace; average

    opposite: involved; affected; complicated; complex; special; rare

Planned: as an architect's blueprint; as the plot of the perfect detective story; as a spontaneous demonstration in a dictatorship

    symbols: Machiavellian; by the numbers; laid out; foregone conclusion

    see also: deliberate; calculating

    opposite: spontaneous; unprepared; random; disorganized; aimless

Plausible: as a perfect alibi; as seeing it for yourself; as the testimony of ten eyewitnesses

    symbols: honest face; a likely story; a leg to stand on

    see also: logical; reasonable; believable

    opposite: illogical; absurd; ridiculous

Playful: as a pack of porpoises; as a puppy with a friend; as a kitten with a ball of string

    symbols: life of the party; kitten on the keys

    see also: comical; nutty; absurd; abandoned

    opposite: dull; serious; sad; gloomy

Pleasant: as the days of wine and roses; as a land of milk and honey; as having money and knowing how to spend it; as good company in happy surroundings; as the far off fields of home

    symbols: Saturnian; Arcadia; Garden of Eden

    see also: congenial; cheerful; genial; gracious; charming; nice; friendly; amiable

    opposite: disagreeable; nasty; mean; rude; cold

Pliable: as picture wire; as soft plastic; as a lover anxious to please; as a candidate who follows the crowd

    symbols: putty; India rubber man

    see also: flexible; adjustable; elastic; adaptable

    opposite: rigid; arbitrary; firm; uncompromising; opinionated

Pointed: as the tip of the needle; as a huntsman's arrow; as a kick on the shin under the table; as a gun aimed at a bullseye

    symbols: on target; on the button

    see also: accurate; sharp; keen; biting; acute

    opposite: dull; inaccurate; vague

Poisonous: as a gossip's tongue; as the sting of an adder; as one man's meat is to another man; as mustard gas; as the doctrines of the devil
>   symbols: dessert with the Borgias; the tongue of the viper
>   see also: lethal; fatal; dangerous; treacherous; harmful
>   opposite: healthy; kind; friendly; harmless

Polished: as the language of diplomacy; as the handle of the big front door (W.S. Gilbert); as a lady's fingernails; as a prize performance
>   symbols: Chesterfieldian; Mayfair; kid gloves; beau monde; savoir faire
>   see also: smooth; glossy; subtle; accomplished; fine; courteous
>   opposite: dull; rough; rude; impolite; awkward

Polite: as a waiter working for a good tip; as a salesclerk to a good customer; as a person of breeding; as a discreet diplomat
>   symbols: Emily Post; Amy Vanderbilt; Alphonse and Gaston; minding one's Ps and Qs
>   see also: courteous; refined; considerate; attentive; kind; cultured
>   opposite: rude; ill-mannered; savage; officious; callous

Political: as a nominating convention; as a campaign speech; as a candidate kissing babies; as a party caucus; as a pork-barrel bill
>   symbols: cloakroom government; party time; vote chasing; a play to the gallery; whistle-stop campaign
>   see also: partisan; selfish; opinionated; prejudiced
>   opposite: impartial; idealistic

Polluted: as the sewage that flows to the sea; as a festering swamp; as a smog-ridden sunset; as spoiled water; as the residue of an oil-tanker spill
>   symbols: Augean stable; poisoned well
>   see also: poisonous; dirty; unclean; impure
>   opposite: pure; clean; healthy; immaculate

Pompous: as a braying jackass in love with the sound of his voice; as a strutting peacock parading for the peahens; as a windbag uttering what he thinks are words of wisdom; as a posturing ham actor sunning himself in the spotlight
>   symbols: Mr. Bumble; stuffed shirt; bag of wind
>   see also: officious; egotistical; rude
>   opposite: meek; quiet; shy; modest; courteous

Poor: as a churchmouse in a rundown parish; as the beggar at the gate; as one with nothing left to sell; as one who cannot afford to dream; as a rich man's opinion of poverty

    symbols: Poverty Row; Queer Street; wolf at the door
    see also: deprived; needy
    opposite: rich; prosperous; wealthy; affluent; privileged

Popular: as cotton candy at the circus; as hot dogs in a ball park; as peanuts with elephants; as going over to the enemy in the war between the sexes; as a prom queen

    symbols: charisma; everybody's sweetheart; bandwagon; matinee idol
    see also: appreciated; sought after; estimable; welcome; prevalent; famous
    opposite: unpopular; objectionable; tarnished

Porous: as a coffee filter; as blotting paper; as a poor excuse; as a gauze bandage

    symbols: sieve; sponge
    see also: open; leaky
    opposite: solid, leakproof

Portable: as a penknife; as a folding umbrella; as a paperback book; as a package of peppermints

    symbols: pocket edition
    see also: light; small
    opposite: heavy; burdensome; big

Positive: as a DNA match; as a fingerprint identification; as a bigot's prejudices; as a test for pregnancy; as the fact that the paths of glory lead but to the grave

    symbols: Sir Oracle; know-it-all; tests prove it
    see also: dogmatic; affirmative; assertive; emphatic; authoritative; certain; sure
    opposite: negative; uncertain; neutral; dubious; doubtful; tentative

Possessive: as a child with a new toy; as a dog with a bone; as the owner of a security blanket

    symbols: Scrooge; silver cord; Linus (Peanuts comic strip)
    see also: affectionate; acquisitive; selfish; jealous
    opposite: generous; open; kind

Powerful: as the iron laws of nature; as the idea whose time has come; as the force of nuclear fission; as the mightiness of right

    symbols: Hercules; Samson; Aaron's serpent
    see also: strong; mighty; overwhelming
    opposite: weak; feeble; frail; delicate; underdeveloped

Precious: as black pearls; as a good name; as time which once past can never be regained; as the gift of life

> symbols: a king's ransom; worth its weight in gold; carved jade yacht
>
> see also: dear; beloved; cherished
>
> opposite: cheap; rejected; little

Precise: as a dictionary definition; as the work of a master watchmaker; as a perfect fit; as a punctilious professor

> symbols: like clockwork; on the button; to a tee
>
> see also: accurate; explicit; certain; fine; flawless; perfect; appropriate
>
> opposite: crude; coarse; gross; vague; uncertain

Predictable: as the Ides of March; as baked beans in Boston; as the timing of the tides; as a total eclipse of the sun; as church bells

> symbols: Pavlov's dog; Big Ben; in the cards; foregone conclusion
>
> see also: certain; sure; inevitable
>
> opposite: uncertain; dubious; vague; doubtful; questionable

Prejudiced: as a kangaroo court; as a bigot with his back to the wall; as one looking for excuses for his own failures; as a bought jury

> symbols: knee-jerk reaction; foregone conclusion
>
> see also: partisan; bigoted; narrow; corrupt; partial; intolerant; opinionated
>
> opposite: impartial; neutral; tolerant; sympathetic; straight

Premature: as a review printed before the show opens; as the claims of victory for Dewey in the 1948 election; as talking about a no-hit game in the seventh inning; as spending the winning before the lottery is drawn

> symbols: jumping the gun; too much too soon
>
> see also: unprepared; hasty; early; young
>
> opposite: mature; ripe; late; old

Pretty: as the flowers that bloom in the spring; as a picture of happiness; as the songs of the birds; as a happy daydream

> symbols: The Graces; sight for sore eyes
>
> see also: attractive; lovely; beautiful; pleasant; handsome
>
> opposite: ugly; frightful; beastly; awful

Prevalent: as the persistence of poverty; as the hope that springs eternal; as fleas in a dog pound; as sunburn on the beach

> symbols: the rage; the reigning influence; trend
>
> see also: popular; common; commonplace
>
> opposite: unpopular; rare; scarce

Privileged: as a trust-fund baby; as a member of the ruling class; as a princess in a golden kingdom; as a boarding school brat
    symbols: born with a silver spoon; the upper crust; the haves
    see also: rich; wealthy; exclusive; prosperous; selective
    opposite: deprived; needy; neglected; forsaken; poor; broke

Productive: as a fertile piece of farmland; as a maternity ward; as sowing seeds in fruitful soil; as an assembly line
    symbols: the horn of plenty; fertile soil; fruitful acres; surplus
    see also: fruitful; fertile; bountiful; profitable; prosperous
    opposite: barren; fruitless; bare; arid; dry

Profitable: as striking gold; as betting on winners; as printing money
    symbols: money in the bank; black ink side of the ledger
    see also: productive; commercial; winning; rich; fruitful; prosperous
    opposite: bankrupt; unlucky; broke; futile

Promising: as a child prodigy; as a number-one draft choice; as a day that starts with a glorious sunrise; as a super salesperson's spiel
    symbols: bright prospect; a comer; a likely; rising star
    see also: hopeful; encouraging; optimistic; engaging
    opposite: hopeless; pessimistic; dubious; doubtful

Prophetic: as a preview; as the lessons of the past; as the handwriting on the wall; as a premonition
    symbols: Cassandra; Elijah; Nostradamus
    see also: predictable; inevitable
    opposite: uncertain; cloudy

Prosperous: as a Hong Kong stockbroker; as the man who broke the bank at Monte Carlo; as a winning mutual-fund manager; as a man with money to rent
    symbols: Golconda; El Dorado; Rockefeller; Croesus
    see also: rich; wealthy; affluent; privileged
    opposite: poor; bankrupt; broke; needy

Provocative: as profanity in church; as an invitation to lust; as a knothole in the fence around a nudist colony; as a preview of pleasure
    symbols: temptation of Eve; Siren song
    see also: inviting; appealing; fascinating; compelling; attractive
    opposite: boring; dull; burdensome; aimless

Prudent: as steering with both hands; as spotting the exits the moment you enter; as looking before you leap; as a squirrel saving nuts for the winter; as worrying more about the hereafter than the heretofore

  symbols: Fabian; weather eye to windward; eye to the future; ear to the ground

  see also: wise; discreet; cautious; careful

  opposite: careless; rash; indiscreet; foolish

Public: as putting it in Macy's window; as a lighted billboard in Times Square; as a Presidential proclamation; as an announcement by the town crier

  symbols: general knowledge; everybody's business; posted on the wall

  see also: open; obvious, free; apparent; available

  opposite: personal; secret; intimate; censored

Pugnacious: as an ugly drunk; as one whose brains are in his fists; as a street bully spoiling for a fight; as a dictator trying to divert his people from their problems; as a cornered rat

  symbols: Ares; Eris; Mars

  see also: militant; threatening; antagonistic; ill-tempered; quarrelsome

  opposite: peaceful; congenial; pleasant; genial; calm; meek; docile; shy

Punctual: as the Naval Observatory; as children for a meal they love; as Big Ben; as the seasons; as the equinox and solstice; as the tides; as the sunrise

  symbols: Johnny-on-the-spot; on-the-button

  see also: timely; accurate; precise; correct

  opposite: late; inaccurate; faulty

Pure: as the driven snow; as the heart of a newborn babe; as Paradise; as water from a crystal spring

  symbols: Sir Galahad; Arcadia; vestal virgin; Artemis

  see also: chaste; immaculate; angelic; flawless; clean; innocent

  opposite: blemished; polluted; tarnished; spoiled; poisonous; doctored; impure

Puzzled: as a mouse in a maze; as a kid trying to figure how they got that great big tuna in that little bitty can; as the audience watching a master magician; as a man trying to understand women's intuition

  symbols: Gordian knot; up a tree; horns of a dilemma

  see also: bewildered; baffling; confused; muddled; uncertain

  opposite: clear; understandable; knowledgeable

Q

Quaint: as a teashop in the tenderloin; as hoopskirts and Hansom cabs; as an assembly-line antique factory; as the contents of the old trunk in the attic

    symbols: Gilbert and Sullivan's world; pure P.G. Wodehouse; E.M. Forster novel

    see also: corny; dated; old-fashioned; queer

    opposite: new; efficient; modern

Qualified: as a politician's promise; as Methuselah would be for social security; as a canary is to sing

    symbols: up to the mark; know-how

    see also: eligible; fit; appropriate; experienced; accomplished; limited

    opposite: amateurish; inadequate; unprepared; absolute

Quarrelsome: as a camel with a nasty disposition; as the two partners in a bad bargain; as Punch and Judy

    symbols: Montague and Capulet; Kilkenny cats; the Hatfields and the McCoys

    see also: argumentative; pugnacious; ill-tempered; disagreeable

    opposite: cooperative; peaceful; genial; congenial; pleasant; calm

Queasy: as a dyspeptic on a loop-the-loop; as a gourmet with a greasy spoon; as a seasick sailor on a stormy sea; as a drunk with dysentery; as lunching at the Ptomaine Tavern

    symbols: bromo bait; the turistas; up tight; Montezuma's revenge

    see also: ill; sick; uncomfortable

    opposite: comfortable; healthy

Queer: as a three-dollar bill; as gravy on ice cream; as a camel's shape; as the people other people marry

    symbols: Alice in Wonderland; Bohemian

    see also: absurd; strange; erratic; irrational; illogical

    opposite: reasonable; normal; average; logical

Questionable: as a hermit's hospitality; as the wisdom of the state; as a plea for mercy by a woman who kills both her parents and then seeks clemency as an orphan; as an anonymous letter; as a confidence man's conscience

    symbols: anybody's guess; fast shuffle; the jury's out; Shady Lane

    see also: arguable; dubious; doubtful; fishy; suspicious; debatable; uncertain

    opposite: clean; honest; clear; certain; sure;

Quick: as the wink of any eye; as the brown fox that jumped over the lazy dog; as a cat's reaction; as cream turns sour
  symbols: Mercury; greased lightning
  see also: fast; brief; nimble; agile; rapid
  opposite: slow; hesitant; left-handed; awkward

Quiet: as the still of the grave; as a stone; as the sleep of the just; as a tiger stalking its prey; as silent prayer; as the wee hours 'til dawn breaks
  symbols: Amyclean silence; still of the night
  see also: calm; placid; relaxed; idle; peaceful
  opposite: loud; deafening; feverish; noisy; boisterous; busy

Quoted: as a favorable review; as the good Book; as a popular joke; as the prices on the New York Stock Exchange; as Bartlett's Familiar Quotations
  symbols: Echo; author credit
  see also: repetitious; corny; familiar
  opposite: original

R

Rabid: as a hound with hydrophobia; as a lynch mob hunting its victim; as a fan who cheers by throwing a temper tantrum
  symbols: mad dog; Corybants; The Furies
  see also: passionate; fierce; inflamed; opinionated; sick
  opposite: aloof; cool; placid; meek; shy; docile; healthy; reasonable

Radiant: as the summer sun; as the light of heaven; as a rainbow after a storm; as a bright new star
  symbols: Milky Way; Great White Way; Roman candle; Hyperion
  see also: brilliant; bright; electrifying
  opposite: dull; dark; gloomy

Radical: as armed revolution; as the red flag; as the bands that throw the bombs; as turning the world on its ear
  symbols: Marxism; nihilism; bolshevism; populism; Left
  see also: revolutionary; extreme; heretical; subversive; innovative
  opposite: cautious; reactionary; docile; peaceful; old-fashioned

Random: as a scattergun; as a lottery; as an arrow shot in air, that falls to earth we know not where (Henry Wadsworth Longfellow); as the rain

    symbols: potluck; luck of the draw

    see also: casual; aimless; accidental; uncertain

    opposite: planned; deliberate; definite; certain

Rapid: as a speeding bullet; as a heat-seeking missile; as the spread of a rumor; as the speed of light

    symbols: Hermes; Mercury; high-tail; wildfire

    see also: fast; quick

    opposite: slow; delayed

Rare: as a day in June (James Russell Lowell); as the fare at a sushi party; as steak tartare; as discretion in a town gossip; as a close-up of the Loch Ness monster

    symbols: one in a million; Ogopogo; hen's teeth

    see also: scarce; sparse; scanty

    opposite: common; familiar; frequent; normal; numerous; abundant

Rash: as teasing a tiger; as Russian roulette; as playing tag with a juggernaut

    symbols: Hotspur; Don Quixote; fire eater

    see also: reckless; bold; daring; adventurous

    opposite: cautious; careful; repressed

Raw: as an open wound; as uncooked kidney beans; as the weather at the North Pole; as a dirty deal; as nature on the half shell

    symbols: nature's nasty side; uncut stone; red meat and green apples

    see also: crude; coarse; immature; painful; rough; harsh

    opposite: smooth; polished; ripe; pleasant

Reactionary: as a reassembly of the Spanish Inquisition; as calling for the resumption of slavery; as turning the clock back

    symbols: Colonel Blimp; the radical right; dinosaur

    see also: backward; changeless; stubborn

    opposite: liberal; modern; flexible

Real: as a rotten apple; as the rocks along the road; as a punch in the nose; as the red of the rose; as the Rock of Gibraltar

    symbols: the McCoy; fact of life

    see also: authentic; true; genuine; honest

    opposite: false; lying; dishonest

Reasonable: as a plausible alibi; as a friendly discussion; as the prices in the bargain basement
>   symbols: Athena; Minerva; golden mean; a likely story
>   see also: convincing; understandable; cheap
>   opposite: illogical; irrational; mad; angry

Rebellious: as an angry adolescent; as a revolutionary; as a thankless child
>   symbols: Ate; Loki; young Turk
>   see also: radical; revolutionary; defiant; subversive
>   opposite: agreeable; docile; meek; placid; reasonable

Reckless: as a jaywalker at rush hour; as a drunken driver; as high-diving into a bathtub; as tasting toadstools
>   symbols: daredevil; brinkmanship; desperado
>   see also: rash; hold; daring; adventurous; careless
>   opposite: cautious; careful; scared; repressed

Red: as a radiant rose; as a boiled lobster; as a third-degree sunburn
>   symbols: rosy dawn; carrot-top; bricktop
>   see also: colorful; bloody; radical
>   opposite: colorless; cautious

Refined: as quality sugar; as the Queen's conversation; as motor oil; as the conversation in a seminary
>   symbols: Attic; The Graces
>   see also: gentle; elegant; polite; courteous; cultured; quiet
>   opposite: loud; coarse; vulgar; rude; boisterous; ill-mannered; tough

Regular: as the ticking of a clock; as a career sergeant in the Army; as a daily routine
>   symbols: clockwork; daily dozen
>   see also: chronic; steadfast; constant; repetitious; changeless
>   opposite: irregular; changeable; uncertain

Regulated: as heating a room with central air; as traffic lights; as shots in a London pub
>   symbols: public utility; under control; computer-run
>   see also: systematic; adjustable
>   opposite: disorganized; mixed up

Rejected: as a bad manuscript; as a slug in the slot machine; as a bad credit risk; as an unsuccessful suitor
> symbols: Ishmael; blackball; sent to Coventry
> see also: forsaken; neglected; deserted
> opposite: sought-after; popular; cherished

Relaxed: as a sleeping baby; as a limp washrag; as a spent spring; as a used-up rubber band; as a pair of old overalls
> symbols: laissez faire; breathing spell
> see also: calm; casual; inert; peaceful; cool; placid; comfortable
> opposite: tense; agitated; edgy; feverish; nervous; active; bothered; worried

Relentless: as the pressure of poverty; as the hounds of hell; as a nagging tongue
> symbols: Javert; avenging angel; bloodhound
> see also: steadfast; pitiless
> opposite: pliable; changeable; kind

Reliable: as money in the bank; as the rotation of the earth; as the Federal Reserve Bank; as the wisdom of Holy Writ
> symbols: real McCoy; steady Eddie; from the horse's mouth
> see also: trustworthy; responsible; steadfast; faithful; authoritative; loyal
> opposite: treacherous; untruthful; false; uncertain; changeable

Repentant: as a crook who cops a plea; as a diner who mistook the hot mustard for mayonnaise; as a sinner caught in the act; as many who marry in haste
> symbols: St. Mary Magdalene; sackcloth and ashes
> see also: sad; apologetic
> opposite: cheerful; callous; indifferent

Repetitious: as a recorded message; as the route of a merry-go-round; as an old man's story-telling; as a stuck needle
> symbols: a parrot; a myna bird; a raven
> see also: dull; boring; familiar
> opposite: new; original; final

Replaceable: as rubber tires; as light bulbs; as a substitute teacher; as golf tees; as an office temporary
> symbols: revolving door; throwaway model
> see also: temporary; transient; changeable
> opposite: permanent; lasting; perpetual; constant; changeless

Representative: as a town meeting; as a random survey; as a secret ballot; as the letters to the editor; as a show of hands

    symbols: John Q. Public; the man in the street; Gallup Poll; straw vote

    see also: normal; average; regular; accurate

    opposite: special; different

Repressed: as a thwarted sneeze; as a Puritan's libido; as dissent in a dictatorship

    symbols: reign of terror; *1984* (George Orwell)

    see also: censored; hidden; concealed; secret; docile

    opposite: open; free; aggressive; reckless; rash; noticeable

Resented: as a new broom in an old mess; as a reformer in a political clubhouse; as the teacher's pet; as a snub at a soirée

    symbols: Dr. Fell; *bete noire*

    see also: hateful; offensive; annoying; disagreeable

    opposite: beloved; dear; lovable; precious; genial; congenial

Resolute: as Columbus sailing into the unknown; as St. George in search of the dragon; as the hunt for the Holy Grail; as a curmudgeon refusing to smile

    symbols: Joan of Arc; never say die

    see also: confident; bold; stubborn; sure; positive; certain

    opposite: hesitant; uncertain; cautious; anxious

Respectable: as high tea at Buckingham Palace; as a pious pilgrim in a church pew; as a pillar of wisdom

    symbols: good name; pillar of the community

    see also: estimable; virtuous; dependable; trustworthy

    opposite: criminal; objectionable; corrupt; rebellious

Restless: as a willow waving in the breeze; as a rolling stone; as an insomniac with hives; as Midas smelling money; as a nervous racehorse at the starting gate; as an adolescent waiting for the phone to ring

    symbols: Ulysses; Gypsy; Flying Dutchman; vagabond

    see also: nervous; edgy; agitated; anxious; feverish; uncertain

    opposite: calm; placid; relaxed; quiet; docile

Revolutionary: as the invention of the wheel; as the sayings of Chairman Mao; as a victory of the downtrodden; as mob law

    symbols: civil war; rabble in arms; tables turned

    see also: radical; rebellious; heretical; subversive; new

    opposite: reactionary; peaceful; old-fashioned; cautious

Rich: as a double dip banana split; as the coffers of Fort Knox; as a butter and sugar diet; as the Comstock Lode

    symbols: Croesus; Rockefeller; El Dorado; Midas

    see also: wealthy; affluent

    opposite: poor; deprived; needy

Ridiculous: as a linebacker dancing the Specter of the Rose; as snowshoes on a swan; as asking a hermit to the Mardi Gras

    symbols: Alice in Wonderland; Momus; crazy quilt; theater of the absurd

    see also: absurd; illogical; incongruous; foolish; comical; strange

    opposite: serious; wise; reasonable; correct

Righteous: as those in the armor of a just cause; as the judgments of the Lord; as the nation which keepeth the truth (Isaiah); as those who walk the straight and narrow path

    symbols: salt of the earth; pillar of the community

    see also: holy; honest, exemplary, correct

    opposite: bad, evil, dishonest, wrong

Rigid: as a steel girder; as the morals of a bluenose; as a cadet's posture; as a contract without an escape clause

    symbols: Procrustean; Draco; Spartan

    see also: arbitrary; uncompromising; stubborn

    opposite: flexible; pliable; accommodating; adjustable

Ripe: as a rich red raspberry; as the cheese that shows its age; as red apples

    symbols: harvest time; heavy on the vine

    see also: mature; perfect; finished

    opposite: raw; crude; underdeveloped; immature

Rotten: as mackerel that shines and stinks by moonlight (John Randolph); as limburger cheese that's past its prime; as a skunk's reputation; as a grouch's disposition

    symbols: Augean stable; gangrene; Sodom and Gomorrah

    see also: decayed; smelly; decadent; objectionable

    opposite: pleasant; agreeable; amiable; good

Rough: as an uncut diamond; as a barroom brawl; as coarse sandpaper; as a rhino's hide; as a walk on a wild waterfront

    symbols: Donnybrook Fair; Vandal; the wild bunch

    see also: boisterous; coarse; violent

    opposite: smooth; quiet; polite; finished; docile

Rude: as the manger where the babe was born; as an insult to Emily Post; as an uncivil servant; as an obscene gesture; as a slap in the face
>   symbols: billingsgate; fishwife
>   see also: insulting; coarse; vulgar; tactless; gross; nasty; impudent; insolent
>   opposite: polite; kind; gentle; courteous; complimentary

Run-down: as a neglected neighborhood; as a ruined reputation; as a broken watch; as an abandoned building
>   symbols: Poverty Row; a shanty in old shantytown
>   see also: abandoned; neglected; forsaken; poor; bankrupt
>   opposite: profitable; prosperous; neat

Rushed: as a short-order cook with a long line of customers; as an emergency operation; as the most popular student on campus; as the umbrella counter in a sudden rainstorm
>   symbols: juggling act; three-ring circus
>   see also: booming; busy; hurried; popular; fast
>   opposite: slow; delayed; relaxed; unpopular

Rusty: as neglected armor; as an old nail; as an athlete gone to pot; as a buried beer can; as a scrap iron dump
>   symbols: overage destroyer; mothball fleet
>   see also: tarnished; blemished; old; dirty
>   opposite: new; clean; polished; flawless; perfect

S

Sacred: as a cow in Calcutta; as the Gospel; as life, liberty and the pursuit of happiness; as the honor of brave and honest folk
>   symbols: Holy Writ; holy of holies; the word of God
>   see also: holy; blessed; dedicated
>   opposite: damned; heretical; idolatrous

Sacrificial: as a burnt offering; as selfless love; as a bunt by a home-run hitter; as dying so that others may live
>   symbols: Alcestis; scapegoat
>   see also: noble; dedicated; devoted; loyal; committed
>   opposite: insincere; negligent; callous; selfish

Sad: as a centipede with foot trouble; as sackcloth and ashes; as the loss of hope; as sudden sorrow
> symbols: Slough of Despond; Acheron; Angerona
> see also: anguished; blue; gloomy; despondent; downhearted; hopeless; discouraged
> opposite: happy; cheerful; amiable; hopeful

Safe: as the vaults at Fort Knox; as a soul in Heaven; as the Federal Reserve; as money in the bank
> symbols: snug harbor; sanctuary
> see also: secure; reliable; trustworthy; dependable; enduring
> opposite: endangered; dangerous; deadly; lethal; disastrous; harmful; fatal

Satisfied: as a lover loved; as a parent who can answer all the children's questions; as a gourmet after a deluxe dinner; as hunger at the groaning board
> symbols: contented cow; cat that ate the canary
> see also: pleased; happy; grateful
> opposite: angry; hungry; anxious; worried; concerned

Savage: as the law of the jungle; as man's inhumanity to man; as a cornered rat; as a Roman circus; as the uncharted wilderness
> symbols: Attila the Hun; jungle beast; beast of prey
> see also: barbarous; cruel; pitiless; beastly; brutal; harsh
> opposite: kind; civilized; cultured; polite; gentle

Scandalous: as the morals of the Marquis de Sade; as gutter gossip; as sin on a silver platter; as a scarlet past
> symbols: talk of the town; whispering campaign; overnight sensation
> see also: notorious; evil; wicked; corrupt; heretical; bad; immoral
> opposite: pure; good; innocent; admirable; clean; nice; chaste; exemplary

Scanty: as a nudist's wardrobe; as a baby's vocabulary; as the dialogue in a pantomime; as a poor man's purse
> symbols: starvation diet; slim pickings
> see also: meager; minimal; scarce; little; poor
> opposite: large; numerous; big; overwhelming; huge; abundant; monumental

Scarce: as bones in ice cream; as water in a wasteland; as the hair on a bald man's head
> symbols: black market
> see also: meager; minimal; sparse
> opposite: numerous; abundant; overwhelming

Scared: as a frightened fawn; as the food taster for the Borgias; as a rabbit on the run; as a new student on the first day of school
  symbols: panicsville; white-knuckle flight
  see also: frightened; cowardly
  opposite: brave; bold; courageous; daring

Scattered: as the stars in the heavens; as the driftwood on the shore; as dust upon the wind; as the applause for a bad act
  symbols: buckshot; blunderbuss
  see also: dissipated; thin; sparse; meager
  opposite: thick; crowded; packed; jammed; abundant

Scornful: as one who wishes he had thought of it himself; as a snob sizing up the hoi polloi; as a skeptic confronted by honest emotion
  symbols: cold shoulder; curled lip
  see also: critical; disagreeable; smug
  opposite: friendly; amiable; agreeable; cooperative; helpful; kind

Secret: as the silence of the grave; as hidden vanity; as the thoughts that cannot be shared; as the history that's told in whispers; as scandal in high places
  symbols: arcanum arcanorum; C.I.A.; "the company"
  see also: anonymous; buried; hidden; concealed; intimate; personal; camouflaged; disguised
  opposite: obvious; apparent; clear; certain; open; noticeable

Seldom: as a borrower remains a friend; as great and good occur in the same person; as the blooming of a century plant
  symbols: once in a blue moon; a sometime thing
  see also: rare; scarce
  opposite: regular; frequent; repetitious

Selective: as a spoiled child's hearing; as a snooty club; as the law of the survival of the fittest
  symbols: choice not chance; Rhadamanthes
  see also: closed; narrow; particular
  opposite: open; broad; hospitable

Selfish: as the practice of me first; as stealing from a baby; as a one-seater automobile
  symbols: looking out for number one
  see also: grasping; egotistical
  opposite: idealistic; generous

Sensitive: as a hair trigger; as a top-secret weapon; as a psychopath with a thin skin; as an allergic reaction
    symbols: litmus paper; pressure point
    see also: delicate; inflamed; painful
    opposite: secure; safe; crude; gross; indifferent; aloof; cold

Sentimental: as a golden wedding; as Auld Lang Syne; as love's old sweet song; as mother love
    symbols: hearts and flowers; tear-jerker
    see also: nostalgic; affectionate; precious; soulful; cherished
    opposite: indifferent; cold; callous; hard; tough

Serious: as a comic's ambition to do tragedy; as the task of being funny; as a doctoral dissertation; as the last rites
    symbols: Old Sobersides; down to cases
    see also: important; urgent; crucial; sober
    opposite: foolish; comical; absurd; nutty; ridiculous

Sexy: as the pros of procreation; as a lesson in love; as the back seat at an X-rated drive-in movie; as the opposites that attract each other; as a matched pair of passion flowers
    symbols: Eros; Casanova; Aphrodite; oomph; Astarte; Venus; the Lorelei; Sirens
    see also: carnal; earthy
    opposite: pure; innocent; chaste

Shady: as an arbor in full bloom; as a con-man under the old oak tree; as a dark night in a pine grove; as a deal with the devil; as a disgraceful past
    symbols: Stygian, Plutonian; Erebus; under a rock
    see also: questionable; immoral; dark; lying; dishonest
    opposite: honest; open; bright; good

Shallow: as a wading pool; as the Los Angeles River in the dry season; as a bird bath; as the conversation in a cocktail lounge; as a hasty judgment
    symbols: Philistine; Babbitt
    see also: superficial; narrow; low
    opposite: deep; cultured; wise

Sharp: as a two-edged sword (*Proverbs*); as the tooth of the tiger; as the eye of the eagle; as the point of a tack; as the tongue of a nag
    symbols: the razor's edge; the needle
    see also: pointed; cutting; keen; biting; harsh
    opposite: soft; dull; kind; friendly

Short: as the simple annals of the poor (Thomas Gray); as the breath of age (William Shakespeare); as an embezzling bank teller; as a sudden stop; as a midget's measurements
  symbols: Tom Thumb; abridged edition; flash in the pan
  see also: abbreviated; brief; condensed; dishonest; simple
  opposite: long; large; excessive; honest; windy

Shrewd: as a rat with a high IQ; as Sherlock Holmes; as the business agent for the business agents' union
  symbols: Machiavelli; David Harum
  see also: wily; calculating; tricky; wise; crafty
  opposite: simple; dull; open

Shrill: as the shriek of fire engine siren; as a whistling teapot with a full head of steam; as a soprano with a head cold; as a scared woman's scream; as the call of the banshee
  symbols: screech owl; glass shatterer; steam whistle
  see also: noisy; loud; deafening
  opposite: quiet; soft; low; silent

Shy: as a modest maiden; as a bankrupt's bank account; as a cautious two-year-old
  symbols: John Alden; shrinking violet
  see also: quiet; meek; docile; repressed; humble; frightened
  opposite: assertive; aggressive; bold; pugnacious; loud; argumentative

Sick: as a dog with dyspepsia; as a soul in torment; as smallpox; as a patient in intensive care
  symbols: Camille; under the weather
  see also: weak; pestilential; inflamed; anemic; feeble
  opposite: healthy; strong

Silent: as the stillness of the grave; as the language of pantomime; as one who has no answer; as the emptiness of space
  symbols: Amyclae; Sphinx; Harpocrates
  see also: quiet; soft; low
  opposite: noisy; loud; shrill; deafening

Simple: as the songs of children; as the plain pleasures of the people; as the basic virtues; as adding one and one; as an honest smile
  symbols: Simple Simon; Tommie Traddles
  see also: plain; commonplace; average; easy; understandable
  opposite: baffling; complicated; difficult; affected

Skinny: as a skeleton on a diet; as bones with binding; as an empty wallet
>   symbols: skin and bones; walking skeleton
>   see also: slim; thin
>   opposite: fat; flabby; padded; ample

Slim: as a streamlined whippet; as a fashion model; as a pauper's pickings
>   symbols: toothpick
>   see also: skinny; thin; flat
>   opposite: fat; flabby; padded; broad; ample

Slippery: as an elusive eel; as a banana peel on a newly polished floor; as a master of disguise
>   symbols: greased pig; Machiavellian
>   see also: sly; elusive; tricky; wily; evasive; loose
>   opposite: catching; open; honest; simple

Slow: as a tortoise taking its time; as a funeral march; as the mills of the gods that grind so small (Henry Wadsworth Longfellow)
>   symbols: molasses in January; snail
>   see also: delayed; hesitant
>   opposite: quick; fast; nimble; instantaneous

Sly: as a superspy; as a sneaky double entendre; as a sneakthief; as a fox in the forest
>   symbols: Machiavelli; Reynard the Fox; Volpone; the Artful Dodger
>   see also: wily; shrewd; artful; calculating; subtle; tricky; slippery
>   opposite: straight; simple; plain; honest

Small: as the hopes of a pessimist; as a gnat's knee; as a single candle in a galaxy of light; as a grain of sand; as home for a humming bird
>   symbols: pocket edition; Tiny Tim; Tom Thumb; Lilliput; the little people
>   see also: little; minimal; meager
>   opposite: big; large; huge; vast; colossal; ample

Smelly: as a pigpen in a high wind; as a fish too long out of water; as a garbage dump
>   symbols: B.O.; halitosis; stinkweed; skunk
>   see also: aromatic; odorous; fragrant
>   opposite: blank; airy

Smooth: as silk and just as gentle; as the soft cheek of a maiden fair; as monumental alabaster (William Shakespeare); as a baby's brow
>   symbols: velvet touch; kid gloves; clear sailing; sweetness and light
>   see also: glossy; polished; fine
>   opposite: rough; coarse; harsh

Smug: as a sophomore sneering at the freshmen; as the cynic who told you so; as a man who makes his own medals; as a self-made man who admires his product; as a reformed smoker; as the cat that swallowed the canary

    symbols: fat cat; Babbitt; the establishment

    see also: patronizing; condescending; arrogant; officious; immodest; vain

    opposite: modesty; humble

Sneaky: as a sidewinder; as a snake in the grass; as a Peeping Tom; as walking on tip-toe

    symbols: Uriah Heep; Pearl Harbor

    see also: deceitful; crafty; wily; tricky; duplicitous; devious; evasive

    opposite: honest; direct; trustworthy; reliable

Sober: as an undertaker's outerwear; as a reformed drunk; as the sound of sorrow; as a judge in the halls of justice

    symbols: water wagon; temperance man

    see also: dignified; solemn; sad; quiet

    opposite: intoxicating; ill-mannered; boisterous; loud

Soft: as a baby's bottom; as the answer that turneth away wrath (*Proverbs*); as the sound of sweet music; as the words that are spoken in love

    symbols: life of Riley; Easy Street; velvet touch; kid gloves; feather bed

    see also: smooth; gentle; kind; gracious

    opposite: hard; pitiless; harsh; austere

Solemn: as a sinner suing for salvation; as a state ceremony; as the Day of Judgment; as the stillness of the unknown

    symbols: Old Sobersides; striped pants

    see also: dignified; formal; holy; sober

    opposite: boisterous; ill-mannered; rude; noisy; loud

Solid: as the Rock of Gibraltar; as a citizen of substance; as stale cheesecake; as a knockout punch

    symbols: money in the bank; 24 carat; old reliable

    see also: firm; strong; hardy; tough

    opposite: frail; weak; feeble; porous; volatile

Soothing: as the charms of music for a savage breast; as a soft word at a tough time; as a mother's touch; as the balm they should have had in Gilead

    symbols: massage; the pause that refreshes

    see also: comforting; soft; calm; relaxed

    opposite: frantic; agitated; anxious; bothered; worried; nervous

Sore: as an aching joint; as a bad loser after a tough decision; as a Sunday driver in a weekday traffic jam
    symbols: Rumpelstiltskin; salt in the wound
    see also: painful; mad; angry; anguished; uncomfortable
    opposite: comfortable; calm; peaceful; healthy

Sought after: as public enemy number one; as a Presidential nomination; as the keys to the kingdom; as the winning ticket in the lottery
    symbols: charisma; matinee idol; oomph
    see also: popular; famous; scarce; rare
    opposite: unpopular

Soulful: as the birth of the blues; as the sweet spirit of sisterhood; as the sighs of love
    symbols: charisma; the inner id
    see also: sentimental; euphoric; cherished; exalted
    opposite: indifferent; callous; downhearted

Sound: as the old dollar; as a healthy horse; as the sleep of the just; as the soul of a saint
    symbols: Salus; Simon Pure; Rock of Gibraltar
    see also: healthy; reasonable; solid; wise
    opposite: sick; ill-advised; dumb

Sour: as spoiled grapes; as the bitterness of a broken friendship; as an off-key symphony; as stale wine; as the grapes of wrath
    symbols: Adullamites; vinegar; spent milk; sourdough
    see also: bitter
    opposite: sweet; happy

Sparse: as waterholes in the wasteland; as compliments in the complaint department; as credit at a collection agency; as a pauper's pennies; as halos in Hell
    symbols: slim pickings; desert
    see also: meager; scarce; scattered; dissipated
    opposite: numerous; abundant; crowded; jammed; packed

Special: as a diamond jubilee; as a pipeline to Santa Claus; as the return of a prodigal; as the gift of grace
    symbols: four-star; red-letter
    see also: rare; original
    opposite: average; common; regular; natural

Spectacular: as the view from outer space; as a moonrise over a mountain; as a rocket rising and soaring into the sky; as Niagara Falls in full flow; as a sunset on the sea

   symbols: Seven Wonders of the World; Roman holiday; Roman candle; Aurora Borealis
   see also: impressive; magnificent; monumental; glorious; beautiful
   opposite: dull; bleak; ugly; colorless; weary

Speculative: as trying to predict which way a fly will jump; as strip poker; as borrowing money to get into a bingo game; as a plunge on the horses

   symbols: toss of the dice; luck of the draw; Fortuna; Lady Luck
   see also: uncertain; changeable; rash
   opposite: certain; sure; definite

Spoiled: as a child that never hears a no; as a burnt offering at a banquet; as rancid butter; as the vines the little foxes find

   symbols: sour wine; rotten apples; snafu
   see also: damaged; decayed; faulty; tarnished; rotten
   opposite: flawless; pure; perfect

Spontaneous: as a burst of laughter; as combustion in a pile of oily rags; as a sudden sneeze; as the tears of a toddler

   symbols: spur of the moment; self-starter
   see also: instantaneous; instinctive; unprepared
   opposite: planned; automatic; constant

Spotless: as a blank sheet; as an angel's reputation; as a broadcast without commercials; as a black leopard

   symbols: Galahad; vestal virgin
   see also: immaculate; pure; flawless; perfect
   opposite: blemished; tarnished; unclean; dirty; polluted

Square: as a box; as the deal you get from an honest man; as old-fashioned virtue

   symbols: old school; old fogy; Fides
   see also: old fashioned; corny; honest; frank; straight
   opposite: new; dishonest; lying

Steadfast: as the spirit of never say die; as a guiding star; as true love through thick and thin; as faithful friendship

   symbols: patience of Job; fidus Achates
   see also: true; constant; changeless; reliable; dependable; trustworthy; loyal
   opposite: changeable; uncertain; volatile; fickle; treacherous

Sticky: as rubber cement; as spilled syrup; as soothing an angry porcupine; as playing catch with a hedgehog

    symbols: flypaper; sea urchin; cactus

    see also: difficult; tough; uncomfortable

    opposite: neat; easy; comfortable

Stingy: as a miser with his money; as a hostess serving a five-portion pie to a table of ten; as a curmudgeon with his compliments

    symbols: Ebenezer Scrooge; pinchpenny

    see also: cheap; tight; frugal; economical; grudging; close

    opposite: generous; open; charitable; kind; helpful

Straight: as the path the crooked cannot walk; as the shortest distance between two points; as the line before the punchline; as an arrow that knows just where it's going

    symbols: the real McCoy; dead level; 24 carat

    see also: direct; honest; neat; pointed

    opposite: crooked; dishonest; subtle

Strange: as the bedfellows of politics; as somebody else's ideas; as the attitudes of adolescence; as tomorrow's fashions looked yesterday

    symbols: one for the books; creature from outer space

    see also: absurd; queer; erratic; different; alien; illogical; incongruous

    opposite: familiar; natural; normal; average; alike

Strong: as a bull moose full of beans; as iron bands (Henry Wadsworth Longfellow); as the scent of gorgonzola; as the staying power of garlic; as Paul Bunyan and his blue ox

    symbols: Atlas; Hercules; Amazon; Samson; John Henry

    see also: powerful; mighty; compelling; overwhelming

    opposite: weak; frail; feeble; overwhelmed

Stubborn: as a Missouri mule with its mind made up; as the fancies of a fool; as a spot that won't come out; as the kid who keeps coming back for more; as a goal-line stand

    symbols: a mule; block of granite

    see also: rigid; balky; obstinate; arbitrary; dogmatic; opinionated; uncompromising

    opposite: flexible; pliable; adjustable; weak

Subtle: as the serpent's slither; as the messages of silence; as the loss of youth; as a pickpocket's touch; as the surgeon's skill
    symbols: Machiavellian; Philadelphia lawyer; Artful Dodger
    see also: artful; calculating; polished; shrewd
    opposite: straight; direct; open

Subversive: as corned beef with lettuce; as working for a rerun of the American Revolution; as a spy in the Oval Office
    symbols: fifth column; Quisling; the underground
    see also: radical; heretical; revolutionary
    opposite: loyal; cooperative

Superficial: as a thin coat of paint; as a surface scratch; as a social lion's small talk; as the forced smile of a harried hostess
    symbols: Philistine; tempest in a teapot; tip of the iceberg
    see also: shallow; thin; contrived; affected
    opposite: deep; wise; authentic

Sure: as the certainty of death; as daylight after the darkness; as the master's touch
    symbols: Sir Oracle; open-and-shut case; lead-pipe cinch
    see also: clear; certain; definite; inevitable
    opposite: questionable; tentative; speculative; doubtful; surprised; dubious; uncertain

Surprised: as a criminal caught in the act; as a mother-in-law by her son-in-law's success; as a drinker who didn't know he was loaded
    symbols: bolt from the blue; bombshell
    see also: miraculous; amazing; baffling
    opposite: predictable; certain; sure

Suspicious: as a smoking gun; as a man who's been offered something for nothing; as one who knows his own guilt; as a copper looking for a clue
    symbols: Doubting Thomas; Sherlock Holmes; Ellery Queen
    see also: fishy; questionable; uncertain; dubious; doubtful
    opposite: aloof; clean; clear

Sweet: as the smell of success; as the satisfaction of revenge; as money to a miser; as sugar and molasses in a honey glaze; as solitude is to a hermit
    symbols: altar of roses; balm of Gilead; honey
    see also: appealing; attractive; fragrant; tasteful
    opposite: sour; bitter

Sympathetic: as a mother's hug; as a helping hand; as a friend who's looking for a favor
  symbols: milk of human kindness; friendly ear; echoing chord; shoulder to lean on
  see also: comforting; soothing; encouraging; partisan
  opposite: indifferent; cool; callous; impartial; antagonistic

Systematic: as the order of nature; as a computer run; as building blocks; as a tax audit
  symbols: by the numbers; by the book; blueprint; assembly-line
  see also: efficient; regulated
  opposite: disorganized; mixed up; messy

T

Tactless: as interrupting the Pope; as a tap dance in a tomb; as tipping a tycoon; as clapping a Queen on the back; as being drunk at a temperance meeting
  symbols: bull in a china shop; foot in the mouth; Philistine
  see also: ill-advised; indiscreet; tasteless; foolish; left-handed; rude
  opposite: exemplary; courteous; tasteful; wise

Talkative: as a teenager on the telephone; as the town gossip; as a parrot who likes the spotlight
  symbols: diarrhea of the mouth; chin music; cave of the winds; magpie; chatterbox
  see also: windy; gaseous; loud
  opposite: silent; quiet

Tame: as a dull party; as a tabby; as a timid toddler; as a tiny titter
  symbols: trained seal; performing dog; pussycat
  see also: docile; meek; gentle; obedient
  opposite: fierce; savage; pugnacious; aggressive

Tangled: as a fishline full of knots; as the web we weave when first we practice to deceive (Sir Walter Scott); as a goat's hair; as an octopus in a fishnet
  symbols: Gordian knot; jumble; snafu
  see also: messy; sticky; mixed; confused
  opposite: smooth; neat; clear

Tarnished: as the town tramp's reputation; as neglected silver; as a rusty nail; as a tainted title

> symbols: damaged goods; mark of Cain; faded halo
>
> see also: blemished; spoiled; rusty; dirty; damaged; impure
>
> opposite: perfect; flawless; polished; pure; clean

Tasteful: as forbidden fruit; as a wine of rarest vintage elegantly served; as a well-turned phrase; as the tact of a true diplomat

> symbols: Attic; savoir-faire; to the Queen's taste
>
> see also: appropriate; elegant; refined; cultured; graceful; correct
>
> opposite: tactless; heavy-handed; foolish; awkward; wrong; tasteless

Tasteless: as well-chewed gum; as promising with crossed fingers; as smacking gum in church

> symbols: Philistine; Roman holiday; X-rated
>
> see also: tactless; ill-advised; indiscreet; rude; heavy-handed
>
> opposite: tasteful; refined; cultured; elegant

Taxing: as the Internal Revenue Service; as Congress at money-raising time; as Social Security; as tiptoeing on a bed of coals; as a tour on the run

> symbols: labors of Hercules; Sisyphian task; hard row to hoe
>
> see also: burdensome; heavy; laborious; difficult
>
> opposite: easy; light; simple

Temporary: as a passing shower; as tomorrow when it comes; as the rooster who rules the roost today; as a permanent wave

> symbols: passing show; One-Shot Willie; ships that pass in the night
>
> see also: momentary; transient; fleeting
>
> opposite: permanent; enduring; perpetual; continuous; timeless; constant; lasting; chronic

Tense: as a snake getting set to strike; as a sprinter at the starting block; as a hermit expecting company; as an expectant father who's been told to expect triplets

> symbols: the jitters; the willies; touch and go; coiled spring
>
> see also: impatient; rushed; nervous; neurotic
>
> opposite: relaxed; casual; carefree; happy

Tentative: as a toe in the water; as the first sip of the soup; as a buyer's first bid; as a poor man's prosperity

> symbols: trial run; dry run; trial balloon
>
> see also: experimental; questionable; hesitant; conditional; uncertain
>
> opposite: positive; affirmative; emphatic; sure; certain

Thick: as autumnal leaves (John Milton); as three in a bed (Sir Walter Scott); as hasty pudding; as thieves in the state pen; as a heavy accent; as an oil slick in sea water
- symbols: laid on with a trowel; Boeotian; pea soup
- see also: heavy; crowded; congested; packed; jammed; numerous; tough
- opposite: thin; sparse; scanty; light; meager; scattered

Thin: as a poor excuse; as a slice of prosciutto; as a touchy person's skin; as a dime in a time of inflation; as the line between self-confidence and sheer conceit
- symbols: walking skeleton; bag of bones; watered soup
- see also: skinny; slim
- opposite: thick; fat; flabby

Threatening: as an angry murmur rising from an unruly mob; as a lawyer's letter that begins with the word "unless"; as an unfriendly fist an inch from your nose; as a black cloud
- symbols: sword of Damocles; handwriting on the wall; storm cloud
- see also: ominous; menacing; imminent; offensive; antagonistic; dangerous
- opposite: friendly; hospitable; safe; kind; helpful

Tight: as a well-tuned drum; as a miser with his money; as a hermit with his invitations; as a two-day drunk; as a closed circle
- symbols: slow on the draw; penny pincher; close shave; Scrooge
- see also: stingy; grudging; cheap; close; leakproof; drunk
- opposite: generous; charitable; loose; open; sober

Timeless: as the sound of the surf at the edge of the sea; as the Ten Commandments; as the laws of nature
- symbols: Rock of Ages; eternity; infinity
- see also: infinite; endless; perpetual; durable; permanent; lasting
- opposite: limited; fleeting; momentary; brief; temporary

Timely: as tomorrow's news; as a birthday party; as a tax refund; as a reminder that today is your wedding anniversary
- symbols: psychological moment; Johnny-on-the-spot; on-the-button
- see also: appropriate; punctual; helpful
- opposite: advised; late; wrong

Tolerant: as a doting sugar daddy; as a psychoanalyst who gets paid for listening; as a patient parent
- symbols: laissez-faire; carte blanche; open society; patience of Job
- see also: understanding; indulgent; permissive; patient
- opposite: callous; intolerant; allergic

Tough: as a hippo's hide; as teakwood; as a Tartar on the Steppes; as a tiger with a titanic appetite; as overcooked steak

  symbols: Amazon; Hercules; bulldog; uphill going; Spartan; Procrustean; Draconian

  see also: strong; hard; hardy; difficult

  opposite: weak; soft; easy

Transient: as a wandering breeze; as a leaf tossed by the wind; as a passing shower; as an idea in an empty head

  symbols: bird of passage; shooting star; flash in the pan

  see also: temporary; fleeting; momentary; replaceable

  opposite: lasting; enduring; permanent; abiding; chronic

Transparent: as window glass; as a miser's greed; as the water in a goldfish bowl; as false modesty; as a peacock's pride

  symbols: an open book; wrapped in cellophane

  see also: obvious; clear

  opposite: hidden; concealed; obscure

Treacherous: as the undertow along the beach; as Lady Luck; as a false friend; as a knife in the back

  symbols: Borgia; Quisling; Vicar of Bray; fifth column

  see also: deceitful; poisonous; false; lying; untruthful; duplicitous

  opposite: friendly; honest; loyal; trustworthy; true

Tricky: as a master magician; as Dicky; as a crooked card game; as a shell game; as outfoxing a cool cat; as a wolf in sheep's clothing

  symbols: Artful Dodger; Till Eulenspiegel; Cagliostro

  see also: artful; wily; contrived; duplicitous; elusive; evasive; sly

  opposite: simple; honest; innocent; trustworthy

True: as many a word spoken in jest; as the words of the wise; as the green of the grass and the blue of the sky; as the fact that fish live in the sea

  symbols: the real McCoy; the way it is; straight goods

  see also: authentic; honest; genuine; real; faithful; steadfast; loyal

  opposite: false; lying; contrived; dishonest; untruthful

Trustworthy: as a faithful friend; as the truth that time has tested; as the love of a loyal dog; as the power of the profit motive

  symbols: square shooter; true blue; fidus Achates

  see also: faithful; reliable; dependable; loyal

  opposite: sneaky; lying; uncertain; fickle; piratical

U

Ugly: as the underside of the rock when you turn it over; as the face of hate; as a grouch's disposition; as the sense of sin

      symbols: Gorgon; Medusa; gargoyle

      see also: tempered; disagreeable; beastly

      opposite: appealing; beautiful; handsome; lovely; attractive

Uncertain: as the glory of an April day (William Shakespeare); as a weather prediction; as the way the cookie crumbles; as the way an egg rolls

      symbols: Buridan's ass; horns of a dilemma; blow hot and cold; thin ice

      see also: questionable; debatable; doubtful; dubious; arguable; incalculable

      opposite: certain; sure; clear; positive; definite

Unclean: as a clogged sewer; as a foul mouth; as a grab-bag of garbage

      symbols: Augean stable; town dump; pigsty

      see also: dirty; messy; blemished; impure; tarnished

      opposite: clean; pure; spotless; neat

Uncomfortable: as a moose at a taxidermists' convention (Bill Leonard); as the sixth year of the seven-year itch; as a hair shirt under a hot sun; as a collision with a cactus

      symbols: Gehenna; gall and wormwood

      see also: burdensome; painful; sticky; tense

      opposite: comfortable; easy; relaxed

Uncompromising: as put up or shut up; as a challenge to a duel; as the man who won't take yes for an answer

      symbols: Procrustean; bulldog; pig iron; stiff-necked

      see also: arbitrary; rigid; stubborn; dogmatic; changeless

      opposite: adjustable; pliable; flexible; changeable

Underdeveloped: as a badly processed photograph; as a country that kept its innocence; as a hermit's hospitality; as an oilfield waiting to be worked

      symbols: stone age; have-not; MTC (more to come)

      see also: raw; crude; immature

      opposite: ripe; mature; old

Understandable: as an outstretched hand; as a fist in the face; as a wolf whistle; as a come-hither wink

      symbols: plain English; words of one syllable

      see also: logical; easy; simple; clear

      opposite: baffling; difficult; complicated; dark

Unfinished: as that symphony by Schubert; as the world on the fifth day; as the mystery of Edwin Drood

      symbols: work of Penelope; task of Sisyphus; rough cut; breadboard model

      see also: endless; underdeveloped; raw

      opposite: finished; final; complete

Unlucky: as a margins investor when the stockmarket crashes; as a florist with rose fever; as the rabbit who lost the foot you carry for luck; as crossing a black cat's path under a ladder on Friday the 13th and breaking a mirror on the way; as a miser with a hole in his strongbox

      symbols: jinx; Jonah; hex

      see also: haunted; damned

      opposite: fortunate; blessed

Unnecessary: as an extra tonsil; as shipping sand to the desert; as sugar in your honey; as icing on the icing

      symbols: coals to Newcastle; appendix; boondoggle

      see also: needless; excessive; irrelevant

      opposite: essential; necessary; crucial

Unpopular: as a polecat in the parlor; as heresy before it becomes orthodoxy; as a skinhead among liberals; as a weasel in the henhouse

      symbols: *bete noire*; rogue elephant; sent to Coventry

      see also: hateful; detestable

      opposite: sought-after; popular

Unprepared: as the student who didn't do the homework; as a sudden gasp; as raw potatoes

      symbols: caught short; wet behind the ears; half-cocked

      see also: premature; raw; spontaneous

      opposite: ripe; mature; planned

Untruthful: as a con-man's come-on; as the winning entry in the contest at the Liars' Club; as the acclaim of a hired claque
    symbols: Ananias; Baron von Munchausen
    see also: lying; false; dishonest
    opposite: true; honest; accurate; correct

Urgent: as an emergency operation; as an SOS from a ship at sea; as a five-alarm fire call; as rescue for a drowning man
    symbols: top priority; a must; matter of life and death
    see also: crucial; serious; essential
    opposite: needless; unnecessary; irrelevant

Useful: as an extra hand; as teeth for a tiger; as tools for a mechanic
    symbols: means to an end; working model; a leg up
    see also: effective; helpful
    opposite: futile; ineffective; useless

Useless: as a pocket with a hole in it; as an extra adenoid; as last year's calendar; as a rain dance in the Sahara
    symbols: exercise in futility; spiked gun; wild goose chase; tilting at windmills
    see also: futile; helpless; inadequate; ineffective; vain
    opposite: useful; necessary; essential; basic; effective

V

Vague: as the shifting sands; as a faint memory; as the outline of a distant shore; as a politician's promises; as an unwilling witness's memory
    symbols: anybody's guess; needle in a haystack
    see also: uncertain; intangible; confused
    opposite: definite; certain; sure; clear

Vain: as a peacock on parade; as a pussycat pretending to be a tiger; as the delights of the flesh; as valor in a lost cause
    symbols: Narcissus; Don Quixote; labor of Sisyphus; wild goose chase
    see also: smug; immodest; arrogant; egotistical; useless; futile
    opposite: modest; simple; humble; useful; productive

Varied: as the vistas in the valley of Kashmir; as the languages in the Tower of Babel; as the faces of the races of the world; as a mixed box of nuts

> symbols: Noah's Ark; the United Nations; salmagundi
> see also: mixed; blended; hybrid
> opposite: pure; straight

Vast: as the endless world of space; as the emptiness of the ocean seas; as the Russian Steppes

> symbols: Atlantean; Antarctica; Sahara; Texas; all over the map
> see also: huge; big; large; colossal
> opposite: small; little; limited; minimal

Versatile: as a one-man band; as a fish that flies; as a triple-threat man in football; as a decathlon champion

> symbols: jack of all trades; Renaissance man; man of parts; Proteus; many strings to the bow
> see also: accomplished; adaptable
> opposite: rigid; ignorant

Violent: as the passions of the poor; as the fury of war; as a battle to the death; as the ability of man to self-destruct

> symbols: The Furies; battle of the Titans; volcano; Juggernaut; Aceldama
> see also: brutal; lethal; destructive; explosive; extreme
> opposite: quiet; peaceful; gentle

Virtuous: as a mortal trying to become a saint; as a Horatio Alger hero; as a blushing bride; as the sweet sisters of charity

> symbols: Xenocrates; Diana; Artemis; Galahad; vestal virgin
> see also: good; chaste; pure; innocent
> opposite: bad; decadent; corrupt; wicked

Visionary: as a dream of glory; as a picture of paradise; as most people's hopes for the hereafter; symbols: castles in the air; Joan of Arc; Utopia; Promised Land

> see also: idealistic; electrifying; ideal
> opposite: cynical; pessimistic; blind

Volatile: as high-pressure gas; as liquid oxygen; as a live volcano

> symbols: Mercury; mercurial; boiling point; vanishing act; full head of steam
> see also: explosive; changeable; moody; hot; gaseous
> opposite: quiet; steadfast; changeless; solid; mild

Vulgar: as the common crowd; as the lowest bunch in town; as the vices of the many; as gutter language in the living room
    symbols: Trimalchio; the great unwashed; nouveau riche; street stuff
    see also: coarse; gross; crass; rude
    opposite: refined; cultured; gentle; polite

W

Warm: as a hero's welcome; as a round of applause; as a sunny day in August; as the glow of friendship; as the heart behind a helping hand
    symbols: torrid zone; the tropics; bubbling over; open arms
    see also: affectionate; comforting; friendly; amiable; hospitable; pleasant
    opposite: cool; aloof; indifferent; callous

Watered: as a well-kept lawn; as a diluted drink; as the sand that meets the surf; as weak soup
    symbols: less than meets the eye; thin stuff
    see also: doctored; thin
    opposite: solid; condensed

Wayward: as the twists of fate; as the primrose path; as the life that moves too fast
    symbols: off the beam; problem child
    see also: loose; dissipated; immoral; bad
    opposite: good; moral; straight; righteous

Weak: as watered tea; as the average person's resistance to flattery; as the fallen sinner; as a man's will compared to a woman's wont
    symbols: jellyfish; creampuff; tired blood
    see also: feeble; anemic; faint; exhausted
    opposite: strong; healthy; stubborn

Wealthy: as Morgan's and Carnegie's fortunes combined; as Howard Hughes in his heyday; as a covey of Vanderbilts; as the man who broke the bank at Monte Carlo
    symbols: Croesus; Midas touch; El Dorado
    see also: rich; affluent
    opposite: poor; needy; deprived

Weary: as the way of the transgressor; as an oldster's aching bones; as a tortoise in a track meet
- symbols: Hercules after his labors; Sisyphus between trips
- see also: exhausted; overworked; jaded; bored
- opposite: eager; dashing; active; busy

Welcome: as a letter from home; as the flowers that bloom in May (Charles Macklin); as Santa Claus at Christmas; as water in the desert
- symbols: open arms; outstretched hand; waiting at the station
- see also: appreciated; popular; desirable
- opposite: unpopular; objectionable

Wicked: as the Devil's disciples; as a dozen dens of iniquity; as the worst of the witches; as evil incarnate
- symbols: Belial; Satan; the serpent in the Garden of Eden
- see also: evil; bad; immoral; hellish; lawless; loose
- opposite: good; righteous; moral; admirable; exemplary

Wily: as a fox in a farmyard; as a weasel at work; as a master spy; as the witch of Endor
- symbols: the Artful Dodger; cutie-pie; Reynard the Fox
- see also: sly; tricky; calculating; crafty
- opposite: simple; plain

Windy: as the weather at the top of the world; as a corner on the Chicago lakefront; as an orator who gets paid by the word; as a blow by blow description; as a filibuster
- symbols: Aeolus; the cave of the winds
- see also: airy; talkative; gaseous; breezy
- opposite: calm; quiet; silent

Winning: as the Superbowl champions; as the prize ticket in the lottery; as a grand slam; as a royal flush; as an angel's smile
- symbols: blue ribbon; championship belt; the laurel wreath
- see also: profitable; lucky; attractive; sought after
- opposite: unlucky; left out; ineffective; futile

Wise: as the sages of the ages; as time; as a wary wildcat; as the word of God; as one who knows when to watch his words; as he who says nothing rather than say something wrong
- symbols: Solomon; the Magi; Athena; Mentor; the Founding Fathers
- see also: prudent; knowledgeable; discreet; learned; cautious; bright; brilliant
- opposite: stupid; dumb; dull; rash; immature

Worried: as a mouse in cat country; as the captain of a leaky boat a hundred miles at sea; as the man who can't pay back the loan shark; as a hypochondriac without symptoms; as an elephant who forgets
>   symbols: weight of the world; cliffhanger; nail biter
>   see also: anxious; anguished; concerned; nervous
>   opposite: calm; relaxed; euphoric; oblivious; indifferent; aloof

Wrong: as the road to Hell; as waterwings on the desert; as a love letter addressed "to whom it may concern"; as the divine right of kings
>   symbols: booby prize; dunce cap; Devil's disciple
>   see also: erroneous; inaccurate; immoral; dishonest
>   opposite: correct; accurate; true; moral; honest

Y

Yellow: as the dying leaves of autumn; as buttercups in bloom; as a canary with jaundice; as cowardice in living color
>   symbols: white feather; streak down the back; lily-livered
>   see also: cowardly; scared
>   opposite: brave; daring; courageous

Young: as first love; as a woman thinks she looks and a man thinks he acts; as everybody's kid sister; as one whose fancy lightly turns to thoughts of love (Alfred Tennyson)
>   symbols: the now generation; the tomorrow generation; small fry
>   see also: childish; youthful; immature
>   opposite: aged; old; ancient; mature

Youthful: as trying to decide what you want to be when you grow up; as growing a beard to look older; as the eternal juvenile; as braces on your teeth
>   symbols: Aeson's bath; Endymion; Juventas
>   see also: childish; immature; young
>   opposite: aged; dated; ancient; old; mature

Z

Zealous: as a bill collector on commission; as Zorro leaving his mark; as a missionary on the scent of souls to save; as the neighborhood gossip keeping tabs on the neighbors

  symbols: mover and shaker; bulldog; bitter-ender; monomania; wearing blinders

  see also: eager; dedicated; anxious; devoted

  opposite: aimless; aloof; apathetic; bored; jaded; indifferent

VOLUME III

THE DAY
AND DATE BOOK

INTRODUCTION

The pages of history are brimming with inspiring, timely pegs on which to hang a speech. This revised version *Speaker's Lifetime Library* volume serves up an even bigger collection of these events along with appropriate angles and speech themes. From January 1st to December 31—including Leap Day—you'll find a wealth of ideas, humorous commentary, and historic facts. Just to get you started on your way to creating scintillating topics and ear-catching intros, we've provided over 1500 events—1180 speech openings including special openings for every month. We've cross-referenced many of the events with corresponding relevant dates, giving you even more angles and insights to spice up your delivery.

Don't forget. Speaking on a particular day doesn't rule out tomorrow or another day as an inspirational source. Today is only the eve of the next day; and a fortnight is only weeks away. But don't stop there. Check the local newspapers for the past five years. You'll never run of out ideas if you enhance your research with events that originated in your own back yard. After all, our entries are finite—limited by this book's publication date. But history never stops happening. New, noteworthy events occur daily, providing even more inspiration. If you keep your eyes open for late-breaking news, and page through this volume, you'll never be stuck for a speaking topic ever again.

JANUARY

INTRODUCTION

Springing forward seems to be the theme of this first month of the year, even though spring is still a few months away. Caesar crossed the River Rubicon in January; and Queen Victoria admitted she wasn't amused. Oscar Wilde declared nothing but his genius; and the U.S. government declared a war on the "demon alcohol" by passing the Eighteenth Amendment. Now, I won't suggest that we get on a soapbox to make wild proclamations; many of our predecessors already have. I do suggest, though, that we take advantage of this first month of a new year by making a fresh start. And here's what we can do...

JANUARY 1

New Year's Day. (See also Volume IV introduction.)

Birthdays of three American Revolutionary heroes: silversmith Paul Revere (1735), flag maker Betsy Ross (1752), General "Mad" Anthony Wayne, (1745).

The U.S. Congress officially prohibited African slave trade, 1808.

The Liberator was first published, 1831.

President Lincoln issued the Emancipation Proclamation, 1863.

Brooklyn merged with Manhattan, 1898.

The Trans-Siberian Railway started its maiden voyage, 1905.

Barry Goldwater was born, 1909.

The colonies of Cyrenaica, Tripoli, and Eezaan united to form the country of Libya, 1935.

Twenty-six nations signed the United Nations Declaration, 1942. (See January 9th and October 24th entries.)

INTRODUCTIONS

Some notable American patriots were born on New Year's Day. Paul Revere, the Bostonian silversmith who rallied American colonists to arms against the arriving British troops; Betsy Ross, maker of the new nation's banner; and General "Mad" Anthony Wayne, who led the charge on many British garrisons, were all born on this day. Outspoken spokesperson for Republican conservatism, Arizona state senator Barry Goldwater, was also a New Year's child. Their dedication to freedom and American ideals are foremost in the thoughts I want to share with you today.

New Year's is a day of both new beginnings and a renewed feeling of commitment to our beliefs. Some great Americans have pronounced their belief on this day that no man can own another. In 1863, President Lincoln issued his Emancipation Proclamation. It reinforced Congress' prohibition of African slave trade which occurred on the same day in 1808. In the first issue of his anti-slavery periodical, *The Liberator*, published on this day in 1832, William Lloyd Garrison proclaimed: "I am in earnest. I will not equivocate; I will not excuse; I will not retreat a single inch; and I will be heard." That sets a pretty high standard for all of us. But it's one which we should hope every person of moral conviction will aspire to in this coming year.

New Year's Day offers us an opportunity to cast aside our differences and resolve to renew our alliances. On this day in 1898, Brooklyn and Manhattan merged to create Greater New York. The Trans-Siberian Railway started on its maiden voyage on this day in 1905, joining a continent. The route united far away Vladivostok, Manchuria, with the world's culture capital—Paris, France. And in 1935, the North

African colonies of Cyrenaica, Tripoli, and Eezaan united to form the country of Libya. In 1942, this feeling of unity was felt worldwide when twenty-six nations signed the United Nations Declaration in Washington, D.C. It's in this spirit of brotherhood that I'd like to speak to you today.

J ANUARY 2

The Spanish army took the city of Granada from the Moors, 1492.

Queen Victoria declared, "We are not amused," 1900.

The first successful human heart transplant operation was performed, 1968.

The Dow Jones Industrial Average rose above the 2800 mark, 1990.

INTRODUCTIONS

Many of you are already spiritually in tune with the attitude voiced by Queen Victoria on this second day of the year in 1900, when she regally declared, "We are not amused." Certainly the Moors would have agreed with her in 1492, when on this date, the Spanish army took their beloved city of Granada. As we look back at those times, our own times certainly seem infinitely simpler. Everything and nothing is shocking or unexpected these days. We could probably sum up our attitude today by saying: "We are not amazed."

Our modern era may be characterized by escalating prices, but it's also elevated by great accomplishments. Dr. Christian Barnard achieved the unthinkable on this date in 1968. He performed the first successful human heart transplant operation, capturing the world's imagination and opening a whole new medical frontier. On the business front this was the day, in 1990, when the Dow Jones Industrial Average topped the 2800 mark for the first time in its history. New limitless boundaries are, indeed, all around us—some much closer than we think. I should like to discuss some of them with you here today.

J ANUARY 3

Cicero was born, 106 BC.

Martin Luther was excommunicated, 1521. (See October 31st and November 10th entries.)

The British seized control of the Falkland Islands, 1833.

Oscar Wilde told U.S. customs officials: "I have nothing to declare but my genius," 1882.

The March of Dimes was organized, 1938.

Alaska was given statehood, 1959.

The United States severed relations with Cuba, 1961. (See January 7th entry.)

Congress usually convenes on or about this date.

INTRODUCTIONS

It may be coincidental that Cicero's birthday occurs around the time when the U.S. Congress convenes in Washington D.C. Today's Senate or House of Representatives may not be oversupplied with golden voices like Cicero's, but it is safe to say that we have more voices, more issues, and probably more listeners. Hopefully, I will be received more gently than Martin Luther, who on this day in 1521, was excommunicated by the Roman Catholic Church for speaking his mind. Therefore, it behooves me to follow some sage rules for public speaking: "Get up, get going, get down to cases, and get off the stand."

When Alaska was given statehood on this day in 1959, it was the first time the U.S. admitted a territory outside of the forty-eight contiguous states. This is also the day when, in 1833, the British seized control of the Falkland Islands off the southernmost tip of South America. There is no telling what borders will change or who will lay claim to a given possession in the not-so-distant future. But in exploring those prospects with you here today, I will try to avoid Oscar Wilde's state of mind on this very day in 1882, when he said, "I have nothing to declare but my genius." I speak to you with no feeling of genius or prophecy whatsoever, but with a sense of deep conviction and a firm knowledge of my own boundaries.

There comes a time when people who have much in common disagree so violently they sever all ties to each other. This was the case in 1521, when Martin Luther, a man devoted to the purity of religious faith, was excommunicated by the Roman Catholic Church, the flagship of Christianity. Luther strongly protested a certain laxness that had become apparent amongst the clergy and the faithful, while the Church strongly objected to his criticisms. Also on this day, in 1961, the United States severed its relations with Cuba. American troops had fought for the island nation's freedom during the Spanish-American War, but the U.S., acting on strong anti-Communist feelings, sanctioned Castro's anti-imperialist government by refusing to trade or communicate—even though the island nation had officially recognized its new leader and government two years earlier. Now I know there are those of you in the audience who might not agree with what I'm about to say, but in a spirit of good relations I sincerely hope you won't disassociate yourself from our otherwise common cause.

The March of Dimes, an organization dedicated to fighting polio, a crippling disease that has affected millions worldwide, was organized on this date in 1938. An outgrowth of President Franklin Delano Roosevelt's Warm Springs Foundation, the

March of Dimes asks everyone to contribute what they can—a nickel, a dime, or a dollar—toward research, prevention, and treatment. A little help given by many people can add up to a mountain of support for a great cause. It is in this same spirit, that I ask you to donate a small portion of your time to listen to what I have to say today.

JANUARY 4

Sir Isaac Newton was born, 1642.

Shorthand inventor Sir Isaac Pitman was born, 1813.

First successful appendectomy was performed, 1885.

President Nixon rejected the Senate Watergate Committee's subpoenas, 1974. (See June 17th entry.)

INTRODUCTIONS

It's Sir Isaac Newton's birthday. Born in 1642, in Woolsthorpe, England, Newton grew up to have an apple fall on his head. This simple event inspired him. He discovered the law of gravity—simply, what goes up must come down. For today, I would like to repeal the law of gravity and impose the law of levity in its place. There is a time for our hearts to be light, and I would like this to be such a time. So I speak of pleasant, happy, and less weighty things.

Dr. William West Grant of Davenport, Iowa, proved on this day that man could live without an appendix. In 1885, he performed the first successful appendectomy. I will join Dr. Grant today. I will prove to you that a speaker can get along fine without an appended flow of extra words.

Inventor of the Pitman shorthand system, Sir Isaac Pitman was born on this day in 1813. His birthday reminds me not to trespass too heavily on your time today; and to extol the virtues of brevity and compactness. Following, so to speak, in his footsteps, I shall endeavor to make my remarks short and sweet.

I hope my remarks today will not be rejected by you in the same way President Richard M. Nixon refused the U.S. Senate Watergate subcommittee's subpoenas on this date in 1974. The subcommittee had requested copies of the President's White House tapes and documents so they could review his actions prior to the Watergate break-in. To ensure that kind of response won't happen here, and in the hope you won't think of this as fifteen minutes of blank tape, I promise to make all of my points public and perfectly clear.

JANUARY 5

Twelfth Night.

Voltaire said, "Opinion has caused more trouble on this little earth than plagues or earthquakes," 1759.

Wilhelm Roentgen discovered the x-ray, 1895. (See March 27th entry.)

Henry Ford announced a $5 minimum wage for an eight-hour workday, 1914.

George Washington Carver died, 1943. (George Washington Carver Day)

Pope Paul VI and Patriarch Athengoras of Jerusalem met in the Holy Land, 1964.

INTRODUCTIONS

Today marks Twelfth Night—the end of the Christmas season. Some of us may feel that in this era of shop-till-you-drop consumerism, Twelfth Night doesn't come soon enough. But today brings inspiration of its own.

George Washington Carver Day commemorates the death, in 1943, of a onetime slave who became a great inventor. Carver proved that the American dream isn't— or maybe is—peanuts. He gave us a hundred and one uses for the humble goober, proving that even simple or common things can provide solutions to greater problems. In that light, let's consider how we can solve our problems today with what we have at hand.

Automobile mogul Henry Ford started a trend on this day in 1914. He announced the establishment of two relatively revolutionary concepts for their time: an eight-hour workday and a $5-a-day minimum wage. As with many new ideas, most people thought he was crazy, heretical, or subversive. That is probably because, as Voltaire said on this very day in 1759, "Opinion has caused more trouble on this little earth than plagues or earthquakes."

A meeting that took place on this date in 1964, reminds me that no difference of opinion needs to permanently sever relations between people who share a common goal. This was the day when, for the first time in five centuries, the Roman Catholic Church met with the Eastern Orthodoxy. Pope Paul VI and Patriarch Athengoras of Jerusalem met in the Holy Land, ending the long-held belief that because they celebrated their Christianity in different ways, they had nothing else to share. Knowing that some of you in the audience have disagreed with me for a long time, I wish to preface today's remarks by asking each of you a simple question: "Are we really that different deep down inside where it counts?"

J A N U A R Y 6

Three Kings Day (Feast of the Epiphany).

Greek Cross Day.

Joan of Arc was born, 1412.

President Franklin D. Roosevelt made his "Four Freedoms" speech, 1941.

Pan Am Airlines completed the first around-the-world commercial flight, 1942.

Sherlock Holmes was allegedly born, 1854.

INTRODUCTIONS

Three Kings Day—also known as the Feast of the Epiphany—is a gift-giving holiday in many parts of the world. In light of this event, consider this: either I am giving you the gift of my eloquently expressed brilliance, or I am much more likely giving you the gift of not taking too much of your time.

Many residents of Tarpon Springs, Florida, and New York City celebrate today as Greek Cross Day. Devout men jump into the waters to retrieve Orthodox crosses in an ancient and always exciting combination of piety and athletics. Much of life—as well as public speaking—is like diving for a Greek Cross. You can get into deep water, and it can be cold. You can jump in quickly or slide in gracefully; then it's time to swim. I believe I have dwelt on this point sufficiently so I'll plunge right in to my prepared remarks.

There's more to life than living in the present. Visions of the future inspire us to live more fully. We are reminded of this simple truth today because it is Joan of Arc's birthday. The Maid of Orleans' visions changed the fate of an entire nation and its leader. Today's visions are often tomorrow's realities. So what do we envision today?

When President Franklin D. Roosevelt addressed the U.S. Congress on this day in 1941, he spoke of "a world founded upon four essential freedoms: freedom of speech and expression, freedom of every person to worship God in his own way, freedom from want, [and] freedom from fear." There is no field of human endeavor where these four freedoms are not—or should not be—the basic starting point of any discussion.

The freedom to travel anywhere in the world expanded its horizons on this date in 1942, when a Pan Am passenger plane completed the first around-the-world commercial flight. It fulfilled the dreams of anyone who ever wanted to see the world but didn't have eighty days to spare. With any luck, what I'm about to say will make some of your dreams and wishes come true just as quickly.

This is the birthday of a famous man who never lived, yet throughout the world, people have enjoyed his exploits, his brilliance, and his talent at deducing solutions. Sherlock Holmes was allegedly born on this day in 1854, according to his creator Sir Arthur Conan Doyle who fashioned the personality of the world's first consulting detective from one of his favorite teachers in medical school. Since I haven't got a clue as to what all of you are thinking right now, I will keep my remarks here today very elementary.

JANUARY 7

The first commercial American bank, the Bank of North America, opened, 1782.

The Baltimore & Ohio Railroad Company began rail service, 1830.

A cracking process to obtain gasoline from crude oil was patented, 1913.

President Harry S. Truman announced that the U.S. had developed a hydrogen bomb, 1953.

The United States recognized Fidel Castro's Cuban government, 1959.

Surveyor VII landed on the moon, 1968.

President Jimmy Carter said he favored a referendum on the future of Palestinians living in the Gaza Strip and West Bank, 1978. (See March 3rd entry.)

INTRODUCTIONS

This is the anniversary of a few newfangled ideas. In 1830, The Baltimore & Ohio Railroad Company started operating out of Baltimore, Maryland. Believe it or not, the first American train was drawn by a team of horses. But nothing can keep a good idea down. In 1968, the manned spaceship Surveyor VII landed on the moon. We have traveled a long, long way indeed. We span the universe as we once dared to span a continent. But we are always looking for better ways to bring people closer together, which is why I came here to speak with you today.

The first commercial American bank, the Bank of North America, opened in Philadelphia, Pennsylvania, on this day in 1782. Doing business strictly in cash is difficult and dangerous, especially if you want to expand your interests beyond your local area. When American businessmen decided to open an institution that could help them trade and negotiate with the rest of the world, they took a giant step toward national economic independence—an important freedom we must never forget. It behooves us, therefore, on this auspicious day to consider a few points that might accrue a little interest of their own.

It was on this date in 1913 that William M. Burton of Chicago, Illinois, was given a patent for a cracking process that enabled him to obtain gasoline from crude oil. His idea changed the way the world moves from one end of the globe to the other. Today, we may not necessarily appreciate the ultimate consequences of Mr. Burton's discovery, but it wasn't his concept that was the problem. It's the way in which it was used by others. For the same reasons, President Harry S. Truman should have heeded sounder advice before he announced the U.S. development of a hydrogen bomb on this same date in 1953. These two volatile inventions bring me to the point I would like to make to all of you: A sound idea is only the tip of the iceberg in any course of action. It's how we carry out that concept that truly judges our ability to think things through.

This is an ideal day to talk about peaceful coexistence. It was on this date in 1959 that the United States recognized Fidel Castro's government in Cuba. And it was on this very day in 1978 that President Jimmy Carter announced that he favored a referendum on the future of Palestinians living in the Israeli-held Gaza Strip and West Bank. Neither of these actions bore the fruit their authors anticipated. But the spirit that spurred them on was filled with the best of intentions. Inspired by these events, I hope to open a new forum for discussion and elicit, hopefully, a more bountiful outcome.

J ANUARY 8

Battle of New Orleans took place, 1815.

President Lyndon B. Johnson declared an "unconditional war on poverty in America," 1964.

INTRODUCTIONS

We don't widely celebrate this day as Battle of New Orleans Day. Some of us might not even know that Andrew Jackson defeated the British army in 1815. The War of 1812 was already over. But this battle was fought because neither side got the news in time. That, of course, is true of many battles in life. They are fought needlessly, because the issue has already been decided, or has disappeared. That is why speakers sometimes address nonissues like the sanctity of motherhood or the importance of kindness. But, even in the Battle of New Orleans, a point was made about the character of those who fought for what they believed was right. And today, without starting a war, I want to discuss some important points that I believe still need to be made.

Perhaps it's part of human nature that we view life as a battleground, but it need not be a combat zone. In 1964, during the Vietnam War, President Lyndon B. Johnson declared on this day an "unconditional war on poverty in America." Some aspects of that still undeclared and most assuredly unfinished war—the battle for a better life—are my topic today.

JANUARY 9

Adrian of Utrecht became Pope Adrian VI, 1522.

William Pitt, the elder, proclaimed: "Where law ends, tyranny begins—Unlimited power is apt to corrupt the minds of those who possess it," 1770.

President Richard M. Nixon was born, 1913.

American forces invaded the Philippine island of Luzon, 1945. (See October 20th entry.)

United Nations headquarters opened, 1951. (See January 1st and October 24th entries.)

Howard Hughes held a telephone news conference, 1972. (See March 13th entry.)

INTRODUCTIONS

It is surprising how time can sometimes jump a century or two, and past words or events can gain new impact. Today is such a day. In 1951, the United Nations headquarters opened in New York City. And in 1913, President Richard M. Nixon was born. But before these two events changed the way we envision world politics and world leadership, in 1770, William Pitt, the elder, told the British House of Lords: "Where law ends, tyranny begins" and "Unlimited power is apt to corrupt the minds of those who possess it." We are in a time when the question of where law ends is very real. And the challenge of the power that corrupts is ever-present. It is against that framework and in that perspective that I welcome this opportunity to speak with you today.

Sometimes, being the only one to accomplish a particular goal means being the last of your kind for a long time, and not everyone has the desire or inclination to be unique. This was the case with Adrian of Utrecht, who became Pope Adrian VI in 1522. This is the anniversary of the consecration of the only Dutch pontiff in history. Adrian VI was also the last non-Italian pope for over four hundred years. Luck sometimes plays a key role in life, but hard work and commitment are the deciding factors that single out certain individuals for a particular status in history's chronicles. Today, I would like to call your attention to someone who, like Adrian of Utrecht, is unique; who will remain unequaled for years to come.

Someone once said that promises are made to be broken. But today marks the anniversary of a promise that was fulfilled. U.S. Army General Douglas MacArthur had promised the Philippine people that he would rescue them from the oppression of Japanese occupation. In October 1944, he stepped on the shore of Leyte just as he had promised. But it was on this date in 1945 that he fulfilled his vow as American forces invaded the main island of Luzon, rescuing the country's capital. Not all promises are delivered in such epic proportions, but even the smallest ones deserve fulfillment. In the shadow of such an event, I stand before you today.

The truth sometimes comes from unexpected sources. And when the truth came from the voice of eccentric billionaire recluse, Howard Hughes, the whole world listened. On this date in 1972, Hughes held a telephone news conference—the first he had granted in fourteen years. He officially denounced the fraudulent biography of his life in that interview. Its author, Clifford Irving, had made a fortune with the book, which he claimed to have written with Hughes. But Hughes branded the book and its author as fakes. In the end, Irving paid dearly for his lies, because the truth became known. I would like to follow in Mr. Hughes' footsteps today.

J ANUARY 10

Ethan Allen was born, 1738.

The Texas oil boom started, 1901.

The first manmade contact with the moon was established, 1946.

Two Soviet cosmonauts were launched into space to dock with the Salyut 6 research station, 1978.

The U.S. and the Vatican re-established full diplomatic relations, 1984.

INTRODUCTIONS

Today is Ethan Allen's birthday. He grew up and became an American Revolutionary War commander. He knew his priorities when he declared, "In the name of the great Jehovah and the Continental Congress...." When he demanded the British surrender of Fort Ticonderoga, Allen regarded himself primarily as an instrument of a supreme Being or will; and as a servant of the Continental Congress. Nature always comes first. We must all apply our thoughts and our efforts in accordance with the larger, supreme laws of existence. My purpose here today is to state some particular thoughts against this broader framework.

We progress; we invest; we change. We are all subject to life's vagaries. And on this day in 1901, oil was discovered in Beaumont, Texas. It started an era of American prosperity and it introduced the world to a new energy source. Today we are very dependent upon finding a new resource because we now know that fossil fuels and other natural reserves are limited; and that no one person or country controls them indefinitely. We have discovered a need to find alternatives. Let us address ourselves today to our own energy and efforts. We must find options that will make things better for everyone.

Each and every one of us should try to keep our lines of communication open. Regular, consistent interaction with friends, associates, and family members provides us with new insights. Communication cements all kinds of relationships. It's a good theme for today, since this is the anniversary of some monumental connections. In 1946, the first manmade contact with our nearest neighbor—the moon—was established when radar signals were bounced off the lunar surface. In 1978, two Soviet cosmonauts were launched into space to dock with the Salyut 6 research station, creating an essential link between man and one of his creations. Even when links are broken, it doesn't mean they can't be mended. In 1984, the U.S. and the Vatican re-established full diplomatic relations after 117 years of silence. Those of us gathered today may not have truly communicated with each other for a long time. But considering these past events, isn't it a good time to renew our lines of communication with each other?

JANUARY 11

Caesar crossed the Rubicon River, 49 BC.

Great Britain held its first lottery, 1569.

Alexander Hamilton was born, 1755. (See July 11th entry.)

France and Belgium occupied the Ruhr Valley, 1923.

Amelia Earhart became the first woman to fly solo across the Pacific, 1935. (She completed the flight on January 12th.)

L. Douglas Wilder became Lieutenant Governor of Virginia, 1986. (See November 7th entry)

INTRODUCTIONS

A great personal life decision is sometimes described as "crossing the Rubicon." Today is the anniversary of Roman emperor Julius Caesar's crossing of the river Rubicon. In 49 BC, Caesar committed himself irrevocably to war against Pompey and the Roman Senate. "The die is cast," he said. For most of us, there is a personal Rubicon that, sooner or later, we have to cross. For whole nations, as well as individuals, this is such a time.

Human destiny is at least in part what we ourselves make it. Amelia Earhart set out to do what no woman had ever done before on this day in 1935. She set out to fly across the Pacific Ocean— from Honolulu, Hawaii, to Oakland, California. She accomplished both her goal and her destiny one day later. As this event proves, progress has a simple motto: Anything can be done. Anything can be done!

Take a good look at the face on a ten dollar bill today because it's Alexander Hamilton's birthday. Born on this day in 1755, this American Revolutionary War hero suffered a fate familiar to many of us. He was mortally wounded in a duel he fought against Aaron Burr. I mention Hamilton's story at the outset of these remarks as a reminder: None of us really knows what lies ahead. We must do what we can—as much as we can—as soon as we can. Tomorrow, after all, depends on what we do today.

Events have consequences that cannot be foreseen. Today is no exception. In 49 BC, Julius Caesar crossed the Rubicon River. In 1935, Amelia Earhart took a chance and became the first woman to fly from Honolulu, Hawaii to California. However, the consequences of an event that took place in 1569 had broader repercussions than the world could have ever anticipated. Great Britain held the world's first lottery in London's St. Paul's Cathedral. Call it luck. Call it calculated good fortune. Today, I hope that I have a winning combination of ideas, and perhaps I won't have to cross the Rubicon or the Pacific Ocean to convince you that they will work.

Failing to keep a promise can have some fatal repercussions. Germany discovered this simple truth in 1923, when France and Belgium occupied the Ruhr Valley after Germany failed to keep up its First World War reparation payments. No action stands isolated from another. And no one can say they don't affect others by their failure to act. I certainly hope that the actions I wish to discuss here will have a better outcome than today's historical event.

L. Douglas Wilder became Lieutenant Governor of Virginia on this day in 1986. What made this such a momentous occasion was that Wilder was the first African-American to become elected and sworn in as a Southern state official since the Civil War. Three years later, he became the nation's first elected African-American governor as well. Public attitudes are not written in stone. They change as regularly and as often as the ocean tides. I would like to look at a few of the ways we, the public, have changed for the better.

JANUARY 12

John Hancock was born in Braintree, MA, 1737.

First U.S. museum was established, 1773.

Jack London was born in San Francisco, CA, 1876.

Mrs. Hattie Caraway became the first elected female U.S. senator, 1932.

(Also see the January 11th Amelia Earhart entry.)

Astronauts aboard the space shuttle Columbia retrieved an 11-ton floating science lab, 1990.

President Bill Clinton signed an agreement to disarm the world's third largest nuclear arsenal, 1994.

INTRODUCTIONS

There are some landmark anniversaries for American women worth mentioning today. In 1935, Amelia Earhart single-handedly conquered the Pacific Ocean by flying from Honolulu, Hawaii, to Oakland, California. And in 1932, Mrs. Hattie Caraway became the first woman elected to the U.S. Senate. Women have come a long way since those days. They have crossed many frontiers: in science, in politics, and in business. You need only look around to find women availing themselves of a wide range of opportunities. Consider, if you will, the vast scope that we enjoy today.

The nation's first public museum dedicated to the preservation of knowledge was founded in Charleston, South Carolina, on this day in 1773. The Charleston Museum was a pioneer effort in the great tradition of public service and education that is the basis of today's remarks.

Signing one's "John Hancock" on an important document wouldn't mean much if, in 1737, John Hancock hadn't been born. He grew to become the first signer of the nation's Declaration of Independence, and unwavering dedication to his beliefs spurred him to make a big statement. He signed his name legibly so everyone could see that he stood by his convictions no matter what the cost. How many of us would be willing to publicly make such a commitment today? This is what I wish to consider with you now.

It's John Griffith Chaney's birthday. He was born in San Francisco in 1876 to a roving astrologer and his spiritualist wife. John's life reads like the plot of a novel. He quit school at the age of fourteen and explored the Bay area in a sloop. He rode the rails as a hobo and was even jailed for vagrancy. At the age of nineteen, he crammed a four-year high school course into one year and entered the University of California at Berkeley. But after a year, he went on the road to seek his fortune in the 1897 Klondike gold rush. He didn't find his fortune until he began writing, but when he did, we became richer for his efforts. We know him by his pen name—Jack London. His romantic adventure tales about the elemental struggle for survival— like *Call of the Wild, White Fang,* and *To Build a Fire*—remind us all that we must respect the indomitable spirit of man and beast alike—a theme I would like to expand on today.

The world as we know it was saved not once, but twice, on this date in history. In 1990, American astronauts aboard the space shuttle Columbia retrieved an 11-ton floating science lab. It was a rescue mission that kept the faltering satellite from plunging to earth. Four years later, in 1994, President Bill Clinton settled an agreement to disarm the world's third largest nuclear arsenal in the Ukraine, saving the entire world from potential manmade decimation. I didn't come here to talk about saving the world in quite the same way, but I do hope my remarks will save some of you from the world's worst threat: boredom.

J ANUARY 13

James Oglethorpe and 130 colonists arrived at Charleston, South Carolina, 1733.

Stephen Foster died, 1864. (Stephen Foster Memorial Day)

Émile Zola's article, "J'accuse," was published, 1898.

Robert C. Weaver became the first African-American cabinet member, 1966.

Michael Jordan became one of thirteen NBA players to accumulate at least 23,000 career points, 1996. (See February 17th and March 9th entries.)

INTRODUCTIONS

Ideas are the most powerful things in the world. Unlike chemical reactions or bombs, ideas that get planted are capable of unlimited growth. Today, on this very day in 1898, the Parisian writer Émile Zola published an article entitled "J'accuse" (I accuse). It was a written to defend the French soldier Alfred Dreyfus, who was being railroaded on treason charges. Zola's ideas aroused the emotions of France and the world. Before the case was over, not only was Captain Dreyfus vindicated, but the French government and military establishment were rocked to their heels and their attitudes drastically changed. This is the power of an idea.

A gentle man died on this day in 1864 at Manhattan's Bellevue Hospital. He rocked no governments; roused no great pangs of conscience. Born in 1826 in Lawrenceville, Pennsylvania, he died at the age of thirty-eight—penniless. He wrote songs, musical images of the American South. This is Stephen Foster Memorial Day—dedicated to the memory of the composer who wrote about the Swanee River; about the old folks at home; and about Jeannie with the light brown hair. Times change, and some of Foster's lyrics are no longer considered politically correct. But the essential bucolic, gentle spirit that he captured remains a part of the American heritage. It is in the shadow of his legacy that I speak to you today.

This seems to be a landmark day for successful beginnings. In 1733, James Oglethorpe and 130 colonists arrived at Charleston, South Carolina, on their way to settling what became the state of Georgia. But overcoming oppressive odds through courage and conviction is not limited to just this event. In 1966, Robert C. Weaver was appointed to the U.S. cabinet. President Lyndon Baynes Johnson made Weaver the Secretary of Housing and Urban Development. He was the first African-American to attain an executive-branch post. I hope our gathering here today is also an omen of good things to come.

On this day in 1996, in a showdown with the highly-touted Philadelphia 76ers rookie basketball player Jerry Stackhouse, Michael Jordan scored a game-high 48 points, making him one of 13 NBA players in basketball history to accumulate at least 23,000 career points. Jordan is a prime example of what one person can do if they aim for the heights. Even though he had left the profession to fulfill a lifelong dream, he returned eighteen months later and achieved even more. Each of us should set our goals that high. Who knows what new heights we could reach as individuals and as a group?

J ANUARY 14

Fundamental Orders of Connecticut were adopted, 1639.

Benedict Arnold was born, 1741.

The first successful, modern-day, Cesarean section was performed, 1794.

Albert Schweitzer was born, 1875.

Henry Ford started his first manufacturing assembly line, 1914.

Iran's Revolutionary Council expelled all American news correspondents, 1980.

President Bill Clinton and President Boris Yeltsin signed the Kremlin accords, 1994.

INTRODUCTIONS

Today is American traitor Benedict Arnold's birthday. Born in 1741, Arnold was a brave American Revolutionary soldier who decided to turn coat. But today is also the birthday of a man who symbolizes the good in human nature—service to one's fellow man, dedication, and sacrifice. In 1875, medical missionary, musician, and philosopher Dr. Albert Schweitzer was born in Kayersberg, Upper Alsace. These two men should remind us that human beings are not cast in a single mold. But we try as a society to reward good, and prevent evil. And in 1639, Americans developed a means of doing just that. The early settlers wrote a constitution entitled the Fundamental Orders of Connecticut. This document established a government by laws rather than by men. Individuals can be Benedict Arnolds or Albert Schweitzers or something in between; but a written constitution—a specific set of fundamental doctrines—to a large extent, saves us from ourselves. Look around us against a backdrop of constitutional doctrine and basic principle, and this is what we see.

Dr. Jesse Bennett of Edom, Virginia, performed the first successful modern-day Cesarean section on this day in 1794. What made this an even more monumental occasion was that he conducted this delicate surgery on his wife and brought their new infant child into the world. It takes a lot of faith, trust, and mutual support between people for some situations to go right. For couples, this simple truth is doubly important. As the lyrics of one popular song remind us: "You've got to stand by your man." You've also got to stand by your woman. Let's talk today about what can happen if you give your spouse that kind of unconditional love.

Henry Ford started his first manufacturing assembly line on this day in 1914. His concept of dividing labor into specialized activities executed by qualified people was not entirely new or original. Organizing a complex project into a series of simple tasks performed by a team of people wasn't unique—it was common sense. But it takes one man to make a sensible solution into a revolutionary trend. I don't think what I'm about to tell you will shock you, but with any luck, I will follow in Ford's footsteps and start a sensible trend.

As a wise man once said: Might does not always make right. On this day in 1980, the Irani Revolutionary Council expelled all American news correspondents from the country. The Shiite Muslim government felt they had the might of religion on their side as they proclaimed a new national order that excluded any other country. But their only reward for their actions was the world's disapproval. On this same day in 1994, President Bill Clinton and President Boris Yeltsin signed Kremlin accords to stop aiming missiles at any nation. After nearly half a century of imposing might, two of the world's largest nations decided peaceful coexistence was truly right. With that in mind, I would like to discuss how we can do what is right without employing might.

JANUARY 15

Reverend Dr. Martin Luther King, Jr. was born, 1929. (Martin Luther King, Jr. Day is celebrated on the Monday closest to this date.)

Kellogg-Briand Pact was ratified by the U.S. Senate, 1929.

INTRODUCTIONS

The Reverend Doctor Martin Luther King, Jr. was born in Atlanta, Georgia on this day in 1929. He did not live to see his vision progress; but certainly, on his day, we can see how far we have come toward the light of his dream. Today we each have a personal and moral obligation to examine the human condition and to ask how we can make it better.

Man is a creature of hope. Back in 1929, on this day when the Reverend Dr. Martin Luther King, Jr. was born in Atlanta, Georgia, the U.S. Senate ratified the Kellogg-Briand agreement for the peaceful settlement of international disputes. It was a general expression of hope. We know how well that worked! Ten years later the world was at war. But this anniversary reminds us that we keep on trying, over the years, and we are trying still.

JANUARY 16

André Michelin was born, 1853.

The Pendleton Act went into effect, 1883.

The Eighteenth Amendment to the U.S. Constitution went into effect, 1920. (See December 5th entry.)

Soviet cosmonauts achieved the first link between two manned spacecraft while in orbit, 1969.

The Commerce Department declared that the nation was in the worst recession since the Second World War, 1975.

Former CIA head Richard Helms reported that the agency was involved in domestic spying, 1975.

The Persian Gulf War began, 1991.

INTRODUCTIONS

Experimentation, we are told, is the road to progress. Today we mark the anniversary of what was called a "noble experiment." It didn't work, but we like to think that it taught us something. The experiment was Prohibition. In 1920, the Eighteenth Amendment, which prohibited the importation and sale of alcohol, went into effect. It was abandoned thirteen years later when the Twenty-first Amendment made liquor legal again. But in the meantime, we learned that in a democracy, the law depends on the people for its effectiveness. Perhaps that lesson was worth the experiment. At least we learned to create a public state of mind before imposing a new law. So it behooves us today to address ourselves to the question of what exactly do we want.

On this day in 1883 we thought we had solved the problem of governmental corruption. The Pendleton Act—a merit system of public employment—was enacted. When this system, known as the U.S. Civil Service, was established, we had no idea what infinite complications and ingenious devices would grow up around it, or that public sentiments toward it would dim. Has life grown more complicated? Or is it merely government that has grown more complicated? That is the question we must ask ourselves today.

A Michelin baby was born on this day in 1853. André Michelin grew to become the French industrialist who first mass-produced rubber tires for automobiles. Thanks to Michelin, our travels are much more comfortable than those of our forefathers who, for centuries, rode on cushionless, metal-rim wheels. Hopefully, my comments to you today will have the same effect that Michelin's rubber tires had on automobile driving: I'd like to take you on a comfortable cruise, and not a bumpy ride.

Getting together for a common cause can sometimes be a complex maneuver. If you were one of the Soviet cosmonauts who achieved the first link between two manned spacecraft while orbiting around the earth on this date in 1969, you'd know what I mean. Luckily, most of us are willing to go to great lengths to communicate with each other. The outcome is always better if we do. Otherwise, we could end up like the allied U.N. forces did on this day in 1991: after a five-month standoff with Iraq and Iraqi-held Kuwait, the Persian Gulf War began with the bombing of military and industrial targets. You and I both know which avenue makes more sense.

It may always be darkest before the dawn, but on this day in 1975, no one was sure if we'd ever see the light of day again. The Commerce Department declared that the nation was in the worst recession since the Second World War. And to add insult to injury, former CIA head Richard Helms reported to the U.S. Congress that the agency had been involved in domestic spying since the late 1950s because of an upsurge in radicalism. As you all know, we lived through those crises. So, what I'm about to present should seem pretty tame by comparison.

JANUARY 17

St. Anthony the Abbot, died, 46 AD.

Benjamin Franklin was born, 1706.

Andrew Hallidie patented the cable car, 1871.

INTRODUCTIONS

Benjamin Franklin, was born on this day in 1706 in Boston, Massachusetts. This American patriot is remembered more as a writer—an inventor, a leader, and a diplomat—than as a speaker, but many a speaker has built his oratory on Franklin's wisdom. He wrote in his publication, *Poor Richard's Almanac*, that: "A word to the wise is enough and many words won't fill a bushel." In that spirit, I shall not try to pile up a bushel's worth of words, but shall speak in full confidence that what I am about to say, as far as this audience is concerned, is most assuredly a word to the wise.

Today is the feast day of St. Anthony the Abbot, the patron saint of animals. On this day, in many parts of the world, animals are formally blessed. It is a fitting commentary on our present way of life, therefore, to look at the way we treat animals. How do we care for our pets? How do we respect the wild beasts? What do we do for the creatures of the earth? I think the answers to these questions can provide an allegory for the quality of life today.

Life is often described as a battle: man against nature, man against beast, man against man. One story that began on this day, in 1871, can be viewed in this light. Andrew Hallidie patented the cable car. In 1869, this 33-year-old wire manufacturer watched a horse-drawn streetcar struggle up a steep hill in the rain. Determined to improve public transport in San Francisco, he finally installed the cable-car system two years later. The public laughed it off as "Hallidie's Folly." San Francisco has buses, subways, and cars now, but every time someone suggests discontinuing the cable cars, San Franciscans insist on keeping them. Life may be a series of struggles and people might call some of the outcomes follies. But it is in the present light where we judge life's events as signs of progress.

JANUARY 18

Captain James Cook discovered the Sandwich Islands, 1778.

Daniel Webster was born, 1782.

Captain Robert Scott reached the South Pole, 1912 (See December 14th entry.)

INTRODUCTIONS

For a public speaker, this is either a very auspicious or a very challenging day. It is Daniel Webster's birthday. Born in 1872, Webster was America's most awesome public orator. You may recall Stephen Vincent Benet's story, "The Devil and Daniel Webster," in which this eloquent speaker argued the case for a man's soul and won. I am no Daniel Webster, but I hope his spirit will at least loosen my tongue as I rise to address you today.

Being second best somehow has never meant quite what it should. This thought comes to mind today because on this date in 1912, a great explorer came in second and, was subsequently forgotten. This was the day when British explorer Captain Robert Scott reached the South Pole. It was a heroic feat, made even more memorable because Scott and his party died on the way back. But Scott's glory was greatly dimmed, because Roald Amundsen had reached the pole a month earlier—and he survived. There is no disgrace in being second; but there is little glory. We all have a tendency to revel in "firsts," perhaps at the expense of those who tried just as hard. And so today I would like to talk about a number of things that we have tried to do and succeeded, even though we weren't the first.

Polynesians had been inhabiting the Hawaiian islands since 400 AD. They had sailed from the Marquesa Islands and Tahiti to find a new paradise. But today's anniversary commemorates another discovery of these inhabited islands. In 1778, British explorer Captain James Cook landed on the Hawaiian Islands and renamed them after his mentor. He called them the Sandwich Islands—after the Earl of Sandwich. It got pretty confusing after that. The British called Hawaii one thing, while the island group's royal kings referred to their land by another. What's in a name, you might ask. Names can be confusing, especially when they refer to exactly the same place or thing. Categories have a similar effect when different groups apply totally different labels to the same person.

J ANUARY 19

James Watt was born, 1736.

Robert E. Lee was born, 1807. (See April 9th entry.)

Tin canning process for food was patented, 1825.

Paul Cézanne was born, 1839.

The Bolsheviks dissolved the Russian Constitutional Assembly, 1918. (See November 7th entry.)

Indira Gandhi became prime minister of India, 1966. (See November 19th and June 6th entries.)

The American Psychiatric Association urged a tightening of the rules for the use of the insanity plea in criminal trials, 1983.

INTRODUCTIONS

Most of us are faced with an important decision at some point in our lives. But few of us ever have the kind of choices that were extended to Robert E. Lee, who was born on this day in 1807. He was offered the command of the Union Army. He decided instead to become the Commander of the Confederate Army. Despite his ultimate defeat in the Civil War, he was a great American. What he so amply demonstrated was that men can find themselves even in lost causes; that nobility of spirit can somehow survive and triumph over defeat. These are certainly things worth remembering as we share here today some thoughts about our own times.

Some people and events stand as milestones in the chronicles of human progress. One such person is James Watt, who was born on this day in 1736. He saw how steam could be harnessed; and he actualized his thoughts by designing a steam engine. Since his time many other types of engines have been produced; but Watt inaugurated our machine-oriented age. On his birthday, it is timely to ask ourselves what we have done with the greater horizons that his concept made possible.

Today I would like to tell you about Ezra Daggett and Thomas Kinsett. Their names are not household words; but their invention is in every household. In 1825, on this day, the Kinsetts of New York City patented a process for canning food in tin containers. They can be said to have pioneered the age of convenience. Not every revolutionary invention enjoys this sort of immortal fame. And so it behooves us to remember that what each of us does can have more of an impact than we know. Today I call your attention to some other little noted examples that have ushered in big changes in our lives.

Some people are not affected by criticism. And Paul Cézanne, who was born on this day in 1839, was one of them. From the day he began to paint, he was severely criticized for the content and execution of his works. But he didn't give in to convention. He continued to search for bold expression rather than realistic representation. At the 1899 Salon des Independents in Paris, he finally achieved the acclaim he deserved. And as the century turned, Cézanne became known as the strongest influence on twentieth-century Cubist painters like Picasso and Georges Braque. Following the tides of public opinion does not necessarily yield masterpieces. To make a mark in this world, one has to forge ahead despite bad reviews from short-sighted critics.

The American Psychiatric Association urged a tightening of the rules for the use of the insanity plea in criminal trials on this day in 1983. So I guess I can't use that as my defense if I do you in with my comments here today.

JANUARY 20

Presidential Inauguration Day, 1937 to present.

The first basketball game was played, 1892.

George Burns was born, 1896.

INTRODUCTIONS

Anyone who rises to speak on this day speaks in the shadow or the glory of some of the most noble phrases ever uttered, phrases spoken by men as they were inaugurated President of the United States. Since 1937, January 20th has been Presidential Inauguration Day. Franklin D. Roosevelt saw "one third of a nation ill-housed, ill-clad, ill-nourished"; John F. Kennedy urged his fellow Americans to "ask not what your country can do for you; ask what you can do for your country"; Harry S. Truman observed that "the supreme need of our time is for men to learn to live together in peace and harmony"; and Dwight D. Eisenhower said that "whatever America hopes to bring to pass in the world must first come to pass in the heart of America." What better introduction than these great words to my humble remarks today?

In a Springfield, Massachusetts meeting hall, on this day in 1892, a YMCA worker named James Naismith introduced a great medium for international communication. It wasn't intended that way. Basketball was simply a game. But Naismith's game did not merely catch on. It took the world by storm. It is played everywhere—from alleys and schoolyards to stadiums and Olympic courts. Basketball has brought glory to its players, and inspiration to its fans. It has the frailties of every sport—the exaggerated competitiveness, the tensions, the unbridled rewards and anxieties. But the game also supersedes language and cultural barriers, creating a common ground that many people understand. This is indeed a worthy theme to explore at this time and in this place.

Few people have ever lived for an entire century, but entertainer George Burns did. Born on this day in 1896, this native New Yorker kept audiences laughing for almost the entire century. Now, without borrowing a line, a cigar, or a martini from Mr. Burns, let's see if I can give you a few pointers to remember, and if not, I'll just say "Goodnight Gracie."

JANUARY 21

Stonewall Jackson was born, 1824.

New York City prohibited women from smoking in public, 1908.

Alger Hiss was convicted of perjury, 1950.

First atomic-powered submarine was launched, 1954.

The supersonic Concorde was put into service, 1976. (See November 22nd entry.)

INTRODUCTIONS

Adversity is a school of hard knocks; but its alumni often shine. Today marks the birth, in 1824, of a man who symbolizes the integrity of stubborn courage. Thomas Jackson is better known to most of us as "Stonewall" Jackson. He was not merely a great Confederate Army leader during the Civil War; he personified strength and steadfastness. At a time when we are called upon to stand fast for fundamental beliefs, it is only fitting to recall the man who, in Robert E. Lee's famous phrase, stood like a stone wall. Who and where are our stone walls today?

Occasionally the act of one individual dwarfs an historical event with the passing of time. Such was the case of a trial which ended on this day in 1950. A confessed Communist, Whittaker Chambers, accused former State Department official, Alger Hiss, of being a Communist agent. Hiss was convicted of perjury, but the trial brought a young California Congressman to even greater worldwide attention. Even though the trial was a cause celebre at the time, it also launched Richard M. Nixon's career. We speak and act, at any given moment, without really knowing what the lasting effect, if any, will be—and so we must be ever-mindful that we are on trial, awaiting a future verdict in history's courtroom. What will history say of us?

The first atomic-powered submarine, the U.S.S. Nautilus, was launched on this day in 1954 at Groton, Connecticut. Atomic power—and we along with it—seem to have been getting into deep water ever since. This is the modern dilemma: How much can and should we venture to make life easier? Not all modern-day inventions have conjured such doomsday premonitions or harbored potentially fatal consequences. On this same day in 1976, the supersonic Concorde passenger jet was put into service in England and France. It took construction of a second one before service was expanded to include New York City. Even though they fly faster, have proven themselves to be safer, and have lasted longer than more conventional passenger jet craft, there were never any other supercraft of this kind built. How much failure to venture forth makes life harder than it should be? Where is the line to be drawn and who is to draw it? These are the broad questions which dominate all others in the world today.

New York City prohibited women from smoking in public on this day in 1908. The lighting and inhaling of tobacco may not be socially correct in today's world, but the point made by early city forefathers was even less in keeping with our present belief that women should have equal rights to succeed or fail in any endeavor they choose to perform—even smoking. My point in telling you this is simple: Laws may be made, but it takes the people's consent to write them into the stones of social acceptance. Fortunately, I can report to all of you that—to coin the phrase of one popular advertisement—"We have indeed come a long way, baby."

JANUARY 22

Great Britain's Queen Victoria died, 1901. (See June 20th and May 24th entries.)

The "Bloody Sunday" massacre occurred in St. Petersburg, Russia, 1905.

Zulu warriors won the battle of Isandlwana in South Africa, 1879.

INTRODUCTIONS

Not too many people give their name to a whole era, but Great Britain's Queen Victoria did. In a literal sense, the Victorian era ended on this day in 1901, when, after ruling the empire for six decades, Victoria Regina died. She personified a way of life, and the spirit of a civilization that believed in virtues like responsibility, dignity, and human obligation. And so, on the anniversary of her death, one may well ask what we have now to take the place of such Victorian values.

A major turning point in history occurred on this date in 1905. The Russian Czar's soldiers fired on a group of peaceful demonstrators in front of the St. Petersburg palace. They were gathered to plead for better living and working conditions. Not only were many killed; thousands were arrested and sent to prison or to Siberian labor camps. We know now that had the Czar's forces been less repressive and their actions less bloody, there might not have been a Bolshevik revolution. The twentieth-century's history might have been different. Yet, as we look around, we also know of more recent "Bloody Sundays" and we have a right to wonder what turning points they are creating in our future.

On this day in 1879, King Cetewayo and 20,000 Zulu warriors overwhelmed a well-trained British military regiment led by Lord Chelmsford at Isandlwana, South Africa. Only forty British soldiers managed to escape. In their push to expand the British empire from "Cairo to the Cape," military and political leaders were unprepared for the strategic brilliance of guerrilla warfare that the spear-and-shield-bearing Zulu warriors employed. The commissioned British troops were also not prepared to fight the courageous spirit and patriotic pride which King Cetewayo had instilled in his people. It took another twenty years before the British adopted the same strategy—but they never nurtured the same spirit. Learning from and adapting to new surroundings takes more than mimicking what you see. It sometimes means acquiring new feelings as well. One never knows when the right spirit will be your best ally as you turn the bends on life's road.

J A N U A R Y   2 3

King Henry VIII took the title of King of Ireland, 1542.

Dr. Elizabeth Blackwell received the first M.D. awarded to an American woman, 1849.

The Soviet government officially severed relations with the church, 1918.

Soviet leaders confessed to an anti-Stalinist conspiracy, 1937.

The Knesset proclaimed Jerusalem as Israel's capital, 1950.

Poll tax was barred in U.S. Federal elections, 1964.

INTRODUCTIONS

Today is a very significant anniversary for women, and for rest of us who would be nothing without women. In 1849, Dr. Elizabeth Blackwell—a native of Bristol, England—became the first female American doctor to receive her medical degree at the Medical Institution of Geneva, New York. This was also a milestone in the annals of the relationship between men and women. It was and still is a topic not just for today's speech but for many more to come.

Today is a good day to remember that no individual or group should control the thoughts of another. On this date in 1937, a group of seventeen Soviet Russian leaders confessed in court to an anti-Stalinist conspiracy allegedly led by Leon Trotsky who had been living in exile for years. Why and how they came to confess brought psychological warfare—"brain washing"—to the world's attention. It's a good time to raise the question of how much we can impose our beliefs on others, and what we can expect in return.

Voting is a right, not just a privilege. And in 1964 on this date, the American government stamped its agreement to this belief. The Twenty-fourth Amendment to the U.S. Constitution went into effect. You no longer had to pay for the privilege of casting your vote; the Federal election poll tax was officially barred. This provides an excellent text for the present day. Citizenship is not merely a privilege; it is a collection of rights. How well are we doing with protecting and advancing those rights?

This seems to be a perfect day for make sweeping proclamations. On this day in 1542, England's King Henry VIII took the title "King of Ireland." In 1950, The Knesset—Israel's parliament—proclaimed Jerusalem as that nation's capital. Both pronouncements were not readily embraced by all. The dissenters did not quietly voice their objections. In light of these events, I promise you, here and now, my proclamation will not be a sweeping generality made on my own behalf. My announcement, it is hoped, will please all of you.

On this day in 1918, the Soviet government officially severed longstanding close relations between the Russian government and the Orthodox Church. All church property including land, houses of worship, relics, and icons were seized by state officials. In return, the church was guaranteed freedom of religious worship in the Soviet constitution, and freedom to be subjected to antireligious propaganda. The segregation of church and state has long been a political issue in many parts of the world. Should government offer support to religious concerns, or should it pay in tribute to Caesar that which is Caesar's? That is a question we still face today.

JANUARY 24

Roman Emperor Caligula was murdered, 41 AD.

John W. Marshall discovered gold at Sutter's Mill, California, 1848.

Edward John Phelps said, "The man who makes no mistakes does not usually make anything else," 1899.

Canned beer first went on sale in the U.S., 1935.

The space shuttle Discovery was launched in the NASA program's first secret military flight, 1985.

INTRODUCTIONS

Today is the anniversary of a death that few people mourned—even when it happened. In 41 AD, the Roman emperor Gaius was murdered by two of his own Praetorian guards. Gaius' nickname was Caligula—or Little Boot—because he was fond of dressing up in soldier's uniforms, but in the end he led no one. The 28-year-old Caligula had just declared himself a god, but his generals, troops, and subjects did not agree. They had been terrorized by Caligula's cruelty and depravity throughout his brief, four-year reign. Becoming a leader does not mean people will automatically obey orders or follow your cause. Effective leaders inspire their followers through sound judgment and good example. I would like to inspire you for a few minutes and I promise not to repeat Caligula's orders.

The lure of gold is a potent force. It enticed European explorers to brave the unknown on both American continents, Africa, and Australia. Today, the prospect of gold attracts nations to claim portions of land near the north and south poles. A landmark gold discovery was made on this day in 1848. John W. Marshall found gold in a millrace of the American River at Sutter's Mill, California. When word got out, thousands of people headed west to seek their fortunes. The '49er gold rush opened the rest of the American wilderness from the Montana mountains to the Mexican deserts. It set the groundwork for the arrival of what we now laughingly call civilization. A few decades later, the Yukon's gold lured men and women to battle the frigid, northwest wilderness. Few things provoke and inspire people like potential wealth—especially the promise of finding a goldmine. And it leaves us to wonder what will lure us to unknown territories in the years to come?

In 1899, lawyer-diplomat Edward John Phelps made a speech on this day in which he said, "The man who makes no mistakes does not usually make anything." That is my text for today. We need to dare. We need to do things. We cannot fear our mistakes.

A great, modern-day convenience first went on sale in Richmond, Virginia, on this date in 1935. It changed the way men relax. This invention meant more wives were saved from abandonment in the evenings by errant spouses. Children were no longer sent off to the local saloon to fill their father's pail. Why? Canned beer first went on sale in the U.S. Not every manmade creation has dire or earth-shaking consequences. Some great ideas just make life a little easier. Though I'm not suggesting we head out for a beer, perhaps my ideas will make life easier, too.

Not all discoveries become public knowledge as quickly as John Marshall's gold strike at Sutter's Mill, California, did on this day in 1848. In fact, the space shuttle Discovery's mission—which was launched on this very day in 1985—was the NASA space program's first secret military flight. Some things are better kept secret amongst a select few. Before I begin my remarks today, I would like to ask all of you: Can you keep a secret?

J ANUARY 25

Robert Burns was born, 1759.

Nellie Bly completed her trip around the world, 1890.

Transcontinental U.S. telephone service began, 1915. (See March 3rd and March 7th entries.)

Pope John XXIII called an ecumenical council, 1959.

American Airlines flew the first scheduled transcontinental Boeing 707 jet flight, 1959.

INTRODUCTIONS

This was a red-letter day for Elizabeth Cochrane, who wrote for *The New York World* under the pen name of Nelly Bly. In 1890, she completed her amazing trip around the world in 72 days, 6 hours, and 11 minutes. On this same day in 1915, Alexander Graham Bell spanned the North American continent without leaving home. He made the first transcontinental phone call from New York to San Francisco. Another giant step toward bringing the world closer together took place on this day in 1959. Pope John XXIII called for the assembly of the Second Ecumenical Council to explore international unity. I think it is fair to say that the echoes of these past events have inspired me to reach out to all of you today.

American Airlines flew the first scheduled transcontinental Boeing 707 jet flight from California to New York on this day in 1959. Life in the corporate world hasn't been the same since. Within three decades, bi-coastal has defined a lifestyle for many ambitious business executives—as well as modern dual-income couples. A quick power breakfast in Beverly Hills or a hard-driving dinner negotiation in Manhattan is a simple red-eye flight away. Who said you can't have your cake and eat it, too? This is one day when it's going to be hard to convince me you can't.

Today is poet Robert Burns' birthday. Born in 1759, this native son of Scotland lived only 37 years, but his words have lived on, finding a place in the hearts of every generation that followed. But it's not in the spirit of Auld Lang Syne that I'd like to speak with you today. Robert Burns loved the simple things in life, and showed the world the nobility of the common man...

JANUARY 26

Australia was settled by the British, 1778. (Australia Day)

Benjamin Franklin wrote to his daughter, 1784.

Daniel Webster replied to Senator Hayne, 1830.

The electric dentist's drill was patented, 1875.

Douglas MacArthur was born, 1875.

INTRODUCTIONS

Today is Australia Day, which commemorates the country's settlement by the British in 1778. Ordinarily, this would only be of interest to Australians, but it has very real meaning for all of us. If the American Revolutionary War had not been raging at the same time, Australia's first settlers—who were all convicts—would have been sent to America, a land settled by people seeking religious and political freedom. Even though these convicts were deemed bad by British law, the goodness in these men emerged. They worked together to overcome a harsh environment and inspired many other strong spirits to join them. Australia Day gives us a timely reminder today that we must have faith that in each of us there is goodness, and working together we can find strength.

The U.S. Senate was the scene of an impartial debate on this day in 1830. At one point in the argument over states' rights and nullification, the eloquent statesman Daniel Webster summarized the cornerstone of our nation's doctrines in a reply to Senator Hayne: "Liberty and Union, now and for ever, one and inseparable." They remain our watchwords—liberty and union. Let us consider what they mean today.

It won't be difficult to convince you that today could be better than it ever was on this same date in history. Benjamin Franklin was very disappointed on this day in 1784. He wrote to his daughter to say that he was unhappy about a sensitive government decision: The bald eagle had been chosen as America's national bird. He thought that the wild turkey—a noble, intelligent bird in Franklin's mind—should be the national symbol. Needless to say, he didn't win. And in 1875, a patent was granted to George F. Green of Kalamazoo, Michigan, for a machine that continues to strike fear in even the strongest of us. The electric dentist's drill was patented. Considering these past events, I certainly hope what I'm about say won't disappoint you or be as painful as having your teeth drilled.

Some people say that people are very much a product of their surroundings. Was this the case with General Douglas MacArthur? Born on this day in 1875 at a U.S. Army barracks in Little Rock, Arkansas, MacArthur grew up with the sights and sounds of military life from the moment he opened his eyes. He grew to become the nation's greatest military leader during the Second World War. If our environment affects our future to such an extent, shouldn't we ask ourselves how we can provide future generations with surroundings that will inspire them to even greater heights?

JANUARY 27

Wolfgang Amadeus Mozart was born, 1756.

Charles Lutwidge Dodgson was born, 1832. (See July 4th entry.)

Samuel Gompers was born, 1850.

The electric light bulb was patented, 1880.

The National Geographic Society was incorporated, 1888.

An Air Force plane dropped a one-kiloton atom bomb, 1951.

France officially recognized the People's Republic of China, 1964.

Three U.S. astronauts were killed in a fire aboard their Gemini spacecraft, 1967.

The U.S. military draft ended when the Vietnam peace accords were signed in Paris, 1973.

INTRODUCTIONS

I doubt that my remarks today will be able to shed as much light as an illuminating event that happened on this anniversary. On this date in 1880, Thomas A. Edison received a patent for his incandescent electric light bulb. It has been easier to shed light in dark places ever since, thanks to Edison's invention; and people have also been seeking to turn off the lights since then. I rise here today to suggest that a more old-fashioned method of shedding light in dark places is still in order. I rise on behalf of that ancient custom of asking questions. Here are a few bright ideas about some areas where I believe we need to shed new light.

Today, we celebrate the life of a musical prodigy. Born on this date in Austria in 1756, Wolfgang Amadeus Mozart went on to write 626 musical compositions—including operas, symphonies, sonatas, and concerti—during his short, 35-year life span. If he had been asked to come before such a group as this, he would probably have written a timeless masterpiece for the occasion. For those of us, however, to whom musical or verbal masterworks do not come easily, there are still opportunities to be heard, and I thank you for giving me an opportunity tonight.

I wonder how much—if anything—these names mean to you: Virgil Grissom, Edward White, and Roger Chaffee. Some of you may recognize them as the three astronauts who were killed in an Apollo spaceship fire at Cape Kennedy, Florida. It happened on this day in 1967. I mention it to remind you that while we have our eyes on the skies, trouble may be right at our feet. These astronauts did not die in outer space; their tragic accident occurred right on the ground. Even though we look far and wide for the causes of our problems, we must also remember to keep our sights on what is happening here at home.

Charles Lutwidge Dodgson was born on this day in Daresby, England, in 1832. An ingenious mathematician and logician who studied at Oxford University, Dodgson achieved his greatest fame when he wrote under the pen name of Lewis Carroll. His two famous novels, *Alice in Wonderland* and *Through the Looking Glass & What Alice Found There*, were written to entertain a pretty ten-year-old whose name was coincidentally Alice Pleasance Liddell. Carroll wrote the perfect introductory verses for my remarks here today, which go: 'The time has come,' the Walrus said, / 'To talk of many things: / Of shoes-and ships-and sealing wax- / Of cabbages-and-kings- / And why the sea is boiling hot- / And whether pigs have wings.'

In the early part of this century, American laborers needed strong representation to attain a humane quality of life in the newly industrialized society. Decent wages, reasonable working hours, and fair treatment were not always easy to get. When Samuel Gompers was born in London, England, on this day in 1850, child labor, low wages, and 14-hour workdays were still common practices in factories. At the end of his nearly forty-year career, Gompers changed that tide in labor. When he emigrated with his family to the U.S. in 1863, he followed his father's trade and became a cigar-maker. He gained his worldwide reputation by leading the national cigar-makers union away from the Knights of Labor to form the American Federation of Labor—the AFL—and by promoting voluntarism. Gompers believed that unions should use strikes and boycotts to achieve their aims. He also encouraged them to apply written trade agreements and to establish national jurisdiction over the numerous local unions that existed. Every great cause has had its champions. Who will be our Samuel Gompers in the future?

On this date, in 1888, the doors to a whole new world opened for many generations of Americans—young and old alike. They led to faraway lands and peoples; introduced us to little-seen portions of the natural world; and showed us glimpses of our past and future through the eyes of great scientists, explorers, and photographers. Thanks to a suggestion made by the telephone's inventor Alexander Graham Bell, these worlds were not just documented in words. There were pictures, pictures, and more pictures. This is the anniversary of The National Geographic Society's incorporation in Washington, D.C., with Bell's son-in-law as its editor-in-chief. In the same spirit in which this organization continues to support exploration and open our eyes to the world around us, I only hope I can also introduce you to some insights into our own human nature—even though I didn't bring any photographs.

Decisive events of war and peace have occurred on this particular day in history. In 1951, a U.S. Air Force plane dropped a one-kiloton atom bomb on Frenchman Flats, Nevada, ushering in another phase in the nuclear arms race. On a more peaceful note, in 1964, France officially recognized the People's Republic of China; and in 1973, the U.S. military draft was discontinued when the Vietnam peace accords were signed in Paris. Since this day also seems to tie in with things that are French, I would like to quote Victor Hugo to open today's remarks: "There is one thing stronger than all the armies in the world, and that is an idea whose time has come."

J ANUARY 28

Edward VI became King of England, 1547.

Wendell Phillips said, "There is nothing stronger than human prejudice," 1852.

The *Yale News* was first published, 1878.

Louis D. Brandeis was nominated to U.S. Supreme Court, 1916. (See November 13th entry.)

INTRODUCTIONS

If we care to measure our nation's progress, today's landmark anniversary provides a convenient yardstick. On this date in 1916, Louis D. Brandeis became the first Jewish-American to be nominated to the U.S. Supreme Court. Today there seems to be nothing particularly remarkable about that appointment. Brandeis' name lives on not only in his historic opinions and dissents, but in the title of a great American university. But in his time, his nomination aroused a tremendous public furor. His ethnic origins and his liberal views made him repugnant to many Americans. Ladies and gentlemen, we have come a long way since then. We have not defeated political, religious or racial prejudice; but we have learned that great men surmount labels. We have learned that healthy nations allow minority beliefs. We know that all peoples need their champions. Times have changed, but how far along the path of mutual respect and open opportunity have we truly progressed?

On this date in 1852, New England orator and abolitionist leader Wendell Phillips said, "There is nothing stronger than human prejudice." How far have we come? Can we rest on our laurels, or is human prejudice still the world's strongest power—and if so, where is it taking us?

It is often said that children are our investment in our future. And today is the anniversary of two events where this saying rang true. In 1547, the nine-year-old Prince of Wales, Edward VI, succeeded his father Henry VIII as king of England. On a more academic note, in 1878, the *Yale News*—the first daily college newspaper—was first published in New Haven, Connecticut. Glimpses into our future can be readily found in the eyes of our youth. Let's discuss how we can help them find themselves before it's too late.

J ANUARY 29

President William McKinley was born, 1843.

John D. Rockefeller, Jr. was born, 1874.

The U.S. Congress established a commission to decide the Hayes-Tilden election, 1877.

INTRODUCTIONS

When I was preparing my remarks for this occasion, I found something both interesting and heartening in the history books. On this date in 1877, the tangle of charges and confusion over the 1876 Presidential election was so thick that the U.S.

Congress established a special Electoral Commission to decide whether Samuel Tilden or Rutherford B. Hayes had been elected. We have had our fair share of political spider webs and special commissions since then. But I speak to you today not as a cynic. Rather, I am one who is convinced that, however slowly, we do move onward and upward.

Not too long ago, a politician criticized a particular concept of public policy as "creeping McKinleyism." That was possibly the only modern reference to the turn-of-the-century U.S. President who was born on this date in 1843. President William McKinley symbolized a totally passé style of laissez-faire conservatism. But he is best remembered because he was assassinated. Teddy Roosevelt became President after McKinley's death. Roosevelt reputedly ushered in modern American politics. We have a great tendency to think in eras; to compartmentalize time into ages. Tonight I propose to challenge that tendency: by talking about present problems. I don't mean to discuss how modern they may be, but rather how long we have some-how failed to solve them.

One of America's greatest philanthropists was born on this day. In 1874, John D. Rockefeller, Jr. was born. Heir to the Standard Oil Company fortune, this only son of founder John D. Rockefeller, Sr., built New York City's famous Rockefeller Center and was instrumental in the selection of the city as the site for the United Nations' world headquarters. He also donated to the construction of the Lincoln Center for the Performing Arts; the restoration of colonial Williamsburg, Virginia; Manhattan's Museum of Modern Art; and the establishment of the United Services Organization which is better known as the USO. As the world's richest man, Andrew Carnegie, once said: "A man who dies rich, dies in disgrace." John D. Rockefeller, Jr. never gave away his entire fortune, but the $250 million he did con-tribute to the arts, education, and charitable aid serves as inspiration for us all. I wish I had millions to give away, but my words will have to suffice. I hope you can find some value in them.

J ANUARY 30

The Articles of Confederation were adopted by Maryland, 1781. (See November 15th entry.)

Richard Lawrence tried to assassinate President Andrew Jackson, 1835.

Franklin D. Roosevelt was born, 1882.

Crown Prince Rudolf of Austria and Baroness Marie Vetsera committed suicide at Mayerling, Austria, 1889.

Adolf Hitler became Chancellor of Germany, 1933.

Mohandas Mahatma Gandhi was assassinated, 1948.

British soldiers shot and killed thirteen civil rights marchers, 1972.

INTRODUCTIONS

Some news anchors like to start off their reports by asking, "What kind of a day has it been?" I thought I might do the same, so I checked to see what kind of a day this has been throughout history. I wonder whether I should have bothered. In 1835, a demented painter named Richard Lawrence tried to assassinate President Andrew Jackson. In 1889, Crown Prince Rudolf of Austria, heir to the Austro-Hungarian empire, and Baroness Marie Vetsera committed suicide at Maylering, Austria, triggering a major revolution in eastern Europe. In 1972, British soldiers shot and killed thirteen Roman Catholic civil rights marchers in Londonderry, Northern Ireland, in an incident that is still referred to as "Bloody Sunday" in the Emerald Isle. But dire as these events were, I have saved the black letter day for last. In 1933, Adolf Hitler became the Chancellor of Germany. That election launched his nation and the world into a full-scale war. Looking back on all these anniversaries, I have come to the conclusion that it's a good day to be here talking to you. Certainly it is good by comparison with the past.

Today commemorates an ironic anniversary. In 1948, the modern world's greatest symbol of peaceful resistance, Mahatma Gandhi, was assassinated in New Delhi, India. The violent death of the father of modern, nonviolent civil disobedience and the major architect of India's freedom reminds us that life is not always what we make it; sometimes life is what other people make for us. With that in mind, let us look at the world that other people are making—and what we are doing about it.

One of history's true giants is a man who was born in Hyde Park, New York, on this date. In 1882, Franklin Delano Roosevelt was born. He brought a nation together; guided its people out of dark economic times; and proved that even in the light of a great physical handicap, any individual can conquer any obstacle. I hope that, in reminding you of his story today, I may proceed to explore with you how and where Roosevelt's kind of courage is needed to inspire us today.

If you think thirteen is an unlucky number, then think again when you remember this day in history. In 1781, the Articles of Confederation were adopted by Maryland. It was the last of the original thirteen states to do so. Americans everywhere should revere the number thirteen: It represents the number of colonies that fought to be a united nation of states; it marks the number of states that ratified the Articles of Confederation that united them; and the American flag's original thirteen stars symbolized the courage and commitment that established our nation. Today, I have a baker's dozen of ideas I would like to impart to you, now that I've assured you thirteen is anything but unlucky.

JANUARY 31

Alexander Selkirk was rescued, 1709.

Jackie Robinson was born, 1919.

McDonald's opened its first fast-food restaurant in the Soviet Union, 1990.

INTRODUCTIONS

Truth, they say, is stranger than fiction. On this date, a true story—which nobody really remembers—provided the basis for a novel that everyone knows. In 1709, a British sailor named Alexander Selkirk was rescued after being marooned for four years on a Pacific island. You may not recognize Selkirk's name, but many of you have heard the story of Robinson Crusoe and his adventures. Somehow, we seem to prefer to deal with facts in fictional—almost mythological—terms. That may be why current social, cultural, and political commentaries all seem more effective when they tell a story. Today I would like to tell you about the facts on which some current story themes are based.

Occasionally one person becomes the living embodiment of an idea; the symbol of a widely held belief. When that happens, the symbol oftentimes works alone. That's the way it was with Jackie Robinson, a great baseball player who was born on this date in 1919. Robinson played for the Brooklyn Dodgers. He broke all-time records throughout his long career. He was also the first African-American major league baseball player. Robinson courageously fought to integrate the all-American sport. And in the end, his dedication helped open the doors for other African-American athletes like Ernie Banks of the Chicago Cubs. That courage, wisdom, and personal dedication to a greater cause are on my mind today. We are in a time when the same challenge falls on many of us—not because of race or religious belief, but because of socially imposed, repressive limitations. The old expression was "quicker than you can say Jack Robinson." Today I would like to rephrase that thought to read "as courageous as Jackie Robinson." We need more people with that kind of courage now.

An American institution took the Soviet Union by storm on this date in 1990. McDonald's opened its first fast-food restaurant in Moscow's Red Square. The golden arches lit up in the famed anti-capitalist capitol. Eyebrows arched in disbelief. No one dreamt détente would be negotiated over hamburgers, yet that taste of America draws hundreds, even thousands, each day; and by now has no doubt served millions. Stranger things have happened in this world. And today I want to let you know about some unlikely, but welcome news a little closer to home.

FEBRUARY

INTRODUCTION:

There are many reasons why February should be a month close to our hearts. First of all, this is American Heart Month—a time to think of our health by exercising and eating smart. St. Valentine's Day is a time for romance; a time to tell those who are close to our hearts that we love them. But February is also American History and Black History Month. For love of our heritage and the brotherhood of man, we have designated this month as a time to remember our past. Now some of you may be anticipating Groundhog Day: Is winter ever going to end? But I ask you here, in the dead of winter, shouldn't you look closer to home for immediate and lasting warmth?

FEBRUARY 1

U.S. Supreme Court convened for the first time, 1790.

"The 400" social elite were named, 1892.

Israelis said they would repatriate about 100 Palestinians, 1993.

INTRODUCTIONS

We observe many anniversaries in the United States. But one that we somehow overlook occurred in New York City on this date. In 1790, the U.S. Supreme Court convened for the first time. The Supreme Court may well be a uniquely American contribution to governmental science: the living symbol of government ruled by laws rather than by men. The separation of powers, the system of checks and balances designed by the Founding Fathers, is part of this country's glory. And today was—and is—a red letter day. So it is in a spirit of pride that I speak to you about the meaning of justice.

In 1892, Mrs. William B. Astor gave a society ball on this day in New York City. Ward McAllister drew up her invitation list which was titled by the number of eligible guests. They were called "the 400." Ever since then, the term "the 400" has been synonymous with the social elite. This prompts me to say that more or less than 400 is probably a far more interesting and challenging audience. I have not counted the house here today, but I am reasonably sure of this audience's quality. And I appreciate the opportunity to speak to you.

There are times when even the best intentions get rejected because past actions have built an impenetrable wall of doubt. Today is the anniversary of such an occasion. In 1993, the Israeli government said they would repatriate about 100 Palestinians who had been deported to Lebanon. Rather than embracing this singular act of kindness, the deportees rejected the plan. It is difficult at times to forgive one action no matter how eloquent the apology. Actions do speak louder than words. But the best actions are prefaced by words, and so I'm here to call you to action.

FEBRUARY 2

Groundhog Day.

Candlemas Day.

The U.S. paid Mexico $15 million for southwestern lands, 1848.

The "Cardiff Giant" was exposed as a hoax, 1870.

The National Baseball League was formed, 1876.

George Halas was born, 1895.

South Africa lifted the ban on the African National Congress, 1990.

INTRODUCTIONS

Today is Groundhog Day. Legend says that if a groundhog—or prairie dog—comes out today and sees his shadow, then six more weeks of winter follow. Of course, if he doesn't see that shadow, winter is supposed to last longer. In some parts of the world, people watch badgers or bears for similar omens. The origins of all these rites stem from a medieval British superstition observed as Candlemas Day. "If Candlemas Day be fair and bright, / Come winter, have another flight. / If Candlemas brings clouds and rain, / go wit and come not again." For speakers, there's no way for you to tell from the way I come out how long my speech is going to be. Some speakers themselves can't tell, until they see how friendly their audience is. But I want to assure you that I will not speak one minute longer than it will take me to finish what I have to say.

Back in 1869, a gigantic, petrified human figure was discovered on a farm in Cardiff, New York. It created a sensation, for about a year. But on this day, the Cardiff Giant was exposed as a hoax. It was neither the first nor the last time people have been asked to put their faith in a falsehood. That is a monumental challenge. What is real? What is true? What is fake? I am not here to overwhelm you with carefully tailored statistics or to play upon your natural fears. I am here to report some relatively simple facts that I think you ought to know—and those are things you can test for yourselves.

As I was preparing today's remarks, I discovered that this was a red-letter day for organized sports. In 1876, eight American baseball teams—Chicago, Boston, Cincinnati, Louisville, New York, Philadelphia, St. Louis, and Hartford—formed the National Baseball League. In 1895, George Halas—the future co-founder of the National Football League—was born in Chicago. Uniting interested parties seems to be the theme for today. In 1848, the U.S. paid Mexico $15 million for lands that eventually became the states of Arizona, California, New Mexico, and Texas. And in 1990, South African President F.W. de Klerk lifted the ban on the African National Congress, and promised to release political prisoner Nelson Mandela. With these events in mind, I would like all of you to consider how we can create an organized league of our own.

FEBRUARY 3

The revolution against the Ottoman occupation of Greece ended, 1830. (See March 25th entry.)

President Lincoln attended a peace conference, 1865.

Four U.S. chaplains died, 1943. (Four Chaplains Day)

Fighting in the Vietnam War came to a virtual halt, 1973.

INTRODUCTIONS

Not too many of you are aware that today has a very special name. It is Four Chaplains Day. It marks the heroic deaths of a Catholic priest, a Jewish rabbi, and two Protestant ministers. They gave their life jackets to other crew members on board the sinking troop transport *Dorchester* and went down with the ship in the North Atlantic during the Second World War. In 1943, Father John Washington, Rabbi Alexander Goode, Reverend George Fox, and Reverend Clark Poling became men to be remembered. Their selflessness should be an example for us all. We should transcend differences of opinion. We should talk together and work together with that sense of common purpose which those four men had in such abundance.

Working together is not always easy. On this date in 1865, President Abraham Lincoln and Confederate Vice President Alexander H. Stephens met aboard a ship anchored at Hampton Roads, Virginia, in an attempt to end the Civil War. The meeting failed because the Confederacy demanded independence. Barely two months later—after more killing and more suffering—Confederate independence was lost anyway. They say talk is cheap; and actions speak louder than words. That was definitely the case when, on this same day in 1973, fighting in the Vietnam War came to a virtual halt. The formal cease-fire had gone into effect. It's always wiser to communicate than to remain silent—unless you're a public speaker, who naturally expects the audience to remain silent while the words fall from his or her lips. You do, of course, retain the option of applauding if the spirit moves you.

FEBRUARY 4

George Washington was elected U.S. president, 1789. (See February 22nd entry.)

The Confederate States of America were organized, 1861.

The Interstate Commerce Commission was established, 1887.

President Nixon ordered all federal agencies to stop polluting the air and water, 1970.

INTRODUCTIONS

As Americans, we seem to have a particular fondness for people who fight hard and gallantly, even if it's for a lost cause. One great example is the Confederate States of America which were organized on this date in 1861. It took a long time to bind up the wounds of the Civil War which pitted the Union in the North with the Confederacy in the South. But out of the ashes of that war and subsequent reconstruction rose great men and heroic acts on both sides. The Confederate cause was lost, but the greater cause of unity was ultimately won. Now, as then, every one of us has a cause that is yet to be won. My remarks today may be judged by the impact they have on your own particular cause. But in the end, decent causes, honest dreams, and devoted advocates find a way to work things out.

Isn't it amazing how times change? Sometimes, the federal government reflects those changes by issuing resolves that appeal to the demands of the people. Today is the anniversary of two examples. In 1887, the Interstate Commerce Commission was established to regulate the transport of passengers and goods across state lines by land and water. America was on the move, and the government wanted to ensure the safe passage of people and cargo throughout the growing nation. But as we later learned, progress has its weak points. Gasoline emissions, industrial growth, and overpopulation took their toll on the nation's roads and waterways. In 1970, President Richard M. Nixon ordered all federal agencies to stop polluting the air and water by 1973. We had become conscious of how delicate our world really is. And once again, the government responded. Let's take a look at how our government is answering our latest demands.

FEBRUARY 5

Roger Williams arrived in America, 1631.

Adlai E. Stevenson, Jr. was born, 1900.

INTRODUCTIONS

More than 300 years ago, on this date, Roger Williams arrived in the American colonies. In 1631, this young British minister had no idea he was to become our first great dissenter. As the founder of American religious tolerance, Williams established religious freedom as the law in Rhode Island. The roots of freedom, it seems, go back to very early days in this land. And what moved Roger Williams still motivates us today: to speak out, to speak our minds. If he had not acted out of conscience as he did, who knows how free we would be to exchange our ideas here today?

The gift of words is a great gift indeed. When one is called upon to speak in public, one walks in the shadow of other great orators. Today is Adlai Stevenson, Jr.'s birthday. Some people questioned his qualifications as a presidential candidate; others commended his talent as an international diplomat; but all agree on his eloquence. Among the many memorable things he said was this: "Eggheads of the world unite. You have nothing to lose but your yolks." We have nothing to lose here today by putting our heads together and finding a solution to our problems.

FEBRUARY 6

College of William and Mary was chartered, 1693. (See December 5th entry.)

Aaron Burr was born, 1756.

George Herman (Babe Ruth) was born, 1895.

The Twentieth Amendment to the U.S. Constitution went into effect, 1933.

The U.S. successfully test-fired a Titan missile, 1959.

The Apollo 14 astronauts prepared to head back to earth, 1971.

Chief Justice Warren Burger asked Congress to ease the Supreme Court's workload, 1983.

Australian Prime Minister Robert Hawke canceled an agreement with U.S. President Ronald Reagan, 1985.

INTRODUCTIONS

If there is a single most notable aspect of our nation's growth, it is probably wrapped up in one word—education. The point is timely today because, on this date in 1693, the country's first college charter was granted, at Williamsburg, Virginia. The institution which opened under that charter is the College of William and Mary. Years later, it became the founding home of Phi Beta Kappa, the national collegiate honor fraternity. As a nation, we have known since those very early times that there is always more to be learned, more to be seen, and more to be explored. Even here today, in our own small way, we carry on that never-ending process.

The Amendment to the U.S. Constitution with the most picturesque name became part of the law on this day in 1933. It is popularly known as the Lame Duck Amendment. You all know what a lame duck is—a politician who has been defeated for reelection but is still in office. Before the Twentieth Amendment was enacted, politicians were elected in November and not sworn in until the following March. In the interim, lame ducks continued to run the government. The schedule was first adopted in the eighteenth century, when communication was slow and changes took time. Today, lame ducks only have two months before they are replaced by newly elected officials. But the media's increased speed and global coverage keeps the public informed of their every move. Consequently, the public can respond immediately. The same holds true when you deal with a live audience. I am not lip-syncing my script and your direct response can stop me. I trust you will not consider me to be a lame duck.

Today is the birthday of one of America's greatest heroes. He was cheered longer and louder than virtually anybody of his time. He never ran for office or starred on Broadway or discovered a cure for a disease. His name was George Herman Ruth, the American baseball player who was the epitome of irreverent, boisterous, happy-go-lucky, party-hearty masculine America. It is worth remembering, on his birthday, that America loves its rough diamonds—people who do whatever it is they do best. Babe Ruth's records have been broken. No record lasts forever. But a lot of young Americans today still harbor the dream of being tomorrow's Babe Ruth. That is what I would like to talk to you about today—the younger generation's constant and usually correct belief that they can do better than their parents' heroes. I have a few suggestions as to where they might concentrate their efforts.

Working overtime is not limited to civilians. Some of our highest-ranking public officials have felt the crunch of a heavy workload. It was on this date in 1983 that Chief Justice Warren Burger asked Congress to create a court made up of federal judges to ease the Supreme Court's workload. This request can be considered in two different lights. Did we have that many cases that needed hearing by the highest court in the land? Or was it because each case needed long deliberation before a final decision was handed down? Either way, they knew when and how to ask for help. So let me get down to the case at hand and lighten your burden of having to listen to my speech.

The ways in which we measure progress successively change with each generation. Three events that occurred on this date in history prove my point. In 1959, the U.S. successfully test-fired a Titan intercontinental ballistic missile from Cape Canaveral, Florida. It was believed that advancements in defense technology would ensure the world's safety. A little over a decade later, in 1971, the Apollo 14 astronauts prepared to head back to earth after spending 33 hours on the moon. Many people postulated that space technology would secure not only the ground we live on, but the skies above us. But by 1985, security took on a whole new meaning when Australian Prime Minister Robert Hawke canceled an agreement with President Ronald Reagan allowing Americans to monitor MX missile tests from Australian military bases. The land down under became the world's first antinuclear nation. Progress must always be measured one step at a time, because when we least expect it, we might find we have moved backward rather than forward. Let's see how we've made true progress on a more local scale.

Today, on the birthday of Aaron Burr, history remembers him simply as the man who mortally wounded Alexander Hamilton in an infamous duel. Only recently has it been suggested that Alexander Hamilton—who founded the *New York Post*—may have done more damage to Burr with a pen in the final days between the duel and his death, than Burr's bullet had done to him. It's doubtful that we'll ever know how or why the man who served as Vice President under Thomas Jefferson came upon his dubious reputation. But I do not doubt that we will part on better terms when I am finished with my remarks here today.

FEBRUARY 7

John Deere was born, 1804.

Charles Dickens was born, 1812.

John L. Sullivan won the last bare-knuckle heavyweight boxing championship, 1882.

Sinclair Lewis was born, 1885.

China's last emperor was born, 1906.

The U.S. Senate voted to form an investigative committee to look into the Watergate break-in, 1973. (See January 4th and June 17th entries.)

INTRODUCTIONS

Back in 1882, the Boston Strong Boy, John L. Sullivan, won the heavyweight championship of the world in Mississippi City, Mississippi. On this date, Sullivan knocked out Paddy Ryan in the ninth round with his bare-knuckled fists. After this fight, boxers fought with their gloves on. Today I propose to make what I will call a bare-knuckle speech. I am taking the gloves off to speak to you bluntly and frankly on issues which deserve that kind of attention.

Today is a double birthday celebration. Two honored writers who were both adept at creating characters that personified attitudes of their times were born on this day. One was Charles Dickens, who chronicled the social conditions of Victorian England; the other was Sinclair Lewis, who penned a graphic portrait of 1920s and 1930s America. They created immortal characters like Fagan, Scrooge, Babbit, and Elmer Gantry. Dickens and Lewis had one particular quality in common; when they saw injustice, they tried to do something about it. It is in that spirit that I rise to speak to you now.

Some men make their name by being the first to do something. Others make their name by doing what they do best. Today is the birthday of a man who was one of the latter. In 1804, John Deere was born in Rutland, Vermont. He and his partner, Major Leonard Andrews, weren't the first men to successfully develop and manufacture a steel plow, but they did produce a better farm tool than their competitors. When Deere went out on his own, he continued making farm implements with that same philosophy in mind. He did his best and was the best at what he did; he was so proud of his work he put his name on everything he built. You might even say he was outstanding in his field. But tonight I'd like to talk about someone even nearer and dearer.

China's last Son of Heaven was born on this day in 1906. When he was two years old, P'u-i [pronounced poo-yee] was taken to Beijing's Forbidden City and was crowned emperor. A regency government ruled in his place as the young monarch grew up in the palace—isolated from his family and his empire. Four years later, his regents abdicated his throne to the Republican Revolution; he didn't know he had lost a 2000-year-old empire. When P'u-i was eighteen, he wanted to move to England or America and the new government wanted him out of the palace. But only the Japanese offered him assistance. He repaid for that help by becoming Emperor K'ang-tee of the puppet Japanese nation Manchukuo—his ancestral home of Manchuria. After the Second World War, he was captured and returned to China where he was re-educated as a citizen of the People's Republic of China. P'u-i's life is the story of lost opportunities: the chance to make his own decisions; the chance to live a life of his choosing. Was this such a unique story? Unfortunately not. But we here have the right to choose our destiny and I propose we do.

F E B R U A R Y   8

Jules Verne was born, 1828.
Three astronauts aboard the Skylab 3 returned to earth, 1974.

INTRODUCTIONS

We like to say that fact is stranger than fiction. Maybe today it would be more accurate to say that fact is catching up with fiction. Jules Verne, who was born in 1828 on this day, was the king of science fiction in his time. He practically invented the form. He wrote about traveling around the world in eighty days and navigating the bottom of the sea. He wrote about voyaging to the moon, and exploring the center of the earth. Of course, these sound more like predictions than fiction now. It is very difficult to tell the difference between fantasy and fact. I hope that tonight we can separate the two, not in matters of science, but in regard to the way we live.

This is the anniversary of a world's—or should I say solar system's—record. The three astronauts manning the Skylab 3 space mission safely returned to earth after spending 84 days in orbit on this day in 1974. We may measure record breaking events on earth by how little time it takes to do something. But record-breaking journeys into orbit are judged by their length and the astronauts' endurance. I think more of us should look to our ability to stay in for the long haul right here on earth. Don't you?

FEBRUARY 9

French colonists arrived in Louisiana, 1718.
William Henry Harrison was born, 1773. (See April 4th entry.)
National Weather Service was established, 1870.

INTRODUCTIONS

Today is the National Weather Service's anniversary. In 1870, this unit of the U.S. Army was officially established to gather and report on the nation's atmospheric conditions. In honor of this occasion I am authorized to give a forecast for this room: the next thirty minutes will be very windy.

I suppose it probably is appropriate for a speaker on this date to take note that today is the birthday of the undisputed record holder for the shortest U.S. Presidential term ever served. In 1773, William Henry Harrison was born. On March 4, 1841, Harrison was inaugurated. Within a few days, he caught a cold. And exactly one month later, President Harrison was dead. The moral for a speaker is clear: say what you have to say while you still have breath. So I will take a deep breath and begin.

Today is New Orleans' birthday—or should I say l'Anniversaire d'Orleans Nouveau. In 1718, Jean-Baptiste Le Moyne and a small group of French colonists arrived at the mouth of the great Mississippi to establish a settlement in the Louisiana bayou country. French-Africans from Haiti—Creoles—soon joined them to work on the plantations. Fifty years later, a band of French-speaking Acadians who were expelled from Nova Scotia—Cajuns—made their home in this thriving port city. Our nation's roots are found in many cultures from a variety of places. And today we celebrate our American heritage with a touch more spice.

FEBRUARY 10

France ceded Canada to England, 1763.

Queen Victoria married Prince Albert, 1840.

Jimmy Durante was born, 1893.

Leontyne Price was born, 1927

The first singing telegram was sung, 1933.

The Gestapo was given a free hand in Germany, 1936.

The luxury liner *Normandie* capsized at pier in New York Harbor, 1942.

INTRODUCTIONS

There is an old newspaper saying that if a dog bites a man, it's not news. But if a man bites a dog, that's news. Today's anniversary made news in much the same way. In 1942, the former French luxury liner, the *Normandie*, drowned—not sank—in New York Harbor. The U.S. Navy was converting *Normandie* into a troopship. It had caught fire the day before, and the firefighters had poured tons of water into its hull. The next day, the waterlogged ship overturned and capsized, like a beached whale. I suppose the moral is that if you water something down too much, it will drown. I have therefore tried to keep today's remarks—if not inflammatory or dry as dust—from being waterlogged.

It came as a great surprise to me to discover that today was the singing telegram's anniversary. It was also surprising to find that there are adults—perhaps even some in this audience—who have never even heard a singing telegram. For their benefit, let me quickly explain. In 1933, the singing telegram service made it possible for customers to have singing messengers deliver their greetings. You could have someone sing "Happy Birthday" to a friend in an another city. It was a cute idea that was even revived in the 1970s and has survived to the present; though now you can place a phone call and sing to anyone you want. "Speak for yourself" is the order of the day. So I apologize. Instead of having your favorite performer sing my message to you, I will deliver it myself.

There are still many nations where the secret police observe no law but their own. In 1936, on this date, the German Geheimstaatspolizei—or Gestapo—was given that power. Their name is still synonymous with evil and repression. It is worth remembering that this kind of gathering—and my remarks to it—probably could not have taken place under Gestapo rule, because it would have been viewed as a conspiracy. I say this not to add solemnity to this moment, but merely to start on the happy note that in this year of our Lord, life is a lot better than it used to be. Now, let us conspire freely.

Canada officially became a British territory on this day in 1763. France ceded the last of its northern holdings in the New World, and New France became Quebec. Fifty years earlier they had lost Nova Scotia and Newfoundland in the Queen Anne's War. They had attempted to expand their holdings into the Ohio and Mississippi River Valleys, triggering the French and Indian War. They lost everything in the push to have it all. An ambitious goal can breed progress. But we must always be mindful that there's a fine line between enterprise and blind ambition. Today, I hope we can devote our time to enterprise.

Every working wife should celebrate today's anniversary. In 1840, Great Britain's Queen Victoria married Prince Albert of Saxe-Coburg-Gotha at London's St. James Palace. Their royal wedding was followed by an equally regal wedding breakfast at Buckingham Palace. But that's when the fairy tale transformed into a more modern reality. Despite the new husband's desire to see the world with his new bride, the young couple's honeymoon was only two days long. As head of the vast British empire, Victoria felt she couldn't spend any more time away from her job. We often hear that women's roles have radically changed from those in the good old days. In the light of this particular anniversary, I hope they never do.

Maybe I should sing my remarks to you today, since this is not only the anniversary of the first singing telegram, it's the birthday of two great American singers. Both Jimmy Durante and Leontyne Price were born on this day. In 1927, internationally-acclaimed opera star Leontyne Price was born in Laurel, Mississippi. And in 1893, Jimmy Durante was born in New York City. He may not have sung his way to the world's great operatic stages like Price did, but he did sing his way from vaudeville theaters to motion pictures and then to television. If you don't think that's something to sing about, then, to quote Jimmy Durante: "Hold on folks, I got a million of 'em."

FEBRUARY 11

The British Parliament first convened, 1254.

King Henry VIII was recognized as the supreme head of the Church of England, 1531. (See November 17th entry.)

The gerrymander was born, 1812.

Thomas Alva Edison was born, 1847. (National Science Youth Day)

Italy signed the Lateran Treaty with the Vatican, 1929.

Margaret Thatcher became the first female head of the British Conservative Party, 1975.

The space shuttle *Challenger* returned to earth, 1984.

Barbara Harris became the first consecrated female Episcopal bishop, 1989.

INTRODUCTIONS

This is the British Parliament's birthday. In 1254, Earl Richard of Cornwall summoned two elected knights from every shire and all of the king's barons to meet at Westminster Abbey while his brother King Henry III was fighting in France. They met to confer on the matter of raising more money for military defense. Before this epic meeting, the king consulted only with his royal advisors and key members of the clergy. The establishment of this parliamentary assembly assured the barons and elected representatives a significant voice in government. I must sadly report that when King Henry returned four years later, he tried to dissolve the parliament. But the barons prevailed. Small beginnings can grow into more productive endings, which is something I would like to plant with you today.

Since Thomas Alva Edison was born on this day in 1847 in Milan, Ohio, I suppose I have a special obligation to be inventive. For some years, the occasion was observed as National Science Youth Day. That sounds like a rather interesting invention itself. Youth is not a science and science is not youth, but I am perfectly willing to go along with the celebration and wish a happy birthday to any science youth I happen to encounter. It seems to me, however, that essentially Edison was a man who was forever asking the question, "Why don't they?", except that the way he looked at things he was more likely asking, "How can we?" I ask all of you to consider adopting the same attitude. Today I propose to talk to you not about why we should do certain things, but rather how.

Back on this date in 1812, the Governor of Massachusetts, Elbridge Gerry, signed a bill setting his state's district lines. A cartoonist looked at the new oddly placed borders and drew a caricature of the redistricting. To him, it looked like a salamander. Combining Governor Gerry's with the map's shape, the cartoonist came up with a new word: gerrymandering. It means distorting a natural contour to suit your own ends. And you can, so to speak, gerrymander a speech as well as a state. You can take a situation and create your own borderlines. That is particularly easy when you have a complicated subject. But I prefer to address myself to what I believe is the central issue, the core question.

This is twice a landmark day for the Episcopal Church. First, in 1531, King Henry VIII was officially recognized as the Church of England's supreme head. The dispute between the king and the Vatican escalated with this radical act. But I'm sure that even the nonconforming Henry would have been alarmed when Barbara Harris became the first consecrated female bishop in the Episcopal Church over four and a half centuries later. In 1989, the ceremony—held in Boston, Massachusetts—signaled the end of the long-held tradition that only male clergy could rise through the Church's ranks. Most traditional beliefs were regarded at one time or another to be radical concepts. I would like to remind you of this simple truth and hope you find that what I have to say is somewhat radical.

In Great Britain, the separation of Church and State had been disputed for nearly five centuries until King Henry VIII declared himself as the Church of England's supreme head on this day in 1531. But reform—both spiritual and political—has occurred more than once on this day. In 1975, Margaret Thatcher became the first female head of the British Conservative Party. And fourteen years later, in 1989, Barbara Harris was consecrated as the first female bishop of the Episcopal Church in Boston, Massachusetts. The war between the sexes went on for longer than the power dispute between man's greatest institutions, and we are privileged to witness its passing. There are other events that we are privileged to witness, and it's those moments I'd like to bring to your attention now.

The Vatican gained its independence on this day in 1929. The seat of the Roman Catholic Church—situated in the center of Italy's capital—was not a separate entity even though its interests spread far beyond the borders of its host nation. But when the Italian government signed the Lateran Treaty, Vatican City gained sovereignty. It was a fortuitous event. In less than a decade, Italy's fascist government expanded its interests and influence in a very different direction. There are times when alliances must be scrutinized in light of personal beliefs. I hope to look at a few of our close relationships with you today.

It wasn't the first time an astronaut walked in space, but on this date in 1984, the space shuttle *Challenger* returned to earth after an 8-day mission that featured the first untethered space walk. Taking the first step in any enterprise requires courage, even when you have allies supporting you all the way. But to be the first to make a move into a new frontier without assistance or means of escape takes more than fortitude. Self-confidence and unconditional faith can transform that first step into a fantastic journey. In that spirit, I've prepared a few words which I'll deliver without a safety net.

FEBRUARY 12

James Oglethorpe landed in Savannah Harbor, 1733. (Georgia Day)

Tadeusz Kosciuszko was born, 1746. (Kosciuszko Day)

Abraham Lincoln was born, 1809. (Celebrated on the closest Monday to February 22nd as President's Day; see February 22nd entry.)

Charles Darwin was born, 1809.

John L. Lewis was born, 1880.

General Omar N. Bradley was born, 1893.

INTRODUCTIONS

This is a special day for many Americans, no matter who they are or where they live. In 1809, Honest Abe Lincoln was born in Kentucky. If you hail from Atlanta or Savannah you know that in 1733 James Oglethorpe and a group of colonists landed in Savannah Harbor. If you are of Polish descent, you probably know that in 1746, the American patriot and war hero Tadeusz Kosciuszko was born. But I'm sure not many of you know that in 1880, John L. Lewis—the founder of the United Mineworkers Union—was also born. It is obviously a perfect time for an upbeat speech about America and I propose to proceed along just that line.

For many Americans, there is a special warmth about this day because it is Omar N. Bradley's birthday. Born in 1893, this native Missourian was known during the Second World War as the G.I.'s general. Bradley was one of the nation's most loved and longest-lived top generals. He was also a plain and gentle man. If we are looking for the model of a dedicated public servant, we don't have to look beyond Omar Bradley. I would like to quote something he said in a 1948 Armistice Day speech: "Humanity is in danger of being trapped in this world by its moral adolescents." That is a pretty good springboard for my remarks today.

Because of one man who was born on this day, the world saw itself in a very different perspective. In 1809, Charles Darwin was born in Shrewsbury, Shropshire. When he was 30 years old, Darwin sailed aboard the H.M.S. *Beagle* to South America to record the unique plant and animal life of the west coast and its surrounding islands. His observations were documented in a book entitled, *On the Origins of the Species by Means of Natural Selection.* Suddenly, the whole world was praising and criticizing his alleged theory that only the fittest survive. But what Darwin really discovered was that only those who are able to adapt to their environment endure and progress. Each and every one of us must adjust our natures to present circumstances at some time or another. As Darwin learned in his travels, endurance through adaptability is the natural key to success. Now it's our turn to adapt.

FEBRUARY 13

The Feast of St. Agabus.

Galileo was detained by the Italian Inquisition in Rome, 1633. (See February 15th entry.)

The Boston Latin School was founded, 1635.

The first state university opened in Chapel Hill, North Carolina, 1795.

Grant Wood was born, 1892.

Tennessee Ernie Ford was born, 1919.

League of Nations recognized Switzerland's neutrality, 1920.

INTRODUCTIONS

Since this is the feast day dedicated to St. Agabus—the patron saint of fortune tellers—I predict that you will not be disappointed with the forecast I'm about to make.

This is an important day for American education. In 1635, the nation's oldest secondary school, the Boston Latin School, opened. America has been dedicated to free public education ever since. In 1795, the nation's first state institution of higher education, the University of North Carolina at Chapel Hill, also opened. We have always encouraged education in this nation. We haven't always succeeded. But we started trying to educate our youth a long time ago. I think there is still room for improvement—even after three centuries of trying. I'd like to make some suggestions today.

Rural America was honored by two men born on this day. In 1892, Grant Wood was born in Anamosa, Iowa. Grant's painting—American Gothic—is still the world's most recognized portrait of American farm life. His vision of the men and women who tilled the soil to feed a nation continues to tell the story of their hardship and their tenacious, hard-working spirit today. In 1919, Tennessee Ernie Ford was born in Bristol, Tennessee. This homegrown country singer painted an innocent, romantic portrait of American rural life with his voice and his guitar. Ford used to finish his shows with a few words that make a great beginning for today's remarks: "Bless your little pea-pickin' hearts."

Remaining neutral on any issue, in any field of endeavor is difficult. In the area of international politics, neutrality is nearly impossible to achieve. But on this date in 1920, Switzerland accomplished just that when the League of Nations officially recognized the alpine nation's neutral position in the political arena. By maintaining their nonpartisan stance, Switzerland has been host to numerous peace conferences; and home to many service organizations dedicated to aiding war and disaster victims throughout the world. Neutrality may not seem like a virtue in this competitive world, but its merits in certain situations cannot be denied—especially when they serve a higher good. I'd like to proclaim my neutrality now, before we begin.

FEBRUARY 14

Valentine's Day.

Thomas Malthus was born, 1766.

Jack Benny was born, 1894.

The first all-electronic computer was introduced, 1946. (See June 23rd entry.)

The Ayatollah Khomeini called for the assassination of Salman Rushdie, 1989.

INTRODUCTIONS

I greet you on Valentine's Day, the celebration dedicated to lovers young and old, greeting-card companies and the people who sell those heart-shaped candy boxes. I too, am here to sell you a bill of goods. I only hope you find it candy for your thoughts.

It is interesting to note that Valentine's Day is also Thomas Malthus' birthday. Born in Surrey, England in 1766, Malthus argued in his *Essay on Population* that populations grow geometrically, while the crops and livestock to feed them grow arithmetically. Because that supply-and-demand ratio never balances, Malthus firmly believed people should marry later in life. According to him, "moral restraint" was the best way to prevent a worldwide famine. You have a not-so-difficult choice to make on this most romantic day of the year. You can follow Malthus' advice and wait a while; or have a romantic evening with the one you love. I know which one I'm going to do. But first I'd like to focus on another thought.

It is said that the pen is mightier than the sword. Today's anniversary clearly demonstrates the strength of words and ideas. But it is also an example of how much trouble words can create for their author. In 1989, Iran's Ayatollah Khomeini called for Salman Rushdie's assassination. The conservative Muslim leader claimed that certain passages of the author's novel—*The Satanic Verses*—ridiculed Islam's essential doctrines. Like a page out of medieval history, Rushdie was marked as a heretic by a religious leader for publishing his thoughts. With any hope, you will not put a price on my head for publicizing my beliefs before you today.

This is Jack Benny's birthday. In 1894, little did the residents of Waukegan, Illinois, know that one of their native sons would grow to become best known for his lack of musical talent. But I don't want to get too carried away, folks; I want to relay a couple of important messages before you quote Jack and tell me to cut it out.

This is the computer's birthday. The world's first all-electronic computer was unveiled at the University of Pennsylvania's Moore School of Electrical Engineering in 1946. The Electronic Numerical Integrator And Computer— ENIAC for short—weighed 30 tons, stood ten feet tall, and could calculate a ballistic trajectory in 30 seconds. It took only nine years for mathematician Alan M. Turing's idea—which he had conceived while taking a walk in a scenic rural English cow pasture—to become a reality. Computers now are much smaller, lighter, and faster. They also serve more peaceful, practical purposes these days. I particularly enjoy preparing my remarks on a computer that allows me to change my mind more than once so you can listen to my more precisely composed ideas.

FEBRUARY 15

Galileo Galilei was born, 1564. (See February 13th and 19th entries.)

Susan B. Anthony was born, 1820. (See December 13th entry.)

The U.S. battleship *Maine* was bombed, 1898.

Cassius Clay became the world's heavyweight boxing champion, 1964.

Great Britain and Ireland switched to decimal-based currency, 1971.

INTRODUCTIONS

I wonder how many of you recall the slogan, "Remember the *Maine!*" Who remembers that these words refer to the bombing of the U.S. battleship *Maine* in Cuba's Havana Harbor? When it happened on this date, in 1898, I wonder how many people were convinced that the Spanish were at fault? Newspaper tycoon William Randolph Hearst had been campaigning for a war. But it was this incident that actually triggered the Spanish-American War. We still seem to need an incident that brings everything to a head, even when there are other, better reasons available. One startling murder can spur much-needed funding for crime prevention; one publicized good deed can win public trust for someone who has privately dedicated a lifetime to performing good works. I would like to ask you today about a number of similar problems that seem to be waiting for a decisive incident to happen.

The story of Galileo Galilei is as important to remember on his birthday as it was 400 years ago. In 1564, Galileo was born in Pisa, Italy. When he created a telescope so he could observe the heavens, the public loaded him down with honors. But when he publicly supported Copernicus' theory that the earth revolved around the sun, he was detained by the Italian Inquisition on the crime of heresy. At the time, the Church still taught that the earth was the center of the known universe. The establishment is not always friendly to ideas which challenge presumed truth. We like to think today that we are much more tolerant than our forefathers. But are we?

He flew like a butterfly and stung like bee; today's the day Cassius Clay became Muhammed Ali. In 1964, the Olympic gold medalist boxer won the first of his world title fights against Sonny Liston. This bout didn't have a colorful name like the Rumble in the Jungle or the Thrilla in Manila. But Cassius Clay did shock the world when he made the announcement he had joined the Nation of Islam and changed his name to Muhammed Ali. Unlike any of the fighters before or after him, Ali's lightning-fast wit and heartwarming charm never failed him—even when the public didn't agree with his political or religious beliefs. But in the face of harsh criticism, Ali's success formula is definitely a winning combination.

Two landmark events occurred on this day that frustrated both bankers and consumers for a number of years. This is the anniversary of Great Britain and Ireland's shift to a decimal-based currency system. In 1971, shillings, bobs, and crowns were replaced by 5, 10, and 50 pence coins. The familiar haypence and sixpence denominations disappeared; a 41 pence chocolate bar sounded so much more expensive than a 7 shilling/6 pence one. But consumers learned to live with the change. In 1820, no one knew that a young girl's birthday would stir up the American currency system over a century later. That was when suffragist Susan B. Anthony was born in Adams, Massachusetts. When the U.S. Treasury issued the quarter-sized Susan B. Anthony dollar, American consumers got confused. People accidentally put the new dollars into quarter slots in the midst of an economic recession. So the first American coin to feature a woman's portrait was discontinued. Traditions are hard to break—especially when it comes to cold hard cash. Without coining phrases, there are a few pieces of change I'd like you to consider right now.

FEBRUARY 16

Ulysses S. Grant demanded the Confederate forces' unconditional surrender, 1862.

Edgar Bergen was born, 1903.

King Tutankamen's burial chamber was opened, 1923. (See November 4th and June 26th entries.)

Fidel Castro became Cuba's premier, 1959.

Mario Soares became the head of Portugal, 1986.

INTRODUCTIONS

Some phrases are far more dramatic and meaningful than others. General Ulysses S. Grant, on this date in 1862, laid down his terms for unconditional surrender to the besieged Confederate forces at Fort Donelson, Tennessee. This phrase, unconditional surrender, is a yardstick by which the totality of victory is still measured. Even from the safety of the speaker's platform, the call to fight until the opposition unconditionally surrenders is sometimes couched as an all-out campaign or a need for constant vigilance. Today I will not rally for unconditional surrender but will speak to you of more reasonable solutions. We face many issues where even a partial victory represents tremendous progress. Let me address myself to that goal now.

Edgar Bergen was born on this day in 1903 in Chicago. He was a star entertainer, but he also did something not too many entertainers do. Bergen contributed to the

English language. When we refer to a Charlie McCarthy or a Mortimer Snerd, we are using names that Bergen gave to two of the ventriloquist's dummies he used in his act. McCarthy and Snerd's names became synonymous with the terms wise-cracking and simple-minded. They remind me that a public speaker's first obligation is not to be either a Charlie McCarthy or a Mortimer Snerd; and the second is not to be too wooden. With that goal in mind, I clear my throat and get going.

Change hallmarks this particular day in history. In 1959, Fidel Castro became Cuba's premier after ousting the pro-capitalist Batista regime. In its desire for independence, Cuba chose to live under communist rule, rather than allow foreign investors free reign over their land and valuable sugar resources. Mario Soares became the first civilian head of Portugal on this date in 1986. After 60 years of military rule, the nation consciously chose to try a new form of government. It's hard to stop the winds of change when the public clamors for relief from the air of stagnation. Hopefully you will find my words refreshing and not too breezy.

FEBRUARY 17

Miles Standish became a military captain, 1621.

Thomas Jefferson was elected U.S. president, 1801.

The Voice of America began radio broadcasts, 1947.

Michael Jordan was born, 1963. (See January 13 and March 9 entries.)

American envoy Henry Kissinger and Chairman Mao Zhedong met, 1973.

INTRODUCTIONS

Back in 1621, news was made this day by a gentleman named Miles Standish. Now you all know who Miles Standish was—or do you? I will wager that most of you assume this was the day he sent John Alden to propose to Priscilla Mullen on his behalf. If Standish is known at all today, it is because Henry Wadsworth Longfellow wrote a poem entitled "The Courtship of Miles Standish." But this isn't the anniversary of that fateful—and fictional—day. This was the day he was made the military captain of the Massachusetts Pilgrim colony. Incidentally, he did end up marrying, not once but twice. This whole story only demonstrates how people can be remembered for the oddest reasons, and how, once set loose, a misconception can be more powerful and widespread than the truth. Today, I am here to set a few facts straight.

Thomas Jefferson was elected the third U.S. president on this day in 1801. This may not be an earth-shaking revelation. But how many of you know that this election ended in a tied vote between Jefferson and Aaron Burr? The final decision was made by the House of Representatives on the 36th ballot. Things that we take for granted, or believe were easily achieved, are sometimes very hard-won indeed. So as we sit here in comfort and luxury, I think we should take a good hard look at the sacrifice and the effort that went into making it that way.

Communications between the U.S. and Communist nations radically changed during the twentieth century—especially on this day. In 1947, the first "The Voice of America" broadcast took place. These radio programs offered news-hungry Iron Curtain nations glimpses of the outside world after U.S.–Soviet relations had ceased. They were officially condemned by Josef Stalin as capitalist propaganda. On this same day in 1973, American envoy Henry Kissinger and Chairman Mao Zhedong met for the first time in Beijing, China. It began an era of détente between The People's Republic of China and the U.S. Communication is essential, whether it's on an international level or simply person-to-person. I certainly hope to establish détente with you today. And I hope you won't label me as a propagandist when I'm done.

FEBRUARY 18

Jefferson Davis said, "All we ask is to be let alone," 1861.

The Adventures of Huckleberry Finn was published, 1885.

The first cow flew, 1930.

Pluto was discovered, 1930.

INTRODUCTIONS

There are any number of earth-shaking events which we file away in our memories. Today marks an anniversary that I think may very possibly have escaped everyone's attention. On this date in 1930, a cow flew—or more exactly—a cow flew in an airplane over the Midwest, and was milked enroute. The reasons for this high-flying dairy exercise are shrouded in the mists of time, but it just goes to show that people will stop at nothing to make a point. Let me assure you that my remarks today will be a little more down to earth.

When Jefferson Davis was inaugurated as the president of the Confederate States of America on this date in 1861, he made a profound statement that is still as worthy of sympathy today as it was then. "All we ask," he pleaded, "is to be let alone." How many of us have felt that same way? Unfortunately, we live in times when it is increasingly difficult to be let alone. There seem to be fewer private compartments on spaceship Earth. And so my subject today is simply this: In times like ours what is there that we can call our own and nobody else's? And is that what we truly desire?

The spirit of adventure seems to prevail on this day throughout history. Mark Twain's novel, *The Adventures of Huckleberry Finn,* was first published on this day in 1885. Youthful adventure was certainly in the minds of the men who, in 1930, helped the first cow fly—in an airplane, of course. Curiosity often leads to adventure. Astronomer Clyde Tombaugh didn't see that flying cow while peering through the Lowell Observatory telescope in Flagstaff, Arizona. But he did discover the planet Pluto on exactly the same day. I hope none of you have lost your own spirit of adventure. I can't offer you airborne bovines or new planets in the sky. So, in the shadow of Huck Finn and Tom Sawyer, I'd like to tell you a tale or two.

When you look up into the nighttime sky, its probably hard to pick out the planets among the stars. But when astronomer Clyde Tombaugh looked through his telescope at the Lowell Observatory in Flagstaff, Arizona, on this day, he found an entity that no one had ever seen. In 1930, Pluto was discovered. According to modern astrologers, the dark planet at the farthest end of our solar system represents the dark underworld—nature's more nefarious side. But I prefer to believe that the planet Pluto represents our irrepressible desire to explore, and the vast potential— even in our modern times—for new discovery. Why not join me in considering some adventurous ideas that reach farther than our eyes can see?

FEBRUARY 19

Copernicus was born, 1473. (See also Galileo, February 15th.)
David Garrick was born, 1717.

INTRODUCTIONS

Did you ever stop to think about what today's world would look like to a man who lived over 500 years ago? Well, Copernicus—who was born on this date in 1473— would not be surprised in the least. If Copernicus hadn't proposed that the earth revolved around the sun, we might still be shortsighted, earthbound creatures today. Galileo would never have invented a telescope. Jules Verne and Arthur C. Clarke would not have written about space travel or moon walks. Ideas are like building blocks. An idea builds on earlier concepts and lays the groundwork for future development. That is why it is so important to encourage thinkers to look beyond what is accepted. For Copernicus, the sky was the limit. We need to encourage more of today's far-reaching thinkers to set their sights even further. Let me give you a couple of examples.

The acting profession has a landmark anniversary today. In 1717, the British actor David Garrick was born. He was not only one of the London stage's greatest actors;

he made the theater a center of culture. He was so revered by the public that he was buried in Westminster Abbey. Garrick reminds us that it isn't what you do, but how well you do it that really counts. I would like to speak out here today for a new emphasis on quality. My theme is simple. What can we do to promote pride in what we do?

FEBRUARY 20

King James I of Scotland was murdered, 1437.

The U.S. Postal Service was created, 1792.

Ansel Adams was born, 1902.

Sidney Poitier was born, 1927.

Anthony Eden resigned as Great Britain's Foreign Secretary, 1938.

Buffy Sainte-Marie was born, 1941.

Council of Economic Advisers was established, 1946.

Astronaut John Glenn orbited the earth, 1962. (John Glenn Day) (See July 18th entry.)

Kurt Cobain was born, 1967.

Radio and television stations nationwide left the air for a national emergency, 1971.

INTRODUCTIONS

Not many people can say there is a national day named after them, but today is such a day. Today is John Glenn Day, which was proclaimed after John Glenn became the first U. S. astronaut to orbit the earth in 1962. This is a good time to remember that each and every one of us might find ourselves opening new frontiers right here on earth when we least expect it. And here are some areas where we seem to be doing just that.

Politics rarely leave room for idealism; but on this day, one politician did put his ideals first. In 1938, Great Britain's Foreign Secretary Anthony Eden resigned in protest to Prime Minister Neville Chamberlain's appeasement policy toward Nazi Germany. It was a gallant gesture. And Eden's public display of conscience may have inspired the entire nation in the hard days that followed. One man's conscience is only symbolic. What counts is its effect on the public. And there are many questions to be asked about the presence or absence of conscience in our world today.

A note in passing. In 1946—on this very day—the Council of Economic Advisers to the President of the United States was established. Obviously, that's why we have not had any economic problems since then. When considering the proliferation of government agencies, just remember that a camel is a horse designed by a committee. And now let us look at a few of our current camels.

Poor leadership is sometimes rewarded with an equally miserable end. This was certainly the case on this day. In 1437, Scotland's King James I had ruled with more than an iron-clad fist throughout his thirteen-year reign. He treated his nobles harshly; and he approved some very unpopular laws. He forbade drinking after 9 P.M.; he banned his subjects from playing football; he ordered his people to wear clothes appropriate to their social status; and he imprisoned any unemployed person who failed to seek a new job. His reforms didn't garner praise or support. While King James was visiting a priory at Perth, his cousin Sir Robert Stewart, Sir Robert Graham, and eight soldiers murdered the unpopular monarch. The moral of King James' story—strict disciplinary measures have never met with popular approval in any century—is the theme for my remarks today.

Communications took some interesting turns on this day in history. In 1792, George Washington signed an act that created the U.S. Postal Service. This federal service and subsequent agencies like the Federal Communications Commission assured that information would flow smoothly from coast to coast. One agency— the National Emergency Broadcast Service—was organized to keep the public informed in the event of a major crisis. Everything seemed to go well until this date in 1971. On that day, radio and television stations nationwide were erroneously given a presidential order to leave the air for a national emergency and a momentary panic seized the nation. No system is absolutely perfect; and this is especially true when discussing communications systems. Our job is to remain mindful of this natural flaw because messages do get misinterpreted or fall between the cracks. With that in mind, I'd like to offer a few kernels of mislaid information which you may not have heard.

Four socially-conscious men and women celebrate their birthdays today. In 1902, naturalist/photographer Ansel Adams was born. His portraits of America's natural majestic wonders served as proof that we must take greater care of our unique and beautiful untamed environment. In 1927, actor Sidney Poitier was born. Throughout his career, Poitier has stressed the individual's right to dignity and respect. In 1941, Buffy Sainte-Marie was born. Pride in aboriginal heritage and personal self-esteem have been recurring themes in this singer/songwriter's work. Lack of social recognition and economic opportunities for today's youth was the focus of singer/songwriter Kurt Cobain's work. Born in 1967, Cobain was the voice of Generation X who was tragically silenced by his own anger and despair. Like the other men and women born on this day, he spoke from his heart and demanded his moment to be heard. Is that more than anyone should ask? I certainly hope not.

FEBRUARY 21

Freedom of worship was established in France, 1795.

Samuel F.P. Morse gave the first public demonstration of his telegraph, 1838. (See April 27th and May 24th entries.)

Lucy Hobbs became the first female American dentist, 1866.

The world's first telephone directory was published, 1878.

U.S. Army accused Senator Joe McCarthy of browbeating, 1954. (See December 2nd entry.)

President Nixon visited Communist China, 1972.

Playwright Vaclav Havel was convicted, 1989. (See December 29th entry.)

INTRODUCTIONS

I am speaking to you on the historic anniversary of Lucy Hobbs' graduation. In 1866, she became America's first female dentist when she received her degree from the Ohio College of Dental Surgery in Cincinnati. This made possible that most unusual of all events—a woman asking a man to open his mouth. In honor of that occasion, I am opening my mouth here today.

Today is the anniversary of one of the U.S. Army's most historic declarations of war. It was a war of ideas, not bullets. That's Congress' department. But on this date, in 1954, the Army accused Senator Joseph R. McCarthy of browbeating Army personnel during his Communist witch hunts. This Army accusation led to the Senate hearings which eventually led to McCarthy's censure. It might be difficult to think of the U. S. Army as a courtroom defender of an individual's civil rights. But like so many complex concepts, perhaps it should be given some open-minded consideration.

It isn't always what is done, but who does it that counts. This point was made clear when on this date in 1972, President Richard M. Nixon, an ardent anticommunist, traveled on a friendship mission to the Peoples' Republic of China. Because of his reputation, only he could have persuaded American anticommunists to sit still for this U.S. policy change. Perhaps we should ask ourselves when, if ever, issues will be decided on the issues themselves, rather than by the force of an individual personality or because of trust in a particular leader. Certainly we are confronted today by issues which should not depend on who is carrying the flag.

Freedom celebrates many anniversaries on this day. In 1795, the religious persecution of the Huguenots and other Protestant sects ended in France when the government established freedom of worship as part of the nation's essential doctrines. Could it happen now? In 1989, freedom of speech and thought was denied to play-wright Vaclav Havel who was convicted on this day for his role in an officially-banned rally. Havel was sentenced in a Prague courtroom to a 9-month jail term for speaking out against a repressive government. When he later became President of the Czech Republic, one of the first freedoms he established for the newly orga-nized nation was the right for each citizen to voice his or her own opinion. Today, I'd like to exercise that freedom if you will allow me.

Samuel F.P. Morse gave the first public demonstration of his telegraph on this day in 1838. This revolutionary device quickly transformed the way people sent and received information. Another new invention, the telephone, made even quicker communication possible. Exactly fifty years after this artist and inventor from Charlestown, Massachusetts, demonstrated his telegram, the world's first telephone directory was published by the New Haven Telephone Company. Anyone who owned a phone could quickly find the number of any other phone user, and the word has been spreading ever since.

FEBRUARY 22

Popcorn was introduced, 1630.

George Washington was born, 1732. (Celebrated on the closest Monday to this date as Presidents' Day. See February 12th entry.)

Jefferson Davis was inaugurated as Confederate President, 1862.

The Dakota Territory was divided into North and South Dakota, 1889.

Calvin Coolidge delivered the first presidential radio broadcast from the White House, 1924.

The U.S. and the Peoples' Republic of China agreed to establish liaison offices, 1973.

INTRODUCTIONS

Today is George Washington's birthday. And although we now celebrate Washington's and Lincoln's birthdays together on President's Day, it doesn't really matter because Washington was not really born on February 22, 1732, anyway. When he was born, America was still on the old Julian calendar. February 22nd was actually February 11th; we added on 11 days when we adopted the Gregorian cal-endar. After many years of celebrating his birthday on February 11, Washington himself finally changed it to the day we all know. I mention this so that you will understand that people had some options we no longer enjoy today. Having your choice of birthdates was a minor option. You also had plenty of open land and sea on which you could build a life. You couldn't take a plane, or a truck, or a railroad train. But it seems that there was more hope for free men. Perhaps we should ask ourselves why.

America has a collection of folkways and family recipes that, put together, have made up our particular way of life. One recipe was given to us by Native Americans on this date in 1630. That was when the locals introduced the Pilgrims to popcorn. Things have been popping ever since.

As this day in history demonstrates, separation can have both positive and negative effects. In 1862, Jefferson Davis was inaugurated as President of the Confederate States of America. Although the Civil War had already begun, Davis' inauguration symbolized the official split between the northern and southern states. But on this same date in 1889, the vast Dakota Territory was divided into North Dakota and South Dakota, creating a more reasonable way to govern this large section of western America. Even in our own time, separation can strain or improve the health of a tense situation. Let me explain.

I am reminded by today's anniversaries that all of us must keep our lines of communication open. In 1924, Calvin Coolidge delivered the first presidential radio address from his White House office. With the advent of radio, relationships between the nation's chief executive and the public became more personal. In 1973, international communication between the U.S. and the People's Republic of China was established. Both countries agreed to establish liaison offices in Washington D.C. and Beijing, China. Keeping with the spirit of this day I would like to start of by saying: You can agree to agree or agree to disagree with anything I'm about to say, but we must keep our lines of communication open.

FEBRUARY 23

George Friedrich Handel was born, 1685. (See September 14th entry.)

The Siege of the Alamo began, 1836.

Electrolytic process for manufacture of aluminum was invented, 1886.

The Rotary Club was established, 1905.

The American flag was raised on the island of Iwo Jima, Japan, 1945.

Canada, Japan, and the European Common Market nations joined the U.S. in economic and diplomatic sanctions against Poland and the Soviet Union, 1982.

INTRODUCTIONS

This is literally a flag-waving day in history. In 1945, the Marines raised the American flag on the Japanese island of Iwo Jima. A famous photograph—taken by Associated Press photographer Joe Rosenthal at the height of the fighting—was the inspiration for the Iwo Jima monument outside the Arlington National Cemetery near Washington D.C. It represents a spirit of valor which continues to inspire all of us today.

Valor is a tradition not at all unique to America; nor is it a unique American custom handed down from one generation to another. But today marks the anniversary of the siege of San Antonio, Texas. In 1836, the city was defended against the Mexican Army by a small band of determined men who were posted in a mission called the Alamo. The gallantry of those men, including frontiersmen Jim Bowie and Davy Crockett, is well remembered. And we Americans have many Alamos to remember.

Sometimes a thing is so commonplace and ordinary today that we pay very little attention to its anniversary. In 1886, Charles M. Hall invented the electrolytic aluminum manufacturing process. If you stop to think of it, his invention made modern aviation possible, and cooking a lot easier. Hall made a fortune from his invention, but he is one of a vast army of relatively unsung Americans—though infinitely better rewarded than most of them—who have made this world better for their presence. Making the world better, of course, is everybody's business, and it is done in many ways.

One way that people attempt to resolve a common cause is by gathering regularly to discuss shared problems or to voice mutual concerns. Today marks the anniversary of the Rotary Club. In 1905, Chicago attorney Paul P. Harris and three of his friends organized a club that is now an international institution. I don't know how many Rotary Clubs around the world have met how many times and heard how many speakers since that first day, but for public speakers what happened on that date has certainly provided a great many platforms.

Friendship is a powerful asset. When you have friends, you have support for your cause—especially if that cause is freedom. It was on this day in 1982 that a number of caring friendly nations stood together to oppose the use of aggression by one nation against another. The Soviet Union had imposed martial law in Poland to suppress that country's growing opposition to outside rule. In support of Poland's fight for freedom, the U.S., Canada, Japan, and the ten nations that made up the European Common Market mutually agreed to impose economic and diplomatic sanctions, cutting off the aggressor's supply connections. The action weakened the Soviets' effort. In the end, Poland won its freedom. Building friendships may take time and effort, but when the chips are down, you can always rely on friends to lend a helping hand.

FEBRUARY 24

The U.S. Supreme Court ruled that one Act of Congress was unconstitutional, 1803.

Honus Wagner was born, 1874.

INTRODUCTIONS

One of the glories of our American heritage is our Constitution—the supreme law of the land. But it wasn't always that way. We owe a great deal to a court decision which marks its anniversary today. In 1803, the U.S. Supreme Court voided an Act of Congress in the case of Marbury v. Madison. It was the first time a law passed by Congress was deemed unconstitutional. This case not only established that the U.S. Constitution held primary jurisdiction, it also crystallized the Supreme Court's power to ultimately rule on questions of constitutionality. So today's landmark anniversary is worth remembering and also a fitting introduction indeed to the consideration of where we stand today.

In professional baseball's early days, there were some very accomplished players who were also popular heroes. Some players were legendary, like the Five Immortals. But there was one who, long after his playing days were over, was a still familiar ballpark figure. Honus Wagner started playing professionally in 1895. He was the Five Immortals' infielder who was first named to the Baseball Hall of Fame. Wagner was also an active baseball coach until the Second World War. Today is his birthday. Born on this date in 1874, Wagner's career reminds us that we may not be as far away from our beginnings as we sometimes think. We would have a hard time today finding his equal in professional baseball. Maybe we should examine what quality in the American lifestyle gave rise to men like Honus Wagner and how we can nurture its growth.

FEBRUARY 25

Great Britain's Queen Elizabeth I was excommunicated, 1570.

Enrico Caruso was born, 1873.

The Sixteenth Amendment to the U.S. Constitution went into effect, 1913.

George Harrison was born, 1943.

INTRODUCTIONS

Today is an anniversary which prompts no great celebration, but is very much worth noting. In 1913, the Sixteenth Amendment to the U.S. Constitution went into effect. This act authorized the income tax. The helping hand of government has been known on occasion to help itself. We all have Uncle Sam as a partner. None of us works alone. But I doubt that the income tax amendment's authors ever had any idea of the tax chunk Uncle Sam would ultimately take. We know about how big that tax bite has become; but how is it being digested?

Two men were born on this date whose careers invite an interesting comparison. In 1873, Italian opera tenor Enrico Caruso was born; and in 1943, George Harrison of the British pop band, "The Beatles," was born. Caruso and Harrison moved in different musical circles, but they both maintained a strong integrity about doing their jobs their own way. They believed in what they were doing. And both men became cultural heroes. The moral seems to be that it is fine to sing for your supper but it is best to sing in your own way. Ultimately, the individual is bound to emerge. We put a tremendous emphasis on teamwork, but as we look around us we depend to a great extent on our individual stars. That is as true today as ever before.

Two grave historic injustices occurred on this day. In 1570, Pope Pius V issued a bill of excommunication against Great Britain's Queen Elizabeth I. In his zeal to right Great Britain's perceived wrongs against the Church, the pontiff not only condemned the young queen's soul; he also declared her deposed from her earthly throne. He then proclaimed that her own subjects were free to murder her without earthly or heavenly condemnation. No matter what someone does against another, an eye for an eye times two does not resolve the problem. I would like to recommend that instead, we turn the other cheek to a current problem that is nearing a similar head today.

F EBRUARY 26

Napoleon escaped from the island of Elba, 1815.

Buffalo Bill was born, 1846.

Fats Domino was born, 1928.

Johnny Cash was born, 1932.

Brian Jones was born, 1943.

INTRODUCTIONS

On this very day in 1815, Napoleon Bonaparte escaped from the island of Elba. He had been exiled after his reign as self-proclaimed Emperor of France. In the one hundred days following his escape, countless lives were lost. It ended with the Battle of Waterloo, and Napoleon was exiled once again, but this time to the island of St. Helena. Human beings are difficult to convince. Ambition and the lust for power die very hard. That can be seen around us today as surely as when Napoleon's legions were gathering for their last futile battle.

Today is Buffalo Bill Day, which "ain't what it used to be." In his time, Buffalo Bill—or Colonel William F. Cody—was the symbol of the American wild west. It didn't matter that a lot of what he presented was purely show business. Buffalo Bill's Wild West Show gave the whole world a thrilling view of the American frontier. Cody was born on this day in 1846. With some help from his press agent Ned Buntline—who dubbed him Buffalo Bill—this Pony Express rider and frontier scout romanticized the adventurous American wild west. The legends did have some negative effects for three or four generations, so I will now set the record straight. Bill himself respected the aboriginal people he encountered on the plains. And in later years, he fairly employed a number of great men like Sitting Bull. Buffalo Bill may have killed some 4280 buffaloes in his lifetime, but he didn't massacre this uniquely American animal wholesale. Like the Native Americans whom he often accompanied on these hunts, he killed only enough for food and clothing for the hunters' families. So, if we want to consider where we are today, we might look at the real lives—not the legends—of our former heroes like Buffalo Bill and make some comparisons. Perhaps we have made more progress than we think.

Modern music has three distinctly different birthdays to celebrate today. In 1928, jazz composer and pianist Fats Domino was born. His inspired songs like "Blueberry Hill" influenced a generation of exuberant, hopeful youth. In 1932, country and western legend Johnny Cash was born. This hard-edged, rough diamond wrote songs dedicated to American rural life, where young men and women only tentatively walk the line and demand the freedom of the open spaces. In 1943, British pop guitarist Brian Jones was born. A member of the not-so-clean-cut rock band—The Rolling Stones—Jones and the rest of the group exemplified youthful rebellion against a conformist social standard. Art may reflect life, but new music is often the collective voice of younger generations. Maybe we should listen more closely to what our future has to say.

FEBRUARY 27

Henry Wadsworth Longfellow was born, 1807.

John Steinbeck was born, 1902.

The U.S. Supreme Court unanimously guaranteed women's suffrage, 1922.

The Reichstag building burned in Germany, 1933.

The U.S. Supreme Court outlawed sit-down strikes, 1939.

The American Indian Movement began the occupation of Wounded Knee, 1973. (See May 8th and December 29th entries.)

The United States accused North Vietnam delaying the release of American POWs, 1973.

INTRODUCTIONS

All the world, Shakespeare wrote, is a stage. But some world events are themselves staged. And today's anniversary sadly reminds us of this truth. In 1933, the Reichstag parliamentary building—the seat of Germany's fragile democracy—burned in Berlin. Adolf Hitler had been elected Chancellor of Germany, but the nation was politically divided. The Nazi party did not have majority rule and it used this incident to incite a public outcry. The party promptly denounced the fire as a Communist plot. Ultimately that public handed dictatorial powers to Hitler. History's verdict is that the fire was probably set by the Nazis themselves. We must always try to look below the surface to examine possible motives. So I shall speak to you today not only about what seems to be happening, but about why.

When we look at America today, we see not only what is before our eyes but also the mythological images that are part of our legacy. Henry Wadsworth Longfellow—who was born on this day in 1807 in Portland, Maine—contributed a great deal to our treasury of American mythology. The legends of Hiawatha and Evangeline as well as the epic tales of the "Wreck of the Hesperus," "Miles Standish's Courtship," and "Paul Revere's Ride" are only a few of the word images Longfellow painted. I wonder how he would view his country today.

John Steinbeck was born on this day in 1902. And like Henry Wadsworth Longfellow who was also born on this day, Steinbeck contributed to America's mythological legacy. Steinbeck chronicled the strength of the human spirit during the Great Depression in his novel, *The Grapes of Wrath*. And he documented the wisdom of the average American in his travelogue, *Travels with Charlie*. Not many of us can observe and capture in words the memorable images we have of our world like Steinbeck and Longfellow could. But on their birthday, we can certainly follow their model and consider what of our world will become tomorrow's legend.

The U.S. Supreme Court marks two important anniversaries today. In 1922, this august body unanimously guaranteed women's right to vote. After years of civil disobedience—including sit-down strikes and hunger strikes—the suffragists won their battle to be heard. But in 1939, the U.S. Supreme Court outlawed sit-down strikes. The civil unrest spurred by the nation's great economic depression had forced the government's hand for too long. To stop the seemingly endless stream of sit-down strikes organized by unemployed workers and union laborers, the court limited their right to protest. No governing body can be so lenient or so indulgent as to breed anarchy amongst its people; it can only serve to create a balance that strives for the good of all. It is a lesson we need to review more often—especially today.

The issue of human rights marks the anniversaries of two controversial events that occurred on this day in 1973. Angered by the government's disregard for the rights of Native Americans, the American Indian Movement began the occupation of the Oglala Sioux settlement at Wounded Knee, South Dakota. The three-month-long siege took place on the site of an 1890 massacre where American cavalrymen killed hundreds of aboriginal men, women, and children. In the meantime, the government was protesting the violation of the Paris Peace Accords. The United States accused North Vietnam of intentionally delaying the release of American POWs and denying those prisoners their rights under the conventions of war. It is a sad commentary that in our own times, the world has not learned to honor the rights of individuals to have the dignity and respect they deserve.

FEBRUARY 28

Bachelors' Day (in nonleap years).

The Republican party was founded, 1854.

Geraldine Farrar was born, 1882.

Linus Pauling was born, 1901.

Mario Andretti was born, 1940.

Zero Mostel was born, 1915.

INTRODUCTIONS

Many of you probably don't know that today is designated as Bachelors' Day. At least that's the case three years out of every four. In leap years, bachelors are given their day on the 29th. I mention Bachelors' Day only for historical reasons, of course. It's based on an old Leap Day tradition in which a lady could propose marriage to a man. Later, it was changed to every year. Period. Luckily, we no longer have to adhere to such preposterous proprieties. Men have been liberated from the grave responsibility of being the one to propose matrimony. And women have been liberated from the anxiety of waiting for this day to arrive each year. With this in mind, I would like to propose a few unrelated ideas to you regardless of your marital status or gender.

Americans never seem to make much of American opera star Geraldine Farrar's birthday. Born on this date in 1882, Farrar grew up amid the prejudice against American opera singers—even in their own country. American singers before and after her often changed their names to sound Italian in order to be accepted on the operatic stage, but Geraldine Farrar paved the way for the end of this senseless bias. As she matured, she brought glamour and some public acceptance to the profession. That is a pretty good reason to remember her. And on her birthday, it carries a lesson for all of us.

Three famous men born in this day devoted their lives to us in very different ways. First was Linus Pauling, the renowned scientist, humanitarian, and advocate of vitamin C. Born in 1901, he spent much of his life helping us live longer by searching for cures to cancer and heart disease. Champion race care driver Mario Andretti kept us on the edge of our seats throughout his career, making life a little more exciting. The third man, actor Zero Mostel, is perhaps best known for his role as Tevye in *Fiddler on the Roof.* As we consider what each of us can offer the world, I'd like to quote Tevye: "To life!"

A new political party was organized on this day in 1854. Their common cause was simply the total abolition of slavery; their candidate for the 1856 presidential election was John Fremont. Their rallying cry was "Free Soil, Free Labor, Free Speech, Free Men, Fremont!" And they lost. But they didn't give up and their next candidate won. His name was Abraham Lincoln, and that group which stood so firmly for freedom and equality was—and still is—the Republican party. When people join together for a righteous cause they—and we—can change the world, little by little.

FEBRUARY 29

Leap Day. (See Bachelors Day, February 28th entry.)

The first Playboy Club opened, 1960.

President's National Advisory Commission on Civil Disorders warned of racism, 1968.

INTRODUCTIONS

We only get a February 29th once every four years, so we better make the most of it. People who are born on Leap Day have the privilege of growing old four times slower than the rest of us do. The flip side of that coin is that they only have birthdays once every four years. Just like many turns of fate, a good stroke of luck can have its drawbacks. I want to discuss some of those hitches with you today.

One of the world's most famous bachelors marked the celebration of Leap Day by opening an establishment dedicated to bachelors worldwide. It seems appropriate since historically, Leap Day was also known as Bachelors' Day. In 1960, Hugh Hefner, the publisher of *Playboy Magazine,* opened the Playboy Club on Chicago's Gold Coast. Though you may know this living symbol of male sophistication and bachelorhood opened a private membership club, you might not know that it gave many famous African-American entertainers their first shot at stardom. The Playboy Club also provided a new forum for a few controversial comedians who went on to become pop icons. On this Bachelor's Day, at least none of us old-maids, bachelors, or married people have to consider what life would have been like if Hef hadn't opened the doors and swept out many outmoded taboos. Let me explain.

In 1968, this was the day when the President's National Advisory Commission on Civil Disorders issued a report about the racial and social problems that were plaguing the nation. I would like to read a brief quotation from that report. It said: "Our nation is moving toward two societies, one black and one white—separate and unequal." What would a similar commission say today?

MARCH

INTRODUCTION

Some people say that if March comes in like a lion, it will go out like a lamb. In the spirit of this old proverb, I want to roar about some great news that will definitely warm your heart while we're waiting for spring to arrive.

MARCH 1

The first U.S. census was authorized, 1790

The U.S. Peace Corps was established, 1961.

INTRODUCTIONS

Did you ever stop to think how much we depend on numbers? Think about it today, because it is the anniversary of the day the first U.S. census was authorized. Since that first day in 1790, we have been counting heads—to determine Congressional districts, to allocate government money, to figure out unemployment rates and so forth. But numbers are part of life, from baseball terms like three strikes you're out; to payment terms such as net thirty days. Life has become so arithmetical that you're probably already counting the moments until my speech ends.

President John F. Kennedy's most notable monument for many years was a noble idea. The Peace Corps was born on this date in 1961. Years later, when Jimmy Carter went to the White House, one of the things that endeared him to voters was that his mother, in her sixties, had been a Peace Corps volunteer in India. The Peace Corps, unlike other American aid organizations, supplies needy nations with shared knowledge, not handouts. Skilled, experienced people traveled to third-world nations and to this nation's depressed areas to impart their know-how; to work side-by-side with inhabitants, to help them help themselves. It is good for us to remember this anniversary of a notable characteristic—the giving of oneself.

MARCH 2

Texas declared its independence from Mexico, 1836.

Hayes-Tilden election was decided by a special Congressional commission, 1877. (See January 29th entry.)

Dr. Seuss was born, 1904.

Vietnam peace treaty was signed in Paris, 1973.

INTRODUCTIONS

I wonder what today's journalists would say if a presidential election took place, and four months later, nobody had been able to decide who was elected? What would they say if a special commission made the decision about which votes counted and which votes didn't? That is a somewhat oversimplified account of exactly what happened in 1876 and 1877. A special electoral commission declared Rutherford B. Hayes as the elected U.S. President over Samuel J. Tilden on this day. It was an era when the population as a whole had a lot more patience. There may be a lesson in this for all of us.

Some of you are only here to listen to me because of an event that took place on this day in 1973. The United States, the Viet Cong, and the North and South Vietnamese signed a peace treaty in Paris, France. The Vietnam War cost many lives; divided Americans into two opposing camps; prompted riots in the nation's cities; affected national and local elections; and—to a frightening extent—disaffected a substantial portion of a generation. But had those negotiatons failed, countless more Americans might have been killed. Before we judge the efforts of current international diplomats, we might look back to this date and ask ourselves what should have been done to end it sooner. Do we now think we should have done something else? As we ponder our future, let us remember our not-so-distant past.

I wonder if it was mere coincidence that on Sam Houston's 43rd birthday, Texas declared its independence from Mexico. The Lone Star Republic had Sam Houston as President; and ultimately when the republic became the Lone Star State, Houston spent 14 years as the state's senator. He only retired when secession from the union became a popular vote. There is a lesson in this for every working politician. The wisest leaders know not only when to stand firm, but also when to move with the times. Take our own times, for example.

One birthday is special for me and for you, and before I am done you'll know who it is, too. He was born Theodor in the year 1904. Born, they say, on this very day. He grew up and drew pictures—pictures galore! He drew Horton and Grinch and the

Cat in the Hat, too. He drew Gerald McBoing Boing, the Lorax, and a Who. He's called Dr. Seuss—Theodor Geisel to boot. Everyone loves him, even owls give a hoot. He reminds us to care in the simplest way. About everything, everyone, every day.

M ARCH 3

"The Star Spangled Banner" became the U.S. national anthem, 1931.

Alexander Graham Bell was born, 1847. (See January 25th and March 7th entries.)

The District of Columbia was organized, 1791.

Congress established the Home Department, 1849.

Czar Alexander II abolished serfdom, 1861.

Apollo 9 was launched to test the lunar landing module, 1969.

INTRODUCTIONS

"The Star Spangled Banner" was written by Frances Scott Key in 1814. But on this date in 1931, this song officially became our national anthem. Congress sometimes lags considerably behind public sentiment and public practice. I imagine everyone here today could recite a list of laws that Congress should have acted on quickly but didn't because we the people didn't want it yet. But we were using "The Star Spangled Banner" as our national anthem long before it became official. There is no law that says we have to wait for Congress to move before we tackle a problem. We pride ourselves on being a nation of doers, on being able to work together voluntarily. Okay. We have plenty of opportunities to dig right in.

The man responsible for the swift delivery of more good news, bad news, and gossip than anyone wants to hear was born today in 1847. When Alexander Graham Bell was a young man he left his home in Edinburgh, Scotland, to teach what he called "visible speech"—a sort of sign language—to the hearing impaired in Boston, Massachusetts. In the course of his work, he experimented with a device that transmitted sound electronically. His tests finally succeeded when he called out to his assistant: "Mr. Watson, come here. I want you." His voice came through a small horn connected to a wire stretched from another part of the house. Bell's telephone eventually knit sprawling cities and the whole world together. It spawned new businesses. It created a new household necessity. And today I ask you to join me in an affectionate but critical look at the communication age that Bell's invention ushered in.

One might think that our nation's capital—including all of its governing departments—were established all at once. But in truth, it took many decades to create what we now take for granted, and today marks the establishment of two key elements. In 1791, the District of Columbia was organized, establishing a nonpartisan home for our federal government. In 1849, the U.S. Congress established the Home Department which is now known as the Department of the Interior. Buildings and nations must be constructed brick by brick, step by step to ensure a solid foundation and a secure structure. It's a formula that also applies to relationships between individuals and groups. Let me present some sound examples.

A wise man tests his concept before making a firm decision on its success. On this day in 1969, some wise men at NASA launched the Apollo 9 space mission to test the soundness of the lunar landing module before having astronauts use it on the moon. Bravery must always be tempered by the wisdom of experience, otherwise brave acts become foolhardy ventures. Isn't it time for us to test a few of our current theories before blasting off into the unknown?

While the Civil War between the northern and southern states over the abolition of slavery was still being waged, Czar Alexander II of Russia issued a manifesto which officially abolished serfdom. On this day in 1861, Alexander decreed that no individual could force another to work in exchange for life and little else. The feudal system that had long been synonymous with peasant life was finally dissolved. No longer enslaved by landowners and nobles, an individual was free to work wherever and for whomever he chose; and had the right to be paid for labor. The terms indentured servitude and slavery have often been equated with the building of great empires. Equal compensation for comparable work is still a hotly debated question, and one I would like to address today.

MARCH 4

Presidential Inauguration Day, until 1937. (See January 20th entry.)

The U.S. Constitution went into effect, 1789.

Knute Rockne was born, 1888. (See November 1st entry.)

INTRODUCTIONS

This is one of those days when a speaker could deliver an entire speech made of quotations from past speeches made on this same date. Up until President Franklin D. Roosevelt's second term, this was Inauguration Day in the United States. In 1801, Thomas Jefferson became the first president to be sworn in at the nation's capital. In 1861, Abraham Lincoln stood on the same spot and said: "This country, with its institutions, belongs to the people who inhabit it. Whenever they shall grow weary of the existing government, they can exercise their constitutional right of amending it, or their revolutionary right to dismember or overthrow it." In 1933, FDR stood before the nation and proclaimed: "The only thing we have to fear is fear itself" and called for "action, and action now." If there is one paramount thread in inaugural addresses, it is that the people ultimately decide their own destiny. That is a pretty good text for our own times.

Today marks the anniversary of the U.S. Constitution's official enactment. In 1789, the entire nation banded together under this important statement of rights and responsibilities. It has been challenged; it has been amended; but it remains the organic, yet supreme law of the land. The Constitution is not a weathervane for current public opinion. But it knows when to bend to the people's everchanging needs. It stands as a bulwark against temporary public passions. But it protects its citizens against governmental encroachment. It is the written chronicle of a constantly maturing relationship. I would like to recall some hills and valleys that were traveled as we the people shaped our relationship with our government.

Today is the birthday of an immigrant who, for many, epitomizes middle America. He was born in Voss, Norway, on this date in 1888. He came to this country with his family when he was five years old. He went to college and became a chemistry instructor, as well as assistant coach of the football team. His name was Knute Rockne. If anyone can be said to have revolutionized American football and put it on the map, it was this man, Notre Dame's Knute Rockne. What Rockne did for America in his time, I am sure, is being done now, or will be done soon, by newer immigrants. We have only to look around us to see that America's immigrant population has a lot to contribute to this nation as a whole.

MARCH 5

The Feast of St. Pirans.

The Boston Massacre took place, 1770.

Rex Harrison was born, 1908.

Winston Churchill delivered his "Iron Curtain" speech, 1946.

INTRODUCTIONS

Since today is the feast day dedicated to St. Pirans, patron saint of miners, I will invoke his name before delivering my remarks. With his protection, I promise not to lead you down a dark tunnel without providing you with a light at the end and some golden insights along the way.

This is the date when, in 1770, British troops fired into an unruly crowd in an incident known as the Boston Massacre. In light of later worldwide developments, it is interesting to know that just five men died in that massacre. At the battle of

Lexington—when the American Revolution started—eight men were killed and ten were wounded. In the Second World War, millions were killed on the battlefield and in concentration camps. But massacre—like so many other words in our language—is a relative term. It can refer to the cold-bloodedness as well as the volume of slaughter. It is a reminder that mere numbers are not the measure of impact. It is the cause and effect of situations that matter most.

Probably no phrase has been a more eloquent summary of an attitude than an expression Winston Churchill coined on this day. In 1946, Churchill delivered a speech in Fulton, Missouri, in which he said: "From Stettin in the Baltic to Trieste in the Adriatic, an iron curtain has descended across the Continent." For nearly five decades, the Iron Curtain separated two hostile ideologies. The rift didn't start with Churchill's speech, but his words crystallized the realization that an international breach was forming. The Iron Curtain has crumbled, but we must never forget how easily opposing doctrines can build walls between people.

On this, Rex Harrison's birthday, I am clearly reminded that this British actor was truly a man's man. Born in 1908, this Lancashire native grew to become a legendary film and stage presence, playing everyone from the King of Siam to eccentric murderers. But as the eccentric Professor Henry Higgins in the musical *My Fair Lady*, Harrison inspired the theme for my remarks today. Why can't a woman be more like a man?

M ARCH 6

Alamo Day. (See February 23rd entry.)

Michelangelo was born, 1475.

The U.S. Supreme Court ruled that the slave Dred Scott could not sue for his freedom in a federal court, 1857.

The Spitfire MK1 took to the air, 1936.

France recognized Vietnam as a free state within the French Indochina Federation, 1946.

Svetlana Alliluyeva announced her intention to defect from the U.S.S.R., 1967.

INTRODUCTIONS

Some people leave their mark on the world in the shape of ideas; some leave a legacy of deeds; and others seem to leave no mark at all. But fewer people still have ever donated their genius. Today we celebrate Michelangelo's birthday. In 1475, this visionary artist was born in Caprese, Italy. When he died he left behind the glorious ceiling and altar of the Vatican's Sistine Chapel; and the immortal statues of David and the Pieta as his heirlooms. He championed a new realism at a time when we were uncertain how to define human proportions—both physically and spiritually. He made us see who and what we really are in relation to the universe that surrounds us. It is that sense of awe and revelation that is my text for today.

Freedom must never be taken for granted. Many people have paid a high price for freedom on this day. In 1946, France recognized Vietnam as a free state within the French Indochina Federation. But in 1857, the slave Dred Scott was denied his freedom when the U.S. Supreme Court ruled that he could not sue for his freedom in a federal court. In 1967, Svetlana Alliluyeva announced her intention to defect from the U.S.S.R. Even though she was the daughter of Soviet dictator Josef Stalin, she was willing to give up her home to gain the freedom she desired. How valuable is your freedom to you?

During the Second World War, England and Germany had unique icons that symbolized their respective might as nations—airplanes. Germany had designed the Messerschmitt which was considered to be the world's fastest fighter plane. But it was on this date in 1936 that a British prototype took to the air—the Supermarine Spitfire. Designed by Reginald Mitchell, the Spitfire was the pride of England's RAF fleet well into the 1950s. It was also a source of jealousy for German pilots throughout the war. You see, the Messerschmitt had been designed to hold the perfect German. And though Hitler was little more than five feet tall—not the average build of the Luftwafte airmen—no one in his ranks wished to tell him he wasn't the perfect German. Their plane was fast, but very cramped. Good ideas can develop and be realized in many ways, but great ideas are developed and realized with a keen understanding of their users' needs. I won't ask you to squeeze into my ideas. Let's work together to find the best fit for all of us

March 7

Luther Burbank was born, 1849. (Burbank Day)

The sewing machine that could stitch buttonholes was patented, 1854.

The telephone was patented, 1876. (See January 25th and March 3rd entries.)

Germany violated the Treaty of Versailles, 1936.

The Remagen Bridge was captured, 1945.

INTRODUCTIONS

Today is Burbank Day. You might not know that it commemorates Luther Burbank's birthday, unless you are a horticulturist. Burbank developed over 200 varieties of fruits and vegetables, as well as hundreds of hybrid flowers at his

California laboratory. The world became a more colorful place and a more delectable place thanks to this man's efforts. Strangely enough, people who work to beautify the land never seem to enjoy the lasting fame of those who lead battles or win elections. Perhaps it would be refreshing for us to look at the gentle art of growing things as a refreshing change of pace.

It has been said that every deed is just another stepping stone on an eternal road. Today marks a number of anniversaries that prove this point. In 1936, Germany violated the Treaty of Versailles by occupying the Rhineland. One single step led that nation on the rocky road to war. In 1945, the U.S. Ninth Armored Division captured Germany's Remagen Bridge. That maneuver changed the course of the Second World War in favor of the Allied powers. No action—however isolated it may appear in the present—ever stands alone. Each deed moves us one step further on life's eternal road. It is up to each individual to decide if that road we all travel is straight or curved; if it crosses a bridge and moves forward; or if it ends at the water's edge.

I certainly hope that one of today's anniversaries will not inspire you to request that I button my mouth. On this date in 1854, Charles Miller of St. Louis, Missouri, was granted a patent. He had invented a sewing machine that could stitch buttonholes. And in 1876, Alexander Graham Bell was granted a patent for his telephone. I hope you will listen carefully in commemoration of buttons and dials. My idea is likewise tightly stitched, and it's even got a nice ring to it.

M ARCH 8

The British House of Lords passed the Stamp Act, 1765. (See March 18th and March 22nd entries.)

Oliver Wendell Holmes, Jr. was born, 1841.

The U.S.S.R. declared that they had built an atomic bomb, 1950.

Arnold Schuster was killed in Brooklyn, 1962.

President Jimmy Carter went on a Middle East peace mission, 1979. (See January 7th entry.)

INTRODUCTIONS

It is Oliver Wendell Holmes, Jr.'s birthday. Born on this date in 1841, Holmes was the son of a New England doctor who was also a famous literary figure. Oliver Junior chose to walk a different path. He became an attorney. As a U.S. Supreme Court Justice, Holmes was famous for the brilliance of his dissents and for the power of his judgments. Like his noted father, he was a brilliant writer. Like his father, he was long-lived. He served on the Supreme Court for over three decades. He resigned when he was well past 90. I begin today's remarks by quoting something Holmes wrote in 1919: "The best test of truth is the power of the thought to get itself accepted in the competition of the market." That is the competition I propose to enter here and now.

Not too many people today recognize the name of Arnold Schuster. But on this date in 1952, this law-abiding citizen recognized the legendary bank robber Willie Sutton; told the police; and was later shot and killed in Brooklyn, New York. Shuster's murder was never solved, and I dare say it discouraged many other law-abiding citizens from turning criminals in to the police. One of today's unsolved problems is how to adequately protect, let alone compensate, those who take the risk of giving public aid to law-enforcement agencies. Time and again we read of cases where a good Samaritan ends up in the hospital or on welfare while the suspected criminal he helped apprehend gets out on bail. The question is not whether to abridge the rights of the accused, but rather how to aid those who find themselves as victims.

As a nation, Americans don't take declarations of any kind lightly. When Great Britain's House of Lords imposed the Stamp Act on this day in 1765, Americans spoke out by boycotting all imported British goods including sugar and tea. This first direct tax placed on the fledgling colonies was supposed to pay for military defense during the French and Indian War. But Americans cried out that taxation without representation was tyranny. In 1950, the U.S.S.R. declared that they had built an atomic bomb, and once again, Americans did not take the declaration lightly. The military built more atomic weapons to balance the power between these two mighty nations. I certainly hope that the declaration I'm about to make will not incite such explosive reactions from you.

Sometimes, the actions of one individual can inspire many to find a reasonable resolution to their problems. On this day in 1979, President Jimmy Carter began a Middle East peace mission. This simple act of diplomacy eventually led to the signing of the first Egyptian-Israeli peace treaty, ending the long-running conflict between the two nations. In the spirit of President Carter's deed, I would like to discuss how we—as a group of individuals—could inspire others to resolve some recent problems peacefully.

M ARCH 9

Amerigo Vespucci was born, 1401.
Benjamin Franklin wrote his creed, 1790.

Napoleon Bonaparte married Josephine de Beauharnais, 1796. (See June 24th entry.)

Artificial teeth were patented, 1822.

Japanese ambassador Niimi Buzennokami arrived in San Francisco, CA, 1860.

The first battle of the ironclads took place, 1862.

Bobby Fischer was born, 1943. (See September 1st entry.)

Alaskan pipeline construction began, 1975.

INTRODUCTIONS

This is Amerigo Vespucci's birthday. In 1401, the man after whom America is named was born in Florence, Italy. I don't pretend to understand why America was given the Christian name of the navigator and mapmaker who placed the continent on a navigational chart, whereas Colombia was named after the surname of the discoverer of the New World. It is hard to imagine the United States of Vespucci. So we celebrate Amerigo Vespucci Day with a feeling which I hope will be strengthened by my remarks, namely that no matter how things are, they could have been worse.

On this day in 1790, Benjamin Franklin took pen in hand and wrote a letter to the Reverend Ezra Stiles, who had asked about Dr. Franklin's religious beliefs. I am grateful to Reverend Stiles for asking, because Franklin's answer is so appropriate today. "I believe in one God," wrote Franklin, "Creator of the Universe. That he governs it by his Providence. That he ought to be worshipped. That the most acceptable Service we render to him is doing good to his other children."

As I was researching my notes for today's speech, I uncovered an interesting tidbit of information. On this day in 1822, Charles Graham of New York City was granted a patent for artificial teeth. Now that I've served up that appetizer, let's chew on a really important piece of news.

Making connections isn't always a simple task, but sometimes persistence pays, as today's anniversaries will attest. In 1860, Japanese ambassador Niimi Buzennokami arrived in San Francisco, California. After centuries of isolation and years of delicate negotiation, Japan finally established diplomatic relations with its eastern neighbor, the United States. In 1975, the Alaskan pipeline was begun, connecting the contiguous United States to its northern sister-state's most valuable resource—oil. It took years of hard work in the wilderness to establish that lifeline for industry. With any luck, I will establish a sound relationship with all of you in a lot less time.

Today marks a few meetings of great minds. On this date in 1796, Napoleon Bonaparte married Josephine de Beauharnais. Their romance inspired an empire, though their reign didn't last. In 1943, another master strategist was born in

Chicago. Chess player Bobby Fischer rose to prominence when he played board champion Boris Spassky for the world chess title. Hopefully, we can all be inspired by strategic meetings rather than following the example of the ironclads. In 1862, two pioneer warships—the *Monitor* and the *Merrimac*—fought a furious battle in the harbor near Hampton Roads, Virginia. Great meetings don't have to become great firefights; they can be a powerful introduction to mutual admiration.

MARCH 10

The U.S. government issued its first paper money, 1862.

Italian women voted for the first time, 1946.

Jan Masaryk was defenestrated, 1948.

Mildred Gillars was convicted of treason, 1949.

Carla Hills became the Secretary of Housing and Urban Development, 1975.

INTRODUCTIONS

You all know how difficult it is toting a pocketful of change around. Imagine what it was like when you had to lug your dollars around in the same fashion. This is the anniversary of a truly ingenious solution. In 1862, the U.S. government issued its first paper money. Instead of carrying bags of five, ten, and twenty dollar coins, the government made it easier to transport and conceal the very same amount. Let's tip our hats to the individuals who made high finance less cumbersome and move on to some even more valuable thoughts.

A question mark hangs over this particular day. It goes back to 1948, when the late Jan Masaryk, son of Czechoslovakia's founder and a champion of democratic self-government fell from a window in Prague and died. Masaryk was his nation's anti-communist Foreign Minister. Many believe he was pushed; and his tragic death did make it easier for the Communists to consolidate their control. History is filled with mysteries that can throw considerable light on larger matters when and if they are ever solved. We face the same type of mysteries today: why certain people behave as they do, why certain leaders choose to make a mountain of some particular molehill. Asking why reveals the extent of this never-ending puzzle.

The world's view of women has changed on this day a number of times in recent history. In 1946, Italian women were allowed to vote for the first time. Their influence was limited to local elections, but that first step was a major one. In 1949, Mildred Gillars was convicted of treason. During the second World War, Gillars was known as Axis Sally. She applied a woman's touch to her Nazi propaganda broadcasts, reminding Allied soldiers that their sweethearts might not wait for them so they should give up the battle and go home. In 1975, the third woman to hold a U.S. cabinet position was appointed. Carla Hills became the Secretary of Housing and Urban Development. Women—like men—can exert their influence for good or bad causes, but their sway cannot be denied. What good cause deserves a woman's touch today?

MARCH 11

The Blizzard of 1888.
Lend-Lease Law was signed, 1941.

INTRODUCTIONS

Everybody talks about the weather, but nobody does anything about it. Ask anyone what subject makes news more often than any other. Chances are the answer will be sports or crime. But the truth is that the weather makes news daily. It definitely was on everyone's mind back in 1888. On this day, a blizzard started in the northeastern United States. The storm lasted for three days, piling up mountains of snow in record proportions. The people who lived through the Blizzard of 1888 talked about it for the rest of their lives. Even today, each generation feels that its great war topped, or bottomed, all other wars; each generation thinks that its challenges are the most severe. We are no different from our predecessors. We view the same world from different perspectives. I think we should try to view our world from someone else's perspective other than our own.

This is the anniversary of the Lend-Lease Law. In 1941, President Franklin D. Roosevelt signed an act that authorized the shipping of war supplies to England and other nations fighting Nazi Germany during the Second World War without physically involving ourselves. We should remember this the next time we equate neutrality and impartiality. We, as individuals, often describe ourselves as neutral when what we really mean is we are nonbelligerent. There is a considerable difference between these two terms. We should ask ourselves: When are we really neutral; when are we simply nonbelligerent; when are we truly in a state of war?

MARCH 12

President Roosevelt gave his first fireside chat, 1933.
Nazi Germany occupied Austria, 1938.

INTRODUCTIONS

When our country was very young, each president was seen by the people only in the few places he had occasion to personally visit. As the nation grew, the chief executive was still seen and heard by a relatively small handful of the electorate, but his picture and words were carried in the nation's newspapers. Then came Franklin D. Roosevelt. In 1933, he tried something new on this date; he broadcast a fireside chat on national radio. Ever since that day, presidents have been brought directly to the people, by television, via satellite, and even via the Internet. Perhaps today will not go down in history books as a key anniversary in the evolution of the democratic process, but maybe it should.

We often find ourselves wondering what would have happened if one deed in a chain of events had been different. And today's anniversary gives us a reason to ponder. In 1938, Adolf Hitler's Nazi Germany invaded Austria and set about what they called Anschluss—the incorporation of Austria into Germany. It shocked the world. But the world did nothing about it. And Hitler occupied more neighboring nations. We will never know whether that chain of events could have been broken; whether other nations could have dissuaded Germany with something stronger than mere verbal protest. We must ask ourselves: Have we stood up as strongly as we might for what we believe is right?

MARCH 13

Joseph Priestley was born, 1733.

Uranus was discovered, 1781.

The first Uncle Sam cartoon was published, 1852.

Czar Alexander II was assassinated, 1881.

World standard time was established, 1884.

Ear mufflers were patented, 1877.

Tennessee outlawed the teaching of evolution, 1935. (See May 5th entry.)

Clifford and Edith Irving pleaded guilty to conspiracy charges, 1972. (See January 9th entry.)

TheArab nations agreed to end their five-month oil embargo, 1974. (See October 17 entry.)

I. King Jordan became president of Gallaudet University in Washington, D.C., 1988.

The House of Representatives unanimously voted to publicly identify 355 current Capitol Hill check bouncers, 1992.

INTRODUCTIONS

As I stand here before you, clocks all over the world are synchronized. It isn't the same time everywhere, but we can look at our watches and calculate the time in Singapore or Moscow or Timbuktu. We've only been able to do that since 1884, when an international conference held on this date in Washington, D.C. established an international time standard based on Greenwich Mean Time. I wonder what would happen if such a conference, for such a purpose, were called today. Would there be a third-world coalition demanding that the base time be moved from Greenwich, England to some spot below the equator? Would the whole idea be denounced as a plot? Would a vast international bureaucracy be created—or at least sought—to regulated its administration? And how long would it take to settle matters? After all, where time is concerned, time is no object.

Uncle Sam is our most popular American relative. He's been around a long time and today's his birthday. In 1802, the lanky Yankee in the star-spangled suit was born in the issue of *The New York Lantern*, a weekly newspaper. Frank Bellew drew the original character that replaced the nation's previous cartoon symbol—Brother Jonathan. We seem to be the only country whose popular national symbol is a public relative. I think that says something about Uncle Sam, his nephews, and his nieces. We are, in a very real sense, everybody's relatives.

Nature played a key role in a couple of events that occurred on this date. In 1733, Joseph Priestley was born in Leeds, England. This Yorkshire chemist's discovery—oxygen—swept the world like a breath of fresh air. But in 1781, British astronomer Sir William Herschel discovered the planet Uranus. We should never take the air we breathe and the skies above us for granted. The universe is filled with so many unsolved mysteries—including the mystery of how to preserve these resources so future generations won't be forced into space to survive.

Isn't it ironic that on the same day the planet Uranus and oxygen were discovered, we would also mark the anniversary of our return to ignorance? In 1935, the state of Tennessee officially outlawed the teaching evolution in schools. The fundamentalist fervor that triggered this action also fueled the famous John Scopes "monkey trial." Clarence Darrow bravely defended the young teacher accused and convicted of teaching a religious heresy. The search for truth does not always follow a simple path. Scopes, Galileo, and many others have been persecuted for seeking answers outside of established dogma. We must keep our minds open and always be willing to weigh every fact if we really want to know the truth.

The struggle to be heard hit a high watermark on this day in 1988, when I. King Jordan became president of Gallaudet University in Washington, D.C. Students of this liberal arts college for the hearing impaired demanded to be heard: They protested the school's tradition of hiring hearing-persons as presidents. When

Jordan became the school's first hearing-impaired president—succeeding Elisabeth Ann Zinser, a hearing person—it demonstrated how much life can change for the physically challenged. This is a national voice that has remained silent for too long.

Hasty actions can be the undoing of well-meaning schemes. On this day in 1881, Czar Alexander III was assassinated by radical terrorists who demanded a constitutional government in Russia. Ironically, the czar had just signed a bill to establish exactly what they wanted. When he died, so did the enactment of the agreement. In their haste to obtain certain freedoms, the conspirators destroyed their own dreams by not waiting for an official response. A more recent example of haste potentially making waste is being played out right now.

When the U.S. House of Representatives unanimously voted, on this day in 1992, to publicly identify 355 current and former members who had overdrawn their accounts at the House bank, public confidence was dampened by a thick atmosphere of mistrust in elected officials. Even if you're not a politician, building public trust and confidence is only the tip of the iceberg; maintaining that trust takes a lifetime of hard and honest work.

Chester Greenwood of Farmington, Maine, was granted a patent on this day in 1877. This fact causes me some level of concern as I stand here before you because Mr. Greenwood invented a pair of ear mufflers. Despite their obvious advantage against winter winds and cold, ear muffs do create a problem for public speakers—they limit the wearer's ability to listen. I'm about to fill the room with hot air so all of you wearing ear muffs might as well take them off and listen to what I have to say.

Dependence on a single resource is a weakness that can enslave and destroy even the mighty. The United States learned that lesson on this day in 1974. The group of oil-producing Arab nations who had imposed a five-month embargo on sales to the U.S. ended their sanction. American dependence on outside oil resources crippled both industry and the economy. They tried to solve the problem by tapping into oil sources closer to home. But even though the world's natural oil supply dwindles year by year, little has been done to find renewable alternatives that will ultimately free us from the slavery of resource dependence.

M ARCH 14

America's first town meeting was held, 1743.
Eli Whitney received a patent for the cotton gin, 1794. (See December 8th entry.)
Albert Einstein was born, 1879.

Philippine military and naval bases were leased to the U.S., 1947.

New York hired a rainmaker, 1950.

INTRODUCTIONS

Today is Albert Einstein's birthday. Born in 1879 in Ulm, Germany, Einstein's life story illustrates quite a few morals. For one thing, the man who is regarded as one of the world's geniuses was not a particularly good student. He was not really a late bloomer, just an individualist who went at his own pace in his own way. He won the 1921 Nobel Prize in Physics for creating a tremendous revolution with his theory of relativity. He also escaped Nazi Germany and immigrated to the United States, where he spent the rest of his life championing the need for atomic research. Einstein even wrote to President Franklin Roosevelt to plead his cause. If there is any truth in the old adage that right makes might, Einstein's story seems to bear it out. This man of peace helped forge the key to the world's most terrible weapon. He was a German exile who became one of his adopted country's great assets. There won't be many Einsteins in our lifetime; but his story is one that we would all do well to remember.

Eli Whitney got a patent for his cotton gin on this day in 1794. The cotton gin patent, however, turned out to be only one of his great contributions. His cotton gin did reduce the need for hand labor which gave a tremendous boost to the South's development. But Whitney also fathered the idea of mass production; the use of interchangeable parts; and the concept of the assembly line. Very few Americans have contributed as much to the nation's economic development as Eli Whitney. The next time you go to your mechanic to have the car fixed, you might stop and think of how much more that repair bill might be if Whitney hadn't come up with the concept of interchangeable parts.

Throughout the United States, town meetings are regularly held to keep local populations informed about and involved in matters directly affecting their community. Today is the anniversary of America's first town meeting. In 1743, a group of concerned citizens met at Boston's Faneuil Hall to voice their opinions on key issues. Town meetings often shed critical light on matters by publicly presenting all sides of the story without editorial bias. In commemoration of this event, I propose we consider this a town meeting here and now, about an issue that affects all of us.

Terminating an agreement is not necessarily a sign of weakness nor the start of an argument. When military and naval bases in the Philippine Islands were leased to the U.S. for 99 years on this day in 1947, the political climate in the Pacific Rim was still shaky. American military presence ensured that nation's security amid great political turmoil. As it is a former American territory, the U.S. government felt a strong allegiance to this large group of islands situated off the Chinese coast. During the 1970s, the agreement was amended several times to suit the needs of both nations. But in 1991, the U.S. terminated its lease and evacuated its bases. It wasn't that U.S. military defense had weakened, or that diplomatic relations between the nations had ceased. Simply, there was no longer any foreign threat to warrant that kind of presence. To cancel an agreement that no longer serves the needs of both parties can sometimes prevent trouble before it begins. It's also a potential solution to another emerging situation that we must confront today.

Desperate times often trigger desperate actions. After months of suffering a severe drought followed by a dry winter, it looked as if there wouldn't be enough water to supply New York through the summer. A crisis was in the making. On this day in 1950, New York hired an old-fashioned rainmaker. Dr. Wallace Howard, director of New Hampshire's Mount Washington Observatory, tried every trick in the book to make it rain. And one month later, it snowed. The crisis was averted. But this story is a good example of how people will resort to any available means to solve a problem. Now before time runs short, let me make my point and leave, before you rain on my parade. And I promise not to try to snow you, or to rain on your parade.

Marcia 15

The Ides of March.

Buzzard Day in Hinckley, Ohio.

Julius Caesar was assassinated, 44 BC.

The world's first blood bank was established, 1937.

INTRODUCTIONS

The Ides of March are upon us. It was William Shakespeare who warned us to beware the Ides of March. We used to think his advice was prophetic, because March 15th—the Ides of March—used to be the day when your Federal income taxes were due. We now have an extra month for that delightful exercise. But there is enough in history to keep reminding us of the Ides of March.

Julius Caesar was forewarned about the Ides of March. It was an accurate warning. He was stabbed to death on that very day in 44 BC by a group of Roman senators including his friend Brutus. Being killed is bad enough, but having it done by a friend is even worse. This also applies to verbal backstabbing. I am not suggesting you had better check up on your friends, because, as Caesar said, the die was cast. Just remember the sage advice of baseball great Satchel Paige: "Don't look back; someone might be gaining on you."

Nature's clock is more reliable than any manmade timekeeper. Today is one of those natural time markers. The town of Hinckley, Ohio, commemorates this day as

Buzzard Day. Like the swallows that return to San Juan Capistrano, the buzzards are scheduled to return on this day to Hinckley. The town sets aside the first Sunday after this date as Buzzard Sunday. So let us remember, with an eye to the buzzards, that there is a time and place for everything.

Today marks the anniversary of a lifesaving bank. The deposits and withdrawals made at this bank spelled the difference between life and death for many people. What's even more surprising is that no one is turned away at the door if they need a loan. Dr. Bernard Fantus established the world's first blood bank on this day in 1937, at Chicago's Cook County Hospital. Both blood and plasma could finally be safely collected, stored, and distributed to patients who did not have family with similar blood types—a breakthrough for surgical procedures and emergency treatment. Isn't it refreshing to know there's a banking system that will save your life without charging you interest?

M ARCH 16

England severed relations with the Roman Catholic Church, 1534. (See February 11th and February 25th entries.)

James Madison was born, 1751.

The U.S. Military Academy at West Point was established by law, 1802.

Harry Houdini became the first man to fly an airplane in Australia, 1910.

The first liquid-fuel rocket was flown, 1926. (Scc March 23rd entry.)

INTRODUCTIONS

This is the anniversary of the day President Thomas Jefferson signed a law establishing a great educational institution. The U.S. Military Academy at West Point, New York was born in 1802 on this date. Throughout its history, it has been far more than a military institute. We sometimes forget that, at a time when higher education was offered only to rich Americans, West Point offered it to those who merited it—regardless of their economic station. The long gray line of cadets produced great generals; but it also produced distinguished presidents, corporate heads, and academic leaders. Its motto stands as solid as its reputation, and I commend it to your attention here and now—duty, honor, country.

The first liquid-fueled rocket was flown on this date in 1926. Dr. Robert H. Goddard succeeded in his experiment in Auburn, Massachusetts. Ironically, few people noticed. But if the U.S. at the time was not interested in rocketry, another country was. While the Second World War was raging, the young German scientist Wernher von Braun pushed the development of Goddard's idea and created rocket-powered weapons like buzz bombs and missiles. After the war, von Braun came to the U.S. and helped guide our historic space program. Goddard's idea finally flowered in his homeland after all. But the story of what happened after this historic day reminds us that we have not always been as ready to accept change—as ready to work on new ideas—as we'd like to think.

On President James Madison's birthday, I would like you to consider how much influence an individual can have on the creation of a nation. Born in Port Conway, Virginia, in 1751, Madison grew to become a key figure in the planning and ratification of the U.S. Constitution. In collaboration with Alexander Hamilton and John Jay, Madison also wrote 29 out of 85 issues of the *Federalist Papers,* a published commentary on the drafting of the Constitution. And as a member of the House of Representatives, Madison was also the sponsor of the Constitution's first ten amendments. Later in life, Madison was elected president of the United States— chief executive of the nation's constitutionally based government. From a single seed a strong healthy plant can grow. We need more gardeners like James Madison in our own times.

On this date in 1910, master magician Harry Houdini became the first man to fly an airplane over the Australian continent. He also drove a car for the first time on that trip. After he left, he never did either again. Just because you've done something once, doesn't mean you have to do it again. Some things only need to be experienced once for lessons to be learned, allowing us to move on to greater things.

MARCH 17

St. Patrick's Day.

Scotland won its independence from England, 1328.

British forces evacuated Boston, Massachusetts, 1776.

Gottlieb Wilhelm Daimler was born, 1834.

Golda Meir became Israeli Prime Minister, 1969. (See May 3rd entry.)

INTRODUCTIONS

Few holidays are as enthusiastically celebrated as St. Patrick's Day. Ireland's patron saint died on this date in the city of Saul in the year 461 AD. Today, everybody in the U.S. puts on the green in honor of the man who reputedly drove the snakes from Ireland. By happy coincidence, the Irish-American city of Boston, Massachusetts also celebrates the 1776 evacuation of the British from colonial shores. But no matter which event is more important to you, I will apply the motto that appeared on the American Revolutionary flag emblazoned with a writhing snake: "Don't Tread on Me." I'll try not to tread too heavily with my remarks today.

Scotland won its independence from British rule on this day. In 1328, a treaty was signed in Edinburgh, ending 32 years of war. The peace only lasted for five years, but British feudal superiority over Scotland did not survive because of the freedom-loving spirit of its people. Oppression can never stand up to courage fueled by a sincere desire for freedom. And with that thought firmly in mind, I won't try to keep you here too long tonight.

Today is the birthday of a man whose name symbolizes precision, quality, and elegance—even though you may not immediately recognize it. In 1834, Gottlieb Wilhelm Daimler was born in Württemberg, Germany. He studied engineering and became well known as an engine designer. In 1885, Daimler designed his first high-speed internal combustion engine; and his first engine-powered bicycle. The next year, he developed a horse-driven four-wheel carriage with a single-cylinder engine option. The following year, he created an engine-powered boat. And two years later, he produced a four-speed-drive, four-wheel, engine-powered carriage for the Sultan of Morocco. With this profit, he opened the Daimler Motor Company. In 1901, Daimler sold the first of his enhanced automobiles which he named after his financial backer's daughter—Mercedes—because he felt a German name wouldn't sell as well in France. You don't have to put your name on your work to be proud of your creations. Just knowing you've done your best is sometimes its own reward.

MARCH 18

Great Britain repealed the Stamp Act, 1766. (See March 8th entry.)

Grover Cleveland was born, 1837.

The North Atlantic Treaty Organization (NATO) was formed, 1949.

Soviet cosmonaut Alexei Leonov became the first man to walk in space, 1965. (See July 17th and May 30th entries.)

INTRODUCTIONS

Four years after the end of the Second World War, the Western Allies, including the United States, Great Britain, and France, formed the North Atlantic Treaty Organization on this date in 1949. NATO was a noble experiment—an attempt to share a common defense responsibility among the member-nations' armed forces. To the amazement of many, and despite defections and dissensions, NATO lasted and stretched its sphere of influence far beyond the North Atlantic Rim. It certainly encourages us today to believe that if people share a common cause, they can work together—despite linguistic, geographic and cultural differences. Perhaps we ought to try to work out a domestic NATO here at home.

Grover Cleveland was a unique President. He was elected for two nonconsecutive terms, as the twenty-second and the twenty-fourth President of the United States. He was also the target of perhaps the most vicious political campaign in American history. During the 1884 election, Cleveland was called the "Rum, Romanism and Rebellion" candidate in a speech given by a supporter of competitor James G. Blaine. As if that were not enough, Cleveland was accused of fathering an illegitimate child. He defused that issue by admitting the charge. If you think that politics plays rough today, bear in mind, the man born on this date in 1837 in Caldwell, New Jersey, went through the mill twice to get elected.

Alexei Leonov became the first man to walk in space on this day in 1965. Flying aboard the Voskhod 2 along with Paul Belyayev, this courageous cosmonaut let himself out of the capsule's air lock about 110 miles above the Crimea, took photographs, and commenced a free fall that lasted 10 minutes before going back inside. Taking the first step on any occasion is a worrisome enterprise. But taking the next step and the next without knowing the outcome requires the fortitude to finish a project through to its conclusion. And it's a virtue we need to discuss here today.

MARCH 19

The swallows return to San Juan Capistrano, California.

Earl Warren was born, 1891.

U.S. Senate rejected American involvement in the League of Nations, 1920. (See June 28th entry.)

Michael Jordan returned to play basketball, 1995. (See February 17 entry.)

INTRODUCTIONS

One swallow does not a summer make, but today the swallows herald a pretty certain sign of spring in an area where spring is not that easy to differentiate from winter. This is the day when, according to tradition, the swallows come back to the San Juan Capistrano mission in California. It is celebrated in legend and song by people who have never been within a thousand miles of Capistrano, but it helps remind them and us that spring is just around the corner. We are at the season when we begin to wonder what will be budding.

When Earl Warren was born on this date in 1891, his hometown of Los Angeles, California, was barely past its frontier days and the U.S. was—so to speak—still in short pants. But before he died, Chief Justice Earl Warren presided over two contrasting chapters in American history that helped this nation mature. One was the case of *Brown v. Board of Education of Topeka*, in 1954, in which the Supreme Court banned racial segregation as public policy, and reversed the previously accepted idea of separate but equal facilities for African-Americans and whites. Justice Warren's other historic role was as Chairman of the Commission that investigated President John F. Kennedy's assassination and decided that assassin Lee Harvey Oswald had acted alone. It was largely because of Warren's tremendous prestige and integrity that this decision remained relatively unquestioned for so many years. His birthday is a welcome reminder that some public servants do serve with integrity. We could always use more integrity.

On this day in 1920, the U.S. Senate rejected the Treaty of Versailles and kept our nation out of the League of Nations. Some historians have contended that if the U.S. had joined the League there might have been sufficient international agreement to prevent the Second World War. That point, of course, is moot. But today we mark the anniversary of the last time the U.S. saw fit to return to an isolationist policy. Soon thereafter, perhaps inevitably, it became impossible for the U.S. to maintain that posture. Today is a good time to remember that as members of a community—local, national, or global—we cannot remain detached from activities and issues around us.

MARCH 20

King George III succeeded to throne of England, 1751.
Uncle Tom's Cabin was published in book form, 1852. (See June 14th entry.)
Mr. Rogers was born, 1928.

INTRODUCTIONS

It has been a long time since the disposition of a king has determined history. The last king whose disposition affected us here in America was George III of England. He succeeded to the throne on this day in 1751. King George thought he could push the colonists around, and he found Prime Ministers who agreed with him. If he had not acted as he did, we might all be British today. Like the late New York mayor, Fiorello LaGuardia, it may be said of King George that when he made a mistake it was a beaut. In pondering what nice things have happened to us since King George's day, let us pause for a moment to remember and to hope that stubbornness such as his will not do for our country what his did for England.

It's Fred Rogers' birthday. And to commemorate the birth of Mr. Rogers on such a beautiful day in this neighborhood. I would like to ask all of you to become good neighbors to the entire world. Won't you please?

MARCH 21

The vernal equinox (the first day of Spring).

Police in Sharpeville, South Africa, fired into a crowd of demonstrators, 1960.

The Reverend Dr. Martin Luther King, Jr., led a civil rights march from Selma, Alabama, 1965 (See January 15th entry.)

INTRODUCTIONS

It can be snowing or freezing but the calendar is very clear about it; today, give or take a few hours for a vagrant vernal equinox, is the beginning of Spring. It colors our outlook; it makes us generally a bit more optimistic; it has us looking for the first buds and blossoms. Maybe the calendar is smarter than we are. Maybe the idea of Spring in our hearts is simply good medicine after a long hard winter—or a short dull winter, for that matter. What kind of Spring can we look forward to today?

On this day in 1965, the Reverend Dr. Martin Luther King, Jr., led a civil rights march from Selma to Montgomery, Alabama, to demand equal rights for African-American citizens. It was neither the first nor the last march, nor the most unusual instance of this remarkable man's leadership. This peaceful demonstration had a better outcome than another civil rights march held on this day in 1960. In Sharpeville, South Africa, police fired into a crowd of peaceful demonstrators, killing 69 people and wounding hundreds of others. But on this first day of Spring, we need to recall these events in light of what was eventually accomplished to renew our hopes for the future. And even in the face of past tragedy, we must remember: Hope springs eternal.

MARCH 22

First American nonaggression treaty was signed, 1621.

The Parliament passed the Stamp Act, 1765. (See March 8th and March 18th entries.)

Edwards Law outlawed polygamy in the U.S., 1882.

Stephen Sondheim was born, 1930.

Andrew Lloyd Weber was born, 1948.

Arab League was formed, 1945.

INTRODUCTIONS

On this date in 1882, the guardians of public morality cheered the adoption of the Edwards Act which outlawed polygamy. Aimed at dissident Mormons who clung to that sect's earlier belief in multiple marriages, this act protected the values of nice people who did not talk about sex; and the virtue of women who didn't have very many rights. In our own times, we have adopted a different version of multiple wives—or husbands. To phrase it in computer terms, marriage is now conducted in serial mode instead of in parallel. An individual is apt to have more than one mate, but not two at the same time. Whether that is a moral improvement I leave to your own communal rather than personal judgment. Morality changes with the times despite the constant dispute between those who think they have it and those who think they are above it. We are still engaged in that altercation today.

If I mention the words nonaggression treaty you probably imagine I am going to talk about modern diplomacy. No. I am talking about the first American nonaggression treaty which was made on this date, in 1621. Governor John Carver of the Plymouth colony and Native American Chief Massasoit made the agreement. And as such agreements go, it was a pretty good one. It lasted half a century. If we can do as well today, we should be happy.

The Arabs have been a great force in history more than once. From the days of the Crusades to the great Ottoman empire, Islam's believers have banded together to defend their faith. While Israel was developing into an independent, non-Islamic nation in 1945, Islamic nations in the Middle East once again formally united on this day as the Arab League. We have a tendency to forget that when pressed to defend their faith, people can and do unite despite any other arguments they may have with each other. It is a good time to remember that essential bond—the bond of shared faith.

The musical theater world has great cause to celebrate on this day. In 1930, the writer and composer of *A Little Night Music,* Stephen Sondheim, was born. And in 1948, Andrew Lloyd Weber, the creator of *Cats* and *Phantom of the Opera,* was born. So without further ado, let me finish my overture and move on to Act One.

MARCH 23

World Meteorological Day.

Patrick Henry uttered: "Give me liberty or give me death!", 1775.

Akira Kurosawa was born, 1910.

Wernher von Brauhn was born, 1912. (See March 16th entry.)

The U.S. Army moved Japanese-Americans to interment camps, 1942.

The Reverend Dr. Martin Luther King, Jr., said: "We must learn to live together as brothers or perish together as fools," 1964.

The U.S. Senate raised the retirement age to 70, 1978. (See April 6th entry.)

INTRODUCTIONS

When the Reverend Dr. Martin Luther King, Jr., said on this day in 1964, that "We must learn to live together as brothers or perish together as fools," he was voicing the spirit which lies behind today's observance of United Nations' World Meteorological Day. Meteorologists and weather experts know that, regardless of national boundaries, we all share the same weather cycles. The storm that starts in one country ends up in another; one land's heat wave is another land's drought. Yet nobody has found a way of fencing in the air we breathe. Let us keep that in mind on World Meteorological Day—and all year long.

On this day in 1775, at the Virginia convention, a fire-breathing lawyer named Patrick Henry rose and spoke the words that generations of Americans remember as the heart of our national heritage: "Is life so dear," asked Patrick Henry, "or peace so sweet as to be purchased at the price of chains and slavery? Forbid it, Almighty God! I know not what course others may take, but as for me, give me liberty or give me death!" Yet, in 1942, The U.S. Army moved Japanese-American citizens from their West Coast homes to interment camps high in the Sierra Mountains because people feared a potential conspiracy based on ethnic origins. As the Reverend Dr. Martin Luther King, Jr., said on this day in 1964: "We must learn to live together as brothers or perish together as fools." What would Patrick Henry set as the price for liberty today?

Today is the birthday of an inspired filmmaker who, in turn, has inspired the film industry. In 1920, Akira Kurosawa was born in Tokyo. Besides being the first Japanese film director to receive international acclaim, Kurosawa's films have inspired some of the world's most famous American and Italian productions. *The Seven Samurai* inspired the western classic *The Magnificent Seven. Yojimbo and Sanjuro* spurred Sergio Leone to create *The Man with No Name* series starring Clint Eastwood, and American production company to produce *Last Man Standing* with Bruce Willis. And Kurosawa's classic, *The Hidden Fortress,* served as the basis for the Star Wars trilogy. We rarely consider how a concept can be translated without diluting its essential meaning. Yet, whether it's a western or an eastern, a classic is a classic because it's got a story worth telling.

M ARCH 24

The crowns of England and Scotland were joined, 1603.

Robert Koch announced discovery of the tubercle bacillus, 1882.

Thomas E. Dewey was born, 1902.

Cat on a Hot Tin Roof opened on Broadway, 1958.

INTRODUCTIONS

If it were just because this was the day German physician Robert Koch announced the discovery of the bacillus that causes tuberculosis in 1882, it would be a significant anniversary. Dr. Koch's greatest discovery paved the way for saving many lives. But above all, it showed the need for applying scientific skills to isolate disease-bearing microorganisms. If this anniversary can give us the message to encourage more scientists to explore the microscopic unknown, it will be a day well worth remembering. It is that unknown, unseen world that continually threatens our existence today.

Thomas E. Dewey was born on this day in 1902, in Owosso, Michigan. He was renowned as a criminal prosecutor, as the governor of New York State and as a two-time presidential candidate; but he will probably be best remembered in history for the 1948 election night when at least one great newspaper, *The Chicago Tribune,* was so sure of the outcome that they printed an edition declaring Dewey's victory over Harry S. Truman. So Mr. Dewey's birthday comes as a reminder not to be too sure—at any time—of what you think is a sure thing.

You never know when opportunity will come knocking on your door and today's anniversary is a prime example. In 1603, Scotland's King James VI awoke to the surprising news that he was no longer King of Scotland; he was the king of both England and Scotland. Sixty hours after Queen Elizabeth I's death, Sir Robert Carey brought the message to James in Edinburgh. James was so excited that he knighted 300 new Scottish and English lords on his way to attend his coronation in London as King James I. Opportunity knocks on everyone's door at one time or another. And the only preparation any of us needs to make is to keep our eyes and hearts open.

On the anniversary of the Broadway premiere of Tennessee Williams' play, *Cat on a Hot Tin Roof* in 1958, I will follow in Big Daddy's footsteps and declare that there has been the smell of mendacity floating around for some time now. It's time to clear to air.

MARCH 25

Greek patriots led an uprising against the Ottoman Empire, 1821. (See February 3rd entry.)

Gutzon Borglum was born, 1871.

The Triangle Shirt Waist Company fire occurred, 1911.

The Canada Act was signed, 1982.

INTRODUCTIONS

It is a sad fact of life that some things that need doing are not done until a shocking event awakens us. That concept comes to mind because today marks the anniversary of the Triangle Shirt Waist Company fire. In 1911, a fire in a crowded New York clothing factory resulted in the deaths of 147 people who had been working in disgraceful sweatshop conditions. The ensuing public outcry spurred a revision of both labor laws and building codes. But it took a disaster to bring the reform. Are we doing any better now?

It is one of history's great ironies that sometimes the work of men is well known while the men who did the work are forgotten. Probably every American would recognize a picture of the Mount Rushmore National Memorial—the huge carvings of George Washington, Abraham Lincoln, Thomas Jefferson, and Theodore Roosevelt protruding from a South Dakota mountainside. But how many of us know that this was the inspiration of Gutzon Borglum? Born in Bear Lake, Idaho, on this date in 1871, Borglum's birthday inspires us to ponder the glories of America and the people who made them a reality.

According to tradition, this is Greek Independence Day. In 1821, Greek patriots led an uprising against the Ottoman occupation of their nation. When Alexander Ypsilantis and other members of the Friendly Brotherhood crossed the Pruth River in Moldavia, they were defeated by a strong military defense force. But the incident triggered a number of anti-Ottoman revolts in the Peloponnese and on several islands. After nine long years of revolution, Greece won its freedom as a sovereign nation. The fight for freedom is often an uphill battle, but for those individuals who believe in its essential spirit, no price is too dear.

Canada had been a self-governing dominion of Great Britain since 1867, but on this day in 1982, Queen Elizabeth II signed the Canada Act which not only ratified the Canadian Constitution, it made that nation wholly independent. Canada's fight for freedom from British rule was won without bloodshed. It may have taken longer to accomplish than America's fight against tyranny, but peaceful settlements always take longer to negotiate. And they are the only revolutions where both sides can win. In my estimation that gives us cause for celebration today.

MARCH 26

Prince Jonah Kuhio Kalanianaole was born, 1871. (Prince Kuhio Day.)

Commercial motion picture film was first manufactured, 1885.

Dr. Jonas P. Salk announced a polio vaccine, 1953.

INTRODUCTIONS

What Prince served in the U.S. Congress? That's a question that might stump some of the experts, unless they know something about today, which happens to be Prince Kuhio Day. This is when the state of Hawaii commemorates Prince Jonah Kuhio Kalanianaole's birthday. This member of the Hawaiian royal family represented the early Territory of Hawaii as a delegate to the U.S. House of Representatives. Prince Kuhio Day reminds us that American roots run back in many directions and at many levels, in many different parts of the world.

This is the anniversary of a communications miracle. On this day back in 1885, George Eastman manufactured the first commercial motion picture film. We all know how the ability to photograph moving pictures of great dramas and of current events created a media revolution. That's what can happen with a simple idea. Indeed, most of the world's progress has come not from complicated concepts but from simple ideas. And so today I want to talk in simple, basic terms.

It was on this day in 1953, that Dr. Jonas P. Salk announced the development of the polio vaccine. Salk's vaccine had a stringent test ahead of it, but this was the day when a long-sought victory against the dreaded disease that caused infantile paralysis appeared likely. It strongly reminds us that for every serious problem there is the potential for a good solution.

MARCH 27

Spanish explorer Juan Ponce de Leon first sighted Florida, 1512. (See April 2nd and April 8th entries.)

Czar Peter the Great founded the city of St. Petersburg, 1703.

President George Washington signed an act to build a U.S. Navy, 1794.

Wilhelm Roentgen was born, 1845. (See January 5th entry)

The first long-distance telephone call was made between Boston and New York, 1884.

Ludwig Mies van der Rohe was born, 1886.

Guglielmo Marconi sent the first radio signals, 1899. (See April 25th and June 2nd entries.)

INTRODUCTIONS

Today marks the anniversary of two media milestones. In 1899, Guglielmo Marconi sent signals through the air via radio waves across the English Channel. It is also the day the first long-distance telephone call was made. In 1884, people in Boston and New York first spoke to each other through a length of wire. Today's worldwide transmissions are descendants of these great events. As I talk to you today, cellular phones and satellite modems make these early miracles seem somewhat quaint. And as for Marconi and Bell's innovations, a savvy 12-year-old can buy a kit and build them both after school. No speaker today is really talking just to his or her audience; the whole world can eavesdrop through press coverage, television and radio broadcasts, and on the Internet. The best motto for any modern-day speaker is that if you have something to say that's meant to be confidential or off the record, your best bet is to keep your mouth shut. You may therefore be assured that since I am continuing to speak, what I have to say is not confidential, not off the record. And I do hope you're listening.

The United States was born as a seafaring nation, and its naval victories began with the American Revolution. But after the Revolution, we had no real navy. On this day in 1794, President George Washington—an old Army man himself—signed the Act of Congress designed to build a navy. I am happy to cite that fine spirit of cooperation as the prelude to my remarks today.

These are intrusive times. X-rays examine the interiors of our luggage, our mail, and ourselves. This may be an appropriate commentary on our times because today is Wilhelm Roentgen's birthday. Born in Lennep, Prussia, in 1845, Roentgen discovered what was originally called the Roentgen Ray. It opened a door through which modern physics has enlarged its view and understanding of the previously unseen. If we have a better idea of what is going on, Wilhelm Roentgen is partly responsible.

Buildings are monuments to civilization. It is interesting to note that today's birthday occurred on the same day Czar Peter the Great founded the city of St. Petersburg. In 1703, the monarch planned and developed the lavish buildings and monuments of Russia's most beautiful city. Then, in 1886, Ludwig Mies van der Rohe was born in Aachen, Germany. This founding father of starkly majestic modern architecture lived and created by a simple yet profoundly inspirational rule—God is in the details.

MARCH 28

The first washing machine patent was issued, 1797.

The Turkish cities of Constantinople and Angora became known as Istanbul and Ankara, 1930.

Fourteen wolves were set free in Yellowstone National Park, 1995.

INTRODUCTIONS

We like to think of our times as the great age of convenience—from precooked foods to numerous labor-saving devices. But it has been a long time coming. For example, it was way back in 1797 on this date, that a U.S. patent was granted to Nathaniel Briggs of New Hampshire for a washing machine. It took more than a century before electricity and human ingenuity produced the labor-saving device we now depend upon. So my message today is one of patience. It takes time to go from the first primitive expression of a new idea to the final, perfected product.

Throughout history, cities and countries have disappeared with a stroke of the pen. They aren't destroyed. Their buildings don't disintegrate. They just change their names. You won't find Zanzibar on the map any more; but you'll find Tanzania where it used to be. You may have misplaced Ceylon which was where Sri Lanka rests now. And it may be decades before Mynamar is simply Mynamar and no longer referred to as Mynamar, formerly Burma. I mention this because two of the world's most ancient cities changed their names on this date, in 1930. The cities were Constantinople and Angora; they are now Istanbul and Ankara. It just goes to show you that a name is less important than what's behind it.

Wolves hadn't roamed the Wyoming wilderness since the 1920s. Their bad reputation had been brought over by European settlers, who carried generations-old misconceptions with them. Explorers Lewis and Clark called the wolf the "shepherd of the buffalo." But when millions of buffalo were slaughtered to near extinction by the settlers, the wolves preyed on the settlers' cattle and sheep. Ranchers, farmers, and bounty hunters trapped or shot the wolf to near extinction in return. But on this day in 1995, 14 western Canadian timber wolves were released into Yellowstone National Park to restore the balance of nature that had existed before the settlers tipped the scales. Their release signalled the defeat of a seven-year battle by the Wyoming and Montana legislatures to stop the reintroduction of the wolf. Traditions can be replaced by new traditions. Nature cannot be replaced, but thankfully it can sometimes be restored.

M ARCH 29

John Tyler was born, 1790.

The first White House wedding took place, 1812.

The British North America Act established the Dominion of Canada, 1867.

Washington, D.C. residents won right to vote in the Presidential elections, 1961.

The last U.S. prisoners of war and armed forces left Vietnam, 1973.

INTRODUCTIONS

This is an anniversary many Americans remember. In 1973, the last American prisoners of war and armed forces left Vietnam. Today, before we crystallize our opinions about U.S. foreign policies, we might get a better perspective if we try to recall how we felt about the Vietnam exodus. No event exists in a vacuum; we can judge the present only by the remembering past.

Until 1961, there was a whole class of law abiding, literate, tax-paying U.S. citizens, who were denied the right to vote in the Presidential elections. It wasn't caused by racial or religious prejudice. It was simply because they happened to live in the District of Columbia, rather than in a state. On this date, the Twenty-third Amendment to the U.S. Constitution finally granted the residents of the nation's capital the right to vote in a presidential election. Democracy sometimes takes a long time to pay attention to its own front yard.

Today is John Tyler's birthday. If you don't immediately recognize his name, perhaps it would help if I recall the phrase, "Tippecanoe and Tyler, too." That's our John Tyler. Born in 1790 in Greenway, Virginia, Tyler was the first vice president to wake up one day and find himself the President of the United States. President William Henry "Tippecanoe" Harrison had died one month after taking office and Vice President John Tyler moved into the White House without much Congressional enthusiasm. We have had all too much experience since then with sudden accessions to the Presidency like Teddy Roosevelt, Harry S. Truman, Lyndon B. Johnson, and Gerald R. Ford. So we should be grateful that the first time it became necessary, in 1840, Tyler was there to make it work. And we should always remember that this country has always been able to get the job done.

Wedding bells rang for the first time in the White House on this day in 1812. Lucy Payne Washington married Supreme Court Justice Thomas Todd at the President's home. Lucy was First Lady Dolly Madison's sister, so it seemed only right that the presidential couple host her wedding to a member of the highest court in the land. But, truly, on that day their status as bride and groom outranked anyone else in attendance. Great and long-lasting unions deserve all the honor, respect, and praise we can give them.

Freedom celebrates a victory without bloodshed on this day. In 1867, Great Britain's Parliament passed the British North American Act. The four Canadian provinces of Quebec, New Brunswick, Nova Scotia, and Ontario were granted the right to form an almost autonomous, but definitely separate dominion. They still owed their allegiance to the queen, and relied on London as the center of ultimate jurisdiction, but in all other respects, Canadians gained their right to independence. The achievement of freedom oftentimes implies the shedding of blood in battle. This anniversary reminds us this doesn't always have to be the case.

MARCH 30

Beau Brummell died in poverty, 1840.

The eraser-topped lead pencil was patented, 1858.

Secretary of State William H. Seward completed the negotiations for the U.S. purchase of the Alaskan territory, 1867. (Seward's Day and Alaska Day)

INTRODUCTIONS

I am encouraged to start my remarks by noting that one of the wisest or luckiest decisions ever made was sealed on this day. In 1867, U.S. Secretary of State William H. Seward completed negotiations for America's purchase of the Alaskan territory from Russia. The price was $7,200,000. Critics at the time called the deal Seward's Folly, but I hope you will join me in prayer that we may commit similar follies in our own time.

And now a word to people who have trouble looking neat or fashionable. On this day in 1840, Beau Brummell—whose name is synonymous with stylish elegance—died penniless in France. There is hope, ladies and gentlemen, that sartorial splendor and good fortune do not necessarily go hand in hand.

What was the world's greatest invention? Some will say the wheel; some will nominate electricity. My own favorite is H.L. Lipman's invention which was patented on this date in 1858. This Philadelphia resident patented the concept of attaching an eraser to the end of a lead pencil. Any man who gives the world a chance to eradicate a mistake deserves to be recognized as a public benefactor. I must tell you that I used his invention many times in composing my remarks for you today.

MARCH 31

Ten-hour government work day was instituted, 1840.

Treaty of Kanagawa opened Japan to U.S. trade, 1854.

The U.S. Congress authorized the Civilian Conservation Corps, 1933.

The province of Newfoundland entered into the confederation of Canada, 1949. (See July 1st entry.)

INTRODUCTIONS

Anniversaries are a convenient way to illustrate how times have changed. In 1840, for example, President James Van Buren established a ten-hour work day for government employees. You may choose your own comment on this landmark. I merely mention it as a backdrop for my remarks on the conditions of life today.

Today marks the anniversary of the signing of the Treaty of Kanagawa in 1854. You may not recognize the name, but most of you will recognize the event. It was the agreement that opened Japanese ports to U.S. ships—the beginning of Japanese-Western trade. One cannot help wondering how different the world's history might have been if this treaty had never been signed, if Commodore Perry had stayed in the North Atlantic; and if the transistor hadn't been invented. The game of "what if" is, of course, an endless one; but the Treaty of Kanagawa reminds us that when we open a door, we never know what is going to be coming through that door or when.

A unique bill was authorized by the U.S. Congress on this day in 1933, which transformed our nation. The Civilian Conservation Corps was established by President Franklin Delano Roosevelt to provide vocational training and jobs for unemployed young Americans. That in itself made the program commendable; the Great Depression had deprived an entire generation of job opportunities. But the CCC—as it better known—also built levies along the Mississippi River to protect its often-flooded valley; constructed campgrounds in our national parks; planted trees in previously logged forests; built badly needed fire lanes in heavily forested wilderness areas; and worked to conserve our already dwindling natural resources. Sadly, the program was abolished in 1942. On the CCC's anniversary, I propose we consider how we can restore the spirit of that program in our own area today.

APRIL

INTRODUCTION:

April showers may bring May flowers, but today I'm not going to rain on your parade. Instead I want to spring ahead to the business at hand; plant some new ideas in your heads; and see which ones sprout.

APRIL 1

April Fool's Day.

The U.S. House of Representatives finally achieved a quorum and convened, 1789.

First wartime U.S. conscription law was enacted, 1863.

INTRODUCTIONS

Today is a difficult day on which to be taken seriously. It is the day when the aquarium receives a lot of phone calls for Mr. Fish, and the practical jokesters go to town. It is hard to be serious on April Fool's Day. But I shall make the effort, secure in the knowledge that even on April Fool's Day life is not all foolishness.

I believe that the April Fool's Day tradition was very much alive in 1789. The newly-established U.S. House of Representatives was finally able to assemble a quorum and get down to business. It had taken them almost a month to get that far. I shall try to get down to business here today just a trifle more speedily.

The United States was not fooling around on this day in 1863, when our first wartime conscription law went into effect. By then we had fought at least three wars—if you count the Mexican War. Conscription is, so to speak, a latter-day American phenomenon since the foundations of our nation were built by volunteer enlistees. That is a spirit worth remembering in our own times.

APRIL 2

Ponce de Leon landed in Florida, 1513. (See March 27th and April 8th entries.)

Congress authorized U.S. Mint, 1792.

Hans Christian Andersen was born, 1805. (International Children's Book Day)

INTRODUCTIONS

Today is International Children's Book Day, which is observed on Hans Christian Andersen's birthday. Did you ever stop to think that the most international of all story forms is the fairy tale? Andersen, who was born in Odense, Denmark, on this day in 1805, created an immortal world of literature as did the brothers Grimm, and Charles Perrault. Dealing with basic emotions and simple confrontations is what their tales have in common. Fairy tales appeal to children because they can clearly understand each message. We have a tendency to talk down to children. But there is a difference between speaking clearly, speaking plainly, and speaking down. Today, in the spirit of clarity, I propose to speak to you about a fairy tale in the making.

On this date, in 1513, the Spanish explorer Ponce de Leon landed in what is now Florida, near the present-day city of St. Augustine. He was looking for the Fountain of Youth; it is an odd quirk that a place known for its number of retired residents should have been first explored in a search for eternal youth. Today, as our largest population segment ages, we are still looking for a fountain of youth. We are caught between two conflicting facts. Our aging population still needs the income derived from work. And apparently the only way to provide enough work for all our young people is to persuade senior workers to retire. That, I dare say, is not what Ponce de Leon had bargained for.

Somebody once said that the difference between a government and a mob is that a government makes its own hard money. I guess from that point of view, today is a notable anniversary. On this date in 1792, Congress authorized the establishment of the U.S. Mint. Ever since then, we seem to have been engaged in a dispute between those who thought we were running out of money and those who thought we could always mint more. As I address this problem before you today, I am afraid I cannot report any greater unanimity than heretofore.

APRIL 3

Washington Irving was born, 1783.

Jesse James was killed, 1882.

Bruno Richard Hauptmann was executed, 1936.

Marshall Plan was enacted, 1948.

President Jimmy Carter decided not to produce the neutron bomb, 1978.

Prime Minister Margaret Thatcher ordered a naval task force to the Falkland Islands, 1982. (See June 14th entry.)

President Ronald Reagan signed a policy directive designed to combat international terrorism, 1984.

INTRODUCTIONS

I am speaking to you today on the anniversary of four decisions with far-reaching consequences. In 1948, Secretary of State George Catlett Marshall's $5 billion European Recovery Program—the Marshall Plan—was enacted by the U.S. Congress. Marshall had proposed the aid package aimed at rebuilding postwar Europe during a Harvard University speech one year earlier. In 1978, President Jimmy Carter decided not to produce the neutron bomb. His decision canceled development of a weapon designed to destroy living beings while leaving buildings intact. But less peaceful decisions have also been made on this day. In 1982, Prime Minister Margaret Thatcher, ordered a naval task force to the Falkland Islands. The islands had been British territory since 1833, and Argentina's seizure of these South American islands was considered an act of aggression. And in 1984, President Ronald Reagan signed a policy directive designed to combat international terrorism. The act gave the U.S. power to launch preventive and retaliatory strikes against foreign terrorists. No decision to act stands alone. Each resolution affects other people's lives. Let us view our own situation against this backdrop.

Today is Washington Irving's birthday. Born in New York City in 1783, Irving created characters like Father Knickerbocker, the Headless Horseman, and Rip Van Winkle. He told the story of Granada's glorious Alhambra. He taught America to laugh at itself. As long as we can look at ourselves and at the world with Irving's combination of good humor, imagination, and wisdom, we will be all right. And as I speak to you today, I shall try to avoid turning any of you into Rip Van Winkles.

There is an interesting contrast brought to mind by this day. It happens to be the anniversary of the outlaw Jesse James' death in 1882 in St. Joseph, Missouri; and Bruno Richard Hauptmann's execution in New Jersey in 1936. By all accounts, Jesse James was a professional thief and killer. Yet he was also an American folk hero of sorts. He was shot by Robert Ford, a member of his own gang. By contrast, Bruno Hauptmann was convicted of the kidnap and murder of Charles A. Lindbergh's baby. He denied his guilt with his last living breath. In both cases the press had a Roman holiday. We may be fascinated with the seamy side today, but so were our parents and grandparents. The only difference is that today the seamy side is an even bigger business.

APRIL 4

President William Henry Harrison died of pneumonia, 1841. (See February 9th entry.)

Daniel Emmett gave a premiere performance of his song "Dixie," 1859.

The Rhodes scholarships were established, 1902.

NATO became official, 1949. (See March 18th entry.)

Reverend Dr. Martin Luther King was assassinated, 1968. (See January 15th entry.)

INTRODUCTIONS

On this day in 1901, the founder of Rhodesia and empire builder Cecil Rhodes set aside $10 million in his will for the establishment of that most coveted of awards to American college graduates, the Rhodes scholarship. Since that day, Rhodes Scholars have come from every part of the country and every walk of life; and their studies in the great English universities have helped both nations to understand each other a little better. It has been suggested that we might explore the possibility of domestic Rhodes scholarships to help the disparate portions of our own nation understand each other better, too. Today I ask you to consider with me how we can promote that kind of mutual understanding in our own community.

There is a certain ironic twist to today's anniversary. In 1859, composer Daniel Emmett first introduced his song, "Dixie" in New York City. Even though he wrote about wishing to be down south in the land of cotton where old times there are not forgotten, he chose to sing for his dinner under the great northern lights of Broadway. I guess passions might occasionally have to take a back seat to the possibility of fame and fortune. But I can assure you that is not why I am standing before you here today.

APRIL 5

First Presidential veto took place, 1792.

Sir Joseph Lister was born, 1827. (See August 15th entry.)

Booker T. Washington was born, 1856.

Alexander Nevsky defeated the Teutons and Livonians, 1242.

INTRODUCTIONS

On this day, in 1792, President George Washington, for the first time, used his power to veto a bill passed by Congress. He rejected a measure apportioning the number of representative districts. It was a Presidential precedent and Washington's successors have been far less reluctant to use their veto power. Our system of governmental checks and balances was designed to give all three branches some kind of governance over the other two. Whether this would have continued if the first President had not chosen to exercise the veto is something we will never know. On the anniversary of that first veto, remember that today, our Congress and our people are not always willing to take no for an answer.

Today is Booker T. Washington's birthday. Born in 1856 in Franklin County, Virginia, Washington emerged from a childhood in slavery to become a pioneer of African-American education and the first head of the famous Tuskegee Institute. He worked to gain the rights for all African-Americans to receive an education. We now take that right for granted, but for many years it was outlawed in this country. His progressive spirit inspired many young people to reach far above public expectations or objections. His legacy reminds us today that we must never take education for granted. We should never deny any individual the right to learn.

Today is the birthday of a pioneer of preventive medicine and the founder of antiseptic medicine. In 1827, Sir Joseph Lister was born in Essex, England. He grew up to become a surgeon at the Glasgow Royal Infirmary. Placing him in charge of a new surgical block in 1861, the hospital's managers hoped that the young doctor and the new facilities would decrease the incidence of "hospital disease" among postoperative patients. This fatal illness was killing nearly 50 percent of Lister's Male Accident Ward patients. Dr. Lister tried many methods to combat the outbreak, but it wasn't until August 12, 1865, that he found a cure. Using an antiseptic barrier to protect surgical wounds from airborne bacteria, Lister reduced patient mortality to less than 15 percent within a year. Miracles still can and do happen in the medical world. Now I'd like to see if we can work some nonmedical miracles here today.

On this day in 1242, Teutonic and Livonian invaders were defeated by a relative handful of soldiers as they advanced on the Russian city of Novgorod. Led by the first non-Mongol czar Alexander Nevsky, the brave yet ill-equipped Russian army stood on the shores of Lake Pepius awaiting their fate. The Battle of the Ice, as it was later called, was just that. As soldiers met in combat, the weight of men and horses weakened the ice on the frozen lake. Miraculously, the ice broke beneath the enemy, taking them to a chilling death. The city was saved. And according to history, the battle signaled the end of the Mongol rule of Russia. No one can predetermine every confrontation. Despite all of our preparations—or lack of them—fate often plays a critical role in the final outcome of any situation.

APRIL 6

First Church of Latter Day Saints (Mormons) was organized, 1830.

The North Pole was first reached by modern man, 1909.

The first African-American reached the North Pole, 1909.

The U.S. entered the First World War, 1917. (See December 7th entry.)

The U.S. launched the Early Bird communications satellite, 1965.

President Jimmy Carter signed legislation extending the mandatory retirement age from 65 to 70, 1978. (See March 23rd entry.)

The space shuttle *Challenger* was launched to recover and repair a damaged satellite, 1984.

INTRODUCTIONS

Religious intolerance and persecution wrote a new and unhappy chapter in the chronicles of American history because of the establishment of a new church. On this date, in 1830, the Church of Jesus Christ of the Latter Day Saints—more commonly known as the Mormon church—was founded by Joseph Smith in Seneca County, New York. Smith was eventually murdered by an outraged mob a few years later. Driven from more than one community, the Mormons ultimately made a heroic transcontinental trek to Utah. Led by Brigham Young, the Mormons built a flourishing community in the Rocky Mountains and thrived. Today, the Mormons are prominent in government and business, and committed to promoting traditional family values. Out of adversity, we are reminded, comes strength—a good point to remember as we face our own problems today.

On this date in 1909, Robert E. Peary and Matthew Henson reached the North Pole with a team of Inuit guides. It marks the first time modern man ever reached the world's northernmost compass point. There is only one aspect of this event that has been rather generally overlooked. Matthew Henson was the first African-American to stand at zero north latitude with Peary. As we contemplate those portions of history we remember, we should spare a few moments for the history that was previously overlooked.

Today marks the anniversary of America's first military involvement in international affairs. In 1917, the United States entered the First World War when the U.S. Congress approved a declaration of war against Germany. It was our first full-scale expedition into armed conflict on continental European soil. Its aim was to protect the rights of our allies. Looking back on this event, we should be inspired to act in the spirit of international friendship for more peaceful pursuits.

Today's key historical events show how much we have changed our view of progress. In 1965, the U.S. launched the Early Bird communications satellite. Progress was measured by a nation's ability to compete in the race for prominence in outer space. Two decades later, progress was measured by man's ability to responsibly maintain what he had established. In 1984, the space shuttle *Challenger* was launched to recover and repair a damaged satellite while in orbit. We are learning to view progress by our ability to protect and maintain our dwindling resources instead of merely finding more efficient ways to extract them. But let's get down to earth and see how we're doing here at ground level.

It was on this date in 1978 that we extended our usefulness a few more years, putting off being put out to pasture. President Jimmy Carter signed legislation extending the mandatory retirement age for most private employees from 65 to 70 years of age. In an age of improved health, it would be sad to think our most experienced workers need to retire before they're ready.

A P R I L 7

The United Nations World Health Organization was established, 1948. (World Health Day) (See November 12th entry.)

John McGraw was born, 1873.

Walter Winchell was born, 1897.

South Pacific opened on Broadway, 1949.

Dag Hammarskjöld, Swedish diplomat, was elected U.N. secretary-general, 1953. (See July 29th entry.)

INTRODUCTIONS

This is World Health Day. In 1948, the United Nations established the World Health Organization to research and prevent disease and improve public health worldwide. Thanks to this organization, smallpox was completely eradicated and the fight continues to eliminate other fatal illnesses in every corner of the planet. The World Health Organization is uniquely privileged; it is concerned with a subject that transcends national borders and prejudices. Medical science does not usually consider its processes state secrets; it does not wage economic warfare; it does not hold human life to be merely a cheap and replaceable commodity. World Health Day is a perfect time to take a good look at the human condition.

The impact some people make is often felt beyond their own time. That was probably true of Walter Winchell who was born on this date in 1897. During the 1930s and 1940s, Winchell was one of America's most influential columnists and broadcasters. But as a lasting influence, he is remembered more as a maker of words than as a rumor peddler. We often hear words and phrases like "scram," or people being "that way." Those are idioms that Winchell not only popularized; he invented most of them. Some of his usages of the English language have faded. But in the end, it isn't what Winchell said; it was how he said it that was significant. I'm not sure I would want my remarks here today to leave that same kind of mark. I hope my meaning will outlast my words.

When John J. McGraw was born on this date in 1873, baseball was a fairly new game. McGraw helped to make baseball the national pastime. He spread its fame and charm worldwide. He was a fine player, and a great manager. McGraw not only developed championship teams and trained outstanding future managers; he led the New York Giants on several international tours. He wrote books about the game and created a whole standard of conduct for the playing field: taking a combative stance; arguing with umpires; and running his ball club with an iron hand that earned him the nickname "Little Napoleon." We were probably fortunate that his passion was baseball—not politics. Is there room today for other John McGraws? Or are we playing by a new set of rules?

Today is the anniversary of a controversial theatrical landmark. In 1949, the musical *South Pacific* opened on Broadway to a shocked audience. The successful team of Rodgers and Hammerstein had written a musical about the affects of racial prejudice! One song struck deep into hearts of theatergoers that night—"You've Got to Be Taught." It reminded people that prejudice often was taught at home. Those lyrics provide the backdrop for my remarks today.

APRIL 8

Ponce de Leon landed at St. Augustine, Florida, 1513. (See March 27th and April 2nd entries.)

Consecration of first synagogue in New York, 1730.

Oleomargarine was patented, 1873.

INTRODUCTIONS

On this date in 1873, a patent was issued for the manufacturing process used to produce oleomargarine. Within a year, laws to protect dairy producers against competition from the butter substitute were enacted. But margarine persisted. If there is a market for a product—or for an idea—you need more than a set of laws to eliminate it. With that preliminary observation, let us proceed to talk about some of our problems which are not synthetic substitutes. They are very real.

A Sephardic Jewish congregation first settled in New York City during the 1650s, but authorities wouldn't permit them to build a place of worship. On this day in 1730, the Spanish and Portuguese Synagogue was officially consecrated. Freedom of worship took a while in colonial America. Even after the enactment of the Bill of Rights, it was still an uphill fight. Maybe that is what makes this basic freedom one that people are still so willing to defend.

APRIL 9

Great Britain's King Henry I was reprimanded for his long hair, 1105.

Robert E. Lee surrendered to Ulysses S. Grant, 1865. (See January 19th entry.)

Hugh M. Hefner was born, 1926. (See February 29th entry.)

The Houston Astrodome opened in Houston, Texas, 1965.

INTRODUCTIONS

America's great leaders are generally remembered for their hours of triumph. Today we remember one who achieved greatness even in the hour of his defeat. Robert E. Lee surrendered his Confederate Army on this day in 1865. He handed over his sword at the Appomattox Court House in Virginia, to a fellow member of Manhattan's Union Club, General Ulysses S. Grant. But after this low point in his career, Lee proved to be a great peacetime leader. His living memorial—

Washington and Lee University—still stands today in Virginia. His life should remind us all to look upward, not down throughout our lives.

When future historians try to figure out when the great American sports explosion really took off, they can start with an event that took place on this day. In 1965, the Houston Astrodome—a huge, enclosed sports stadium—opened in Texas. Spectator sports became impervious to inclement weather, making big-time sports an unassailable year-round institution. The only challenge remaining is the same one I face here with you today. The physical surroundings are fine. My job is to supply the quality product.

History often repeats itself, and an event that occurred on this day proves my point. In 1105, King Henry I of England and his entire court were verbally reprimanded in church by Bishop Serlo of Seiz during the Easter service. He complained that the assembled wore their hair like women. It was fashionable for men in the English court to grow waist-length, flowing tresses. After the service, the king begrudgingly allowed the bishop to shear his locks. Fashion trends have split generations and social groups for as long as we can remember. Isn't it time we find more serious differences to criticize and resolve?

Today is Hugh M. Hefner's birthday. From the day he was born in 1926, Hefner exercised his imagination—inventing adventure games for his friends and drawing cartoons. We all know that he built the *Playboy Magazine* empire and a worldwide chain of private clubs. But did you know that Hef was also a champion of civil rights, equal opportunity employment, and numerous other causes that he contributed to through his Playboy Foundation? We often remember the more sensational stories about famous people rather than their finer points. There are a few more individuals I'd like to mention here who also deserve our praise rather than our snickers.

APRIL 10

The U.S. Patent law was approved, 1790.

The safety pin was patented, 1849.

American Society for the prevention of Cruelty to Animals (ASPCA) was chartered, 1866.

Buchenwald concentration camp was liberated, 1945.

INTRODUCTIONS

Today marks a few important anniversaries for those who have built better mousetraps. In 1790, the first U.S. patent law was approved to protect inventions against piracy. And in 1849, the safety pin was patented by Walter Hunt of New York, thanks to that law. No one has a patent on honesty, but the right to safely secure ownership of one's own inventiveness—even if it's a quick solution for securing diapers—helped build the world as we know it. Intellectual property rights even allow me to copyright today's remarks. Whether I do so is highly moot. It may be determined by your reaction. Don't say you haven't been warned.

Some enlightened New Yorkers obtained an important charter on this date in 1866. They founded the American Society for Prevention of Cruelty to Animals. The mistreatment of animals, particularly cart horses and beasts of burden, was so commonplace that it wasn't generally regarded as cruel behavior at the time. More than a century later, the ASPCA is still championing the rights of abandoned pets; and the safety of wild animals that have been abused. It is a sad commentary that we have not yet learned as a species to nurture our relationships with other living beings.

Cruelty is not peculiar to a particular era. Seventy-nine years after the New York anticruelty movement began fighting for animal rights, the victorious Allies in the Second World War came upon the horror of the Nazi concentration camps. Today marks the anniversary of the liberation of the Buchenwald concentration camp in Germany. In 1945, the U.S. Army's 80th Division found piles of corpses, living skeletons, crematoria, gas chambers, and paraphernalia which made the tortures of the Inquisition look like kindergarten. On this day, civilization discovered that barbarism was not dead. But it was not the last time such atrocities against human beings were discovered. It is time to ask ourselves once again, what makes some people so barbarous and what makes the rest of us turn our heads in denial until it's too late?

A PRIL 11

Jackie Robinson played his first major league baseball game for the Brooklyn Dodgers, 1947. (See January 31st entry.)

President Harry S. Truman removed General Douglas MacArthur from command, 1951. (See April 19th entry.)

Washington state employees won a suit requiring the state to pay women as much as men for comparable work, 1986.

INTRODUCTIONS

President Harry S. Truman once said: "The buck stops here." On this day, in 1951, the buck stopped with a vengeance when President Truman removed General Douglas MacArthur from his command during the Korean War. The two men had disputed American involvement in that war from the very beginning. MacArthur came back to a hero's welcome. He spoke before a joint session of Congress and told the nation that old soldiers never die, they just fade away. But the power of the Presidency did not fade away. And so today brings another reminder that those who are elected—not those who are commissioned—bear the ultimate responsibility of government.

Today we salute a landmark victory for women's rights. In 1986, Washington state employees won a lawsuit that hit the state below the belt. The decision required the Evergreen State to dig deep into its pockets and pay women as much as men for comparable work. Equal pay for equal work is still a matter of dispute in many areas today, but isn't it refreshing to know that some of the battles in this war between the sexes have been resolved?

A PRIL 12

Great Britain adopted the Union Jack, 1606.

The American Civil War began, 1861.

Franklin Delano Roosevelt died, 1945. (See January 30th entry.)

The Salk vaccine was declared safe and effective, 1955. (See March 26th entry.)

Yuri Gagarin became the first man to fly in space, orbit the earth, and make a safe landing, 1961.

Senator Jake Garn became the first U.S. senator to fly in space, 1985.

Harvard University was granted first animal life-form patent, 1988. (See June 16th entry.)

INTRODUCTIONS

Fort Sumter stands in the harbor of Charleston, South Carolina, and on this day in 1861, it was the hub of history. The Confederate Army fired on this Union garrison, and the Civil War began. As we consider that bloody fratricidal conflict, I feel we are all determined that no matter what the differences among Americans today, violence and war cannot be the answer.

Space travel played an important role in two events that occurred on this date. In 1961, Soviet cosmonaut Yuri Gagarin became the first man to fly into space, complete one full orbit around the earth, and make a safe landing. Twenty-four years later, in 1985, a U.S. Senator made space travel history. Senator Jake Garn of Utah became the first senator to fly into orbit as a passenger on the space shuttle *Discovery*. There is still room in the vastness of space for us to reach far beyond ourselves and find monumental achievement in what are considered routine acts on earth.

This is the anniversary of a unique patent. It wasn't the design for building a better mousetrap. In fact, quite the opposite. In 1988, Harvard University was granted a patent for building a genetically engineered mouse. The first animal lifeform ever patented marked the beginning of a new scientific frontier—which some of you may or not agree—increases man's understanding of nature. But like all great inventors, we must review our dabblings in light of their ultimate consequences.

Flags have served as visible identities of individuals, groups, and nations. Soldiers and civilians alike still swear allegiance to causes that are often represented by banners. One very familiar flag created a debate over the cause it represented—the Union Jack. In 1603, King James VI of Scotland had become King James I of Scotland and England. He commissioned a new national flag that reflected this union and that would serve as a standard for his shipping and naval fleets. On this day in 1606, Great Britain adopted the Union Jack—a banner which combined the Scottish cross of St. Andrew with the British cross of St. George. It wasn't always the happiest of unions: Scotland feared British exploitation; and England feared a flood of Scottish immigration. But King James immediately managed to convince his people to swear an undying allegiance to a Scottish game which involves manuveuring a ball between flags on a course. Of course, that game is golf. Now that's something to which even some of us swear an undying allegiance nearly four hundred years later.

A PRIL 13

King Henry IV of France signed the Edict of Nantes, 1598.

Handel's *Messiah* premiered in Dublin, Ireland, 1742. (See September 14th entry.)

Thomas Jefferson born, 1743.

Frank W. Woolworth was born, 1852.

The Metropolitan Museum of Art was founded, 1870.

The Illinois state legislature voted to allow women to serve on juries, 1923.

Van Cliburn won Moscow's Tchaikovsky International Piano Contest, 1958.

INTRODUCTIONS

Today is Thomas Jefferson's birthday. Any time Americans meet freely to hear an uncensored comment by someone exercising the right to speak his or her mind, we are reaping the rewards of that joyous event which took place on this day in Shadwell, Virginia in 1743. Jefferson became the principal author of the Declaration of Independence. He also contributed essential concepts to the U.S. Constitution and the Bill of Rights. He bequeathed funds and his entire book collection to the establishment of the Library of Congress—our nation's depository for every copyrighted work. Those are just a few of the reasons why Jefferson's birthday is every American's celebration.

New York's Metropolitan Museum of Art is world famous for its magnificent collections. It was founded on this date in 1870, when America was considered a cultural backwater. At the time, the idea that an American art museum would eventually be of equal stature to the Louvre in Paris or the Prado in Madrid seemed a bit ambitious. But on this same date in 1958, the international music world lost its long held and very similar feelings about American musicians. Texas-born pianist Van Cliburn won Moscow's Tchaikovsky International Piano Contest. My remarks to you today are based on the unalterable conviction that people are not simply at the mercy of their surroundings; people can exceed expectations.

It's ironic that on the same day New York's Metropolitan Museum of Art was founded in 1870 and Texas-born pianist Van Cliburn won Moscow's Tchaikovsky International Piano Contest in 1958, we would also celebrate the birth of the man who created an American icon—the five and dime. This is Frank W. Woolworth's birthday. Born in 1852, the creator of the five-and-ten-cent store launched his empire with a shop in Rodman, New York. Woolworth's concept was so successful that it soon became a nationwide chain. His dime stores not only sold inexpensive perfumes, toys, candies, record albums, and housewares, they offered patrons refreshing soda fountain specialties and snacks as well. Quite a few Americans have seen the Metropolitan's art treasures, and many have heard a live opera. But millions of Americans fondly remember their first childhood visits to Woolworth's. Has our appreciation of art and culture changed for the better? It is something I'd like to consider with you today.

The cause for civil rights celebrates two notable anniversaries on this day. In 1598, King Henry IV of France signed the Edict of Nantes, granting civil rights to the Protestant Huguenots—a religious minority who had been persecuted by the Catholic majority for their beliefs. And in 1923, the Illinois state legislature voted to allow women to serve on juries. This august body decided that women were capable of responsibly deliberating a set of given facts and reaching a final decision without changing their minds. It still amazes me how many areas of business, government, and religion still refuse to recognize the basic tenet that all individuals are created equal and are equally capable no matter what their creed or gender may be.

APRIL 14

Wales became part of England, 1536.

President Abraham Lincoln was shot, 1865.

The Pan-American Union was founded, 1890. (Pan American Day) (See November 18th entry.)

President William Howard Taft threw the first ball to start the major league baseball season, 1910.

The passenger liner S.S. *Titanic* hit a North Atlantic iceberg, 1912. (See April 15th entry.)

INTRODUCTIONS

Today is Pan-American Day. In the context of recent times, perhaps I should make clear that this is a day designated to remind us that we are not the only Americans; that in South, Central, and North America there are many American nations. In 1890, these neighboring nations founded the Pan-American Union. We need to be reminded every now and then of the spirit of the Good Neighbor, as President Franklin D. Roosevelt put it; or the Alliance for Progress, as President John F. Kennedy saw it; or NAFTA—the North American Free Trade Agreement—as President Bill Clinton recognized it. Under any title, it is important for us to look at our intercontinental relations, and Pan-American Day is a good time to let our camera pan north and south and remind us of our longtime neighbors.

There are a number of real-life tragedies which have been repeatedly subjects of drama. Two such events occurred on this day. In 1865, President Lincoln went to Ford's Theatre to see a play. John Wilkes Booth, an actor from an illustrious theatrical family, went to the theatre that night, too. Need I recall the rest? Years later, in 1912, the S.S. *Titanic*—a gigantic luxury liner making its maiden voyage from England to New York—struck an iceberg in the North Atlantic. Out of the 2200 people on board, 1523 died. There were, of course, many good events that also happened on this date, but somehow they do not appeal to our dramatic sensibilities in the same way.

President William Howard Taft started a tradition on this day in 1910. He threw the first ball onto the playing field to start the major league baseball season. Some presidential duties never die, but it's nice to know that some of their traditional tasks are as pleasant as this.

Wales became part of England on this day. In 1536, King Henry VIII gave his consent to an Act of Parliament that officially established the union between the neighboring nations. Even though they had lived in relative independence for over three centuries, Henry felt he had to gain further control over the Welsh clergy. And this act further restricted Welsh freedom. Twenty-four new shires had been created to parcel the nation. And newly elected representatives for each of those districts were admitted to Parliament, but no Welsh-speaking citizen was allowed to be nominated under the new restrictions. So consequently, the citizens had no voice in government. Unions between parties can serve a mutual good, but if improperly negotiated, one side or another runs the risk of losing certain, valuable freedoms. It's a topic we should consider carefully while we discuss our future.

APRIL 15

U.S. income tax filing day. (National Hostility Day)

Leonardo da Vinci was born, 1452.

President Abraham Lincoln died, 1865. (See April 14th entry.)

The passenger liner S.S. *Titanic* sank, 1912. (See April 14th entry.)

INTRODUCTIONS

Some years ago, a gentleman with a penchant for designating special days and weeks announced that April 15 was to be known as National Hostility Day. It makes sense. After all, this is the day when you file your Federal income tax return. Every year on this day, American post offices are packed with people filling out forms, writing in their checkbooks, buying stamps, and mailing their returns. Frowns and furrowed brows sometimes become sighs of relief as these citizens exit the building. Keeping that example in mind, wouldn't it be a great boon for mankind if hostility could be limited to one day that ends at midnight?

On this day in 1452, the village of Vinci in Italy's Tuscany was the site of a great event. Inventor, designer, painter, and sculptor Leonardo da Vinci was born. The world became a richer place as da Vinci's genius grew and took form. So today I address you cheerfully on the subject of nurturing the power of imagination. And if you can't do any better, at least give me a Mona Lisa smile.

APRIL 16

The Rush-Bagot agreement was ratified, 1818.

Bernard Baruch spoke of "a cold war," 1947.

INTRODUCTIONS

This is a perfect day to study contrasts. On this date in 1818, the U.S. Senate ratified the Rush-Bagot agreement between the United States and Canada which led to the creation of the world's largest demilitarized, unfortified national border. The agreement was the result of meetings between British minister to the U.S. Charles Bagot and Acting Secretary of State Richard Rush one year earlier. Despite their differences in the War of 1812, these two nations forged a peaceful settlement. If every now and then we feel beleaguered by the throws of international politics, we have the comfort of knowing our longest border is a friendly one. But on this same day in 1947, Presidential advisor Bernard M. Baruch made a speech to the South Carolina state legislature in which he said "Let us not be deceived—we are today in the midst of a cold war." Some have contended that this was not so much a diagnosis as a self-fulfilling prophecy. Unfortunately, we have a tendency to attack some of our problems as if we were fighting a cold war rather than settling our differences peacefully. Which way should we choose today?

APRIL 17

Richard the Lionhearted returned to England, 1194.

Giovanni da Verrazano discovered New York Harbor, 1542. (Verrazano Day)

J. Pierpont Morgan was born, 1837.

Nikita Khrushchev was born, 1894. (See September 12th and October 30th entries.)

Bay of Pigs incident ended in Cuba, 1961.

INTRODUCTIONS

A king was crowned for the second time on this day. In 1194, Richard the Lionhearted was reaffirmed as England's monarch, ending an epic journey that began with his victory over the Moslem leader Saladin during the Third Crusade. On his way home from Palestine, he was taken prisoner by Duke Leopold of Austria and Holy Roman Emperor Henry VI. Richard's abductors demanded a ransom of 100,000 marks for his release. To make matters worse, his brother John had seized the throne in his absence with the help of King Philip II of France. John did little to help his brother, but Richard's loyal followers prevailed. The final proof of Richard's greatness came when he forgave his ambitious brother after he regained his throne. Courage should be moderated with an equal amount of compassion. Without the ability to forgive, bravery can all too quickly become brute force.

I wonder whether many of you are aware what an important role harbors played on this day in history. In 1524, Giovanni da Verrazano discovered New York Harbor. And in 1961, Cuba's Bay of Pigs was the scene of the defeat of a U.S.-supported invasion force of Cuban exiles by Fidel Castro's army. Finding and maintaining a safe harbor in our personal lives can be just as easy or as difficult as it was in these two historic events. Today I want to discuss the former rather than the latter.

An archetypal capitalist and an archetypal socialist were both born on this day. In 1837, J. Pierpont Morgan was born. He grew up to be the personification of American ruthless wealth and self-serving philanthropy. And in 1894, one of the cold war's leading protagonists, Soviet Premier Nikita Khrushchev, was born. This is, therefore, an auspicious day to discuss the strength of our own personal character and belief systems.

Aꜱᴘʀɪʟ 18

Paul Revere made his legendary ride, 1775. (Paul Revere Day) (See January 1st and April 19th entries.)

A 60-day-long rainfall began in Chicago, 1858.

The San Francisco earthquake occurred, 1906.

Simon & Schuster published the first crossword puzzle book, 1924.

The first laundromat opened, 1934.

Iɴᴛʀᴏᴅᴜᴄᴛɪᴏɴꜱ

On this day in 1775, Paul Revere rode to Lexington and Concord, Massachusetts, with the message that the British were coming. Even though Henry Wadsworth Longfellow's epic poem centered on this patriotic silversmith's feats, the truth of the matter is that Revere didn't ride alone. He and William Dawes both rode to Lexington; Revere was captured by the British on the way to Concord, and Dawes was not. Perhaps Longfellow decided that there weren't enough words that rhyme with Dawes. In any case, I believe that we should remember the name of William Dawes, who on a famous night, it's clear, had a longer ride than Paul Revere.

I want to come clean about today's anniversaries. First of all, I want to salute the opening of the first laundromat. In 1934, the great American pastime of literally washing your dirty linen in public started in Fort Worth, Texas. Luckily, in 1924, Simon & Schuster published the first crossword puzzle book, which meant you could at least do something more thought-provoking while your clothes got clean than watch them tumble dry. These are indeed glorious anniversaries, and a fitting occasion to talk about cleaning up a few puzzles of our own.

This is the anniversary of the 1906 San Francisco earthquake. The tremor's center was actually located in the small town of Olema, California, north of the city. Olema grew another 40 feet north to south as the earth shifted. But the greatest damage occurred in the bayside metropolis where the quake and subsequent fires razed the city. All seemed lost on this day in 1906, but it is heartening to note that only a few years later, San Francisco was the site of a great World's Fair. It reminds us all, that—like a Phoenix rising from the ashes—we can rise above the greatest personal disasters and achieve new heights.

This day marks the anniversary of a rainfall of biblical proportions. The spring rains started in Chicago, Illinois, on this date in 1858. A few days later, citizens began to worry when it didn't stop. It poured for forty days and forty nights. Fifty days went by without a break. Sixty days and sixty nights later, the rains that had drenched both body and spirit stopped. Is anyone ever prepared for the unexpected? Not really. The only thing we can do in the sight of the unforeseen and unforseeable is to have patience and never give up hope.

APRIL 19

The American Revolutionary War started, 1775. (Celebrated as Patriot's Day and Boston Marathon Day on the third Monday of the month.)

General Douglas MacArthur gave his farewell speech, 1951. (See April 11th entry.)

Grace Kelly married Prince Rainier of Monaco, 1956.

Astronauts Sally Ride and Guion Bluford, Jr. became the first woman and first African-American selected for the NASA program, 1982. (See June 24th and August 30th entries.)

INTRODUCTIONS

Today is the anniversary of "the shot heard round the world." In 1775, British troops were met in the village square at Lexington by Captain John Parker and a prepared group of armed farmers. They were ready to fight because they had been warned by Paul Revere and William Dawes the night before that the British had landed. Historians now believe that the British did not mean at all to start a war, and that the start of shooting was not only unpremeditated but almost accidental. But men were killed, and the British moved on from Lexington to the Battle of Concord where as Ralph Waldo Emerson wrote, "once the embattled farmers stood, And fired the shot heard round the world." Patriot's Day is also the anniversary of another test of strength: the annual running of the Boston Marathon. This seems to be a good time to think about how tests of strength and fortitude, as a group or an individual, are fertile grounds for achievement.

Today an old soldier bid his farewell. On this date in 1951, General Douglas MacArthur addressed a joint session of the U.S. Congress. Removed from his command by President Harry S. Truman, MacArthur's military career ended with a few memorable words. He recalled the song about old soldiers that never die, saying: "like the old soldier of that ballad, I now close my military career and just fade away." MacArthur was a brilliant leader for whom there was no middle ground. During his career, he aroused strong feelings both for and against him. His accomplishments were tremendous, but were often followed by controversy. We do not seem to have many—if any—men of that stature around these days, and we could use some.

We often equate love with storybook romances. On rare occasions, fairy tales do happen in real life. Today marks one of those once in a lifetime incidents. In 1956, a glamorous Hollywood actress married a royal prince. When Grace Kelly was joined in holy wedlock with Prince Rainier of Monaco, the whole world watched a storybook ending come true. Unfortunately, real-life fairy tales are not too plentiful. Instead, we seem to make up our own fairy tales and try to persuade ourselves that they are true. Today I address myself to some of those stories in search of the real-life truth.

APRIL 20

Asser Levy and Jacob Barsimson were granted full citizenship, 1657.

Adolf Hitler was born, 1889.

The Supreme Court ruled that federal courts could order low-cost housing for minorities in white urban suburbs, 1976.

INTRODUCTIONS

History is filled with ironies, and a few events that occurred on this day prove my point. In 1657, Asser Levy and Jacob Barimson were granted full U.S. citizenship in the city of New Amsterdam, which was later renamed New York. This nation was first settled by those seeking religious freedom, though with each new group of immigrants, the battle was renewed. And on this day, settlers of Judaic origin won their contest. Coincidentally, on this same day in 1889, freedom's most notorious enemy, Adolf Hitler, was born in Branau, Austria. Facism's rise and fall taught us that we must protect freedoms in the same way the U.S. Supreme Court did in 1976. They ruled that federal courts could order low-cost housing for minorities in white urban suburbs to ease racial segregation on this day. Freedom does have its consequences, but they seem minor in comparison to those implied by the denial of freedom.

APRIL 21

Rome was founded, 753 BC.

Sam Houston's army defeated the Mexican forces at San Jacinto, Texas, 1836. (San Jacinto Day)

John Muir was born, 1838. (See September 25th entry.)

Woodville Latham demonstrated motion picture projection, 1895. (See March 26th entry.)

Elizabeth Alexandra Mary Windsor was born, 1926. (See June 2nd entry.)

INTRODUCTIONS

In 1836, Sam Houston's forces defeated the Mexican army at San Jacinto, Texas. This decisive battle occurred less than two months after the fall of the Alamo and turned the tides for Texas in its war for independence. I dare say only Texans seem to remember San Jacinto Day. The rest of us remember the Alamo. Victory can be sweet, but heroism and personal sacrifice are memorable. The human spirit is our most lasting strength. That fact is important to remember, especially in the dark moments before ultimate victory. If each of us is true to the memory of his or her own particular Alamo, we too shall win the later battles.

When moving pictures were invented, they were a private sort of entertainment. You watched images move by peeping into a box where a huge wheel flipped one card after another. They were called peep shows back then. Woodville Latham changed all that when he demonstrated a process of projecting moving pictures onto a screen. On this day in 1895, he showed an amazed New York audience the first projected motion pictures. Ten years earlier, George Eastman had invented motion picture film, but it took Latham's invention to complete the chain of events. A whole new era of mass entertainment was born that day. Eventually, more inventions improved the lighting and the sharpness of the images projected with Latham's machine and Eastman's film. Successful inventions often trigger more creations and eventually make one great advancement. We should all look at our personal contributions in this same light, and review if we, as individuals, are helping our world progress.

Rome may not have been built in a day, and it might not have been founded by twin brothers raised by a nurturing wolf. But on this day in 753 BC one of the ancient world's greatest cities was founded on a site surrounded by seven hills. Rome was the hub of an empire that stretched as far as Constantinople to the east and Ireland to the west. Roman forces conquered Egypt and Palestine. The Roman senate created roads, waterways, and monuments across Europe. And in later centuries, Rome also became the seat of Christianity. All roads led to Rome, until their governmental system became so complex they were no longer able to control their empire. The rise and eventual fall of Rome are lessons to remember when we analyze our own world today.

John Muir's birthday gives us cause to celebrate our nation's natural wonders. In 1838, this naturalist and author was born in Dunbar, Scotland. When he was eleven years old, his family emigrated to Portage, Wisconsin, where he studied engineering. In 1867, an industrial accident nearly cost Muir his eyesight. Temporarily blinded, he vowed to devote his life to witnessing God's work in nature if only his sight would return. It did, and he did. Muir walked through woods and fields from Wisconsin to the Gulf of Mexico observing the solemn beauty of the forests and hills. The next year, he walked through California's majestic glaciers and forests in Yosemite Valley. He walked north through Humboldt County's giant sequoia forest; and south through the exotic Joshua tree desert. After a decade of walking, Muir fulfilled his destiny when he urged the federal government to adopt a national forest conservation policy. And in 1903, he shared his vision with President Theodore Roosevelt as they camped together in Yosemite National Park. The Muir Woods National Monument—a redwood forest with trees nearly 2000 years old—was dedicated by a grateful nation in his honor while he was still alive. The spirit of John Muir can only endure if we continue to protect our unique wilderness for the generations to come.

APRIL 22

Pedro Alvarez Cabral discovered Brazil, 1500.

Nikolai Lenin was born, 1870.

Alexander Kerensky was born, 1881. (See September 15th and November 7th entries.)

Homesteaders swarmed into the Oklahoma Territory, 1889.

J. Robert Oppenheimer was born, 1904. (See July 16th entry.)

The Army-McCarthy hearings were televised, 1954. (See February 21st entry.).

INTRODUCTIONS

History—like politics—makes strange bedfellows. Today, for example, marks the birth of two post-Czarist Russian leaders. Born in 1881, Alexander Kerensky led the revolution that displaced Czar Nicholas II in 1917, and established a moderate democratic government. Born in 1870, Bolshevik leader Vladimir Ilyitch Ulyanov—better known as Nikolai Lenin—returned from exile to overthrow Kerensky and his moderates and to establish a socialist regime. Kerensky himself was exiled by Lenin. We must remember that no one should be ostracized for their beliefs no matter how much we may disagree. I hope you will keep that in mind while I speak.

Land ownership seemed to be a hot topic on this day in history. In 1500, explorer Pedro Alvarez Cabral discovered the territory of Brazil and claimed this vast area of South America for Portugal—a nation who was not about to lose its claim to the New World to either Spain or England. In 1889, the great Oklahoma Land Rush took place. Homesteaders and carpetbaggers gathered at the border days earlier, and at the sounding of a gun on this day, the assembled crowd of covered wagons, horses, carts, carriages, and shoe leather swarmed into the Oklahoma Territory staking—and sometimes jumping—claims to the free land. Next to gold, land has impassioned people to risk everything more than any other commodity. As populations grow and land gets scarcer, this passion will surely grow. But now I'd like to shift to a topic that I— personally—feel even more passionate about. That is, if you'll allow me to stake a momentary claim on your attention.

It was on this day in 1904, that a peaceful, soft-spoken man was born in New York City. This son of a successful textile merchant excelled in physics, chemistry, and Oriental philosophy at Harvard University. He became fascinated with atomic structure while studying at Cambridge University's Cavendish Laboratory. He worked on the first atomic power experiments and later became director of the Los Alamos Laboratory in New Mexico. On July 16, 1945, this theoretical physicist introduced the world to an awesome power that had the potential of serving humankind for both good and evil. On that day, Almogordo, New Mexico, became the site of the world's first nuclear explosion. On J. Robert Oppenheimer's birthday, it is wise for all of us to remember that all great discoveries have the potential for both good or evil. It is up to individuals and governments to make sure that knowledge is harnessed to serve the betterment of the whole of humankind.

APRIL 23

The feast day of St. George.
William Shakespeare was born, 1564; and died, 1616.

INTRODUCTIONS

This is the feast day of St. George, the patron saint of England. George was not British; and there is no indication that he ever crossed the English Channel. According to accounts, he was born in the Middle East and died in Palestine around the fourth century. Hundreds of years later, he turned up as a saint whose name was invoked in England before the Norman conquest. The stories about his slaying of a dragon emerged centuries after that. The facts surrounding the man don't matter in this case, as much as the fact that the myths about him have come to personify a national heritage. If we examine our own thoughts, each of us will find we have our very own St. George. What is important is that, once we have chosen a moral mentor, we should at least emulate that mentor's values.

If there is one name that symbolizes the written word and the glow of theater lights, it is William Shakespeare. He was probably born on this date in 1564, and very definitely died on this same date in 1616. Every now and then, life itself lives up to Shakespeare's dramatic and historical sensibilities. Certainly, our own lives remind us that "all the world's a stage." Look around you. There are still Hamlets, King Lears, Julius Caesars, and even Macbeths serving as heads of state. There are contemporary comedies of errors and a great deal of much ado about nothing. Shakespeare's writings, ladies and gentlemen, are excellent training grounds for the realities of life, including the realities of life today.

APRIL 24

First regularly issued American newspaper started publication, 1704.

The Library of Congress was established, 1800.

The soda fountain was patented, 1833.

Spain declared war on the U.S., 1898. (See April 25th entry.)

MIT executed the first satellite relay of a TV signal, 1962.

China launched its first satellite, 1970.

INTRODUCTIONS

If there are any newspaper people present here today, I want to wish them a happy birthday—not for themselves, but for the institution they represent. In 1704, the first regularly issued American newspaper, the *Boston News Letter,* started publication. Newspapers continue to inform us, to educate us, and to help us wrap our packages. Greater versatility we cannot ask. Naturally, I look forward to having these remarks printed in tomorrow's edition.

Jacob Ebert and George Dulty are not exactly household names. I mention them because, on this very day, in 1833, they received the first patent for the soda fountain. Ours is a soda fountain society. We've made major advances in the bottling and canning of soft drinks. And new flavors continue to hit the market each year. Did you ever stop to think that the soda is one of the ways America has colonized the world? The soda fountain psychology has shaped our social life—it's the "pause that refreshes," the elixir of youthful masses. But I wonder what its inventors, Jacob Ebert and George Dulty, would say if they knew they had created an international pop icon? And what would they have done about ridding the world of all those cans and bottles?

The Library of Congress was established on this day in 1800 with $5000 in funding and Thomas Jefferson's entire book collection. Today, this vast depository of American literature, letters, sound recordings and photographs stands as a monument to our intellectual heritage—a precious asset we should cherish and enjoy.

The world got a little bit smaller on this day in 1962. Scientists at the Massachusetts Institute of Technology successfully transmitted the first satellite relay of a television signal sent from Camp Parks, California, to Westford, Massachusetts. This momentous achievement made it possible for the entire world to sit back and watch a live event as it happened in one small corner. Knowledge and information should never be limited to a select portion of a given population. And satellite technology obviously wasn't, because in 1970, the People's Republic of China launched their first satellite. Many winning ideas achieve success because individuals are willing to share their thoughts and experiences toward furthering a common cause. It's a concept I would like to explore with you today.

A PRIL 25

Guglielmo Marconi was born, 1864. (See March 27th entry.)

The U.S. formally declared war on Spain, 1898. (See April 24th entry.)

Ella Fitzgerald was born, 1918.

U.S. and U.S.S.R. troops met in friendship, 1945.

The United Nations Conference opened, 1945. (See January 1st, January 9th, and October 24th entries.)

INTRODUCTIONS

This is a particularly appropriate day to be standing up here communicating with you. Today is Guglielmo Marconi's birthday. Born in 1864 in Bologna, Italy,

Marconi was the father of the wireless radio—which revolutionized worldwide communications. And in 1945, as the Second World War was drawing toward a close in Europe, American and Soviet soldiers met at the Elbe River, and a group of international dignitaries met in San Francisco at the opening of the United Nations Conference. At that magic moment, the east and west joined forces on two separate fronts, despite the language barrier. In 1918, a female diplomat who never worried about speaking any particular language was born. Jazz legend Ella Fitzgerald communicated to international audiences through her singing, bringing diverse peoples together in a common love of jazz. Common causes don't need words to communicate their meaning. And that seems to me to prove something that is the theme of my remarks here today. In communication, action speaks louder than words.

APRIL 26

Confederate Memorial Day in the southern United States.

John James Audubon was born, 1780.

INTRODUCTIONS

Confederate Memorial Day, is still observed in the South. It honors those who sacrificed their lives in hopes of changing the future for their successors. A nation's grief is of almost epic proportions; a region's grief is somehow part of a familial heritage. Let us consider on this day the sacrifices our predecessors made for us, and remember that we must also sacrifice our own comfort sometimes for our successors.

John James Audubon was in love with America's birds. Born on this day in 1785, he drew and wrote about the uniqueness of North American wildlife with a master's touch. But some generations later, the society that bore his name—the Audubon Society—was regarded as a membership of oddballs. Bird watchers at that time had no place in a world that revered only artificial or contrived beauty. That attitude, praise be, is now recognized as being—if you will pardon the expression—for the birds. Luckily, many of us have come to share Audubon's view of natural beauty.

APRIL 27

The U.S. Social Security System made its first benefit payments, 1937.

Ulysses S. Grant was born, 1822.

Samuel F.P. Morse was born, 1791. (See February 21st and May 24th entries.)

INTRODUCTIONS

This is an historic anniversary for the United States. But in 1937, I don't think many Americans realized how historic it was going to turn out to be. On this day, the first insurance payments were made to retired and unemployed individuals under the Social Security Act of 1935. It is difficult to contemplate what would have happened in the ensuing generations if there had been no pension system. Regardless of its problems and defects, it was the first time the United States had committed itself to do something for citizens in need other than provide outright charity for those unable to work. Today we are entitled to wonder how we can do more, but only after we recognize how much has already been done.

Today is the birthday of a man who changed his name and went on to fame—Hiram Ulysses Grant. He was born in 1822. And when this Ohio native entered West Point, he mistakenly enrolled as Ulysses S. Grant. He kept that name for the rest of his life. Grant commanded the Union army during the Civil War and became a U.S. President in 1868. To put it kindly, history records his presidency as undistinguished. Afterwards, in private life, he was bilked in an investment scam and spent the rest of his private life writing his memoirs. Royalties from his writings at least paid off his debts and provided for his family. Grant was an honest man who reinforced the latent American belief that great generals don't necessarily make good Presidents. It was 66 years before another professional soldier, Dwight D. Eisenhower, lived in the White House. But Grant's birthday reminds us that even great men, like lesser mortals, can be miscast.

APRIL 28

A mutiny took place on the H.M.S. *Bounty,* 1789. (See September 9th entry.)

James Monroe was born, 1758. (See December 2nd entry.)

Rush-Bagot Agreement was written, 1817. (See April 16th entry.)

The first "Take Our Daughters to Work Day" took place, 1993.

INTRODUCTIONS

I guess everybody knows the story of the mutiny on the H.M.S. *Bounty.* It was on this day in 1789 that Fletcher Christian led an uprising of the H.M.S. *Bounty*'s crew against its captain—William Bligh. After the facts became legendary and the bestselling book was transferred to the motion-picture screen, Captain Bligh's name became synonymous with an imprudent adherence to rules and regulations. Bligh and 18 crew members survived being set adrift on the open sea by Christian and his mutineers. But Breadfruit Bligh, as he was later called, never learned an all-important lesson: that executives should have some level of compassion for employees' needs. Placed in a managerial role two more times, Bligh encountered mutinies at each of his posts. I mention this on the anniversary of the mutiny on the H.M.S. *Bounty* as a reminder to all managers: Never mistake kindness for weakness, nor compassion for stupidity.

A unique twist on an old tradition was established in Manhattan on this day in 1993. The first "Take Our Daughters to Work Day" was celebrated in offices, stores, factories, and everywhere else mothers work. The New York-based Ms. Foundation established the day to boost the self-esteem of the nation's young women and to open a world of opportunities to them. Fathers had been taking their sons to see where they worked for decades. But according to tradition, mothers were not expected to do more than to show their daughters around the house. Women make up a large portion of the nation's workforce these days. And this designated day recognizes the significant contribution made by women to the nation's economy.

APRIL 29

William Randolph Hearst was born, 1863. (See February 15th entry.)

Coxey's Army marched on Washington D.C., 1894.

Emperor Hirohito was born, 1901. (See November 10th entry.)

The zipper was patented, 1913.

President Herbert Hoover received the King of Siam, 1931.

INTRODUCTIONS

If you think times have changed, I bring before you the story of Coxey's army. In 1894, on this day, an Ohioan named Jacob S. Coxey led a group of about 400 unemployed men on a march to Washington, D.C. Coxey was arrested for trespassing at the Capitol Building, and his army subsequently dispersed. Coxey's Army became a symbol for raggedy groups and parades that marched on behalf of lost causes. But let me tell you what Coxey really wanted. He wanted the government to finance a public-works program. He thought this could be done simply by printing five hundred million dollars in new money. Jacob Coxey may be gone; but proposals similar to his keep popping up—and everyone still seems to look to Uncle Sam for help.

On this date in 1863, William Randolph Hearst was born in San Francisco. Some historians believe Hearst helped to start the Spanish-American War. Hearst's newspaper, the *New York Journal,* kept calling for a confrontation until it was officially declared. The war was a success for the U.S. and for Hearst. But in later years, the Hearst newspaper chain shrank, and the lands that had won their liberty from

Spanish rule did not prove to be islands of political serenity and happiness. The war for circulation in New York between Hearst and Joseph Pulitzer produced a whole era of sensationalist journalism. It was sardonic that the press had a field day in the 1970s when Hearst's granddaughter, Patty, was kidnapped. Sensationalism in the reporting of the news has not changed much since Hearst's heyday. But hopefully we have learned to be a little more suspicious than passionate about the so-called "facts" presented in the news.

Today was the beginning of Japan's Showa—or bright peace—dynasty. In 1901, Emperor Hirohito was born at Tokyo's Aoyama Palace. He was the 24th direct descendant of Jimmu, Japan's first emperor, but Hirohito distinguished himself as Japan's first modern emperor. He broke the age-old precedent of Imperial silence in 1945, when he broadcast Japan's acceptance of the Potsdam Declaration on the radio. He broke a 1500-year tradition in 1959, by allowing his son, Crown Prince Akhito, to marry a commoner. And during the 1970s, he became history's first reigning Japanese monarch to tour both Europe and the United States. It's up to unique individuals such as Emperor Hirohito to define when and how outmoded customs should be broken so nations can progress. Just as it's up to us, the public, to review our customs now and then.

It was a historic day at the White House, in 1931, when President Herbert Hoover welcomed the King of Siam. It was the first time an absolute monarch traveled to the United States and entered the doors of the White House. In light of this event, I want to inform you that my own arrival to speak with you here is not history in the making. But hopefully, you will receive my words with a reasonable modicum of respect.

Gideon Sundback of Hoboken, New Jersey, received a patent on this day in 1913. This simple event gives me some reason for concern because Mr. Sundback had invented a separable fastener. The zipper made getting dressed and undressed a lot easier than meddling with buttons. But it can also lead to some embarrassing moments, especially for someone standing up in front of a crowd. So, to avoid undue exposure, I'll get right on with my briefs..

A PRIL 30

George Washington was inaugurated as President of the United States, 1789. (See January 20th and March 4th entries.)

INTRODUCTIONS

Today is a memorable American anniversary. It was on this date in 1789 that George Washington was sworn in as President of the United States on the balcony of Federal Hall in New York City. The first inaugural speech in America was uttered at that ceremony. Although many more followed, Washington's words are worth hearing once again: "The foundation of our national policy will be laid in the pure and immutable principles of private morality." We should search these words within ourselves and take a closer look at the state of our personal values and our public morals.

M A Y

INTRODUCTIONS

The month of May derives its name from Maia, the goddess of spring and fertility. But in the United States, May has been designated as Older Americans Month, honoring the nation's senior citizens, the fastest growing segment of our population. One cannot help wondering about the whole concept of setting aside a month to remind us of our older generations. This spurt of solicitude, I suspect, would not be necessary if we revered our elders in the same way earlier civilizations did and some other cultures still do. Let this Older Americans Month be a reminder that with each passing year, each of us ages just a little bit more, and there's a ring of truth to the golden rule, which is as you know, "Do unto others as you would have them do unto you." How do you want to be treated in your golden years?

May is Mental Health Month. The human mind is an intricate, organic computer. Each of us is the sole owner and operator of a semi-intuitive, parallel processor of cognitive data. We take pride in our geniuses; we all believe we are a little smarter than our predecessors. We still hide our fears of those whose minds have been painfully affected by genetic malfunctions, physical injury, disease, or chemical abuse. Many of us maniacally exercise to keep our outer bodies physically fit, but this is a time to seriously consider the fitness of gray matter that makes all of us different from any other creature on earth.

M A Y 1

May Day observed throughout the world under a variety of names.

Great Britain was formed, 1707.

Mozart's *The Marriage of Figaro* premiered, 1786.

Construction of the first skyscraper began, 1884.

The Empire State Building was dedicated, 1931.

INTRODUCTIONS

May Day has traditionally been a day of celebration. In Europe, it was celebrated by peasants with garland festivals and dances around May poles. In former Soviet Russia, the May Day Parade in Moscow's Red Square was a show of military and political might. In America, it is sometimes observed as Loyalty Day; but our principal observance is called Law Day, which is dedicated to respect for the law and its enforcers. No matter how you personally perceive today—as a festival of flowers; as a show of proletarian prowess; as a day to show respect for those who protect and defend the laws of the land—remember, May Day comes but once a year. I will hurry with my remarks so you can return to your celebrations.

Today is an anniversary dedicated to great unions. In 1786, Mozart's *The Marriage of Figaro* premiered in Vienna, Austria. But a much more historic—yet harmonious—union took place in 1707. England and Scotland formed the nation of Great Britain on this date, and although it was not always a marriage made in heaven, the association did make Britain truly great. The best marriages combine give and take; weaknesses and strengths; and loads of respect. Whether it's between people, companies, or countries, marriages take a lot of work.

Touching the sky doesn't always mean your feet have to leave the ground, as today's anniversaries will attest. In 1884, construction of the first skyscraper—the Home Insurance Building—began at the corner of LaSalle and Adams Streets in Chicago, Illinois. The first building to be called a skyscraper was only ten stories tall. But on this same date in 1931, the Empire State Building was dedicated in New York City. Taller skyscrapers have been built since those days; and even taller structures have already been conceived. But one thing they all have in common is a firm foundation planted deep into the ground. Ideas may seem like they're reaching for the stars. If they're built on firm facts, who knows how high they can reach.

M AY 2

The German city of Berlin surrendered to the Russian Army, 1945.

The first jet airplane passenger service was launched, 1952.

INTRODUCTIONS

On this day in 1945, the German city of Berlin surrendered to the Russian Allied forces during the Second World War. It is important to remember this high-water mark in history. Russia, which had been invaded and occupied in two World Wars, became a conquering nation when it entered Germany's capital. The Russian forces went on to conquer the Japanese troops in Manchuria soon after. This anniversary reminds us that past defeat can sometimes inspire incredible strength in the future. The losers of battles won't necessarily be victims in a war's final outcome.

Commercial jet airline passenger service marks its anniversary today. In 1952, the first passenger flight took off from London, England, and landed in Johannesburg, South Africa. Little did anyone on that flight know, at the time, that jet-setting would become a way of life. No one ever dreamed that business executives, students, and vacationing families would hop on jets as quickly and easily as they get into cars. Sometimes it is hard to imagine how one single action can inspire the world to follow suit.

M AY 3

Niccolo Machiavelli was born, 1469.

The first U.S. medical school was founded, 1765.

Golda Meir was born, 1898. (See March 17th entry.)

United States Chief Justice Evans Hughes said: "The Constitution is what the judges say it is," 1907.

Nellie Taylor was sworn in as the first female director of the U.S. Mint, 1933.

Margaret Thatcher became England's first female Prime Minister, 1979.

INTRODUCTIONS

The first U.S. medical school opened on this day in 1765, at what is now called the University of Pennsylvania. Our nation's medical system has progressed by leaps and bounds ever since. Even though we have improved the state of health care in this country, there is still room for improvement. We must now consider how tomorrow's medical students will afford the rising cost of their education; and how we, in turn, will afford their services once they become professional practitioners. Good health is a terrible thing to lose, but we must find answers to these questions before we also lose our future caregivers.

On Niccolo Machiavelli's birthday, it is worth noting that his recipe for dictatorial rulership remains as valid today as when he wrote it. Born in Florence, Italy, in 1469, Machiavelli wrote that morality had to yield to political power. To him, the reality of politics was that anything goes. Every now and then, we are surprised to find contemporary politicians who agree with him. I don't think politicians should read Machiavelli; voters should. Machiavelli, after all, wrote his masterwork, *The Prince,* long before people were allowed to govern themselves. The only way we can continue to govern ourselves is if we ourselves stand as the guardians of more positive, honest values.

Laws are fine, and the U.S. Constitution is one of the finest. But it was one of our great jurists—Chief Justice Charles Evans Hughes—who said on this day in 1907, that "the Constitution is what the judges say it is." Justice, in the end, depends not simply on the law but on the way people construe the law.

Today is a triple-header landmark in women's history. It's Golda Meir's birthday. Born in Kiev, Ukraine in 1898, Meir grew to become an ardent Zionist. She eventually emigrated to the Land of Milk and Honey—Israel—and became its first female prime minister. In 1979, Margaret Thatcher became England's first female prime minister. She had already set a new precedent by becoming the Conservative Party's first female leader, but Thatcher broke all the rules of tradition by being elected to the nation's highest political position. And the international political arena was not the only gentlemen's club rousted on this day. In 1933, many people believed women couldn't handle money. That is, until Nellie Taylor was sworn in as the first female director of the U.S. Mint. There are only a few areas of international business and politics where women are still excluded from the highest positions. I'd like to talk about those last bastions today.

M A Y 4

Pope Alexander VI divided the New World, 1493. (See June 7th entry.)

The Ancient Order of Hibernians was founded, 1836.

The Academy of Motion Picture Arts and Sciences was founded, 1927. (See May16th entry.)

Al Capone entered a federal penitentiary, 1932.

Four students were killed at Kent State University, 1970.

INTRODUCTIONS

On this day in 1836, one of America's many minorities founded a fraternal brotherhood in New York City called the Ancient Order of Hibernians. I expect that if they were founding it today, they might have simply called it the Ancient Order of the Irish. The Irish emigrated to America to escape religious and political oppression and a devastating famine. They fought racial prejudice once they landed in Boston and New York. Eventually, the Irish not only won respect and tolerance; they rolled up their sleeves and helped to build their new country. Immigrants from other lands soon followed in their footsteps. Thank goodness, there is no longer a sign in any American workplace saying: "No Irish need apply." On the anniversary of the founding of the Ancient Order of Hibernians, I salute what is still and must always be a land of opportunity and of tolerance.

Violence is unfortunately part of American life. On this day in 1970, four students were killed by National Guardsmen on the campus of Kent State University in Ohio. Student unrest, over America's involvement in the Vietnam War and the national draft policy, had erupted. Student takeovers of campus buildings, demonstrations, and manifestos were all too common, as was the violence on both sides of the protests. The incident at Kent State brought the nation up short. Years later, there was another confrontation on the site of the incident. The demonstrators sought to prevent the construction of a building on a site they felt should be preserved as a memorial. We must not forget such somber historical events, but we should not memorialize them in bitterness. Those events should only inspire us to find a better way.

Al Capone was the king of organized crime in 1920s Chicago; there seemed to be no way to bring him to justice during that heated decade. But there was. On this day in 1932, Al Capone entered the federal penitentiary at Atlanta, Georgia. He had not been convicted for any of his principal and obvious crimes: He went to jail for income tax evasion. One way or another, lawbreaking can be punished. The moral of this story is simple: Don't give up. There is more than one way to catch a thief. And there is more than one solution for almost every problem.

M AY 5

Karl Marx was born, 1818.

Nicola Sacco and Bartolomeo Vanzetti were arrested, 1920.

John Scopes, a biology teacher, was arrested, 1935. (See March 13th entry.)

Denmark was liberated from Nazi occupation, 1945. (Liberation Day in Denmark)

INTRODUCTIONS

In 1977, the Governor of Massachusetts held a public ceremony to admit that the prosecution of the cobbler Nicola Sacco and the fish peddler Bartolomeo Vanzetti had been improperly conducted. The event occurred 50 years too late. The Italian immigrants, Sacco and Vanzetti, were arrested on this date in 1920, for manslaughter committed during a payroll robbery. It was felt by many at the time, and by more subsequently, that they had been tried, convicted, and executed by a hostile court and jury in an unfair trial because they were anarchists. The Sacco-Vanzetti case was a widely known cause celebre in American judicial history. Today will always be a question mark on the American conscience.

Today is Liberation Day in Denmark, which commemorates the end of the Nazi German occupation of that country in 1945. It also recalls the Danes' behavior under that occupation. When the Nazis took over, they wanted to force Danish Jews to wear yellow stars of David and be subjected to the same indignities suffered by victims in other Nazi-occupied lands. The Danes refused to comply. Ultimately—at the risk of their own lives—citizens succeeded in smuggling every Danish Jew out of the country to neutral Sweden. Yes, when so challenged, there is such a thing as the exercise of national conscience. It happened there. It has happened here. Indeed, I think it is happening here right now.

Today is Karl Marx's birthday. Born in Treves, Prussia in 1818, Marx became the de facto patron saint of the proletariat. Like many of the other "isms" that emerged during the nineteenth century, Marxism subscribed to Darwin's theory of survival of the fittest. In Marx's case, he believed the working classes, not the social elite and royalty, should ultimately rule. Society has, for the most part, learned that utopian extremists only breed counter-extremes, not ideal or real social conditions. Let us look at some of the other idealistic "isms" that we seem to be clinging staunchly to today.

M A Y 6

First postage stamps were issued, 1840.

Sigmund Freud was born, 1856.

Rudolph Valentino was born, 1895. (See August 23rd entry.)

Roger Bannister broke the four-minute barrier for the mile run, 1954.

INTRODUCTIONS

Today is the postage stamp's birthday. In 1840, the British postal service issued the "black penny" stamp. It was the first stamp of its kind. Since then, postage stamps have become big business both as a means of mailing letters and as valuable collectibles. They are still the same small adhesive-backed pieces of paper, but most cost a great deal more than a penny. And, like many honorable institutions, postage stamps are at risk of pricing themselves out of the market—because there are now alternatives. Indeed, the number of ways we can send a message today deserves to be examined.

Humanity seems to be constantly setting and resetting goals for itself. For generations, runners aimed for the four-minute mile, which it seemed would never be conquered. Then, on this date in 1954, an Oxford University medical student named Roger Bannister ran the mile in 3 minutes, 59.4 seconds. The barrier had been broken; the goal had been achieved. In the years thereafter, top runners routinely beat the record. This is a common attribute of ours. What we once regarded as miraculous becomes commonplace in time. But life is full of what I suppose we must call routine miracles. We are surrounded by miracles to which we should pay more attention.

Sigmund Freud was born on this day in 1856, in Freiberg, Moravia. Few men have explored new frontiers like Freud's pioneering encounters with the subconscious. He was obsessed and extreme in his views. But without his unyielding efforts, others might not have been impelled to follow his example. Some people suggest that the world would be better off if Freud had not delved into man's psyche. But his pioneering efforts directed other men toward the discovery of reasons why we act and react the way we do. Freud's birthday is a perfect time to reflect on those same matters here today.

M AY 7

Johannes Brahms was born, 1833

Peter Illyich Tchaikovsky was born, 1840.

The *Lusitania* was sunk by a German submarine, 1915.

Nazi forces surrendered to General Eisenhower, 1945.

INTRODUCTIONS

The British ocean liner *Lusitania* was not the first civilian ship sunk by German submarines during the First World War. But it was the first major passenger ship attacked in that war. When it was torpedoed in the Atlantic Ocean on this date in 1915, it played a major role in turning American sympathies toward the Allies and away from Germany. I prefer, on this anniversary, to remember it for a remark made by the American theatrical producer Charles Frohman, who was aboard the *Lusitania*. He allegedly said, as he was going to his Maker, "Why fear death? It is the most beautiful adventure in life." I would hope that we could all travel through life with the feeling that the most beautiful adventure remained ahead. The best ingredient for a happy life today is the hope of tomorrow.

In 1945, the surrender of the Nazi forces to General Dwight D. Eisenhower's army took place on this day in Reims, France. The cease-fire and proclamation of VE Day—Victory in Europe Day—didn't take effect until the next day, but I promise not to talk as long as that.

If we really wanted to enter into the spirit of this day, I shouldn't be speaking to you. We should simply be listening to music, because it's the birthday of two of the world's greatest composers. In 1833, Johannes Brahms was born in Hamburg, Germany. And in 1840, Peter Illyich Tchaikovsky was born in Votkinsk, Russia. Brahms and Tchaikovsky—what a birthday pair! It leaves me with no alternative but to hope that at least my words will be music to your ears.

M AY 8

Jean Henri Dunant was born, 1828. (World Red Cross Day)

Harry S Truman was born, 1884.

Victory in Europe was declared during the Second World War, 1945. (VE Day) (See May 7th entry.)

American Indian Movement militants surrendered to government officials at Wounded Knee, South Dakota, 1973. (See February 27th and December 29th entries.)

INTRODUCTIONS

Today is World Red Cross Day which is observed on this service organization founder's birthday. Jean Henri Dunant was born in 1828 in Geneva, Switzerland. His merciful efforts toward helping those in distress throughout the world earned him the position of co-winner of the first Nobel Peace Prize. Due in part to Dunant's work, mercy became an international language. We have only to look around us to realize that we need more of that global vocabulary in the world today.

For President Harry Truman, his 61st birthday in 1945 was an unforgettable one. He had only been President of the United States for 38 days, and on this birthday, the war in Europe ended. For Truman—who was born in Lamar, Missouri, in 1884—it was quite a day. People have disagreed about his role in world history, although he generally receives quite high marks. There is no disagreement, however, about the fact that Truman was the author and the exemplar of the most terse description ever given of the U.S. Presidency. Truman said: "The buck stops here." You and I can stand up and criticize, or applaud, or suggest, or oppose—and I propose to do some of the foregoing on this rostrum here today. But it is the President we choose who ultimately has to face up to the fact that the buck stops here.

M AY 9

John Brown was born, 1800. (See October 16th entry.)

Mother's Day was proclaimed, 1914.

Lt. Commander Richard E. Byrd flew near the North Pole, 1926. (See May 12th and April 6th entries.)

First eye bank opened, 1944.

Newton N. Minow referred to the quality of television programming as a "vast wasteland," 1961.

INTRODUCTIONS

Seventeen years after Robert Peary and Matthew Henson reached the top of the world, two men attempted to fly over the same point. Today marks the anniversary of this event. In 1926, Lt. Commander Richard E. Byrd and Floyd Bennett flew near the North Pole in a Fokker monoplane. They reached 87.75 degrees north before they turned back. The press and public heralded them as heroes. But there were those who doubted they had achieved their goal. They had not dropped the American flag from the plane as they had promised. Three days later, Roald Amundsen, the famous South Pole explorer, flew over the 90 degree mark in a dirigible. But his achievement went relatively unnoticed. Many times, history discovers the truth after the fact. This was the case 70 years later, when Byrd's diary revealed that he might not have made it. In light of this story, let us consider today that we should applaud not only those who we believe have achieved, but also those who have tried.

A new kind of bank opened on this day in 1944. It was the eye bank at New York Hospital. Now we are able to transplant other body parts, like kidneys, livers, and hearts. But on the anniversary of the first eye bank, I want to salute the world's greatest mechanics, the doctors who do so well at patching up human beings. The trouble seems to be that we are constantly finding new ways to give them more human beings to patch up.

Right and wrong are relative terms. If they are hard to define at times, it is even harder when the goal is worthy but the methods are extreme. That was certainly true in the case of John Brown, who was born on this date in 1800 in Torrington, Connecticut. Brown fought against slavery. He felt so strongly about it that he killed for his convictions. He created a new land known as "bloody Kansas," and he met his Waterloo at Harper's Ferry, where a U.S. military unit captured him. The unit's commander was Robert E. Lee, who went on to command the Confederate Army while the Union Army sang "John Brown's body lies a-moldering in the grave but his soul goes marching on." Yes today is John Brown's birthday, and I think that until we can achieve equality for all people, his soul still goes marching on.

On this day in 1961, Newton N. Minow, who was chairman of the Federal Communications Commission, referred to the quality of television programming as a "vast wasteland" during a speech. The vast wasteland has become an ocean of information and customized news delivery since his day, thanks to the establishment of cable television networks. I'd like to tell you now about the abundance of information I've found on this rich resource.

Isn't it refreshing to know that among the many holidays we celebrate in this nation which commemorate great deeds—Columbus Day, Memorial Day, Veterans Day, and President's Day—there is a special day set aside for the great deeds accomplished by the women of our nation—Mother's Day. On this day in 1914, President Woodrow Wilson proclaimed the designation of a national Mother's Day. It's surprising how long it took for the nation's leaders to recognize the importance of mothers in everyone's life. After all, where would they have been, if they hadn't had mothers? So today, I would like to salute the conscientious President Wilson for making such an important and worthwhile proclamation by discussing American mothers and the changing face of motherhood in this nation today.

M AY 10

First transcontinental railroad link completed, 1869.

Fred Astaire was born, 1899.

Nazis burned books, 1933.

Winston Churchill became Prime Minister of Great Britain, 1940.

Nelson Mandela was sworn in as South Africa's first native-African president, 1994. (See July 18th entry.)

INTRODUCTIONS

There were big doings at Promontory, Utah, on this date in 1869. They drove a golden spike into the ground, completing the first full transcontinental railroad connection. If covered wagons helped open the West, the railroad made it mature. We Americans aren't very impressed by railroads today; but it was the railroad that sparked the nation's industrial development. And in some ways, the clock is turning back. Confronted with mass-transportation problems in big cities, many people are urging not merely the continuance but the expansion of commuter rail service. We may yet see celebrations for the driving of a few more golden spikes.

Human beings are mortal; they don't live forever. But their ideas can be immortal. Printed books and oral storytelling traditions store ideas that later generations can discover. On this date in 1933, a group of fanatics thought they could change that. The German Nazis burned all the books of which they disapproved—20,000 copies. It was the book burners' golden hour. And of course it didn't work. The Nazis were ultimately ground into the dust. The messages of those books were remembered. There is a lesson for today in this sad anniversary. Book burning is in the same family as censorship, and both are kissing cousins of ruthless conformism. We need the stimulus of differing opinions and opposing ideas. It would be very flattering for me, as your speaker here today, if you were to agree with everything I said. But it would be far more rewarding if what I said started you thinking about why you agree or disagree.

Do the times make the men or the men make the times? The man who took office as Great Britain's Prime Minister, on this date in 1940, is a case in point. He had been a successful author and lecturer, but more of a gadfly than a politician. Winston Churchill was 66 years old when he was offered his nation's highest office. Did those challenging times make Winston Churchill? Or was he responsible for inspiring England and the free world's finest hour? I suspect the truth is a little, or a lot, of both. Great men not only rise to an occasion, they make an occasion. Would England have fought so gallantly in the Second World War without Churchill's eloquence and bulldog determination? We will never know. What we do know is that whenever the times have called for that kind of leadership, sooner or later, one person has emerged. Do we have it now? That is for each of us to answer for ourselves. Will we have it in the future? I hope so, because we know now that we will continue to need it. Look around you and see the reasons why.

Even though Fred Astaire was born on this day in 1899, I won't tap dance around today's topic. But don't feel sad or blue. The fact is that it's such good news, you must excuse me while I put on the Ritz.

An historic turning point occurred on this day in 1994. Since its early settlement by the Boers and the British in the 1800s, South Africa had maintained its rule of apartheid-segregation and discrimination between races. Native Africans were considered third-class citizens as were East Indians, who had emigrated to South Africa in the late 19th century. Bitter clashes, demonstrations, and political arrests were part of daily life. One political prisoner, Nelson Mandela, had spent years in a South African jail for opposing apartheid. He was eventually released in the 1980s as that nation began to lift its bans because of international political pressure. On this par-

592 / Volume III

ticular day, the former political prisoner Nelson Mandela was sworn in as South Africa's first Native-African president. No tradition is written in stone. We as a society can always instigate change where it is needed. The first step to making a significant change in policy or tradition is to recognize its existence, and that is what I wish to present to you today about a long-standing tradition I think we should abolish.

M AY 11

Ottmar Mergenthaler was born, 1854.

Irving Berlin was born, 1888.

Glacier National Park was established, 1910.

INTRODUCTIONS

Every time we sing "God Bless America" or hum our dreams for a "White Christmas" we pay tribute to Irving Berlin's genius. "God Bless America" was written by a man who was born in Temum, Russia, in 1888, and raised in New York's Lower East Side tenements. Berlin's songs also express America's hopes, aspirations, and attitudes from "Oh, How I Hate to Get Up in the Morning" to "You're Not Sick, You're Just in Love." What is the American spirit? I submit it is the spirit that welcomes an immigrant boy and makes him its poet laureate. That is the spirit I still see in our nation today. Let me tell you about it.

In the late 1800s, this country had an absolute explosion of print. Newspapers flourished; the book business boomed. All this was largely due to Ottmar Mergenthaler, who was born on this date in 1854, in Hachtel Germany. Mergenthaler emigrated to the United States when he was 18 years old. As a young man, he invented a machine that mechanically set printing type. It was called the Linotype. In one fell swoop, Merganthaler's machine changed printing from a slow, hands-on trade into a mass-production enterprise. The Linotype increased daily newspaper circulation and made books more affordable. We think of America as a very inventive land, which it is. But America is inventive because it has attracted inquisitive and inventive people. Let us hope that this spirit of inventiveness continues. Let us do what we can to insure its continuance.

On this day in 1910, a spectacular parcel of American wilderness nestled on the northern border of Montana was designated as a national park. Active glaciers continue to shape the craggy mountains, lush alpine meadows, crystal-blue lakes and green valleys. The million-acre Glacier National Park is a monument to North America's natural beauty: a cherished heirloom we can all appreciate. There are intangible beauties we hold just as dear, and those are my topic today.

MAY 12

Roald Amundsen reached the North Pole in a dirigible, 1926 (See May 9th entry.).

Soviet land blockade of West Berlin ended, 1949.

INTRODUCTIONS

Today is the anniversary of a significant western victory. In 1949, after 11 long months, Soviet troops stopped their blockade of all land routes to West Berlin, Germany. It did not occur as a result of any sudden upsurge of conscience, but simply because the Western powers had rendered the blockade useless by operating the world's greatest airlift. That was the kind of victory we can all appreciate: victory without shooting, victory by ingenuity over intransigence. We could use more victories like that one.

We use the term Florence Nightingale as a synonym for a kind, ministering angel. The real Florence Nightingale was born on this date in 1820 in Florence, Italy. She was an indomitable British lady who transformed nursing into a noble profession; contributed greatly to the organizational structure of the modern hospital; and changed the general concept of medical care. On her birthday, the least we can do is to keep alive the kind of progress she worked so hard to achieve.

MAY 13

Jamestown, Virginia, was founded, 1607.

Winston Churchill rallied England to battle, 1940.

INTRODUCTIONS

We meet on the anniversary of the first permanent English settlement in continental America. In 1607, Virginia's Jamestown colony was established on this date. We have a tendency to concentrate on New England's Pilgrim colony, but Virginia was settled first. Pocahontas and Captain John Smith were an item way before Priscilla Mullen met John Alden and Miles Standish. As a matter of fact, history records that the Pilgrims themselves were planning to settle in Virginia when they boarded the Mayflower. We are glad they didn't. It might have taken longer to establish the thirteen colonies if everyone had settled in one place. Our regional diversity might not have become as unique. America would have been much different today.

Great Britain's Prime Minister Winston Churchill, speaking to the House of Commons, said on this day in 1940: "I have nothing to offer but blood, toil, tears and sweat." Blood, toil, tears and sweat—that is the human investment. That is any free nation's basic investment. How is our investment doing?

MAY 14

The Lewis and Clark expedition began, 1804.

Women's Auxiliary Army Corps (WAACs) was founded, 1942.

INTRODUCTIONS

In 1942, on this date, the Women's Auxiliary Army Corps was established as a U.S. Army unit. The WAACs were enlisted into noncombat units during the Second World War. In later years, women were recognized as regulars rather than auxiliaries, and their military career opportunities broadened considerably. Back in 1942, as today, the question remains: "Where do we go from here?"

The Lewis and Clark expedition left St. Louis, Missouri, to explore the western frontier on this date in 1804. After mapping much of what was to become the great American west, Meriweather Lewis and William Clark returned to St. Louis in September, 1806. Commissioned by President Thomas Jefferson, Lewis and Clark were the pioneers of American government-financed exploration. In our time, that same funding has landed men on the moon and researched the stars beyond. America is founded on the spirit of exploration. We have much to explore not only in outer space, but in the inner space of our own cities, as well as in the secrets of the earth we plow and the oceans we navigate. In that spirit, there are a few issues I'd like to explore today.

MAY 15

Peace Officers' Memorial Day.

Nylon stockings went on sale, 1940.

First experimental airmail route in the U.S. was started, 1918.

United Airlines began using stewardesses, 1930.

The U.S. Congress instituted immigration quotas, 1924. (See May 19th entry.)

INTRODUCTIONS

Today is Peace Officers' Memorial Day which commemorates the men and women who devote their lives to keeping the peace. American peace officers don't make the laws, they protect the laws passed by the people. They are not a Gestapo or a secret police playing by their own rules. Keeping the peace is a high-risk occupation; peace officers deserve more than a memorial day. Above all, they deserve the public's cooperation. Any policeman will tell you that, in the last analysis, law enforcement depends more on how law abiding the people are, not on how vigilant or tough the police themselves are. Maybe if we all keep that in mind there won't be as much need in future for a Peace Officers' Memorial Day.

On this day, in 1940, the age of synthetics really began when nylon stockings first went on sale. Since then we have had dacron, rayon, polyester, kevlar, polar fleece, and a great number of new household words. The only trouble is that as fast as we learn to duplicate or improve upon a natural substance, we start to run into shortages of the raw materials to make the synthetic versions. Man's ingenuity may be infinite, but we have learned that our resources are very finite.

Today marks the anniversary of some airworthy experiments. In 1918, the first experimental U.S. airmail service began carrying mail to and from New York, Philadelphia, and Washington, D.C. The new system was an overnight success as more and more executives demanded to have their letters and packages airmailed for fast delivery. In 1930, United Airlines' stewardesses began serving passengers on their San Francisco, California, to Cheyenne, Wyoming, flights. This idea also caught on like wildfire. More and more executives demanded to take business flights so they could be served by these amiable hostesses. The loftiest ideas can succeed if they fulfill a public demand, and you don't have to pilot a plane to find out why.

M AY 16

William H. Seward was born in Florida, New York, 1801. (See March 30th entry.)

The impeachment of President Andrew Johnson failed, 1868.

First Oscars were presented at the Academy Awards, 1929. (See May 4th entry.)

The Cultural Revolution began, 1966.

Junko Tabei became the first woman to reach the summit of Mt. Everest, 1975. (See May 29th entry.)

INTRODUCTIONS

Today marks an anniversary that was chronicled in President John F. Kennedy's book, *Profiles in Courage*. In 1868, President Andrew Johnson faced impeachment proceedings as a result of a dispute with the U.S. Congress over withdrawals that the president made from the Bank of the United States. Senator Edmund G. Ross of Kansas, a man who opposed much of Johnson's political thinking, stood up and voted according to his conscience. His was the deciding vote that saved the president. It meant the end of Senator Ross's political career, and he knew it. But he did what he felt was right. Ironically, few people today even know his name. But I hope that there are still public servants facing the issues today with the same courage and honesty that Senator Ross displayed when the chips were down.

Today is Oscar's birthday. Oscar, as if you didn't know, is the award presented by the Academy of Motion Picture Arts and Sciences. In 1929, five Oscars made their debut at a Hollywood dinner. And Oscar has been imitated everywhere ever since. There's hardly an art form or an industry does not have its own equivalent of the Oscar—the Emmy, the Grammy, the Tony, the Desi, the Coty. I think Oscar had a good idea. Recognition by one's colleagues is sometimes the sweetest recognition of all. As a matter of fact, I'd like to use this occasion to present a couple of Oscars of my own.

On this day in 1975, Mount Everest was conquered. If this sounds incorrect to all of you, let me qualify my statement further. On this day in 1975, Mount Everest was conquered by a woman. An experienced Japanese mountaineer, Junko Tabei, took to the Himalayan slopes and climbed the world's tallest mountain, reaching its summit on this date. This event proves one very profound point: there are few places and fewer deeds that exclusively belong to a man's world.

A dark decade began on this day in 1966, when the Communist Party's Politburo approved an edict authored by Chairman Mao Zhedong. It started The Great Proletarian Cultural Revolution. Schools were closed and the Red Guard—an elite troop of young, zealous students—was formed to attack traditional values and so-called bourgeois thinking. The people—according to Mao—had to learn to live by a pure interpretation of Chairman Mao's original manifesto. Intellectuals, military leaders, business people, and politicians were dragged out into the streets, forced to wear dunce caps, and were publicly criticized by Red Guardsmen. An entire nation was tortured and terrorized into submission by this young army. At the end of its ten-year purge, tens of thousands had been killed and millions of lives ruined. Childhood and adolescence are times for growth and learning. It is up to adults to teach their children how to use their energies for the common good. Placed in the wrong hands, youthful exuberance can become a lethal weapon.

MAY 17

Edward Jenner was born, 1749.

New York Stock Exchange was founded, 1792.

Racial segregation in public schools was declared unconstitutional, 1954.

INTRODUCTIONS

Today is the New York Stock Exchange's birthday. Since it opened in 1792, the Exchange has sometimes been castigated as the speculators' playground; a stock manipulators' oasis. It has had its share of intrigues and conspiracies, but its birthday is a good time to be reminded that the concept of public stock ownership—transacted through the stock exchange—has given a higher percentage of people a "piece of the action." Stock ownership has made it possible for the small investor to be a significant factor in the nation's economic life. So, as we look at major American corporations, let us remember that we are looking at the investments and financial futures of millions of small shareholders.

On this date in 1954, in a unanimous decision written by Chief Justice Earl Warren, the U.S. Supreme Court swept away America's ancient heritage of racial segregation and declared that "separate educational facilities are inherently unequal." It was the dawning of racial equality in American education. It's an age that had a long, long way to go. On the anniversary of that historic decision, how far have we come, and how far is the path yet before us?

This is Edward Jenner's birthday. Born on this date in 1749 in Berkeley, England, Dr. Jenner developed a new medical concept called vaccination. Thanks to his discovery, smallpox ceased to be a worldwide plague, and numerous diseases have been prevented or mitigated by immunization processes based on Dr. Jenner's idea. If only for the birth of Edward Jenner, today is a pretty healthy day in the annals of time.

MAY 18

Napoleon became Emperor of France, 1804.

Haley's comet was seen from the earth, 1910.

The Tennessee Valley Authority (TVA) was authorized, 1933.

Mount St. Helens erupted, 1980.

INTRODUCTIONS

Napoleon Bonaparte was a Corsican soldier enlisted in the French army who became the First French Republican general after the French Revolution. But that was not enough for this ambitious young man. On this date in 1804, Napoleon became the Emperor of France. Under his reign, France attempted to conquer Europe and the world—an occupational disease that affects many self-made monarchs and dictators. We should always beware of political or military leaders who talk of the nation's destiny when it is clear that they have only their own ambitions in mind. Somehow the lesson of Napoleon never really seems to sink in. Even here and now, we seem to have candidates for defeat as in Waterloo.

The Tennessee Valley Authority was authorized on this date in 1933, to develop the hydroelectric and water resources of the Tennessee River including the power dam at Muscle Shoals, Alabama; and to assist in the economic and social development of the entire valley. Despite bitter opposition from both public and private interest groups, it can be conservatively said that the TVA changed the face of the South. On its anniversary, let us not be afraid of change nor the risks it brings. After all, our country's worth it.

Nature certainly made its presence known on this day in history. This is the anniversary of a visit from Haley's Comet. In 1910, the enormous comet was seen from the earth as it moved across the sun. It was a spectacle few people who witnessed it would ever forget. But the fearsome power of nature has also been evident on this date. In 1980, Mount St. Helens erupted in Washington state. It was the mountain's most powerful eruption in 123 years. People were evacuated from their homes for hundreds of miles around as volcanic ash rained down upon them. Unfortunately, 60 people died during the spectacular event. We must never take nature for granted. We may be fascinated by its beauty, but if we don't respect its power, we only delude ourselves as to who is the master.

MAY 19

Anne Boleyn was beheaded, 1536.

Immigration quotas were established, 1921. (See May 15th entry.)

INTRODUCTIONS

Over the course of history, many people have lost their heads. And on this day a queen lost hers. In 1536, Henry VIII of England's second wife and mother of Elizabeth I—Anne Boleyn—was beheaded in the Tower of London. In case you want to measure the world's progress, just reflect that if Henry and Anne had a similar falling out today, it would have been solved by a divorce and Anne would probably have been awarded custody of their child. You may recall that both Henry VIII and his daughter had rather nasty ways of disposing of people they didn't like. I am therefore very grateful to be appearing to talk today before a group of modern-day commoners, and I trust that what I am about to say will not move you to boo or hiss, and certainly not to shout, "Off with his head!"

On this date in 1921, the U.S. Congress decided to limit America's "open door" policy somewhat, by establishing immigration quotas. To this day, immigration continues, though thankfully some of the ethnic discriminations built into the quota system were eventually eradicated. But one of the unforeseen results of these restrictions has been a tremendous increase in the number of illegal aliens. Maybe we should have remembered that another one of our oldest traditions, along with hospitality, is gate-crashing. For all I know, I may be speaking to a few gatecrashers here today. If so, I can only say I am flattered. I'd rather have you sneak in before I talk than sneak out before I finish.

M AY 20

Mecklenburg County, North Carolina, declared its independence from British rule, 1775. (Mecklenburg Independence Day)

Charles Lindbergh began his solo transatlantic flight, 1927.

Amelia Earhart took off on her first solo flight, 1932.

First airborne invasion took place, 1941.

The first railroad timetable was published, 1830.

INTRODUCTIONS

Today is Mecklenburg Independence Day. From the looks on your faces, I gather that some further explanation is in order. In 1775, Charlotte, North Carolina—located in Mecklenburg County—was the site of a convention which adopted a declaration of independence from British rule. The participants sent words to that effect to the North Carolina delegation at the Continental Congress meeting in Philadelphia, Pennsylvania. So today marks the anniversary of a brave step in our nation's history—and therefore a very good time to talk about some other brave steps which seem to be needed these days.

On this day in 1927, the young American aviator Charles A. Lindbergh took off from Roosevelt Field, New York, and headed for Paris, France. It seemed like an incredible risk. Hour after hour, the world held its breath and waited for news of the *Spirit of St. Louis*. Lindbergh—later nicknamed the Lone Eagle—was supposed to land at Le Bourget at 7:30 P.M. the following evening. He didn't. But news came that he had been seen over Ireland and then over England. He finally landed shortly after 10 P.M. What happened thereafter is a story for another day. Today's anniversary serves to remind us that American initiative and American success are based on one basic ingredient—American self-confidence. As a nation, you do not discourage Americans by warning us of the risks. Today I want to talk about a few chances we should be taking now.

It is a sardonic twist of fate that, on the anniversary of Charles A. Lindbergh's first transatlantic flight, a less heroic aviation first was also achieved. In 1941, Nazi Germany captured the island of Crete in history's first totally airborne invasion. The whole face of warfare—and its costs—changed. The menace of a surprise attack became infinitely greater. When we contemplate today's cost for national defense, or the effect of that cost on other areas of our life, we should remember why, no pun intended, they are sky-high.

This is the anniversary of the day man—and woman—conquered the skies above. In 1927, American aviator Charles A. Lindbergh took off from Roosevelt Field, New York, bound for Paris, France. And in 1932, American aviatrix Amelia Earhart took off from Newfoundland and headed for Ireland. Both Lindbergh and Earhart took incredible risks to be the first of their kind. But today's anniversaries only show that there never was and never should be a gender gap when it comes to measuring a person's ability to surmount a challenge.

Before this day was marked with memorable events in aviation history like Charles Lindbergh and Amelia Earhart's first solo transatlantic flights, another event changed the way we thought of land-based travel. In 1830, the first railroad timetable was published in a Baltimore, Maryland, newspaper. The arrival and departure times of the nation's first railroad train—the Baltimore & Ohio—were of critical importance to passengers and cargo shippers wishing to take advantage of this new, luxurious means of locomotion. Airplanes have their allure, but generations of Americans have had a love affair with trains.

M AY 2 1

American National Red Cross founded, 1881.

Charles Lindbergh landed in Paris, France after completing the first solo transatlantic flight, 1927. (See May 20th entry.)

INTRODUCTIONS

Today is the American National Red Cross' birthday. In 1881, Clara Barton founded the organization in Washington, D.C. Today the Red Cross may be the world's best-known symbol. And in America, the Red Cross symbolizes one of the ways good neighbors help each other. The only people the American National Red Cross doesn't help are public speakers who get into trouble by shooting off their mouths. So I will try to avoid any rash statements that may get me in trouble with this distinguished audience here today.

MAY 22

Richard Wagner was born, 1813.

The American steamboat Savannah made the first transatlantic crossing, 1819. (National Maritime Day)

Sir Arthur Conan Doyle was born, 1859. (See January 6th entry.)

The Truman Doctrine went into effect, 1947.

INTRODUCTIONS

On this day in 1819, the American-built steamboat *Savannah* was launched from Savannah Harbor, destined for an Atlantic crossing. This anniversary is commemorated every year as National Maritime Day. Somebody recently said that if you don't think the U.S. is still a seagoing nation, how do you explain the frequency with which we find ourselves in deep water. On National Maritime Day, I propose to steam right into my subject, and since we have signaled the engines to go full speed ahead we don't need a lot of wind.

Today marks the anniversary of the Truman Doctrine's enactment. Outlined by President Harry Truman in 1947, the Truman Doctrine was intended to limit and contain Soviet expansion by providing U.S. aid for countries threatened by Communist takeover. The passage of this legislation approved an initial appropriation of $400 million for aid to Greece and Turkey. Since then, historians and revisionist historians have argued over the Truman Doctrine's wisdom and effectiveness. But nobody has ever doubted that it made the United States' position absolutely clear in its time. For speakers, the Truman Doctrine is a simple one. Stand up and be counted; then count on sitting down. I shall endeavor to tell you where I stand, and trust you will not tell me to stand down.

German composer Richard Wagner was born on this day in 1813. Inspired by ancient Teutonic legends of gods, heroes, and heroines, Wagner was a man with definite opinions in many fields besides music. That is true of many of us who don't happen to have Wagner's musical genius. Today I propose to speak on a topic which I do not think Wagner covered. And when I am through, I will be happy to face the music.

MAY 23

Benjamin Franklin created his own pair of bifocals, 1785.

The play *Abie's Irish Rose* opened on Broadway in New York City, 1922.

INTRODUCTIONS

Benjamin Franklin was a man of many talents, including invention. And today is the anniversary of his most famous creation. In 1785, he described his design in a letter. It was a very simple idea. Franklin needed two pairs of spectacles: one pair for reading, one pair for seeing at a distance. He got tired of switching from one pair to another, so he constructed a pair of spectacles that had both types of lenses in each frame: the upper portion worked for seeing at a distance and the lower portion worked for reading. Our problem ever since, of course, has been to make sure we are looking through the right lenses for the correct purpose. Today I want to address myself to the bifocular way we look at the world.

I don't know how many of you have ever heard of the play, *Abie's Irish Rose*. The title pretty much tells you the plot. I mention it because today is the anniversary of its premiere. In 1922, the critics gave it a rather unfriendly reception. As a result, it only ran for 2327 performances and became one of the longest running plays in theatrical history. My point in recalling the bad reviews is not to throw rocks at the critics. They are entitled to their opinions. What this story illustrates is something that has happened time and again. The public has a habit of making up its own mind. We are often told that the media can make or break an artist, a politician, or a supermarket product. That seems to be a pretty lame excuse. I believe that most products stand or fall on the basis of their own performance. Of course, if I fail to get the reaction I hope for my remarks today, you understand I intend to blame it on the critics.

MAY 24

Queen Victoria of England was born, 1819. (celebrated on the Monday closest to the date as Victoria Day) (See January 22nd and June 20th entries.)

Samuel F.B. Morse sent first telegraph message, 1844. (See February 21st and April 27th entries.)

The Brooklyn Bridge opened, 1883.

INTRODUCTIONS

"What hath God wrought!" Samuel F.B. Morse, an artist born in Charlestown, Massachusetts, sent those words in the first message telegraphed from Washington, D.C. to Baltimore, Maryland, on this date in 1844. The 53-year-old Morse was being devout and modest. The telegraph was what Morse himself had wrought. I have always felt that people who make God the author of their bright ideas are subconsciously hedging—rather like saying, "Now, if it doesn't work out the way we think it will, remember He did it." Nobody had to apologize for the telegraph. It united the nation and eventually the world. It furnished the basis for an international language—the language of dots and dashes known as Morse Code. I mention today's anniversary because I intend to practice a virtue first taught to Americans by the fact that telegrams were priced by the word. In the spirit of the telegram, I intend to keep my remarks short and to the point.

This is the Brooklyn Bridge's birthday. In 1883, the Brooklyn Bridge which links Brooklyn to Manhattan was opened. It also paved the way to a glorious opportunity for generations of con men thereafter. Nobody will ever know how many times the Brooklyn Bridge has been sold to a gullible visitor. America has crossed a lot of other bridges since then, but none has been the subject of as many nefarious transactions as this one. I promise that what I offer you today is straightforward, honest, and real. I'm not here to sell you the Brooklyn Bridge.

Victoria Regina as born on this day. In 1819, Great Britain's monarch and India's empress, Queen Victoria, was born in Kensington, England. Few monarchs have reigned as long or have been as revered as Victoria. Few people have left their imprint on an entire era. Her popularity was based on what she stood for: integrity, responsibility, and duty. The lesson here is clear. First, above all, stand for something; better still, stand up for something. Right now I am standing up before you; if you can stand me, I intend to stand up for something.

MAY 25

St. Bede died, 735 AD.

First session of the Constitutional Convention convened, 1787.

Ralph Waldo Emerson was born, 1803.

INTRODUCTIONS

Today is the anniversary of the U.S. Constitutional Convention's first session. In 1787, the representatives that gathered in Philadelphia eventually adopted a final draft of the nation's Constitution. I mention this event because of one particular point. This was not supposed to be the convention's first session. It had been scheduled to convene on May 14th. But only the representatives of Virginia and Pennsylvania were there on time. A quorum didn't convene until this day. Legislatures seem to have had that same problem ever since. I am grateful to see from the few empty chairs here today that, ladies and gentlemen, we seem to have a quorum.

This is Ralph Waldo Emerson's birthday. He was born in Boston, Massachusetts, in 1803. It is very hard to make a speech without quoting something from Emerson, who said: "Nothing great was ever achieved without enthusiasm." I believe we have great things yet to achieve, and I am here to win your enthusiasm for those great things that lie ahead.

The final act of a great man is often more memorable than any other deed executed during his life. On this day in 735 AD, the Anglo-Saxon scholar Bede awoke in his monk's cell at the Jarrow monastery. He was ready to dictate the last chapter of his latest translation—the Gospel according to St. John. "Take up your pen and ink and write quickly," he told his scribe. Upon completion of his translation, Bede knelt down to pray and died. Only a small handful of individuals ever live to complete everything they set out to accomplish. So I will follow good St. Bede's final orders by speaking quickly to you now.

M AY 2 6

Asa Yoelson was born, 1886.

The Egyptian Pharaoh Cheops' funeral ship was found, 1954.

Israel formally returned El Arish to Egypt, 1979. (See May 27th entry.)

INTRODUCTIONS

The Pharaoh Cheops ordered the construction of Egypt's Great Pyramids thousands of years ago. When he died, he was buried in a funeral ship built for his other-world journey. On this date, in 1954, Cheops' funeral ship reached another world. It was uncovered near the Pyramid of Giza. Our world is certainly different from that into which the remains of Cheops were supposedly consigned. But I doubt that ours is the world Cheops' heirs had in mind for their king. It is hard to achieve one's goals in this lifetime, let alone to accomplish them in another. So let me speak today about some things we can do during our lifetimes instead of building funeral ships for an unknown future journey.

When Asa Yoelson was born on this day in Srednike, Russia, in 1886, Asa's parents had no idea they would emigrate to the United States. But they soon did. They never could have dreamt that their son would become a jazz singer—they hoped he would become a cantor at the local synagogue. But Asa Yoelson changed his name to Al Jolson. He sang his way up from Rialto vaudeville theaters to Ziegfeld's Follies and finally to the motion picture screen. Jolson was the first singer to be heard on film. And his famous line is the perfect introduction to my remarks to you today: "You ain't heard nothin' yet, folks."

Actions speak much louder than words, as an event that happened on this day clearly proves. In 1979, Israel formally returned El Arish to Egypt under the terms of a peace pact. The capital of the Sinai peninsula had been occupied by Israeli forces for over a decade. This deed showed both Egypt and the world that Israel meant to keep its promise to instigate a peaceful coexistence between the two nations. The next day, the border between Israel and Egypt was opened. It is a lesson we must always keep in mind when negotiating with others. Actions cannot be broken. They are like promises written in stone.

M AY 2 7

Achsah Young was hanged as a witch in Massachusetts, 1647.

Amelia Bloomer was born, 1818.

Julia Ward Howe was born, 1819.

Dashiell Hammett was born, 1894.

Henry Kissinger was born, 1923.

Egyptian President Anwar Sadat and Israeli Prime Minister Menachem Begin announced the opening of the border between Egypt and Israel, 1979. (See May 26th entry.)

INTRODUCTIONS

Achsah Young is not a particularly famous figure. Let me tell you why. Achsah Young was the first person inscribed in the annals of colonial America for being executed as a witch. It happened on this date in 1647. Some people dispute this fact. Margaret Jones—who was executed in 1648—is given the dubious honor by a few historians. But using Achsah Young's demise as the starting point and today as the anniversary date, I rise to note that we don't hang witches anymore. We organize cults around some of them, and suggest sanity tests for others. Please notice that I never said we don't believe in witches any more. The fact is that we may call witchcraft by many other names, but we continue to give it credence, and at times, we continue to fear it. Sometimes it is easier to declare "witchcraft" is responsible and to flee unpleasant situations. I am not here to blame anything on witches. Indeed, some of the things that confront us suggest that so far, we have been leading a charmed life. Let me explain.

Amelia Bloomer is primarily remembered in history for an old-fashioned article of feminine apparel. In 1818, Amelia Jenks was born on this date in Hiram, New York. She grew up, married, and became Mrs. Bloomer—an outspoken suffragist who felt that feminine apparel was a handicap. She took to wearing trousers and bloomers. Mrs. Bloomer was ridiculed for her stance on women's rights, but it didn't stop her from fighting. Today is also Julia Ward Howe's birthday. Born in New York City in 1819, Ms. Howe was not only a suffragist; she fought for the abolition of slavery and wrote the lyrics to the "Battle Hymn of the Republic." I salute America's greatest fighting force—America's women. And I'd like to suggest a battle that all of us—men and women—can fight together.

Art often mirrors real life. This statement was never truer than in the case of author and screenplay writer Dashiell Hammett. Born on this day in 1894, Hammett was the originator of the hard-boiled school of fictional detective writing. He had a lot of experience from which to draw his characters. Before enlisting in the First World War, Hammett had spent eight years working as a Pinkerton detective. While receiving treatment for tuberculosis—which he contracted during the war—Hammett started writing short stories and novellas. In 1930, his novel about a detective named Sam Spade was published. *The Maltese Falcon* won Hammett critical acclaim. Two years later, the first of the Thin Man novels hit the best-seller lists. The hard-edged Nick Charles and his gutsy society wife Nora were America's favorite sleuthing couple. And it's often been said that Nora's character was based on Hammett's real-life love, playwright Lillian Hellman. Life is an inspirational experience that can become art in itself if we only stop for a moment to appreciate it.

This is Henry Kissinger's birthday. In 1923, Kissinger was born in Furth, Germany. If history had taken a different turn, this masterful diplomat would have stayed in Germany; and later on, history would —no doubt—have taken a very different turn. But the fact is he and his family emigrated to the United States. Kissinger grew up to become one of history's most celebrated diplomats. He made history when he was appointed Secretary of State. He was the first Jewish-American to hold the position; and he was the first Secretary of State to speak with a German accent. Kissinger also made history by breaking away from precedents; by being aware that public opinion was a powerful force; and by working about three times harder than most people. I propose to celebrate his birthday by urging us all to take a leaf or two from that particular Kissinger book.

MAY 28

The Dionne quintuplets were born, 1934.

The Dunkirk evacuation began, 1940.

INTRODUCTIONS

Most of us are born alone, so to speak; some of us are born twins; fewer of us are born triplets. On this day in 1934, Mrs. Oliva Dionne gave birth to quintuplets. The Dionne Quints were a wonder of the modern world. Their family doctor became a world celebrity. Nobody would have dreamed that, thanks to new fertility drugs, multiple births would become more numerous in later years. What seems to be a natural miracle in one generation sometimes becomes a commonplace scientific procedure in the next. Let us address ourselves to some of today's miracles which we would like to see become commonplace tomorrow.

In a period of about a week in 1940, more than 300,000 Allied Forces were evacuated from the French shores near Dunkirk, a bitter defeat by the Nazis on the European continent during the Second World War. Ships, fishing boats, sailing craft of every shape and size crossed the English Channel to rescue the stranded troops in one of the world's largest volunteer missions. The Dunkirk evacuation did more than bring the fighting men out of what seemed a final, inescapable trap. It also gave new heart to the British people who gave their time and effort toward the cause. When I look at the world today, I find it in far better shape than right before the evacuation at Dunkirk. We have a lot of challenges to face, but if we can summon up only a fraction of the spirit of Dunkirk we will prevail.

MAY 29

Patrick Henry was born, 1736.

Bob Hope was born, 1903.

John F. Kennedy was born, 1917. (See November 22nd entry.)

Edmund Hillary and Tensing Norkay scaled Mount Everest, 1953. (See May 16th entry.)

INTRODUCTIONS

Today marks a high point in history. I hope you will not think I am indulging in extravagant language about this gathering. I am talking about this day in 1953, when

Edmund Hillary and Tensing Norkay climbed higher than any human beings had ever been before. They became the first men to scale the world's tallest peak high in the Himalayas—Mount Everest. I find myself wondering what it must be like climbing Mount Everest. But coming back down to earth, my subject today is not up in the clouds. It's right down here with the rest of us.

When I began to prepare my remarks for today, I did a bit of research. I found that today was the birthday of both Patrick Henry and John F. Kennedy, two eloquent American speakers. It's also the birthday of another great spokesman, Bob Hope. Even though he was born in England, Hope embraced and embodied the American spirit as much as native sons Henry and Kennedy. And he took that spirit on the road to American radio and television audiences as well as American military bases around the world. It occurred to me that the best thing I could do on these three birthdays was simply to practice the three G's of public speaking—get up, get down to cases, and get off. I have done the stand up; that leaves two G's left to go.

M AY 30

Memorial Day (celebrated on the last Monday of the month).

Joan of Arc burned at the stake, 1431. (See January 6th entry.)

The Hall of Fame was dedicated in Bronx, New York, 1901.

Alexei Arkhipovich Leonov was born, 1934. (See March 18th entry.)

INTRODUCTIONS

Today used to be Memorial Day when it was defined by a date. Memorial Day is now celebrated on the last Monday in May. That gives us a three-day weekend, which may or may not add to our commemoration of the men and women of the armed forces who died in service to our country. But it does add somewhat to the pleasure of the moment. Regardless of this date change, I would like to hope that future generations will be spared from making these sacrifices. And we can all do something about that.

This is the Hall of Fame's anniversary. It is some measure of fame itself that most people now are likely to ask which hall of fame— baseball's, football's, rock 'n' roll's or what? The sad fact is that the Hall of Fame that was dedicated in The Bronx on this day in 1901, is less famous than some of its namesakes. Fame is fleeting—unless we are interested in keeping it alive. The same is true of progress. It is not automatically self-sustaining. If you like the way things are, you can't sit back and expect them to keep on going; and if you don't like the way things are going, you've got to help change them. If my remarks today make no other point but that one— and make that one clear—then I will be content.

Ma y 3 1

President Dwight D. Eisenhower spoke about revolutionaries and rebels, 1954.
Adolf Eichmann was executed, 1962.

INTRODUCTIONS

This is the anniversary of Adolf Eichmann's execution by the State of Israel. Eichmann was hunted down as the Nazi mass murderer of Jews during the Second World War. His hanging wrote a new chapter in international law and terrified other fugitive Nazis hiding in various places around the world. But it didn't seem to have a broad enough impact. The crime of genocide has not ended. But neither has our desire to stop its perpetrators.

It was on this date in 1954 that Dwight D. Eisenhower made a speech at Columbia University's bicentennial. The President of the United States and the former President of Columbia University said: "Here in America, we are descended in blood and in spirit from revolutionists and rebels—men and women who dared to dissent from accepted doctrine. As their heirs, we may never confuse honest dissent with disloyal subversion."

Ju n e

INTRODUCTION:

April showers may bring May flowers, but June heralds the end of the school year and the beginning of summer vacation. This particular month is also traditionally the Marriage Month. More brides step up to the altar in June than in any other month in the year. But enough about an obvious subject, I'd like to propose a marriage of head and heart to resolve a few issues here today so we can all take a well-deserved summer break.

J UNE 1

Brigham Young was born, 1801.

Captain James Lawrence said: "Don't give up the ship," 1813.

Norma Jean Baker was born, 1926.

J. P. Morgan was photographed with a midget on his lap, 1933.

Cable News Network made its debut, 1980.

INTRODUCTIONS

Of all the watchwords chronicled in American history, none has been quoted more than the immortal words: "Don't give up the ship." According to reports the U.S.S. *Chesapeake's* Captain James Lawrence uttered them as he lay dying aboard his ship on this day in 1813. Some record the statement as the U.S.S. *Franklin's* Captain James Mugford's dying words in 1776. Generally, Captain Lawrence is regarded as the revered author of this ringing cry that became the U.S. Navy's motto. The fact is that Lawrence's vessel was not only defeated by the British ship *Shannon* but was also boarded and captured. Despite the Captain's fighting words, we did give up the ship. I mention this not to poke holes in an eloquent battle cry, but simply to point out that, while words are fine, you still need to back them up. My word to you today is that words simply aren't enough.

Public attention is easily diverted. If you doubt this, I refer you to a case in point. During a U.S. Senate hearing held on this date in 1933, one of the world's greatest financiers—J. Pierpont Morgan, Jr.—was waiting to be questioned about the current economic state. It was the Depression, after all. A circus press agent suddenly placed a midget woman on Morgan's lap and took a photograph. You won't find much in the history books about that Senate hearing, but you'll find Morgan and the woman in one history book after another. They say a picture's worth a thousand words. Undaunted, however, I shall continue relying on words in my appearance before you today. I will nevertheless keep one eye peeled for a circus press agent with a charming little person in tow.

Today is Brigham Young's birthday. He was born on this day in 1801 in the green hills of Whittingham, Vermont. Young not only believed in miracles, he led one: the epochal Mormon trek across the wild continent to Utah's Great Salt Lake. High in the Rocky Mountains, Young and his followers founded Salt Lake City. Young was both a religious leader and a doer. He had 27 wives and was survived by 47 children. While he lived, polygamy was still an accepted Mormon practice, although it was outlawed in the rest of the nation. On his birthday, we are reminded that doing and teaching often go hand in hand. Those who speak with faith in the rightness of their cause are often made more eloquent by their faith. You understand, of course, that I hope to persuade you by assuring you that I wholeheartedly believe in what I am about to say.

The icon of 1950s American femininity was born on this day. In 1926, Norma Jean Baker was born in Los Angeles, California. She always wanted to be an actress, and when she grew up she dyed her hair blond and changed her name to Marilyn Monroe. People noticed Marilyn. She had all the charm, innocence, and sex appeal that was necessary to be the ideal all-American bombshell. She rose from a cameo role in a Marx brothers film to stardom in less than five years. She was *Playboy Magazine's* first cover girl. And when she married the all-American male, baseball player Joe DiMaggio, her fans loved her even more. Sadly, real life never lives up to the myths we create around our heroes and heroines. Some people question whether we aren't deluding ourselves by worshipping or emulating popular idols. But youthful hopes and dreams inspired Norma Jean Baker to become Marilyn Monroe. Well I certainly don't picture myself on the cover of *Playboy,* but I, too, have a dream. And I'd like to share that dream with you.

Back in 1980, people didn't think there were many frontiers left to explore. But they changed their minds when Cable News Network made its debut on this day. CNN was the world's first all-news cable television station. Within a decade, the network surpassed television giants like ABC, NBC, and CBS at getting the news first; they also set a precedent by delivering the news and commentary 24 hours a day. CNN brought the realities of the Persian Gulf War into the world's living rooms. It continues to be on the scene throughout the nation and the world. There may not be much that's new under the sun. But there are certainly a lot of unique opportunities that still haven't been explored.

J UNE 2

Marquis de Sade was born, 1740.

Great Britain granted Guglielmo Marconi the first wireless radio patent, 1896. (See March 27th and April 25th entries.)

The U.S. Congress granted Native Americans citizenship, 1924.

Queen Elizabeth II was crowned at Westminster Abbey, 1953. (See April 21st entry.)

INTRODUCTIONS

Today is the Marquis de Sade's birthday. Cynicism is not necessary to observe that de Sade was born before his time. I can't decide whether this French nobleman, born in 1740, would have been a contemporary cult leader, a porno film producer, an adult magazine publisher, or a romance novelist. Maybe he would have done all of the above. In real life, he spent his last decade in a lunatic asylum. In today's world, he might have had prominence in some circles. I intend, today, to strike a blow against what he preached. Not being a sadist, I shall not inflict cruelty upon this audience by trying your patience and continuing to speak after I have made my point. My point is simply this.

Today marks the anniversary of the second Elizabethan age. In 1953, Great Britain's Queen Elizabeth II was crowned at Westminster Abbey. Surrounded by heads of state, princes and dukes, lords and ladies, Elizabeth's coronation followed a tradition that dates back to the Middle Ages. But Elizabeth II also broke new ground: She allowed the ceremony to be televised. Tens of thousands of her loyal subjects became the first British commoners to attend a royal coronation. Some traditions seem to live on unchanged, while others seem to continue with some alteration. Today I would like to propose a few enhancements to another long-held tradition.

An unusual footnote was written into the annals of American history on this day. The aboriginal peoples of North America have inhabited the continent from coast to coast for thousands of years. But in 1924, the U.S. Congress granted Native Americans their right to national citizenship for the first time. Treaties had been made since the establishment of the Jamestown and Plymouth colonies—and many of them were broken at one time or another. I want to establish a treaty with all of you that cannot and will not be broken.

J U N E   3

The Dutch West India Company received a charter for Nieue Amsterdam, 1621.

Jefferson Davis was born, 1808.

P.T. Barnum's circus made its first tour of the United States, 1835.

Josephine Baker was born, 1906.

The National Defense Act was authorized, 1916

Edward, Duke of Windsor, married Wallis Warfield Simpson, 1937. (See June 19th and June 23th entries.)

INTRODUCTIONS

This is the anniversary of the National Defense Act. It was neither the first, the last, the biggest, nor the smallest defense legislation in our history. But in 1916, this act established the Reserve Officers Training Corps. The ROTC. has certainly had its ups and downs, but through it all there has been one concept worth commending here today: the idea of a civilian-officer. It meant that the armed forces could benefit from having officers who were not strictly military academy officers. We are a nation of laypeople; we are not content to leave anything entirely to the experts. Sometimes I think we should establish a reserve training corps for active citizenship. Today, as a matter of fact, I want to talk to you about what we are doing to train our citizens to be good citizens.

When Great Britain's King Edward VIII dramatically abdicated in 1936 to marry the woman he loved, the world gasped and sighed. On this day, in 1937, that historic love story reached its moment of romantic glory in Mons, France. Edward, Duke of Windsor, married his love, Mrs. Wallis Warfield Simpson. They did indeed live happily ever after until his death in 1972. Happiness can be achieved by those who are willing to make sacrifices. That is the kind of happiness I want to talk about today.

Jefferson Davis was the President of the Confederate States of America. Since today is his birthday, I will quickly tell his story. Born in Christian County, Kentucky, in 1808, Davis was a West Pointer and a brilliant military leader in the Mexican War. He was a Mississippi state senator and later became the U.S. Secretary of War. Then he went back to the Senate. He was not considered an extremist even when he reluctantly followed his state out of the Union. After Robert E. Lee's surrender, he tried to continue the war long enough to negotiate more favorable terms, but he was captured in May, 1865. Held prisoner in Virginia, he was shackled until public outcry ended that barbarism. He was indicted for treason in 1866, released on bail in 1867, and never brought to trial. Until he died in 1889, the U.S. continued to revoke his citizenship. I have told this bit of American history not just because it's his birthday. If you see parallels or contrasts with the aftermath of other wars, so be it. But on this day, I think we should consider our present in terms of our own past.

Today marks the anniversary of the greatest show on earth. In 1835, P.T. Barnum's circus made its first tour of the United States. Barnum had made his name by presenting the most unique individuals and deeds at his Manhattan museums. After two fires leveled those structures, he set his sights on the big top. The circus he created was as much a childhood heirloom as soda fountains and five-and-dime stores for decades. And life under the big top continues to fascinate both young and old audiences alike in such sophisticated metropolises as New York, Paris, Moscow, and London. It is refreshing to reflect on the fact that we never seem to lose our childlike sense of wonderful and innocent pleasures like the circus. I hope we never grow up.

When the Dutch West India Company received a charter to establish a New World settlement called Nieue Amsterdam in 1621, neither the government nor the trading company had any idea what would develop from this simple act. On this day, New York City was born. The Dutch West India Company's settlement quickly outgrew its original boundaries at the southern tip of Manhattan island which had been purchased from the natives for $24 worth of trinkets. Soon it stretched across five boroughs. More than likely, Manhattan's founders would shake their heads in wonder if they saw what they had wrought. But my point in telling you this story is this: Sometimes an ambitious idea grows larger than you could ever imagine.

A talented actress, comedienne, singer, and dancer who could laugh at herself was born on this day in 1906. Josephine Baker's long legs, lanky figure, and funny faces didn't hold much promise in American eyes. It didn't get her down. She landed a job as blues singer Bessie Smith's dresser and toured Harlem's thriving 1920s night-club scene though she saw more face powder than footlights. When she was offered a job as a dancer in a jazz revue that was bound for Paris, naturally, she took the job. Baker quickly became the toast of Paris' Follies Bergere. Audiences loved the uninhibited way she sang and gyrated. During the 1940s and 1950s, French film-going audiences flocked to see her. Josephine Baker never became the toast of America, but France proclaimed her their national treasure. I could never repeat one of her performances, but let's see if I can hold your attention anyway.

JUNE 4

Old Maids' Day. (See February 28th entry.)
King George III of England was born, 1738.

INTRODUCTIONS

Today used to be celebrated as Old Maids' Day, which was originated in 1946. It doesn't get much attention anymore. This is not a manifestation of a mere alteration in vocabulary to satisfy feminists. It is simply that singleness is no longer regarded as a debility. We have come to believe that people are entitled to choose their own lifestyles. In my remarks today, I start with the assumption that people can have options, choices, and the opportunity to choose his or her own path through life. I hope today I can be helpful to some of you in making that choice.

Great Britain's King George III was born in London on this date in 1738. It is somewhat due to his stubbornness and ill-temper that the American colonies first rebelled and then declared their independence. Perhaps America should celebrate George III's birthday; but I do not come here to make that suggestion. Rather, I come to point out that we should be grateful to the man who would have been our King George. There were those who thought George Washington should take that role. Thank goodness he refused. Now we have regular election days. Without a king, we need not simply debate national policy. We can influence it. Here is what I have in mind.

JUNE 5

Adam Smith was born, 1723.

Joseph and Jacques Montgolfier demonstrated their hot-air balloon, 1783. (See November 21st entry.)

William Tecumseh Sherman refused the presidential nomination, 1884.

Women's suffrage was introduced in Denmark, 1915.

The Marshall Plan was proposed, 1947. (See April 3rd entry.)

The Six-Day War began, 1967.

The Suez Canal was reopened, 1975.

INTRODUCTIONS

Thomas Carlyle called economics the dismal science. If it is a science at all, we can thank, among others, Adam Smith, who was born on this day in 1723, in Kirkcaldy, Scotland. Smith was not the first political economist, but he put the subject all together in 1776 in his book which was entitled, *Inquiry into the Nature of the Causes of the Wealth of Nations.* We have had a number of economic debates since then. Economics has become not so much the dismal science as the disputatious one. It may be that I am going to make a contribution to the science today, or perhaps merely to the continuing disputes. So here I go.

The great Civil War general, William Tecumseh Sherman, was asked to run as a presidential candidate. But on this date in 1884, he sent a clear, profound message which went something like this: "If nominated, I will not accept; if elected, I will not serve." Once you accept an invitation, you can't be quite that terse thereafter. So, since I have accepted your kind invitation to talk here today, I shall be saying a few more words than General Sherman.

It is an ironic twist of fate that the Six-Day War's anniversary also marks the day the Suez Canal was reopened. In 1967, the Six-Day War began between Israel and its neighboring Arab nations. After the six days were over, the ideological and political battles didn't end. That took years to amiably negotiate. In 1975, The Suez Canal reopened for the first time since the Six-Day War. International shipping lanes between the Mediterranean and the Indian Ocean were once again operational. History sometimes seems to create ironies such as this to remind us that no event stands alone. In the final analysis, all events are both the coincidental cause and the effect in a never-ending cycle.

J U N E 6

Nathan Hale was born, 1765.

The Allied forces landed on the beaches of Normandy, 1944. (D-Day)

Senator Robert F. Kennedy was assassinated, 1968.

Professor Hiram Bingham set sail in search of the last Incan city, 1911. (See July 24th entry.)

The Indian army attacked Sikh extremists at the Golden Temple of Amristar, 1984. (See January 19th and November 19th entries.)

INTRODUCTIONS

Today is the anniversary of D-Day: the landing of the Allied Forces on the beaches of Normandy in 1944. We had been told, long before the reality of the Second World War, that warfare had changed, that the days of mass land battles were over. There were no more trenches, we were told. There would be fierce engagements in the air and on the sea, but no more infantry waves on the battlefield. D-Day was not the only battle of its kind; the infantry was also a valuable asset in the Pacific theater. Will there ever be another D-Day? It would be rash to expect us to find that elusive answer. But I do not mean to strike a pessimistic note on this day. If it had not been planned and carried out, I might not be here talking to you; indeed, there might not be meetings like this. D-Day ensured our freedom. Things have grown more complicated since then, but we at least still have our freedom. I propose to use that freedom here today to do some shooting—but I will only be shooting off my mouth.

In war, millions have been killed; millions of bullets have found their mark. Yet, the bullet which found its mark on this day in 1968, shocked the world. New York Senator Robert F. Kennedy died in Los Angeles, California, from bullet wounds. Robert Kennedy's assassination was the overture to America's long, hot summer of civil discontent. The fact that now we can and do talk together, that we have regained a degree of public tolerance, is a comforting one. So let's talk.

It's Nathan Hale's birthday. Born on this date in 1775 in Coventry, Connecticut, Hale was executed as a spy when he was 21 years old. According to legend, as he stood on the gallows, he said: "I regret that I have but one life to lose for my country." Unfortunately for hapless speakers, one can find any number of famous dying words, but not many equally effective opening lines. Perhaps it will comfort you in the audience today, however, to know that I begin my remarks with the awareness that the end should be in sight. Nathan Hale's eloquent dying words were brief. I shall try to do the same, though very definitely with a different ending.

JUNE 7

Freedom of the Press Day.

Spain and Portugal signed the Treaty of Tordesillas, agreeing to divide the new World between them, 1494. (See May 4th entry.)

Henry D. Thoreau wrote: "Man stands to revere, he kneels to pray," 1841.

INTRODUCTIONS

Today is Freedom of the Press Day which was originated by the Inter-American Press Association. Freedom of the press—whether as a special day or as an institution—has not often been observed throughout the Americas. Freedom of the press and freedom of speech must go hand in hand. Obviously, to a speaker, freedom of speech is a matter of some importance. It is a freedom that I plan to make some use of here and now.

In this day in 1841, the author Henry D. Thoreau noted that: "Man stands to revere, he kneels to pray." One stands up to man; one kneels to God. Prayer is a noble institution, and I certainly am not here to disparage it. But I am here to say that we must not confuse reverence and prayer. Reverence is a sign of respect; prayer is a plea for divine intervention. Today I wish to speak about our relationship to our government—a relationship which, I submit, demands reverence but not prayer. We elect our representatives; we do not anoint them. So let's talk about rendering unto Caesar.

When Spain and Portugal signed the Treaty of Tordesillas, agreeing to divide the new World between them on this day in 1494, it never occurred to them that eventually, the settlers and residents of the New World would have their own opinions of who should govern them. And today I'm here to voice a few revolutionary concepts myself.

JUNE 8

Frank Lloyd Wright was born, 1869.

The suction vacuum cleaner was patented, 1869.

The U.S. Postal service delivered the mail by missile, 1959.

Former President Dwight D. Eisenhower addressed the National Governors Conference, 1964.

U. S. forces were authorized to go into combat in South Vietnam, 1965.

INTRODUCTIONS

On this date, in 1965, President Lyndon B. Johnson authorized U.S. forces to go into combat against the Vietcong in South Vietnam. It was neither the first nor the last step in our escalated role in that conflict. And Johnson was neither the first nor the last President to deal with it. Hindsight tells us that we kept trying to be just a little bit pregnant. And, of course, that can't be done. If you are involved in something, it's best to either to dive in or bow out. I won't get into a debate over which course might have best changed the final outcome. But I have a speech to make today on a somewhat different subject even though I'm faced with a similar challenge. I will dive in with both feet. Otherwise it might take years—or at least hours. So, without further ado, let me say ...

Not many architects achieve Frank Lloyd Wright's fame. Born in Richland Center, Wisconsin, on this day in 1869, Wright's most famous works include Tokyo's Imperial Hotel, Manhattan's Guggenheim Museum, and striking homes like the Robie House and his own Talliesin. He pioneered the concept of synthesizing a structure to its surroundings. For him, architecture was a design for living. Life should be approached in much the same way—as a design for living. To a large extent, we can't count on finding a Frank Lloyd Wright to design our lives. So we have to be our own architects. That is the idea I want to address here today.

On this day, in 1964, former President Dwight D. Eisenhower delivered an address to the National Governors Conference. In his speech, he said: "Our best protection against bigger government in Washington is better government in the states." I will elaborate on that statement by saying: our best protection against government is the better governing of ourselves. Repressive laws are all too often prompted by the excesses of individuals and the failure of others to stand together. Let me give you some concrete examples of how we can and should better govern ourselves.

The United States Postal Service has been dedicated to finding faster more efficient means of moving our mail since it was established in the 1700s. It successfully experimented with a number of new modes of transportation while the public was still trying to figure out how it worked. Trains, trucks, and planes were all employed by the pioneering postal service almost as quickly as it was invented. But on this day in 1959, this efficient government department tried delivering letters by what appeared to be the fastest means possible—by missile. Officials gathered in Mayport, Florida, to view the momentous occasion. The U.S.S. *Barbero* naval submarine launched a guided missile containing 3000 letters from its post at the Naval Auxiliary Air Station. It promptly dove to the bottom of the sea. I certainly hope none of you were waiting for a letter from Florida on that day in 1959, because if you are—I've got some good news and some bad news for you. Now, I'd like to launch straight into my main topic.

A windbag took center stage on this day in 1869. No, not before an audience, though this one was brought into the world to make it a cleaner, brighter place. That windbag was and is the suction vacuum cleaner, patented by Ives McGaffey of Chicago. In that spirit, I'll take a deep breath and start cleaning house of some cluttered thoughts.

JUNE 9

John Howard Payne was born, 1791.

Cole Porter was born, 1892.

The Jonkers Diamond was sent by transatlantic mail, 1935.

INTRODUCTIONS

This is the day when, in 1935, the fabulous, 700-plus-carat Jonkers Diamond was mailed from England to the United States for 35 cents postage. I bring this matter to your attention not to make us all miserable about today's postage rates, but rather to suggest that every point in time is different. We can recall the past but we cannot relive it. What we can do with the present is to plan for a better future. I have no solution for the postage rates, but I do have some thoughts on some other matters that I'd like to share with you.

This is John Howard Payne's birthday. He was born on this date in 1791 in New York City. Payne was the author of dozens of plays and an actor of some repute, but most people only remember his one claim to fame. Payne wrote the song "Home Sweet Home." One success can outlive a parade of lesser efforts. So, be it ever so humble, there's no place like the top. Payne didn't get there often, but he did make it once. There is hope for all of us. That optimistic note is what persuades me to address you here today.

Cole Porter was born on this date in 1893 in Peru, Indiana. His Broadway hits were innumerable: his lyrics were sophisticated; his music was catchy and clever. Merely reciting the titles of some of his songs provides a selection of themes for my remarks here today: "Anything Goes," "Just One of Those Things," "Don't Fence Me In," "Wake Up and Dream," and "You're the Top." But my personal favorite sums up my opinion on today's topic: "Let's Do It."

J U N E   1 0

Judy Garland was born, 1922.

Italy attacked France, 1940.

Lidice, Czechoslovakia was wiped out, 1942.

Mussolini was overthrown, and Italy became a republic, 1946.

INTRODUCTIONS

Today marks the anniversary of both a low and high point in Italian history. In 1940, Italy joined forces with Nazi Germany in attacking France. Under Mussolini's dictatorship, Italy's action was described by President Franklin D. Roosevelt as, " ... the hand that held the dagger has stuck it into the back of its neighbor." But in 1946, the same country overthrew its dictator, and formally became a republic. We like to remember the happy events. But we can better appreciate our current blessings if we look at both sides of the coin.

Do you recognize the name Lidice? Do you have to stop and think about it? Don't be disturbed if that is the case, because Lidice is not a happy memory. On this day, in 1942, after Gestapo leader Reinhard Heydrich was killed, Nazi forces wiped out the entire town of Lidice, Czechoslovakia. Even in the midst of the Second World War, this was a shocking event. In light of what has happened since, is it shocking anymore? I suggest that we ask ourselves what causes the vengefulness that destroyed Lidice and other towns since then. How do we exorcise that spirit?

The human spirit is a complicated entity. We are taught to think that material success is the road to happiness. Frances Ethel Gumm was born on this date in 1922. This young girl from Grand Rapids, Minnesota, changed her name to Judy Garland and became a star before she even entered high school. Few people have enjoyed so much professional success and personal unhappiness. Garland brought the world laughter and pleasure, but gained little of the same in return. Perhaps we should all be less worried about material success and more concerned with the happiness that we and others might find over the next rainbow.

JUNE 11

Stalin's great Soviet "purge" ended, 1937.

Ben Hogan made his comeback on the professional golf circuit, 1950.

Jacques Cousteau was born, 1910.

INTRODUCTIONS

This was the day, in 1937, when Josef Stalin's great Soviet "purge" reached its climax. After a secret military trial, Marshal Tukhachevski and seven other high-ranking officers were convicted of conspiring with the Germans and sentenced to death. They were shot the next day. Earlier in the year, thirteen civilian leaders who had fallen out of favor with Soviet Premier Stalin, had been convicted and executed. With this execution, Stalin managed to terrorize and suppress all opposition to his call for pure socialism. He also branded any concept that was not his own as anti-socialist, Leninist, Trotskyite, or simply traitorous. What makes this case even more interesting is that Stalin signed a nonaggression treaty with Germany two years later. The U.S.S.R. remained conveniently neutral until it became more convenient to side with the Allies. The lesson to be learned is that actions speak louder than words; and actions of convenience speak only of treacherous intents.

Every act of athletic heroism is memorable. That is particularly true when an athlete makes a comeback. Today is the anniversary of such an event. In 1950, professional golfer Ben Hogan thrilled the nation when he won the U. S. Open Golf Championship. Hogan had been a champion long before then. But more than a year earlier, he had been seriously injured in a car accident. It appeared he would never play again. But Hogan was determined. He worked. He struggled. He exercised. He kept trying. And he won. The physically challenged do the same thing every day of their lives, but they are not always publicly applauded for their achievements. We who are able-bodied don't always understand how much courage and how much strength goes into seemingly ordinary tasks. So today, I ask you to remember Hogan's comeback for what it symbolizes. Remember also that for today's physically challenged, every step is a giant one. It is easy to say we simply cannot do something. It is much harder to say we can and we will.

We often think of pioneering explorers as individuals who discover uncharted lands, scale the highest peaks, or reach for the stars. But today is the birthday of an explorer who discovered uncharted lands and solved many mysteries under the sea. French naval officer and undersea explorer Jacques Cousteau was born on this day in 1911. Besides crossing deep into this mysterious frontier, Cousteau also developed a process for using television underwater and invented the aqualung diving apparatus. That's a lifesaver. Now I can take a deep breath knowing that I won't run out of air while I dive into my speech.

J U N E 1 2

The Virginia Convention adopted a Declaration of Rights, 1776.

The Baseball Hall of Fame opened, 1939.

The Alcan Highway was opened to traffic, 1943. (See November 20th entry.)

Bryan Allen flew the first man-powered aircraft, 1979.

The Chicago Bulls won their first NBA title, 1991. (See June 19th and June 20th entries.)

INTRODUCTIONS

Today's anniversary has been largely overlooked. It's a shame, because it was really a red-letter day in American history. It was on this date, in 1776, while the Continental Congress met in Philadelphia, that the Virginia Declaration of Rights, largely written by George Mason, was adopted by the Virginia Convention. Perhaps if I read you a few passages you will see why I find this precursor to the Declaration of Independence so important. And I quote. Article One: "That all men are by nature equally free and independent and have certain inherent rights . . . the enjoyment of life and liberty . . . and pursuing and obtaining happiness." Article Two: "That all power is . . .derived from the people." Unquote. They must have overheard this in Philadelphia. But the Virginia Declaration of Rights made some other points as well, like insistence on freedom of the press and freedom of worship. All in all, this remarkable document's influence is obvious. Our great heritage has many roots, but one of the greatest is this 1776 document. It is a privilege to be able to get up and speak your mind. And to speak one's mind on this day is particularly appropriate.

Today is the day when the Baseball Hall of Fame opened in 1939 in Cooperstown, New York. Some of you may think this Hall of Fame is silly, or frivolous. I hail it as an example of America's desire to recognize and honor accomplishment. So why don't we have a fund-raisers' hall of fame, or a charitable volunteers' hall of fame? There are so many unsung heroes in this world. I come to you today to speak in favor of more recognition for more good people who do good things .

The Alaskan Highway, linking our northernmost state to points south, had taken years to complete and was officially opened in the dead of winter on November 20th, 1942. On this day in 1943, the Alaskan Highway—which winds its way through the northern wilderness between Dawson City, British Columbia, in Canada, and Fairbanks, Alaska—had its first traffic. The road was bumpy and potholed in places from the climatic extremes that part of the world experiences annually; and it wasn't completely paved until 1994, but the highway we now call the Alcan has become a legend. And the 25,000 cars, jeeps, vans, RVs, and trucks that brave the trip each summer attest to our growing love of wilderness adventure. In 1979, on this very same day, an adventurous spirit named Bryan Allen flew the man-powered aircraft across the English Channel. The 26-year-old cyclist braved the piercing winds and cold in the Gossamer Albatross to prove that gas engines weren't a necessity to air travel. Not all of us are willing to brave driving the Alcan or flying the Channel in a man-powered aircraft, but I have an adventurous idea I hope you'll be willing to try.

J UNE 13

Alexander the Great died, 323 BC.

The Yukon Territory entered into the confederation of Canada, 1898. (See July 1st entry.)

Missiles were first used in warfare, 1944. (See March 16th entry.)

The U.S. Supreme Court issued the Miranda decision, 1966.

First African-American Supreme Court Justice was nominated, 1967.

President Jimmy Carter proposed a superfund to clean up hazardous waste, 1979.

INTRODUCTIONS

This is the day when Alexander the Great was proven right for saying he had no more worlds to conquer. In 323 BC, he died of a fever. He felt he had done it all. There isn't one of us—neither the greatest scientist nor the richest financier nor the most successful explorer—who cannot find another hill to climb, another challenge to overcome, another world to conquer. Whether you call the enemy of progress fear, complacency, or apathy, this is no time to give up trying.

The anniversary of a landmark nomination is always a cause for celebration. In 1967, Thurgood Marshall was nominated to the U.S. Supreme Court by President Lyndon B. Johnson. It was a long time in coming, but it came. Marshall became the Supreme Court's first African-American justice in America, and went on to a truly distinguished career. What needs doing ultimately gets done. We are still picking up more polish, more substance. And, speaking of some things taking longer to gain substance than others, I want to assure you that I was not referring to my speech here today. I don't expect my remarks to be short and sweet, but I do expect them to be short.

This is the anniversary of a landmark decision that ensured the rights of those suspected of committing a crime. In 1966, the U.S. Supreme Court handed down the Miranda decision which stated that a criminal suspect could not be questioned without his consent; that he or she had the right to an attorney; and that he or she had to be advised of his or her rights before being questioned by authorities. Before I begin my remarks, I would like to advise all of you that you have the right to remain silent while I am speaking; you have obviously consented to listen; and even though I didn't bring my attorney you do have the right to question me after I'm done.

Our nation's natural resources are fragile and finite, and in the course of our industrial progress, suffered greatly from mismanagement and misuse. On this day in 1979, President Jimmy Carter joined the ranks of conservation-minded Executives in Chief like Theodore Roosevelt, Franklin D. Roosevelt, and Richard M. Nixon when he proposed a superfund to clean up hazardous waste. He also set aside vast tracts of land as wilderness areas to be preserved for future generations. Those were the acts of a president. But today I am here to talk about what we ourselves can do for the environment.

JUNE 14

Flag Day.

The U.S. Army was founded, 1775.

Harriet Beecher Stowe was born, 1811.

Donald Trump was born, 1946.

President Dwight D. Eisenhower spoke at Dartmouth College, 1953.

Argentine forces surrendered the Falkland Islands, 1982. (See April 13th entry.)

INTRODUCTIONS

Today is Flag Day. It's the anniversary of the day we adopted the Stars and Stripes as our national banner. Since 1777, the Stars and Stripes have waved over the land of the free and the home of the brave. It is a very comforting and very inspiring icon. We don't need to have the flag waved in our faces, but we are comforted to know that what it symbolizes is still there, still whole, and still worth preserving. One thing the flag represents is free speech. The flag stands there for all to see, and the speaker is free to speak his mind. With thanks to flag, the nation, and to you here we go.

Today is Harriet Beecher Stowe's birthday. In 1811, Harriet Beecher Stowe was born in Litchfield, Connecticut. As an adult, she wrote a book whose alternate title was, *Life Among the Lowly*. You never heard of it? Yes you have. The full title was, *Uncle Tom's Cabin* or, *Life Among the Lowly*. Her story first appeared in book form in 1852. It whipped up abolitionist sentiments in the North long before the Civil War. And its influence lasted long after that war. Today, when we call someone a Simon Legree, we are recalling one of Stowe's characters; and if Uncle Tom does not mean today what it did to Mrs. Stowe, it is still drawn from her book. Not too many authors or speakers can create that kind of impact. But we continue to use her symbolism. In fact, I am relieved that this is a friendly audience; otherwise I would feel like little Eliza crossing the ice.

There are those among us who have a fear of books. That thought was on President Dwight D. Eisenhower's mind on this day in 1953 when he addressed an audience at Dartmouth College. "Don't join the book burners," he warned. "Don't think you are going to conceal faults by concealing evidence that they ever existed." Speeches—like books—cover the entire spectrum from good to bad. Naturally, I hope my remarks fall in the first category. At least I am secure in the knowledge that, along with book burning, the hook has been outmoded as a method of dealing with speakers. Thus heartened, I turn to my text for the day.

Since it's Donald Trump's birthday, I would like to reflect on a few words from this Manhattan real estate developer who was born in 1946. Trump once said "if you're going to be thinking anyway, you might as well think big." I certainly hope all of you are ready to invest a few moments to consider an idea that could reap big benefits for all of us.

This is the birthday of the U.S. Army. The Army was founded on this day in 1775, when the Continental Congress in Philadelphia authorized the recruitment of 10 companies of riflemen to serve for one year. I am reminded of an old Army addage: If it moves salute it, if it doesn't move, paint it. Not wishing the latter, I will now move right along into my main topic.

J UNE 15

The feast day of St. Vitus.

The second installment of the U.S. estimated tax is due.

King John I of England signed the Magna Carta, 1215.

British peasant revolted against the poll tax, 1381.

Benjamin Franklin proved that lightning contained electricity, 1752.

Vulcanized rubber was patented, 1844.

The first settlers arrived in Idaho, 1860.

Harry Langdon was born, 1884.

The Second International Peace Conference opened, 1907.

The cork-centered baseball was patented, 1909.

Pioneer Day was declared a state holiday in Idaho, 1911.

New Yorker Carrie Chapman-Catt opened the first Women's Suffrage Congress, 1913.

A New York City ordinance requiring cab drivers to wear white collars on the job went into effect, 1925.

Mario Cuomo was born, 1932.

Jim Belushi was born, 1951.

INTRODUCTIONS

Today is the feast day of St. Vitus. In Germany, it is said that if you dance before a statue of St. Vitus on his day, you'll be assured a year's good health. This patron saint of comedians, dancers, and Sicilians is invoked against epilepsy, lightning, snakebite, attacks by wild animals, and oversleeping. Certainly people who were born today like silent-screen comedian Harry Langdon, former New York Governor Mario Cuomo, and comedic actor Jim Belushi have been blessed by St. Vitus. And Ben Franklin definitely picked the right day to prove that lightning contained electricity. At least he became enlightened instead of lighted by his discovery. Hopefully, with good St. Vitus watching over me, I'll have the same affect on you today.

If you want to tell me to go fly a kite, then you should know that this is a good day do it. It was on this day, in 1752, that Benjamin Franklin flew a kite with a key tied to its string and proved that lightning contained electricity. Franklin's accomplishment does me about as much good as the cork-centered baseball that was patented on this very day in 1909. But it does remind me of a Franklin proverb which every speaker should remember: "A word to the wise is enough, and many words won't fill a bushel." I am not here to fill a bushel. In fact, I'm hoping to knock the first one out of the park and head for home.

We all have something in common with King John of England, on this, the anniversary of the day he begrudgingly signed the Magna Carta in 1215. The last article of the document read: "that the men in our kingdom shall have and hold all the aforesaid liberties, rights, and concessions well and peacefully." In essence, King John lost some of his power without recourse when he signed the Magna Carta. This is also the day when you write a check for the second U.S. estimated income tax installment. So here we are on the day a king signed away part of his power, and you may have to sign away part of your income for taxes plus listen to me. But perhaps, you'll find my words less taxing.

If you think that writing a check for the second U.S. estimated income tax install-ment—which, by the way, is due today—is cause for revolt, perhaps another event that occurred on this day might give you cause for thought. In 1381, a bloody peas-ant revolt ended in London. For three days, peasants descended upon the city of London to protest the poll tax. King Richard II had imposed a one-shilling levy on every person over 14 years of age. It was the third tax leveled on the common peo-ple in four years. It took no account for each individual's means or circumstances. So the overtaxed public went on a rampage. The rioting ended when the king him-self rode into the angry crowd, revoked the tax, and promised to abolish serfdom. It is up to the people to voice their opinions about government. But in return, it's also up to the people to listen carefully to their leaders' response.

The citizens of Idaho call today Pioneer Day. In 1860 the first pioneering settlers arrived in the territory that soon became the state of Idaho. Other pioneering efforts have also happened on this day. In 1907, pioneers in world politics convened at the Second International Peace Conference in The Hague, Netherlands. And six years later, the women's rights pioneer Carrie Chapman-Catt opened the first Women's Suffrage Congress in Budapest, Hungary. It's a groundbreaking day for pioneers, now let's see if I can lead you to some new ground.

Since Charles Goodyear received a patent for vulcanized rubber on this day in 1844, I promise to make my speech a smooth ride for all of you who are listening. The most I can hope for is that your patience won't wear too thin if I tread a few tired lines before burning a little rubber. But I just feel driven to it.

J U N E 16

The Black Prince—Edward, Prince of Wales—was born, 1329.

John Quincy Adams began a three-week speech, 1838.

Abraham Lincoln warned of a house divided, 1858.

The Wizard of Oz opened, 1902.

The U.S. Supreme Court ruled that scientists who developed new life forms in lab-oratories could patent their creations, 1980. (See April 12th entry.)

INTRODUCTIONS

History records that on this very day in 1838, former U.S. President John Quincy Adams—then serving in the House of Representatives—rose and began a speech opposing the Texas annexation. The history books tell us that his speech lasted three weeks. I assure you that my remarks today will be somewhat shorter.

On this date in 1858, the Republican Party assembled in Springfield, Illinois. It had just nominated Abraham Lincoln as a candidate for the U.S. Senate. He lost that particular election, but his words on that day still echo through the corridors of time. Lincoln said to his audience: " 'A house divided against itself cannot stand.' I believe this government cannot endure permanently half slave and half free." Those who doubt the power of words would do well to remember these memorable phrases. His words captured the attention and the imagination of a nation that led him onward to the Presidential nomination and election two years later. A great many speakers —who do not use words quite as well—share similar objectives. Today I stand before you with no illusion of Lincolnian eloquence. But I do share his wish not to see a house divided. So today, I will not try your patience with a long oration. As Lincoln once said, though not directly referring to my remarks, "People who like this sort of thing will find this the sort of thing they like."

Since today is the anniversary of *The Wizard of Oz's* stage premiere, I won't lead you down the yellow brick road for too long. We all know that even though it's a beautiful day and we might have a few adventures during the next few minutes, when all is said and done there's no place like home. So if you've got the courage to hear me out, I think you'll discover that I've got a brain—or at least a lot of heart.

Today is the Black Prince's birthday. In 1329, Edward, Prince of Wales, was born. He gained his dark nickname partially because of the color of his armor. But Edward also earned his dubious title for his ruthless brutality toward his enemies and his relentless cruelty on the battlefield. Even on his deathbed, Edward refused to forgive his enemies. Isn't it ironic that we still award our villains more colorful titles than we give to our heroes? There have been many Black Princes and Red Barons in our past, and even a few who could still wear the label today. Where are our White Knights when we really need them?

J UNE 17

The Battle of Bunker Hill occurred, 1775. (Bunker Hill Day)

Billy Barker was born, 1816. (See August 21st entry.)

First round-the-world airline service commenced, 1947.

Army-McCarthy televised hearings ended, 1954. (See February 21st and April 22nd entries.)

A break-in at the Democratic National Headquarters in the Watergate complex was discovered, 1972. (See January 4th and February 7th entries.)

INTRODUCTIONS

This is the anniversary of the day when an American commander said, "Don't fire 'til you see the whites of their eyes." It was said in 1775, at the Battle of Bunker Hill in Boston, Massachusetts. A wise old speaker once told me that the time to stop speaking is when you can't see the whites of your audience's eyes. So I want you all to know I shall be watching you closely.

Listening is on the rise. I can remember the time before portable radios, cassette and CD players, cellular phones, talking computers, and canned music—when you could walk on the street or fly in a plane without an aural accompaniment. I started thinking about this when I discovered that today was the anniversary of the first round-the-world passenger airline flight. A Pan-American Airline plane took off from New York's LaGuardia Field. It didn't take 80 days to fly around the world, but it did take a lot longer than the same trip takes today by jet. The flight was noisy. But the sounds were those of engines and propellers, not the soundtrack of a movie or of pretaped musical selections. Perhaps sooner than we think some speakers will be talking to groups assembled in front of their individual home computers. One advantage over a live audience, of course, is that an individual can sign off line, without offending the speaker. But I am here, as are all of you, live and in person. I shall devote the next few minutes to not turning you off.

JUNE 18

Robert Goodloe Harper gave his "millions for defense" toast, 1798.

The Battle of Waterloo took place, 1815. (See February 26th entry.)

INTRODUCTUONS:

I wonder what would happen here today if a speaker toasted the guest of honor in the way Robert Goodloe Harper did at a dinner held for diplomat John Marshall who had just completed a mission to France. On this date, in 1798, Harper declared: "Millions for defense, but not a cent for tribute." Of course, the figure would be revised to billions if it were quoted today. I have a feeling that with that amendment, his policy would still be generally palatable. My point is that we are not necessarily as far removed from our past as we sometimes think—at least, in terms of sentiment. An interesting sidelight is that Harper himself was eventually elected to the U.S. Senate. But he soon resigned because he couldn't afford it. He did much better in business and with his law practice. But, as you can see from the way his words have come down to us, he talked a pretty good case. I shall now endeavor to do the same.

J UNE 19

The Statue of Liberty arrived in the United States, 1885.

Bessie Wallis Warfield was born, 1896. (See June 3rd and June 23rd entries.)

Lou Gehrig was born, 1903.

The royal British family adopted the name Windsor, 1917.

Federal Communications Commission was created, 1934.

Michael Jordan was signed to the Chicago Bulls, 1984. (See June 12th and June 20th entries.)

INTRODUCTIONS

There are few symbols more closely related to the spirit of America than the Statue of Liberty. Today is the day when "Lady Liberty" arrived. In 1885, she landed at Bedloe's Island in New York Harbor. This noble symbol was a gift from France. She was created in Paris by Frederic Bartholdi around a metal skeleton designed by Alexandre Eiffel. She was transported by ship in parts; and reassembled on the spot where she still proudly stands. We like to think of our nation as the source of all inspiration, but even our symbol is an immigrant. "Lady Liberty" personified the rest of the world's perception of us as a nation. What do you think our image is in the world today—if it is a single image? Let me give you some food for thought on that point.

Back in 1934, on this date, Congress created the Federal Communications Commission to regulate interstate and international communcations by radio, telephone, telegraph, and cable. That started me thinking about how communications have expanded since then: television, fiber optics, remote networks, modems, cellular and satellite phones, one could go on and on. We are still in the midst of a media explosion. But thank goodness no license is required for me to address you, as long as I do my talking in the old fashioned way. That is what I plan to do, including the old-fashioned idea of keeping it short and sweet.

Two events that were part of major news headlines in the 1930s began on this day. In 1917, Great Britain's royal family adopted the name Windsor to replace Saxe-Coburg-Gotha. When Queen Victoria married Prince Albert, the nation's union with a royal house of Germany was sealed. But during the First World War, political and public sentiments changed; so King George V made that unprecedented name change to disassociate the royal family from its German origins. All succeeding monarchs from that day forward have had the last name of Windsor. George's successor, King Edward also made news when he abdicated his title, became the Duke of Windsor, and married a woman who was born on this day in 1896. Bessie Wallis Warfield became the famous divorcée Mrs. Wallis Simpson, and as you all know she eventually bore the title Duchess of Windsor. You've all heard the question: What's in a name? This story definitely gives us food for thought.

When Michael Jordan was signed to the Chicago Bulls basketball club on this date in 1984, the team's general manager was quoted as saying, "Jordan isn't going to turn this franchise around." But the University of North Carolina at Chapel Hill varsity player, Olympic gold medalist, and the NBA's number one draft pick, took the team from last place to win three consecutive championships between 1990 and 1992. Maybe Jordan just wasn't listening. Today I'm going to tell you that you are just as capable. And I hope you are listening intently.

A great American who became the inspiration for millions was born on this day in 1903. Baseball player Lou Gehrig joined professional sports and quickly rose to fame. Nicknamed the "Pride of the Yankees," Gehrig played with another all-time hero, Babe Ruth, but before he could beat the Babe's career high, he was stricken with the debilitating nervous disorder ALS and retired from the game. But what Gehrig the man and Gehrig the baseball player taught all of us is that each individual must work hard to achieve his goals in life and one of those ultimate aims should be living itself. That Yankee pride of purpose is the subject of my remarks here today.

J UNE 20

123 British prisoners suffocated at the Black Hole of Calcutta, 1756.

The Great Seal of the United States was adopted by Congress, 1782.

Lizzie Borden was acquitted of murder, 1893.

Victoria became Queen of England, 1837. (See January 22nd and May 24th entries.)

The Chicago Bulls became the first team to win three successive NBA championships in 27 years, 1993. (See June 12th and June 19th entries.)

Lillian Hellman was born, 1907.

INTRODUCTIONS

I stand here surveying this room on the anniversary of an incident known as the Black Hole of Calcutta. One hundred forty-six British soldiers were placed in a tiny dungeon that was so crowded only 23 survived the night. The Nawab—or governor—of Bengal, Suraj ad Dawlah, had ordered his army to overtake the East India Company's garrison in Calcutta to protest Great Britain's expansion into India. The date for this horrific event was 1756, but it is not too late to be grateful that your condition is somewhat less crowded here today.

The Great Seal of the United States was adopted on this very day by the U.S. Congress back in 1782. That was before we even had a constitution! The nation's symbol featured an eagle holding an olive branch, and the legend, "E Pluribus Unum," which, in Latin, means "one from many." That still has numerous connotations; not just one nation of many states, but one people of many origins; or one freedom of many freedoms. I must tell you, however, when used by a loquacious speaker, that can also mean only one thought out of many words. I will not practice that kind of e pluribus unum here today. At least I will try not to.

Every generation has its crime of the century. Today we have the anniversary of a not-guilty verdict handed down for such a crime. This verdict did not, however, put an end to the strangely persistent legend. In 1893, Lizzie Borden was acquitted in New Bedford, Massachusetts, of the murders of her father and her stepmother. You may not know that she was acquitted. You are more likely to know the children's rhyme which goes: "Lizzie Borden took an ax. / Gave her mother forty whacks. / When she saw what she had done. / She gave her father forty-one." Thus is folklore born. Well, I am not here to add to the folklore—or to the ledger of crime. I am here, however, to plead a case before you, ladies and gentlemen of the jury.

On this day in 1905, a champion of human rights was born in New Orleans. Playwright Lillian Hellman became a well-known playwright and screenwriter penning stories that blatantly attacked injustice, exploitation, and selfishness in human nature. *The Children's Hour, Little Foxes,* and *Watch on the Rhine* exposed the effect a malicious child, a manipulating family, and an irresponsible, carefree generation had on individual lives and on their surroundings. We often speak of human rights in broader terms than the impact of one individual on another; or one family on a town; or one generation on a world. But it's about this more personal designation I would like to speak with you today.

JUNE 21

The summer solstice begins.

The reaping machine was patented, 1834.

The long-playing record was demonstrated, 1948.

INTRODUCTIONS

Although the summer solstice isn't always precisely punctual, today is often the first day of the summer season. In observance of that occasion, I shall endeavor not to get this audience hot under the collar. When "summer is icumen in," as the Scottish poet Robert Burns put it, our major purpose in life is, or should be, to keep cool. At the same time, however, there are issues to which we cannot turn a cold shoulder. I shall try to maintain a moderate temperature in the climate of my remarks today.

Today is a record anniversary. In 1948, the long-playing record was demonstrated by CBS Laboratories' Dr. Peter Goldmark. The LP—with its high-fidelity recording and its extended playing time—ushered in the advent of new medium for recording sounds and launched a 40-year tidal wave of gold and platinum records. The LP—and its smaller cousin the 45—have since been replaced by cassette tapes and compact discs. However, I mention the LP merely to point out that if you had brought in a turntable instead of a live speaker, you might be getting a longer and louder—and perhaps funnier—set of remarks than I am about to present to you.

As the old saying goes: "Ye shall reap what ye shall sow." And today's anniversary reaped a good profit for inventor Cyrus McCormick. In 1834, McCormick received a patent for his reaping machine. To honor both Mr. McCormick's invention and an old proverb, I shall sow a few ideas here today and hopefully, you will reap some benefit.

JUNE 22

Henry Hudson was set adrift, 1611. (See August 3rd and September 3rd entry.)

Joseph Papp was born, 1921.

Joe Louis became world heavyweight boxing champion, 1937 and 1938.

Three civil rights workers were slain in Mississippi, 1964.

The voting age was lowered to eighteen by law, 1970.

President Reagan honored the remains of four Marines, 1985.

INTRODUCTIONS

There is a story about an old vaudevillian whose act was falling flat—so flat that he was yanked off the stage and a local youngster was brought in as an emergency fill-in. The youngster was a smash hit and the next day the local critic wrote that the old vaudevillian's act "had died that others might live." We are inclined to take some martyrs' deaths that lightly. On a more somber note, I want to remedy that here today by recalling that on this date in 1964, three civil-rights workers disappeared in Mississippi. Comedian and activist Dick Gregory requested and got publisher Hugh Hefner to post a $25,000 reward and eventually their murderers were found. The bodies were discovered two weeks later. These martyrs in the cause of African-American civil rights, in essence, died that others might live. Today, I want to ask all of you how we may live so that others may live.

One reason not all people are alike is that we come from different generations. In 1970, on this day, President Richard M. Nixon lowered the voting age from 21 to 18 years old. There were those who saw disaster ahead. After the Twenty-sixth Amendment ratified the law on June 30, 1971, young adults could vote not only in national elections, but state and local elections as well. Critics believed it was the end of the electoral system. It didn't work out that way. Young Americans demonstrated just about the same degree of callowness and sophistication as their parents. They listened to the candidates, the media, their peers, and their parents—then made up their own minds anyway. And so we discovered that young people can be both different and much like their elders. So today I will not talk about people in general or by generation. I will talk, instead, about things which affect our assembly of widely assorted and variable individuals.

If it's worth doing well, it's worth doing twice, and today's anniversary will prove my point. Joe Louis became world heavyweight boxing champion on this day in both 1937 and 1938. He won the title when he knocked out James Braddock in Chicago. The next year, he knocked out German contender Max Schmeling in New York City. It takes fast work and a bit of luck to gain the title of champion in any field of endeavor. But it takes real persistence to keep one's title from being grabbed by strong competitors. That's not too different from what a public speaker faces. Now that a little fast talk has gotten your attention, let's see if I can hold it.

On this day in 1611, Henry Hudson, his son, and six other crew members were set adrift by mutineers in what is now called Hudson's Bay. The explorer had been commissioned by the Russian Muscovy Company and the Dutch East India Company to find the fabled Northwest Passage to Asia. He had discovered the island of Manhattan and the Hudson River. But drifting aimlessly around this huge inland sea—which eventually bore his name—tempers flared among crew of his ship, *Discovery,* during a long, harsh winter. A mutiny resulted. Hudson and his crew were never found. The mutineers sailed back to England, but the ringleaders did not return. They were killed in a battle with the Inuits. When the chips are down, it's difficult for leaders and followers to keep a clear sighting of their ultimate goal. I want to reset our own sights today and sail right on through before we have a mutiny on our hands.

On this day in 1985, President Ronald Reagan received the coffins of four Marines killed in an attack on a San Salvador café. At the ceremony, the president solemnly vowed that the slayers of these brave man would "not evade justice on earth any more than they can escape the judgment of God." Individuals are judged for their acts not only by an earthly court of laws and taboos; they are also arbitrated within the context of a higher consciousness, a Supreme Being, a God. No matter what religious creed one follows, at the final moment of each individual's existence there comes an accounting of one's deeds in life—the pluses and the minuses are weighed against the sum total of existence. On this solemn anniversary, can each of us here today say that our accounts are balanced for future judgment?

When Joseph Papp was born on this day in 1921, most Americans still thought of Shakespeare's plays as generally unentertaining, long-haired, intellectual stuff. But when Papp opened New York's Public Theater and produced the acclaimed summertime Shakespeare in the Park series, a lot of Average Joe's changed their minds. Papp's productions brought Shakespeare and other playwrights' works to modern audiences in much the same way Shakespeare himself presented his plays at the Globe Theater. The sets weren't elaborate; the actors were talented but relatively unknown; the tickets didn't cost a fortune. As a result, American theater gained a whole new audience. I would like you to imagine how many other opportunities there are to popularize great work, and how many people would welcome it.

J UNE 23

Luxembourg became a principality, 963 AD.

The capital letter typewriter was patented, 1868.

Edward VIII, Duke of Windsor, was born, 1894. (See June 3rd, June 19th, and December 10th entries.)

Alan M. Turing was born, 1912.

Aviators Wiley Post and Harold Catty took off from New York for a flight around the world, 1931. (See July 22nd entry.)

U.S. Congress created the Civil Aeronautics Authority, 1938.

The International treaty of scientific cooperation and peaceful use of Antarctica was signed, 1961.

INTRODUCTIONS

Won't you join me in wishing a happy birthday to the principality of Luxembourg which was founded on this date in 963 AD? The birthday has to be happy because

Luxembourg has survived occupations and invasions by more powerful neighbors—and every other country is more powerful than Luxembourg except in its ability to survive. Good countries, like good speeches, sometimes come in small packages.

Today we commemorate a chilly subject—Antarctica. On this date in 1961, an international treaty for scientific cooperation and the peaceful use of the Antarctic continent was signed. It will be a cold day when that treaty ends. Meanwhile, we can benefit from knowing that none of the treaty nations are planning a mass migration of their populous there in the near future. The Antarctica treaty is like my speech today, designed to keep the pot warm and the friendly fire going.

History records that on this date, in 1868, Christopher Sholes, a Wisconsin journalist and state senator, received a patent for a contraption called a "Type-Writer." This particular typewriter printed only capital letters—it didn't have a shift key. I will endeavor today to follow its example. I plan to make a few big points and take a position from which I shall not shift.

A lot of controversy has arisen over Edward VIII, Duke of Windsor, in the past few years. Was the son of Great Britain's King George V really a German spy? Born on this day in 1894, it was a well-known fact that before Edward took the throne he wanted to sign a friendship agreement with the German government. The royal house of Windsor did have German connections which his father officially declared as severed during the First World War. Did Parliament really allow him to abdicate his title and marry a commoner just to get rid of him? The mystery has not yet been solved, though new evidence is still being uncovered. The truth of historical events sometimes takes years to uncover. Though I am here to speak and not to spy, and with any luck I'll leave you today with more answers than questions. I would like to present to you today. . . .

During the 1930s, America took to the skies. On this day in 1931, aviators Wiley Post and Harold Catty took off from New York City for their epic flight around the world. And seven years later to the day, the U.S. Congress created the Civil Aeronautics Authority to regulate air traffic. The skies had become crowded with airmail routes, passenger flights, and barnstorming stunt pilots in the thirty years following the Wright Brothers' first flight at Kitty Hawk, North Carolina. Now known as the Federal Aviation Administration, this arm of government continues to monitor the thousands of aircraft that fly in America's crowded airspace. Luckily, I don't need to wait for clearance from air-traffic control to fly my idea past you today.

No one had ever heard of digital computers when British mathematician Alan Mathison Turing was born in 1912. Artificial intelligence was just a wild-eyed fantasy in a few obscure science tests. While studying for his masters degree at Cambridge University's King's College, Turing took long walks through the riverside meadows down to the village of Grantchester. On one of his afternoon strolls, he conceived of a universal computing machine; and in 1937, he published his theory entitled "On Computable Numbers." After the Second World War, Turing headed a project to create the ACE—Automatic Computing Engine. Three years later, he directed the construction of the Manchester Automatic Digital Machine. And in 1950, Turing predicted that computers would eventually think like humans. Sadly, he never lived to see his prophecy come to the fruition it has reached. But Turing's habit of strolling through Grantchester Meadows changed the world. Maybe more of us should learn to get out from behind our PCs with their CRTs and LCDs and follow in Turing's footsteps once in a while.

J UNE 24

John Cabot sighted land between Halifax and southern Labrador, 1497.

Empress Josephine of France was born, 1763. (See March 9th entry.)

Flying saucers were reported near Mount Rainier, Washington, 1947.

The Berlin Blockade began, 1948. (See May 12th entry.)

Sally Ride became America's first female astronaut, 1983. (See April 19th entry.)

INTRODUCTIONS

We are meeting on an historic anniversary. In 1947, flying saucers were sighted over Mount Rainier, Washington. Kenneth Arnold of Boise, Idaho swore that he saw "shining saucer-like objects . . . Not just one, but nine." That was it. In later years, the reports were considerably more detailed, up to and including accounts of alien abductions, descriptions of "gray men" and so forth. There is little evidence that these people were deliberately trying to con the public, but the government explained the sightings as marsh gas mirages, weather balloons, or atmospheric phenomena. People didn't seem terribly anxious to believe those explanations either. This event reminds me of the story of the flying-saucer commander who came home to his own planet and reported that he had landed on earth and walked into Times Square. "What did you see there," he was asked. "Well," he said, "there were a lot of little creatures moving about and at every corner there was a big creature with red and green eyes bending over and winking at them. I think the big creatures were making speeches." So please consider me today as your resident traffic light—the "Don't Walk" sign is now flashing.

The space shuttle *Challenger* safely landed on this day in 1983, at Edward's Air Force Base. This may not seem that newsworthy until you consider that one of the crew members was Sally Ride, our first female astronaut to travel into space. Some people speak of the "glass ceiling" that many women encounter as they rise up through their given profession. They see the top, but they can't break through the invisible barricade of gender discrimination to reach their goal. Sally Ride obviously broke through and reached the stars. That should be the goal for each of us, in every endeavor. Shoot for the stars.

Five years after Christopher Columbus reached the New World, exploring the islands in the Caribbean, and returned to Spain to report his discoveries, a courageous British navigator sighted the coastline between between Halifax, Newfoundland, and southern Labrador. On this day in 1497, John Cabot made the first recorded discovery of the North American mainland. History tells us that the Vikings had landed on this continent five centuries earlier, but they had left no written record of the epic journey. John Cabot did. I guess the moral of this story is that if you want to go down in history as the first to discover something, keep a detailed record of the event. Transcripts of what I'm about to announce will be available in the lobby.

JUNE 25

General George Armstrong Custer made his last stand, 1876. (See December 5th entry.)

George Orwell was born, 1903.

The Korean War began, 1950.

INTRODUCTIONS

I am mindful as I stand before you today that even a speaker given a cordial greeting should be wary of assuming that the audience has already been won over. Today is the anniversary of Custer's Last Stand. In 1876, General George Armstrong Custer and his entire command of over 200 men were wiped out by the Sioux nation at Little Big Horn, Montana. Only one horse—who was named Comanche—survived. Do not misunderstand me. I have no fear that Custer's Last Stand will be repeated here today with me as Custer. It is simply that, remembering Custer's blustering overconfidence, I do not start with any blissful assumption that what I am about to say will automatically win your support. In brief, I am here to sound my own little big horn and to hope that you will find my message to your liking.

Some anniversaries leave stern memories. Long after Custer's Last Stand took place in 1876, another questionable military event occurred. In 1950, North Korea invaded South Korea, sparking the Korean War. Countless casualties and a relatively unaltered border resulted. And the battle continues across opposite sides of international conference tables—featuring streams of speeches from both sides. Today, these anniversaries remind us that when the bullets stop, the war of words goes on unabated. I am not here to take part in any war of words; I shall not assail your ears with a verbal barrage. Instead, I shall speak to you in what I hope will be measured tones for a measured amount of time, on behalf of a very peaceful cause.

George Orwell, who was born on this day in 1903, kept his feet planted firmly on the ground as he wove prophetic visions of civilization's future right here on earth. His prophecies concerning life in the year 1984 were not far from wrong; and his commentary on civilization's degeneration in his novel, *Animal Farm,* provide the theme for my remarks here today. The animals in his story fought for and won their freedom from a tyrannical farmer, establishing an egalitarian government based on equal rights and the democratic process. The lust for power overtook some of the pigs, and slowly the social scales shifted from absolute equality to a privileged class structure where some animals became more equal than others. We certainly don't have to worry about a beastly revolt in our near future, but I think we should consider the obvious imbalance in our democratic society that favors some individuals more than others.

J UNE 2 6

Abner Doubleday was born, 1819.

George Edward Carnavon was born, 1866. (See November 4th and February 16th entries.)

The United Nations Charter was signed in San Francisco, California, 1945. (See January 1st, January 9th, April 25th, and October 24th entries.)

The Berlin airlift began, 1948. (See May 12th entry.)

INTRODUCTIONS

Today is Abner Doubleday's birthday. He was born in 1819, in Ballston Spa, New York. There are those who claim that the sport which Abner Doubleday reputedly invented became the national pastime for a reason other than its athletic prowess. Perhaps even when he was playing baseball, some of the game's charm may have been confrontations with the umpire. There are few games as susceptible to on-field disputes as Doubleday's game of baseball. After all, every pitch is subject to the umpire's judgment. Today we find some overtones of baseball in our immediate situation. You—the audience—will be the umpires who make judgment calls on my every pitch. Shall we play ball?

JUNE 27

Helen Keller was born, 1880.

Mormon leaders Joseph and Hyrum Smith were murdered by a mob in Carthage, Illinois, 1844. (See April 6th entry.)

President Franklin D. Roosevelt delivered his "rendezvous with destiny" speech, 1936.

Patrons at Manhattan's Stonewall Inn clashed with police during a raid, 1969.

INTRODUCTIONS

We generally think of courage in terms of combat—either on the battlefield or on the playing fields. Today we should be thinking of a far greater kind of courage. Today is Helen Keller's birthday. Born in 1880, in Tuscumbia, Alabama, Helen Keller was diagnosed blind, deaf, and mute. In her time, many physically challenged people were placed in lunatic asylums. But thanks to inventor Alexander Graham Bell—whose wife was hearing-impaired—and her visually-impaired teacher Anne Sullivan, Keller learned to speak. She learned to read lips by touching the lips and throat of the individual speaking. She learned to read Braille. She became a professional writer and crusaded for better treatment of visually- and hearing-impaired individuals. People are courageous when they conquer one handicap. Helen Keller conquered many. And I cannot help thinking, as I stand here speaking to you and you sit listening to me—how much we really take for granted.

When President Franklin D. Roosevelt was renominated on this day, in 1936, he sounded a rallying call for his time. "This generation," Roosevelt proclaimed, "has a rendezvous with destiny." I don't think that generation had a monopoly on such a rendezvous. We too, in our time, have our own rendezvous with destiny. The question is: Will we recognize it when we get there?

Today marks some somber footnotes in the history of America's fight for freedom. In 1844, Mormon leaders Joseph and Hyrum Smith were murdered by a mob in Carthage, Illinois. The First Church of Latter Day Saints had been exiled from New York State and a number of other places before attempting to settle in the Midwestern town. But local people were enraged by the idea of having these so-called heretics who practiced polygamy in their Christian town. The Mormons were run out on a rail once again. In 1969, patrons of Manhattan's Stonewall Inn clashed with police during a raid. Homosexuality was treated as a crime in New York City and the incident at this bar became the focal point for gay rights' advocates for years to come. Our nation's forefathers guaranteed its citizens the right to live peacefully and without discrimination based on ethnic or religious or even sexual orientation. We, the public, still need to be reminded of this basic American doctrine. After all, whether or not we share the views of the group whose freedom is threatened, we must stand up and protect their rights to freedom. If we don't there may be no one to stand with us when it's our freedom at stake.

J UNE 28

Henry VIII of England was born, 1491.

Richard Rodgers was born, 1902. (See July 12th entry.)

Gavrilo Princip assassinated Austria's Archduke Francis Ferdinand, 1914.

The Treaty of Versailles was signed, 1919. (See March 19th entry.)

Terrorists hijacked a passenger jet to Entebbe, Uganda, 1976. (See July 4th entry.)

INTRODUCTIONS

Today is Richard Rodgers' birthday. Born in New York City in 1902, he started out writing songs for amateur boys' club shows. His music quickly matured to familiar, yet haunting, melodies that made him a giant in the theatrical world. The music "Slaughter on Tenth Avenue" and "My Funny Valentine" soon gave way to the scores for groundbreaking musicals like *Oklahoma, South Pacific, The King and I,* and *The Flower Drum Song* which were written with lyricist Oscar Hammerstein III. Youthful promise is sometimes the gateway to remarkable achievement. We must all seek to nurture talent in our children while it is blooming. Who knows? The next Richard Rodgers could be writing a song after school right now.

I wonder how many of you know the name of Gavrilo Princip. It is one of history's quirks that some of the people who kindled epic flames are so little recognized. Gavrilo Princip was a Serbian revolutionary who fought for his nation's freedom from Austro-Hungarian rule. We should remember his name because today is the anniversary of an incident that triggered the First World War. On this day, in 1914, Princip assassinated Austro-Hungary's heir apparent Archduke Francis Ferdinand and his wife Sofia in Sarajevo, Bosnia-Herzegovina. Today we should be mindful that individual names and events are often major elements of a larger canvas. It is against the world's larger canvas rather than the small group assembled here today, that I have prepared my remarks on this occasion.

The fact that the anniversaries of both the beginning and end of the First World War occur on the same day is poetic justice. In 1919, most of the nations involved in that great war signed the Treaty of Versailles and agreed to organize an international League of Nations, except one—the United States. Sometimes, even the best solutions are disputed by those who could benefit from them. I hope my remarks here today will offer a reasonable solution we can all approve.

On this date in 1976, terrorist hijackers seized an Air France plane and flew it to Entebbe, Uganda. They held the passengers—mostly Israelis—as hostages. The world was aghast. A week later, a daring Israeli raid freed the hostages and quashed the terrorists' plans. The moral of this story—for speakers as well as doers—is not to overplay your hand. I promise not to hold any of you hostage.

The Lord, it's said, works in strange and wondrous ways. An event in 1491 was perhaps more of the former and less of the latter. The founder of the Church of England was born on this day. Great Britain's King Henry VIII was born in Greenwich, England. Henry VIII had more wives than most monarchs; was a glutton for good food; reputedly wrote songs like "Greensleeves;" and generally did more of everything than most people—including fighting with the Catholic Church. But he had one attribute which speakers like myself must always envy. No two ways about it: When he spoke, people listened.

J U N E 2 9

The Stationers Company was granted a monopoly, 1566

Peter Paul Rubens was born, 1577.

Britain passed the Townshend Revenue Act, 1767.

Antoine de Saint-Exupéry was born, 1900.

Al Smith was nominated as a presidential candidate, 1928.

British authorities arrested more than 2700 Zionists, 1946. (See August 31st and September 29th entries.)

Israel united east and west Jerusalem, 1967.

The space shuttle *Atlantis* linked up with the *Mir* space station, 1995.

INTRODUCTIONS

A monopoly was created on this day in 1566. Great Britain's Queen Mary had granted the Stationers Company guild the power to be the nation's sole booksellers eight years earlier. But on this date they gained a total monopoly on the business of publishing. The guild consisted of printers, booksellers, and publishers nicknamed for the stalls or stations they set up to sell their wares. Their monopoly meant that every book title had to be registered in the company's roster in advance. "Illegal" books were confiscated and burned. No guild member was allowed to publish the same book as another member. Healthy competition wasn't even considered. No edition could exceed 1250 copies. Best-sellers had to be reset and reprinted so printers would have steady work. Book prices soared in the absence of competition. Soon no one could afford to buy their products. Economic health relies on a certain amount of competition. In that spirit, I invite you to challenge my ideas after I've presented them. After all, even a speech can benefit from a little competition.

Peter Paul Rubens was born on this date in 1577, in Westphalia to a Flemish family. Unlike many starving artists of his time, Rubens did very well indeed—not merely in the mastery of his art but also in the size of his purse. If you visit Rubens' house in Antwerp, you will see quite an establishment. It is fair to say that, even though so many people have delighted in his work, in a material sense he got a lot more out of it. There is one school of public speaking that operates on a similar equation. The speaker gets more out of a speech than the audience. But I have heard me many times before. What I hope to get out of today's remarks will come to me not from your immediate response; it will come from what you say or do in the days, weeks, and years to come.

We are generally familiar with the reasons for the Boston Tea Party in 1773. This so-called party protested the import tax levied by Britain on its colonies. But few remember that the whole thing really began on this date. In 1767, King George III gave his approval to the Townshend Acts which had been proposed by Chancellor of the Exchequer Charles Townshend. The acts taxed imports of glass, paper, lead, paints and tea to the colonies. The tea tax was retained long after the colonists boycotted and successfully repealed the other levies. Slowly but surely the resentment against "taxation without representation" laid the groundwork for the American Revolution. As your speaker today, I must be more mindful than King George was of taxing people unfairly—so I will be careful not to tax your patience.

It was considered almost revolutionary that John F. Kennedy, a Catholic, was elected President. But before that day, another Catholic candidate had won a major party Presidential nomination and today is the anniversary of that event. In 1924, Alfred E. Smith was denied the Democratic nomination because he was a Catholic. In 1928, he was not rejected. Another bastion of religious differentiation in America was breached. Thank goodness our history is filled with these small steps forward. And so today, I should like to be so bold as to suggest some other small but potentially powerful steps we should take.

An adventurer with a romantic soul was born on this day. In 1900, Antoine de Saint-Exupéry was born in Lyon, France. His escapades as a test pilot, military reconnaissance pilot, and aviator were enough to fill a hundred adventure novels; and he penned quite a few of them himself. Saint-Exupéry wrote popular books like *Night Flight; Wind, Sand, and Storm;* and *Flight to Arras,* when he wasn't involved in real-life adventures. But his most famous work was a children's fable entitled *The Little Prince.* The moral of this classic story provides a perfect theme for my remarks today: The best things in life are the simplest ones. The real test of wealth is one's ability to give to another.

The first joint American-Russian space mission had taken place during a thaw in the Cold War, in 1975. The ice finally melted away twenty years later. And on this day in 1995, the U.S. space shuttle *Atlantis* linked up with Russia's *Mir* space station in outer space. It was the first of seven scheduled missions to prepare both nations for a joint pioneering effort—the contruction of an international space station. Its purpose sounds like something from the pages of a science fiction novel: the station will serve as a scientific laboratory and launching platform for a planned expedition to Mars. In less than three decades, we have seen science fiction become reality: man has walked in space, landed on the moon, and photographed the birth of a new star. Is any dream so farfetched anymore that we can't make it come true?

Many Arab nations resented Great Britain's involvement in the Holy Land following the First World War. But as the Second World War came to an end, troubles in British-held Palestine escalated. Tens of thousands of displaced European Jews moved to overtake the Holy Land in the name of Zionism—a radical religious and political movement that had originated in eastern Europe. Terrorism erupted in Jerusalem, and on this day in 1946, British authorities arrested more than 2700 Zionists in the hope that it might end the plague of bombings and sniper attacks. It didn't. Two years later, Great Britain was forced to leave Palestine, and Israel was born. Jerusalem was split in half so that Islamic holy places would not fall under Zionist jurisdiction. On this same day in 1967, Israel ignored international protests and united the city. The incident ignited a full-scale war. Neither side was willing to compromise their religious beliefs for the sake of political peace. Religion has ignited violent defense of this powerful common cause many times in many parts of the world. Today I propose to initiate a movement toward *using religion for more peaceful pursuits.*

J UNE 30

Great Britain's Poor law was passed, 1572.

Gone with the Wind was published, 1936.

The Twenty-sixth Amendment to the U.S. Constitution was enacted, 1971. (See June 22nd entry.)

The Pure Food and Drug Act became law, 1906.

The Meat Inspection Act became law, 1906.

Ada Kepley became the first female law school graduate, 1870.

INTRODUCTIONS

Welfare reform has been instituted in many different ways throughout history. On this day in 1572, Great Britain's Queen Elizabeth I instituted that nation's first Poor Law. This system gave statutory assistance to the poor who were unemployed or vagrant. Church parishes were responsible for distributing this government-funded aid. Those applicants who were willing and able to work were given tools and placed in paying jobs. Those who couldn't work—such as the elderly or infirm—were cared for in their own homes. Able-bodied individuals who were work-shy were publicly punished as vagrants. Great Britain's welfare system radically changed with the times, and so has ours. Let's discuss our own welfare.

Probably the world's most popular Civil War novel was written generations after the actual incident. Margaret Mitchell's epic *Gone with the Wind* was first published on this date in 1936. The novel was an all-time best seller and the film adaptation was a box office sensation more than once. Some novels are indeed gone with the wind, but not *Gone with the Wind*. It was a very long book, and a very long motion picture, too. But do not be alarmed. On its anniversary I will do it homage by delivering a considerably shorter speech.

This nation prides itself on providing its people with foods and medicines which are safe to consume. And today marks the anniversary of the reason why. In 1906, the U.S. Congress established both the Meat Inspection Act and the Pure Food and Drug Act. Scientists and doctors had discovered that poorly prepared or mishandled ingredients, foods, and medications had killed many Americans. Not all producers were following sterile or standardized methods of processing, packaging, or storing these vital commodities. By enacting strict guidelines and regular inspections, the government ensured the public's safety. Thanks to these measures, botulism and other preventable illnesses were nearly eradicated; the physically deforming effects of drugs like Thalidamide were discovered; and the public was educated on how to properly cook and handle raw meats and poultry. Before I arrived here today, I got a Grade A prime inspection stamp to prove that my remarks will be safe for you to digest. And I've limited the dosage.

One talent many American women have is the ability to outtalk any American man. And on this day in 1870, Ada Kepley became one of the first American women to take professional advantage of that talent. She was the nation's first female law school graduate. Even in Ms. Kepley's day, people knew that women could bring men to their knees by preparing and delivering a strong verbal defense. So if any of you plan to contest my remarks here today in a court of law, I'll have you know my attorney is in the audience and she's making notes for my defense.

J U L Y

INTRODUCTION

While most of us think of July as the middle of vacation season—a time for back-yard cookouts and napping under a shaded tree in a hammock—the world seems to revolve around the word freedom. The list of nations that gained their freedom during this particular month attests to this seasonal trend. From Canada and the United States to Peru and other points south, the July watchwords were independence and freedom. The echoes of "liberté, egalité, fraternité" chimed through France, Belgium, and the north African coastal nation of Algeria. During the month of July in 321 AD, freedom from work was proclaimed by the Roman emperor Constantine. Now that's something for which we can all hum the V for victory theme as Winston Churchill did in 1941. But I'm quite sure that some of you agree with Horace Greeley who said in July: "Go west, young man! Go west!" The freedom of the wide open spaces are near and dear to my heart as well. So without further ado, I will get on to my remarks, so you can enjoy your freedom when I'm done.

J U L Y 1

Freedom Day.

Canada Day.

The U.S. Post Office issued the first adhesive-backed stamps, 1847.

The provinces of Nova Scotia, New Brunswick, Quebec, and Ontario officially became the Dominion of Canada, 1867.

The Battle of Gettysburg began, 1863.

The province of Prince Edward Island joined into the confederation of Canada, 1873.

Theodore Roosevelt and the Rough Riders charged San Juan Hill, 1898.

The U.S. Post Office inaugurated the postal zip-code system, 1963.

Medicare went into effect, 1966.

INTRODUCTIONS

Today is Freedom Day. Many nations—including our own—gained their freedom during this particular month of the year. Canada became a self-governing British dominion on this day in 1867. France had its first revolution on July 14. Nations such as Algeria, Argentina, Colombia, Belgium, Peru, Liberia and Venezuela also gained self-government and freedom during this month. So our theme today is freedom. How do we keep our freedom? What do we do with our freedom? How strongly are we committed to the concept of freedom?

Today marks the anniversary of the Battle of Gettysburg, a three-day-long confrontation that took place in 1863. President Abraham Lincoln said we must remember this battle so that from its honored dead "we take increased devotion to that cause for which they gave the last full measure of devotion." In the largest sense, their cause was to fight for what Lincoln described as a "government of the people, by the people, for the people [that] shall not perish from the earth." It is in that context that I speak to you today.

The concept of providing health care for senior U.S. citizens became a reality on this date. In 1966, Medicare became part of the services offered to American citizens. In the intervening years Medicare has been accused of making a few people rich; it has also been credited with helping more people to live healthier and longer lives. The greatest medicine in the world—for old and young alike—is the knowledge that someone cares. Let us dedicate ourselves to that goal both individually and as a nation. To that end, I should like today to call your attention to a number of current opportunities and challenges.

Today is Canada Day, a day to commemorate this northern nation's freedom from British rule. In 1867, the provinces of Nova Scotia, New Brunswick, Quebec, and Ontario became a confederation under an Act of Parliament known as the British North America Act. Canada's representatives sat down at the bargaining table and negotiated a peaceful step-by-step settlement which guaranteed them self-government. Neighboring territories like Prince Edward Island soon joined them. As a dominion, Canada still owed its allegiance to the British crown and to Parliament, eventually receiving total independence in 1982. But unlike its southern neighbor—the United States—Canada did not bear arms to gain its freedom. There was no "shot heard round the world." A fight for independence does not always imply a call to arms, the loss of lives, or the embittered severance of a long-standing relationship. And I hope all of you will be inspired by this story as we discuss the issues I'm bringing to the table today.

I would like to open my remarks today by saluting the U.S. Post Office, who issued the first adhesive-backed stamps on this day 1847, and kept us from searching for a pot of glue while mailing out our bill payments. In 1963, the Postal Service made it easier for our creditors to get our checks when it inaugurated the postal zip-code system. My reason for mentioning these particular events is simple. When are we going to end this reign of revolving credit; and stop echoing Theodore Roosevelt's immortal cry heard this day in 1898 when he and the Rough Riders took Cuba's San Juan Hill—"Charge!"

J U L Y 2

The Continental Congress declared American independence, 1776.

President Lyndon B. Johnson signed the Civil Rights Act into law, 1964.

INTRODUCTIONS

Some of you are undoubtedly getting ready to celebrate Independence Day in two more days. I am happy to point out that, since we are already gathered here today, we can celebrate right now, because today is the real anniversary of our independence. On this day in 1776, the Continental Congress declared that the colonies "are, and of right ought to be free and independent States." Congressional member John Adams wrote to his wife that, quote: "The Second of July, 1776, will be the most memorable epoch in the history of America. I am apt to believe that it will be celebrated by succeeding generations as the great anniversary festival . . . It ought to be so solemnized with pomp and parade, with shows, games and sports, guns, bells, bonfires and illuminations, from one end of this continent to the other, from this time forward, forevermore." And of course we have done just that, but not on July 2. After passing this resolution, the assembly decided to adopt a full declaration on July 4. But we have every right to celebrate both days. So I rise with a birthday salute to the past and to the future of a free and independent nation.

A century after the Battle of Gettysburg—and almost to the day—a law was enacted that ensured equal freedoms for all Americans. On this date in 1964, President Lyndon B. Johnson signed the Civil Rights Act. It was not the end of the fight for equal rights that had pitted neighbor against neighbor, brother against brother during the Civil War. But the Civil Rights Act did win the battle for government recognition that there had been a denial of full citizenship for certain segments of our population. The lesson to be learned today is that no justice system is written in stone. Modifications and enhancements can always be made for the betterment of all.

J U L Y 3

Sunday was designated as a day of rest, 321 AD.

George Washington took command of the Continental Army, 1775.

George M. Cohan was born, 1878.

INTRODUCTIONS

On this date in 1775, a 43-year-old Virginia country gentleman and soldier named George Washington assumed command of the Continental Army at Cambridge, Massachusetts. He did not make a particularly spectacular start, but ultimately, Washington turned out to be a pretty good man for the job. On this anniversary, we should recall the spirit with which he and his troops proceeded to fight against seemingly overwhelming odds. No matter how bleak a situation may look today, the odds are better than those Washington and his army faced in 1775.

George M. Cohan was one of America's top song-and-dance men. This unashamed and effervescent flag waver wrote "You're a Grand Old Flag" and "I'm a Yankee Doodle Dandy." Now today happens to be George M. Cohan's birthday. Born in Providence, Rhode Island, in 1878, Cohan's father decided to designate his son's birthdate as July 4th. So George M. became in his own words "a real live nephew of my Uncle Sam, born on the Fourth of July." Let us then give a great entertainer his due and celebrate today as Uncle Sam's real live nephews and nieces. Even if it isn't the Fourth of July—it's mighty close.

We should all take a rest and reflect today on an important event that took place centuries ago on this very day. In 321 AD, the Roman Emperor Constantine proclaimed *dies solis*—or Sunday—as a day of rest and religious observance so his Christian soldiers could attend services and his pagan troops could offer prayers to their gods. It is an ancient tradition and one I hope never changes. Everyone needs at least one day a week away from the battlefield—including me. So rather than making you toil through a long speech, I'll give you a break and quickly make my point.

J U L Y 4

Independence Day in the United States.

Three Presidents died and one President was born.

Stephen Foster was born, 1826. (See January 13th entry.)

Giuseppe Garibaldi was born, 1807.

Henry D. Thoreau went to live near Walden Pond, 1845. (See July 12th entry.)

Lewis Carroll first told Alice Liddell the story of Alice in Wonderland, 1862.

Israeli commandos raided Entebbe airport in Uganda and rescued 103 hostages on a hijacked airliner, 1976. (See June 28th entry.)

INTRODUCTIONS

Of all the days of the year, none has more glorious starting points for an American speaker than today—Independence Day. Maybe that is why some speeches are described as "a real Fourth-of-July piece of oratory." It refers to the usual flag waving, chest pounding, heart beating invocation of our glorious heritage. Well, one glory of our heritage is that we don't always have to be a captive audience. After all, Independence Day is a celebration: a day to enjoy the unalienable right to the pursuit of happiness. So I will not waste your time telling you what you already know about our founding fathers or the blessings of our noble land. I will simply ask you to consider those blessings and try to put them to good use. Back in 1776, the men who signed the Declaration of Independence on this date said, and meant it literally, that "we mutually pledge to each other our lives, our fortunes, and our sacred honor." Think how much less is asked of us today.

Is history a matter of chance or is there some great director guiding its course? When we consider this day, we find some interesting facts. Two of the men who signed the Declaration of Independence died years later on exactly the same day in 1826. President Thomas Jefferson and President John Adams—whose lives were so closely intertwined in both destiny and friendship—died fifty years to the day after they signed the Declaration of Independence. And five years later, President James Monroe—author of the Monroe Doctrine—passed away in 1831. But in 1872, future President Calvin Coolidge was born in Plymouth, Vermont. Isn't it interesting that so much Presidential history is associated with this day? Is there some special meaning that remains unknown? Even if there were not, it is a very special day based on these facts alone. This should be a day of inspiration and renewal for all of us; a day that reminds us that a nation is as great as its people.

The father of Italian independence and unity was born on this date. In 1807, Giuseppe Garibaldi was born in Nice, France. He tried, in vain, to incorporate his birthplace into Italy rather than France. But even for Garibaldi the Fourth of July commemorated another event. When his fortunes were at a low ebb and his patriotic efforts got him into trouble, Garibaldi found refuge in America. This story serves to remind us that independence is not strictly American. Many people have fought for and won their freedom. The spirit of the Fourth of July, then, belongs to the world.

The story of Alice's adventures underground was first told on this date. In 1862, Lewis Carroll and an Oxford University schoolmate, Robinson Duckworth, took Lorina, Alice, and Edith Liddell on a boating trip to the town of Godstaw. Carroll entertained the group by relating his story while they lunched on the riverbank. In the six months that followed, Carroll wrote down his tales; and—at Alice's request—entitled his work *Alice's Adventures Underground*. Inspiration comes from many sources and blooms in many forms. It is up to each of us to derive what we can from those moments and share our creations with the world.

JULY 5

P. T. Barnum was born, 1810.

Venezuela gained its independence, 1811.

William Booth founded the Salvation Army in London, 1865.

INTRODUCTIONS

Today is Phineas T. Barnum's birthday. Born in 1810 in Bethel, Connecticut, Barnum is still regarded as America's greatest showman. He very adroitly followed his own maxim: "There's a sucker born every minute." But despite this flippancy, Barnum greatly contributed to America's vitality, excitement, education, and even its sophistication. He created a circus that became known as "the greatest show on earth"; he brought soprano Jenny Lind to America; and he tried to palm off Jumbo the African elephant as the world's last surviving mastodon. He brought his customers flocking. But when he wanted to get rid of them, he pointed them to a door marked "Egress." Only after they had gone through it did they realize that egress meant exit. Barnum didn't take life seriously, and as a result, he succeeded in persuading others to enjoy it a little more. I suspect that wherever P.T. Barnum is today, he is looking down on us; waiting for me to finish talking; and then hoping we will all egress.

On this day in 1811, Venezuela became the first South American nation to declare its independence from Spanish rule. Native son Simon Bolivar led the fight for his country's freedom, and the virus of freedom spread to the rest of the continent. So today, I ask you to remember that we have no monopoly on the tradition of independence and freedom. Everyone in the world deserves it.

We are gathered here today on the anniversary of a meeting that changed the lives of many good Christian men and women. In 1865, a Methodist minister named William Booth held the first meeting of the Christian Revival Association in London's East End. His mission was to establish "stations" where the poor and homeless could be fed and housed. This somewhat militarist movement—of one fervent evangelist—is better known as the Salvation Army. And that's the name Booth chose for his troops in 1878. Throughout 80 nations, Booth's soldiers still volunteer their services and sign the Articles of War against degradation, depravity, and despondency. Today I promise not to drum my beliefs into your head, but I cannot guarantee I won't blow my own horn for a good cause.

JULY 6

John Paul Jones was born, 1747.

The first all-star baseball game was played, 1933.

Louis Pasteur successfully used his antirabies vaccine, 1885. (See December 27th entry.)

T.E. Lawrence and a small group of Arab revolutionaries captured the Turkish garrison at Aqaba, 1917.

INTRODUCTIONS

If the average American were asked to name our greatest naval heroes, John Paul Jones would be high on the list. Because today is Jones' birthday, I'd like to begin my remarks with the brief saga of our first great naval hero. To begin with, John Paul was not named Jones. In 1747, he was born simply as John Paul, in Kirkcudbrightshire, Scotland. As commander of his own British ship he had been charged with flogging a seaman to death and murdering a mutineer. With the law hot on his tail, he fled to Virginia; and changed his last name to Jones. During the American Revolution, he took a commission in the infant American Navy. He became the only American to bring the Revolution to England, raiding towns and harbors along the coast. The high point of his career was the epic battle between his ship, *Bonhomme Richard,* and the British warship *Serapis.* In the heat of this confrontation, Jones allegedly declared: "I have not yet begun to fight!" When the Revolution was over, Jones became a forgotten man. After the war comes diplomacy—which was not one of Jones' virtues. So he lived out his life in Paris, waiting for another American commission. He died in 1792 at the age of 45. His new commission arrived one month after his funeral. In 1905, his remains were discovered and brought to the final honor of a resting place at the U.S. Naval Academy at Annapolis. That is the not always heroic saga of John Paul Jones. Sometimes our heroes have feet of clay—and sometimes we fail to give them their due. Perhaps that is because we all live in the present. Memories of former glory don't pay today's bills; or solve today's problems. Yesterday's heroism may have made things easier today, but our eyes are always on tomorrow.

Americans pride themselves on being team players. Baseball, basketball, football, and hockey are all team sports. Therefore, when the first major league baseball all-star game was played on this day at Chicago's Wrigley Field, it was regarded as a sort of circus attraction. The concept of all-star games bloomed after this event took place in 1933. A number of sports now hold annual all-star events. I'd like to think that it's not only because of the big names, but because Americans want the best. A contest between all-star teams often replicates the classic confrontation between champions. As a people, we always aspire to be the best. It's an idea worth pursuing with you here today—an all-star hope for tomorrow.

On this day in 1885, Louis Pasteur successfully used his antirabies vaccine to treat a young boy who had been bitten by a rabid dog. I want to remind all of you about this event because some of you might foam at the mouth over my remarks here today. But at least I can assure the rest of you—as well as myself—that there is a cure.

Mind can win over matter despite the odds. An event that occurred in 1917 illustrates my point. Turkey was allied with Germany, fighting against the British during the First World War. At the same time, Saudi Arabia and Palestine were fighting for their freedom from Turkish rule. Both British troops and Arab rebels needed supplies, but no one could pass the watchful eye of the two huge long-range guns that monitored the route. The heavily armed garrison at Aqaba overlooked the shipping channel from Cairo to Palestine. With a relative handful of Arab horsemen, a British officer named T.E. Lawrence captured the garrison on this date. Better known as Lawrence of Arabia, it was he who deduced that the Turkish army never anticipated a desert attack. So he took advantage of the garrison's unarmed side. Thorough analysis of a problem can lead to surprising solutions, and it's in that spirit I would like to consider here today a solution to our present situation. If we analyze our position carefully, we can beat the odds.

J ULY 7

Sir Thomas More was executed, 1535.

Commodore John D. Sloat proclaimed California for U.S., 1846.

John D. Rockefeller (1839) and Nelson Rockefeller (1908) were born.

INTRODUCTIONS

Everybody has his or her own personal definition of utopia. The original concept of a utopia—that is to say, the word "utopia" itself—was created by Thomas More. For most of his life, it seemed that More had not only coined the word but found his own ideal world. More's novel, Utopia, centered around a mythical island named—you guessed it—Utopia. His mythical paradise was a metaphor for England. Utopia was filled with creature comforts but lacked individual freedom. The book was received as a satire on government and humanity, not as an idealistic vision at all. Real life seemed a lot kinder to More. He was knighted. He became King Henry VIII's favorite; the royal chancellor's favorite; and the people's favorite. But his troubles began and ended when Henry VIII named himself the supreme head of the Church of England. More felt the king could not rule both church and state. On this day in 1535, More was beheaded. Standing fast on matters of conscience does not a Utopia make; but it does ultimately make this world a better one. With the example of Sir Thomas More, let us then examine some matters of our own conscience.

On this day in 1846, U.S. Naval Commodore John D. Sloat landed at Monterey and claimed California for the United States. The Mexican War was on, and there was a good bit of fighting before the annexation took hold. But when gold was discovered at Sutter's Mill less than two years later, California was an American territory and the boom was on. Today is a good time to remember that California didn't just happen to join the union—America took it. As we contemplate our place in the world, we should not regard ourselves as plaster saints. We have not always practiced what we preached. In fact, I want to raise a question to you here. Should we practice what we preach, or preach what we practice?

Both John D. Rockefeller, Sr. and his grandson and Nelson A. Rockefeller were born on this day. The founder of the Standard Oil Company, John D. Rockefeller was born in 1839. As a young man, this ambitious entrepreneur switched from dealing grains, meats and commodities to selling a new product—crude oil. His business rapidly grew as the machine age became more dependent on fossil fuel, and eventually it became the first great U.S. business trust. It wasn't long before that monopoly came under fire with the passing of the Sherman Anti-Trust Act in 1890. But around that same time, Rockefeller turned his remarkable drive toward more charitable causes including the establishment of the University of Chicago and the Rockefeller Foundation. By contrast, his grandson—Nelson Rockefeller—rose to greatness in the political arena. As director of a Standard Oil affiliate in Venezuela, Nelson became fluent in Spanish. That asset landed him an appointment at the State Department during the Second World War. From there, he became leader of the Republican Party's moderate wing; New York's governor for four terms; a presidential candidate; and U.S. Vice President under Gerald Ford. Like his father and grandfather, Nelson was also a patron of education and the arts, founding New York's Museum of Primitive Art and serving as a trustee for the Museum of Modern Art. Sometimes the best source of inspiration for younger generations is found right at home. It's up to each and every one of us to provide our children and grandchildren with supportive standards to live by that they can see for themselves in our own daily actions. As in the case of the Rockefellers, actions spoke louder than words.

JULY 8

The Liberty Bell cracked, 1835.

The Declaration of Independence was first read to the public, 1776.

The Wall Street Journal was first published, 1885.

William Jennings Bryan gave his "cross of gold" speech, 1896.

INTRODUCTIONS

On this day in 1835, the Liberty Bell cracked while it chimed in honor of Chief Justice John Marshall who had recently died. This day is now observed as Liberty Bell Day. The Liberty Bell stands silent in Philadelphia. It rings only in our memories and our hearts. Maybe that's where it should really ring, even if it had no cracks at all. Do we really believe in what the Liberty Bell stands for—not merely for ourselves but for others as well?

We sometimes forget how different our times are from those in the past. Today brings a reminder. In 1776, the Declaration of Independence was signed, but it took four more days before it was publicly read. Today marks the anniversary of that first public reading in Philadelphia. It took two days to prepare copies for shipment to all the colonies. It took another month until all the copies were signed. Today, a document of equal importance is faxed or e-mailed, and broadcast within minutes. We may move faster and more expeditiously today. But the Declaration of Independence's authors not only put their necks on the line—they kept on doing so. They didn't change their minds; call a press conference to complain about being misquoted; or send a massive e-mail retraction. We should remember that fact. I certainly will today. I will say what I came here to say. And like those who read the Declaration of Independence to the people of Philadelphia, I will thank all of you for your attention.

Today marks the anniversary of a speech made at the 1896 Democratic National Convention. At this assembly, Nebraska delegate William Jennings Bryan said: "You shall not press down upon the brow of labor this crown of thorns; you shall not crucify mankind upon a cross of gold." His oratory electrified the convention. A few days later this 36-year-old Demosthenes was nominated as the Democratic presidential candidate. I want you to know that I do not expect any similar reaction to my remarks here.

I have a bit of interesting financial news. Or rather, news about financial news. Today, in 1885, was the day that the first *Wall Street Journal* was published. Even the daily that generations of financial wizards have relied upon to forecast the future couldn't have predicted the state of the world today. But as it has already established an Internet edition, it is once again showing us the direction the world is heading. But what of this world of technology? Should we invest ourselves? That's what I'd like to talk about.

JULY 9

Elias Howe was born, 1819.

Millard Fillmore became President, 1850. (See March 31st entry.)

INTRODUCTIONS

Today is Elias Howe's birthday. Just in case that makes you feel like asking "how now," let me tell you about Mr. Howe. You may not recognize his name. He was the man who invented the sewing machine. Born on this day in 1819 in Spencer, Massachusetts, Howe wasn't a comedian, but he has certainly kept us in stitches. On his birthday, I am moved to observe that we could use his talents once again right now, since so many things seem to be coming apart at the seams.

Some U.S. Presidents have been more famous than others. One past President is so little remembered that a presumably tongue-in-cheek society was organized to remind the nation that he ever existed. I am referring, of course, to Millard Fillmore—our thirteenth President. He acceded to office when President Zachary Taylor died on this day in 1850. Millard Fillmore decided that the Union must be preserved, so he supported the Fugitive Slave Act just to keep the nation together. After that, his own party refused to renominate him. In 1852, he sent Commodore Matthew C. Perry to Japan in order to negotiate a trade agreement. In 1856, he tried to get back into the White House as the Know-Nothing party's candidate. He lost that election and went back home to Buffalo, New York. I don't know why fame eluded Millard Fillmore, but I feel that on this anniversary we should celebrate those Americans who contributed to their nation, however unsung their efforts may be.

JULY 10

John Calvin was born, 1509.

INTRODUCTIONS

On this day in 1509, an influential religious leader was born in Noyon, France. John Calvin's religious ideals, which became known as Calvinism, influenced the development of Puritanism, the Protestant work ethic, and the concept of congregationalism—with a small "c." John Calvin believed in austerity, and America's founding fathers lived according to that Puritan ideal. We may not exemplify all of Calvin's concepts in the same way our forefathers did. But when the chips are down, our Protestant work ethic remains a bedrock of our American strength.

J U L Y 1 1

Robert the Bruce was born, 1274.

John Quincy Adams was born, 1767.

Alexander Hamilton challenged Aaron Burr to a duel, 1804. (See January 11th entry.)

Sir Wilfrid Laurier became the first French Canadian Prime Minister of Canada and opened up the Canadian Prairies to immigration, 1896.

E.B. White was born, 1899.

The Skylab space station fell to earth, 1979.

INTRODUCTIONS

John Quincy Adams— whose birthday is today—was not your usual U.S. President. Born in 1767, in Braintree, Massachusetts, Adams was the only President who was the son of another President. After he left the White House, he served in the House of Representatives until his death. The Adams family has played a remarkable role in American history; and John Quincy Adams was one of its prime protagonists. On his birthday, we are reminded that public service very often runs in the family; if we want our children to carry this legacy, we must first furnish them with excellent examples.

As you may or may not recall, Scotland's king—Robert the Bruce— was about to give up the fight for independence from British rule when he saw a spider spinning its web. At first, the spider failed. But it continued to spin and spin and spin until it finally finished its web. Robert realized that if a little spider could prevail, then he could do the same. He continued to fight and ultimately won. That's the story of Robert the Bruce, who was born on this day in 1274, in Turnberry, Scotland. When we get discouraged and need to be inspired, we don't have to sit down and watch a spider. We can remember the story of Robert the Bruce.

When journalist and author E.B. White was born on this day in 1899, the world was entering a drastic transitional phase that challenged every fiber of what society felt was right or wrong. Adventure, war, and automation rapidly became part of White's world. After the First World War, he went to Alaska as a reporter for *The Seattle Times,* and while still in his twenties, he became a writer for *The New Yorker* and

Harper's magazines. Famous for his indignant commentaries, this naturalist who preferred Thoreau's view of life and the environment reveled in scrutinizing a peculiar species called modern human. White deplored mechanization, automation, and modernization, voicing a weariness that many people at the time experienced. As one of his characters once commented: "No wonder I'm sitting here in this dreary joint at the end of this woebegone afternoon, lying about my bizarre thoughts to a doctor who looks, come to think of it, rather tired." I hope none of you share that sentiment right now.

Picture wagon trains streaming across endless prairies past seas of plains buffalo; sodbusters literally raising houses from the soil; and filling fertile land with waving grain. America? Yes, but this happened in Canada as well. Today is the day, in 1896, that Sir Wilfrid Laurier became the first French Canadian Prime Minister of Canada. During his term in office the Canadian Prairies were opened up to immigration. To quote Horace Greeley, "Va ^ l'ouest jeune homme, va ^ l'ouest!" Settlers arrived from Scotland, the Ukraine, France, and Great Britain, braving the bitter-cold winters and torrid tundra summers of the Canadian wilderness in the hope of establishing a new life. That pioneering spirit is the theme of my remarks today: the pursuit of a better quality of life for all of us.

Chicken Little was right. It was on this day, in 1979, that the abandoned Skylab space station burned up in the atmosphere and showered debris over the Indian Ocean and Australia. Well, I'm not here today to tell you that the sky is falling...again. In fact, I've got much better news.

J ULY 12

Julius Caesar was born, 102 BC (See March 15th entry.)

Henry D. Thoreau was born, 1817. (See July 4th entry.)

U.S. Congressional Medal of Honor was established, 1862.

Oscar Hammerstein was born, 1895. (See June 28th entry.)

INTRODUCTIONS

On this date in 1862, the Congressional Medal of Honor was authorized. It still remains America's highest recognition of valor in the cause of freedom. Today I wish to salute those Americans who found within themselves an extra measure of devotion that made them national heroes. And I should like to take this occasion also to take note of the many Americans whose heroism is a daily occurrence. Their efforts enable our nation to prosper and grow. We do not give ourselves enough credit for this kind of contribution. So today I urge us to look at some of the energy that has been expended for the sake of maintaining American peace and prosperity—and in defending those concepts.

Julius Caesar built the Roman empire. Born on this day in 102 BC, Caesar was the first monarch of this vast ancient empire. But in the end, he fell prey to the same lust for power that had led him to the top. He died at the hands of assassins—one of whom was his closest friend. But Julius Caesar's story reminds us that those who use government for their own ends—those who disregard the will of the people—often underestimate the resilience and the resistance of those people.

Henry David Thoreau was an escapist. The philosopher from Concord, Massachusetts, was born on this date in 1817. Thoreau did not want to be governed; and he did not want to be part of government. Thoreau wanted to live a natural existence without human intervention. In 1845, he chose the Fourth of July as the day when he moved into a rustic hut on Walden Pond. His deed reaped some of America's most influential literature. If we can find the peace and inspiration together which Thoreau found in solitude we will be doing pretty well. And we can start by remembering that both then and now, this nation needs to allow individuals to march to a different drummer.

J ULY 13

The Northwest Ordinance was enacted by Congress, 1787.

Horace Greeley wrote: "Go west young man, go west ...," 1865.

The second New York blackout paralyzed the city, 1977. (See November 9th entry.)

INTRODUCTIONS

In 1787, the United States was still an infant nation governed by a loose code known as the Articles of Confederation. But on this date a law was enacted that became the basis of our geographical and national growth—the Northwest Ordinance. The law outlined how the territory north of the Ohio River should be governed; and how those lands would evolve into states. It established territorial self-government as a step toward statehood. And it required all U.S. territories to grant their citizens the right to freedom of worship, trial by jury, and opportunities to receive public education. All in all, it wasn't a bad day's work. If we can contribute however slightly to what the Northwest Ordinance's authors started, we can consider ourselves fortunate.

It is sometimes both comforting and shocking to recall what some wise men have said in the past. On this day, in 1865, Horace Greeley delivered a few comments I think you might be interested in hearing. He wrote in *The New York Tribune* that "Washington is not a place to live in. The rents are high, the food is bad, the dust is disgusting and the morals are deplorable. Go West, young man, go West, and grow up with the country." Have times really changed that drastically?

J U L Y 1 4

French Revolutionaries stormed the Bastille, 1789. (Bastille Day)

Nicola Sacco and Bartolomeo Vanzetti were convicted of manslaughter, 1921. (See May 5th entry.)

Woody Guthrie was born, 1912.

Gerald R. Ford was born, 1913.

INTRODUCTIONS

Today is Bastille Day which commemorates the storming of the Bastille prison in Paris during the French Revolution. In 1789, the incident at the Bastille was seen as a great victory for the rights of the common man. But it also marked the beginning of the infamous Reign of Terror. There have been times when independence has brought out the darker side of human nature. And on Bastille Day, I rise to say that freedom is a right that cannot be used for personal gain.

Sometimes, a person's place in history is secured by accident—not only by design. Today is Gerald R. Ford's birthday. He became President of the United States during a time of crisis precipitated by an absolutely unprecedented series of events. But his demeanor in office helped to ensure further peaceful chapters. Born on this day in 1913 in Omaha, Nebraska, Gerald Ford was not elected President; he wasn't even elected Vice President. He was the Republican minority leader in the House of Representatives when Vice President Spiro Agnew pleaded no contest to charges of falsifying tax returns, was fined, and resigned his office. Two days later, on December 6, 1973, President Richard M. Nixon nominated Ford to succeed Agnew, and Ford took the office. Less than a year later, Nixon himself resigned because of the Watergate impeachment hearings and Ford acceded to the presidency. It was quite a shock for the nation—and for Gerald Ford as well. But he put the country back on an even keel. And so today we can all take heart from remembering the way one American unexpectedly moved into the White House and the way the nation unexpectedly kept its cool. With those surprises far behind us, we should be well prepared for any more surprises ahead.

Woody Guthrie was a staunch advocate of the common man, composing songs about the hardships and achievements of both farmers and factory workers during the Great Depression. This travelling American minstrel—who was born on this day in 1912—also wrote some inspiring lyrics about the grandeur of this great nation which also serve as the theme of my remarks here today: "This land is your land / This land is my land / From California / To the New York Island / From the redwood forest / To the Gulf Stream waters / This land was made for you and me."

J ULY 15

The feast of St. Swithin's.

Rembrandt Harmens van Rijn was born, 1606.

The provinces of Manitoba and the Northwest Territories entered into the confederation of Canada, 1870. (See July 1st entry.)

INTRODUCTIONS

Today is St. Swithin's Day. Legend has it that if it rains today it will continue to rain for 40 days. If, on the other hand, it remains fair today, it won't rain for 40 days. No rain for 40 days in England is a veritable impossibility. And for St. Swithin—who was the Bishop of Winchester, England—the idea of no rain for 40 days was obviously the expectation of a miracle. For us here today I see another significance in this day. What this legend says to me is that we cannot expect the world to change overnight. What exists today may—and in all likelihood will—be the same next week and the week thereafter. Changes can sometimes be so subtle as to go unnoticed for a long time. We live in a world quite different from what it was ten years ago; but most of the changes happened one small step after another. As a matter of fact, if we look at some of those steps, we can perhaps do our weather forecast not for the next 40 days, but for the next decade.

Rembrandt Harmens van Rijn was born in Leyden, Holland, on this date in 1606. He came from a well-to-do family, and in his time he was a highly acclaimed painter. But he outlived his time. He went bankrupt. He kept on painting, producing some of his greatest work. But the public had passed him by. When he died, his greatness seemed to be behind him. Of course it didn't work out that way at all. In the intervening centuries, his greatness grew and flourished. And so today I suggest that we remember that our own judgment of our own times may not be history's final verdict. Let us try to step back a bit and look at our own world from history's broader perspective. That is what I propose to try to do here now.

J ULY 16

The first atom bomb test took place in New Mexico, 1945. (See April 22nd entry.)

Apollo 11 space mission was launched, 1969. (See July 20th entry.)

The Nixon tapings were revealed, 1973. (See January 4th entry.)

The Chicago Black Sox Trial began, 1921.

INTRODUCTIONS

Two scientific miracles that changed the world occurred on this day. They both were prompted by war, but eventually were used in the name of peace. The first atom bomb was tested at Los Alamos, New Mexico, on this date in 1945. Less than a month later, this device proved to be man's deadliest weapon. And as one of its inventors—Richard Oppenheimer—later mused upon his discovery: "I have become death, killer of millions." We now harness this power to energize the world. Also on this date, in 1969, Neil Armstrong, Edwin Aldrin, Jr. and Michael Collins, blasted off from Cape Kennedy, Florida in the Apollo 11 space capsule. Their destination was the moon. The rockets used to bomb Europe in the Second World War were transformed into the engines that help us reach for the stars. Science itself is neither good nor bad; it is a tool that builds both swords and plowshares. Our goal as a society today is not to discourage science itself, but to decide how we should apply it.

It was on this day in 1973, that the existence of tape-recorded versions of President Nixon's White House conversations was disclosed. Nixon's refusal to surrender those tapes led to his resignation a year later. Our lives are affected by a series of interlinking events. We must always consider our actions not simply in terms of isolated decisions, but rather in the context of their consequences. Our motto should always be "Where do we go from here?"

It's an appropriate day to wear black socks. On this day in 1921, the Chicago Black Sox Trial began. Eight White Sox baseball players were accused of throwing the 1919 World Series. It was considered a dark day for baseball, but I disagree. Had the crime gone unnoticed and unpunished, it would certainly have been a victory for the forces of ethical decay. But honesty didn't win the series that day. In fact, that game is still on. Today, I ask you to set an example that future generations will know that the only way to win the ballgame is by knocking one out of the park.

J ULY 17

Disneyland opened in Anaheim, California, 1955.

Douglas Corrigan flew in the wrong direction, 1938.

Arco, India became the first city to have atomic-powered electrical service, 1955. (See July 16th entry.)

The Soyuz 19 linked with Apollo 18 in space, 1975. (See March 18th entry.)

INTRODUCTIONS

It's Disneyland's birthday. The world-famous amusement park opened in Anaheim, California, on this date in 1955. What a glorious opportunity to comment on how life seems to imitate Disneyland! I certainly won't let this opportunity pass me by. Disneyland is a seemingly simple world, filled with mechanical marvels, safe adventures, and nostalgic surreality. It is what all of us, I suspect, secretly wish the real world would be. And one reason Disneyland is that way is that they work very hard to keep it that way. That's a lesson we can all learn.

Douglas Corrigan was just another American airplane pilot until he took off from New York on this day in 1938. He was supposed to fly to California, but the next day he landed in Dublin, Ireland, instead. From that point, Douglas Corrigan was nicknamed "Wrong Way" Corrigan. The world strongly suspected that "Wrong Way" Corrigan knew where he was going all along even though he swore he didn't. It's rare to find people who are willing to reverse themselves and to be called "Wrong Way" Corrigans. As Ralph Waldo Emerson said, a foolish consistency is the hobgoblin of little minds. "Wrong Way" Corrigan wasn't bothered. And the world in its time has been advanced by others who did not hesitate to take a sharp turn in a different direction.

On this day in history, progress took a peaceful turn exactly ten years and one day after we feared the worst. In 1955, the world witnessed the establishment of the first atomic-powered electrical service in Arco, India. It had taken the world a decade to realize that the first atomic bomb explosion at Los Alamos, New Mexico, was not the sole use for atomic energy. This event proved that the awesome power of a volatile scientific discovery could be harnessed for peaceful, productive purposes. Scientists are often accused of opening Pandora's box. But the truth is that it isn't wrong to make new discoveries, but we do need to seriously consider how they are applied.

There was a thaw in the Cold War in 1975. On this day, the Soviet Soyuz 19 space craft linked with the U.S. Apollo 18 space craft. The first cosmonaut to walk in space, Alexei Leonov, and his crew member Valery Kubasov not only met astronauts Thomas P. Stafford, Donald K. Slayton, and Vance D. Brand, they worked together over the next 44 hours to conduct scientific and technical experiments that were of mutual benefit. Meetings such as this don't happen often enough. Everyone has a lot to learn from each other if we can only put aside our differences and get down to some real work, and that's precisely what I propose to do.

J ULY 18

Rome burned and Nero fiddled, 64 AD

Nelson Mandela was born, 1918. (See May 10th entry.)

John Glenn was born, 1921. (See February 20th entry.)

President Franklin D. Roosevelt was nominated for a third term, 1940.

INTRODUCTIONS

There were two times in American history when we came closer to having a king than most of us suspect. The first time was when some people proposed George Washington should be crowned the king of the United States. Washington himself disapproved. The second time occurred on this day in 1940, when President Franklin Delano Roosevelt decided to defy the old two-term tradition and accepted the nomination for a third term of office. Roosevelt was re-elected, and was later elected to a fourth term. Soon after his death, an amendment to the U.S. Constitution limited the Presidential incumbency to two elected terms. There is, of course, a provision for a little elasticity when a President dies in office. Generally, the Vice President is entitled to two elected terms in addition to his period of accession. But the installation of a permanently indispensable man or woman as Chief Executive is specifically unconstitutional. Thus we are destined to continue our search for new candidates. That means that higher aspirations are firmly built into the American dream. Where do we go from here?

We are all familiar with the story of Nero's fiddling while Rome burned, and today marks that anniversary. It started on this day in 64 AD, and when it was over, there were those who blamed the fire on Nero himself. But the emperor picked a likely group of scapegoats—the Christians. It was the perfect excuse for persecuting them. Even now, when it seems that some corner of the world is always in flames, too many of us keep imitating Nero. First we fiddle, then we look for scapegoats. Let us consider some of our current fires as cases in point.

J ULY 19

The Sisters of Charity was founded, 1813. (See August 28th entry.)

The first women's rights convention convened, 1848.

Lizzie Borden was born, 1860. (See June 20th entry.)

V for victory theme was introduced by Winston Churchill, 1941.

INTRODUCTIONS

One of history's longest battles has been the fight for women's rights. Today marks a milestone in that struggle. On this day in 1848, the first women's rights convention was held in Seneca Falls, New York. At this assembly, Elizabeth Cady Stanton declared that "man cannot fulfill his destiny alone" and Amelia Bloomer wore her signature garments. Today, we can see how far that battle has come, and even though we still have a way to go, I believe we can feel hopeful and confident that in the end, equality will prevail.

Except for national anthems, we do not normally associate a specific musical piece with a specific state of mind. But about this day in 1941, Great Britain's Prime Minister Winston Churchill conceived the idea of using a musical Morse code theme to symbolize the letter V for victory. It was recognizable on the air and yet somewhat undetectable because it was a familiar succession of musical notes. It was, in fact, the first four notes of the theme of Beethoven's *Fifth Symphony*. Ever since, that theme has meant V for victory. During the Second World War, it signified hope to thousands of Europeans listening to their radios in Nazi-occupied nations. Today it reminds us that hope is an intangible concept that the arts can translate for the entire world.

J U L Y 2 0

The province of British Columbia entered into the confederation of Canada, 1871. (See July 1st entry.)

Sir Edmund Hillary was born, 1919. (See May 29th entry.)

Neil Armstrong walked on the moon, 1969. (See July 16th entry.)

INTRODUCTIONS

On this day in 1969, a human being first set foot on the moon and walked on its surface. That "one small step for man, one giant leap for mankind" was taken by Apollo 11 astronaut Neil Armstrong. A few moments later, his teammate Edwin "Buzz" Aldrin, Jr., took that same giant step. It was a heady experience not only for the men who did it, but for everyone back on earth. We have learned that few things are impossible in this world— except to understand and control our own destiny. But it is no longer fantasy to speak of reaching for the stars.

J U L Y 2 1

Paul Reuter was born, 1816.

The Confederate Army won the Battle of Bull Run near Manassas VA, 1861.

Ernest Hemingway was born, 1899.

Marshall McLuhan was born, 1911.

The first time a battleship was ever sunk by an airplane, 1921.

U.S. Veterans Administration was established, 1930.

INTRODUCTIONS

We are so accustomed to air-powered warfare that it is sometimes surprising to recall that an aviator had to sink a battleship during peacetime to get America's military leaders to pay attention. On this very day in 1921, aviation pioneer General Billy Mitchell flew off with a payload of makeshift aerial bombs and sank the former German battleship *Ostfriesland* off Hampton Roads, Virginia. That momentous display of air power didn't fully persuade his superiors. Consequently, when the Second World War broke out, there weren't enough aircraft carriers to maneuver what had become regarded as the greatest weapons of that war—fighter planes. We know now that no single weapon is supreme, but control of the skies remains a very decisive factor. Since that day, we have had far more dramatic weapons demonstrations. But the tradition of "Colonel Blimpism" is a difficult one to erase. Colonel Blimp, for those of you who haven't heard of him, was a fictional British officer who never achieved greatness because he commanded strictly by the book. Military matters have always been complicated by disputes between the visionaries and the picket fencers. We have that same dilemma with us today.

Author and adventurer Ernest Hemingway was born on this day in 1899, in Oak Park, Illinois. He lived in the disillusioned post-First World War world of the 1920s and 1930s, capturing those few precious moments in time and recording them for posterity. He became an anachronism thereafter. *A Farewell to Arms* and *For Whom the Bell Tolls* assured his place in literary history, but it was *The Old Man and the Sea,* the story of an elderly Cuban fisherman's struggle to catch a giant fish, that earned him a Pulitzer and then a Nobel Prize. Hemingway's life was as dramatic as the fiction he wrote. The illusion and disillusionment; the heroism and the frailty; the emotions he experienced and described seem as real and relevant today. Circumstances may change; but Hemingway reminds us that people do not. We might remember that when we try to improve our quality of life. Human nature is the only constant.

If you were asked what group has grown the most in our times, you probably would say it was the elderly. And maybe that's right. But suppose you were asked what single group that encompasses both young and old has grown? The answer would be veterans. On this date in 1930, the Veterans Administration was established to preside over the rights and welfare of our millions of First World War veterans. That was before the Second World War; before the Korean War; before the Vietnam War; before the Persian Gulf War. If the veterans were a large group in the 1930s, think about their numbers today. They may not be enrolled in the American Legion or the VFW as they were in the past, but they are still a sizable constituency indeed. On this anniversary, we should consider how we can create a future without military veterans. Not because we don't like military veterans, but because it takes a war or simply the threat of war to create them.

The Confederate Army won the Battle of Bull Run on this day in 1861. The bloody confrontation that occurred near Manassas, Virginia, spurred a flood of news reports that elicited a number of publicized comments. The world's richest man—Andrew Carnegie—uttered one of them. He was reported as saying: "War should become as obsolete as cannibalism." Its a humane declaration I would like to promote today.

As writer Marshall McLuhan—who was born on this day in 1911—once said: "The medium is the message." I'm sure that Paul Reuter, founder of Reuters News Service, agreed. Born on this same day in 1816, it was Reuter who realized that news should be delivered in a timely fashion. He tried everything, including homing pigeons to move latebreaking news items across Europe for publication in the growing number of newspapers. We come a long way from newspapers and teletype machines as the sources for news. Besides radio and television broadcasts, fax machines, the internet, and the WorldWide Web have opened new frontiers in communications. News transmission and delivery happens within nanoseconds these days, making the new lightning-fast, computerized media the real message of my remarks here today.

JULY 22

Pilgrims set out from Holland destined for the New World, 1620. (See November 19th and November 21st entries.)

Settlers arrived on Roanoke Island, Virginia, 1587.

Sir Alexander Mackenzie arrived at Canada's Pacific coast, 1793.

Rose Fitzgerald Kennedy was born, 1890.

Wiley Post completed the first around the world airplane flight in 7 days, 18 hours, and 45 minutes, 1933. (See June 23rd entry.)

John Dillinger was killed in Chicago, Illinois, 1934.

INTRODUCTIONS

In 1620, the exiled British Pilgrims started out from Holland for the New World on this day aboard the ship *Speedwell*. They landed at Plymouth, England, where they transferred to the *Mayflower*. The rest is history. One wonders what would have happened if they had followed their original plan and landed in Virginia. They never would have sighted Cape Cod and Plymouth Rock nor established the first British settlement on the northeast American coast. Interestingly, on this same day, in 1587, another group of British settlers landed on Roanoke Island, off Virginia. They expected to be welcomed by a group that preceded them. But there was no one left. And when a third group arrived some years later, the second company had also disappeared. The story of Roanoke's Lost Colony is still a mystery to this day. There is no mystery about the Plymouth Pilgrims except for what might have happened if they had sailed to Virginia. History is full of big "ifs." What happens if we do this, or if we do that? We have some pretty big "ifs" on our immediate horizon.

Today marks the anniversary of John Dillinger's death. In 1934, Public enemy number one was shot down by FBI agents as he left Chicago's Biograph movie theater. That event captured the public's imagination. The media's enthusiasm for the criminal "hall of fame" fanned the flames of sensationalism—making heroes out of villains. Public enemy number one had to work harder to maintain his dubious position. The dilemma in dealing with crime is that we have to talk about it to deal with it; and when we talk about it we invariably glamorize it. This isn't simply the media's fault. Violence and crime sell newspapers and television news shows. Instead of just asking what we can do about crime, we ought to ask what we can do about the public's insatiable interest in this subject.

A great American matriarch—Rose Fitzgerald Kennedy—was born on this day in 1890, in Boston, Massachusetts. Rose Fitzgerald Kennedy saw her son John rise to the Presidency and be assassinated. She lost another son, Robert, who was on the road to Presidential nomination when he was assassinated. She lost a son and daughter earlier, before these two tragedies. But through it all she carried on, providing inspiration and encouragement. Long after her death, Rose Fitzgerald Kennedy remains a symbol of courage, of dedication, and of determination for American women and men alike.

An epic journey ended on this day in 1793, when Sir Alexander Mackenzie stood for the first time on the Canadian Pacific coast. He had walked across the entire breadth of the uncharted North American continent, exploring the natural wonders of Quebec's rolling hills, Ontario's lakes and rivers, Manitoba and Saskatchewan's lush prairies, Alberta's majestic mountains, and British Columbia's ancient coastal rain forests. As he stood along the shore of the mighty Pacific Ocean, he realized his journey had come to a successful end. But ours is just beginning. I'd like to take you on a journey across some uncharted territory a little closer to home.

J ULY 23

Steve Brodie jumped off the Brooklyn Bridge and survived, 1886.

Ice cream cone was invented, 1904.

INTRODUCTIONS

On this day, in 1886, saloon keeper Steve Brodie jumped off the Brooklyn Bridge and lived to tell the tale. The fact that there is and was a Brooklyn Bridge; and a Steve Brodie who lived to tell the tale are all established facts. The only uncertainty is whether he ever jumped off the Brooklyn Bridge as he claimed. True or not, Brodie contributed an American colloquialism. A "brodie" is a blunder. To "make a Brodie" is to make a mistake. These contributions to our popular language may not have been what Brodie had in mind when he was fished out of the water below the bridge and claimed to have survived a jump. It just goes to show that history can be made by taking a dive—or claiming to have done so. Even as I stand here talking to you, the world is full of Steve Brodies. The truth of their claims we may never be able to find.

The ice cream cone is said to have been invented on this day in 1904, in St. Louis, Missouri. When you stop and think what the ice cream cone has done for the dairy business and retail trade, not to mention the dispositions of human beings, you've got to regard today's birthday as a blessed event that most assuredly deserves a place in history. Let's face it. It's very nice to have something around that is made to take a licking.

J ULY 24

Simon Bolivar was born, 1783.

Brigham Young and the first Mormons arrived at Salt Lake, Utah, 1847. (Utah Pioneer Day) (See January 6th and June 1st entries.)

Machu Picchu was discovered, 1911.

Kellogg-Briand Treaty declared in effect, 1929. (See January 15th entry.)

INTRODUCTIONS

Simon Bolivar has been called the George Washington of South America. The nations of Venezuela, Colombia, Ecuador, Panama, Peru and Bolivia officially named him "Libertador"—The Liberator—and Bolivia was named after him. Simon Bolivar, who was born on this date in 1783, in Caracas, Venezuela, led a continent to independence. You never can tell where, when, and how something that will change the course of history will begin; or who among us will accept the call to lead us to the other side.

Sometimes when you search hard for something; you don't always know you've reached your goal when you're there. That was the case when Hiram Bingham climbed to a Peruvian mountain top with a native guide and walked through a mysterious city in the clouds. On this day in 1911, Bingham discovered one of the last Incan cities—Machu Picchu. The young Yale history professor had been searching for this mythical place ever since he read about it in the accounts of the Spanish explorers who had failed to uncover its whereabouts. But Bingham didn't know he had succeeded in his quest as he surveyed the vine-covered stone walls and buildings. It wasn't until he had searched a few other places and returned to New York that he realized his search was over. The next year, Bingham returned to the city in the clouds and documented his findings for the National Geographic Society. Sometimes it is difficult to see the forest for the trees when you have your mind set on a particular goal. Expectations and preconceived notions can play tricks on you, clouding the reality around you. I'm happy to report to all of you, however, we have reached our goal without ever doubting we've arrived.

JULY 25

National Farm Safety Week.

Puerto Rico became a self-governing commonwealth of the United States, 1952. (Commonwealth Day in Puerto Rico)

Louise Brown was born, 1978.

Soviet cosmonaut Svetlana Savitskaya became the first woman to walk in space, 1984.

INTRODUCTIONS

This is the beginning of National Farm Safety Week. We think back so fondly to the bucolic, rustic charms of the country farm that we forget the risks. Farming is a physically and financially risky business. Even when farming ran on horse-and-donkey power, it was physically taxing and dangerous. Urban dwellers believe that cities are dangerous. But cities have no monopoly on risk. Perhaps it would be helpful to remember, at least during National Farm Safety Week, that where the grass is greener it is also apt to be slipperier as well.

On this day in 1952, the Commonwealth of Puerto Rico became a self-governing territory of the United States. The designation was just short of statehood status. At the time, this change was expected to solve the island's status problem. But we learned soon enough that the hope was premature. Commonwealth Day certainly deserves to be considered a noble attempt and a good start. And any day that celebrates a noble attempt and a good start has to be considered a pretty special one.

The world was awestruck when Louise Brown was born in England on this day. Obviously, many of you don't know who she is, so let me explain. In 1978, Louise

Brown became the world's first known test-tube baby. After a number of disappointing attempts, Louise's parents chose to try this new and radical form of conception. The experiment was an overwhelming success. The world's hope is in its children, and Louise's birth gave hope to many potentially great parents.

There are few things in this world that only men can do; and walking in space is not one of them. On this day in 1984, Soviet cosmonaut Svetlana Savitskaya became the first woman to walk in space. We have made great progress since the days when women were treated like fragile porcelain dolls and more like the equal partners we really are. Today, I'd like to open up a few other frontiers.

J ULY 2 6

George Bernard Shaw was born, 1856.

Carl Jung was born, 1875.

The Federal Bureau of Investigation was established, 1908.

U.S. Department of Defense was established, 1947.

Fidel Castro led a futile attack and was captured in Cuba, 1953.

INTRODUCTIONS

Today is the FBI's birthday. Established by Attorney General Charles J. Bonaparte on this date in 1908, the Federal Bureau of Investigation did not acquire its Napoleonic complex until some years later. Today's FBI is a far cry from what it used to be, and—for the most part—I think we can regard the current edition as the best. We can credit the FBI with assuming an important role in modernizing the science and methods of crime prevention, crime detection, and law enforcement. On the FBI's birthday, we can be secure in the knowledge that we have a lot better protection than we might have without it.

In 1947, this was the day that the U.S. Department of Defense was established under the Armed Forces Unification Act. It signaled the recognition that there had to be one combined overall military command. Let us hope that the totality of war will not be the ultimate confirmation of the wisdom of the Armed Forces Unification Act now or at any future time.

Fidel Castro has ruled Cuba for so long that today's anniversary seems like an echo from another planet. On this day, in 1953, the young revolutionary led a futile attack on a Cuban Army barracks at Santiago. He was captured and sent to prison. But this adventure gave his movement its name—the July 26th movement—and the next time he struck he succeeded. So today should be a good day to heed the warnings around us. Perhaps, if others had heeded the signs on this day, history might have been different.

Thanks to a man who was born on this day in Kesswil, Switzerland, the world realized that the human mind was influenced by far more than potty training and unrealized childhood fantasies. In 1875, the founder of analytic psychology, Carl Jung came into this world. His theories delved deeper into the human psyche than Freud's psychoanalytic methods. He proposed the concepts of extroverted and introverted individual personalities. He believed that man's institutions such as religion, literature, and oral tradition were provocative manifestations of a collective consciousness that was stimulated by social interaction. Jung helped us to realize that for every individual's action there is a potential for a similar, synchronous action taking place somewhere else in the world. With this thought in mind, let's see how many of us are thinking similarly about a topic I've been mulling over all morning.

When George Bernard Shaw was twenty years old, he decided to become writer, and moved from his birthplace—Dublin, Ireland—to the great city of London where his mother and sister already lived. Born on this day in 1856, Shaw did not have a promising start to his chosen career. In fact, he failed so miserably as a novelist he was starving and penniless. But just as he was ready to quit, he was offered a job writing book reviews for the *Pall Mall Gazette*. Then he got offers to write art criticism for *The World* and theater reviews for *The Saturday Review*. Twenty years after he had made his fateful decision to become a writer, his first play—*Arms and the Man*—premiered on the London stage. Shaw was an overnight success. During the next twenty years he created a body of memorable plays including *Major Barbara* and *Pygmalion* which was eventually remade into the musical *My Fair Lady*. Some individuals take longer than others to achieve their dreams. But no matter how much time it takes, all great achievers share two things in common: persistence and self-confidence. Those are two themes I would like to address today.

J ULY 27

The Atlantic telegraph cable between England and the U.S. was completed, 1866.

The Korean War armistice was signed in Panmunjom, Korea, 1953.

INTRODUCTIONS

The Atlantic telegraph cable between England and the United States was completed on this date in 1866. From that day forward, news crossed the ocean instantly. And that, in turn, speeded up the tempo of world events to a relatively rapid pace. Perhaps we were better off when news traveled slowly. That, however, is one piece of information we will never know. Meanwhile, we now operate knowing that what we say or do here will—if it makes news—be out in nanoseconds across the globe via the internet. With that in mind, I've chosen my words carefully.

On this day in 1953, an armistice agreement was signed at Panmunjom, on the border between North and South Korea. After more than two years of seemingly endless negotiations, this agreement allegedly ended the Korean War. This still chilly and tenuous truce reminds us that a tense peace has only one positive facet—it is better than a hot war. So, in our everyday affairs, we must not always hold out for the ideal if we can settle for a step forward. The hardest part often is trying to decide whether the settlement is really a step forward at all.

J ULY 28

The Fourteenth Amendment was ratified, 1868.

The First World War began when Austria-Hungary declared war on Serbia, 1914. (See June 28th entry.)

A U.S. Bomber crashed into Empire State Building, 1945.

Terry Fox was born, 1958.

INTRODUCTIONS

Today marks the anniversary of the Fourteenth Amendment to the U.S. Constitution. This is the amendment that guarantees due process of law to all citizens. Announced on this date in 1868, the Fourteenth Amendment was enacted after the Civil War to extend the federal guarantee of due process to govern state as well as federal matters. It was an extension of Constitutional supremacy; and a forerunner of the further protection of civil rights. It took another century to move from this amendment to the civil rights legislation of the 1960s, but it was an historic step well worth noting today.

On this day in 1945, the Second World War was coming toward its end. But at home, a U.S. bomber crashed into the Empire State Building in New York City. The building stood firm. The bomber was destroyed. It was Saturday, so only 13 people were killed on the ground. Designers had been improving airplanes and skyscrapers for years, but nobody ever imagined that one would crash into the other. And so today, one cannot help wondering what strange, unexpected events lie ahead that nobody—not one of us—has ever anticipated.

Terry Fox was born on this date in 1958. The story of this remarkable Canadian's life was all too short, but his courage serves as eternal inspiration for us all. When Terry was 19 years old, he started a marathon run at the Mile 0 marker of the Trans-

Canada Highway in Victoria, British Columbia. His goal was to run the full length of the highway to Prince Edward Island on the east coast to raise the nation's and the world's awareness of cancer. This would have been a monumental task for any runner. But Terry Fox wasn't just another marathon runner. Fox himself had fallen to the disease; and the disease eventually cut short his heroic Run Against Cancer and his life. His run was cut short in Thunder Bay, Ontario, when the cancer spread to his lungs. Faith, deep-set desire, and compassion for humankind seem like abstract words until you set them against the backdrop of this courageous story. And then you are reminded that one young man ran to save the world's life.

J U L Y   2 9

Sir Francis Drake and the British fleet routed the Spanish Armada, 1588.

Benito Mussolini was born, 1883.

Dag Hammarskjöld was born, 1905. (See April 7th entry.)

President Eisenhower signed the National Aeronautics and Space act, creating NASA, 1957.

INTRODUCTIONS

Although the story of David and Goliath encourages us to believe that a little guy can sometimes be more than a match for a big one, we don't usually apply that rule to military encounters. But every time a military machine gains too much confidence, it is a good idea to think of the Spanish Armada which was reputedly the mightiest war machine ever assembled. It turned out to be somewhat less than that. On this day in 1588, thanks to the indomitable spirit of Sir Francis Drake, the British fleet under his command, and inclement weather, the Spanish Armada was totally routed and Great Britain was saved. So, even if you are not planning a military engagement, you can take a leaf from this story. The Armada was over-publicized to the point where its reputation spurred the British on to an unprecedented effort. Please be assured that today I have not assembled an Armada of fancy phrases or superficial superlatives. Instead of sailing a mighty man-of-war—oratorically speaking—I propose to do no more here today than to paddle my canoe.

This is Benito Mussolini's birthday. This father of modern fascism and classic demagogue, was outdone at his own game by his neighbor, Adolf Hitler. Together, they tried to move the world back into the dark ages. Beware of politicians who tell you to beware of politicians; beware of political leaders who love uniforms; beware of those who stand on balconies above the crowd and talk for hours. If Mussolini's birthday means nothing else, it reminds me that only a dictator can get away with talking too long. In his lifetime, Mussolini also was famed for supposedly getting the trains to run on time. Posthumously, his memory will get this speaker, at least, to finish on time.

One of the world's most influential peacemakers was born on this day in Jonkoping. The second Secretary-General of the United Nations, Dag Hammarskjold was born, in 1883, to Sweden's Prime Minister Hjalmin Hammarskjold. While on a peace mission to meet President Moisi Tshombe of Katanga in the African Congo in 1961, Dag Hammarskjold died in a plane crash. But before his fateful death, he had presided over numerous international conflicts that were on the brink of igniting new world wars. The Suez Canal controversy; the Belgian Congo's fight for independence; the border crisis between Lebanon and Jordan; and the continuing conflicts between the Arab nations and the newly formed state of Israel all came within the diplomatic jurisdiction of this protagonist of international peace. His efforts won him a posthumously awarded Nobel Peace Prize and the respect of the entire world. Too often we honor our military leaders rather than our peacemakers. Today, I think we should make steps to change this policy.

A remarkable step upward was made on this day in 1957. President Dwight D. Eisenhower signed the National Aeronautics and Space Act which created the NASA program. Rather than setting our sights on new frontiers right here on earth, we began to look into the skies for new worlds to explore. We should all take a cue from this momentous occasion and redirect our goals to greater heights than we ever thought possible, then work doggedly toward them until we reach the stars.

JULY 30

First representative assembly convened in America, 1619.

Henry Ford was born, 1863. (See October 1st entry.)

Thorstein Veblen was born, 1857.

C. Northcote Parkinson was born, 1909.

The MGM lion roared, 1928.

The Strategic Arms Reduction Treaty was signed, 1991.

INTRODUCTIONS

We meet here today on the anniversary of the first legislative assembly held in America. The representatives met at Jamestown, Virginia, on this day, in 1619. It was a brief meeting, which in itself makes this legislative session even more unique. I shall, of course, take my inspiration from it today, and get right down to business.

On this day in 1863, Henry Ford was born near the town of Dearborn, Michigan. The man who did more than any other person to mass produce and popularize the automobile in America was famous for saying that you could have your car in any color you wanted—as long as it was black. Ford turned out millions of black Model Ts between 1908 and 1927. A lesser-known fact is that Henry Ford also had a passion for soybeans. Certain they were versatile enough to feed the world and all its appetites, he once served a sixteen-course banquet of dishes made with soybeans, and he always kept a few pitchers of soymilk on hand. When he found a good thing, he held on to it. I suggest that we look around at the good things we have today and devote a little bit more of our energy to holding onto them.

I want to say a few words today about Thorstein Veblen, the scholar who, in 1899, gave us the "theory of the leisure class." Veblen's theory—if I may oversimplify it—was simply that he was against consumerism. As he remarked, "Conspicuous consumption of valuable goods is a means of reputability to the gentleman of leisure." Today is Veblen's birthday. So in honor of this man who was born in Wisconsin in 1857, I will conspicuously consume a portion of your time for a few remarks here today about the consumer habits of the not-so-leisure class.

Sometimes I wonder where the world would be if C. Northcote Parkinson had not discovered "Parkinson's Law." I wonder about that particularly on Professor Parkinson's birthday, which happens to be today. Born in 1909 in Durham, England, Parkinson brought us up short in the 1950s with his basic law of human behavior which states that "work expands so as to fill the time available for its completion." Applied to the work of a public speaker, that means speakers will continue to spout for as long as you let them. Fearful of Parkinson's Law, I took pains to check how much time I had for today's remarks. I then took pains to plan a speech that was shorter than that. I figured that if talk—like work—expands to meet the time available, I have to be more profound in order to find enough words. And if I find enough words I may not find enough audience left and if—but enough! You see the sheer logic of Parkinson's Law. And so, let me be brief.

The MGM lion roared for the first time on this day in 1928. The famous film production company—MGM—had added sound to its roster of special effects. So as a way of launching the world's first "talkie" they let their lion introduce the feature attraction. I wish it were that easy for me to spice up my speech for today, but unfortunately the local zoo doesn't loan out its inmates. I'll have to roar about my good news without assistance.

The Cold War melted down on this day in 1991, when the Strategic Arms Reduction Treaty was signed by U.S. President George Bush and Soviet Premier Mikhail Gorbachev. The nuclear arms race didn't just come to a halt. Both nations agreed to disarm and disband projects like Star Wars, Minutemen missiles, and other doomsday mechanisms. It's a relief to know that within half a century, the world's most powerful nations went from nuclear frenzy to nuclear limitation—and that I don't have to worry about you pushing a panic button.

J ULY 31

Whitney M. Young, Jr. was born, 1921.
Apollo 15 astronauts drove a car on the moon, 1971.

INTRODUCTIONS

Today marks the anniversary of history's strangest automobile ride. In 1971, Apollo 15 astronauts David R. Scott and James B. Irwin began three days of exploration on the moon's surface driving a specially designed electric car. Millions of earthlings watched the trip on television via satellite transmission. In one respect, the moon's first car drivers were like a speaker in front of an audience. Nobody knows in advance exactly where they are going—and they can't wait to get there. Mindful of this, I shall immediately shift into high gear and get rolling.

Whitney M. Young, Jr. was born on this date in 1921, in Lincoln Ridge, Kentucky. This outstanding African-American leader is remembered for many events in his life, but his remarks in a 1970 speech which he made in New York City, serve as inspiration for my theme today. "We may have come over in different ships," said he, "but we're all in the same boat now."

A UGUST

INTRODUCTION

In some parts of this country, the days of August have a special name: the dog days of summer. Not to demean the canine species, this designation is an apt description of the doggedly hot temperatures most regions encounter during this sweltering month. And summer heat does seem to raise people's tempers. It's not uncommon to hear people barking about the heat and the humidity, nipping at comments as if they're meant to be insults. So rather than reciting some dog-eared verses to you, I'll dog the trail of my remarks and get down to my point.

A UGUST 1

The Republic of Switzerland was founded, 1291. (Swiss Independence Day)

The British Parliament moved to Oxford, 1625.

William Clark was born, 1770. (See May 14th entry.)

First U.S. Census was taken, 1790.

Herman Melville was born, 1819.

INTRODUCTIONS

Today is Swiss Independence Day. I mention it, not because there is anything novel about the concept of Swiss independence, but rather, because the reverse is true. This anniversary marks the founding of the Republic of Switzerland in 1291. That, in turn, makes this country the oldest such government still in existence. The Swiss are not a notoriously talkative people—which may be why they have been able to keep their government running so long. It may also be long lasting because there is no mountain too high for the Swiss to climb. I plan to keep all this in mind today and follow the Swiss example. Limit the talk, keep looking up and oh, yes—stay as neutral as possible.

The first U.S. census was taken on this day. In 1790, the government discovered there were four million Americans. We seem to have been counting something or other ever since. Mark Twain said there are three kinds of lies—lies, damned lies, and statistics. I will try, therefore, to state my case here today not with figures, not with statistics, but simply by reminding you of what you can see and hear for yourselves.

The British Parliament made an unprecedented move on this day in 1625. The members of this august governing body had been convening in London for hundreds of years. But on this day, they assembled sixty miles north—in the university city of Oxford. It wasn't a wartime security measure per se, but it was meant as a preventive action mounted against a lethal invasion. The black plague had been raging through London, killing thousands of people per week. Parliament moved in an attempt to save itself from decimation. No amount of military defense or political negotiation can stop our worst enemy—the spread of disease. So why don't we spend as much on medical research as we do on less important preventive measures?

American author Herman Melville was born on this day in 1819, in Caroll County, Maryland. He didn't create volumes of monumental work during his lifetime, but he did write a voluminous piece of literature entitled *Moby Dick*. The tale of

Captain Ahab and the great white whale epitomized man's unending battle with his own unnatural nature. But unlike its narrator Ishmael, I promise to relate my story without divining an epic fish tale.

Since today is William Clark's birthday, I will quickly tell you the story of the man who was born on this day in 1770. William Clark was appointed by President Thomas Jefferson to join Meriweather Lewis on an expedition to explore the recently acquired Louisiana Territory. Lewis and Clark's observations of this vast northwestern wilderness—its indigenous people, wildlife, and terrain—are well known. In return for his services, President Jefferson made Clark a brigadier general of the Louisiana Territory militia and awarded him a vast section of the new land. He also made Clark the territory's superintendent of Indian Affairs. Throughout the remainder of his career, Clark regularly appealed to the federal government for the just and humane treatment of Native Americans. Some heroes rest on their laurels while others take their position and apply it to the greater cause of human rights. There are other present-day heroes like William Clark who I would like to honor here today.

A UGUST 2

Andrew Hallidie operated his first cable car in San Francisco, 1873. (See February 23rd entry.)

The U.S. War Department purchased its first airplane, 1909.

Alexander Graham Bell died, 1922. (See January 25th, March 3rd, and March 7th entries.)

Albert Einstein wrote a letter to President Franklin D. Roosevelt, 1939. (See March 14th entry.)

Gulf of Tonkin incident took place, 1964.

INTRODUCTIONS

The future of the world sometimes changes without our even realizing it. That may well have happened on this day back in 1909, when the U.S. War Department bought the first airplane from Wilbur and Orville Wright. Did the airplane's military capabilities speed up aviation's development? Many people think so. On the other hand, the automobile developed pretty well without military intervention. But after this initial purchase, the relationship between the airplane and the military grew by leaps and bounds. One man's luxury can be another's necessity, and after all, necessity is the mother of further invention.

On this day in 1964, the North Vietnamese attacked a U.S. destroyer within the international waters of the Gulf of Tonkin. That's the way we were told it happened thereafter by President Lyndon B. Johnson and his aides. As a result, the U.S. Congress adopted the Gulf of Tonkin Resolution a few days later, which gave the President broad powers to use the armed forces without a declaration of war. This was followed by deeper U.S. involvement in Vietnam. Americans have been urged to remember the Alamo and remember the *Maine* and remember Pearl Harbor. It might be well for us, on this day at least, also to remember the Gulf of Tonkin. If we occasionally look back, we can look ahead with a much clearer view.

When the telephone's inventor, Alexander Graham Bell, died on this day in 1922, he did not receive a 21-gun salute nor a final trumpet call. But the United States phone system did shut down for two whole minutes. It might be the only time in history that telephones throughout this nation went silent in unison for more than two whole seconds. So before I begin my remarks, I would like to lobby for an annual commemorative system shut down in honor of Alexander Graham Bell's death. It would give all of us a much-needed break.

AUGUST 3

James II of Scotland was killed, 1460.

Christopher Columbus sailed from Spain, 1492.

Henry Hudson entered the inland sea that was later named Hudson's Bay, 1610. (See June 22nd entry.)

Whittaker Chambers accused Alger Hiss, 1948. (See January 21st entry.)

INTRODUCTIONS

On this day, in the year 1492, Christopher Columbus set out from the port of Palos, Spain, to look for a sea route across the Atlantic to India. What a glorious failure he had! And how many other discoveries—like that of the New World—were made by people who were really looking for something else. Coincidentally, Henry Hudson entered Hudson's Bay on this same day in 1610. Hudson and the crew of the *Discovery* were searching for the Northwest Passage from the Atlantic to the Pacific. Curiosity—once aroused—is a very driving force. And so I am here not simply to utter a few platitudes, but rather to raise a few questions and to give you some information which, I hope, will raise your curiosity.

On the anniversary of King James II of Scotland's death, I promise to pay due respect to the solemnity of the moment. In 1460, James II and his army were laying siege to the English garrison at Roxburgh Castle. The 29-year-old monarch's wife sent word that she was coming for a visit. Elated at his wife's arrival, he ordered his artillery men to prepare a special salute. As Queen Mary made her way to the encampment, the cannon salute began. But unfortunately, James was standing in front of one of his own cannons and was killed instantly. With any luck, dear audience, I will not be blasted off the stage by my salute to you.

A UGUST 4

John Peter Zenger was acquitted, 1735.

The Revenue Marine Service was founded, 1790. (Coast Guard Day)

England declared war on Germany; and the United States declared its neutrality, 1914.

INTRODUCTIONS

One of the great pleasures of American life is our right to criticize our government and its leaders. That right really began on this day, in 1735, when Governor William Crosby of New York acquitted John Peter Zenger—a printer and publisher of the *New York Weekly Journal*—of libel charges. Zenger's defense was that the statements he had printed in his newspaper about New York's royal governor were true. His acquittal was regarded as an evolutionary landmark in America's freedom of expression. The case set no legal precedents, but it did establish the tradition that public office is a valid subject for public criticism. Thanks to Zenger, we can go in for a zinger now and then. While I do not plan to sling any mud here today, it's nice to know that I'm not being censured.

Today is Coast Guard Day which celebrates the founding, in 1790, of the Revenue Marine Service. We now know this branch of the Department of Transportation as the U.S. Coast Guard. It isn't in the news very often. The Coast Guard just doesn't have time, considering the length of the coastlines it patrols. On its anniversary, it is nice to note that, as of this moment—and let us hope for the future as well—the coasts are clear.

After Austro-Hungary declared war on Serbia, Germany declared war on Russia and on France and then invaded Belgium. The First World War had begun. When England declared war on Germany on this day in 1914— because of its commitment to its allies and because of Germany's invasion of Belgium—the German Chancellor made a classic, self-righteous statement about its British cousin. German Chancellor Theobald von Bethmann-Hollweg said, "…just for a scrap of paper, Great Britain is going to make war on a kindred nation.…" In one respect, he was not far from wrong. King Edward of England had close German relatives. But England's loyalty to its neighbors ran deeper. And definitely deeper than that of the United States who declared neutrality. It is the glory of civilization—certainly not excluding Germany—that we do not take our so-called "scraps of paper" lightly. At least we should not.

AUGUST 5

Admiral David Farragut damned the torpedoes, 1864.

Cornerstone of Statue of Liberty laid, 1884. (See June 19th entry.)

The comic strip Little Orphan Annie first appeared, 1924. (See October 7th entry.)

American Bandstand was first televised, 1957.

INTRODUCTIONS

Most of our battle cries are either appeals to our memory or blunt questions—like "Remember the Alamo!" or "Do you want to live forever?" However, one battle cry that was first uttered on this day seems to summarize a pretty general American attitude. It was said by Admiral David Glasgow Farragut at the Battle of Mobile Bay during the Civil War in 1864. What he said was: "Damn the torpedoes, full speed ahead!" That is my speech plan for today.

It is often said that art reflects the times in which it was created and today's anniversaries are sparkling examples of this statement. In 1924, the comic strip Little Orphan Annie first appeared in daily newspapers. The optimistic little girl—with her dog Sandy—never let tragedy get the best of her. She uplifted readers who found themselves sunk in the depths of despair during the Great Depression era that soon followed. Also on this date, in 1957, American Bandstand premiered on the relatively new medium of television. Its host, Dick Clark, introduced generations of young audiences to a new musical form called rock 'n' roll. Every week, the hottest bands played the latest tunes while a live audience danced the newest steps. The program quickly galvanized a generation who felt increasingly detached from the rest of society. As we look toward tomorrow, none of us are orphaned by circumstances anymore. Moral support can be found in many places reaching out to us and bringing us together.

AUGUST 6

John Cabot returned from the New World, 1497.

Alfred Lord Tennyson was born, 1809.

Sir Alexander Fleming was born, 1881.

Warner Bros. Studios premiered the first talking pictures, 1926.

Andy Warhol was born, 1927.

The Enola Gay dropped the first atomic bomb on Hiroshima, Japan, 1945.

INTRODUCTIONS

Today was a very big day in 1926. The world discovered that the movies could talk. The Warner Brothers motion-picture company premiered two short films with live sound called Vitaphone films in New York City. Actors could finally be heard as well as seen. All of a sudden, silent screen actors had to worry about their voices—not just their looks—and they had to memorize their lines. They learned what it feels like to be a public speaker. Now if I could only learn what it feels like to be a movie star. …

Today marks the anniversary of the Hiroshima bombing. When the atom bomb was dropped by the crew of the Enola Gay on this Japanese city in 1945, it was more than the shattering premiere of a brand new weapon. The world did not stand still thereafter. In Hiroshima, we learned the real effects of atomic power on something we had not tested at Los Alamos, New Mexico—real people. We learned the horrifying effects of radiation not just days but years later. We learned that man had no control over the terrible might of the microscopic atom.

I wonder how many of you recognize the name of Sir Alexander Fleming—not because he happened to have been born on this day in 1881, in Lochfield, Scotland—but because he grew up to discover a lifesaver. Fleming isolated penicillin. In a world given to celebrating anniversaries and birthdays of military heroes, statesmen, and mechanical geniuses, I think that Alexander Fleming's birthday also deserves a kind word. Having given you that word, I now proceed to problems for which, alas, there is no miracle cure like penicillin.

"Men may come and men may go, But I go on forever." Do not be alarmed. That is not the keynote of my remarks here today. It is a quotation from Alfred Lord Tennyson. Today is his birthday. Great Britain's poet laureate was born in 1809 in Somersby, England, and it is Tennyson who inspired me as I came here to speak today when he wrote, "My strength is as the strength of ten, because my heart is pure." What I am about to tell you comes from the heart.

On this day, in 1497, the Genovese navigator John Cabot returned from his voyage aboard the *Matthew*. Licensed by Great Britain's Henry VII, Cabot had sailed to the New World and claimed Nova Scotia in the name of his mentor as he planted the Tudor flag on its shores. The entire voyage cost the king £10, plus an annuity of £20 to Cabot. Expeditions are far more expensive to finance now than in Cabot's days, but modern explorers still need outside support to continue the work of discovering the unknown.

Andy Warhol was born on this day in 1927. At one point this pop art master and experimental filmmaker declared that, in the future, everyone will have at least fifteen minutes of fame. I certainly hope he was right because what I'm about to announce to you will take about that long to explain. Here goes...

AUGUST 7

The Whiskey Rebellion took place, 1794.

Battle of Guadalcanal, 1942.

The Gulf of Tonkin Resolution, 1964. (See August 2nd entry.)

The feud between the Hatfields of West Virginia and McCoys of Kentucky erupted, 1882.

INTRODUCTIONS

Today was the day, in 1794, when President George Washington issued a proclamation telling a group of Western Pennsylvanian farmers to go peacefully back to their homes and to stop their Whiskey Rebellion. Washington's words were not enough. He had to issue a second proclamation a month and a half later and sent troops to persuade the rebels. It is worth noting that, even though the fight over excise taxes imposed on whiskey-making was quelled that time, the Internal Revenue Service is still engaged in games of wits with some rural whiskey makers. I trust that this brief historical note will put you in good spirits for my remarks here today.

When the U.S. Marines landed at Guadalcanal on this day in 1942, it was more than merely the start of a bitter battle between U.S. and Japanese forces. It was the turning point in the Pacific theater confrontation during the Second World War. It was the first time the United States had taken the offensive. So today there's a built-in historical reminder that the best defense is a good offense.

It all started in 1878, when Randolph McCoy accused Floyd Hatfield of stealing a hog. But when Ellison Hatfield was fatally stabbed by three McCoys on this day during the 1882 election, animosity turned into a desire for revenge. During the next eight years, the fiery feud between the Hatfields and the McCoys raged across state borders. Their legend even had its Romeo and Juliet—Rosanna McCoy and John Hatfield. When equal sides find themselves at loggerheads no one comes out a winner. So before I begin, I want to call a truce with all of you here. And not to offend any Hatfields in the audience, but I'd like to say my pleasure at speaking here today is the real McCoy.

AUGUST 8

Battle of Britain began, 1940.

President Harry S. Truman denounced repression of freedom, 1950.

President Nixon announced his resignation, 1974. (See July 16th entry.)

INTRODUCTIONS

The theater of war used to play out its acts to a select audience. War was conducted on a battlefield by fighting men, while the civilians waited for the results. That changed in modern times. And on this day in 1940, a major random attack began—the Battle of Britain or "The Blitz." The German air force waged a sustained series of daytime air attacks against both British home territory and the Royal Air Force. Their targets were not strictly limited to airfields or army bases. They rained bombs on British cities as well. The Blitz eventually ended because the British people responded with a new burst of determination. It was their spirit that ultimately defeated the purpose of the attacks. When you find yourselves in a war—even a war of words—it is wise to remember that an aggressive offense cannot defeat a fortified spirit. And there is no greater rage than that which is in response to an assault on innocents.

Government is a double-edged sword. Devised to protect its people, it can also stifle the rights of individuals in the desire to work for the common good. President Harry S. Truman warned us of these consequences on this date in 1950, when he said: "Once a government is committed to silencing the voice of opposition, it has only one way to go, and that is down the path of increasingly repressive measures, until it becomes a source of terror to all its citizens and creates a country where everyone lives in fear." The same watchwords apply to each of us as individuals. We must take care not to deny any person the right to oppose our opinions. So I hope you will lend me a moment of your time to listen to my opinion today.

AUGUST 9

Gerald R. Ford succeeded Richard M. Nixon as President, 1974. (See July 14th entry.)

Jesse Owens became the first Olympian to win four medals, 1936. (See September 12th entry.)

INTRODUCTIONS

Sometimes we are told that an individual cannot fight city hall. Today I want to remind you of just how much one person can affect the world. When Adolf Hitler hosted the 1936 Summer Olympics in Berlin, he wanted to prove that Aryan superiority was not limited to intellect—it included athletic prowess. In front of thousands of spectators and the world media, African-American runner Jesse Owens became the first person to win four Olympic medals. He stood on the winner's platform as living proof that individual achievement can outweigh perceived group strength and transcends racial, political, and economic barriers. Let us discuss today how we as individuals can succeed despite the alleged odds.

AUGUST 10

Chicago was incorporated as a village, 1833.

The Smithsonian Institution was established, 1846.

President Bill Clinton was born, 1946.

INTRODUCTIONS

When Chicago was incorporated as a village on this day in 1833, nobody could have foreseen that it would become a major American industrial hub; that it would burn to the ground and rise again as a metropolis; that it would be the capital of crime during the Prohibition; and it would be watched by the whole world when it hosted the 1968 Democratic convention. It is a city that is known for its colorful local politics; and known for the themes it has inspired in American literature. All great cities have grown from humble beginnings and—despite their problems—have invigorated not only their residents, but the world. People can be like cities. Let us look today at how each of us can rise to greater personal heights.

The Smithsonian Institution was approved by an Act of Congress on this day in 1846. Its establishment was the dying request of James Smithson of London, England, who had bequeathed its initial funding. Since then, various units of the Smithsonian have been endowed by other private philanthropists—the Freer Gallery, the Mellon and Kress Collections, the Hirshhorn and many, many others. Public and private funds have built this jewel in the crown of American museums. Private initiative started it. Public enthusiasm followed. In doing good deeds, we do not need to wait for the government to take the initiative.

William Jefferson Clinton was born on this day in 1946. Legend has it that Bill Clinton's uncle brought him into town once when Bill was still an infant, leaned his nephew up in a cardboard crib on the general store counter; and said to the people around him: "Take a good look at that boy, 'cause some day he's gonna be governor of Arkansas." Well, some day came, and Bill was governor. But he didn't stop there. Whether this story is true or just modern myth isn't important. While not every child will grow up to become president—despite every parents' wishes—there is no achievement more American than to exceed expectations.

AUGUST 11

Vietnam was partitioned, 1954.

Riots broke out in the Watts district of Los Angeles, California, 1965.

INTRODUCTIONS

King Solomon was asked to judge between two women each claiming to be the mother of a certain baby. Solomon suggested that the solution was to cut the baby in half and divide the remains between the two parties. One woman said, "No, let her have the child." Solomon knew that she was the real mother. She cared enough to give of herself to save her child. Partitions of wealth or of land can be like this tale of King Solomon. Those who agree to divide may not do so to be reasonable. On this day, in 1954, the French withdrew from what was French Indochina. Under the terms of a Geneva agreement, the territory was divided into two separate nations. The people of the two Vietnams voiced their opinions soon after. Many of them left Communist North Vietnam to take refuge in South Vietnam. All too soon, there was war. And when it ended, the North ruled all of Vietnam. Partition is rarely the final settlement; it is the intermission. We always seem to have an intermission or two someplace .

On this day in 1965, six days of rioting began in the Watts district of Los Angeles, California. It came as a surprise to most of the country that the idyllic dream factory—the land of the lotus eaters—had the same social problems as less-glamorous cities. It also shocked residents of the city itself. Unfortunately, problems arise even in the most ideal situations. If no one takes notice, those small problems can erupt into large disasters. Watching for signs, listening to grievances, and resolving what may seem to be inconsequential matters are simple ways to ensure the best conditions for everyone. On that note, why don't we clear the air today before situations begin to smolder.

AUGUST 12

Julius Rosenwald was born, 1862.

Cecil B. DeMille was born, 1881.

The Berlin wall was built, 1961. (See November 20th entry.)

Mrs. Kasenkina jumped from a window to escape deportation, 1948.

INTRODUCTIONS

Dictatorships are sometimes like long-winded speakers. They prefer a captive audience. On this day, in 1961, Communist East Germany literally created a captive audience. Overnight, the Communist government put up a wall sealing off East Berlin from West Berlin. The purpose was obviously to keep East Germans from leaving. But some brave people leapt to their freedom over the heavily fortified barricade. Like the Walls of Jericho, in 1989, the Berlin Wall came tumbling down. The city once again became whole, and its people were free to choose where they lived. No matter how large or strong a barricade you erect, you cannot stop people from choosing their own destinies.

The struggle for personal freedom has many times meant jumping over walls to escape oppression. Not all attempts were successful, I fear. Mrs. Olga Kasenkina had been sent to America to teach Soviet diplomats' children in New York City. Then she was ordered to return home. As she was being deported on this day in 1948, she broke away from consulate officials and leapt through a window at the Soviet embassy. Rather than spending her life in Stalinist Russia, she chose freedom at all costs. This happened long before a rash of defectors became an international embarrassment for Soviet Russia and other socialist nations. For a closed society, a window on the world can be a difficult thing. For an open society, there have to be windows, so speakers like me can sound again that ancient call: open the windows!

Julius Rosenwald was born on this day in 1862, in Springfield, Illinois. His name may not mean much to many of you, but his mail-order business helped build a growing nation. Rosenwald's Sears, Roebuck, and Company brought the luxuries of civilization to remote settlements when America's west was young. He amassed a fortune as he built his company into a huge retail institution. With his goals achieved, Rosenwald started sharing his success with the nation. He became a great philanthropist in his later years. Rosenwald's life reminds us that we should always view our personal successes with some consideration of what it can do to help others.

Cecil B. DeMille was born on this day in 1881, in Ashfield, Massachusetts. Real life has always been hard put to equal the sheer spectacle of a DeMille production. And I sometimes get the impression that life would be a lot more interesting if it could be staged by a Cecil B. DeMille. So today, I would like to talk to you about the spectacle of life and the competition for the role of Moses.

AUGUST 13

Lucy Stone was born, 1818.

Alfred Hitchcock was born, 1899.

The 3,000-mile welcome for Apollo 11 astronauts, 1969.

INTRODUCTIONS

Whoever said that you can't be in two places at once must have felt foolish on this day in 1969. Three Apollo 11 astronauts—Neil Armstrong, Edwin Aldrin and Michael Collins—flew to New York, Chicago, and Los Angeles on the same day to attend civic receptions in their honor. One thing Michael Collins said during the course of that day deserves to be said again now. He said: "We share with you the hope that we citizens of Earth who can solve the problems of leaving the earth can also solve the problems of staying on it."

Alfred Hitchcock was born on this date in 1899, in London, England. This master of the thriller once remarked: "In the entire history of sadism, the television commercial is the only instance where man has invented a torture and then provided the victims with an escape. What is interesting is that so few people avail themselves of the opportunity." I hope to take advantage of this fatal flaw in all of you today.

When Lucy Stone married Mr. Henry Blackwell she became known as Mrs. Lucy Stone. Born on this day, in 1818, in West Brookfield, Massachusetts, this women's suffrage movement leader was particularly interested in enabling women to keep their maiden names. It was a long hard fight. And when she died in 1893, the battle still had not been won. Little did anyone know that nearly a century later, professional women everywhere would follow Mrs. Stone's example. So today, it is timely to remember that the hardest thing to keep is a good name.

AUGUST 14

The Boxer Rebellion ended, 1900.

The Social Security Law was established, 1935. (See April 27th entry.)

The Atlantic Charter was signed by England and the United States, 1941.

VJ Day, 1945.

INTRODUCTIONS

When the leaders of two great nations meet at sea and issue a statement of principle, it has to have a certain element of drama. The situation was very dramatic when on this date in 1941, President Franklin D. Roosevelt and Prime Minister Winston Churchill issued the Atlantic Charter simultaneously in Washington D.C. and London. They had held a three-day conference aboard the British fighting ship H.M.S. *Prince of Wales* and the U.S. cruiser *Augusta* to discuss their potential postwar goals: no more territorial aggrandizement; respecting the wishes of territorial inhabitants as to territorial changes; recognizing the people's right to decide on their own form of government; easing restrictions on international trade and insuring equal access to raw materials; cooperating to provide better economic security for people all over the world; freedom from want and fear; freedom of the seas; and the ultimate establishment of a permanent structure of peace. Fifteen nations—including Soviet Russia—endorsed the Atlantic Charter in less than two months. Now let's look at the results of that charter today.

Today marks a critical a landmark in Second World War history. In 1945, this was VJ Day. Japanese forces formally surrendered on September 2nd aboard the U.S. battleship *Missouri,* but this was the day the Japanese stopped fighting. It was a euphoric moment for the winning side. Since then, there seems to have been a long time between euphorias. We have found new battles to fight.

The Boxers were put down on this day in 1900. After a 56-day siege of European and American families living in Beijing and other parts of China, the Boxers ended their bloody rampage when 10,000 British, American, French, and German forces marched into the capital city to rescue the stranded diplomats, missionaries, businessmen, men, women, and children. The Boxers were members of a patriotic martial arts society that strongly protested the western influences that had swiftly spread throughout the nation in less than 50 years. More than 1500 Europeans had been killed before the rebellion ended. But the event was only the beginning of the rapid demise of the western occupation of Asia. Neither independence nor dominance come easily, but it seems neither groups nor individuals consider the eventual cost.

A UGUST 15

Macbeth died, 1057.

Napoleon Bonaparte was born, 1769.

Sir Joseph Lister discovered the antiseptic process, 1865. (See April 5th entry.)

T.E. Lawrence was born, 1888. (See July 6th entry.)

The Panama Canal was opened, 1914.

INTRODUCTIONS

When the Panama Canal opened on this date in 1914, it was considered one of the wonders of the modern world. Countless laborers had suffered in the dense Central American jungles—battling heat, humidity, snakes, and malaria—to build it. A half century later, people realized that the canal wasn't wide enough for modern freighters and cruise ships to pass through. Forgetting the political wrangling and maneuvering that centered around the canal, it became a monument to the rapidity of change. On its anniversary, let us remember that today's superhighway is tomorrow's Route 66.

Today is Napoleon Bonaparte's birthday. Born in 1769 in Ajaccio, Corsica, Napoleon was a small man who cast a gigantic shadow. In his honor, I plan to make a short speech and let the shadow shift for itself. A lot of people have imagined themselves to be Napoleon and succeeded only in meeting their Waterloo. As the saying goes, if you want to meet your Waterloo, bite off more than you can chew. My ambition today is considerably more modest.

A notable anniversary that inspired a tragic play marks this date. In 1057, Macbeth of Moray was mortally wounded by Malcolm near Aberdeen, Scotland. Macbeth had placed his claim on the Scottish throne because he was married to King Kenneth III's granddaughter. In 1047, he had killed Duncan, his only rival, in battle and grabbed the throne. As the saying goes, violence begets violence. Macbeth's death did not end the fight for the Scottish crown—it continued for generations. The question I put to you is this. Have leaders really changed so much in our time?

On this day, in 1888, an enigma was born. Thomas Edward Lawrence came from a middle class Edwardian background and showed great promise as an archaeologist when he studied at Oxford University. He had fallen in love with the desert after bicycling from England to Palestine, and his passion grew as he joined an excavation team in Saudi Arabia at the beginning of the First World War. Lawrence joined the British army as a cartographer and expert in Arab culture when the war reached the desert. A spark of inspiration spurred him on to lead a handful of Arab rebels and overtake a Turkish garrison at Aqaba; and from that day forward, he was known as Lawrence of Arabia. His fame grew as news of his exploits reached Europe and America. But instead of reaping glory's benefits, he hid in the shadows. He changed his name and joined the RAF, working on motorcycle and hydrofoil designs; and writing his epic chronicle, *Seven Pillars of Wisdom.* He found peace in obscurity until he died in 1935, when he was laid to rest in Britain's highest place of honor— Westminster Abbey. An average person would have reveled in fame, but Lawrence was no ordinary man. His accomplishments transformed the Middle East's future, but he never perceived his deeds as historical turning points. He had not chased his destiny, it found him. With Lawrence's story in mind, I would like to address with you today a question each of us should ask ourselves. If fate comes knocking on your door, are you ready to rise to the occasion without expectations of fame and glory?

AUGUST 16

George Meany was born, 1894.

A gorilla saved a young child, 1996.

INTRODUCTIONS

George Meany, who was born on this day in 1894, was the American Federation of Labor's vigorous and vital leader well into his eighties. As a matter of fact, labor seems to have more elder statesmen in its leadership than any other walk of life. I know that labor leaders are apt to make more speeches. So, although I'm not a labor leader, I welcome this opportunity to make a speech to you; if it makes me live longer it is a double pleasure. On the other hand, if it just makes things seem longer…

Many people are convinced that wild, untamed animals are a danger to humans. That's why zoos build deep moats or put up shatter-proof glass around their exhibits to protect visitors from harm. I do begin wonder about this attitude when I recall an incident that happened on this day in 1996. A 3-year-old boy accidentally fell 15 feet into the gorilla pen at the Brookfield Zoo near Chicago, Illinois. As he lay unconscious, a rare female western lowland gorilla named Binti-Jua picked up the child, cradled him in her arms, carried his unconscious body to the cage door, and protected him until his rescuers arrived. A similar incident took place at the Great Britain's Jersey Zoo a few years earlier. A dominant male silverback gorilla gently patted and then stood guard over a young boy who fell into that exhibit. Naturally, the question is this: Are our so-called human virtues limited to our species or are we only deluding ourselves?

AUGUST 17

Davy Crockett was born, 1786. (See February 23rd entry on the Alamo.)

Mae West was born, 1892.

Gold was discovered in Klondike territory, 1896.

INTRODUCTIONS

Not too many women have given their name to a distinctive garment. In the case of bloomers, they were named after the first person who wore them. In the case of Mae Wests, they're named after the shape of the woman they resembled. The Mae

West was an inflatable life preserver widely used during the Second World War. For reasons I needn't go into the soldiers and seamen who wore them nicknamed them for the raunchy blonde bombshell who had graced the silver screen since the 1930s. For Mae West, it was a lovely salute. Born on this day in 1892—or thereabouts—in Brooklyn, New York, Mae West put more innuendo into a few words than anyone after her. "Come up and see me some time" always seemed steamier when delivered with West's classic style. In honor of her birthday, I am here to sound an optimistic note. As long as there's a Mae West keeping us afloat, the world isn't in too bad a shape.

There is a four-letter word that has inspired more hope in mankind and opened more new lands than any other. I will not keep you in suspense; the word is gold. The search for gold started the settlement of California in 1849; of British Columbia in 1856; and of Alaska and the Yukon territories on this day in 1896. This was the day that George Carmack, Skookum Jim and Tagish Charlie discovered gold on Bonanza Creek in the Canadian Klondike. Officials were barring fortune-hunters from crossing the border into Canada unless they had enough funds and provisions to stake themselves for a full year in the wilderness. But that didn't stop the 100,000 adventurers who sought their fortunes during the next two years. Thanks to the Klondike gold rush, Alaska became an American territory. Some brave-hearted people still search for the pot of gold at the end of the Arctic rainbow. But the key word always has been that four-letter one—gold. One way or another, gold is rich and rich, well, rich.

A UGUST 18

Virginia Dare was born, 1587.

The milk condensation process was patented, 1853.

Pope Leo XIII declared his law of history, 1883.

INTRODUCTIONS

On this day, in 1853, Gail Borden received a patent for an improved process for condensing milk. His invention ultimately led to the foundation of the Borden Company. But it has also led me to an important decision here tonight. If Gail Borden could condense milk into a more convenient form, there is no reason why I can't condense the three-hour speech I had originally planned into a more manageable length. So rest easy; what I am about to give you is the condensed version.

When Pope Leo XIII opened the Vatican Archives on this date in 1883, his remarks condensed a great deal of morality into a very small package. He said, "The first law of history is not to dare to utter falsehood; the second is not to fear to speak the truth." History is not the only arena in which those laws should apply. I do not plan to break them here today.

Today is Virginia Dare's birthday. The first child born to English parents in the New World was born on Roanoke Island, North Carolina, on this day in 1587. Virginia, her parents, and the whole Roanoke colony, disappeared shortly after that off the face of the earth. It is interesting that the history of American settlement started with a lost child. Interesting because one of our abiding problems today—on Virginia Dare's birthday—is still the problem of lost children. They are not lost not in the literal sense, but rather in terms of lost potential, lost opportunities, lost souls. Let us take a moment to consider what this loss means to each of us.

AUGUST 19

Captain Gennadi Nevelskoy raised the Russian flag on Sakhalin Island, 1851.

Bernard M. Baruch was born, 1870.

Orville Wright was born, 1871 (celebrated as National Aviation Day).

Malcolm Forbes was born, 1919.

INTRODUCTIONS

Since this is National Aviation Day, I may be entitled to try a few flights of fancy— but I'll resist the temptation. National Aviation Day commemorates the birth of Orville Wright. Born in 1871, in Dayton, Ohio, Orville and his brother Wilbur invented the airplane. When they set out to make a heavier-than-air propeller-driven machine fly off the ground, they looked for a place with a big wind. I guess I am to be the big wind today.

Bernard M. Baruch was probably America's most notable elder statesman. Born on this day in 1870, in Camden, South Carolina, Baruch advised every President from Woodrow Wilson to John F. Kennedy. He would sit on a park bench and hold impromptu press conferences as easily as he moved within the inner circles of power. In his last years, he was hard of hearing and wore a hearing aid. There was always a suspicion that one of his assets in delicate conversations was that he could decide what he wanted to hear. Selective hearing is a marvelous tactic in negotiations. It isn't quite as marvelous when encountered by a public speaker especially if audiences fall asleep or start talking to each other. I figure that the way to avoid that problem is either to have the sound volume on the public address system turned up so high so that nobody can fall asleep; or to make the speech short and sweet. Since the latter is also a lot easier on the speaker, you will be relieved to know that I have chosen my second option.

Sakhalin Island, just north of Japan, has been the scene of a number of international incidents. But on this day, in 1851, one event not only led to a naval captain's demotion, it spurred a tidal wave of Russian expansion. Czarist Russian military and political leaders believed that the Amur River in Siberia emptied into the Sea of Okhotsk. Naval Captain Gennadi Nevelskoy had been sent to explore the region for future settlement. But he discovered that his superiors were wrong; this mighty river actually ended at the Pacific Ocean. In his excitement, Nevelskoy raised the Russian flag on the eastern shore of Sakhalin Island directly across from the river's mouth. On his return, he was demoted to the post of sailor because he had acted without orders from his superiors. They did, however, take advantage of this revelation. Nearly a decade later, Manchurian China ceded that portion of the Amur River region; and the Russian city of Vladivostok was established at the river's mouth. Japan eventually ceded Nevelskoy's island to the Czar as well. Independent actions don't always yield the best results for the individuals who do them, but that doesn't mean no one will come along to take advantage of the situation. Remember that while I tell you about a recent incident that has occurred right in our own backyard.

Since it's Malcolm Forbes' birthday, I would like to reflect on a few words this eloquent publisher, who was born in 1919, once said. "I don't waste too much time philosophizing about wealth," Forbes commented, "I just recommend it to everyone." And I agree. I don't want to waste too much time philosophizing about our future. I just recommend we do something about it.

A UGUST 20

Alaska was discovered, 1741.

Benjamin Harrison was born, 1833.

INTRODUCTIONS

About this time of the year, in 1741, the Danish explorer Vitus Bering discovered Alaska while heading a Russian expedition through the Arctic. Little did Bering realize that a century later his discovery would become known as Seward's Folly; and would be the site of a third rush for gold. I don't think Bering could have foreseen that two centuries later this peninsula would still be one of the last relatively uninhabited wildernesses left on earth—a place where nature stills reigns supreme.

Most American Presidents have some particular claim to fame, and I have a particular liking for the uniqueness of Benjamin Harrison's right to that honor. Born on this day in 1833, in North Bend, Ohio, Harrison was the grandson of the President William Henry Harrison, who served the shortest term in history. But that was not Benjamin's particular claim to Presidential distinction. It was simply that Benjamin

Harrison—who succeeded Grover Cleveland as President—also preceded Grover Cleveland as President. He beat Cleveland in one election, then lost to him the next time around. This would have been inspirational if you happened to be Grover Cleveland; and rather irritating if you were Benjamin Harrison. But it's a concept that every public speaker should bear in mind. Just because they are on your side when you start, don't think they won't turn on you. I want you to know I will be watching you very carefully.

AUGUST 21

Billy Barker struck gold in western Canada, 1862. (See June 17th entry.)

German-Russian nonaggression treaty was announced, 1939.

Construction of the first nuclear submarine was ordered, 1951.

The Hawaiian Islands achieved American statehood, 1959.

INTRODUCTIONS

Aloha! That may seem like an odd sort of greeting in this nontropical setting, but I believe it is timely, because today is the anniversary of Hawaii's admission as the 50th state—and the first state outside the North American mainland. So I say again, Aloha! It probably would have been nice—in honor of the occasion—if you had been given the opportunity to witness Hawaiian traditions such as hula dancers in grass skirts, or a few thrilling surfing demonstrations. I guess the only Hawaiian tradition I could emulate would be to lecture you like a missionary, but I feel I would be miscast. So, instead...

On this date in 1939, the Soviet Union (which had been claiming to be the only true opponent of Nazism) and Nazi Germany (which had set itself up as the prime enemy of Communism) announced that they had agreed to a ten-year nonaggression treaty. It was signed formally three days later. The so-called nonaggression treaty proved to be the fuse that ignited the Second World War. In no time, the Nazis and the Communists greedily divided Poland between them. Not too long afterward, they fought each other. The moral to this story is clear: Actions speak louder than words. But words can sometimes lead to action; and perhaps my words here today may have some constructive effect in their own way.

Back on this day in 1951, the U.S. ordered the construction of the first nuclear-powered submarine. The same power used in the atomic bombs during the Second World War was ordered to be harnessed as an alternative energy source. Why is war a more powerful motivator than peace? And why has it taken war to produce alternatives for problems that exist in peacetime, like electricity shortages and cancer treatment? I do not come here today with the answers to those questions. I come, rather, to urge that we renew the search for the answers.

A British canal man and sailor named Billy Barker struck gold in western Canada on this day in 1862. When Barker arrived in British Columbia's northern Cariboo mountains, a few thousand other adventurers had already staked their claims in the 1856 gold rush. He couldn't find a plot anywhere near the big veins that were already discovered, so he decided to try his hand below the canyon on Williams Creek. Other prospectors gathered to laugh at Billy's folly, as he dug deeper and deeper. Fifty-two feet later, he struck one of the area's richest finds. It was worth $600,000 when gold was only $20 an ounce. Billy went through his fortune fairly quickly. So he dug up another strike equally as rich a few miles south. But his beautiful second wife frittered that fortune away. In the end, Billy Barker died penniless. Opportunity does knock more than once for some people. The question each of us must ask, of course, is what do we make of it when we have a great opportunity right in our hands?

A UGUST 22

George Friedrich Handel started writing *Messiah,* 1741. (See September 14th entry.)

The America's Cup was first won, 1851. (See September 18th entry.)

Theodore Roosevelt became the first U.S. President to drive an automobile, 1902. (See October 27th entry.)

Baseball's World Series was first suggested, 1903.

Ray Bradbury was born, 1920.

INTRODUCTIONS

Yacht racing is not your average spectator sport, but a particular yacht race has captured the public's fancy for more than a century—the America's Cup. On this day in 1851, the U.S. schooner *America* won the race against the British schooner *Aurora* to win a silver cup trophy in British waters and international honors. From that day forward the race has been known as the America's Cup. It was defended by American sailors and yachts for well over a century thereafter and remained in U.S. possession until recently. Great Britain's Sir Thomas Lipton tried many times; he lost the races but his great sportsmanship won American hearts. To many people, the America's Cup races seem to be an anachronism in an age of jet travel and mass spectator sports. But some traditions never lose their charm. Today, on the anniversary of the America's Cup, it's good to know that there are still people who appreciate the art of handling a favorable wind. And now, if you will supply the appreciation, I will supply the wind.

Barney Dreyfuss used to own the Pittsburgh Pirates baseball team. This may not give him a resounding claim to fame. But we are told that Dreyfuss wrote a letter on this day, in 1903, that entitles him to a place in history. Writing to an American League club owner, this National Leaguer said, "The time has come for the National and American Leagues to organize a World Series." And later that year the first World Series was held. Now, of course, we have world series in one sport after another. And if you look at them, you'll find that most of them are misnamed since they are actually restricted to one country. We sometimes mistake our world for the entire world. Today I'd like to resist the temptation to mistake a narrow focus for the big picture, and look at both.

Author Ray Bradbury was born on this date in 1920, and grew up in Waukegan, Illinois and Los Angeles, California. While he was in high school, he launched his own magazine—*Futuria Fantasia*. Within a few years he was selling his stories to pulp magazines; and later, to major publications like *The New Yorker* and *The Saturday Evening Post*. Bradbury's fantasy and science fiction narrate the interrelationship of technology, society, and the individual in terrifyingly precise detail. But one story—which was first featured in *Playboy Magazine* because other publishers were scared to print it—told of a world where firemen burned books because the government decided their contents made a television-addicted, pill-popping society unequal and unhappy. One of *Fahrenheit 451*'s characters—an old English professor—describes books in a particularly profound way: "This book has pores. It has features. This book can go under a microscope. You'd find life under the glass, streaming past in infinite profusion...They show the pores in the face of life." We cannot deny the power of well-written ideas; nor the empowerment great books inspire in a receptive audience.

AUGUST 23

The first American women's college held its first graduation, 1838.

Rudolf Valentino died, 1926. (See May 6th entry.)

Nicola Sacco and Bartolomeo Vanzetti were executed, 1927. (See May 5th entry.)

INTRODUCTIONS

On this day in 1926, the great romantic film idol Rudolph Valentino died in New York City. His passing—at the age of 31—plunged countless females of all ages into an orgy of public grief. It reminds us that people can be just as concerned over actors as over war and peace; and that we have an infinite capacity for hero worship. Before we smile condescendingly at what now appears to be silliness, we might take a look at ourselves—not the lunatic fringes and fan club extremists—but the things that otherwise normal adults go crazy over.

The sad case of a misconducted trial and appeal ended on this day in 1927. Two Italian immigrants—Nicola Sacco and Bartolomeo Vanzetti—were executed for the alleged murder of a guard during a payroll robbery. During the long period before they met their end, Vanzetti wrote to Judge Thayer: "Never in our full life could we hope to do such work for tolerance, for justice, for man's understanding of man as now we do by accident." Their trial, execution, and Vanzetti's profound words should stand in the forefront of our discussion of human rights today.

When the first American women's college, Mount Holyoke Female Seminary, opened in South Hadley, Massachusetts, the public generally felt women needed refinement, not higher education. On this day in 1838, the college graduated its first students. This may not have had a profound effect on the male population in their day, but to twist a famous line that was written nearly a century later: For today's women, men bend on their knees to women with degrees.

AUGUST 24

The city of Pompeii was destroyed, 79 AD

Great Britain reminted its coins, 1562.

British forces burned Washington, D.C., 1814.

The North Atlantic Treaty went into effect, 1949. (See March 18th entry.)

Daniel K. Inouye of Hawaii was sworn in as the first Japanese-American in the House of Representatives, 1959.

Hiram L. Fong of Hawaii was sworn in as the first Chinese-American in the U.S. Senate, 1959.

INTRODUCTIONS

Back in the year 79 AD, on this day, Mount Vesuvius erupted. Before it was finished, two Roman cities—Herculaneum and Pompeii—were wiped out. The ruins of Pompeii remind us how suddenly and how thoroughly a living city can cease to exist. Most of the time cities don't go that fast, but they do change. If they don't change, they run the risk of becoming like Pompeii—not by being buried under rivers of lava—but simply by falling apart. Sometimes I ask myself, if I had a choice of having my hometown permanently preserved as it is or starting all over from scratch, which would I want? The answer, of course, is that neither way really works. Let's talk today about the way things do work.

On this day in 1814, Washington, D.C. was burned to the ground by the British. It happened during the War of 1812. And unlike Mount Vesuvius' destruction of Pompeii, or General Sherman's razing of Atlanta, the British Army was infinitely more selective. They didn't burn the whole city; they concentrated on the White House and other government buildings. Then they marched north to Baltimore, where they were repulsed at the Battle of Fort McHenry. The nation's capitol was rebuilt, and after a suitable lapse of time, Great Britain and America became the best of friends. It has been said that the only thing that separates the British and the Americans is their mutual illusion that they speak the same language. Sometimes that is also a speaker's illusion. I hope that today my words will not disguise my meaning. I must say I have the feeling—which is a nice one as I stand before you— that you and I do indeed speak the same language.

Saving a penny here and a nickel there makes good sense in most cases, but in 1562, it was a source of embarrassment to the British government. In an attempt to economize on the cost of minting money, King Henry VIII had coins made from metals like iron and lead that were worth less than the face value they represented. The public felt its money wasn't worth the metal it was minted on and refused to accept it. So on this day, the government finished reminting all of the nation's coins worth their face value in solid silver. Cutting costs and investing well are always a balancing act but as every good manager knows, you can't cut corners when it comes to the quality of perceived value.

Americans are descended from many different groups that immigrated in hopes of attaining a better life. On this day in 1959, two native sons of immigrant parents achieved some pretty high goals. Daniel K. Inouye of Hawaii was sworn in as the first Japanese-American congressman to the U.S. House of Representatives; Hiram L. Fong of Hawaii was sworn in as the first Chinese-American U.S. senator. Asian-Americans have made considerable contributions to every field of endeavor including scientific research, business, law, and politics. Yet few people have hailed those achievements—an oversight which I intend to correct right now.

AUGUST 25

The National Park Service was established, 1916.

Leonard Bernstein was born, 1918.

Bret Harte was born, 1836.

INTRODUCTIONS

Today is the National Park Service's birthday. In 1916, this department was established to protect tracts of our nation's wilderness from development. In the course of reviewing what this event means to the nation, I discovered that the first National Park Service director was paid $4500 a year. That says a lot about inflation. It also says a lot about the increased popularity of our national parks. These protected areas get more crowded each year, and the job of maintaining and protecting them gets more and more difficult. The wide open spaces just aren't as wide or as open as they used to be. So I guess you might as well resign yourselves to staying here for a while. Just sit back and watch your humble servant spout like Old Faithful.

One of America's most famous composers and conductors was born in Lawrence, Massachusetts, on this day in 1918. At the age of 25, Leonard Bernstein was already known as the famous symphony conductor who brought the New York Philharmonic to new glory. He was also an accomplished composer. His *Jeremiah* symphony brought him public acclaim. And, in his spare time, he wrote the scores for popular musicals like *West Side Story* and *Candide*. Bernstein moved with ease between these two facets of the music world. It makes me feel very guilty because I can't compose or conduct for you. All I can do is stand and talk.

Some talented people rise and shine brighter as the years go by, while other rise like meteors and fall the same way. One of writing's meteors was Bret Harte, who was born on this day in 1836, in Albany, New York. Harte wrote exciting and grubbily humorous accounts of Western life like "The Luck of Roaring Camp" and "The Outcasts of Poker Flat." Within a decade, he burned himself out as an author, while friends and colleagues like Mark Twain kept shining, burning brighter with each new work. Bret Harte's example is one every speaker—and every writer—should keep in mind. And I plan to keep an eye on you today to make sure that I don't hold the podium so long that you end up like a Bret Harte character who he described as follows: "...he smiled a kind of sickly smile, and curled up on the floor, / And the subsequent proceedings interested him no more." So, moving right along...

AUGUST 26

Lee DeForest was born, 1873.

The Nineteenth Amendment to the U.S. Constitution was ratified, 1920.

INTRODUCTIONS

Today marks a milestone in the fight for women's rights. On this day in 1920, the Nineteenth Amendment to the U.S. Constitution—giving women the right to vote—

was ratified. It did not end discrimination against American women, but it armed them with a new secret weapon. Later on, they found out that it wasn't only talk that hadn't been enough—the vote wasn't enough either. Ultimately, they moved into consciousness raising and public awareness. Both, of course, are things treasured by every speaker. So if my remarks today make you more conscious or even keep you conscious—I will be content. Conscious of what, you may ask? Even if you don't ask, I will tell you.

American inventor Lee DeForest was one of a relatively small group of brilliant men who took Marconi's radio and developed it into the device that transmits sight and sound signals into your home—the television. He was also a pioneer in the development of talking pictures. Today is Lee DeForest's birthday. He was born in Council Bluffs, Iowa, in 1873. And I think it is safe to say that Lee DeForest was instrumental in giving an awful lot of people a chance to sound off to more people than they could collect in any one place. Dr. DeForest, wherever you are, thank you. And now a few words for my sponsors.

AUGUST 27

The first hydrogen balloon was tested, 1783.

Colonel Edwin L. Drake dug the first oil well, 1859.

Sam Goldwyn was born, 1882.

Lyndon Baynes Johnson was born, 1908.

Bill Brock flew the *Pride of Detroit* over London, 1927.

George Eyston set an automobile land-speed record, 1938.

Captain Erich Warshitz flew the first jet plane, 1939.

The first white men crossed the Northwest passage from the Atlantic to the Pacific, 1954.

The Soviet spacecraft Soyuz 15 went into orbit and met with a Soviet space station, 1979.

INTRODUCTIONS

When Colonel Edwin L. Drake struck oil in Pennsylvania on this day in 1859, the world had its first oil well. The world got the better end of the deal. Colonel Drake was broke within 15 years. He kept producing oil, and waiting, but it just wasn't a precious commodity in those days. His story is quite different from the one about the two desert prospectors who struck it rich. They were looking for gold and found water. You see—as Thomas Edison put it—everything comes to him who hustles while he waits. So, with all due respect for Edwin Drake and the first oil well, I won't keep you waiting.

President Lyndon Baynes Johnson, who was born on this day in 1908, came to office when John F. Kennedy was assassinated. This first Texan president ushered us into the space race, signed the Civil Rights Act, and declared a war on poverty during his terms in office. He once said: "Presidents learn—perhaps sooner than others—that our destiny is fashioned by what all of us do—by the deeds and desires of each citizen—as one tiny drop of water after another ultimately makes a big river." I hope my words here today will add a few drops to that river.

Today is Sam Goldfish's birthday. You all know who he is. As a young man, Sam moved to the U.S. from Poland and got into the glove business. He did pretty well, but then he discovered the movies. He and his new partners hired Cecil B. DeMille, a young untried director. Their gamble was a hit. Then Sam Goldfish joined Edgar Selwyn and started Goldwyn Studios. The name stuck. He became Sam Goldwyn, one of Hollywood's greatest producers. Opinionated and honest, he coined comments like: "A verbal contract isn't worth the paper it's written on." When asked once for his opinion of a film script, he replied: "I read part of it all the way through." In his honor, I'm here to give you part of my thoughts all the way through.

Historically, this has been a good day for reaching new frontiers. It all started in 1783, when J.A.C. Charles tested the first hydrogen balloon. His experiment paved the way for modern aviation. In 1927, Bill Brock flew over London in the *Pride of Detroit* on his way to completing the first flight around the world. Back on land, race car driver George Eyston set a 345-miles-per-hour land-speed record in 1938. The next year, German pilot Erich Warshitz flew the first jet plane through the skies. During the summer of 1954, the Arctic Circle's Northwest Passage was finally conquered in a pair of icebreakers. And in 1979, Soyuz 15, a manned Soviet spacecraft, went into orbit and rendezvoused with a space station. While I'm not expecting to set any endurance records or verbal speed today, I'd like join the others who have gone before me on this date, and "boldly go where no man has gone before."

A UGUST 28

Mother Elizabeth Seton was born, 1774.
The first radio commercial was aired, 1922.

The New York Times broke the TV quiz show scandal story, 1958.

A civil rights march took place in Washington, D.C., 1963.

Antiwar demonstrators harassed the Democratic convention in Chicago, IL, 1968.

INTRODUCTIONS

Today marks the anniversary of two demonstrations that altered the course of American history. In 1963, an inspiring civil rights march was held in Washington, D.C., led by the Reverend Dr. Martin Luther King, Jr. This demonstration is well-remembered because of his eloquent "I have a dream" speech. The Civil Rights Act was passed less than a year after this peaceful event. In 1968, an antiwar demonstration held in Chicago during the Democratic National Convention ended in a violent confrontation between protesters and police. After a shocking mediafest which was fueled by dramatics— like one of the alleged Chicago Seven conspirators being bound and gagged at his own trial—two generations of Americans learned an eye-opening lesson about the communications gap that had grown between them. Taking a lesson from these two events, I have decided today to ask you to heed the words of President Lyndon Johnson who once said, "Let us reason together."

It is recorded in some history books that on this day in 1922, the commercial message was born. It aired on WEAF—a New York radio station—and the world hasn't been the same since. So it is only fitting that I should be here before you today to say that I will be back after a word from my sponsor.

On this day, the television industry marks black-letter day in its history. The producers of the popular quiz show 21 had routinely given contestants the answers to questions in advance. The show was so convincingly rigged that participants like college professor Charles Van Doren were transformed into national heroes overnight. In 1958, *The New York Times* broke the scandal wide open with a front-page story. The news injured the viewing public's faith in heroes, and changed broadcasters' minds about what should be televised. An old adage says: "You can't believe everything you see." But I assure you, you can believe everything you hear from me today.

America's first Roman Catholic saint was born on this day in 1774. Mother Elizabeth Seton was a native New Yorker. After she had married and started a family, her husband passed away from a chronic illness in 1803. Mrs. Seton converted to Roman Catholicism a few years later; and opened an elementary school in Baltimore, Maryland, where several young women were entrusted to her care. From that beginning, America's first religious society, the Sisters of Charity was formed in 1813, with Sister Seton as its first mother superior. Saint Elizabeth Seton didn't start America's first Catholic elementary school, but she is considered the founder of the American parochial school system. Her life's work gives us cause enough to consider the educational system's future here today.

AUGUST 29

Chop suey was invented in New York City, 1896.

Carry Nation tried to visit John L. Sullivan, 1901. (See November 25th entry.)

W.A. Dwiggins defined advertising, 1922.

INTRODUCTIONS

We like to think that the United States is a pacesetter among the world's nations, but until recently we rarely considered American cuisine as one of our high points. But on this date in 1896, a truly American dish was invented—chop suey. It's true. According to the record books, chop suey was first concocted in New York City by visiting Chinese ambassador Li Huang-Chang's chef. Let me say that I am glad that Americans have discovered real Chinese cuisine since that momentous occasion. I must also commend the man who devised this stir-fry dish for opening up our eyes to something new and different.

It's been a long time since anybody went around the country smashing saloons with a hatchet, crusading against the evils of alcohol. I don't know how many of you have heard of Carry Nation who left Kansas at the turn of the century to put everyone on the wagon. On this day, in 1901, Ms. Nation was in New York City, and she was on the war path. We are told that she paid a well-publicized visit to a saloon run by John L. Sullivan, the former heavyweight boxing champion. John L. was nowhere in sight. He sent her a message that he was sick in bed. Since I am not carrying a little hatchet—and you're not sick in bed—I hope we can have a more meaningful discussion here today.

It was on this day in 1922, that illustrator and designer W.A. Dwiggins was quoted in the *Boston Transcript* as defining advertising design as "the only form of graphic design that gets home to everybody." With any luck, my words will form a convincingly graphic idea that gets home to all of you.

AUGUST 30

The hotline between the U.S. and Moscow was established, 1963.

Thurgood Marshall took his seat on the U.S. Supreme Court, 1967. (See June 13th entry.)

Guion Bluford Jr. became the first African-American astronaut in space when he blasted off aboard the space shuttle Challenger, 1983. (See April 19th entry.)

INTRODUCTIONS

In 1963, a favorite prop for screenwriters of the time was established—the hotline between the White House in Washington, D.C., and the Kremlin in Moscow. I have no inside information as to when and how that hotline has been used. But I come before you today convinced that I'd much rather talk to you than to the Moscow or Washington end of that phone line. The hotline may be technically perfect, but this is a much better connection.

Two men took gigantic steps in their given professions on this day in history. In 1967, Thurgood Marshall took his seat on the U.S. Supreme Court. Appointed by President Lyndon Baynes Johnson, Marshall was the first African-American justice to step up to the nation's highest court bench. In 1983, astronaut Guion Bluford, Jr., took off as a member of the space shuttle Challenger's crew. Bluford was the first African-American astronaut to take a giant leap into space. No individual can be denied his or her right to reach the heights if he or she is determined to be best. I may not scale the highest peaks before you today, but the people I wish to speak to you about certainly have.

AUGUST 31

A Packard automobile completed the first transcontinental car trip, 1903.

Thomas Edison patented the kinetoscope, 1887.

The U.S. Investigating Committee recommended that Great Britain give up control of Palestine, 1947. (See June 29th and September 29th entries.)

INTRODUCTIONS

In 1887, Thomas Edison invented something called the kinetoscope—or at least he had it patented. This was the day the patent was granted for his device which allowed an individual to peer through a peephole to watch images that appeared to move. I come before you today to give you a peek at some events that are rapidly moving all around us.

A monumental feat was accomplished on this day when, in 1903, a Packard automobile reached New York City from San Francisco, California. It was the first time anyone had ever attempted to drive across the country without a horse. The trip took 52 days—not the 4 or 5 days it takes us now. Then again, the Packard averaged about 10 to 20 miles per hour. They say that time is relative, yet time surely seems accelerated and relevant in our own times. Let's slow down for a moment and consider where we have been.

SEPTEMBER

INTRODUCTION:

Now is the time when we traditionally conclude the rites of summer with the long Labor Day weekend. Labor Day was intended to be a salute to working people. But what it has become is a celebration of the end of the vacation season—a signal that it's time to go back to work. It's also a warning to children that it's time to hit the books. Somebody once said that the principal reason for Labor Day speeches was to give the picnicking crowds a chance to digest their food quietly. Therefore, I shall enter into the spirit of this occasion by giving you a few modest thoughts to chew over and hope I produce nothing too hard to swallow.

SEPTEMBER 1

James J. Corbett was born, 1866.

Edgar Rice Burroughs was born, 1875.

The provinces of Saskatchewan and Alberta entered into the confederation of Canada, 1905. (See July 1st entry.)

The Second World War began, 1939.

Bobby Fisher won the international chess championship against Boris Spassky in Reykjavik, Iceland, 1972. (See March 9th entry.)

INTRODUCTIONS

On this very day in 1939, Germany invaded Poland and ignited the Second World War. You may think that this anniversary hardly makes an inspiring jumping-off point for a speech. But if you compare today with the one in 1939, you must admit that things have changed. Somehow, slowly and uncertainly, we do seem to learn something from our past mistakes. Tomorrow is the heir of yesterday; and today is the legacy we leave for tomorrow. The world fell apart on this day in 1939, and had to be mended with blood, sweat, toil, and tears. What do we need to do for tomorrow? That's a broad question, and I'll only deal with a few aspects of it today.

Gentleman Jim Corbett was well-dressed, eloquent, and moved gracefully in polite society. He was the man who beat the legendary John L. Sullivan for the world heavyweight boxing title. He was a superb boxer—not a slugger or brawler. This native San Franciscan was also a new kind of professional fighter who played by the

Marquess of Queensberry rules. Born on this day in 1866, James J. Corbett became a successful lecturer and actor after his pugilistic career ended. We've had a succession of accomplished, articulate fighters since Corbett's day, but it was Gentleman Jim who broke the old thick-headed mold. He demonstrated that technique and style could be more than a match for brute force. You don't always have to win by a knockout. All you need is to score enough points. And so to my first point.

Today is the birthday of Tarzan's creator, Edgar Rice Burroughs, who was born in Chicago in 1875. As much as we may be fascinated with the concept of conversing with our animal friends, I do believe that we have a lot to learn first as humans about communicating with each other. Of course, if you find areas of disagreement with what I am about to say, you can always decide that my remarks were for the birds.

SEPTEMBER 2

U.S. Treasury Department was established, 1789.

U.S. Vice President Theodore Roosevelt gave his "speak softly and carry a big stick" speech, 1901. (See October 27th entry.)

Japanese forces formally surrendered to the Allies, 1945. (See August 14th entry.)

INTRODUCTIONS

The U.S. Treasury Department was established on this day in 1789. The Constitutional government had been operating for five months or so before the Treasury Department came into existence, which shows that our priorities have certainly changed since that day. Apparently, when this nation started, we were less convinced that money talks. In the beginning, of course, government was not big business; the income tax was more than a century away. People could, and many did, live off the land. The services provided by the government were minimal. But times have changed. The U.S. Treasury Department today, thanks to the Internal Revenue Service, has fingers in a lot of pies. As someone remarked, they have so many forms of taxes all over the world these days that they even tax your patience. That, indeed, is a tax on which the government has no monopoly. Today, however, I will defer to Uncle Sam. I am not here to tax your patience. I don't find my appearance before you taxing in the least. And I greatly appreciate the opportunity to share some deductible reasoning with you.

"Speak softly and carry a big stick." Vice President Theodore Roosevelt made that famous statement about his foreign relations policy on this day, in 1901, at a

Minnesota state fair. I guess it worked. Certainly when he became President the next year, he wasn't the last person in that office to softly warn an aggressor nation, and then send in the marines. But I didn't bring a stick tonight, so I hope you'll understand if I speak up.

SEPTEMBER 3

Henry Hudson discovered the island of Manhattan, 1609. (See June 22nd and August 3rd entries.)

Treaty of Paris ended the American Revolutionary War, 1783.

Louis Henry Sullivan was born, 1856.

The first municipal electric power station was built by Thomas Edison, 1882. (See September 30th entry.)

George Eastman patented his roll film camera and registered his Kodak name, 1888.

Britain and France entered the Second World War, 1939.

INTRODUCTIONS

According to history, sometime around this date in 1609, explorer Henry Hudson discovered Manhattan Island. One reason there is some uncertainty about the date is that when he first saw Manhattan, he really wasn't sure that it was an island. In that respect, Hudson was no different from many recent visitors. The only way to figure out how Manhattan works is to be there for awhile. The same thing is true of conclusions. The only way to reach them is to take one step at a time. That is what I propose to do here today. I'll give you my conclusion and you have every right to wonder how in the world I got there.

Today commemorates a sort of microcosm of extremes—an anniversary of one war's end and the start of another. On this day, in 1783, the American Revolution formally ended when Great Britain and the U.S. signed the Treaty of Paris. But in 1939, Great Britain and France declared the war against Germany. What this says to me is that life presents a constant stream of alternatives, but we aren't always in a position to make the choice for ourselves. Today I want to talk about alternatives—not absolutes like war or peace—that we may choose to accept or reject. After all, I had to choose what I would talk about today; so I think it is only fair to present you with some options as well.

In the past century or so, we have renovated the earth, the shape of the cities, and the whole concept of architecture. The man who influenced this facelift in the twentieth century was the architect Louis Henry Sullivan, who was born on this day in 1856 in Boston, Massachusetts. Sullivan built the prototype of the modern skyscraper back in 1890, in St. Louis, Missouri. He trained future modern designers like Frank Lloyd Wright; and pioneered the concept that a structure's form is dependent upon its function. It is appropriate on Louis Sullivan's birthday for us talk about the shape we are in as well as the shape of things to come. While I do not intend to cover all of that broad canvas, I at least hope to lay down a cornerstone.

Electrical lighting was on everyone's wish list after its inventor, Thomas Edison, introduced it to the world. To meet the demand in New York City, Edison built and put into operation the first municipal power station—the Pearl Street Station. It happened on this day in 1882. Hundreds of thousands of power stations have been built since then. Some run on conventional turbine engines, while others use water or nuclear energy to supply electricity. Now that everyone can access electricity to turn on lights, watch televisions, work on computers, and listen to me over this microphone, I certainly hope no one finds the "off" switch.

It is said that punning to an audience is like checking a lion's tonsils: It only hurts the first time. But you know how some things just seem to click? While I was preparing to speak today, I discovered that on this day in 1888, George Eastman patented his roll film camera and registered his Kodak name. In light of this picturesque historic moment, I won't overexpose you to what's framed up in my mind. I'll focus on flashing you a few verbal snapshots instead. Now, without further puns, I will develop the contents of my photographic memory. Oh yes, if you have any negative remarks, please feel free to slide them in afterwards when we rewind. And if you miss anything, don't worry, there will be prints available.

SEPTEMBER 4

The village of Los Angeles was founded, 1781.

11,000 Boy Scouts held their first parade, 1909.

The first transcontinental live television broadcast was aired, 1951.

INTRODUCTIONS

I want to start by wishing El Pueblo de Nuestra Senora de la Reina de los Angeles de Porcincula a happy birthday because it was founded on this day in 1781. I also want to thank whoever was responsible for shortening its name to Los Angeles.

Because of its spectacular growth in the twentieth century, we like to think of Los Angeles as a totally modern phenomenon born of the movie business—a lotus land described as "seventeen suburbs in search of a city" and "an asylum that's run by the inmates." But the fact is that for most Americans, Los Angeles—rightly or wrongly—symbolizes the good life. Los Angelenos have to work for a living just like the rest of us; and they worry about water and smog just like the rest of us. Nevertheless, we seem to need a symbol of the good life and we have one. I'd like to look at life in general and tell you what I find that really is good about it.

On this day in 1951, Americans on both coasts were able watch the same live television picture at the same time. The first nationwide broadcast featured President Truman's speech at the Japanese Peace Treaty Conference in San Francisco. I am happy to tell you that my speech today is on a far less weighty level—and, of course, presented to a distinctly more selective audience.

Scouting proudly salutes an important anniversary today. In 1909, the Boy Scouts held their first national parade at London's Crystal Palace. Less than two years after its conception, great Britain's Boy Scouts Organization was 11,000 members strong. Lord Robert Baden-Powell's Scouts participated in wholesome activities like water safety, camping, hiking, and wood crafting. According to its founder, scouting built strong bodies, keen minds, and sound character. In 1907, Baden-Powell had taken 20 boys from various backgrounds on a camping trip to Brownsea Island. That autumn, the first troops were formed. You can't keep a good idea down, especially when it incorporates ideals and values that both young and old can appreciate.

SEPTEMBER 5

The first Continental Congress convened, 1774.

INTRODUCTIONS

A cynic once remarked that when nobody talks it's a crisis and when everybody talks it's a Congress. Today marks the anniversary of a lot of serious talks—the start of the first Continental Congress. Most Americans know that the Second Continental Congress adopted the Declaration of Independence. But the first Continental Congress flowered on this day in 1774, and fathered the historic gathering that met the following year. If you search diligently enough, you can find something good and constructive every day of the year. Today is no exception. To those who say, "what's so good about today?" I'm happy like to reply— just listen.

SEPTEMBER 6

The first coeducational college opened in Oberlin, OH, 1837.

Jane Addams was born, 1860.

INTRODUCTIONS

The first full admission of women to an American college filled with men happened on this day. In 1837, Oberlin Collegiate Institute—now called Oberlin College—which is located in Oberlin, Ohio, became America's first coeducational institution of higher learning. Four women and thirty men began their studies together. It took a long time for other rights and privileges to be extended to the distaff side, but this was a notable beginning. And it makes a pleasant backdrop against which to speak about matters in which women and men have an absolutely equal stake and concern.

There used to be a saying that women's work was never done. Fortunately, a good deal of progress has been made by women who went beyond the limits of what used to be regarded as women's work. One pioneer was Jane Addams, who was born on this day in 1860 in Cedarville, Illinois. Addams devoted her life to making life better for others. She founded Chicago's Hull House; she was a women's rights leader; and she fought for world peace. In 1931, she and Columbia University's President, Nicholas Murray Butler, were jointly awarded the Nobel Peace Prize. Addams was the first American woman to receive that honor. Men have both wartime and peacetime heroes. With women—given their chance—peace has predominated. So, given the chance, I wish to say that whether or not my remarks prove to be educational, I am glad that the audience itself is coeducational.

SEPTEMBER 7

Great Britain's Queen Elizabeth I born, 1533. (See November 17th entry.)

James J. Corbett beat John L. Sullivan, 1892. (See September 1st entry.)

The Boulder Dam (Hoover Dam) went into operation, 1936.

INTRODUCTIONS

You may not know it, but England's Queen Elizabeth I was born on this day in 1533. During her reign William Shakespeare and others made the English language positively sing. Apparently this lyrical language was not lost on her. When Sir

Walter Raleigh wrote to her , "Fain would I climb, yet fear I to fall." Elizabeth replied, "If thy heart fails thee, climb not at all." Is that where we are today—with hearts that have failed us so we climb not at all? I doubt this greatly. I don't expect to be that eloquent today; but I have borrowed those words from the Queen as today's theme. Let me tell you why.

Electrical power is a prime necessity in this nation. It was the same back in 1930. Growing cities and settlements in the west needed electricity as much as their eastern counterparts. So to meet their demand, the government spent six years harnessing the power of the Colorado River as it rushed through the Black Canyon at the Arizona-Nevada border. In 1936, Boulder Dam—which was later renamed Hoover Dam—was completed and went into operation on this very day. Besides supplying the west with much-needed energy, the project that President Herbert Hoover had authorized created a new body of water. Lake Mead has been a cool, relaxing oasis for vacationers ever since. Progress seems to change the face of our environment. Now we've come to a point where we need to assess our past work before we forge further ahead.

SEPTEMBER 8

King Richard the Lion-Hearted was born, 1157. (See April 17th entry.)

The first permanent European settlement in North America was established, 1565.

INTRODUCTIONS

This is King Richard the Lion-Hearted's birthday. Born in Oxford, England in 1157, Richard spent most of his time outside of his kingdom, and didn't quite have a glittering historical record to match his reputation. Maybe some of his reputation rested on his fondness for troubadours and his talent for writing lyrics. Maybe the troubadours that spread his legend considered him to be one of their own. Possibly the moral of this story is that if you write your own legend maybe history will be good to you. I don't plan to sing for my supper today, but the words you are about to hear are mine—all mine. Somehow I doubt that entitles me to be remembered as lionhearted, but wait until you have heard the words. Then decide for yourself.

It was on this day that the first permanent European settlement in North America was established at St. Augustine, Florida in 1565. Spanish explorers had been landing in the New World for over five decades before this momentous event. But this day marked the first time settlers came to build homes in this unknown land. Pulling up roots and laying new foundations in strange territory takes a lot of courage. Fear of the unknown stops a lot of us from taking steps that could change our lives for the better. Let's take our inspiration from these courageous men and women who risked everything to find a new life, and begin exploring the frontiers that lie before us.

SEPTEMBER 9

William Bligh was born, 1754. (See April 28th entry.)

The United Colonies became the United States, 1776.

California became a state, 1850.

INTRODUCTIONS

This is California's birthday. Or more exactly, this is the anniversary of California's admission to the United States as the 31st state. Apart from anything else, this event was a great service to public speakers who can liberally indulge in that extra oratorical flourish of referring to a nation that spreads from coast to coast—from Maine's rocky coast to California's sunny shores. Gold had been discovered the year before California became a state, in 1850, and the rush continues today. I do not expect to strike gold in my remarks today. But I may strike a nerve or two. And now, as they say in California's most famous city, "roll 'em."

We generally observe the United States' birthday on the Fourth of July. But if you want to be technical, we didn't become the United States until this day. In 1776, the Continental Congress decided to change the name of the rebellious United Colonies to the United States. So today is indeed the United States' birthday—at least in name. Not every name for our nation requires an act of Congress. As a matter of fact, we don't know all of our names. People do talk behind our backs—as it were. Today I would like to talk face to face about some items that rarely make the news but are nevertheless things people are talking about. For example...

SEPTEMBER 10

The Scottish defeated the British at Sterling, 1297.

U.S. Naval Commodore Oliver Perry defeated the British, 1813.

The first coast-to-coast paved road in the U.S. opened, 1913.

Arnold Palmer was born, 1929.

INTRODUCTIONS

The Battle of Sterling took place on this day. In 1297, Scottish rebel forces, led by William Wallace and Andrew Murray, ambushed the Earl of Surrey's army on the bridge at Forth near Sterling. The Earl's 300 cavalrymen and 10,000 foot soldiers were quickly defeated by a handful of highlanders. The fight for a personal cause has spurred many people to victory despite the odds. Let me present a few more recent examples.

This may be hard to believe, but today, back in 1913, the first coast-to-coast paved U.S. road was unveiled. Up to that time, portions of our transcontinental highway were just dirt roads. This smooth throughway was named the Lincoln Highway. Of course, a paved highway made cross-country travel a great deal easier. Getting from one point to another is not always that easy for a speaker. The oratorical highway is often more like a backcountry road than a modern-day interstate. Both motorists and speakers have to be concerned that they don't use up too much gas along the way. Now that my engine is warmed up, let me shift into high gear, and proceed.

Not all great naval battles took place on the open seas. In fact, a critical U.S. naval battle occurred on a lake—the Battle of Lake Erie. On this day in 1813, Commodore Oliver Hazard Perry described his defeat of the British fleet in a succinct message that has been a model for clarity and brevity ever since. I have every intention of keeping it in mind as I address you here today. "We have met the enemy," Perry said, "and they are ours." Now I don't plan to be quite that brief, but I will try.

Today is Arnold Palmer's birthday. Born in 1929, this great golfer who hails from Youngstown, Pennsylvania, is known for his playing efficiency and style. Those talents won him a regiment of admirers—Arnie's Army. In speaking to you here today, I plan to emulate Arnold Palmer's classic method—to tee off properly, aim true, and finish with as few strokes as are necessary to do the job.

S EPTEMBER 11

Benjamin Franklin wrote about the Treaty of Paris, 1783.

O. Henry was born, 1862.

D.H. Lawrence was born, 1885.

INTRODUCTIONS

William Sydney Porter was born on this day in 1862, in Greensboro, North Carolina. Under his pen name—O. Henry—this American writer narrated unforgettable stories about Manhattan life. He also wrote equally unforgettable short stories about cowboys and about Latin America. But his most famous setting was the city that he called "Baghdad on the subway." O. Henry was a master manipulator of trick endings and surprising twists. It's a great temptation for a speaker to use the same trick on his audience. You'll have to wait until the end to see whether I would do that to you.

Benjamin Franklin was 77 years old when—with John Adams and John Jay—he negotiated a peace settlement with Great Britain in Paris France. On this date in 1783, shortly after the Treaty of Paris was signed, Franklin wrote to a friend that, "There never was a good war or a bad peace." He didn't waste words. I shall try to follow his example here today and not take too much of your time. After all, as Franklin observed, time is money.

Lady Chatterley's Lover—for those of you who might be unfamiliar with the title—is a classic romantic tale that was banned for decades due to its graphic content. Today is its author's birthday. D.H. Lawrence, who also wrote *Women in Love,* was born on this day in 1885. While my own remarks today might raise a few eyebrows, I hope that rather than censoring me, you will look past that to the message.

SEPTEMBER 12

The Black Crook premiered in New York City, 1866.

Nikita Khrushchev became Soviet Russia's Premier, 1953. (See April 17th and October 30th entries.)

H.L. Mencken was born, 1880. (See December 28th entry.)

Jesse Owens was born, 1913. (See August 9th entry.)

INTRODUCTIONS

This was the day, in 1866, when a new form of American entertainment premiered in New York City. The show was entitled *The Black Crook.* It was the first American presentation to feature beautiful showgirls. The idea spread like wildfire after that. There has been a tendency ever since to bring on the dancing girls, so to speak, as attractive window dressing to help sell a concept. You can see I am no dancing girl nor do I have any waiting in the wings. I hope that you will find what I have to say worth the price of admission on its own merits.

Back in 1953, this was the day when Nikita Khrushchev became the First Secretary of the U.S.S.R.'s Communist Party, a position which automatically brought him front and center. Khrushchev loved to talk, and in one of his famous public appearances, he brought a new technique to the public forum when he pounded his shoe on the table to add emphasis to a point in the course of a United Nations discussion. I trust there are no Khrushchevs in the audience here today. For my part, I plan to rely on the tongue in my mouth and not the one in my footwear.

On December 28, 1917, the long-defunct *New York Evening Mail* ran an article purporting to give the history of the bathtub. It was an obvious spoof. It discussed the invention of the bathtub at length, alleging that the tub was invented in Cincinnati in the 1840s, that Millard Fillmore had been the first president to take a bath in the White House, and an entire litany of other absurdities. The trouble was, the article's author, H.L. Mencken, had written the article so convincingly that even after he printed an explanation of the hoax, his article continued to be quoted by medical men, professional journals and societies as a factual study on the advancement of personal hygiene. Bits and pieces of the myth he created still exist as fact and custom. I mention this, not because I emulated Mencken while preparing my notes for today, but because today is the anniversary of his birth, in 1880. I may not be as persuasive as he was in that article, but I can assure you from the outset, that everything I'm about to say is true.

SEPTEMBER 13

The Battle of Quebec took place, 1759.

First U.S. national election was authorized, 1788.

Yitzhak Rabin of Israel and Yasser Arafat, PLO chairman, signed the Middle East peace accord, 1993.

INTRODUCTIONS

The Battle of Quebec marks the day when General Wolfe defeated General Montcalm. On this day in 1759, this battle between British and French forces became a turning point in Canadian history. I mention this battle here today not so much for its tremendous historical importance but because in the end, both leaders were killed. That is not the normal course of events for a military encounter. We have always had some leaders who lead the way and others who simply point the way. The same is true of speakers. We have a choice. We can stand up and say "this is the cause, follow me;" or we can far more easily say, "this is the situation, now what do we do about it?" One need not have the answers to sound the alarm or raise the question. So I am emboldened to speak to you today without necessarily having any solutions or panaceas.

When the U.S. Congress, on this day in 1788, decided that the first national election would take place on the first Wednesday in January, 1789, they were mindful that many people would want to make speeches. So they gave them plenty of time. In all the intervening years, we haven't done very much to render speechmaking any less long-winded. Even today, when someone is invited to speak, the first question he or she asks is, "how long shall I talk?" I wonder why no one ever asks how short the talk should be. Since so many speeches are delivered to captive audiences, I regard a long speech as cruel and unusual punishment. Being humane, I shall not inflict such punishment upon you here today.

Today marks the anniversary of an historic meeting between Israeli Prime Minister Yitzak Rabin and PLO chairman Yasser Arafat. In 1993, these two leaders, whose peoples had been at war for nearly half a century, met in Washington, D.C., signed a peace accord and shook hands. It took a remarkable diplomatic effort on both sides, as well as the United States, to bring the two together. Since that time there has still been terrorist violence between the two countries; Yitzak Rabin was killed by one of his own people who disagreed with the peace effort; and things haven't changed that much. But no effort toward peace—which generally implies a cessation of the killing of soldiers and other innocents—is unimportant. Changing societies may take generations, but every moment made toward the goal of change is another building block in its solid foundation.

SEPTEMBER 14

George Friedrich Handel completed *Messiah,* 1741. (See August 22nd entry.)
Francis Scott Key wrote "The Star Spangled Banner," 1814.
Ivan Pavlov was born, 1849.
Margaret Sanger was born, 1883.

INTRODUCTIONS

Very early in the morning on this day in 1814 at Baltimore Harbor, Francis Scott Key wrote the words to a song as he watched and waited to see whether the American flag was still flying—a signal that the United States had turned away the British invaders in the War of 1812. "Oh say can you see, by the dawn's early light," Francis Scott Key wrote, asking whether the flag was still there. When those lines were written, the British had burned government buildings and the White House in our nation's capital. If they had succeeded in taking Baltimore, it would have been the end. Francis Scott Key wrote of the rockets' red glare and bombs bursting in air. We have learned how to make more powerful weapons. But I like to think that we have also improved the way we communicate with each other. It is in that spirit that I want to discuss a few current aspects of "the land of the free and the home of the brave."

The German composer George Friedrich Handel had held his "farewell concert" in the spring of 1741. But somehow, toward the end of summer he was inspired to write another work. Many consider it to be his greatest achievement. He started writing on August 22nd, and finished on this day. Handel's *Messiah* wasn't given its first performance until the next spring, but I assure you that I won't wait as long to perform the speech that I spent as many days preparing. Plus, it's a lot shorter than his masterpiece. We can all sing a "Hallelujah Chorus" for that.

Many reactions are the result of what we call conditioned reflexes. Some people's hearts beat faster when the flag goes marching by. Some people get hungry when they hear the dinner bell ring. Some products have a particular odor deliberately applied to trigger a craving or an appreciation. The scientist who pioneered the study of conditioned reflexes was Ivan Pavlov, born on this day in 1849 in Ryazan, Russia. Pavlov showed the world how a dog could be trained to react one way or another to two distinctly different styles with which he rang a bell. There are those of us who immediately fall asleep when a preacher begins his sermon. Public speakers sometimes clear their throats because—as Winston Churchill once admitted—this form of habitual pause gives one time to collect and organize one's thoughts. But the most dangerous conditioned reflex of all is to close our minds to what we do not wish to hear; or to close our mouths when it would be better to speak. I will make a deal with you. I will open my mouth and talk if you will open your minds and listen.

Margaret Higgins Sanger, who was born on this day in 1883, was trained as a nurse. But she devoted her life to birth control, until her death in 1966. When Sanger began championing her cause, birth control was a dirty word. Contraceptive information was classified as obscene and censored by the post office. She was arrested on obscenity charges—although the case never went to trial. The dispute continued even after her death, but at least the issue was discussed with a freedom that had been previously denied. Thanks to Sanger's single-minded efforts, people can speak more freely today about birth control. The most important testimonial to Ms. Sanger is that she helped to make freedom of speech a reality. I do not plan to test the limits of free speech today. But it is nice to know you and I can speak and listen without being sent to jail.

SEPTEMBER 15

William Howard Taft was born, 1867.
Agatha Christie was born, 1890. (See November 25th entry.)

Russia was proclaimed a republic by Alexander Kerensky, 1917. (See April 22nd and November 7th entries.)

INTRODUCTIONS

Not too many people in U.S. history have been chosen to serve as President and as Chief Justice. William Howard Taft—who was born on this day in 1857, in Cincinnati—was President for four years and Chief Justice of the United States for nine years. He also headed a distinguished Ohio political family. I thought it might be appropriate to start off my modest set of remarks with a quote from Taft, but when I paged through the quotation anthologies, I discovered that William Howard Taft had another distinction. He wasn't in most of them. In fact, most of his printed quotes were judicial decisions. You are being spared from that, and instead I shall present a subject that obviously has arisen since Taft's days. At the risk of a bad pun, let me say that my speech is without president.

One of the world's greatest mystery writers was born on this day in 1890. Agatha Christie was educated at home by her mother and spent her childhood growing up in the Derbyshire countryside. She began writing detective stories while working as a nurse during the First World War. She continued honing her craft after the war as her first—and short-lived—marriage disintegrated. In 1920, she introduced the world to the Belgian detective Hercule Poirot in *The Mysterious Affair at Styles*. Later, her loyal fans were treated to the exploits of Miss Marple. It's certainly no mystery why her books sold over 100 million copies in numerous languages. And it is beyond a shadow of a doubt that you haven't got a clue as to what I'm about to tell you.

Alexander Kerensky was an idealistic attorney in Czarist Russia who frequently defended revolutionary intellectuals accused of political offenses. He entered politics and championed concepts like freedom of speech, freedom of the press, the right of assembly, freedom to worship, universal suffrage, and equal rights for women. But unlike some of his clients and political peers, Kerensky supported Russian involvement in the First World War. In 1917, Kerensky urged the dissolution of the monarchy during the February Revolution. And on this day in 1917, Russia was proclaimed a republic by Alexander Kerensky after Czar Nicholas II abdicated his throne. Kerensky's dream came true—but it was short-lived. He was ousted during the October Revolution and Vladimir Lenin took his place as the voice of the people. The public often cheers great ideas, but the voice of the people can be a fickle one. It's a lesson every public speaker must remember while standing at the podium. You never can tell when an audience will send you into exile.

SEPTEMBER 16

The settlement of Shawmut was renamed Boston, 1630.

Esperanto was first taught at a college, 1908.

Two dozen nations signed the Montreal Protocol, 1987.

INTRODUCTIONS

Many immigrants to the United States have chosen new names. On this day in 1630, a community of new arrivals did just that. The Massachusetts settlement of Shawmut changed its name to Boston, in honor of a British town. I wonder whether the language or the history of America would have been the same if Boston had remained Shawmut. Would we be remembering the Shawmut Massacre or the Shawmut Tea Party? Would Shawmut baked beans taste as sweet? Names—like other words—create mental images and impressions. I hope my words here today can be as successful in conveying a message and an impression as the imprint of Boston on the American conscience. It's a difficult act to follow.

Many years ago, a language called Esperanto was devised to enable people worldwide to speak to each other. On this day in 1908, Clark University—located in Worcester, Massachusetts—initiated a course in the universal language of Esperanto. I don't know how long the course remained in the Clark curriculum. But Esperanto—though still alive—was not as widely accepted as its sponsors had hoped. English and French are common diplomatic languages. Besides, it's hard enough to communicate in one's own language, as we all know. Let me say that in any language I am happy to be here.

On this day in 1987, two dozen nations signed the Montreal Protocol, designed to save the earth's ozone layer by urging nations to curb harmful emissions. Our atmosphere is a precious and finite commodity. These delegates did their part by enacting these measures. Now, for my personal contribution I will try to clear the air while employing a minimum of gas. Plus, you'll be happy to know that most speakers are wind-powered anyway.

SEPTEMBER 17

George Washington gave his farewell speech, 1796.

INTRODUCTIONS

Having lived through a number of presidential farewell addresses, I always find it difficult to understand one thing about George Washington's parting speech. The content is no problem. The puzzle is that he dated it September 17th, but never delivered it. Instead he published it on September 19th, in 1796. So maybe today is its anniversary—and maybe not. But since we know that Washington never told a lie, I assume it was on this day that he said, "Citizens by birth or choice of a common country, that country has a right to concentrate your affections." We are indeed citizens by birth or choice of a common country, and it is that community of interest that is the basis of my remarks here today.

SEPTEMBER 18

Samuel Johnson was born, 1709.

George Washington laid the Capitol Building's cornerstone, 1793.

The New York Times published its first issue, 1851.

Greta Garbo was born, 1905.

The Air Force was established as a separate branch of the military, 1947.

Ted Turner won the America's Cup in his yacht *Courageous,* 1977. (See August 22nd entry.)

George Meegan finished a 6-year walk, 1983.

INTRODUCTIONS

This is the anniversary of a very solemn and important event in our nation's history. In 1793, President George Washington placed the cornerstone on the Capitol Building in Washington, D.C. Unfortunately, the history book that I consulted did not document what the President said on that momentous occasion, so I can only assume that he expressed pleasure at being present at the ceremony; and complimented the assorted dignitaries in the audience. And so, as George Washington may have said...

British author Samuel Johnson—whose birthday we don't seem to be celebrating here today—was nevertheless born on this day in 1709. I mention this because one of Dr. Johnson's quotations preys on my mind when I speak in public. Johnson once criticized the poet Dryden by saying: "He delighted to tread upon the brink of meaning." I hope today to make my meaning—and the reasons for it—both on the cutting edge and crystal clear.

Greta Garbo was born on this date in 1905, in Stockholm, Sweden. Apart from her impressive screen performances, she was also famous for her constant search for solitude. "I want to be let alone," were supposedly Garbo's watchwords. I have always found that difficult to understand because, frankly, the opportunity not to be alone—the chance to be here addressing a warm and friendly audience—seems to me to be something special. I thank you in advance for your kind attention.

In the words of the motto of *The New York Times,* which published its first issue on this day in 1851, I am about to deliver "all the news that's fit to print."

As a popular song commented, walk a mile in my shoes. But on this day in 1983, a British adventurer named George Meegan finished a 19,021-mile walk from the southernmost tip of South America to Prudhoe Bay, Alaska. It took him six years to reach his goal. I am certainly not going to walk in his shoes to deliver my speech. At this rate, I'll be lucky if I can run the 10-minute mile.

The Air Force joined the ranks of the Armed Forces on this day in 1947. Previously a division of the Army, air combat had played such a major role in the Second World War, it was decided that the time had come to recognize the importance of our defense strength in the skies above. In honor of this event, I have selected a topic out of the blue, and would like to chart a course with some twists and turns, and possibly a loop or two. Today is a day to reach great heights and finish with a smooth landing.

SEPTEMBER 19

Washington's farewell address was printed, 1796. (See September 17th entry.)

Mickey Mouse made his debut, 1928.

Great Britain and China announced their agreement to transfer Hong Kong in 1997 to Chinese rule, 1984. (See December 19th entry.)

INTRODUCTIONS

I suppose that one of the most well-known characters of our time is Mickey Mouse. Well, today is his birthday. He was born in the 1928 animated cartoon "Steamboat Willie" which premiered on this date. Mickey was the first Disney character to speak in a distinctive voice—although not nearly as distinctive as his later sidekick, the irascible Donald Duck. Today I find myself wondering how the Disney studios got Mickey to laugh and got Donald to babble. But let me state my case, and then you can cast the roles for yourself.

SEPTEMBER 20

President Harry S. Truman asked Secretary of Commerce Henry A. Wallace to resign, 1946.

Billie Jean King beat Bobby Riggs, 1973.

INTRODUCTIONS

Back in 1973, this was expected to be a very exciting day. Veteran tennis star Bobby Riggs was scheduled to play the outstanding woman player, Billie Jean King. It was touted as the battle of the sexes. Naturally, what the match proved was that a great young female champion could beat a once-great, over-the-hill male champion. That is rather like the less-than-profound truths that we hear from some public speakers. Today—to the best of my ability—I hope that the only deuce I raise is vocal. I will try to serve up a few winners in the process. Today, speaking is my racket.

In 1946, Secretary of Commerce Henry A. Wallace delivered an address on September 12th in which he strongly criticized America's policy toward Russia. Eight days later, on this date, President Harry S. Truman reacted. He asked Mr. Wallace to resign. I am quite mindful that what I say here today may be held against me. I am also hopeful that what I say may meet with your approval. I guess the only way to find out is to begin.

SEPTEMBER 21

The invernal equinox generally occurs.

H.G. Wells was born, 1866.

The editorial entitled "Yes, Virginia, there is a Santa Claus," was published,1897.

INTRODUCTIONS

Although the invernal equinox sometimes plays games with the calendar and autumn sneaks in a day late or a day early, this is the usual day for welcoming the new season. Autumn, as you know, is apt to bring big winds, and I hope that wasn't why I was asked here today. If that were the case, I would find it a painful blow. So let me abandon that line of dubious speculation and say what I came here to say.

In 1897, an editorial was published in *The New York Sun* newspaper on this day entitled, "Yes, Virginia, there is a Santa Claus." It was a little early for Christmas, but it is never too early to keep a pleasant thought alive. I am not here today to reaffirm the positive existence of good old Saint Nick, but there are some other jolly thoughts I would like to share with you.

One man is largely responsible for a Martian invasion, invisibility, and time travel. Science fiction writer H.G. Wells was born on this day in 1866, in Bromley, England. His works have thrilled generations of readers. Perhaps little that took place in *The War of the Worlds, The Invisible Man,* or *The Time Machine* will ever take place in real life, but his writings did contain elements of the Internet and other predictions which have subsequently come true. But that is not what I've come here to discuss today. I have another purpose. To quote Wells' time traveller, "You must follow me carefully. I shall have to controvert one or two ideas that are almost universally accepted."

SEPTEMBER 22

Nathan Hale was hung, 1776. (See June 6th entry.)

The U.S. Post Office was established, 1789.

The world's fastest train took its inaugural run, 1981.

INTRODUCTIONS

The U.S. Post Office was established on this day in 1789. I was tempted to refer to it as a red-letter day, but I will refrain. Delivering the mail in those years was an arduous and uncertain task. I guess this illustrates that not every problem is a brand new one. In fact, as we computerize communications, we seem to have just as much trouble getting messages across on the Internet as our forefathers did with horse-driven technology. Somebody once defined progress as finding new ways to mess things up faster. That is a dismal view which I am prepared to challenge here today. To me, progress is the development of options. And I think we have options. Let me elaborate.

The world's fastest train took its inaugural run from Paris to Lyons, France at 156 mph for 300 miles on this day in 1981. Though I promise not to speak at a comparable speed, I shall endeavor to honor that historic moment by keeping my thoughts on track and reaching my conclusion as quickly as possible.

SEPTEMBER 23

The Royal College of Physicians was established, 1518.

Harvard University held its first commencement, 1642.

John Paul Jones uttered his famous battle cry, 1779. (See July 6th entry.)

Neptune was discovered by German astronomer Johann Gottfried Galle, 1846.

INTRODUCTIONS

During the reign of Great Britain's King Henry VIII, the craft guilds were in flower. Each profession had its own local union, where apprentices learned their craft, journeymen refined their technique, and master craftsmen handed down their skills. From bootmakers to printers, every craft was protected by a chartered guild. In 1518, Henry VIII granted Thomas Linacre a guild charter to establish a guild of craftsman trained in the diagnosis and treatment of disease. The Royal College of Physicians was established to protect citizens from medical charlatans and quacks who often applied cures that were more fatal than the disease being treated. Barbers and surgeons soon followed, creating their own guild. But that's another story. The diagnosis and treatment of disease has become more than a time-honored profession, and a lifesaver—literally. It's big business. But the question remains: at whose expense?

The first American college commencement took place on this day in 1642. It wasn't the same kind of convocation ceremony that we are partial to these days. But for the new graduates of Harvard College, it was a great event. Whether the event was highlighted by a brilliant keynote address I do not know. Whether our events here today will be highlighted by a glowing address is highly doubtful—since I'm your speaker. But, like most commencement remarks, I hope mine will send you away happy.

It's amazing what you can do when you set your sights on the stars. On this day in 1846, German astronomer Johann Gottfried Galle discovered the planet Neptune. Perhaps there are no more planets left to discover. I say perhaps, because no one will know until another one is discovered. There's a lesson in that thought that goes far beyond astronomy, and into every facet of life. Life is discovery and exploration. While I don't have a planet to add to the world's sky charts, I'd like to advance a few thoughts about a recent discovery that might encourage you to do some exploration of your own.

SEPTEMBER 24

John Marshall was born, 1755.

The Chicago Seven trial began, 1969. (See August 28th entry.)

INTRODUCTIONS

This is Chief Justice John Marshall's birthday. He was born in Midland, Virginia, on this day in 1755. "The people made the Constitution," Justice Marshall said in an 1821 decision, "and the people can unmake it. It is the creature of their own will, and lives only by their will." I quote Chief Justice Marshall in salute to the will of the people. The opposite of people's will—as far as I am concerned—is the won't of the people. I am here today to discuss both.

It was more than a year after antiwar demonstrations erupted into a riot during the 1968 Democratic National Convention, that the demonstration leaders—the Chicago Seven—went on trial. On this day in 1969, attorney William Kunstler began his opening remarks. About the only thing the trial seemed to prove was that the human tongue can be a blunt instrument. I have made a conscientious effort to make mine smooth around the edges today.

SEPTEMBER 25

Vasco Nuñez de Balboa discovered the Pacific Ocean, 1513.

First American newspaper was published, 1690.

Bill of Rights was submitted to the states, 1789.

The U.S. Congress established Yosemite National Park, 1890. (See April 21st entry.)

The Ford Motor Company instituted an 8-hour, 5-day work week, 1912.

Sandra Day O'Connor became the first female Supreme Court Justice, 1981.

INTRODUCTIONS

The Bill of Rights, which guarantees so many of our basic freedoms wasn't in the Constitution when the first Congress met, so the Congress did something about it. On this day in 1789, Congress sent each state twelve proposed Amendments to the Constitution. Ten of those amendments, constituting the Bill of Rights, were ratified. It is thanks to the Bill of Rights that we can assemble here, and that I can say what I choose from this rostrum. Now all I have to do is to remember what I came here to say.

The first American newspaper was a rather modest three-page publication entitled *Publick Occurrences, Both Foreign and Domestic,* which was published on this day in 1690 in Boston. It was never published again, because the Massachusetts Governor didn't like it. In those days what the Governor didn't like was neither published nor speechified. I am happy, therefore, to be making this speech here and now rather than in the good old days. I hope you like it, but in any case, I'm glad to know that neither you, nor I, nor my remarks are in danger of being suppressed. Indeed, the reverse is true. Today, you have to wonder if and how what you say will be reported in the press. Since there is only one way to find out, here goes.

Back in 1513, Spanish explorer Vasco Nuñez de Balboa and his crew were tracking through the thick hot jungle environment of the Isthmus of Panama. Like his predecessors, Balboa was searching for a passage to Asia and the riches of the New World. However, on this particular day, Balboa discovered a seemingly placid body of water. He stood in the shallows on the beach and, on behalf of the king, claimed the Pacific—meaning calm and quiet—Ocean for Spain. We now know that this vast, roaring ocean is anything but a calm or quiet segment of the world. But today, amid this pacific setting, I hope that for a few moments I can offer you tranquil seas and a calming wind.

Besides a being a transportation pioneer, Henry Ford proved to be an innovator in business management as well. He adapted some of Eli Whitney's production concepts, like the assembly line and interchangeable parts. But on this day in 1912, Ford's motor company instituted something we can all appreciate—an 8-hour, 5-day work week. Cutting the work week nearly in half is certainly my idea of progress. Now let's see if I can cut the time for my speech just as easily.

A long-standing injustice came to an end on this date in 1981. Sandra Day O'Connor became the first female U.S. Supreme Court justice on this day in 1981. If there is one point she has demonstrated since that time, it is that gender plays no role in the process of justice. As far as what is worn under the robes, justice can be blind. Given an equal chance, that same point could be proven by women in many other professions. But society, like the wheels of justice, grinds exceedingly slow. But the wheels do grind, and it's that daily grind I'd like to talk about.

SEPTEMBER 26

Johnny Appleseed was born, 1774.

The Act of the Holy Alliance was signed, 1815.

George Gershwin was born, 1898.

President Woodrow Wilson collapsed, 1919. (See December 28th entry.)

The first Nixon-Kennedy debate was televised, 1960.

INTRODUCTIONS

This was a very big day for the spoken word, back in 1960. The first televised Presidential debates were aired nationwide. John F. Kennedy and Richard M. Nixon started a trend in national election campaigns with their televised, face-to-face confrontation. The power of words and their delivery—not to mention a close shave—were never more dramatically illustrated. Perhaps that is a good omen for my remarks here today. At any rate, I am grateful to you for providing a podium but omitting an opponent. It's much better being able to pontificate without having to compete.

Anyone who rises to make a public speech on this day would do well to take it easy—as I plan to do in my remarks here. In 1919, on this day, President Woodrow Wilson collapsed. He had been on the road conducting a 40-date speaking tour. His mission was to garner the nation's support for the Treaty of Versailles. It's also a reminder that speaking can sometimes be more of a strain on the speaker than it is on the listener. So today I will try to be easy on you—with very selfish motives.

In the name of Christianity, many politically directed activities have taken shape. The Crusades, the Spanish conquest of the Americas, and the European Inquisitions are just a few of those deeds. On this day in 1815, the Act of the Holy Alliance was signed by the Czar of Russia, the Emperor of Austro-Hungary, and the King of Prussia. The agreement stated that: "They will consider themselves as members of one and the same Christian nation." Gradually other Christian monarchs through-out Europe signed the act with the exception of two key figures: Great Britain's king and the pope himself. Church and state have often crossed their intentions in the annals of history. Isn't it time for us to clearly define each other's goals and, as the Bible said, "Render unto Caesar that which is Caesar's?"

When Jacob Gershowitz's parents bought a piano for his brother Ira, they quickly discovered that Jacob had a remarkable talent: he could listen to a song, then sit down in front of the keys and tentatively play it. Encouraged by his parents, he took lessons. Born on this day in 1898, Jacob Gershowitz found a career in music under the name George Gershwin, and went on to write such masterpieces as *Rhapsody in Blue, An American in Paris,* and *Porgy and Bess*—an opera which was highly controversial when it opened, as it dealt with the issue of black poverty in the South. Though he passed away in 1937, his music lives on. Isn't it amazing what a little encouragement can do?

Today marks the birth, in 1774, of a simple American icon. According to popular legend, John Chapman—better known as Johnny Appleseed—slung a sack of apple seeds over his shoulder and set out from his home in New York State. He headed for the frontier, planting trees which would not bear fruit for his consumption, but for anyone who might happen upon them in the future. Chapman gave saplings to the natives and new settlers. In addition to the apple trees and a coterie of medicinal herbs, he planted seeds of a different sort. He would sit under the shade of one of his trees, and invite passersby to join him while he read passages from the Bible and other books. As I speak to you today, I'd like to think I'm following in his footsteps. I didn't bring any seeds, but instead I'd like to sow a few thoughts in the hope that they too might take root, and grow to bear fruit sometime in the future.

SEPTEMBER 27

Samuel Adams was born, 1722.

The first locomotive to haul a passenger train was operated by George Stephenson in England, 1825.

Thomas Nast was born, 1840. (See November 7th entry.)

INTRODUCTIONS

I'll have you know it's Samuel Adams' birthday. He was a firebrand in his time: the leader of the Stamp Act resistance and a prime instigator of the Boston Tea Party. John Adams' second cousin from Boston was born in 1722. And one thing is certain. When Sam Adams spoke, things happened. This can be very encouraging to some speakers and very frightening to others. I prefer to steer a middle course. I'm certainly hoping that what I say here will have some influence and will prove to be right. I will definitely bear in mind Sam Adams' injunction: "Let us contemplate our forefathers, and posterity, and resolve to maintain the rights bequeathed to us from the former, for the sake of the latter."

Every time you see the Democratic donkey or the Republican elephant, you are viewing the inspiration of the great political cartoonist, Thomas Nast, who flourished at the turn of the century. This was the day Thomas Nast was born, in 1840, in Germany. His family emigrated to America when he was six years old. Nast's creations—like The Tammany Tiger and Boss Tweed cartoons—did a great deal to harden public opinion against the corrupt Tammany Ring that controlled New York City politics in the late nineteenth century. Nast knew the power of images. Today, I have to paint my pictures with words; but word pictures can tell a story, too. And there are some stories that need telling today.

When, on this day in 1825, the first locomotive to haul a passenger train was operated by George Stephenson in England, there was more than passengers and cargo on board. The industrial future was there—perched atop the billowing stack—never once looking back at the agrarian past which was quickly enveloped by the thick coal smoke. The past may have been the good or bad old days, but one thing's certain, there's no going back. We cannot live in the past, but we can learn from it, and a number of lessons are particularly important today.

SEPTEMBER 28

Friedrich Engels was born, 1820.

INTRODUCTION

The reason why Karl Marx's name is known everywhere is largely because of a man who is relatively unknown. Friedrich Engels coauthored the *Communist Manifesto* with Marx, and edited a considerable portion of Marx's writings. This German author was born on this day back in 1820. I think that makes it appropriate for me to point out that very few people work alone. Most of life is actually a collaboration. Today, I want to enlist all of you to collaborate on a project. Not for the writing of a manifesto or the organization of a new "ism," but to do something good that needs doing.

SEPTEMBER 29

U.S. Navy Admiral George Dewey received a hero's welcome in New York, 1899.

Great Britain began ruling Palestine under a League of Nations mandate, 1923. (See June 29th and August 31st entries.)

The Munich Agreement was signed, 1938.

INTRODUCTIONS

This was a very festive day in 1899. New York City gave a hero's welcome to Admiral George Dewey on his return from the Spanish-American War. Dewey became famous for his historic naval victory at Manila Bay. He also became famous for saying to his flagship's captain, "You may fire when you are ready, Gridley." Nothing Dewey said later ever dimmed the flame of that one short sentence. I plan to keep my sentences short today. But I don't expect the kind of results that Admiral Dewey got. It's my modest hope that when I am done, none of you will be tempted to fire when ready.

Four men met in Munich, Germany, on this day in 1938: British Prime Minister Chamberlain, French Premier Daladier, Italian Premier Mussolini and German Reichfuehrer Hitler. They negotiated and agreed to the partitioning of Czechoslovakia. Neville Chamberlain announced it was the beginning of "peace in our time." That peace—and Chamberlain's job—lasted less than a year. I hope that today will prove somewhat more constructive or, at the very least, a lot less damaging. With that modest goal, let me proceed.

SEPTEMBER 30

Ether was first used as an anesthetic, 1846.

The first American hydroelectric plant opened in Appleton Wisconsin, 1882. (See September 3rd entry.)

Porgy and Bess premiered in Boston, 1935.

INTRODUCTIONS

Although ether was introduced as an anesthetic on this day in 1846 by dentist William Morton, it has never seemed to be as widely effective as that particular soporific—a long, dull speech. I am, therefore, very mindful of my obligation not to intrude on ether's territory. In other words, no boring sermon today, folks.

The easiest way to avoid becoming a bore is to startle people by challenging some of their favorite assumptions. Indeed, one of the big hits in the musical *Porgy and Bess*—which premiered in Boston on this day in 1935—was a song entitled "It Ain't Necessarily So." A lot of things we assume fall in that category. They "ain't necessarily so." And what ain't necessarily so is exactly what I propose to talk about now.

OCTOBER

INTRODUCTION:

Right between the lazy days of summer and the chilly days of autumn, there's a time when the days are sunny and warm, but the nights are crisp and cool. It's called Indian Summer. Summer's green leaves begin to change their hue to yellow, orange, and burnt red; pumpkins and maize ripen in the fields. I don't know who coined the term Indian Summer, but I'm glad they did. The name also serves to remind us of the days when Native Americans harvested nature's bountiful array of nuts, fruits, and vegetables; fished its clear running rivers for salmon and trout; hunted the herds of wild buffalo; and stalked the mountains for bear, moose, and deer. Nature had blessed these people with everything they needed just before the winter snows began to fall—in Indian Summer. And the people respected and nurtured nature's gifts throughout the year in return. During this month of October, we should give thanks for the natural beauty and bounty that surrounds us as our predecessors did, and pray that there will always be an Indian Summer.

OCTOBER 1

Henry Ford introduced the Model T, 1908. (See July 30th entry.)
The Lost Battalion was trapped in the Argonne Forest, 1918.
Winston Churchill made a mysterious forecast, 1939.

INTRODUCTIONS

There was a famous American First World War fighting unit known as the Lost Battalion. It earned its name when trapped in the Argonne Forest of France—surrounded by the Germans—on this day in 1918. The unit members held out against unbelievable odds until they were rescued on October 8th. So here I am at the podium—a standing target—on the Lost Battalion's anniversary. Let me tell you right now that I intend to speak my way out. And I can assure you my battle plan does not include waiting a week to be rescued. Since I feel surrounded by friends rather than enemies, I thank you for your kind attention. And now to business.

On this day in 1908, Henry Ford introduced the Model T automobile, known affectionately as the Tin Lizzie. Model T manufacture employed assembly lines, interchangeable parts, and mass production—unlike its custom-built European counterparts such as the Mercedes and the Bugatti. I want you to know I didn't use Ford's assembly line mentality to prepare today's remarks. There is a Model T type of speech, but it takes an awfully long time to crank it up and it doesn't go very far or very fast these days. So we will leave the Model T's birthday saluted and undisturbed today.

History records that on this date in 1939, Winston Churchill said, "I cannot forecast to you the action of Russia. It is a riddle wrapped in a mystery inside an enigma." A riddle wrapped in a mystery inside an enigma. You can apply that description to a few of today's situations. In fact, a speaker sometimes looks out on an audience and finds a riddle wrapped in a mystery inside an enigma. So, I prefer not to regard myself as a super sleuth. I don't set myself up to tell you things you never knew 'til now. Instead, I propose to express some opinions, state some facts, maybe point out some conclusions—but I will leave others to solving riddles.

OCTOBER 2

Mohandas K. "Mahatma" Gandhi was born, 1869.

Groucho Marx was born, 1890.

INTRODUCTIONS

Mohandas K. Gandhi was the great modern apostle of nonviolent civil disobedience. The Mahatma used those tactics to gain respect for East Indians living in South Africa. He used the same strategy to lead his native India to independence from British rule. Gandhi was born on this day in 1869. In a strange twist of fate, he himself met a violent death, in New Delhi, in 1948. But Mahatma Gandhi taught the world that if you speak peacefully and make sense, people will listen and will act on what you say. I plan to speak very peacefully here today, and I hope to make sense. Beyond that, you are on your own.

Groucho Marx was legendary for his wit. Like other famous actors, Groucho listed different years for his birth at different times in his life. We are certain that he was born in Manhattan on this day, but we're not to sure if it was in 1890, 1891, 1889, never mind. It was Groucho who said once that he would never join any club that would accept him as a member. I've known speakers who had a similar attitude. They're not interested in speaking to an audience that's willing to listen. I have a higher opinion of audiences in general. The truth is I'm really impressed with your choice of speaker today. As a matter of fact, I can hardly wait to hear me.

O C T O B E R 3

Thanksgiving Day proclamations were made, 1789 and 1863.

Johns Hopkins University opened, 1876.

Gore Vidal was born, 1925.

INTRODUCTIONS

It's a little early for Thanksgiving, but this day has a very clear connection with that occasion. In 1789, President George Washington proclaimed the first national Thanksgiving Day. It was to be observed on November 26th in honor of the adoption of the U.S. Constitution. On the same day in 1863, President Abraham Lincoln designated the last Thursday in November as Thanksgiving Day. If Washington and Lincoln considered this to be an auspicious day to make proclamations, I'm not going to argue. I'll make one, too.

I don't think there is a university in this country whose name is misstated more often than Johns Hopkins. This institute of higher learning opened in Baltimore on this day in 1876. There's a story about a distinguished Johns Hopkins University president who was asked to speak in Pittsburgh. He was introduced most generously and graciously as the President of John Hopkins University. That's the usual error—no "s" in the first word, which is Johns, not John. So he thanked the gentleman who had introduced him. As he started his speech he commented how happy he was to be in "Pittburgh." The moral of this story is that the greatest comfort for a speaker is the knowledge—as he rises to deliver his remarks—that he has the last word. And that brings us to my first words.

With your permission, I would like to begin by quoting author Gore Vidal, who was born on this day in 1925. He commented once in an interview that "Literature takes a skill beyond just listening. You have to be able to take a line of prose...and become as one with the other end of that prose. A great writer can do that for you, and a great reader can do that for any writer." I feel the same way about our meeting here today. With the energy that's percolating in this room, we could create a bestseller right here.

O CTOBER 4

Rutherford B. Hayes was born, 1822. (See March 2nd entry.)

The Sputnik satellite orbited the earth, 1957.

Transatlantic jet plane service began, 1958.

Turkey declared war on Russia, 1853. (See October 25th entry.)

INTRODUCTIONS

On this date in 1957, the Russians launched the first Sputnik satellite into orbit around the earth. It was a startling scientific achievement. The event jolted the United States into an all-out effort to expand its limited space technology. It also provided new topics for speakers—visions of a new era, blue-sky dreams—literally. Nowadays, nothing that science does shocks us. And consequently, speakers are hard pressed to present miraculous visions that haven't already been announced. So I will put speculation aside and devote myself to a more down-to-earth theme.

A British airline company put the first transatlantic passenger jet service into operation on this day in 1958. It's interesting that it took longer to launch that service than to put a satellite into orbit. I guess it's similar to the answer Walter Pitkin—the author of *Life Begins at 40*— gave when asked about the difference between a 200-word article and a 1500-word article on the same subject. He simply replied, "the 1500-word article you can have tomorrow; the 200-word one will take a week." An article's length is not necessarily a measure of its difficulty. The same holds true with speeches, too. I hope that my remarks here today will have the merit of brevity rather than the vice of empty glibness.

Most wars end with a settlement of the conflicts that ignited them. Today marks the start of a war which ended in a stalemate. On this day in 1853, Turkey declared war on Russia. The discord had erupted over who had ultimate control of the Middle East—particularly the Crimean Peninsula. Russia, an orthodox Christian empire, demanded its right to protect Christian subjects living in the Islamic Ottoman-Turkish empire. The declaration soon exploded into an international free-for-all. Russia had been arguing with France over the control of certain holy places in Palestine. So, France sided with Turkey. Great Britain was determined to gain control of the Suez Canal which was also in the Ottoman Empire. It sided with Turkey. Russia's long-time ally, Austro-Hungary, just wanted to be on the winning side. It sided with Turkey. In the end, thousands of lives were lost and no one won the

Crimean War. One nation, however, lost more than soldiers' lives. Austro-Hungary lost Russia's much-needed military and financial support when the war ended. At the end of every war, there is always a loser. But the question I want to put to you today is this: In any conflict or war, is there ever really a winner?

O CTOBER 5

President Chester Alan Arthur was born, 1830.

President Franklin Delano Roosevelt spoke about world peace, 1944.

The first presidential television broadcast was made from the White House, 1947.

Raoul Wallenberg was granted honorary U.S. citizenship, 1981.

INTRODUCTIONS

Back on this day, in 1947, Harry S. Truman became the first U.S. President to televise a speech from the White House. There weren't too many television sets yet, and the President's speech was not the hit of the week—he was asking the nation to observe meatless Tuesdays, eggless and chickenless Thursdays, and to eat one less slice of bread daily for the sake of providing food for postwar Europe. But the public responded favorably. I want to believe it was because President Franklin D. Roosevelt had made a speech on this same day, in 1944, in which he said: "We owe it to our posterity, we owe it to our heritage of freedom, we owe it to our god, to devote the rest of our lives and all our capabilities to the building of a solid, durable structure of world peace." Let's see if we can muster that same spirit for peace and cooperation today.

In 1880, Chester Alan Arthur was placed on the Republican presidential ticket with James A. Garfield as a sop to the old-line spoils-minded party wing. When President Garfield was assassinated, everyone thought a crass political phase was automatically going to follow. But President Arthur turned out to be something else again. He prosecuted dishonest officials; secured the passage of the Civil Service Act; and did what historians generally regard as a good job. Chester Alan Arthur was born on this day, in 1830, in Fairfield, Vermont. His story reminds us that you can't simply apply past performance as a basis for future deeds. After all, if history was always repetitive, we wouldn't have much of a future. So today, I rise to speak on a hopeful note. There may be more Chester Alan Arthurs around than we think. The question is, what should they do?

The United States has rarely granted individuals honorary citizenship. And on this day in 1981, the nation awarded this rare honor for the second time in its history to former Swedish diplomat Raoul Wallenberg. During the Second World

War, Wallenberg was credited with saving thousands of Hungarian-Jewish lives by issuing them Swedish identification papers in Nazi-occupied Hungary. The award was posthumously given to this courageous war-hero who disappeared in 1945. Because he was living in Hungary when Soviet troops overtook Nazi forces, he was arrested by Stalinist officials and vanished into the Soviet prison system. Heroes don't always personally receive medals and awards, but that superficial element doesn't diminish their courage nor their greatness. There are a few heroes like Raoul Wallenberg that I would like you to join me in honoring right now.

OCTOBER 6

Thomas Edison showed his first motion pictures, 1889.

Al Jolson spoke in *The Jazz Singer,* 1927.

Michael Jordan announced his retirement from professional basketball to play professional baseball, 1993. (See February 17th entry.)

INTRODUCTIONS.

Today is a double-feature anniversary. In 1889, inventor Thomas Edison showed his first motion pictures in West Orange, New Jersey. And 38 years later, in 1927, singer/actor Al Jolson spoke in the first "talkie"—*The Jazz Singer* which premiered in New York City. We learned to see—via the camera and film—before we learned to speak on celluloid. The same thing holds true for each of us as individuals. A baby sees before speaking a word or understanding a word. In elementary school, show always comes before tell. And so today, I want to speak with you about things that we have all seen. Having seen them, we now have to decide what to do about them. So let's have the pictures in our minds as I provide the soundtrack.

OCTOBER 7

The first gravity-powered railroad went into operation, 1826.

James Whitcomb Riley was born, 1849. (See August 5th entry.)

Great Britain's Prime Minister William Gladstone commented on civilization's resources, 1881.

Marian Anderson became the first African-American opera singer to join New York's Metropolitan opera, 1954.

INTRODUCTIONS

Today is the birthday of the first American railroad. In 1826, the Granite Railway—powered by a horse and the force of gravity— began operation. It ran from Quincy to Milton, Massachusetts, carrying granite rock down to the waterfront. Gravity is a one-way force; it doesn't pull you uphill. And a speech which takes its gravity too seriously ends up going downhill. So, as I think of the Granite Railway, I remind myself that gravity isn't enough. I'd rather work up to something than coast down to it. And today I want you to get worked up with me.

The Hoosier poet James Whitcomb Riley was born on this day in 1849, in Greenfield, Indiana. He was Little Orphan Annie's creator and warned that the goblins'll get you if you don't watch out. Public speakers have been stealing that last story line for generations. It is a nice suspense-filled touch to put the blame on unidentified goblins; but remember that Pogo's creator Walt Kelly pointed the finger a lot closer to home. "We have met the enemy," Pogo said, "and he is us." Today we don't need to worry about the goblins. All we have to do is to look in the mirror. I have looked. Let me tell you what I saw.

Back on this date in 1881, British politician William E. Gladstone stood up and said, "The resources of civilization are not yet exhausted." This was obviously not a prophecy. Some of us are pretty tired and our resources—we have sadly discovered—are not renewable. Let's talk about some conservation measures here and now, before it's too late.

You may not be familiar with Marion Anderson, but she opened a stage door on this day in 1954, and changed the face of opera, much to the delight of opera fans around the world. As the first African-American to join New York's Metropolitan Opera, Anderson must have had plenty of butterflies in her stomach when she made her debut; a feeling which, oddly enough, I can identify with right now. But her phenomenal vocal ability quickly won audiences. I don't have a dulcet soprano voice, and I don't plan to sing to you today, but perhaps what I have to say will have a similar effect on you.

OCTOBER 8

John Hay was born, 1838.

The Great Chicago Fire started, 1871. (celebrated as the start of Fire Prevention Week)

The Reverend Jesse Jackson was born, 1941.

INTRODUCTIONS

Let us pause for a moment to remember Mrs. O'Leary's cow. That cow supposedly kicked over a lantern in Mrs. O'Leary's barn on this day in 1871, and started the Great Chicago Fire. In sixteen hours, 3.5 squares miles of that growing city was razed to the ground. I don't know whether that story libeled an innocent animal. But a story—like a fire—is very hard to stop once it gets started. And so is a public speaker.

John Hay combined a distinguished diplomatic career with an equally distinguished career as a poet and author. Since he was born on this day in 1838, I am reminded of some of his more famous maxims. For example, he once wrote: "Who would succeed in the world should be wise in the use of his pronouns. Utter the you twenty times where you once utter the I." He wrote something else which is very good advice for the public speaker. "True luck," he said, "consists not in holding the best of the cards at the table; luckiest is he who knows just when to rise and go home." I will keep that in mind as I address you here today.

America's first African-American presidential candidate was born in Greenville, South Carolina on this day in 1941. During the civil-rights movement in the 1960s, Jesse Jackson was asked by the Reverend Dr. Martin Luther King, Jr. to head the Chicago branch of the Southern Christian Leadership Council's economic arm— Operation Breadbasket. Jackson quickly became the project's national director. He had convinced African-American businesses to supply employment for young people and to feature African-American products in key neighborhoods. In 1968, Jackson was ordained as a Baptist minister at the Chicago Theological Seminary. And three years later, Jackson headed Operation PUSH which was dedicated to combating racism, and promoting scholarship and hard work among youth. In 1983, he became the nation's first African-American presidential candidate; and although he didn't win the election, Jackson made his point to the entire world. Opportunities are abundant for those who work hard to be there when they come knocking on the door. I'm here knocking on your door. Are you willing to listen to what I have to say?

OCTOBER 9

Leif Erikson landed in North America, 1000 AD.

Yale University was chartered, 1701.

John Lennon was born, 1940.

INTRODUCTIONS

Today is Leif Erikson Day which commemorates the supposed landing of the Viking explorer on the North American mainland in 1000 AD. Who knows how many people discovered America before Columbus, starting with Native Americans? It is safe to say, however, that the first Europeans who landed in North America were apparently not greatly impressed. They apparently felt it might be a nice place to visit, but... I must say that I feel the same way about the speaker's podium: It's a nice place to visit, but I wouldn't want to live here. So I will try to make my visit a brief but happy one.

This is the day when, in 1701, the Collegiate School of Connecticut was chartered. This institution of higher learning was later named Yale University. I dare say, Yale has turned out some of America's greatest leaders—and turned down some of America's great leaders as well. That's the hazard of any selection system. There are those who deplore procedure as it applies to the college admissions process. But no matter what educational or social system exists, every individual is called upon to make a judgment or a choice. I had to select the thoughts I plan to share with you today. You, in turn, will decide whether to accept or reject them. Yale's motto speaks of "light and truth." Yet, each of us sees the truth in our own light.

Today is John Lennon's birthday. The boy who grew up to be a Beatle, was born in Liverpool in 1940. In honor of his all-too-short life, I'd like to take a moment to imagine; to imagine where his life would have taken him were he alive today. Before he died, he had been devoting more and more time and energy to a number of worthy causes, using the fame and influence he'd accumulated in music toward a hope of world peace. You might say he was a dreamer, but he wasn't the only one. I share his dreams, as I'm sure many of you do. And I'd like to borrow a few more words from him as my topic today: "Imagine all the people, living life in peace."

OCTOBER 10

Giuseppe Verdi was born, 1813.
The tuxedo was born, 1886.

INTRODUCTIONS

Back in 1886, on this date, an autumn ball was held at a very elite retreat known as Tuxedo Park, New York. Some of the male guests wore a new type of dinner jacket. The garment eventually took its nickname from this elegant setting: The tuxedo was born that night. I don't know if this information thrills you, but I regard it as a sort of warning. It tells me that our gathering here may be remembered more for what somebody wore than for anything I say. And so I speak to you today unburdened by any illusions of profundity.

Today is Giuseppe Verdi's birthday. In 1813, this operatic composer was born in Le Roncole, Italy. Even if you are unfamiliar with the opera *Aida,* you have to be impressed by this composer's name alone. I wonder if we would be equally amused by his name's English translation. Somehow, a Joseph Green opera doesn't sound quite the same. We hear a name—or a word—and it plants an idea in our minds. There is a difference among being asked to deliver an address; or being asked to make a speech; or being asked to say a few words. I will try to live up to the assignment given to me here today. I can only hope I do so well that other speakers turn Verdi with envy.

OCTOBER 11

Great Britain's King Henry VIII denounced Martin Luther's teachings, 1521.

Brigadier General Casimir Pulaski died, 1779. (General Pulaski Memorial Day)

Eleanor Roosevelt was born, 1884.

The Democratic National Committee sponsored a television program, 1932.

Pope John XXIII's Ecumenical Council convened, 1962. (See January 25th entry.)

INTRODUCTIONS

Casimir Pulaski was a hero in the fight for Polish independence before he came to the United States in 1777. Two years later, Pulaski led a charge against British forces in Savannah, Georgia. He was mortally wounded and died two days later. Today is General Pulaski Memorial Day which commemorates the passing of Brigadier General Casimir Pulaski. It is a good time to remember that the freedom we enjoy today cost both blood and tears. We can talk freely today because of the sacrifices and the courage of men like General Pulaski.

It's Eleanor Roosevelt's birthday today, so I'd like to take a few moments to speak about this great lady. Mrs. Roosevelt elevated the role of First Lady to a stature on par with that of the Commander in Chief. Anna Eleanor Roosevelt was born in 1884 in New York City. She was President Theodore Roosevelt's niece, and married her cousin, Franklin D. Roosevelt. She was an awkward public speaker all her life. But if today I can be one-tenth as effective as Mrs. Roosevelt was in winning public attention for both civil and human rights at home and abroad, I will be grateful indeed.

Christianity's defenders often made strange bedfellows in history's final analysis. Great Britain's King Henry VIII publicly denounced the teachings of Martin Luther in a book entitled, *Assertion of the Sacraments*. On this day in 1521, King Henry presented a published copy to Pope Leo X. But the king's printed reprisal of Martin Luther's teachings didn't stop Cambridge University scholars and British printing presses from spreading the Protestant founder's word. The moral of this story comes from an old adage: People who live in glass houses shouldn't throw stones. Since I live in a high-rise, I'm going to tread carefully for the next few minutes.

The first political telecast took place on this exact day in 1923. Sponsored by the Democratic National Committee, it was broadcast from New York. I could spend some time dwelling on it; but for now, I'd like to return you to your regularly scheduled programming.

OCTOBER 12

Christopher Columbus discovered the New World, 1492.

Lions International was founded, 1917.

INTRODUCTIONS

Christopher Columbus arrived in the Bahamas on this day in 1492, so you might logically suppose that this would be Columbus Day. It used to be that simple, but it isn't anymore. Columbus Day is now observed on the second Monday of October. It is customary, on Columbus Day, to salute Columbus' Italian heritage; to spare a fond memory for Queen Isabella of Spain who financed his exploration for a new route to India; and perhaps to sympathize with the Native Americans who were perfectly happy until Columbus landed. I would like to suggest another form of celebration. I propose that each of us set out to discover America all over again. I've tried to do just that, and I'd like to tell you what I've found.

In 1917, on this very day, the Lions International was founded in Dallas, Texas. For some reason—which escapes me—our fraternal organizations seem to adopt animal names like the Lions, Moose, Golden Eagles, and Elks. Having equated ourselves to animals, we proceed to do one thing that animals don't. We make speeches. And those of us who make speeches always hope that what we are saying is not the same old stuff. In keeping with our love of animal analogies, I hope you will find this speech to be a horse of a different color.

Oｃｔｏｂｅｒ 13

The U.S. Naval Fleet was authorized, 1775.

President George Washington laid the cornerstone of the President's Mansion, 1792.

INTRODUCTIONS

On this day in 1792, President George Washington laid the cornerstone of the Executive Mansion in Washington, D.C. He started the project, but he wasn't around to see it completed. He died in 1799. John Adams became the mansion's first resident in 1800. Some people lay down cornerstones for others to build upon. I'm here to lay down a cornerstone by pontificating on a few topics. It's tempting to lay it on with a trowel. But I will try to be aware of these obvious hazards as I speak to you here today.

The United States Navy was officially authorized on this day in 1775. To honor today's anniversary, I shall try to leave the deep water to the Navy and avoid finding myself at sea. And in honor of the sailing ships that constituted our first seagoing line of defense, I shall furnish my own wind.

Oｃｔｏｂｅｒ 14

The Battle of Hastings took place, 1066.

William Penn was born, 1644.

President Dwight D. Eisenhower was born, 1890.

U.S. Air Force Captain Chuck Yeager became the first person to fly faster than the speed of sound as he tested a rocket-powered research plane, 1947.

The Reverend Dr. Martin Luther King, Jr. (1964) and Elie Wiesel (1986) won the Nobel Peace Prize for their work in promoting human rights.

INTRODUCTIONS

In 1890, Dwight D. Eisenhower—military leader and the 34th U.S. President—was born on this day. Ike was not regarded as an outstanding public speaker, but he spoke in eloquent terms at Columbia University's Bicentennial Celebration in 1964. He referred to "the revolutionary doctrine of the divine rights of the common man." I don't think that can be improved upon as the idyllic definition of modern American life. We've given royalty its chance in the past, and luckily we now place the emphasis where it rightfully belongs. My question today is: What will be the common man's, or woman's, rights tomorrow?

Today is William Penn's birthday. Pennsylvania's founder was born in London in 1644. When he arrived in the colonies, Penn made peace with the Native Americans; established a tradition of brotherhood and decency; and built Philadelphia—The City of Brotherly Love. Ironically, after he returned to England, the people who supervised his colony didn't do a very good job. As a matter of fact, Penn went to debtor's prison for a while. History tells us that he was about to sell Pennsylvania when he suffered a stroke. What if he had sold Pennsylvania to another entrepreneur? The game of "what if" is always fascinating; and we could play it from now to the end of time. But I'd rather play another game with you: the game of "how come?" I am puzzled about why a few things are happening right now.

One of history's turning points occurred on this day—the start of the Norman Conquest of the British Isles. In 1066, William the Conqueror defeated the Anglo-Saxons at the Battle of Hastings. The conquest was aided by conflicts among the Anglo-Saxons themselves, but this confrontation sealed their fate. The Normans' true conquest of Britain took many more years as words and traditions blended together, ultimately creating a rich heritage. In the last analysis, conquest by force is far less enduring than conquest by ideas. So today, I shall try to conquer your previous assumptions with a few strong ideas.

Two noble heroes in the fight for human and civil rights were honored on this day when they received the Nobel Peace Prize. In 1964, The Reverend Dr. Martin Luther King, Jr., received this coveted award for his work in championing African-American civil rights. And in 1986, Romanian-American activist Elie Wiesel won the award for internationally promoting human rights. It doesn't matter where you were born or what corner of the world you call home, respect for human rights—as individuals or as a group—is a common cause we can all support.

Today is the anniversary of a landmark in aviation history. In 1947, test pilot Chuck Yeager flew an X-1 rocket plane into the history books as the first man to break the sound barrier. Though I'm not a pilot, in honor of that event, I'd like to spend a little time today disturbing that barrier in another way, by telling you about...

OCTOBER 15

P.G. Wodehouse was born, 1881.

The Graf Zeppelin made the first commercial transatlantic flight, 1928.

First draft card burned, 1965

INTRODUCTIONS

Author P.G. Wodehouse was a nonagenarian when he passed way in the 1970s. He was born on this day in 1881, in an England that passed away when he was still young. Scatterbrained Lords like Bertie and impeccable butlers like Jeeves disappeared from Wodehouse's world during the Second World War. Yet the innocent, civilized universe he created continues to entertain millions of readers. We all have worlds that we fondly remember. Some of us consider our parents' and grandparents' times as the good old days. We probably imagine those days as being quite different from the way they really were. Did you ever stop to think how our children will reminisce about our good old days? Ask yourself now. Or better still, come stroll with me down a future memory lane. Some of you might say, what's good about these good old days? I'm going to answer now.

You may not know it, but today is the aniversary of the day in 1928 when the Graf Zeppelin, a predecessor of the infamous Hindenburg, made the first commercial transatlantic air flight. For passenger travel, the airships were a luxurious marvel. But for transoceanic communications, it meant that documents could cross the ocean in three days, instead of the seven or eight it took by ship. It may not seem very fast by our modern standards, but the Graf Zeppelin set a record in its day. Like that dirigible, I'm here today full of hot air and ready to deliver a message. And don't worry, I fully intend to beat that three-day record.

Today is quite a day to make a statement. After all, it was on this very day in 1965 that the first draft card was burned in protest of the United States' escalating military involvement in Vietnam. And on this same day in 1969, those flames of protest swept across the nation in the form of demonstrations and a candlelight vigil outside the White House. Now, I'm not here today to encourage civil disobedience or rebellion; but I do have some burning ideas of my own that I'd like to share with you.

OCTOBER 16

Noah Webster was born, 1758.

Oscar Wilde was born, 1854.

Abolitionist John Brown staged a raid on the U.S. arsenal at Harper's Ferry, Virginia, 1859. (See May 9th entry.)

INTRODUCTIONS

If public speakers have a patron saint, they must be particularly mindful of this day; for today is Noah Webster's birthday. Noah—the unabridged—Webster of dictionary fame was born in 1758 in West Hartford, Connecticut. Thanks to him, no speaker is honestly ever at a loss for words. I have a fair stock of Mr. Webster's wares that I have assembled for you today. And so to work.

Oscar Fingall O'Flahertie Wilde may have been the most adept wordsmith of the English language. Born on this day in 1854, Wilde was not only a great playwright; he also authored a few notable epigrams and pithy sayings. If he had been born in 1954, he would have been publicly honored and lionized in the publishing world. But Oscar Wilde was born out of his time. His refusal to abide by society's sexual standards brought him vilification, persecution, and eventual infamy. In his novel *The Picture of Dorian Gray,* Wilde wrote that "the only way to get rid of a temptation is to yield to it." I was tempted to speak to you today, and I am happy to yield to that temptation.

OCTOBER 17

Albert Einstein emigrated to the U.S., 1933. (See March 14th entry.)

A group of Arab nations started an oil boycott, 1973. (See March 13 entry.)

Mother Teresa was awarded the Nobel Peace Prize for her work with the destitute of Calcutta over three decades, 1979.

INTRODUCTIONS

On this date in 1973, the western hemisphere woke up to a critical energy shortage when the oil-producing Arab states imposed a boycott. We've been looking for ways to conserve our own oil resources and find new energy alternatives ever since. But have we taken sufficient heed? Have we had so many Cassandras and so many dire warnings of impending calamity that we simply don't pay attention? Let me try to answer these questions.

It has been said that there is no greater charity than to give selflessly to those who have no means to repay. Compassion and charity are particularly appropriate topics for today, as this is the anniversary of the day in 1979 when Mother Theresa received the Nobel Peace Prize in recognition of her three decades of work with Calcutta's most destitute citizens. I'm not here to suggest that each of us should abandon our lives to the service of others, but we should recognize that there is no patent on miracles. Every person in this room, and everyone outside of it as well, is capable of bettering the cause of humankind. And that is miraculous. Today, I'd like to talk about some of the ways in which we can do just that.

OCTOBER 18

First American labor organization was founded, 1648.

The Mason-Dixon Line was established, 1767.

The U.S. officially took ownership of the Alaska territory, 1867. (See March 30th entry.)

INTRODUCTIONS

The Mason-Dixon Line was officially adopted on this day. In 1767, the border between Maryland and Pennsylvania became the border between the North and the South and it's been that way ever since. When you draw a good line, it works. The question always is how you decide where to draw that line. Today I want to draw a new line or two.

Both trade associations and labor unions have their roots in the medieval guilds. On this day, in 1648, Boston's shoemakers, barrelmakers, and tubmakers were given official permission to set up their own guild. They eventually went their separate ways when they no longer shared a common cause. We tend to forget what all crafts-people have in common, emphasizing only their differences. I'm reminded of the illustration Eric Sevareid sometimes used to stress the common interest. He pointed out that when two people are sitting in a boat, it doesn't make much sense for one of them to point an accusing finger at the other and say, "Your end of the boat is sinking." Let's not put ourselves in that position now. Let's take a look at both ends of the boat.

OCTOBER 19

Sir Thomas Browne was born, 1605.

Lord Cornwallis surrendered at Yorktown, VA, 1781.

Journalist H.R. Ekins completed an around the world flight in 18.5 days, 1936.

INTRODUCTIONS

Today marks the anniversary of Lord Cornwallis' surrender at Yorktown, Virginia. This event, in 1781, ended the American Revolutionary War. Why isn't that momentous occasion better remembered? How can Americans single out days like the

Fourth of July and forget the day that saved the Fourth of July? Truly, we remember what we want to remember; see what we want to see; hear what we want to hear. Fortunately, we don't all remember, see, or hear the same things. And by telling each other of our own perceptions, together we see and hear a little more. So I welcome the opportunity to share some of my perceptions with you today.

When H.R. Ekins—a reporter for *The New York World Telegram*—completed an around-the-world airline trip in 18.5 days on this day in 1936, his story made headlines all over the world. It was especially newsworthy because he beat two other competing journalists to both the finish line and the scoop. Going around the world in less than three weeks by passenger plane was a rare feat back then. We have certainly speeded up since then. The only thing we may not have accelerated is the art of public speaking. Conscious of that fact, I shall try to go through my subject—not around it—as quickly as the topic will allow.

This is the birthday of the seventeenth-century physician and writer, Sir Thomas Browne, who was born in London in 1605. His name is not very well known today, but some of his thoughts and phrases are immortal. It was Thomas Browne who wrote, "There is no road or ready way to virtue," and "Charity begins at home." I would like to take as my text today another of Sir Thomas Browne's observations: "The whole world was made for man." The whole world was made for us. And what are we doing with it?

O CTOBER 20

George Washington wrote about religious differences, 1792.

Benjamin Disraeli wrote about change, 1867.

General Douglas MacArthur stepped ashore at Leyte, in the Philippines, 1944. (See January 9th entry.)

The "Saturday night massacre" occurred in Washington, D.C., 1973.

INTRODUCTIONS

While writing a letter about this time of year in 1792, President George Washington made some observations about the causes of the world's troubles, and came to a decisive conclusion. "Of all the animosities which have existed among mankind," he wrote, "those which are caused by a difference of sentiments in religion appear to be the most inveterate and distressing, and ought to be deprecated." Most disputes are not between good and evil, but between two opposing sides who are convinced that they are in the right and that the Lord is on their side. But the biggest problem arises from those who don't believe there is a right and wrong; who think life is a free-for-all. I think it's time we look at what we as a nation believe in, and what perhaps should be called the ethics of survival. Every year another "how-to-survive" book hits the shelves. Let's take a look at why that happens.

British Prime Minister Benjamin Disraeli lived in a time of whirlwind changes—and a lot of people were afraid of them. Back in 1867, as the late October landscape showed its seasonal alterations, Disraeli commented that "Change is inevitable in a progressive country. Change is constant." That is the eternal contradiction: Change is constant. Once we accept that fact we can get on with the business of figuring out what we can do about it. How are things changing and what can we do about it?

In 1973, the "Saturday night massacre" took place at the White House. This may seem a rather lurid description, but it's not far from wrong. On that Saturday night, President Richard Nixon fired the special Watergate prosecutor Archibald Cox, Attorney General Elliot Richardson, and Deputy Attorney General William D. Ruckelshaus. To many people it signaled the beginning of President Nixon's end. Everything went downhill from then until he resigned. It's hard to define the domino effect that some singular events take; and we don't always immediately recognize their significance. Right now, for example, there are world events occurring that may hold the key to our future. So we look around us; try to keep informed; and you are patient enough to listen to what I think is worth noting.

OCTOBER 21

Whale Watching Week

Alfred Nobel was born, 1833. (See December 10th entry.)

Thomas A. Edison demonstrated the incandescent electric lamp, 1879.

Timothy Leary was born, 1920.

INTRODUCTIONS

Today is Edison Lamp Day, the day that Thomas A. Edison demonstrated the incandescent electric lamp in 1879. In honor of that bright occasion, I shall endeavor to shed a little light of my own.

A number of years ago, the Honolulu-based First Society of Whale Watchers ordained this day as the start of International Whale Watching Week. This designation has a very real meaning for public speakers because we and the whale have so much in common. Whale watchers and audiences both come to see the subject spout. In honor of Whale Watching Week, I shall now rise to the surface to sound off.

Alfred Nobel was born on this day in 1833, in Stockholm, Sweden. He made his fortune as an inventor and manufacturer of high explosives and detonators. When he died, he left his fortune for the establishment of the Nobel Prizes for the advancement of the peaceful arts and sciences—including the fine art of peace itself. It's interesting that he is remembered for his legacy and not for his explosives. I guess this proves that last impressions are the most important. And that, in turn, suggests that the conclusion of my speech here today is what you will take away with you; so I hasten toward that end.

On the anniversary of the day Thomas Edison turned on an incandescent lightbulb, a controversial figure who also believed in turning things on was born. It's Timothy Leary's birthday. The psychologist who coined the beat generation mantra, "Tune in, turn on, and drop out," was born in 1920. On this day, I'd like to attempt to expand your minds a little myself, though not with contraband substances. My words and thoughts are all I brought. And if, as a song by the Moody Blues said, Timothy Leary isn't dead, but just "outside, looking in," I hope he'll approve of our more moderate approach to his idea. I will not, however suggest that you "drop out." In fact I'd like to begin by thanking you for dropping in.

OCTOBER 22

André Garnerin demonstrated the parachute, 1797.

The Great Influenza Epidemic began, 1918.

INTRODUCTIONS

André J. Garnerin is not one of those names that rings bells. I doubt that even his French countrymen and women have him enshrined in their hearts. But on this day, in 1797, André Garnerin gave the first public demonstration of his invention: the parachute. He jumped from a balloon to show how his creation worked. And luckily, it did work. The parachute was originally designed to enable people to escape from the early balloons during an emergency, and to land safely. Those early balloons were literally filled with hot air. This makes this anniversary particularly important for speakers. Since, as you know, speakers are also filled with hot air, the importance of landing on your feet from a great height cannot be overestimated. So, that being understood, let us take off.

At this time, in 1918, a worldwide influenza epidemic went on a rampage. During the First World War, over 18 million people died from the flu virus—not from guns or grenades. For years afterward, we patted ourselves on the back. We thought that medical science had found a way to diffuse microscopic bombs like influenza. Then, as you may recall, in the 1970s, the U.S. government instituted a nationwide swine flu vaccination program. It reduced fatalities, but there was some question about the vaccine's harmful effects. And in the early 1990s, another influenza epidemic swept through the U.S. so severely that it reduced our national average life expectancy by a few points. Sometimes we really don't know if the cure is worse than the disease. We have some miracle drugs whose side effects require other miracle drugs. We establish welfare programs to care for the needy; and then we have organizations that ferret out welfare cheats. I'd like to speak with you about some of these contradictions today.

OCTOBER 23

The swallows leave San Juan Capistrano. (See March 19th entry.)
Johnny Carson was born, 1925.

INTRODUCTION:

Although Nebraska claims him as a native son—and he has returned that compliment—the fact is Johnny Carson was born in Corning, Iowa, on this day in 1925. He grew up in Nebraska and aged gracefully in the nation's bedrooms as the host of television's "Tonight Show." Johnny Carson's birthday is a comfort to a speaker. It reminds us that talk doesn't always put people to sleep. It has kept millions of people awake. I am probably a poor substitute here today for Johnny Carson, which—I presume—is why the job went to Jay Leno, but here goes.

OCTOBER 24

National Popcorn Week. (See February 22nd entry.)
The George Washington Bridge opened, 1931.
The United Nations' charter was adopted, 1945. (celebrated as United Nations Day) (See January 1st, January 9th, April 25th, and June 26th entries.)

INTRODUCTIONS

For reasons best known to popcorn manufacturers, the last week of October was designated as National Popcorn Week. Since today is also United Nations Day, which marks the U.N. Charter's adoption in 1945, I can safely say that things have been popping ever since. But popcorn is an American legacy and National Popcorn

Week is literally an event you can take with a few grains of salt. I hope my remarks today will not be taken that lightly. And I promise that I won't try to butter you up.

Adlai Stevenson remarked on United Nations Day in 1963, that "The journey of a thousand leagues, we say, begins with a single step. So we must never neglect any work of peace that is within our reach, however small." Stevenson then added that "Our efforts will be erratic, and the world will remain a dangerous place to live." I have no argument with this statement. But I will let the United Nations handle that kind of talk. Today, I'm going to concentrate on the price of popcorn and other luxuries.

A wonderful event took place on this day in 1931. An event that alleviated the traffic crush on rush-hour traffic crossing the Hudson River to Manhattan. The George Washington Bridge opened, with four lanes going each way on two levels. That was an enormous amount of space. Of course, it didn't take long for commuters to fill those lanes to the point where traffic there is worse than ever. Speakers will often do the same. Give a speaker half an hour, and it's not quite enough. Make it an hour, and it's still not quite enough. Well, before I begin, I'd like to thank you for the opportunity to bridge my thoughts to you, and I promise not to use any more of your time than it takes to drive my point safely home.

OCTOBER 25

St. Crispin's Day.
The charge of the Light Brigade took place, 1854. (See October 4th entry.)

INTRODUCTIONS

Today is the feast day of St. Crispin, the patron saint of shoemakers. Since more of us are working out daily in running shoes and crosstrainers; rediscovering nature in our hiking boots; and scaling walls and cliffs in climbing shoes, there ought to be a major resurgence of festivities honoring this guardian of the footwear manufacturers who protect our feet from bruises, bunions, and blisters. I like occasions such as this—they are a welcome stop along the way. So while you rest your weary feet I will exercise my active tongue and try not to put my foot in my mouth. Then—with due regard for St. Crispin—we can put our shoes on and go about our business.

In 1854 on this day, the doomed British Light Brigade charged into the valley of death. It's a lot easier to quote Tennyson's poem than to remember the details of the Crimean War's Battle of Balaklava. We remember lines like "Theirs not to make reply, / Theirs not to reason why, / Theirs but to do and die." Even today, we are often asked to do things without question. But if mankind is to progress "half a league, half a league, half a league onward," we had better start asking for reasons why and learning to say no.

$\mathbf{O}$ C T O B E R 2 6

The first jackasses arrived in America, 1785.

Hillary Rodham Clinton was born, 1947.

The U.S. Air Force officially reported that there were no such things as flying saucers, 1955.

A shoot-out took place at the OK Corral, 1881.

INTRODUCTIONS

Every now and then, history turns up an anniversary that has not had its proper due. Today is such a day. In 1785, we are told, two jackasses arrived in Boston Harbor from Spain. These were not ordinary jackasses. They were a gift from the King of Spain to President George Washington. They were sent to the fledgling nation so they could be mated with mares to produce America's first native mules. The roots of American stubbornness and mulishness go pretty far back. But it's a comfort to know that jackasses had to be imported; we didn't start off growing our own. Are we any smarter today? Let's take a good long look at ourselves.

On this day, in 1955, the U.S. Air Force officially proclaimed that flying saucers were nothing more than delusions and myths. But the public went right on seeing flying saucers and describing visits with mysterious space creatures. It takes more than an official denial to defeat the power of folklore. From the days of dragons to flying saucers, history has shown us that people believe what they want to believe. And so I come to you today to tell you what I want to believe, what I do believe, and what I hope I can persuade you to believe as well.

Today is First Lady Hillary Rodham Clinton's birthday. In honor of this occasion, I'd like to take a moment to examine the role of U.S. Presidents' wives. It might come as a surprise to many of you that in most other nations—including our northern neighbor, Canada—the spotlight doesn't fall on elected officials' spouses. Polls which include questions about leaders' wives are as American as the phenomenon of First Ladies publicly influencing government policy. This is hardly new. George Washington, John Adams, James Madison, and Franklin D. Roosevelt—to name just a few—all had strong partners working with them in the White House. Eleanor Roosevelt even became a United Nations ambassadress after she left office. Born in 1947, Hillary Rodham Clinton joins a long and distinguished list of truly American heroines. There are a few "first ladies" who've never been to the White House, but deserve to be mentioned here today.

The infamous shoot-out at the OK Corral took place on this day in 1881. It's a rather romantic notion: a high-noon shoot-out between Sheriff Wyatt Earp— accompanied by his two brothers, and Doc Holliday—and members of the Ike Clanton gang. But in reality, this bloody incident in Tombstone, Arizona, left three men dead and two more ravaged by gunshhot wounds. I'd like to think that if that incident were replayed today, law enforcement officials would've captured the Clanton gang without firing a shot; and they'd all be serving sentences for weapons possession, conspiring to commit manslaughter, as well as their previous felonies. Though we like to think of these as uncertain and violent times, we have made remarkable progress. It's that progress I'd like to talk about today.

O C T O B E R   2 7

President Theodore Roosevelt was born, 1858. (See August 22nd entry.)

Dylan Thomas was born, 1914.

DuPont announced the invention of nylon, 1938.

John Cleese was born, 1939.

Menachim Begin and Anwar al-Sadat won the Nobel Peace Prize, 1975. (See November 11th entry.)

INTRODUCTIONS

Theodore Roosevelt—who was born in New York City on this day in 1858—exemplified his own policy. He spoke softly and carried a big stick. As Governor of New York, he was a trust-busting, anticorruption crusader. He was so hated by political bosses, they persuaded him to run for the vice-presidency just to get rid of him. President McKinley was assassinated six months after the 1900 election and Roosevelt found himself in the White House. As U.S. President, big business found him to be a tough opponent and nature conservationists discovered that he was their strongest advocate. Good people can't be kept down and good causes can't be swept under the rug. So, on Teddy Roosevelt's birthday, I'd like to raise my voice, as he might have done, and say "Bully for the honest man."

Dylan Thomas is best remembered for the lines, "Do not go gentle into that good night, / Old age should burn and rave at close of day; / Rage, rage against the dying of the light." I am not here to discuss the problems of aging, but I would like to take a leaf from Dylan Thomas, who was born on this day in 1914, in Carmarthenshire, Wales. I will raise my voice to ask why so many people are willing to "go gentle into that good night" of sloth, bureaucracy, and indifference that perpetuate the myth that you can't fight city hall. A generation or two ago, some people found out that the best way to stand up and be counted was to sit down. If you care enough, you can do enough. That's my reason for speaking with you today.

As today is British comedian John Cleese's birthday, I will talk a bit about his strife. I mean wife. No. I mean life. He was born on this day in 1939. In England, of course, you silly people. Pay attention. He wrote and performed with Monty Python's Flying Circus. So to celebrate this gentleman's terrific talent, I will now go on to something completely different.

You could say the fabric of life changed on this day in 1938. Dupont Chemical Company research teams based in New York and London and led by Dr. Wallace Carothers, introduced a new fiber. Named for the two international cities that cooperated in bringing this synthetic into existence, nylon—which stands for New York and London—was born. Stretching far beyond hosiery and leisure suits, nylon and its successors have found their way into our daily lives in a myriad of ways. Ideas capable of such momentous change don't come along very often. But today I've got one, and I'd love to share it with you.

O CTOBER 28

The feast day of St. Jude.

Thomas Jefferson wrote about natural aristocracy, 1813.

Statue of Liberty was dedicated, 1886. (See June 19th entry.)

The U.S. Congress overrode President Wilson's veto and enacted the Volstead Prohibition Act, 1919.

INTRODUCTIONS

Today is the feast day of St. Jude, the patron saint of the impossible. You've seen those classified ads thanking this saint for helping them through trying times. I don't know if it had anything to do with your inviting me to speak here today. But I welcome the opportunity to share with you some thoughts and some reflections. With all due respect I wish to thank St. Jude in advance, and I trust you will not find my remarks to be too impossible.

Writing to his friend and colleague John Adams on this date in 1813, Thomas Jefferson had a few kind words to say about the aristocracy. "I agree with you, " he wrote, "that there is a natural aristocracy among men. The grounds of this are virtue and talents." Today, I should like to salute its current members—the men and women whose virtues and talents epitomize our greatest strengths.

Today marks the anniversary of a day when the U.S. Congress put politics ahead of government. On this day in 1919, Congress overrode President Wilson's veto and enacted the Volstead Prohibition Act. The law lasted eight years. What it proved was not only that an unpopular law would be rebeled against, but that it was simple to make criminals out of a large segment of the population. I'd like to propose a toast to the more level heads that prevailed in 1927. Though I wonder, in these increasingly litigious times, just how much we learned.

O CTOBER 29

Sir Walter Raleigh was executed, 1618.

Robert G. Ingersoll commented on property ownership, 1896.

Wall Street crashed, 1929.

INTRODUCTIONS

History remembers Sir Walter Raleigh as a great courtier—the man who spread his coat over the mud to protect a noble lady's shoes. But Raleigh was a far more adventurous man than that. This pioneering explorer of the New World got into serious trouble with the Crown. When he was executed on this day in 1618, he became increasingly popular in memory. That, of course, was small comfort to the late Sir Walter Raleigh. Mindful of the need for immediate rather than long-term approval, I stand before you totally uninterested in posterity's verdict of my next remarks. I am more concerned about keeping my head right at this moment.

On October 29, 1929—as the show business paper *Variety* so tersely noted—Wall Street laid an egg. Stock market prices collapsed, and the twentieth century's worst economic depression rose from its ashes. Many people believe that the Great Depression ended because the Second World War began. Everybody who lived through that depression tells their descendants that no matter how bad things are they were worse then. However slowly progress moves, we do make progress. Let me illustrate.

A former Illinois Attorney General and eloquent orator Robert G. Ingersoll said on this day in 1896, "Few rich men own their property, the property owns them." Has that sentiment really changed in the past century? Ask yourself how much of what you do today is dictated by what you own, what you have to protect. Are we the property of our property? With every asset, do we buy another liability? And what can we do about it?

OCTOBER 30

Orson Welles and the Mercury Theater broadcast *The War of the Worlds,* 1938.

Nikita Khrushchev ordered the de-Stalinization of the U.S.S.R., 1961. (See April 17th and September 12th entries.)

INTRODUCTIONS

It started out as a radio dramatization by a young actor-director named Orson Welles, who had adapted a version of H.G. Wells' novel, *The War of the Worlds.* It aired on this evening, in 1938, over a coast-to-coast network. *The War of the Worlds* was so realistic that part of the nation actually believed Martians had invaded New Jersey. Telephone lines were jammed; people contemplated suicide; and some took ill with anxiety. It took days to persuade the public that it had only been a radio show. We are always ready to believe the strangest things. Man is the most credulous beast. For some speakers, this is a great comfort. For others, like myself, it's a warning. My speech today—I must assure you—will not be a dramatization. It will be a documentary.

When Soviet Premier Nikita Khrushchev chose to emphasize his regime's break with Josef Stalin's previous dictatorship, he chose a very simple strategy. He ordered Stalin's name edited out of books and magazines. On this day in 1961, he also ordered that Josef Stalin's remains were to be moved from his mausoleum in Red Square. We may laugh at this sort of incident when it happens elsewhere. But all of us can be diverted from the real issues through arguments over where the bodies are buried; or who should be credited with this or that. I am not here today to empty tombs or to remove names from the history books. Instead, I would like to direct your attention to the issues at hand.

OCTOBER 31

Halloween.

National UNICEF Day.

Martin Luther posted his 95 Theses, 1517. (See January 3rd and November 10th entries.)

U.S. Navy Rear Admiral G.J. Duefek became the first person to land an airplane at the South Pole, 1956.

INTRODUCTIONS

Today is Halloween, and I hope that my appearance here was not arranged as part of a Trick or Treat joke. There are a lot of Halloween superstitions and traditions that have survived, even though witches floating around on their brooms probably need an air-traffic controller today. So, with all due deference to the occasion, I will try to keep you all in good spirits while the goblins and ghouls roam outside.

When Martin Luther posted his 95 Theses on the church door in Wittenberg, Germany, on this day in 1517, he started a revolution: a Protestant Revolution. History does not provide for retakes. We will never know whether a little less intransigence might have prevented or delayed for centuries the schism between Catholicism and Protestantism. What we do know is that those who are unwilling to accept the status quo often change it more than they intended. The one unchanging rule of life is change. Nature changes. People change. But thanks to kind audiences like you, today we can describe our changes in words, not manifestoes. I thank you for the opportunity to do so here today.

This is National UNICEF Day which is observed on behalf of the United Nations Children's Fund. Children speak a direct, uninhibited, single-minded language of their own. In many ways, the job of a speaker is to think like a child. Decide what you want, tell the audience what you're after, and wait for somebody else to do something about it. I have just given you the structure of my speech. Now for the details.

It was no trick, on this day in the spring of 1956—yes, October 31, 1956—that U.S. Navy Rear Admiral G.J. Duefek entered the aviation record books. He became the first person to land an airplane at the South Pole. Now, unfortunately, I don't have any tricks up my sleeve for you today either. But before I begin I would like to say what a treat it is to be here.

NOVEMBER

INTRODUCTION

November is when the north winds begin to blow and herald the coming of winter. This month is also a time of migration: whales swim south to the warm waters of Mexico; ducks, geese, cranes, and even monarch butterflies fly south to escape the ice and snow; and many people now fly south to Florida and Arizona to warm their weary bones. Now before I convince all of you to call your travel agents, I have a few warm words to share with you about a hot topic.

NOVEMBER 1

The U.S. Continental Congress closed, 1788.

The U.S. Post Office introduced the money order, 1864.

The U.S. Weather Bureau made its first observations, 1870.

Notre Dame beat Army 35-13 at West Point; popularized the forward pass; and brought team captain Knute Rockne to fame, 1913. (See March 4th entry.)

The Hapsburg monarchy came to an end, 1918.

Charles Cooper of the Boston Celtics became the NBA's first African-American player, 1950.

The U.S. tested their first H-bomb, 1952.

INTRODUCTIONS

This is the day when, in 1870, the United States Weather Bureau made its first observations. It wasn't called the weather bureau back then because it was part of the U.S. Army Signal Corps. On this particular day reports were telegraphed from 24 places around the U.S. and the first national weather report was born. Unfortunately, most weather people are relatively unappreciated until they are wrong. They are not alone in this respect. The perceived bad work gets more attention than good work. It's always tempting for a speaker to talk about bad news and bad people. Audiences react to that sort of thing. But today my news is good; my words are calm; and my audience looks sunny.

In 1952, the United States conducted a test explosion of a hydrogen bomb at Eniwetok Island in the Pacific. It was such an awesome test that it probably strengthened the resolve of sensible people everywhere never to employ such a weapon. Later developments and events proved that anyone could make one anywhere. We were not privileged. Today's anniversary is a reminder that it's not our weapons but our spirit that sustains us. And today, as I look around me, I find much sustenance for that spirit.

Two governments went out of business on this day in history. In 1788, the U.S. Continental Congress closed after conducting business for fourteen years. It was later replaced by the House of Representatives and the U.S. Senate. In 1918, the Hapsburg monarchy which had ruled the Austro-Hungarian empire for centuries also came to an end. Two separate republics were proclaimed to replace the old system. The Hungarian Republic was proclaimed in Budapest; and the Austrian Republic was proclaimed in Vienna. Governments may seem like legacies that never die. But in truth, they evolve and dissolve as public demand prescribes. Let's take a look at a local legacy that's due for transformation.

It got a whole lot safer to send money through the mail on this day in 1864. The U.S. Post Office introduced the money order. Besides being safer, it was money you could take to the bank. This provided a great measure of security in the days before credit cards and electronic funds transfers. Now here's an idea you can take to the bank.

A professional basketball milestone took place on this day, which opened the doors for a number of its greatest heroes. In 1950, Charles Cooper of the Boston Celtics became the NBA's first African-American player. Since that day, many great players—inspirational heroes to basketball fans and aspiring players—have stepped on and off the professional basketball court. Wilt Chamberlain, Julius Irving, Magic Johnson, Michael Jordan, Isaiah Thomas, and Kareem Abdul-Jabar are just a few of the men who were given the opportunity to play the game thanks to Charles Cooper. If one individual has the courage to cut a path, others can surely follow. I'd like to introduce you to another groundbreaker today.

NOVEMBER 2

Marie Antoinette was born, 1755.

Warren G. Harding was born, 1865.

Warren G. Harding was elected U.S. President, 1920.

Radio reported Harding-Cox election results, 1920.

INTRODUCTIONS

Marie Antoinette was an Austrian princess who married France's crown prince in 1770. Naturally, she became queen when he succeeded to the throne in 1774; and she was guillotined during the French Revolution in 1793. She was born in Vienna on this day in 1755, and is remembered not for any of the events I have recited, but for a line she allegedly said when told that the people had no bread. "Let them eat cake," Marie Antoinette replied. The fact is that long before Marie Antoinette was born, "Let them eat bread" was a wisecrack similar to "Tell them to go into the garden and eat worms." Her remark was also attributed to a French queen of a previous century. I mention this because it shows how people can be remembered for the wrong reason. How do you think our time and we ourselves will be remembered? Will we be remembered at all? Let me tell you how I see us being described by some future historian.

Very few American homes had radios on this day in 1920. But the ones who did were able to follow the Presidential election results from the comfort of their own homes. It was the first modern radio news broadcast of an election, and the start of general public interest in national affairs. In recognition of that anniversary, there are a few pieces of public business that I would like to broadcast to you here and now.

The 1920 presidential election had one rather unusual aspect. Born in 1865, in Corsica, Ohio, Republican candidate Warren G. Harding was celebrating his birthday. On his 55th birthday, he was elected President of the United States. I think history will record that as a far better birthday present for Warren G. Harding than for the American people. During his term, the Teapot Dome scandal broke. When he died—and was succeeded by Vice President Calvin Coolidge—few people felt the nation was the loser. Harding was the candidate who was allegedly nominated in "a smoke-filled room" by a group of political bosses. Now it may seem very strange for me to be recalling these events, but I hope they will suggest to you—as they have to me—that we can look forward to doing better in the future than we ever did in the past. On this November 2, I turn my eyes resolutely forward, and I will tell you why.

N OVEMBER 3

Karl Baedeker was born, 1801.
President Lyndon Baynes Johnson won by a landslide, 1964.

INTRODUCTIONS

On this day in 1964, Lyndon B. Johnson—who had succeeded President Kennedy after his assassination—won the Presidential election over Senator Barry Goldwater by the largest popular vote plurality in the nation's history. Four years later, LBJ faced up to the facts and announced he would not run for re-election. If he had run, he might easily have been defeated because of the events in Vietnam during his term. From the most popular President ever to one whose chances of re-election were dubious was quite a change. It doesn't make public opinion seem particularly stable. And it reminds us that opinions are triggered by events. As to the events that affect the ebbs and flows of the tides of public opinion today, let me give you my own first-person-singular assessment.

Karl Baedeker made a career of selling his opinions. Born on this day in 1801, in Essen, Germany, Baedeker was the pioneer writer and publisher of a popular international travel guide series. Indeed, his name became synonymous with the word guidebook. Today, I'd like to give you my own Baedeker for our world.

NOVEMBER 4

The first vessel to traverse the Erie Canal arrived in New York, 1825.

Will Rogers was born, 1879.

The cash register was patented, 1879.

Walter Cronkite was born, 1916.

The entrance to King Tutankhamen's tomb was discovered, 1922. (See February 16th and June 26th entries.)

INTRODUCTIONS

Today is Will Rogers birthday. Born in Oolagah, Oklahoma, in 1879, Rogers began his career as a vaudeville trick-rope artist, but he soon discovered that audiences liked to hear him talk. Government and politics were his targets. He went on to a brilliant career as a monologist, lecturer, newspaper columnist, and movie actor. When the U.S. Congress makes a joke, he once said, it's a law, and when they make a law it's a joke. He also said, "I do not belong to any organized party. I am a Democrat." At first, when he said these sorts of things on network radio in the 1930s, people were shocked. But his good-humored and brilliant delivery made the needling of sacred institutions a popular mass entertainment. It still is. We may take government seriously, but not solemnly. That's the spirit I want all of you to apply to my remarks today.

Walter Cronkite was by no means the first television news broadcaster; he was, however, the first to become a national institution. When Cronkite concluded his report by saying that's the way things were, we believed him. During his vintage years, television became the prime news medium for millions of Americans. Broadcast news was still a dream when Walter Cronkite was born on this day in 1916, in St. Joseph, Missouri. Now that medium is our window on the world. I have been looking through that window rather closely lately, and I'd like to tell you what I see.

The cash register was granted a patent on this day in 1879. A lot of time slipped by between the cash register's invention and the emergence of the computer. But I think that the machine became the answer to business' prayers on this day in 1879. We started punching keys instead of handwriting receipts. The trouble is, machines seem to have enhanced our capacity to enlarge and compound human error, instead of reducing human error. I am not suggesting that we become Luddites. But I do suggest that we strike a new balance between striving to make machines more error-free and devoting more time to thinking things through manually.

An historic event revealed the secrets of one man's past on this day. In 1922, archaeologist Howard Carter and his patron George Edward Carnavon did not heed the curse of the pharaoh inscribed on the tomb entrance which said: "Any man who enters this tomb I will pounce upon like a cobra." The next year, they didn't heed the words engraved on the burial chamber: "May he inside remain uninjured, the son of Ra." The discovery of King Tutankhamen's tomb in Egypt's Valley of the Kings was an immediate media sensation—the world contracted mummy fever. Even though a cobra did not pounce on the archaeologists, the Egyptian government did. Officials accused the team of grave robbing, and eventually forced Carter to donate his finds to the Cairo Museum. A mosquito bit Carnavon while he was visiting the tomb. He died from infections and complications less than two months after the burial chamber's seals were broken. Any undertaking needs to be driven by more than greed, ambition, or a desire for the limelight. There is a lesson for all of us in the mummy's curse.

Is anyone here familiar with Clinton's Ditch? No, it isn't a Presidential bailout. In 1825, the Erie Canal—nicknamed for its creator, General Clinton—provided a vital connection from the Hudson River all the way across New York State to Lake Erie. At first, most people thought the idea was absurd and potentially disastrous. But on this day, the first vessel to traverse the Erie Canal arrived in New York City. The trip from Buffalo took nine days, which may seem long in these times, but it was a vast improvement over the weeks of grueling overland travel it took before Clinton's Ditch was built. This brings me to my theme for today. In our modern age, there are still doubters and Luddites who perceive every step made in the name of progress as an omen of doom or a signal of civilization's demise. But without innovation, none of those doomsayers would have time to criticize, they'd still be on the road from Buffalo.

NOVEMBER 5

Guy Fawkes Day.

Eugene V. Debs was born, 1855.

The first American automobile patent was granted, 1895.

INTRODUCTIONS

Guy Fawkes Day is the basis for lighthearted celebration throughout Great Britain, even though it commemorates a very serious event. The leader of the Gunpowder Plot, Guy Fawkes, was captured by authorities on this day in 1605 as he was about to blow up the House of Lords. He and a number of coconspirators were tried and executed. Over the centuries, the serious nature of Guy Fawkes' arrest has faded into childhood whimsy. That does happen sometimes, and I cannot help but wonder whether the things we take so seriously today—such as professional sports, or high fashion—are not truly whimsical. Aren't we taking the outrageousness of some current levels of taste too seriously? Let me give you a few examples.

The first U.S. patent for an automobile was issued on this date in 1895, to George B. Selden who had actually invented his creation much earlier. He held off filing his patent while he tried to find backers. He still hadn't gotten either the money or the patent when other people started building automobiles. His patent did garner funding from a few manufacturers. But Henry Ford refused to pay him. He claimed his Model T wasn't based on Selden's design. In the end, Ford made more money. The moral of this story is: Don't hide a good idea while you look for backers. Get it going as fast as you can. I'm going to practice what I just preached right now.

The name of Eugene V. Debs is not well known today. In the early 1900s, his name was both honored and reviled. Born on this day in 1855 in Terre Haute, Indiana, Debs was a labor leader, a socialist, and a Socialist Party presidential candidate. In his time, socialism was not only regarded as an extreme left-wing movement, it was absolute treason in America. What made matters worse was that Debs was an American working man—not a foreign intellectual. He contradicted popular belief. He later became a venerated figure among liberals and even nonsocialists; some of his ideals were eventually incorporated into modern American political platforms. His story reminds me that people with good intentions often have differing opinions. But those differences shouldn't create ill will or passionate reprisals. The latter only creates martyrs, not solutions.

NOVEMBER 6

John Philip Sousa was born, 1854.

Abraham Lincoln was elected U.S. President, 1860.

The first intercollegiate football game took place, 1869.

INTRODUCTIONS

As we consider our present political assets, we may not see another Lincoln on the horizon. But even if we don't, we see a nation less divided, stronger, and a great deal larger than it was in Lincoln's time. Did you know that two days after the election, Lincoln wrote to Vice President Hannibal Hamlin, suggesting that it might be a good idea if they met? They had been elected on this date in 1860, without ever meeting each other. Yes, we have made progress since Lincoln's time. Please be mindful of that as we view the contemporary political scene together in my remarks here today.

On this day in 1869, Rutgers University and Princeton University played the first intercollegiate football game, in New Brunswick, New Jersey. Football, like basketball, has been the great "democratizer" of American college education. It has financed the expansion of student bodies and facilities; given college educations to those who might not have otherwise afforded them; and inspired a great deal of alumni loyalty. Today, on college football's anniversary, I would like to address myself to a question college football coaches and faculties alike are asking themselves. What is the future of America's college system?

American marching bands and march music owe a great deal to John Philip Sousa, who was born in Washington, D.C., on this day in 1854. Nicknamed the "March King," Sousa wrote a number of high-energy, emotion-filled themes like "The Stars and Stripes Forever," and led some of the greatest marching bands of his time. I challenge any American who claims not to be moved by Sousa's music. And on his birthday, I intend to march right into my topic. So here I go. Are you ready to face the music?

NOVEMBER 7

Abolitionist Elijah P. Lovejoy was murdered by a mob, 1837. (See November 9th entry.)

Madame Marie Curie was born, 1867. (See December 21st entry.)

Harper's Weekly featured a Republican elephant, 1874. (See September 27th entry.)

The Bolshevik Revolution began, 1917. (See April 22nd and September 15th entries.)

Billy Graham was born, 1918.

President Richard M. Nixon was re-elected, 1972. (See January 9th entry.)

L. Douglas Wilder of Virginia became the first elected African-American governor, 1989. (See January 11th entry.)

INTRODUCTIONS

On this day in 1917, Vladimir Lenin and his Bolshevik followers started a revolution against Alexander Kerensky's provisional democratic government. The Russian Revolution did not begin as a Communist movement; the Czar was overthrown and replaced by a democratic coalition. But that government seemed to be content to make only a small portion of the reforms the people demanded. They had tasted power. Czar Nicholas II had been blind to public demand—so was Alexander Kerensky. On this day in 1917, the Bolsheviks opted for armed force as the people's weapon of change. Today is a day to remember that with power comes responsibility. Leaders must never forget the people who granted them power. And as a speaker, I will not take that power lightly.

Billy Graham came a long way in the world from Charlotte, North Carolina, where he was born on this day in 1918. As the greatest evangelist of his time, Graham became the friend of presidents and a missionary to the world. The results seem to have been mutually rewarding. Those who find religion are usually willing to put their money where their mouths are. So evangelism is still a consistently self-sustaining effort. I commend it to you as an example of a basic truth. If we believe in something, we should be prepared to do something for that belief. And so I come to you today with a call to believe as well as a call to act.

The world of science is oftentimes thought to be a man's domain. But Madame Marie Curie—who was born on this day in 1867—was a definitive exception to that myth. This dedicated Polish-born French physicist won two Nobel Prizes. In 1903, she shared this most coveted award in physics with Henri Becquerel and her husband Pierre Curie for their research and discovery of radioactive elements and properties. And in 1911, Madame Curie was the sole honoree in the field of chemistry for her successful isolation of pure radium. The grueling hours and years of often solitary dedication deterred many women from pursuing a career in science, almost as much as the men who told them they were not up to the job. Today I wish to honor those courageous women who—like Marie Curie—turned a deaf ear to such absurd theories.

NOVEMBER 8

The Nazi beer hall putsch took place, 1923.

Franklin D. Roosevelt was first elected President, 1932. (See January 30th entry.)

U.S. and British forces invaded Nazi-occupied North Africa, 1942.

INTRODUCTIONS

On November 8, 1923, Adolf Hitler and his followers broke into a Münich beer hall and proclaimed a new German government. They had a few thousand adherents, but they had miscalculated both the government's and the public's attitude. Not only did the announcement fail to garner applause, Hitler was arrested a few days later and sent to prison. Some people thought that was the end for Hitler, but you cannot stop ideas—even bad ones—by imprisonment. You can only stop bad or reckless ideas by spreading better concepts. That is my subject for today.

In 1942, U.S. and British forces invaded Nazi-held North Africa. This day was a major turning point in the outcome of the Second World War. The Allied forces switched roles from a defensive to an offensive posture. It's very important to take the initiative in a situation, rather than passively waiting to react to whatever comes. You and I can do that today. I'd like to give you a few examples.

NOVEMBER 9

Elijah P. Lovejoy was born, 1802.

Carl Sagan was born, 1934.

CrystallKnacht took place, 1938.

New York had its first blackout, 1965. (See July 13th entry.)

The U.N. General Assembly approved ten resolutions condemning South African apartheid, 1976.

The Berlin Wall crumbled, 1989. (See August 12th entry.)

INTRODUCTIONS

Back in 1966, on this day—or, more exactly, this night—most of the northeastern United States, and New York City in particular, experienced a massive power failure. It was a black night in the city, but it proved to be peaceful and cooperative. In fact, nine months later, there was a baby boom on the eastern seaboard. Twelve years later, during the long, hot summer of 1977, New York City had another blackout; but that time looters had a field day. Was it because people had changed, or because the weather was different, or because times were harder? We will never really know. We do know that things are much better in the light than in the dark, and so I am here to try to shed a little light on some items that I hope you will find of interest.

Elijah P. Lovejoy was a newspaper editor. He was also a fiery abolitionist. Born on this day in 1802, in Albion, Maine, Lovejoy established a newspaper in Alton, Illinois. His coverage of the abolitionist movement irritated some of the people in the town, and his presses were destroyed many times. On November 7, 1837, he was murdered by a mob while trying to defend his newspaper. Newspaper publishing and public speaking are both somewhat less hazardous today. And so, with consummate bravery, I leap into the fray.

Apartheid has had many faces in our long history. And it played a major role on this day for the worse and the better. In 1938, Nazi rabble-rousers roamed the streets of German cities looting and destroying Jewish-owned buildings. Shattering glass rang throughout the night and littered the paths of horrified passersby the following morning. CrystallKnacht was the overture to a reign of terror that accelerated from apartheid to genocide. The solemn memory of CrystallKnacht still echoed in 1976, when the U.N. General Assembly approved ten resolutions to condemn a century-long tradition of South African apartheid. We enjoy luxuriating in pleasant memories of our past. But we often learn much more from solemn, sobering moments; their ghosts can spirit us to change and to progress.

Mankind has been seeking the origins of life on this planet for seemingly billions of years. One American astronomer uncovered a very relevant clue to the puzzle. He replicated in a laboratory the creation of a key element found in all living things by exposing water and gases to ultraviolet light, duplicating the sun's life-supporting energy. His experiment yielded that vital life source—amino acids. Born on this day in 1934, Carl Sagan is better known to the public for his highly acclaimed television series, *Cosmos,* than for his pioneering efforts in the laboratory. But then there are billions and billions of things in this universe you don't know about me. So let me begin.

NOVEMBER 10

Martin Luther was born in Eisleben, Germany, 1483. (See January 3rd and October 31st entries.)

The U.S. Marine Corps was established, 1775.

Henry M. Stanley found David Livingstone, 1871.

Hirohito became emperor of Japan, 1926. (See April 29th entry.)

INTRODUCTIONS

Today is the U.S. Marine Corps' birthday. Established by the Continental Congress in 1775, the Marines have seen plenty of action and succeeded in getting many situations "well in hand." But today, I plan to tell you about some things that do not fall into that popular category of "Tell it to the Marines." By the way, did you know that the expression originated with Sir Walter Scott? He had a character say, in his novel *Redgauntlet*, "Tell that to the marines—the sailors won't believe it." So, fellow civilians…

A momentous meeting took place on this day deep in the African jungle. In 1871, journalist Henry M. Stanley met missionary David Livingstone. I have always thought that when Mr. Stanley said, "Dr. Livingstone, I presume," the good doctor should have answered, "You certainly do presume." You see, Dr. Livingstone was far from being lost or in need of rescue. In fact, he remained in Africa long after Stanley returned to civilization and glory. I assure you that I'm not here to play

Stanley to your Livingstone. I do not believe you are lost or need me to find the way. But perhaps I can put up a signpost or two.

NOVEMBER 11

Margaret Hunt revealed the secrets of her medical practice, 1528.

Armistice was proclaimed during the First World War, 1918.

Kurt Vonnegut, Jr. was born, 1922.

"God Bless America" was first sung, 1939.

Egypt and Israel signed a cease-fire agreement sponsored by the U.S. and began peace discussions, 1973. (See October 27th entry.)

INTRODUCTIONS

On this day in 1918, the First World War came to an end. The guns fell silent. And the world waited to assess the destruction of the world's first mechanized, bio-chemical, impersonal war. Unfortunately, the silence did not last as long as the world hoped. Today, as we remember those who died in that first world war, we might give some thought as to how we can prevent those events from ever happening again.

Today, "God Bless America" is so well known as a sort of semi-official national anthem, that it may come as a surprise to you to learn that the song was 22 years old before it was heard in public. Irving Berlin wrote it during the First World War, but it was not publicly sung until this day, in 1939, when Kate Smith introduced it on a radio broadcast. As you may recall, the last line of the song refers to our land as "home, sweet home." Today I propose that we examine what we can do to keep our land that way.

In 1528, a "sorceress" by the name of Margaret Hunt revealed the secrets of her medical practice before the bishop of London's commissary. On this day, she explained how she used a combination of natural herbs and prayers to heal the sick—powerful cures she had learned from a wise woman named Mother Elmet. In Margaret Hunt's day, most people couldn't afford to consult a physician when they were ill. Many more trusted in the old ways of folklore cures and traditional medicine. Surprisingly, the bishop didn't condemn Ms. Hunt for heresy or witchcraft. He was simply curious about the methods that had gained her a popular reputation among the common folk during a time when doctors were generally mistrusted. We still see this age-old battle today. Should we trust tradition or science? I think a healthy balance of both would be the best prescription. Let me tell you why.

Wouldn't be fun to travel through time just by thinking? Imagine what you could do if you could see the future in one place; go back to the past somewhere else knowing things turn out fine; and take a quick break in the present on another planet. Obviously, author Kurt Vonnegut, Jr. thought about it, too. Born on this planet, on this calendar coordinate, in the year allocation 1922, Vonnegut described the highs and lows, the joys and sorrows, the adventures and personal moments of a time traveler who did all of the above in his novel *Slaughterhouse Five*. What if we were all gifted with the ability to observe, experience, and relive every moment at will? But as Vonnegut wrote: so it goes. Let me go back to the present and tell you about our future.

NOVEMBER 12

Elizabeth Cady Stanton was born, 1815.

Grace Kelly was born, 1929.

The U.S. Supreme Court ruled that segregation on public buses was unconstitutional, 1956. (See December 1st entry.)

The World Health Organization announced that Asia was free of smallpox for the first time in history, 1975. (See April 7th entry.)

INTRODUCTIONS

Elizabeth Cady Stanton, who was born in Johnstown, New York, on this day in 1815, was an early feminist leader and author of the historic "Declaration of Sentiments" which was presented at the first Women's Rights Convention in 1848. Stanton spearheaded the successful efforts to give New York State women joint guardianship of their children, the right to own property, and the right to sue in court. Just listing the rights she fought to win is an indication of how bad things were for women before she came along. She did not live to see women win the right to vote. But on her birthday, she deserves to be saluted by both women and men alike. She championed common causes that have no gender—equality and justice. Today I want to talk to you about a few human rights issues that I think Ms. Stanton would have defended if she were alive today.

I don't know how many girls these days dream of becoming royal princesses. It's an old fashioned idea, but it happened once in our own time. Grace Kelly, born on this date in 1929, was a young woman from Philadelphia, Pennsylvania, who became a movie star. That would have made most young women pretty happy. Then she married a monarch—Prince Rainier. As Princess Grace of Monaco, she embarked on a journey that took her a world away from her childhood home. Dreams sometimes do come true. So today I would like to talk about the dreams of some other young American women.

NOVEMBER 13

Louis Brandeis was born, 1856. (See January 28th entry.)

The Holland Tunnel was officially opened, 1927.

Vietnam War Moratorium demonstrations occurred nationwide, 1969.

INTRODUCTIONS

On this day in 1927, the Holland Tunnel was officially opened. This major through-way between New York City and New Jersey runs under the Hudson River. Before it was built, the only way to get across in an automobile was by ferry. There was an earlier railroad tunnel, but the Lincoln Tunnel and George Washington Bridge were yet to come. I must confess that I have never understood why the Hudson River tunnels preceded the Hudson River bridges, but I assume that there was some irrefutable logic afoot. Perhaps the moral of this story is that if you want to get somewhere, you have to dive into deep water. On that note, I'll jump straight into my remarks right now.

Over a three-day period that began on this day in 1969, hundreds of thousands of Americans participated in nationwide demonstrations. Despite fears of violence, the Vietnam Moratorium demonstrations were peaceful, and hence, far more impressive. We are a proud people; we do not like to be threatened; peaceful persuasion is more to American taste. Even the best of causes suffers in America when it is advocated violently. I don't know whether what I am an advocate of is the best cause, but I think you'll be a lot more receptive to clear, simple words than to placards and chants. In that hope, I will now proceed.

NOVEMBER 14

Moby Dick was published, 1851. (See August 1st entry.)

Nellie Bly set out to go around the world in 80 days, 1889. (See January 25th entry.)

INTRODUCTIONS

Herman Melville had written five novels before the one which was published on this day in 1861. As you may have guessed, I'm referring to *Moby Dick,* which begins with the words, "Call me Ishmael" and goes on to say, "I love to sail forbidden seas, and land on barbarous coasts." The imagery of Ishmael's world—the great white whale Moby Dick, and Captain Ahab's grim pursuit—gives me today's theme. The world is full of Ishmaels who are disenchanted with what is around them and who seek forbidden seas and barbarous coasts. It is that state of mind, that human condition, that I wish to address here today.

NOVEMBER 15

The Articles of Confederation were adopted by Congress, 1777. (See January 30th entry.)

Pike's Peak was sighted, 1806.

Antiwar protesters gathered in Washington, D.C., 1969.

INTRODUCTIONS

On this day in 1777, the Continental Congress—facing up to the fact that 13 separate colonies were engaged in a war with England—adopted the Articles of Confederation. Copies of this document were distributed two days later for ratification. The thirteen Articles which provided a framework for uniting the colonies were not completely ratified for four years. And as we know from the history books, it took a while to work out the kinks. Today, I rise to suggest that we as individuals consider chartering our own nonpolitical confederation—an interdependence declaration. How are we mutually interdependent? I'm glad you asked.

A young Army officer named Zebulon Montgomery Pike sighted a high mountain and decided to climb it. Before he got to its base, he was arrested by the Spanish authorities for trespassing on Spanish territory. He didn't climb the mountain. But Pike's Peak in Colorado still bears his name, and this was the day, in 1806, that he first sighted his goal. The moral of Pike's story is simple. The person who reaches for the heights doesn't always get there. But at least that individual identified the goal. By aiming for the heights, we spur ourselves and others to greater achievements. Let me be specific about what I have seen and what we all stand to achieve.

Protest demonstrations are usually limited to single-minded special interest groups banded together by a single cause. But on this day in 1969, passionate protesters representing a variety of interests gathered together in Washington, D.C. Under most circumstances, these 250,000 people would not have united in solidarity for a common cause. But this particular issue—American involvement in the Vietnam War—affected many Americans from many different walks of life. Their assembly did not garner an immediate response from the government, but it did enlighten a large portion of the nation. On that day, many Americans learned that not all wars are fought for patriotic reasons; and not all patriotic Americans advocated the Vietnam War. We, as a nation, are a passionately independent group with as many diverse opinions as we have people. But given a common cause, sometimes we forget our differences and unite to create a powerful tool—the voice of the people. Today, I'd like to address an issue that needs the people's voice to cheer it on to becoming a reality.

November 16

The Incan empire fell to Spain, 1532.

General William Sherman made his march to the sea, 1864.

The U.S. and U.S.S.R. established diplomatic relations, 1933.

INTRODUCTIONS

Back in 1933, this was the day when the United States and Soviet Russia established diplomatic relations. They finally agreed to talk to each other. I am happy to establish diplomatic relations with this audience today, and I hope we will both remain diplomatic after my speech is over.

A bitter residue was all that was left after General William Tecumseh Sherman marched with his troops from Atlanta to the sea. It began on this day, in 1864, and in its wake a broad scar of ruin and destruction marred the South; and tainted the memories of later generations. That memory only recently seems to be fading. We need to remember the details of important events, but we also need to lose the bitterness that some memories leave behind. Otherwise, memories become ghosts that haunt our dreams, never allowing them to be realized. We must always look forward and place the past where it belongs: as a reflective reference for the future; not a stained mirror of what could have been.

For want of a nail, a shoe was lost. For want of a shoe, the horse was lost. For want of gold, an empire was lost—all in the name of greed. As explorers arrived in the New World, they heard tales of riches beyond the imagination—stories of golden cities. They were lured by the lust for gold. Spanish explorer Francisco Pizarro was no exception when he landed in South America. He destroyed entire Incan cities which had been built by an advanced civilization that worshipped the sun and treated gold as a gift from their god. On this day, in 1532, the Incan empire fell. Pizarro took the Incan emperor Atahualpa prisoner and demanded a ransom of gold. The Incans paid, but Pizarro murdered his prisoner in the name of Christianity. What Pizarro didn't destroy on that day was a treasure that remained concealed high up in the clouds, protected by the sun god—Machu Picchu, the last city of the Incas. Some of you may argue that gold built nations, including our own. But every civilization, every tribe, every nation has contributed to the world's treasury of wisdom, and it takes great wisdom to know how to use and preserve the world's blue, green, and golden riches.

NOVEMBER 17

The Act of Supremacy—which declared King Henry VIII as head of the Church of England—was passed by Parliament, 1534. (See February 11th entry.)

Elizabeth I ascended to the British throne after the death of Queen Mary I, 1558. (See September 7th entry.)

John Peter Zenger was arrested for libel, 1734. (See August 4th entry.)

The SALT talks began in Helsinki, 1969.

The U.S. House of Representatives approved the North American Free Trade Agreement: 238 to 200 votes, 1993. (See April 14th entry.)

INTRODUCTIONS

On this day in 1969, the United States and Soviet Russia began the strategic arms limitation talks. In one sense, SALT proved to be a smashing success: The two nations were still talking eight years later. Perhaps they should have considered having strategic talk limitation talks. At any rate, I am imposing my own talk limitation here today. This is not an open-ended discussion and I shall limit the extent to which it is an open-mouthed one as well.

NOVEMBER 18

L.J.M. Daguerre was born, 1789.

U.S. Navy Captain Nathaniel B. Palmer discovered Antarctica, 1820.

W.S. Gilbert was born, 1836.

Standard Time was adopted in the U.S., 1883.

INTRODUCTIONS

Until this date, every locality in America set its own time preference. My time was not necessarily your time. In 1883, Standard Time was adopted in the United States and the resulting time zone system made life a lot simpler. Now we have time in common. I will try to be careful with your time as I proceed to use mine.

Most of us have an ancient photograph or two of ancestors. Most of us own at least one camera. All of this traces back to a man who was born on this day in 1789 in Cormeilles, France. Louis Daguerre gave his name to the daguerreotype—an early type of photograph. It was Daguerre who popularized photography; who first proved that a picture was worth a thousand words. But I was not asked here today to take your picture. So instead I will offer you a thousand words, more or less.

On W.S. Gilbert's birthday, I can be forgiven—as a speaker—for treating my assignment a bit lightly. Gilbert, of Gilbert and Sullivan fame, was born on this day in 1836, in London. He viewed life with a sometimes ironically lighthearted view; and wrote satirical operettas with Sir Arthur Sullivan that reflected the not-so-subtly humorous side of Victorian morals and mores. Gilbert once wrote that "when everyone is somebody, then no one's anybody." He also felt that "things are seldom what they seem, skim milk masquerades as cream." And he duly noted that "the Law is the true embodiment of everything that's excellent; it has no kind of fault or flaw, and I, my lords, embody the Law." I have no original philosophical gems to offer here today, but now that W.S. Gilbert has set the facts straight, I shall proceed.

Not to bring up a chilly subject, but on this day in 1820, U.S. Navy Captain Nathaniel B. Palmer discovered the last continent: Antarctica. This desolate land of ice and snow may not be fit for man's habitation, but it is still the home to a unique collection of birds and beasts. Elephant seals wallow on the rocky shores; but Antarctica's more famous residents are the penguins. Majestic emperor penguins proudly stand in their colorful suits; eccentric rockhoppers, with their lime-green and shocking pink headdresses leap from boulder to boulder; and king penguins, uniformly stroll in groups to the beach in their trademark tuxedos, and patiently wait for one brave soul to dive into the water before the rest follow in unison. It's a great relief to know that Captain Palmer didn't think Antarctica was a future settlement site. I guess he thought the place was already overrun with enough layabouts, strutting dandies, eccentrics, and meek conformists without adding on humanity's unique species. Who knows what would happen to the neighborhood if they moved in?

NOVEMBER 19

The *Mayflower* arrived off the coast of Cape Cod, 1620. (See July 22nd and November 21st entries.)

Peregrine White was born aboard the *Mayflower,* 1620.

Lord Chesterfield wrote about wisdom, 1745.

President Lincoln delivered the Gettysburg Address, 1863.

Indira Gandhi was born, 1917. (See January 19th and June 6th entries.)

The Alaska Highway was formally opened, 1942. (See June 12th entry.)

The U.S. Senate voted 61 to 38 in favor of the North American Free Trade Agreement, 1993. (See November 17th entry.)

INTRODUCTIONS

On this day, in 1620, the *Mayflower* arrived off Cape Cod. I imagine the Pilgrims aboard that ship had somewhat the same feeling as the audience here today—wondering why they got into this and what in the world was going to come up next. I'm quite sure Peregrine White, the first English child born in new England, who was born on this day aboard the *Mayflower,* wasn't expected to make such a dramatic debut. I don't think I have any great surprises for you. But I do have a few thoughts and observations which I hope you will find of interest.

The Earl of Chesterfield was a fountainhead of good advice for his son; and he wrote most of his suggestions in a journal. On this date, in 1745, Lord Chesterfield's advice was this: "Be wiser than other people if you can, but do not tell them so." Never were wiser words placed in the mind of a speaker. I speak to you today with absolutely no illusions of superior wisdom on my part—and the hope that my audience feels the same.

On this day in 1863, President Abraham Lincoln dedicated a national cemetery with a few brief remarks. He stood at the site in Gettysburg, Pennsylvania, and delivered an address that he had written on a paper bag during the train trip from Washington. I am planning to make a few brief remarks myself here today. And I assure you, in advance, that there is no further resemblance between what I am about to say and Lincoln's immortal address. On the anniversary of the Gettysburg Address, we have the opportunity to dedicate ourselves. I hope that what I have to say can provide a target or two.

Jawaharlal Nehru, independent India's first prime minister, headed a government caught in a political whirlwind. Freedom from British rule was not followed by peace; extremists representing numerous political and religious sects demanded to be heard—and sometimes violently. Nehru's daughter Indira Gandhi—who was born on this day in 1917—entered an equally unsettled world during her four terms as India's prime minister. During her last term in office, Sikh extremists instigated riots and used terrorist tactics in an attempt to be heard. Gandhi sent armed forces to their holiest shrine—the Golden Temple of Amristar in the Punjab—where reportedly 600 lives were lost in a violent confrontation. To avenge the death of their compatriots, Gandhi herself was assassinated by Sikh terrorists who took full responsibility. It is difficult to find common ground in a diversely opinionated world, but we must always try lest we become martyrs to nothing and victims of all.

NOVEMBER 20

Robert F. Kennedy was born, 1920.

International War Crimes Tribunal trials began, 1945.

The Hubble Space Telescope photographed the Eagle Nebula, 1995.

INTRODUCTIONS

Today is Robert F. Kennedy's birthday. Born in 1925, in Brookline, Massachusetts, Kennedy once said, "Some people see things as they are, and say why. I dream things that never were and say, why not." Today I propose to speak of things that could be, and say, why not?

An International War Crimes Tribunal was set up to try suspected Nazi war criminals on this day in 1945, in Nuremberg, Germany. The trial process was not endless and the verdicts were prompt; but many decades later, in our own country and elsewhere, war criminals were still being sought, extradited, or simply died while still in hiding. And there had been several wars in between. Second World War crimes were followed by other crimes committed in later conflicts; and it is time to wonder what has been learned. That, indeed, is my subject today. What, in terms of human justice, have we learned in our time?

An awe-inspiring image was sent back to earth on this day in 1995. In its exploration of our universe, the Hubble Space Telescope sighted and photographed the birth of a star. The image of the Eagle Nebula's towering mass expanding and taking shape reminds us how powerful and majestic life truly is. Out of nothing more than air, ideas also take shape like the stars in the sky. Let's take a closer look at a few ideas with star potential right now.

NOVEMBER 21

The Mayflower Compact was signed, 1620. (See July 22nd and November 19th entries.)

Voltaire was born, 1694.

The first manned balloon flight took place, 1783. (See June 5th entry.)

INTRODUCTIONS

The first human flight in a free-floating balloon took place on this day. Back in 1783, Joseph and Jacques Montgolfier had already demonstrated their hot-air balloon with a 10-minute flight over Annonay, France. Their project interested the King of France, who decided to approve a manned-flight demonstration. Jean Pilatre de Rozier and the Marquis d'Arlandes thought it would garner some personal notoriety in the history books if they volunteered to fly. They got their wish. I wonder how many other times glory has sparked accomplishment. I'm not only the passenger in my own hot-air balloon here today—but the design and the hot air are all my own.

Self-government in America actually began in deep water aboard the *Mayflower* off Cape Cod on this day in 1620, when the Pilgrims signed the Mayflower Compact for what they called "a civil body politic." Self-government, I am happy to say, is not in deep water these days. And I have a few suggestions to offer to keep the waters calm.

François-Marie Arouet was born on this day in 1694, in Paris. This fact becomes a little more meaningful when I add that François-Marie Arouet adopted the pen name Voltaire. Among this playwright and author's observations was his remark that "The way to be a bore is to say everything." Since I do not want to bore you here today, I will try not to say everything. That will make both the task of talking and the task of listening somewhat more bearable.

NOVEMBER 22

SOS was adopted as the international distress signal, 1906.

The flying boat, *The China Clipper,* left San Francisco on the first transpacific airmail flight, 1935.

President John F. Kennedy was assassinated, 1963. (See May 29th entry.)

The supersonic Concorde jet began service to New York from London and Paris, 1977. (See January 21st entry.)

INTRODUCTIONS

November 22 is a date that will always be remembered by the generations who lived through it in 1963. It was the fatal day President John F. Kennedy was assassinated. So much of what transpired after that was seen on television throughout the world, vividly engraved in millions of minds. Questions about the incident have persisted ever since. It is the nature of human beings to ask questions, to wonder, to be skeptical. It was President Kennedy's nature to stand back and look at himself—and sometimes to be amused. I would like to think that in this regard he was a typical American; that, while we are serious in our purposes, we don't take ourselves too seriously. As Kennedy said months before he died, "...if we cannot end now our differences, at least we can make the world safe for diversity." So if you find you disagree with what I am about to say, remember the Kennedy injunction, and together we will make the world safe for diversity.

It's rough enough when people from different parts of the world attempt to talk to each other. Luckily, there is one universal phrase. Ever since this day, in 1906, the letters SOS—spelled out in wireless code—have been used as the international distress signal. I wonder why we can have a universal distress call and still not be able to convey happy news to each other in the same easy fashion. I'm not signaling an SOS to you today. Instead, I owe you much happier, and hopefully, safer signals from my post at this podium.

The act of flying over deep waters saw two high points on this day in history. In 1935, Pan-American's flying boat—*The China Clipper*—left San Francisco carrying the first air-mail load across the Pacific Ocean. And in 1977, the supersonic Concorde jet expanded its service across the Atlantic Ocean to New York City from London and Paris. *The China Clipper* was eventually mothballed as faster planes were developed, but neither it nor the Concorde added to the air-crash statistics. With a safety record like this, I think it's reasonable to suggest we fly over some fairly deep subjects without bailing out. Here goes.

Nᴏᴠᴇᴍʙᴇʀ 23

Abigail Smith Adams was born, 1744.

The Female Medical Educational Society was established, 1848.

INTRODUCTIONS

When Abigail Smith was born in Weymouth, Massachusetts on this day in 1744, she never dreamed that she would celebrate her birthday in 1800 in the new Executive Mansion as the nation's First Lady. When Abigail Smith married John Adams, she became the wife of one President and the mother of another. She also became one of the first major spokespersons for women's rights in America. After the Declaration of Independence was signed, she wrote to her husband, "In the new code of laws which I now assume will be needed—please give a thought to the ladies and see to it that it is put beyond the power of the vicious and lawless...to treat us with cruelty and indignity with impunity. Don't forget that all men would be tyrants if they could." On Abigail Adams' birthday today, I think it is only fair to point out that the Adams family's amazing contributions were not those of men alone. American men and women make an unbeatable combination, and it is that combination whose common efforts I salute today.

Today is the anniversary of the founding of the first women's medical society in America, in 1848. The organization was called the Female Medical Educational Society of Boston. What I found interesting was that it was established in the same year as the all-male American Medical Association; and that the Female Medical Educational Society's officers were all men! I want to talk today about our changing times, and times have certainly changed since the men organized the Female Medical Educational Society.

November 24

Lee Harvey Oswald was killed, 1963. (See November 22nd entry.)

Chief Justice Earl Warren spoke at President Kennedy's memorial service, 1963.

Barbed wire was patented by Joseph Glidden of DeKalb, IL, 1874.

The U.S. Congress passed the Brady handgun control bill, 1993.

INTRODUCTIONS

Probably no homicide has ever been witnessed by more people than the shooting of President Kennedy's accused assassin Lee Harvey Oswald. He was shot by Jack Ruby at the Dallas city jail in front of national television cameras, on this day, in 1963. The whole world saw it happen; but we have yet to fully understand how and why. Ironically, on this same day in 1993, the U.S. Congress passed the Brady handgun control bill, a long-needed measure that was triggered by the attempted assassination of President Ronald Reagan and the shooting of one of his aides. It often challenges our sense of logic to see how much time goes by before we react to a serious situation. Sadly, it sometimes takes more than a single incident to make us face the truth and move forward. That issue is the theme for my remarks today.

I can think of no better way to begin my remarks here today than to quote what Chief Justice Earl Warren said at President Kennedy's memorial tribute on this day in 1963. He said: "If we really love this country, if we truly love justice and mercy, if we fervently want to make this nation better for those who are to follow us, we can at least abjure the hatred that consumes people, the false accusations that divide us and the bitterness that begets violence." In peace and good will, my friends, I humbly raise my voice.

Before I begin, I'd like to set the record straight on a common misunderstanding. When our national poet laureate Robert Frost penned the phrase "good fences make good neighbors," he also went to say that walls were only good for tearing down. But on this day in 1874, Joseph Glidden of DeKalb, Illinois, received a patent for barbed wire, which has proved useful in agriculture, security, and defense. I'd like to say good fences make good boundaries, and for public speakers, time boundaries keep audiences from running out.

NOVEMBER 25

The feast day of St. Catherine.

Andrew Carnegie was born, 1846. (See December 24th entry.)

Carry Nation was born, 1846. (See August 29th entry.)

Great Britain's Prime Minister Benjamin Disraeli described his times, 1864.

Russia had its last free election for more than half a century, 1917.

The world's longest-running play, Agatha Christie's *The Mousetrap,* opened in London, 1952. (See September 15th entry.)

INTRODUCTIONS

According to tradition, today is when young Parisian seamstresses are supposed to go out on a carnival manhunt. Why? Because that's how they celebrated the feast of St. Catherine for centuries. Some young American men may say this is an anachronism. Young American women don't need a St. Catherine's Day—and neither do young American men. But I am not here to tell you things about American men and women that you already know. Rather, I'm here to take a look at some other matters that good old St. Catherine could never have encountered.

On this day in 1917, there was a free election held in Russia to select a constituent democratic assembly after Czar Nicholas II abdicated. Russian voters chose an assembly in which less than a third of the deputies were Bolshevik Communists. So the Bolsheviks suppressed the assembly when it convened the following January. Since I am going to be talking today about some American political problems, I thought it might be helpful to remember that we solve our problems a little differently. To live and speak in a climate of freedom, I remind you, makes every problem just a little smaller.

Great Britain's Prime Minister Benjamin Disraeli viewed his times with a very critical eye. On this day in 1864, he noted that "the characteristic of the present age is craving credulity." I suspect that if Disraeli were alive today, he would say the same thing. "Craving credulity"—the ardent eagerness to find things to believe in—is also part of our time. Young and old alike follow false leadership and waste their substance on false illusions. Will this change? Is it a phenomenon of our times or of all times? Today I want to share with you some thoughts about what people are looking for—and where.

The world's richest man, Andrew Carnegie, once said, "A man who dies rich, dies in disgrace." On this day in 1835, Carnegie was born into a working-class family in Dunfermline, Scotland. When they emigrated to the United States, the young nation was just emerging as an industrial giant; and Andrew Carnegie's wealth grew right along with it. He built a steel-manufacturing empire which he sold in 1901 to another industrial giant, J. Pierpont Morgan, for what was at that time $250,000,000. That sale of the Carnegie Steel Company not only made Carnegie the richest man in the world, it allowed him to do whatever he wanted. So he built and stocked hundreds of free public libraries across the United States, Canada, and Great Britain. He established social-assistance programs in Scotland. He founded universities and educational foundations which are still in existence today. Carnegie was still rich when he died, but he certainly did not die in disgrace; and his life serves as the framework for my remarks today.

NOVEMBER 26

A lion was first exhibited in America, 1716.

The first presidentially proclaimed Thanksgiving Day was observed, 1789. (See October 3rd entry.)

INTRODUCTIONS

Among the more obscure annals of American history is the saga of the first lion ever seen on these shores. The exhibition of this king of beasts was announced in Boston on this day in 1716. I feel somewhat as that lion must have felt: quietly gauging your mood as you, in turn, wait expectantly for me to roar. I hope you won't mind if I speak in more gentle tones. I may not roar like a lion, but I assure you I'm not sheepish about saying what's on my mind.

NOVEMBER 27

Pope Urban II called for a crusade, 1095.

Chaim Weizmann was born, 1874.

The Army War College was authorized, 1901.

New York City's Pennsylvania Station opened, 1910.

INTRODUCTIONS

On this day, in 1901, the Army War College was authorized. With this act, our nation officially recognized that the art of warfare had become much more complex. If they thought it was complicated in 1901, what would its founders think today? Now, more than ever, the most important weapon of offense or defense is not hardware, it's knowledge. Admittedly, some of today's knowledge incorporates an understanding of hardware usage. But the human mind is still the most potent instrument of all. And so today, I would like to explore what lies in the American mind—the attitudes with which we approach the world in which we live.

During the First World War, an émigré scientist was director of the British Admiralty laboratories. In 1874, Chaim Weizmann was born on this day in Russian Poland. This brilliant scientist helped synthesize some of the elemental ingredients needed for the manufacture of explosives. He was also an active Zionist. Years later, when Israel became a nation, Weizmann was elected to be its first president; and a great scientific institute bears his name today. Weizmann's birthday reminds us that scientists are not all isolationists; they can also be political leaders. I don't know how you feel about these facts, but I find them very encouraging. Let me tell you why I think public life today needs all the talent it can get.

This is the anniversary of the crusades. In 1095, Pope Urban II called for a crusade to free the Holy Land from Islamic occupation. The supreme head of the Catholic Church promised that every soldier who participated in this holy war would be absolved of his sins. Many requests for the defense of the Byzantine empire and the Holy Land had come from lords and ambassadors. But it took Pope Urban's plea to inspire armies to take up the sword for their faith. Defense of a common belief can motivate many to act. I hope my remarks today concerning some of our mutually held beliefs will ignite you to act.

By 1910, the nation's railroad system had grown from horse-drawn trains to a gigantic web of locomotives streaming down steel roads from coast to coast. It had taken nearly a half century for this invention to became the backbone of the nation's transportation system. And on this particular day, the world's largest railroad station opened. In its time, New York's Pennsylvania Station soon had more trains, more passengers, and more cargo passing through its maze of tracks and platforms than the world had ever seen. It helped make that city the nation's eastern hub. In a world that is clamoring for a return to public transportation, I think it's time to reflect on what Pennsylvania Station and the railroad systems it serviced meant to people in its heyday. Its importance might inspire us in our own time.

NOVEMBER 28

Ferdinand Magellan reached the Pacific Ocean from the Atlantic, 1520.

Commander Richard E. Byrd started his flight over the South Pole, 1929.

Communist China was turned down for admission to the United Nations, 1967.

INTRODUCTIONS

Down at the tail end of South America is a rough body of water known as the Straits of Magellan. The Straits were discovered by Ferdinand Magellan in 1520, as he was trying to find an eastern route to the Moluccan Islands in the Pacific. On this day, Magellan reached the Pacific Ocean. I think it is fair to say that he did it the hard way. Today my goal is not to reach the Pacific, but rather to unveil something specific; and I shall try not to circumnavigate the globe to get there.

When Ferdinand Magellan went through the Straits that now bear his name he must have thought he was at the bottom of the world. But four centuries later, Commander Richard E. Byrd actually hit bottom. On this day in 1929, Byrd took off with copilot Bernt Balchen and a flight crew from their Antarctic base, called Little America, and headed for the South Pole. Byrd showed the world that Antarctica could be conquered. But at what consequence? Let's discuss this today.

On this day in 1967, the United Nations assembly voted on the question of admitting the People's Republic of China into its organization. And for the eighteenth time, that nation was turned down. This sounds like ancient history, now, because the People's Republic of China has been an active United Nations member for quite a few years. But I mention it to emphasize that times change; and we change with them. We are changing right now. May I give you some examples?

NOVEMBER 29

Karl Marx wrote to Abraham Lincoln, 1865.

The First Army-Navy football game was played, 1890.

Busby Berkeley was born, 1895.

Commander Richard E. Byrd flew over the South Pole, 1929. (See November 28th entry.)

INTRODUCTIONS

This day marks the anniversary of a bitter, continuing battle between two major armed forces—the Army and the Navy. The battle began in 1890, and I see no sign of its ending. What I am talking about, of course, is the annual Army-Navy football game. In other countries, armed forces get caught up in rival juntas and cabals, competing for government control. I find it comforting that our military's power plays and deceits occur on the athletic field. And now, it is only fitting that we go into a huddle to discuss our nation's next move.

In the course of preparing today's remarks, I came across a letter dated November 29, 1865, which was supposedly sent to Abraham Lincoln. The year is obviously wrong, because Lincoln died in April of that year. But if the text of the letter is accurate, it is rather interesting. The letter read, "From the commencement of the titanic struggle in America, the working men of Europe felt instinctively that the Star Spangled Banner carried the destiny of their class." I say this letter is rather interesting not only because of its content but also because of its author. We are told the letter was sent by Karl Marx. We have come a long way from the days when America was considered the mecca of radicalism; but it may put things in a better context to realize that the American concept of freedom was pretty radical back then; and, indeed, is still considered pretty radical today in some quarters. I begin my remarks, then, with the premise that we represent the wave of the future. Now let's see how it works.

In the dark days of the Great Depression, many people went to the theater to forget their troubles for an hour or two in front of the flickering silver screen. Thanks to filmmaker Busby Berkeley who was born on this day in 1895, audiences got what they wanted: light comedy and pretty girls; hit songs and pretty girls; tap dancing and pretty girls; and oh yes, I almost forgot, pretty girls. Berkeley nicknamed them and titled many of his films as the "Golddiggers." Of course, the prettiest, most talented member of Berkeley's star-studded Golddiggers cast was his wife Ruby Keeler who, along with costar Dick Powell, tap-danced and sang their way into America's hearts. Now, I certainly can't tap-dance or sing. And I can assure you that I'm no golddigger. But with any luck, I can talk my way into your hearts.

NOVEMBER 30

Mark Twain was born, 1835.

Winston Churchill was born, 1874.

The U.S.S.R. invaded Finland, 1939.

INTRODUCTIONS

On this day, in 1874, Winston Leonard Spencer Churchill was born in Oxfordshire, England. His sometimes adventurous, but always distinguished career as a writer and politician didn't end when he reached retirement age. In fact, he embarked on a new career—at a time when most people would rest on their laurels—as Great

Britain's Prime Minister during the Second World War. Churchill's eloquent words rallied a nation bombarded by bombs. And on his 80th birthday, in 1954, Churchill fudged a bit, for the first time, when he said, "I have never accepted what many people have kindly said, namely that I inspired the nation. It was the nation…that had the lion heart. I had the luck to be called upon to give the roar." Churchill certainly did roar, but luck had little to do with it. The audience gives a speaker the chance to sound off, but the sound itself is up to the speaker. I thank you for the opportunity you have given me here today. Now let's see what I can do with it.

Back in 1835, Samuel Langhorne Clemens was born on this day in Florida, Missouri. People didn't think Samuel would amount to very much while he was growing up along the Mississippi River valley. He never held down a job for very long, or put much effort into the ones he held. But Samuel was just a late bloomer. In fact, when he took the pen name of Mark Twain, the whole world opened its doors and its hearts to him. "Thunder is good," he once wrote, "thunder is impressive; but it is lightning that does the work." Perhaps I can raise some thunder today about the foolhardy notion that you have to be young to be a success. Fresh ideas—like lightning bolts—have been known to strike even old oaks like me.

In 1938, a lot of people tried to find excuses for Soviet Russia's actions when that nation signed a treaty with Nazi Germany. But excuses were hard to find when, on this day in 1939, Russia invaded Finland. The world cheered when that nation held off the invasion for three months. Ultimately, of course, Russia imposed its own peace on Finland. We should learn to judge people and nations not by what they say, but by what they do. Of course, in my case what I do is stand up here and speak to you. It's your job to judge my intentions.

DECEMBER

INTRODUCTION:

Christmas comes but once a year, and unluckily the Christmas shopping season only lasts that long as well. There was a time when Christmas advertising didn't appear in newspapers, magazines, or on television until the first week of December. Slowly but surely, the kickoff date was moved to the day after Thanksgiving. Nowadays, you'll find Christmas gift-giving ideas and advertising making an appearance right after Halloween. At this accelerated rate, in another century, we'll be Christmas shopping all year long! But before I make all of you anxiety-ridden over Christmas and the Christmas shopping season, let me give you a few pieces of good cheer and then send you on your merry way.

DECEMBER 1

A telephone was first installed in the White House, 1880.

The first drive-in gas station was opened in Pittsburgh by the Gulf Refining Co., 1913.

Boys Town was founded, 1917.

Lady Astor joined the British Parliament, 1919.

Skywriting was introduced, 1922.

Rosa Parks refused to give up her seat on a city bus, 1955. (See November 12th entry.)

President Jimmy Carter placed more than 56 million acres of Alaska's federal lands into the national park system, 1978.

INTRODUCTIONS

In 1917, Father Edward Flanagan founded a unique institution on this day in Omaha, Nebraska. It was called Boys Town. Its basic concept centered on Father Flanagan's firm belief that, in his words, "There is no such thing as a bad boy." Father Flanagan was no starry-eyed dreamer. He defined a serious problem that faced the nation; it wasn't that there were bad boys being born, it was the conditions they lived in that created their problems. Flanagan tried to put friendless boys into an environment where they could have an opportunity to grow up as good citizens. That isn't a bad idea for the rest of us. Today, I'd like to address myself to what we can do to bring out the good in everyone.

We first saw the writing in the sky instead of on the wall, I am told, on this day in 1922, when a pilot flew over New York City and released a trail of white smoke that spelled out the friendly word "hello." Since then, skywriters have announced everything from "Eat at Joe's" to "Will You Marry Me?" Certainly the British Parliament saw the writing on wall on this day, in 1919, when Lady Astor was sworn in as their first female member. Since I'm not a licensed pilot, nor a stone mason, nor a member of Parliament, I guess I'll have to make today's announcement verbally.

This was certainly an historic day, in 1880, when the first telephone was installed in the White House. This invention assured the public, in no small way, that the President of the United States could keep in touch with the needs of the nation. In 1913, those needs had certainly changed. On this day, the nation's first drive-in gas station was opened for business by the Gulf Refining Company in Pittsburgh, Pennsylvania. But the nation's chief executive must always remain mindful of the nation's future needs, not just those in the immediate present. And also on this same day, in 1978, President Jimmy Carter responded to the needs of future generations when he placed more than 56 million acres of Alaska's federal lands into the national park system to protect them from mineral or oil development. Progress has taken many turns, but as long as we make careful decisions at each fork, we can be assured safe travel on the road to our future.

Some people say that one small individual can't make a difference in this huge world. But today marks an anniversary that proves those naysayers are wrong. In 1955, Miss Rosa Parks had finished a long, exhausting day of work. She got on a city bus in Montgomery, Alabama, but rather than walking to the back and taking a seat, she chose to sit toward the front. This African-American seamstress was arrested when she refused to give up her seat to a white person. It was a crime back then, not only in South Africa, but right here in America. And this was the incident that sparked a citywide boycott; that progressed into a court battle; and eventually ended in a U.S. Supreme Court ruling that decided against the racial segregation of public transportation throughout the nation. The story of Rosa Parks should remind all of us that each individual can make a difference no matter how great the odds. I certainly am going to try in my own small way to make a difference here right now.

D ECEMBER 2

President James Monroe declared the Monroe Doctrine, 1823. (See April 28th entry.)

The Manhattan Project achieved the first man-made atomic chain-reaction, 1942.

Senator McCarthy was censured by the U.S. Senate, 1954. (See February 21st entry.)

The Archbishop of Canterbury visited Pope John XXIII, 1960.

INTRODUCTIONS

In 1823, on this day, President James Monroe told the European powers to stay out of the western hemisphere. We may remember that portion of the Monroe Doctrine, but most of us don't recognize the other statement from that document, in which President Monroe declared that "In the wars of the European powers, in matters relating to themselves, we have never taken part, nor does it comport with our policy to do so." All living beings like to protect what they regard as their territory. Today, I'd like to suggest taking a closer look at what can be deemed as our territory. I don't mean this world, this hemisphere, or this nation. I'm talking about our cities and our homes. Christmas, like charity, starts at home, and I have a few suggestions for the season.

Some years ago, a small plaque was placed on the wall at Stagg Field, the University of Chicago's football stadium. Inscribed on this marker are the following words: "On December 2, 1942, man achieved here the first self-sustaining chain reaction and thereby initiated the controlled release of nuclear energy." In a secret laboratory below the stadium, the Manhattan Project research team created the first man-made atomic chain reaction from uranium ore. Its success exploded into the public's consciousness three years later at Hiroshima and Nagasaki; and later still on Bikini Atoll in the South Pacific. One of the Manhattan Project's leaders, J. Robert Oppenheimer, fought for the peaceful use of atomic power for the rest of his life. Other team members, like Enrico Fermi, sought to build bigger and better weapons from the knowledge gained under the football stadium. The chain reaction caused by this singular event reminds me that no one is ever sure how his or her actions will affect the future of others. Let's discuss those consequences today.

Precedents are often made to be broken. And this day marks the anniversary of a long-held precedent that stood on a flimsy foundation for nearly four hundred years. In 1960, The Archbishop of Canterbury visited Pope John XXIII at the Vatican. The two heads of two major Christian religions broke a senseless tradition that had been set back in the 1500s by Great Britain's King Henry VIII and Pope Leo X. Sometimes a serious rift can occur between people who, in reality, share a lot in common. There's one closer to home that's been nagging at me for a long time. I hope all of you will join me in working to break that precedent right here and now.

DECEMBER 3

John Paul Jones hoisted the first seagoing American flag, 1775.

INTRODUCTIONS

On this day in 1775, Lieutenant John Paul Jones raised the American flag aboard the flagship of the newly formed Continental Navy, the *Alfred*. The banner he proudly flew bore 13 stripes and the British Union Jack in place of our stars. It was called the Grand Union flag. John Paul Jones' days of glory were still ahead of him; but this day was a glorious beginning. I have modestly raised the flag here today by appearing before all of you. So now let's weigh anchor and test the wind.

DECEMBER 4

The first Thanksgiving celebration took place in America, 1619.
The phonograph was invented, 1877.

INTRODUCTIONS

When we think of Thanksgiving, visions of the Pilgrims sitting down to a groaning board of food come to mind. But the Pilgrims weren't even at the first American Thanksgiving. That historic event occurred on this day in 1619, at Berkeley Plantation in Virginia—a year before the Pilgrims landed in Massachusetts. Obviously we've been giving thanks for longer than most of us thought. But it's really not important because the spirit of thankfulness should be timeless and calendarless. And since this is the season of timeless and calendarless sentiments, I am happy to have so pleasant an occasion to speak to you.

In 1877, on the night of December 4, some of Thomas A. Edison's co-workers sat up until the wee dawn hours in his New Jersey laboratory at Menlo Park. They were playing with a new device that had just been completed—the phonograph. Edison and his assistants weren't really playing; they were recording and testing their presentation for a public demonstration that was held a few days later. History does not record how early in the game they had trouble with a needle stuck in a groove. But I take the occasion of the phonograph's anniversary to raise my voice in person. This is not a recording and I hope you won't think I'm a broken record.

DECEMBER 5

Phi Beta Kappa was organized, 1776. (See February 6th entry.)

General George Armstrong Custer was born, 1839. (See June 25th entry.)

Walt Disney was born, 1901.

Otto Preminger was born, 1906.

The Twenty-first Amendment, which repealed the Eighteenth Amendment, was passed by the U.S. Congress, 1933. (See January 16th entry.)

INTRODUCTIONS

Today is Walt Disney's birthday. In 1901, the man who introduced Mickey Mouse and Donald Duck and Sneezy and Dopey and Goofy to the world was born in Chicago. Disney's contributions went a lot deeper than his talents as an animator. Did you ever hear the song, "Who's Afraid of the Big Bad Wolf?" That came to us courtesy of Walt Disney, who created a park just south of Los Angeles where parents and children could have fun living out their fantasies of frontier life, exploring fairy tale castles, and touring snow-capped alpine mountains. I can't speak in anger before you today without reminding myself of Donald Duck's tirades; so I will approach my subject with the Disney touch for making all of you feel happy.

Even though today is Otto Preminger's birthday, I will avoid making a spectacle of myself here on the podium. Preminger, who was born in 1906, was known for making spectacles—megabudget films presented on the big screen. From the looks of this audience, we do seem to have a cast of thousands.

D ECEMBER 6

The feast day of St. Nicholas.

Gerald R. Ford was appointed Vice President, 1973. (See July 14th entry.)

Joyce Kilmer was born, 1886.

INTRODUCTIONS

Today is the feast of St. Nicholas, patron saint of children and sailors. In many parts of the world, this day is considered a pleasant prelude to the Christmas season. St. Nicholas was a bishop who lived in Asia Minor during the fourth century; who has become the worldwide personification of kindness and good will. Stories of his legendary deeds grew over the years until he became a sleigh-riding, jolly gentleman named Santa Claus. But no matter which version of this saint's life you fondly remember, I hope St. Nicholas' spirit lives in your hearts and minds today.

"I think that I shall never see / a poem lovely as a tree" was a sentiment written by a poet born on this day in 1886. Joyce Kilmer wrote that immortal contemplation while serving as a soldier during the First World War. I would like to rewrite this line as the theme for my remarks here today: I hope that I shall live to see, a world as peaceful as this one could be. But to complete this speech in my allotted time, I think I'd better cease to rhyme.

D ECEMBER 7

Delaware became the first state to ratify the U.S. Constitution, 1787. (Delaware Day)

The U.S. declared war on Austro-Hungary, 1917. (See April 6th entry.)

Japanese air forces attacked the U.S. naval base at Pearl Harbor, Hawaii, 1941.

The U.S. formally announced that all 6 Japanese aircraft carriers involved in the attack on Pearl Harbor were sunk, 1944.

INTRODUCTIONS

How many of you are aware that today is Delaware Day? Outside of Delaware, that is. On this day in 1787, Delaware became the first state to approve the contents of the U.S. Constitution. In my book, that makes today pretty significant. We can take pride in the good things about our nation both past and present. So I wish to speak to you out of that pride and with a sense of optimism about our future.

On the morning of this day in 1941, the Japanese Navy launched a sneak attack from the air over the U.S. Naval Base at Pearl Harbor, Hawaii. An oil embargo had been imposed on Japan by numerous nations—including the U.S.—because of their aggressive actions in China and Manchuria. That sanction provoked a conflict; and broke a peaceful trading agreement between the Americans and Japanese. When the war ended, Americans and Japanese worked together to resume a close relationship. Today we have proven that it is possible for nations to forgive, if not to forget. Now all we have to do is inspire that same reasoning among individuals. And so I rise to speak on behalf of peace and goodwill among neighbors both near and far.

For every action, there is a reaction, as a pair of anniversaries which occurred on this day will prove. In 1941, Japanese air forces launched an attack on the U.S. naval base at Pearl Harbor, Hawaii. In 1944, America formally announced that all six Japanese aircraft carriers involved in that raid were sunk. This is a pretty drastic example, but their cause-and-effect relationship also has its peaceful side. Before and after Pearl Harbor, both nations actively engaged in the trade of imports and exports. The United States contributed to Japan's postwar reconstruction; and Japan contributed to America's knowledge of transistors and microchips. The U.S. introduced modern western culture to this Pacific Rim giant and as advertising man Jerry Della Femina once wrote: "Now, from the folks who brought you Pearl Harbor…"

D ECEMBER 8

Horace was born, 65 BC

Eli Whitney was born, 1765. (See March 14th entry.)

American Federation of Labor was founded, 1886.

James Thurber was born, 1894.

The U.S. and Great Britain declared war on Japan, 1941. (See December 7th entry.)

INTRODUCTIONS

On this day in 1886, an assembly of labor union leaders met in Columbus, Ohio, and organized the American Federation of Labor. It wasn't the first collaboration of labor unions, but it proved to be the one that worked for many generations. There has been much dispute about union power. But there is no disputing that, before unionism gained its strength, the lot of the average working person was a good deal harder. History is a sort of pendulum; when it swings too far in one direction, it eventually swings back in the other direction; ultimately it reached its own gentle balance. The AF of L has been part of that delicate balance for a long time. On its birthday, I rise to salute the idea of decent pay for honest work, and to suggest how we can ensure more of the same.

The great Roman poet Horace was born in Venusia in the Roman Empire on this day in 65 BC. For many generations, Latin students struggled through Horace's writings. Today I will not quote passages from his works, but I will quote one line which seems appropriate: "Brevis esse laboro, obscurus fio." Translation: "It is when I am struggling to be brief that I become unintelligible." So today I will speak just a bit longer.

Writer and cartoonist James Thurber had a lot in common with his fictional characters like Walter Mitty. Born in 1894, Thurber lived a mild-mannered childhood in Columbus, Ohio, until he lost one eye in a bow-and-arrow accident. This twist of fate kept him from pursuing a life of wild adventure, but it encouraged him to spend more time observing the mechanized, automated, modern world emerging around him. His cynical wit graced the pages of *The New Yorker*. He aimed his critical pen at the war between the sexes, the fate of the average man caught in the bureaucratic whirlwind, and the far more intellectual life of dogs. As Thurber once wrote: "Open most heads and you will find nothing shining, not even a mind." I assure you I do not agree with Mr. Thurber as I stand here before you. If fact I see your lights shining at the end of my own mind's tunnel.

DECEMBER 9

John Milton was born, 1608.

The first sermon was delivered in New England, 1621.

Noah Webster established New York City's first daily newspaper, *The American Minerva*, 1793.

Ball-bearing roller skates were patented, 1884.

INTRODUCTIONS

John Milton was born in London on this day in 1608. This great British poet was the author of the lines: "Peace hath her victories, no less renowned than war." He also wrote, "Give me the liberty to know, to utter, and to argue freely according to conscience, above all liberties." But let me reassure you, unlike Milton's comment that "with thee conversing I forget all time," I will not abuse my welcome here today with lengthy oratory. I am acutely conscious that, as Milton wrote, "they also serve who only stand and wait." While you are sitting—not standing—you shouldn't be kept waiting. So let us go immediately into our subject for the day.

In 1621, the first sermon in New England was delivered on this day at Plymouth, Massachusetts. What I find most interesting about this event was not its status as the first sermon so much as preacher Robert Cushman's topic for that day, which was "The Sin and Danger of Self-Love." That is a very appropriate reminder for a speaker—particularly after a generous introduction. The sin and danger of self-love can lead a speaker into the self-delusion that the audience is hanging on every word. In reality, every word may be hanging the speaker with the audience. I hope that neither you nor I find ourselves in that predicament. So I speak to you today in thoughtful humility.

When Noah Webster established Manhattan's first daily newspaper, *The American Minerva,* in 1793, he started a media ball rolling in that city. Newspapers have come and gone, but the news and the media's delivery of it never stop. It's like the U.S. patent which Levant M. Richardson received on this day in 1884. Richardson's invention—ball-bearing roller skates—have rolled through the generations. They've since been replaced by in-line skates, but the concept keeps rolling down the road. In that spirit of progress, I'd like to get a new idea rolling with all of you today.

DECEMBER 10

The Nobel Prizes are awarded. (See October 21st entry.)

The first recorded sighting of the Aurora Borealis took place in New England, 1719.

Wyoming became the first state to adopt women's suffrage, 1869.

Great Britain's Duke of York became King George VI when his brother, Edward VIII, abdicated, 1936. (See June 23rd entry.)

The United Nations adopted the Declaration of Human Rights, 1948.

INTRODUCTIONS

Today is United Nations Human Rights Day which commemorates the adoption of the United Nations Declaration of Human Rights in 1948. Among other things, that Declaration says that "All human beings are born free and equal in dignity and rights...Everyone has the right to freedom of thought...Everyone has the right to freedom of opinion and expression." To which I can only add—as your speaker here today—try and stop me.

The world's great achievements are notably recognized on this day when—in accordance with the late Alfred Nobel's will—the Nobel Prizes are presented for achievements in world peace, in literature, and in science. As I contemplate the stature of the Nobel recipients, I must say that I have the feeling that while Oslo and Norway draw the winners, you good people have found yourselves with the booby prize! But I will do my best.

On this day in 1869, a great victory was won for western women. The Territory of Wyoming became the first government to adopt women's suffrage, giving both genders the right to vote. Out in the Wild West where men were men, Wyoming was a half century ahead of the rest of the world in giving women equal rights. On Wyoming Day, I rise to express the hope that we can be as farseeing and wise in our time as the men of Wyoming were in 1869.

Romantic fairy tales don't usually happen in real life—they are the stuff of fiction. But on this day in 1936, Great Britain's King Edward VIII abdicated his throne to marry the woman he loved, the American divorcée Wallis Warfield Simpson. Love, my friends, can conquer all. And so today, I would like to talk to you about love: love of nation, love of neighbor, love of justice, and love of freedom.

In 1719, an awesome sight appeared in the nighttime skies over New England. This natural wonder regularly occurs throughout the northern hemisphere, but it was on this day that the first New England sighting of the spectacular Aurora Borealis was recorded for posterity. According to ancient legends, the Great Northern Lights are said to be the spirits of gods or ancestors; and children conceived under this brilliant nocturnal display are supposedly blessed with remarkable talents. Modern science has told us that the Aurora Borealis is actually a phenomenon created by light refraction. But that's not as exciting or inspiring as the stories told by the people who have witnessed the dancing lights on dark winter nights. I prefer to follow ancient traditions today as we meet under northern skies. Maybe what is born from my words to you today will blessed by the gods with your positive response.

DECEMBER 11

Alexander Solzhenitsyn was born, 1918.

Plans for a dirigible mooring tower on the Empire State Building were unveiled, 1929.

INTRODUCTIONS

Today is Alexander Solzhenitsyn's birthday. Born in 1918 in Rostov, Russia, Solzhenitsyn grew up to become an eloquent author and human rights' advocate in the midst of an inhuman Soviet system. His talents won him government persecution and a place in the Siberian labor camps. But Solzhenitsyn proved that one true voice raised in protest can become a chorus. Words can be a mighty weapon. I regret that—as regards to that weapon—I do not come as heavily armed as Solzhenitsyn. But I welcome the opportunity to raise my voice here today.

In 1929, the Empire State Building was a long way from completion when an announcement was made on this day. The building's sponsors unveiled their plans to top the skyscraper with a mooring tower, because it seemed likely that there would be regular worldwide zeppelin service in the near future. I believe that one zeppelin did actually tie up briefly, but the tower's major effect was that it gave the building a good deal more height—and another observation deck. I guess the moral of this story is that if you aim high you are bound to stand taller; but there are better things to do than latch on to a large bag of hot air. So I will try not to be a windbag today.

DECEMBER 12

The golf tee was patented, 1899.

The Ford Foundation contributed $500 million to U.S. colleges and universities, 1955.

INTRODUCTIONS

I did not realize how modest an offering I was bringing to you with my remarks until I checked on what notable events have occurred on this day in history. I found out that, in 1955, the Ford Foundation gave the largest philanthropic contribution package ever assembled: $500 million in funding for U.S. colleges and universities. I don't know what my words of wisdom are worth, but it certainly doesn't come within hailing distance of that wisdom. But, of course, my friends, money isn't everything. So I stand before you to offer something else.

There are unsung events in mankind's history, and one such occasion occurred on this day. In 1899, a patent was issued to George F. Grant of Boston for a wooden golf tee. Can you imagine the state of the world without golf tees? Don't laugh. Without golf tees, the game of golf might have been replaced by croquet, and then what would have happened to country clubs and corporate negotiations? I could go on, but you see my point. For want of a tee, the game could have been lost. Now a speech—like a golf game—has to tee off somewhere. What you have just heard was my opening drive. Now if I can only stay out of the rough, we will be on our way.

DECEMBER 13

Sir Francis Drake set out to sail the world, 1577.

Abel Tasman discovered New Zealand, 1642.

Dartmouth College was chartered, 1769.

Robert E. Lee's wise words, 1862.

George Gershwin's *An American in Paris* was publicly performed for the first time, 1928.

The Susan B. Anthony dollar was issued, 1978. (See February 15th entry.)

INTRODUCTIONS

When Moor's Indian Charity School was rechartered as Dartmouth College at about this time of year in 1769, its founder, Eleazar Wheelock, became the college's founding father. It's a fact duly celebrated in Dartmouth song and legend. Some years ago, there was a brouhaha over the fact that Dartmouth athletic teams were nicknamed the Indians. A few people complained that Dartmouth's teams weren't really Native Americans; and neither was the Dartmouth student body. Now, I am not here to analyze the logic or the justice of college nicknames. But I recall this story for one particular reason: unchallenged traditions are eventually challenged. And no matter how minor those disputes are, we must look for the broader concerns that they often represent. Today I should like to talk about some prevalent symptoms.

Robert E. Lee, on this day in 1862, said, "It is well that war is so terrible, or we should grow too fond of it." The same is true of all wars: those fought by armies; those fought in courts of law; those fought in the news media. Contention and competition often spur the adrenaline and stimulate progress. But there can be a cost. Today I am here to say a few words for peace and quiet—and how we can keep them.

Isn't it fascinating how human beings as a species seem to be born with a nonmigratory wanderlust that's not evident in any other living creature? A few anniversaries that are marked on this day will prove me out. In 1577, the British explorer Sir Francis Drake set out to sail around the world. He was the first Englishman to attempt that daring feat. In 1642, the Dutch navigator Abel Tasman discovered New Zealand in the relatively uncharted waters of the southern hemisphere. In 1928,

American composer George Gershwin completed his symphonic narration of his European travel experiences. He gave *An American in Paris* its first public performance on this day. Even though wanderlust is obviously in our blood, I hope you will all sit patiently while I tell you some great news from abroad.

DECEMBER 14

Nostradamus was born, 1503.

Roald Amundsen reached the South Pole, 1911. (See May 9th and January 18th entries.)

INTRODUCTIONS

Back in 1911, the Norwegian explorer Roald Amundsen became the first human being—as far as we know—to reach the South Pole. I suppose that was the ultimate in getting to the bottom of things. Today, on the anniversary of Amundsen's accomplishment, we still have a few poles to reach. Perhaps it would be more correct to say that too much of the world still stands poles apart. And when you stop to think of it, the North Pole and the South Pole, however far apart, have a lot in common. I'm going to stand on my soapbox right here and now to establish some common ground that won't leave either of us standing at opposite poles.

On December 14, 1503, Michel de Notredame was born in the Provence region of France. He became a physician and then wrote down hundreds of visions that came to him about future events using the pen name Nostradamus. It would be all too easy on Nostradamus' birthday to wax prophetic. Admittedly, the temptation is strong; and if I could be as vague or ambiguous as some past prophets, I would certainly take the chance. But vagueness and ambiguity are themselves high art. I guess, I'll have to settle for present truths as I understand them.

DECEMBER 15

Nero was born, 37 AD.

INTRODUCTION:

On any list of bad kings, Nero's name is pretty prominent. The emperor who fiddled while Rome burned was born in Antium on this day in 37 AD. Four years after Rome's slums went up in flames, Nero went down in disgrace and was branded by the Senate as a public enemy. He committed suicide—which may have been the only thing he really did well. On Nero's birthday, I am tempted to say that I didn't come here to set the world on fire. But for your sake, I will refrain because when the speaker fiddles around, the audience burns. So let us leave ancient Nero and get on with the business at hand.

DECEMBER 16

Ludwig van Beethoven was born, 1770.

Boston Tea Party took place, 1773.

Noel Coward was born, 1899.

Arthur C. Clarke was born, 1917.

Battle of the Bulge began, 1944.

INTRODUCTIONS

We meet here today on the anniversary of history's most memorable tea party. In 1773, The Boston Tea Party took place in Boston Harbor. The incident was staged as a protest against British taxation. It was a picturesque demonstration, but we had to do a good bit more to get rid of British taxation in this country. Today, I remind you of the Boston Tea Party to make the point that tea parties rarely solve anything. Nevertheless, they do get people talking. I'd like to accomplish that same end today in the hope that I can also get you thinking.

Whenever I mention the Battle of the Bulge, people think I'm talking about waistlines. But the real Battle of the Bulge began on this day in 1944, when German forces launched a counterattack against the U.S. 101st Airborne Division lead by Major General Anthony McAuliffe in Bastogne, Belgium. The incident created a dangerous bulge in the battle line; and stubborn courage was the weapon that ultimately stopped the German threat. Whether the bulge is on a battle line or a waistline, it calls for prompt and strong measures. This also holds true for speakers and audiences. If there is too much fat in a speech or in the speaker's head, it creates a bulge that loses not only the battle, but the audience as well. So I will try to keep my lines lean and battle-ready here today.

German composer Ludwig van Beethoven was probably born on this day, in 1770. It has been said that what Shakespeare was to drama, Beethoven was to music. The composer himself said that "true art is selfish and perverse—it will not submit to the mold of flattery." In that sense, my friends, I regard you collectively and severally as true, unselfish artists who are anything but perverse and who cannot be swayed by flattering remarks. Now, I'll skip the sugar coating, and head directly into the substance of my remarks.

There is an old tradition that the show must go on. It goes back for many generations. But Noel Coward—who was born on this day in 1899, in Teddington, England—once wrote a song entitled "Why Must the Show Go On?" He pointed out that if one packed up one's talent, there were plenty more to step into the breach. There are times when a speaker echoes Noel Coward's question. There are also times when the speaker doesn't ask the question, but the audience certainly does. Today, therefore, I will try not to prompt the question, but perhaps I can offer an answer. I think I know why this particular show must go on, and I would like to share that information with you.

A modern-day visionary was born on this day in 1917. When author Arthur C. Clarke was a child, he made his own telescope so he could observe the stars. His fascination grew, and even though he couldn't afford to get a university education, he was honored with a membership in the British Interplanetary Society—a select group of astronomers who kept their well-trained eyes on the skies. During the Second World War, Clarke joined the R.A.F. so he could get a closer look at the world above us. And in 1945, he wrote his first science-fiction story which predicted in amazing detail the transmittal of television and radio signals via satellite. Readers thought Clarke was a little outlandish in his description. But twenty years later, when the first Early Bird satellites were launched, they realized his ideas weren't so farfetched after all. According to Clarke's Third Law, which was stated in his book *Profiles of the Future: An Inquiry into the Limits of the Possible:* "Any sufficiently advanced technology is indistinguishable from magic." The scientific world began consulting with this teller of tales from our not-so-distant future on other projects like the Apollo 11, 12, and 15 space missions which Clarke broadcasted with Walter Cronkite. Clarke's story should provide all of us with the inspiration to encourage our youth to look up at the skies and dream their dreams. Someday they may become realities.

DECEMBER 17

Wilbur and Orville Wright made their first airplane flight, 1903.

INTRODUCTION:

This is an auspicious day for flights of fancy and for airy promises. That's because today marks the anniversary of the Wright brothers' historic first flight at Kitty Hawk, North Carolina. We first learned on this day, how to take off into the wild blue yonder in a flying machine. Wilbur and Orville Wright's flights were short and not too lofty, and I shall endeavor to make my remarks here today follow that same pattern.

DECEMBER 18

Edwin Armstrong was born, 1890.

Steven Spielberg was born, 1947.

First commercial nuclear power plant in America was placed in operation, 1957.

The first communications satellite broadcast was made, 1958.

INTRODUCTIONS

Edwin Armstrong, who was born on this day in 1890, created FM—or frequency modulation—which eliminated radio static. In honor of this native New Yorker's birthday, I will make every effort to eradicate any static from my remarks today. Besides, we are at the Christmas season which I trust will be static-free for one and all.

On this day in 1958, a voice from outer space was heard over radios worldwide. It was a very human voice that had been sent from earth out into space; and then transmitted back to this planet via a communications satellite. The voice belonged to President Dwight D. Eisenhower, who delivered a Christmas message to everyone on the planet. Today, I don't have such an elaborate way to deliver my message to all of you. So I hope you will forgive the absence of satellite technology as I proceed on my simple way.

In 1957, America's first commercial nuclear power plant began supplying electricity to the town of Shippingport, Pennsylvania, on this day. It was a pre-Christmas present of sorts. As you know, electrical energy is generated by the interaction of positive and negative poles. The long dispute over nuclear energy produced a lot of both. We have a tendency to be positive even when we are being negative. Today I would like to remove the electricity from the air and talk about more static subjects.

The Christmas season seems to bring out the child in all of us—young and old alike. Perhaps that is one of the reasons why we find Steven Spielberg's films so appealing. Born on this day in 1947, Spielberg has generously shared his childhood visions of extraterrestrials, gremlins, and dinosaurs with us on the big screen. He's retold the heroic myths and adventures we read as children with characters like Luke Skywalker, Princess Leia, and Indiana Jones. Wouldn't it be wonderful if all of us could maintain that spirit of childlike wonder, adventure, and imagination every day of the year? What sort of a world would we create for ourselves?

D ECEMBER 19

Great Britain passed a vagabond law, 1547.

Thomas Paine published "The American Crisis," 1776.

The Continental Army went to their winter quarters at Valley Forge, 1777.

A Christmas Carol was first published, 1843.

Corrugated paper was patented, 1871 by Albert L. Jones of New York.

Great Britain and China signed an accord to return Hong Kong to China in 1997, 1984. (See September 19th entry.)

INTRODUCTIONS

"These are the times that try men's souls." Thomas Paine published those words on this day in 1776, in the first of his essays on "The American Crisis" which appeared in *The Pennsylvania Journal.* Paine also wrote, "The summer soldier and the sunshine patriot will, in this crisis, shrink from the service of his country; but he that stands it now, deserves the love and thanks of man and woman." And he added, "Those who expect to reap the blessings of freedom, must, like men, undergo the fatigue of supporting it." In all fairness, I don't think I can improve on that brief presentation of patriotism, so I won't try. Instead, I will speak to you today, in the season of peace and goodwill, about blessings. It is, I think, a good time to count our blessings.

On this day in 1777, General George Washington led the Continental Army into their winter quarters at Valley Forge, Pennsylvania. According to historical records, Valley Forge was not exactly a winter vacation resort. Now if the Continental Army could endure Valley Forge, listening to me shouldn't be too bad.

Back in 1547, homeless vagabonds were considered a source of embarrassment which "soiled the nation's social fabric" in the British government's eyes. So to stem this rising tide, Parliament passed a law which decreed that vagabonds who refused to return to their hometowns and find gainful employment would be publicly whipped. Second-count offenders would be whipped and branded with a "V." Third-time offenders would be enslaved for two years. Chronic homelessness was punishable by death before this day, so this new, stringent law seemed lenient to the many dispossessed peasants who had lost their lands in tax foreclosures. I guess the problem of homelessness has been with us for a long time. So why can't we find a reasonable cure for those suffering the effects of this debilitating and demeaning social disease, rather than creating panaceas that only seek to launder this issue from our sight?

On this day in1843, a Christmas tradition was born. Tiny Tim and Bob Crachit came to life when Charles Dickens published his delightful tale of miser Ebenezer Scrooge's Christmas epiphany entitled, *A Christmas Carol*. Though I could never hope to match Dickens' eloquence or entertainment value, I'd like to try my hand at the roles of the Ghosts of Christmas' Present and Future for a few minutes. Perhaps when I'm finished, we'll discover a little of that spirit for ourselves.

It may interest you to know that corrugated paper was patented by Albert L. Jones of New York, on this day in 1871. Now whether or not you found that bit of news enthralling, I can assure you it only gets better from here.

DECEMBER 20

New Orleans first flew the American flag, 1803.

Electric lights were installed on Broadway, 1880.

The pneumatic tire was patented, 1892.

The Union of Soviet Socialist Republics was formed, 1922. (See December 21st entry.)

INTRODUCTIONS

This is the day when, back in 1892, the pneumatic tire was patented. It demonstrated that an air-filled hollow surface could provide a cushioned ride. Apparently, I was selected to commemorate this anniversary by providing some hot air of my own. I will endeavor to do so without running the risk of overinflation.

In 1880, the electric lights went on throughout Broadway's theater section for the first time on this day. The event was followed shortly by the saying that "there's a broken heart for every light on Broadway." We do a great many more things with electric lights today. Light, we have found, is not simply a source of illumination. It also has a cutting edge and can burn and even obscure. If you shine a light that's very bright, it can have a blinding effect. So, if today I attempt to shed a little light on a subject or two, I will try to make it neither cutting nor blinding nor burning. Let us say that it will be light, but certainly not heavy.

In 1803, on this day, the city of New Orleans flew the American flag for the first time. This simple act signaled a transfer of ownership as the Louisiana Territory was handed over to the United States who had purchased it from France. Another transfer of ownership occurred in 1922, when 14 eastern European republics merged to form the Union of Soviet Socialist Republics. Ownership is a serious responsibility. It doesn't matter if you're discussing real estate, a work of art, or an entire nation;

to have ownership over something implies that you are liable for the future of that which you possess. I would like outline our mutual responsibilities as owners of an intellectual property that we all possess: our freedom to voice our opinions.

DECEMBER 21

Snow White and the Seven Dwarfs premiered, 1937.

Radium was discovered by Marie and Pierre Curie, 1898. (See November 7th entry.)

Eleven Soviet republics proclaimed the birth of the Commonwealth of Independent States, and the end of the U.S.S.R., 1991. (See December 20th entry.)

INTRODUCTIONS

Back in 1937, Walt Disney premiered the animated cartoon feature film, *Snow White and the Seven Dwarfs*. Even thought it was based on the famous fairy tale by the Brothers Grimm, Disney had added some of his own touches to his production. I don't recall that the Brothers Grimm had given the seven dwarfs individual names, but Disney certainly did. Doc and Happy and Grumpy and Sneezy and Sleepy and Bashful and Dopey were all cartoon profiles of human nature. Dopey never talked, but that might have made him less dopey than the others in the long run. But I am here to talk, which may make me more like Doc or Happy or Grumpy. I'm definitely not Bashful. And you'll have to decide for yourselves if I'm Sleepy after I've finished my remarks.

DECEMBER 22

Esek Hopkins took command of the Continental Navy, 1775.

INTRODUCTIONS

On this day in 1775, a new naval fighting force came into being as Esek Hopkins took command of the Continental Navy. The military fleet consisted of seven ships. It has grown somewhat since then, and its commanders have been greatly distinguished. Esek Hopkins himself turned out to be a controversial figure, and was suspended from command early in 1777. But on this particular naval anniversary, I am delighted to have the opportunity to weigh anchor and see where my wind carries me.

DECEMBER 23

Maryland donated land for the creation of the District of Columbia, 1788.

"A Visit from St. Nicholas" was first published, 1823.

The transistor was invented, 1947.

INTRODUCTIONS

Today marks the anniversary of the invention of the transistor. On this day in 1947, John Bardeen, Walter H. Brattain, and William Shockley saw the fruition of their research at the Bell Telephone Laboratories in New Jersey. The transistor's inventors won the Nobel Prize for their discovery, which not only made equipment miniaturization possible, it ushered in a tidal wave of electronic miracles including the personal computer. We have not yet completely transistorized the basic process of human communication. That action still requires a speaker and an audience. Of course, there are transistors that condense a speaker's comments into a tiny capsule and deliver them to an intended audience via the internet. Conversely, transistors can deliver an audience to a speaker in the same way. But I'm old-fashioned. I am delighted to have this opportunity to come before you in person to speak my mind.

In 1788, on this day, the state of Maryland gave ten square miles of its territory to the United States for the establishment of a national capital city. The U.S. Congress finally got around to voting on the issue of what to do with this gift in 1790. The pace of government in those days was rather leisurely. But times have changed; government has become just about our largest growth industry. Since government is generally a process of talking things over, talk seems to have become a very large growth industry. I'm not about to make any undue contribution, though I am here to talk to you. And I appreciate the opportunity. At the same time, I shall keep in mind poet James Russell Lowell's advice: "No, never say nothin' without you're compelled tu, / An' then don't say nothin' that you can be held tu."

Rather than boring you with the solemn details of a sobering historical event, I will open my comments today by telling you that on this day in 1823, Clement Clarke Moore's "A Visit from St. Nicholas" was first published. For those of you who don't recognize it by its title, it begins: "Twas the night before Christmas / And all through the house..." This simple poem, which appeared in the *Troy Sentinel* newspaper reminds me that as we grow and mature we oftentimes forget the exuberance, the innocence, the joy we experienced in childhood. We replace enthusiasm with serious, often harsh logic. Today I intend to resist the trend in the hopes I can inspire all of you to wish and to dream.

DECEMBER 24

Christmas Eve.
Thomas Wolsey became Chancellor of England, 1515.
Andrew Carnegie became the Laird of Pitton Green, 1902.
Howard Hughes was born, 1905.

INTRODUCTIONS

A butcher's son became the Chancellor of England on Christmas Eve. In 1515, Thomas Wolsey was appointed by King Henry VIII to this high political position. Wolsey had advanced his station before this date. At fifteen years of age, he was an Oxford graduate, and quickly became the vicar of two parishes. Wolsey's reputation as a hard worker preceded him throughout his life. Within a few years, he was promoted to archbishop of York. Known for putting in 12 hours a day, Wolsey not only impressed his king, he proved that even a poor man's son can rise to greatness if he's willing to work. I'm sure Wolsey would agree with my simple theme today: Persistence pays. An aside about Thomas Wolsey: As archbishop, he built a magnificent palace outside London. He had a great passion for architecture and soon, word spread that his palace was more impressive than the king's. Henry came to see for himself. Apparently he agreed, because shortly after his visit, he moved Wolsey out and moved in himself. The moral of that incident, if there is one, might be that people who live in grand houses might as well stow thrones.

I can't think of any speech made on this day that didn't draw at least some of its inspiration from the fact that this is Christmas Eve. I don't refer to today's sectarian religious significance. I refer instead to the faith, the love, and peace that seem to manifest themselves around this time of year. I thank you for the opportunity to speak with you about such wonderful gifts of the heart today. To echo words which have been spoken many times before, but still bring a sense of delight and wonderment: "Twas the night before Christmas..."

On Christmas Eve in 1905, an enigma was born in Houston, Texas. During his life, Howard Hughes' personal activities and professional practices raised many unanswered questions. The tangle that he left as his legacy proved once again that real life has a more complex plot than any fictional work. Howard Hughes managed to avoid public speaking throughout his entire life, which wasn't too difficult since he also totally avoided the public. Those of us who have less of an aversion to such chores have always been puzzled by Howard Hughes' shyness. I regard speaking to you here today as both a privilege and a pleasure, and I thank you for your attention.

As an impoverished child, Andrew Carnegie grew up across the street from the Pitton Estates which had a beautiful park that was open to the neighborhood children and families for their enjoyment on Sunday afternoons. But Carnegie wasn't allowed to enter the park because his uncle, Tom Morrison, had been publicly harassing important local and national politicians including the Laird of Pitton Green. On Christmas Eve in 1902, Andrew Carnegie—the world's richest man—became the Laird of Pitton Green. He purchased the estate and permanently opened the park for the enjoyment of all children. Christmas Eve is the perfect time to remember a comment Carnegie once made which also states my theme for today. He remarked, and I quote: "A man who dies rich, dies in disgrace."

DECEMBER 25

Christmas Day.

Pope Adrian IV was enthroned, 1154.

George Washington crossed the Delaware, 1776.

INTRODUCTIONS

I know there are some of you who feel Christmas was created by department-store owners and advertising agencies, but the truth is that this gift-giving holiday has been celebrated throughout the world for a long, long time. The early Christians celebrated the first Christmas in Rome back in 336 AD. It was the perfect counter-balance to the weeklong pagan celebration of Saturnalia, a Roman festival that was highlighted by merrymaking and gift-giving. The ancient Persians celebrated this very day as the birthday of their mystery god, Mithra, who was also represented as the Sun of Righteousness. During this same time, the Celts and Teutons celebrated their Yule rites by decorating their homes with greenery and lights and sending gifts and greetings to family and friends. Traditions are hard to break, so if any of you are feeling like old Ebenezer Scrooge, then all I can say is "bah humbug" to you. Christmas is here today. And Christmas is here to stay.

When I think of miracles and civilization, I recall an event which took place on this day during the First World War. Not that I feel this event was civilized or miraculous, because it represents the failure of negotiation. But on Christmas Day, in the Argonne Forest, German soldiers from one side and British, Scottish, Canadian, and American soldiers on the other—men who had spent months shooting at each other from muddy trenches—rose from their foxholes; met each other face to face; and played soccer. I hope we can all emerge from the trenches of our lives and hardships on this one day, and share in the miracle that is humankind.

On Christmas Day, the greatest speeches are those found in people's hearts. But when one is called upon to deliver an address on this day, the temptation to merely quote from the Bible is best resisted. Few of us can improve on passages from the New Testament. What we can do, and what I propose to do here today, is to move from prayer to pragmatism. We have thought today of how the world should be. Let us not meanwhile forget how the world is—and here is how I see it.

It was on Christmas night, back in 1776, that George Washington led his troops across the Delaware River to attack the British the next day in New Jersey. For all the calm solemnity of Christmas day, the world is still with us on Christmas. And we are still of this world, perhaps a little better for having paused to catch our breath. Most of us still have our own Delawares to cross. Perhaps, if we remember Washington's example, we will be inspired today to get moving. My own particular Delaware is the assignment to speak here today, and so I am ready for the river. Shall we cast off?

An English cardinal made history on Christmas Day. In 1154, Cardinal Nicholas Breakspear of Albano was enthroned as Pope Adrian IV. He was history's only British pope. While the English monarchy continued its long battle with the Vatican over the supremacy of state over church, the accession of this "by-the-book" cardinal seemed a most auspicious decision. Ironically, it was Pope Adrian IV who officially sanctioned King Henry II's invasion of Ireland five years later. But it is Adrian IV's enthronement which serves as the inspiration for my remarks today. Sometimes success is achieved because an individual is in just the right position at just the right time. All seems to be in order for a successful conclusion to the matters at hand. Let me present you with the signs.

DECEMBER 26

Boxing Day.

Mao Zhedong was born, 1893.

The coffee percolator was patented, 1865.

INTRODUCTIONS

Today is Mao Zhedong's birthday. Born in Hunan province of northern China in 1893, Mao became a sort of prophet to his people. Even more than the thoughts of Lenin, the sayings of Chairman Mao have been extensively quoted in the Communist world. I won't be quoting from Mao's *Little Red Book* today, nor will I be packaging what I have to say in pocket-sized volumes. And, unlike the Chairman, I'll try to be brief.

In Great Britain, today is known as Boxing Day. The story goes that this is the day when presents are given in boxes to the postmen and -women, the gardener, the family doctor, and so forth. Other versions of the story tell a tale of neatness. This is the day when all good Englishmen and -women throw away their boxes or return gifts. Nevertheless, it is nice to know that the spirit of giving or receiving need not end on Christmas Day. It's also a great idea to have a day devoted to recovering from the Christmas excesses. Therefore, on this Boxing Day, I rise to celebrate with you a new coming of peace—the end of the Christmas shopping season.

Mr. James Nason of Franklin, Massachusetts received a belated, but very welcome present on this day in 1865. He was granted a patent for his invention—the coffee percolator. I know there are a few of you out there who need a cup of freshly perked coffee after yesterday's festivities. But if you can just have patience, I've been brewing a few ideas that might perk up your spirits better than two cups of coffee. Let me serve them up right now.

D ECEMBER 27

Flushing Remonstrance was issued, 1657.

Louis Pasteur was born, 1822. (See July 6th entry.)

The song "Sweet Adeline" was first publicly performed, 1903.

INTRODUCTIONS

In 1657, Peter Stuyvesant was the governor of New Amsterdam. And as governor of this fledgling Dutch colony, Stuyvesant ordered the people of Flushing, Long Island, not to extend their hospitality to Quakers. On this day, the people of Flushing sent a petition to the governor known as The Flushing Remonstrance, which stated: "we are bounde by the law of God and men to doe goode until all men and evil to noe one." More than 300 years later, I believe this reminder is still in order. We are bound to do good to all and evil to none. The big question, of course, is how. I come here with no sensational new panaceas, but perhaps a suggestion or two.

Louis Pasteur—who was born on this day in 1822, in Dole, France—discovered that diseases can be produced by various bacteria. This remarkable discovery laid the groundwork for future research in the areas of antisepsis, sterilization, and the prevention of infection. Pasteur also lent his name to the purification process he discovered while trying make milk safe to drink—pasteurization. On Louis Pasteur's birthday, I find myself concerned with devising preventive measures against a different kind of infection. I speak here today of infections of the mind; of the hates and lunacies that afflict the world. What can we do about this rampant form of disease?

The first public performance of the song "Sweet Adeline" took place on this very day in 1903, in New York City. "Sweet Adeline" has been the flower in the hearts of every barbershop quartet ever since. It is interesting that a barbershop quartet can perform the same song in the same way year after year to the delight of the crowd. But a speaker has to constantly keep up with the times. I must admit that there are occasions when I would rather be up here singing "Sweet Adeline" than pontificating. Today, however, I can reassure you. I will neither sing nor pontificate. What I have to say is not meant to be profound, but I hope you will find it of interest.

DECEMBER 28

President Woodrow Wilson was born, 1856. (See September 26th entry.)

Chewing gum was patented, 1869.

H.L. Mencken published the great bathtub hoax, 1917. (See September 12th entry.)

INTRODUCTIONS

Today marks the anniversary of a major addition to the American lifestyle. On this day, in 1869, William F. Semple of Mount Vernon, Ohio, received a patent for chewing gum. We had various kinds of gums before then, but Mr. Semple's patent covered "the combination of rubber with other articles" for "an acceptable chewing gum." I don't know if there were any gums made with real rubber—although it sometimes seems that way. The chewing gum's virtue is that it is still there when you finish. The problem is that it sticks around. The same problems can exist with that other form of chin exercise known as public speaking. It can be rubbery and elastic; it can be stretched to meet a time frame; it is often hard to get rid of; and it can get very sticky. I shall keep those dangers in mind as I invite you to chew over a few thoughts with me.

Back on December 28, 1917, H.L. Mencken published an article in *The New York Evening Mail* describing the origin of the great American bathtub. He described how it was first installed in a Cincinnati mansion by a Mr. Adam Thompson, in 1842; and how various cities and states passed laws to regulate or tax it. The article was a pure hoax. Mencken never intended it to be taken seriously, but it was. To this day, you can probably find articles relaying as fact the items of Mencken's imagination. The great American bathtub hoax reminds us all to be skeptical. I hope that while you should take my remarks seriously here today, that you will remember that saying something is so does not make it so.

DECEMBER 29

Archbishop of Canterbury Thomas á Becket was assassinated in his cathedral, 1170.

Texas became a state, 1845.

The Battle of Wounded Knee took place, 1890. (See February 27th and May 8th entries.)

Charles Goodyear was born, 1800.

Vaclav Havel was elected president of the Czech Republic by the nation's Federal assembly, 1989. (See February 21st entry.)

INTRODUCTIONS

History books tell us that on this day in 1845, Texas joined the United States as its 28th state. Considering the size, riches, and political wiliness of the Lone Star State, people have reversed the phrase from time to time, and said that the U.S. joined Texas. In any case, the combination proved to be a rewarding and stimulating one. On this anniversary, I hope that our coming together here today will also prove productive. Or, at the least, like Texas, provide some entertaining moments.

The Battle of Wounded Knee occurred on this day, in 1890. When it was over, 25 U.S. cavalrymen were dead, and so were about 150 Native American men, women, and children. It took years for the battle to be more aptly described as a massacre. This was the last major engagement between Native Americans and the U.S. Army. It aroused the conscience of Americans then and even more so years later. Perspectives being what they are, it is understandable that what one view sees as a battle, another view sees as a massacre. Our perspectives sometimes vary with our distance from an event; and sometimes with our sympathies. The important thing is to recognize that we do speak from perspective and not from absolute divine revelation. It is in that spirit and that form of awareness that I admit to having no patent on total truth as I rise to give you my view here today.

A close friendship ended in murder on this date in history. In 1170, the Archbishop of Canterbury, Thomas á Becket, was murdered in his cathedral during vespers by four barons of King Henry II's court. The king and the archbishop had been close friends until Henry made Becket—who was his chancellor at the time—into an archbishop. Henry had hoped to settle the battle between church and state by stacking the odds in his favor. What Henry hadn't calculated was that Becket would take his new duties very seriously. The questions of jurisdiction over a crime allegedly committed by a priest divided these two friends; and in an emotional outburst, the king vented his anger over dinner with his barons. The rest of the story became the stuff of legend. The moral is clear: one misplaced word can have fatal results. Its lesson provides my theme for today.

Today is the day in 1800, when Charles Goodyear was born. Please forgive me if I attempt to retread a few tired remarks off the rim. Mr. Goodyear developed and patented a process called vulcanization which rendered India rubber less sticky and able to withstand temperature extremes. Despite this revolutionary achievement, he died penniless. However, in honor of his birth, I'd like to bounce a few ideas around today, and perhaps despite Goodyear's best efforts, we can get a few of them to stick.

DECEMBER 30

The Gadsden Purchase was signed, 1853.

Frank Sinatra began a singing engagement at the Paramount Theatre, 1942.

Kiss Me Kate opened on Broadway, 1948.

INTRODUCTIONS

Now that we are mercifully past the Christmas shopping season, I find we are assembled on the anniversary of a great shopping expedition. On this day in 1853, James Gadsden signed an agreement with the Republic of Mexico to purchase the southern portion of Arizona and New Mexico for ten million dollars. That was by no means America's biggest land purchase. There was the Louisiana Territory; there would be Alaska; and there would also be the Virgin Islands. It is interesting how much of what is now the United States was purchased from other nations. We may not have the world's best record around the conference table, but we seem to do very well over the counter. America's greatest success has been in the peaceful marketplace—and not the least of that success has been in the marketplace of ideas. If you put your concepts on the counter, and take your chances, the odds are in your favor that they will be bought. So here I go, putting an idea or two on the counter.

On December 30, 1948, William Shakespeare made it to Broadway with a little help from Cole Porter and Bella and Samuel Spewack. The immortal Shakespearean farce *The Taming of the Shrew* premiered at the New Century Theater under the title *Kiss Me Kate*. In 1948, this essentially antifeminist classic became a smash hit with Cole Porter's music. Looking back on it—and also on the year we are about to end—I find the gender battles are still raging.

Frank Sinatra began a singing engagement at the Paramount Theatre on this day in 1942. The New York City police reserves had to be called in to cope with the swooning, crushing, and enthusiastic screaming of the hordes of teenage girls who flocked to see and hear their idol. The offspring of that generation did the same thing for another generation of singers. It seems to happen regularly as part of the preservation of the species. To its elders, each time seems worse than the times before. I find myself wondering how the next generation will report the year we are now concluding. Let me make a few guesses.

DECEMBER 31

New Year's Eve.

INTRODUCTIONS

Well, we made it. We got ourselves through another year and have arrived at its last rites. Tomorrow we will look toward the future. Today, we should look back to see how far we have come. We should assess what the year meant to us. I will not presume to intrude upon anyone's personal memories, but I find it a very easy measuring stick to use: Just think back to last year at this same time. Do you remember last year at this time, and the shape we were in? Let me refresh your memory.

VOLUME IV

THE SPECIAL OCCASION BOOK

INTRODUCTION

For each of the occasions covered in the following pages, there are a number of paragraphs which can either be used in sequence as the outline of a full speech or as separate introductions, useful individually for any speech on the subject.

The paragraphs are all of a general nature. That is, they deal with the particular subject in general terms, leading into the special information or acknowledgments the speaker wishes to include.

Some of the subjects have a certain degree of overlap. If you are making a speech of acceptance for a nomination, you may find something suitable not only under the category "Acceptance," but also under "Acknowledgment" or "Responses."

Please be sure, therefore; to consult the list of subjects that follows to locate all the categories that may apply to what you want to talk about.

LIST OF SUBJECTS

Acceptance speeches

Acknowledgment of honor

Appreciation

Armed Forces Day

Armistice Day

Artist's unveiling

Award presentation

Bachelor party

Birthday

Bon voyage

Candidacy announcement

Christmas party

Columbus Day

Commencement

Cornerstone laying

Easter

Election Day

Father's Day

Fundraising

Funeral

Graduation

Greeting

Groundbreaking

Inauguration

Independence Day

Induction of new members

Introduction

Invocation

Jubilee

Keynote address

Labor Day

Lincoln's birthday

Long service

Membership meeting

Memorial ceremony

Memorial Day

Moderator

Mother's Day

New Year's Party

Opening

Political campaign

Promotional event

Recruitment

Responses

Retirement

Reunion

Sales meeting

Self-introduction

St. Patrick's Day

Statement of position

Testimonial

Toastmaster

Veterans Day

Washington's birthday

Wedding

Wedding anniversary

Welcome

Acceptance
(OF GIFT, NOMINATION, ETC.)

(See also Acknowledgment; Responses)

I am delighted to be in the presence of so blessed a company. We have it on very good authority that it is more blessed to give than to receive. Since you have been kind enough to give so notably, and to make me the recipient of your favorable attention, you are surely blessed for your generosity. I am deeply honored to be the subject of your generous attention.

There is a story of a graduation at which the mothers of two of the students were sitting together, when a third student was singled out to be saluted as the finest all-around member of the class. The speaker recited the student's feats of scholarship, deeds on the athletic field and notable leadership achievements. As the trophy was being presented, one of the mothers leaned over to the other and whispered, "That's all very fine, but what else has he done?" Only the most immodest of recipients of an honor is free from wondering that same thing.

Your recital of the reasons for this occasion has been flattering and overwhelming, but nevertheless, in all modesty, I recall the comment often made about feats of legerdemain: "There's less to this than meets the eye." Your citation—focusing wholly on the positive—is most kind, and I would be happy to accept it as total truth. But I must add that in reciting my qualifications you have given me a goal for the future, and for that in particular, I thank you.

Through the centuries, people have been selected for various kinds of designations on many different standards of evaluation. Some are based on the drawing of straws, some based on purity, and even on virginity. Some forms of recognition are the result of knowing the right people or the wrong people. We have all seen deserving people toil away unrecognized, in the shadows of the rising stars. I prefer, of course, to regard your choice of me here today as either divine inspiration or the reward of virtue.

The fact is that some things come to the man who waits, some things come to the man who seeks them, some things seek the man. If a person of political bent begins pursuing the spotlight, and making appearances with established members of the same party, it is likely that person will soon be running for office. If a manufacturer subtly scents a product to attract buyers, the chances are that it is a case of the reward seeking the customer. And if the gift comes in the form of a Trojan Horse, we must beware of those bearing the gift. The late Groucho Marx, not the most gracious recipient of honors, once said "I don't want to belong to any club that will accept me as a member." Suffice it for me to say, then, that I am not here as a product of any political desires, nor as the result of the blandishments of a well-wrapped package, nor as a sucker falling for a Trojan Horse. Finally, and most importantly, I feel truly honored to be accepted by this club and present company.

I have looked the gift horse you have presented me straight in the mouth, and there's no doubt about it, it's a thoroughbred. I thank you for your kindness. I appreciate the honor you have paid me and the graciousness that accompanied it.

Thank you very much.

Acknowledgment (of honor)

(See also Acceptance, Responses)

On occasions such as this, I am reminded of the old story about the man who was being tarred and feathered and ridden out of town on a rail. Asked how he felt about it, he said, "If it wasn't for the honor of the thing, I'd just as soon walk." I certainly don't feel that I am being tarred and feathered or ridden out of town on a rail here today. Quite the opposite. I must tell you that once the realization of this moment sinks in, I am going to be walking on air for some time to come. The honor you have done me is one I shall long remember and prize .

It was Yogi Berra, you may recall, who, upon being honored at a special night in the baseball park for his distinguished career, responded to the acclaim and tribute of the crowd by saying, "I want to thank everybody who made this night necessary." I won't presume to define this happy occasion as necessary, but it is most certainly one for which I would like to extend my heartfelt gratitude.

There are some who react to honors in the same way as the psychologist who, upon being greeted in most friendly fashion by a longtime colleague, started muttering to himself, "What did he mean by that?" I will not search for ulterior motives for the way you have received me here today. If my efforts have been in any way supportive of the objectives and/or needs of this group, suffice it to say that it is not a coincidence nor an ulterior aspect. If my participation has aided the cause, I can only say I am grateful for the opportunity.

There is a saying—or should be—that the greater the gratitude, the shorter the speech of thanks. If that were the rule on this occasion, I must confess I would have completed my remarks by now, because words cannot convey the fullness of my appreciation. I shall not take up your time with a long litany. Suffice it to say that I shall endeavor to justify your vote of confidence.

In listening to the remarks preceding mine, I had difficulty realizing that some of the references were to me. You have portrayed me, I think, with all the warts removed and the rough edges smoothed over. It is a portrait that not only touched me—I fear it retouched me. That, as much as the honor itself, is what makes this occasion so moving for me.

Robert Benchley used to tell the story of the temperamental actress who was complimented by a child performer on the set in the studio. "My," said the child, "you look so beautiful today." The actress replied insecurely, "What am I supposed to say to that?" And the child, as sweet as ever, said. "Thank you's okay." Nobody needs to prompt me on that line. Thank you—very much.

APPRECIATION
(OF CONTRIBUTION, SERVICE ETC.)

There are three basic types of occasions that bring people together—not including, of course, the occasions that bring two people together. In larger groups, the three occasions that bring people together are (1) To take note of something that has already happened—either to celebrate it or to deplore it en masse; (2) to take note of something that hasn't happened either to try to make it happen or to prevent it from happening, and (3) to salute someone we hold responsible for any of the above. And that is the nicest kind of get-together. It is why this occasion today is so special.

Celebrating events can be a very joyous time, but it is always better when we celebrate the people who are responsible for the events. Today is a doubly gratifying occasion because we are saluting someone as well as something. We are saying thanks and well done and congratulations. Our presence here is the beginning of that salute. We are here not because we had to come but because we wanted to come, and we wanted to come because we wanted to be part of this occasion.

For many years, at historic Cooper Union in New York, there was a series of free lectures, followed by questions from the audience. Every night, no matter what the subject, the same little man would show up and sit listening intently while the lecturer talked; and when the question period came, every night, the same little man would raise his hand to ask a question. No matter what the subject, the question he asked was always the same. "What you have spoken about tonight," he would say, "is it good or bad for the working man?" There was no doubt in his mind what life's goal should be. And I suspect, from the wonderful record of the person we are honoring here tonight, that there is something of that same single-minded attention to a single all-important goal, too.

We are here to honor one who has been successful and inspirational in a chosen field. Eddie Cantor once said that it takes twenty years to make an overnight success, and Nathan Bedford Forrest, the Confederate general, said it was simply a matter of "git thar fustest with the mostest men." Perhaps Booker T. Washington was wiser still when he wrote that "success is to be measured not so much by the position that one has reached in life as by the obstacles which he has overcome while trying to succeed." Success, indeed, comes in different forms at different times for different people. But it is sweetest when it comes with the approval, the applause, the rewards freely given by the people. And that is why we are here today.

In the spirit of the occasion, I am reminded of the story of a professional toastmaster presiding over ceremonies honoring a local celebrity, who was given a piece of paper with the honoree's name on it so that he could pretend to know the man. Well, as luck would have it, the little slip of paper fell through a crack on the rostrum just as the guest toastmaster arose to introduce the guest of honor. Without a moment's hesitation, the toastmaster said, "And now it is a pleasure to present our guest of honor, a man whose name is on everyone's lips, just as his accomplishments are on our minds today."

And so today, I ask you, in the spirit of this momentous event, to join me in honoring what's-his-name.

ARMED FORCES DAY

Rudyard Kipling wrote a salute to the professional soldier, many years ago, which deserves to be recalled as we observe Armed Forces Day. Kipling wrote of the British enlisted man, better known as Tommy Atkins. He wrote in an era of simpler times—no airplanes, no tanks, no nuclear bombs. But what he said is, I believe, as true today as it was then. He wrote: "For it's Tommy this, an' Tommy that, an' 'Chuck him out, the brute!'/But it's 'Saviour of 'is country ' when the guns begin to shoot."

There are great divisions of opinion in peacetime about the level of armament, the size of the armed forces, the pay and perquisites of the soldiers and sailors and air force and marines. But should the nation be attacked, our priorities, of course, would be rearranged. There is no doubt that the armed forces would be at the top of the list. Wouldn't it be wonderful if we could strike a balance, and achieve that form of patriotic pride without having somebody shooting at us?

Our armed forces are unique in the world—unique in their tradition, unique in their relationship to the government and the people; and rare in their volunteer spirit. These branches of the military are the lineal descendants of the citizen soldiers and sailors who fought the American Revolutionary War, led by a Virginia planter named George Washington. The officers of our armed forces come through great educational institutions to which they are admitted on merit, not by privilege of birth. And the command of our armed forces rests at the top with the chief executive elected by the people. The funds that maintain the armed forces are voted annually by the people's representatives assembled in Congress. We are not a nation where the armed forces are one camp and the rest of the nation another. It is not a case of "them" and "us." We are part of them, and they are part of us.

There is a singular bond of cooperation and admiration between our armed forces that binds us together in times of war and peace. Knowing that the person protecting your flank is as highly trained as you are can be more than a comfort. It has been, and no doubt will be in the future, a life saved.

The armed forces are insurance. And no matter how much you have, some salesperson insists you need more; and, on the other hand, no matter how much you have, if the occasion comes to use it, you always need more. That is why, whichever side of that equation you happen to find yourself on, it is comforting on Armed Forces Day to salute the conscientious men and women who represent our first line of insurance.

What is the secret weapon of our armed forces? Or perhaps it might be wiser to ask, what is the invisible weapon shared by our Army, Navy, Air Force and Marines? I am not giving away any deep, dark military secret when I answer that question, because the invisible weapon of our armed forces is a very simple one. It is nothing less than the confidence of the free citizens of a free nation. It is the fact that our armed forces are the servants, not the masters of the nation. It is the fact that we recognize the soldier, the sailor, the air-force man or woman and the marine as people, citizens, sons and daughters of America, not as outside help. On Armed Forces Day, it is fine to take pride in the machinery of defense, but I salute, first and foremost, the people of the armed forces.

I have a particular request to make to the nation on Armed Forces Day. Today I suggest we extend to the people of the armed forces a special courtesy. I propose that we salute them for a change and—though it fills me with national pride—not just to see them salute back.

ARMISTICE DAY

(See also Veterans Day)

Some of you may recall a headline which appeared on a momentous day years ago in the *New York Daily News* and was reproduced elsewhere because it said something so profound and yet so succinct. It came at the end of the Second World War, and it read, very simply, "Peace Breaks Out." Not simply peace, but rather peace breaks out. It was particularly appropriate because peace is precisely that—a break-out, or a break-away, from the grinding horror of war. Armistice Day commemorates the cease-fire in a war that, until then, had been the most terrible war of all time—the First World War. Today, we remember all those occasions when the shooting stopped and the bombing ceased.

Wars sometimes end with a whimper, sometimes with a bang; sometimes with an unconditional surrender, sometimes with a cease-fire painfully negotiated over a bargaining table. What is important about Armistice Day is not how the fighting ended, but simply that it ended at all. We have yet to see the time when an armistice proved total and eternal. And when we celebrate Armistice Day we express the unfailing hope that no further anniversaries of this kind will be created or that, if fighting rages anywhere as we meet, it too will swiftly reach an Armistice Day of its own.

Benjamin Franklin, at the end of the American Revolution, was a wise old man who had labored long and hard in the struggle for our nation's independence. He wrote, in 1783, that "There never was a good war or a bad peace." I don't believe he meant totally to condemn the violent struggle for independence, in which he himself had played so great a role. What he meant, I believe, was that at its best war is nothing more than a necessary and avoidable evil, and that mankind was meant to live in peace. Armistice Day reminds us that a world at peace is better than a world at war, that the silencing of the guns of war is the only true victory.

On this day, we remember—whether from having taken part or from the history books—the struggle that has been carried on to preserve our world. We remember the joy of finding the nation at peace. We remember the people who made that possible. And we remember, also, how brief, in the long march of time, was the particular Armistice we commemorate today. Less than 25 years after Armistice Day 1918, the world was aflame again with weapons of destruction far more terrible than those of the First World War. The dictionary defines an armistice as a temporary suspension of hostilities by mutual agreement. Perhaps one day, instead of celebrating an Armistice Day, we shall truly celebrate a Peace Day, when the suspension of hostilities is not merely temporary, but permanent.

As yet, nobody has found a way to arrange a lasting armistice in the war against terrorism, the pinpoint conflicts that underlie so much of the politics of the world today.

As yet, nobody has found a way to turn all the world's swords into plowshares. Armistice Day is a day that reminds us not to give up trying, not to give up that fight— the fight for lasting peace.

"The mere absence of war," said John F. Kennedy in the year he died, "is not peace." And John Milton, hundreds of years earlier, gave us the true meaning, the true significance of Armistice Day when he wrote, "Peace hath her victories, no less renowned than war." And so today we celebrate the best of victories.

A RTIST'S UNVEILING

There is probably no torture ever devised by the ingenious mind of man or woman more excruciating than what a painter or a sculptor is subjected to when he does his work out in the open. An idler passes by and asks, "What are you making?" The artist is distracted; if he tries to reply, he will probably be further distracted by the reaction of the questioner who, as often as not, will say something like "What's the point of that?" or "I don't quite see what you mean." The torment of prejudgment by amateurs has driven many an artist into seclusion. It is bad enough to go through the anxiety of revealing a completed work to an uncertain public without having that public looking over your shoulder and breathing down your neck while the work is being done.

It has always seemed to me, therefore, that the artist whose talent was reserved for himself or herself alone was in many ways the wisest. He or she alone knows to the full what the creation was conceived to be and what has gone into it. To share that finished product with the world is—in some cases—an act of courage, and in every case an act of generosity. For, no matter what the material rewards for a work of art, that work of art is essentially a giving of oneself, a personal confession by the artist, a deliberate invitation to the judgment of strangers.

We here today are not merely spectators. Art essentially is a form of expression, a type of communication, a means of establishing a rapport between artist and audience. Some artists communicate with words, some with clay, some with cameras, some with paint, some with rock or mortar or with seeds and soil. All great works, no matter what the medium, come to that point when they reach fruition, and are—whether or not the artist is—ready for unveiling.

The time has now come to draw back the curtain, to unwrap the package, to exchange the joy of anticipation for the pleasure of perception. Art in its truest sense does not exist in a vacuum. The sole purpose of art is to convey the essence imbued into the work by the artist. Its unveiling is, in one sense, the beginning of its life. It is in that spirit, with that feeling of welcoming a new addition to the ageless family of the arts, that we now open this work to public view.

I believe it was Sam Goldwyn, years ago, who said he had found the perfect formula for commenting on a new work without necessarily committing himself. He would simply say, "What a picture!"—leaving the interpretation to the imagination of whoever heard him. I remind you, however, that what you say about a work of art is not necessarily as important as what you take away with you after seeing that work. With that thought in mind, I am happy to declare this exhibit open.

AWARD PRESENTATION

Many years ago, there was a summer camp for boys which found itself unhappy with the competitive aspects of camp activity. Awards were given for proficiency in various sports, and inevitably, some campers who were natural athletes won batches of medals and others won none at all. The director of the camp tried to solve this by creating new categories for awards skills in various arts and crafts, for example. But even this failed to achieve his goal of finding at least one award for every camper. Finally, for every age group, he established a new medal. It was called the Improvement Medal, and it always went to a camper who had no other claim to glory. The result, unfortunately, was not quite what the camp director had intended. The winner of the improvement medal, and the whole camp, knew that he had been singled out as the saddest apple in the basket. His award was in fact a consolation prize that didn't console at all, but instead aggravated the injury. Today, I am happy to say we are presenting no improvement medals.

Today's award presentation is very simple in its concept. It is meant to be, and is, formal recognition of excellence, as determined by a process of selection that reflects the accomplishments of outstanding people. I want to make that clear, because we live in a time of so many award presentations that one can sometimes be entitled to a healthy dose of skepticism about the whole idea. I recall, for example, the story of the famous writer who was called upon one day by the head of a literary organization, Mr. Jones. Said Mr. Jones, "Your work is so distinguished, your influence on the literature of our times has been so profound, and your reputation throughout the world is so unique, that our society has decided to have you as our guest of honor and award winner at our annual dinner two months from today." The great writer thanked him but said he would be unable to attend on that day since he would be out of the country. "In that case," said Mr. Jones, "do you know any other writer that might fit the qualifications and be able to attend?" Suffice it to say that today's awards were not determined by the honoree's ability to attend.

Virtue may be its own reward. After all, as Aristotle once said, "Dignity does not consist of possessing honors, but in deserving them." However, we believe that virtuosity deserves some more concrete and tangible form of recognition. From the time of the laurel wreath awarded by the ancient Greeks, we have recognized that in every field of endeavor some people are outstanding in their particular work, and some people are outstanding simply as people. Very often, in saluting these outstanding people, we do more than merely honor them; we help them to set standards for emulation from this time forth. These are achievements that deserve recognition, and this is the recognition that comes as just reward for achievement.

When the Academy of Motion Picture Arts and Sciences began giving out what came to be known as the Oscars, they were relatively unique. Since then we have had Emmies, Tonys, Cleos, Grammys and Edgars and so many Halls of Fame that fame itself has become a honeycomb of niches. But it would be impossible to categorize the people we are honoring today or the reasons for their selection. By any measure, they have given us cause to celebrate their successes. So let me get down to particulars.

BACHELOR PARTY

We are here tonight in honor of what Benjamin Franklin called "an incomplete animal." Yes, that was the way old Ben defined a bachelor. "A single man," Franklin wrote, "has not nearly the value he would have in state of union. He is an incomplete animal. He resembles the odd half of a pair of scissors." Now it is rather unusual for half a pair of scissors to spend the night clipping down the road to perdition, but that is the agenda for tonight.

It is traditional to have a very special party on the night before the end of bachelorhood. It is traditional in the same way as making sure that the condemned man eats a hearty meal. The purpose in both cases is to make sure the man of the hour knows what pleasures he is about to give up.

You've heard of trial by fire and trial by ordeal. Tonight it's a case of trial by association. Anybody who brings out this kind of crowd is clearly going to have to change his ways. But that change, of course, won't come until tomorrow. And meanwhile, the night is still young.

Years ago, tradition had us believing that before the wedding, the groom spent his last waking hours carousing and the bride spent them blushing. Actually, both of them—if they are like most normal human beings—are probably wondering what they have gotten themselves into and worrying about it. The truth is, the bachelor party's purpose is getting the future bridegroom's mind away from the worries of the morrow. We call it one last fling, but the flinging is usually more on the part of the people who are throwing the party. And the future groom is the party of the first part.

So tonight I call upon all and sundry present to join in saluting one who is doing his best to bring a small truce to that most ancient of conflicts—the war between the sexes. One small segment of that war, you see, is due to end tomorrow in mutual surrender. But in the meantime, the instructions are simple—come out swinging.

Tonight we are celebrating what Ralph Waldo Emerson and Montaigne saw as a very contradictory institution, the state of matrimony. Matrimony is what those outside want to get into and those inside want to get out of. For our guest of honor tonight, I commend the wisdom of Emerson and Montaigne. You are about to enter a new state, which I am reliably informed is the result of a temporary madness called love. I refer to this as a temporary madness because I am told that it rarely lasts more than 50 or 60 years. Or is it that it just seems like 50 or 60 years?

On the night before the wedding, a man and his friends are soon partied. Tonight we rejoice—for tomorrow is somebody else's turn. And remember the wise words of that ancient seer who said, "Keep your eyes wide open before marriage and half shut afterwards."

Birthday

Mark Twain, who sometimes had a rather somber view of life, said that we rejoice at a birth (and grieve at a funeral) because "we are not the person involved." Others have noted that, in the course of our lives, we are annually being congratulated for the one thing we did not do for ourselves—a birthday. But that is not totally correct. For a birthday is also celebrated as a feat of survival, and that each of us can view as a very individual accomplishment.

Thoroughbred horses at the racetrack all grow a year older on January 1; they don't have individual birthdays. For people, birthdays have sometimes been far more complicated than they are today. George Washington, for example, was born on February 11, 1732. In his early manhood, the old-style calendar was abandoned, making his birthday February 22. For most of his life, however, he continued to observe the 11th as his birthday. Then February 22 became the accepted date, for about a century and a half, until somebody got the bright idea of celebrating Washington's birthday on a Monday to give us all a three-day weekend. For most of us ordinary people nowadays, however, the day we were born is the birthday we keep for the rest of our lives. Sometimes we are tempted to try to fuzzy up the exact year, but we don't generally fiddle around with the day of the month. And there are always people around, of course, to remind us what day it is. Sometimes they are friends; sometimes they are enemies. You'll have to decide which is which or who is who today.

On the average, about 20 million people have their birthdays on any given day of the year; if they decided to celebrate together, they'd have to have a birthday country. We prefer, of course, to concentrate on a somewhat smaller and more modest constituency. Instead of wishing happy birthday to 20 million people, we have decided to single out our own birthday star.

Birthdays are more than just the odometers of our lives. They mark a very different sort of passage as well. As Albert Einstein once said, "As I grow older, the identification with the here and now is slowly lost. One feels dissolved and merged into nature. It makes me feel happy. The greatest experience we can have is the mysterious." Is there any greater mystery—or greater opportunity—than what lies ahead?

It is appropriate to remind this gathering, on this day, of the words of I Timothy 6:7, "For we brought nothing into this world, and it is certain we can carry nothing out." Birthday parties are designed to take care of that gap between coming into the world with nothing and going out the same way. In between, your friends and admirers take pleasure in loading you down—or is it loading you up—with expressions of their esteem.

On some birthdays, it has been said, you take the day off; on others, you take a year off. As far as your friends are concerned, it's okay either way.

Bon voyage

In the ancient days of humankind, travel was usually a hard necessity, not a pleasure. Instead of wishing the traveler bon voyage, the people who stayed behind were more likely to be the ones who forced the traveler to move on. But times have changed. Today we speed the parting guest or the prodigal son with good wishes and good cheer.

We wish bon voyage to people we like, in the hope that they will enjoy the trip; but we also wish bon voyage to people in the hope that their journey returns them safely to us. Except, perhaps, in the case of the perennial houseguest, when bon voyage takes on an entirely different meaning. But that's clearly not the case today.

In the old days, wishing a traveler bon voyage was a very serious expression of hope and good will in a truly uncertain world. Caravans were apt to be raided, ships sailed sometimes unknown and always dangerous seas; wherever you were going, the natives were apt to be unfriendly. The people who set out on such trips faced, at the very least, sudden storms and lots of surprises.

Things are different for the modern traveler than they were in the old days—or are they? Today's tourist may not have to worry about sudden storms; instead she has to worry about sudden transport strikes or overbookings. Instead of possibly losing her way, she has to beware of losing her luggage. So travelers now, as in the past, go with those age-old good wishes for a safe journey and happy return! And may you and your luggage travel to the same destinations at all times.

Probably no nations have been more travel-minded or mobile than the English-speaking ones. All the modern means of transportation except the railroad virtually began in the United States—the airplane, the steamship, the automobile. We commute greater distances to work—or to play—than any other people since the dawn of time; and our British cousins, in their time, traveled and ruled the four corners of the earth. But when we wish the traveler well, we use a French term, not our own English language. That is because the language of international relations and diplomacy, until our own time, was French. When important people were traveling to or from foreign climes, they received good wishes in the language of diplomacy—the French bon voyage. But today, bon voyage crosses all language barriers. It isn't just French. It is universal.

Somehow, it sounds more festive than the simple "have a good trip" and it is considerably shorter than that ancient Irish blessing, "May the wind be at your back and the sun light the paths ahead."

No matter how you say it, the message is the same: "A safe and happy journey be yours." Sometimes we urge the traveler not to eat the food and not to drink the water, but of course that too is part of our expressing the hope that nothing will interfere with an enjoyable trip. In other words, "Bon voyage!"

CANDIDACY ANNOUNCEMENT

The act of running for office in the United States is one that is surrounded with symbolism. You throw your hat in the ring, or you dicker in "a smoke-filled room" or you coyly let yourself be "drafted" in response to popular demand. All the terminology—and the accompanying circumstances—cannot alter the basic single fact that a candidate, in the cold language of the dictionary, is one who seeks or aspires to be elected or appointed to an office, or is put forward by others. Not many candidates are aware that the word itself—candidate—means "clothed in white," from the old Roman custom of wearing a white toga to signify the seeking of office.

I am fresh out of white togas, so I should like to signify my quest for popular support by simply announcing that I am a candidate for the office of _____. I am neither a "favorite son" candidate nor a "dark horse" candidate nor, at this early juncture, "the people's choice." I submit myself to popular consideration in great confidence that, when they come to choose, I will indeed be the people's choice. But that comes at the end, the climax of the campaign. And I believe at this time we can state in all earnestness, that this is just the beginning.

A candidate in this country *runs* for election; in England, he *stands* for election. Either way, he runs or stands on a platform. A platform is designed to let the voter know how the candidate proposes to use the office once he is elected. In announcing my candidacy here today, I assume the immediate obligation to make public, before the election, how I propose to carry out the duties of the office for which I am running, and why I believe my candidacy deserves your support. In the course of this effort, I propose to talk about positive principles and programs. I remember, and I am sure you do too, the story of the candidate who swore that he wouldn't base his campaign on his opponents' shortcomings but instead would try to make his case on his own. Well, I am not going to maintain that I am that rarest of species, the candidate wholly without shortcomings. I am sure that I need not dwell on them because others will. So I will confine myself to trying to acquaint you with my positive qualifications, which I think—and trust—you will find outweigh by far any other considerations.

It has been written that some people pretend to see the light when what really happened is that they felt the heat. My candidacy is neither the result of my suddenly seeing the light or suddenly feeling the heat. It is neither a sudden decision nor one undertaken recklessly. Nor is it the other type of candidacy—the one prompted by the candidate's desire to receive title for title's sake. I am committed to this candidacy simply because I think I can do the job well and I would like to do it. I don't believe in drafted candidates. Someone who has to be coaxed or cajoled into running simply doesn't bring to the office the enthusiasm and the confidence which any office requires if it is to be done well. So I am here with my own enthusiasm, my own confidence and my own candidacy, eager for the campaign and ready for action.

Christmas party

One of the things that makes a Christmas party so delightful is that it is everybody's party. Most other parties are in honor of some friend, relative or colleague. We celebrate and salute the guest of honor's great new achievement or anniversary. We come together to congratulate a particular individual for a notable accomplishment. But Christmas is something else.

Christmas, of course, is a birthday party, but it is an idea, a symbol and above all a spirit of fellowship. At the same time, a Christmas party has another unique attribute we cannot ignore. Christmas is a gift-giving occasion. The old adage that says it is not the gifts so much as the thought that counts, rings remarkably true. More than any other time of the year, we hold dear our friendships and relations, as we come together to celebrate. If we can hold these feelings into the coming year, it is sure to be a joyous one.

I think it is only fitting to remember that Saint Nicholas, who is more celebrated at this time of year as Santa Claus, is not only the patron saint of children and of sailors but also of pawnbrokers, suggesting that it is all right to go into hock at Christmas time. But prudence argues as strongly against that course as against overestimating one's capacity for Yuletide wassail. Think before you drink and remember why credit has a limit.

A great many of the things we accept as ancient Christmas customs are a lot younger or much older than we think. It was little more than a hundred years ago that Americans began sending each other Christmas cards. The night before Christmas was a fine time for the kids long before Clement Moore wrote a poem about it in 1822. The Christmas tree, however, is a good deal older than Christianity itself, and so is the Christmas party. But successive generations have propagated traditions by handing down the most enjoyable aspects of the festivities; and we are the blessed recipients of their bequest to us.

Christmas, of course, is the time for strange gifts, and the day after Christmas is the time for many happy returns. As far as commercial enterprise is concerned, Christmas starts the day after Thanksgiving—or seems to—and when it finally ends on Twelfth Night, the milk of human kindness is apt to have become a bit skimmed. So we must cherish the high points and weather the low ones. That is the Christmas spirit.

I can't think of a more thankless task for a speaker than trying to talk when the audience either wants to get down to exchanging gifts, toasting the season or singing carols. Even Santa Claus is not expected to make a speech at Christmas time. All he says is just what I am about to end my remarks by saying: "Merry Christmas to all, and to all a good night!"

To this I can only add the sage advice an old friend gave me many Christmases ago. "Don't shoot off your mouth, because you can never tell whether you're loaded."

Columbus Day

On a Monday close to October 12, Americans celebrate the discovery of the New World by Christopher Columbus. There are those who contend that the Norse Vikings or Manchurians or the ten lost tribes of Israel somehow discovered America before Columbus did; but the fact is that Columbus—though it's widely accepted that he never reached the Americas—got back to the old world and spread the word about new lands in the west. He also gave history something good to say about 1492, which otherwise would have been remembered mainly for the flowering of the Spanish Inquisition.

In recent years, Columbus Day has become a very special day of celebration for those of Italian descent, because Columbus, although in the service of Spain, was an Italian himself. Just as St. Patrick's Day has a very special meaning for those of Irish heritage, Columbus Day is an Italian-American tradition. But it may surprise you to know that a man named William Mooney founded an organization called the Society of St. Tammany that had what is generally regarded as the first American celebration of Columbus Day back in 1792. Later on, of course, Tammany turned to other things and this celebration became more closely affiliated with an organization aptly named the Knights of Columbus. Columbus Day owes a great deal to the Knights.

It is one of the sardonic jests of history that the world Christopher Columbus introduced to Europe does not bear his name, but rather is named after Amerigo Vespucci. The basis for calling it America was that Vespucci was the first European to reach the continental mainland—in 1497 to be exact—about eight days before Sebastian Cabot, another Italian who was in the service of the English crown. No matter who deserves the credit, he was an Italian. But if Vespucci got the continent, history has certainly made it up to Christopher Columbus. And how many cities in the U.S. are named Vespucci?

The celebration of Columbus Day seems to me to be far more significant for what Columbus symbolized than for how the credit was distributed for his discovery. He refused to be diverted from his goal by the conventional wisdom of his time. He was gifted with courage, and with the patience to stick to the course he had laid out for himself. "Every ship that comes to America," Ralph Waldo Emerson wrote, "got its chart from Columbus."

In the words of Joaquin Miller's memorable poem "What shall we do when hope is gone?/The words leapt like a leaping sword/Sail on! sail on! sail on! and on!" There are always new dimensions to be explored, new worlds to be discovered. On Columbus Day, we honor his memory by remembering to sail on, with our eyes alert for the far horizon.

COMMENCEMENT

(See also Graduation)

A commencement address is usually delivered by someone who commenced a long long time ago, and whose audience waits hopefully for the finish. It is supposed to offer sage words of wisdom or inspiration to young people about to commence their next phase of mortal existence. With the shape the world keeps getting itself into, the thought keeps occurring that the new generation might do best to work up its own helping of conventional wisdom.

But, despite the tremendous advances in education which make this, I truly believe, the finest generation yet, I must carry to you the perhaps sad word that you are all doomed to have more schooling—this time in the school of experience. They used to call it the school of hard knocks, but it doesn't always live up to that billing these days. As a graduate of the school of experience, I am called upon here and now to welcome the commencement of a new class. In the words of mathematician Buckminster Fuller, "You are getting ready to go out into the game of life, to graduate into reality. I don't see this as some sort of side exercise, but as part of the absolute frontier—the frontier of whether we are going to survive on our planet or not. Every minute is counting now."

Although what we celebrate here is a commencement, it is also an ending, the climax of years of education. Some of you may feel a real glow of accomplishment, some an equally satisfying sense of relief, and some of you may even be a bit uncertain about what lies ahead. That all goes with the territory. I am a good bit older, and I must confess that I begin each day much that same way—remembering good things from the past, relieved to have gotten through some of the not-so-good things and wondering what's coming next.

That legendary baseball pitcher, Satchel Paige, once counseled his public in these words: "Don't look back; someone might be gaining on you." I would like to amend that advice somewhat. Don't be afraid to look back; but try to look ahead with the advantage of past experience. That, rather than to see whether anybody is gaining on you, is why man was designed to be able to turn around and look in any direction.

Above all, as you move on, remember that human attribute: the ability to turn around and look in any direction. Blinders are for horses, not for people. If education has any single goal, it is to encourage people to ask questions and to know how to search for the answers. It is not enough in life to be a listener, a passive member of the audience. It is not enough to look straight ahead and never look around. It is not enough to breathe a sigh and figure that your learning days are over. "Growth," as John Henry, Cardinal Newman once said, "is the only evidence of life."

This is your Commencement Day. And it is only fitting to say to you, as we salute your accomplishments, that, truly, this is only the beginning. And I conclude with this final observation. One of the greatest achievements of graduation is sitting through the commencement exercises.

CORNERSTONE LAYING

I have it on the hallowed authority of the Encyclopaedia Britannica that a cornerstone today need not be what it originally was, "a support, a corner or a key part of the foundation of a building." All it needs is a message—sometimes carved on it, sometimes ceremoniously placed inside it—entrusted to stone for the information or possible amazement of a future generation. My function here today is probably first to make sure we all know where the cornerstone is, second to tell you the message we are asking this stone to convey to those who pass this way in future times, and third, and perhaps most important, to give us another good reason to finish the building.

One thing that always worries me about the kind of cornerstone inside which documents and mementos are placed, is the question of whether, when, how and why the documents will ever be seen again. If a date for having the stone opened is specified at the time we have the cornerstone-laying ceremony, how do we know the stone will be around for the unveiling on that specific date? How do we know the building will still be around?

We don't know—we hope. And in modern times we have been able to add some new twists as forms of insurance. We take pictures of the cornerstone; we keep copies of the messages and/or mementos of the occasion.

Cornerstones are almost as old as the oldest buildings known to civilization. They existed even in buildings that didn't have corners. They signified offerings to the gods, prayers, threats to deter people from disturbing the building, and sometimes simply identification of the builder or owner of the establishment.

Cornerstones can be dedicated, troweled, prayed over, inscribed, sprinkled, or used as the setting and occasion for human sacrifices. Even these days, a nervous speaker at a cornerstone ceremony every now and then gets the strange feeling of being brought forth for that honor.

Beyond the obvious, the cornerstone serves a second essential purpose. Any building, or every building, represents the flowering of an idea, the collaborative effort of many people. This building represents something more, in terms of what it means to the community. In dedicating this cornerstone, I hope it will be a symbol of permanence and of strength in this community. For this cornerstone, we all know, represents more than meets the eye.

I am honored to be invited to participate in this ceremony. It is always gratifying to be in on the start of something new, and particularly so when what you are taking part in is the challenge of building for the future.

EASTER

Easter is, of course, a profoundly religious occasion, but it is also associated with so many different customs and traditions that an Eastertime speaker has a wide range of topics from which to choose the subject of discourse. For the fashion-minded there is the life and times of the Easter parade, or the latest crop of Easter bonnets. For the artistic there is the decorated egg; for the philosophical, there is birth and rebirth; for the competitive, the egg roll; for animal lovers, the Easter rabbit. As you can see, people have been observing Easter in lots of ways.

Easter derives its name, it is believed, from an ancient Teutonic deity, the goddess Eostre. A festival in honor of the goddess Eostre was celebrated every Spring, and when the Resurrection of Christ became a movable Christian celebration, it seems to have taken the popular title of an established seasonal occasion. But, by any name, it is a time to rediscover the miraculous joy of life.

This is the time of the year when the life-giving breath of Spring begins to cause the grass to grow and the leaves to open and the buds to blossom. "All the veneration of Spring," said Emerson, "connects itself with love." It is a lovely sentiment, and an ideal to which we all aspire.

It is customary, at Christmas, to exchange gifts, and at New Year's to exchange resolutions. Easter seems to be the season of hope and good wishes and moral communion—in many ways the most spiritual of the year's many traditional occasions. And so it seems appropriate for me today to speak of some of the difficult moral issues of our time.

Perhaps one of the most important is faith. I speak not of faith in the formal religious sense nor in terms of the relationship between humankind and its Maker, but rather of the kind of faith on which the greatest of human progress has always been based—faith in others and in ourselves. It is so easy to contemplate the things which divide us—the prejudices, the distrusts, the suspicions, the isolation, the insecurities—that we are apt to lose sight of the extent to which humanity means compassion, love, family in its most encompassing sense, sympathy, and a helping hand.

Look around you. Examples of that kind of faith are not hard to find or to emulate and honor. Easter reminds us that, however difficult things may seem, faith will be rewarded.

The truth shall rise again.

ELECTION DAY

The trouble with a speaking engagement near Election Day is that whatever you say is likely to be regarded as at least subtly partisan. In a time of picking sides, the burning question too often is, "Whose side are you on?" I am here to make a few frankly political statements, but they are concerned with the election process itself and not with who is to be elected.

First and foremost, I am here to say there are very clearly two opposite sides on the question of voting, and I am an unabashed partisan. The two opposite sides are those citizens who exercise their right to vote—and indeed regard it not merely as a right but as an honor and a duty—and those who choose not to be represented in our representative government. It is guaranteed in the Constitution that one has the right of free speech and free assembly and all the other basic freedoms; how sad it is that so many millions of Americans, enjoying the blessings of liberty, have opted out of the fundamental process of free democracy in a free republic. As the population grows, we're tempted to wonder how much our individual vote counts. Ask the gentleman who, not so long ago, not only lost an election by one vote, but had neglected to cast his ballot that day. Every person who neglects to vote scores a point for everyone and everything they oppose.

Election time is also an appropriate occasion for speaking out about the sad fact that so many people of outstanding attainments and great qualities of leadership avoid elective office like the plague. Such public office used to be a great achievement and honor. But the risk and discomfiture of running for office, and the potential embarrassment of having one's private life publicly dissected in the scrutiny gauntlet of the media, have discouraged all too many good people. There is a great contradiction between our increasing recognition of the right of privacy and our increasing and understandable curiosity about the personal and private lives of candidates. This, as much as greater income opportunities for outstanding people in the business and professional world, has created for our times a problem which previous generations did not have to face—the problem of persuading more people to try for public office. I have no easy solution to offer; but I believe it is something about which we all might do some thinking.

Lest I seem to be using this occasion to view things through dark glasses, let me say a few words in praise of an ancient and honorable American election tradition—the tradition of the good loser and the gracious winner. There are so many places in the world where peaceful elections are virtually impossible, that it is only fair to salute the good temper, good faith and good judgment of our domestic winners and losers alike. We have a great respect in this country for the voice of the people—even when we may think the voice has been wrong.

Henry D. Thoreau said that "Even voting for the right is doing nothing for it," and Franklin D. Roosevelt said "Nobody will ever deprive the American people of the right to vote except the American people themselves." So, while everyone who votes deserves credit for keeping the breath of life in our way of life, everyone who abides by the decision of the voters is making a further contribution. After all, reflect on what might happen if we held an election and nobody came.

FATHER'S DAY

You may recall that ancient saying that every dog has his day. Father's Day is of somewhat more recent vintage—and so, in all fairness, is Mother's Day as well. In bygone times, the idea of setting aside a day to honor your father and your mother would have seemed to be a feckless dilution of the ancient Commandment. As I recall, it said

"Honor thy father and thy mother," not "set aside one day each year to honor one, and reserve another day for the other."

So I prefer to think that the real purpose of Father's Day is to make public what we hold in our hearts all year long. And in that spirit, I am here to celebrate the idea of fatherhood in general and one father in particular.

There are two maxims—or two sides of one maxim—that make a very important point about fatherhood in general. It's a wise father who knows his own child, and a wise child who knows his own father. As babies, we begin with the assumption that father knows everything; as teenagers we are apt to lean more to the theory that father knows nothing; as adults we finally come to the point where we know our father, what makes him tick, how much he means to us—and how much he has put up with in the process of our growing up.

Kids find it easy to excuse their own mistakes because every next step in life is still new to them. But fathering is also an experience where every step as the children are growing up is also a new one for good old Dad. In a family relationship, part of what makes it memorable is the process of learning together—the joy of a father suddenly realizing that somehow or other he has helped to bring up somebody of whom he can be proud, and/or fond—and who is proud of and concerned about him in return.

Fatherhood basically is a long battle to make a dependent independent. It is a steady battle to keep the next generation from making the last generation's mistakes. Today, I am happy to salute one of the winners—I hesitate to use the word survivors because the process of fatherhood, while trying, is not fatal. All of us are children, many of us in our time become parents and grandparents, and some of us have the happy occasion to salute or be saluted by another generation along the way. Some of us are chips off the old block and some of us are regarded more as splinters and driftwood. But all of us can join in saluting fatherhood.

Fundraising

Years ago, the famous publisher, M. Lincoln Schuster, attended the planning session for a big fund drive on behalf of a distinguished educational institution. One of the campaign planners said that, although he recognized that big business should not take part in the management of education, he felt it would be productive to invite major corporations to take part in running the fund drive. "In other words," said Mr. Schuster, "you want to drive the money changers back into the temple."

Almost every fundraising campaign these days has a little of that spirit in it. That's almost inevitable, because the hard fact of life today is that before a campaign can do good, it has to do well. The business of raising money, even for charitable and public purposes, is precisely that—a business, not merely because there are professional experts who make a living by running fund campaigns but because a successful campaign today, whether run by amateur volunteers or by a professional organization, still has to be run using basic business guidelines. You are dealing with "customers" when you seek contributions just as much as when you sell goods across the counter. Before a contributor makes a gift, he or she has to be convinced that the donation is worthwhile, the cause praiseworthy and the administering organization deserving of trust and confidence.

Some people think that these considerations only apply if you are asking for and receiving a multifigure contribution from the aforementioned "customer." But that is not necessarily the case. Any of you who have been stuck with the responsibility for selling charity raffle tickets for a mere pittance or for getting the neighbors to chip in a buck apiece for a local animal shelter can probably testify to the fact—noted in one of Parkinson's laws as a matter of fact—that people are sometimes even more persnickety about small expenditures for which they are responsible than they are about huge ones. No matter what the size of the gift, nobody likes to feel it is being thrown away.

Anyone who sets out to raise funds without believing in the cause, but simply as a matter of duty, is giving himself a doubly difficult task. It is hard enough to get people to open up their hearts and their pocketbooks when you are talking to them with all your heart and soul. So I ask you to remember that when a dedicated campaign worker asks for your charitable "investment" in a worthy cause, that campaign worker is already contributing to what is usually a larger investment of time and effort and commitment.

I have always felt that the gift of money—while forever needed cannot tell the whole story. The most precious gift, always, is the message that you care. There are, in practical terms, only two ways of showing how much you care about a particular cause. One is the amount of work you do for it; the other is the amount of your substance you give to it.

We live in times when, thanks both to the complications of modern life and the generosity of the human spirit, the number of worthy causes seeking contributions grows with every passing day. Very few, if any of us, can afford to give to a great many of these worthy causes. That is why the concept of the United Way became popular, to enable the individual giver to let somebody else divide the gift among the various needs. But virtually every nonprofit organization also needs primary funding of its own, and virtually every such organization needs to know that it can depend on the steady interest and support of a specific constituency.

One of the nicer aspects of personal giving in the United States is that a substantial portion of what you give turns out to be somebody else's money. Depending on your income-tax bracket, you save a varying percentage of the taxes you would otherwise have to pay Uncle Sam, because contributions up to a rather substantial proportion of your income are tax-deductible. If you don't make contributions, you may have to pay more in taxes; so it is Uncle Sam's money, as well as yours, that you are donating.

I hope for the help that will enable this campaign to do well. Only then can the money do good.

FUNERAL

When we assemble to note the passing of one who, until so recently, lived among us, we do not mourn for the deceased. Indeed, most religions regard death as passing on to another reward and those without religion see death simply as a mortal's final chapter. We mourn our loss; we sympathize with the sorrow of the bereaved. We search for the good things to remember as solace. If we understand the nature of the occasion, it may serve to give us comfort.

Traditionally, a memorial address searches out and takes note of the good and noble things in the life we are remembering. It is this remembrance that remains when the curtain falls. But each of us, in our own life, is the sum total of many memories. Each of us learns from what we remember fondly. Each of us, in some measure, looks back to the departed and chooses that which is worth remembering. Even in the act of remembering, we are moved somewhat to emulate or to avoid, depending on the memory. Generally, what we choose to remember is the best of the past life—and the best is always a model that we try to emulate.

"No man is an island," John Donne wrote. But we do not simply share the tolling of the bell. We share a learning process, a degree of inspiration, a lasting lesson of friendship for some, love for others. And when we say that something of the departed remains with us we are not speaking allegorically. We are speaking of part of the experience of our own lives.

One of the comforting things that can always be said to those who come to extend their last respects is that they are not your last respects to _____. You have remembered; and forever filed away in your spirit is the memory of whatever tie it was that connected you with (him) (her). You have also come to be part of this community of mourners—to add to the mutual comfort that arises from knowing that grief is shared and understood.

Most of the richness of the human experience is in what is handed down from one life to the next—not simply things of mortar and stone, but memories of what this one did or that one said or this one felt. That is why we remember the good things, because they are worth remembering, and because we, the living, have a need to remember. And we have much to remember about _____.

The departed never wholly leave us. We never wholly leave each other. And we remember.

Graduation

(See also Commencement)

The word "graduation" has several meanings. The primary meaning is the state of being arranged in steps or degrees. It is worth pondering that an inanimate thing, as well as a human being, is subject to graduation. Anything which comes in an orderly progression is a process of graduation. We graduate from one phase of life to another, because life is a series of progressions which we achieve through learning and growth.

Some of the young people taking part in today's ceremony may be saying to themselves, "Wouldn't I have graduated to the next phase of life without going to school? Wouldn't I graduate from being a child to being an adult when I get old enough without having to earn a diploma or take tests?" The answer, of course, is that growing up is a series of graduations. Some are simply the result of your physical growth over the course of years, which is not under your own control; and some are the result of studying and learning, which is aided by teachers and parents but is principally your own accomplishment. What we are here to celebrate today is what you have accomplished—what came about not simply because you grew older but because you learned.

Today is generally thought of as a vacation from learning. That which we derive from landmark personal experiences—the experiential learning we do—is integral to our progression. As a matter of fact, human beings keep on learning until the day they die. They learn from what they read and what they see and what they hear and what they do. The hope is that your schooling and your teachers have been able to prepare you to know how to continue learning independently.

The graduation ceremony and the diploma you receive announce to the world that you are ready to go ahead to the next step in your lives. You have passed through an important part of the learning process. If it has been completely successful, it has taught you how much more there is to learn. An American writer of the nineteenth century—Bayard Taylor—said something very wise about this whole subject: "Learn to live, and live to learn."

Every time you graduate, you go on into a bigger world, where there are more people to know, more difficult jobs to do, more experiences to have than you have yet gone through. One of the things which graduation says is that you are now ready to get more out of life. When you learn to read, a whole new world opens up. When you learn to understand the way a machine works or how a government works or why a plant thrives in the sunlight, other worlds open up to you. And as you continue to learn, seemingly unrelated discoveries begin to reveal common threads; basic truths emerge from beneath the veil. We always speak of people growing up; we don't simply mean that they reach physical adult stature. We also mean that they move on to higher understandings of the world, like climbing up a mountain so you can see farther, and suddenly realizing that the separate mountains make a range, and are—like the foundation of knowledge you have developed—a single entity capable of limitless growth.

You have climbed up the mountain. It was easier for some of you than for others. But for all of you, it is an accomplishment that your parents and friends applaud. We congratulate you. You have completed an important phase of your education. Use it well.

GREETING

I rise to express the spirit of this occasion, to greet and welcome you. It has been said that human beings are the only living creatures who ever ask themselves, "Why are we meeting here like this?" Even though we have herding instincts in common with many other inhabitants of the planet, we also have more personal and more uplifting motivations—friendship, affection, appreciation, a sense of justice, a sense of beauty.

It is particularly pleasant to meet to share in these rewards. Happiness is one of those things that seems to grow when it is shared. For that matter, even misery loves company.

My function here today is rather like that of the orchestral overture, to let you know that what you have come for is about to start—and also to begin to get you in the appropriate mood. It isn't a difficult job, because you all know the purpose of the gathering. In that sense, no overture is needed.

If I may paraphrase a remark of Yogi Berra's, which he is supposed to have made when he was the guest of honor at a civic celebration, "I want to thank everybody who made this occasion necessary."

Of course there are many ways of extending greetings, salutes and hospitality. Sometimes, there is that strange symbol known as the key to the city. Sometimes there is a toast; sometimes there is a commemorative monument. Always, and this is my function at this juncture, there are the words of welcome and the official starter who says, as I do now, "it's time to settle down to the pleasant business of the day."

GROUNDBREAKING

I suspect that there is some rather ambiguous symbolism in the fact that, when we launch a great new building project, the two tools we use are a shovel and a speech. If your comment when this is over is that this was a ceremony where we really "shoveled it," there will always be a certain element of doubt as to what the comment really meant to say. Or to look at it another way, life is a process of digging a hole and then building your way out of it.

Groundbreaking as a ceremonial event goes back to the early roots of man. It goes back to the time when the idea of digging, of interfering with the natural order of things, seemed terribly daring—a sort of defiance of the gods. So when we dug—which was then about our only form of civil engineering—we thought it wise to say a few appropriate words of veneration for the gods, to be sure they knew we were not intending to commit a malicious act.

We wouldn't begin to build until we asked the gods for their blessing on our enterprise. And, if you stop to think about it, that's what we still are doing today. A groundbreaking ceremony is designed to celebrate the start of a project which we think deserves to be smiled upon by the Supreme Power. The ceremonial turning over of the soil is our signal of hope for a new enterprise.

It also reminds us that nothing is stronger, nothing is firmer than the ground on which it is built, and I suppose that where you choose to build is as important as what you choose to build.

Finally, we should remember that the ceremony of breaking ground is also the signal that it is time to go to work, to prepare the land for whatever we are hoping to do with it. Being asked to preside at a groundbreaking ceremony, like being chosen to throw out the first ball at the start of the baseball season, is a great honor; but to me it has always seemed that it was also a means of doing honor to the worthiness of a project. In a certain sense, building new constructions is also an American national game. From the quonset hut to the skyscraper, we have been originators and doers in the field of construction. We attach a spirit of good citizenship to the idea of building. Breaking ground is thought of as a sign of progress. So I am happy to have the privilege of being part of this ceremony.

And as we press our tools into the earth to break the ground, we should remember that for all the countless centuries that we have taken sustenance from the soil, we have also built upon it. The land is good and, Fate willing, we shall use it well.

INAUGURATION

For as long as there have been leaders among humankind, there have been formal procedures for installing new office holders. Everything from human sacrifice to majestic coronation rites has been used to celebrate the advent of a new regime. I am happy to note that we are going to be somewhat between those two extremes of human sacrifice and majestic coronation here today.

In the old days, loyal subjects used to prostrate themselves as a sign of allegiance to the new top brass. Then, when democracy came along, there was a certain fear that candidates for the top brass would prostrate themselves before an arbitrary electorate, reversing the old custom in search for votes. In the old days, the big day was highlighted by the show that was put on for the new official—the parade, the dancing girls, the gifts from far places. That got turned around too. The big show, for example, in the case of U.S. presidential inaugurations, has been the speech made by the new chief executive. And some of those speeches have been most memorable. President Franklin D. Roosevelt said "we have nothing to fear but fear itself." John F. Kennedy suggested that we "ask not what your country can do for you; ask what you can do for your country." Lincoln reminded us that "This country, with its institutions, belongs to the people who inhabit it."

It has been said that, in this country, people who run for office to win a seat in the government often win in a walk because of their popular stand, and spend a good part of their term riding high. That last is certainly the hope as we inaugurate today's standard bearer. I remind you of the words of Matthew, 22:14: "For many are called, but few are chosen." To be chosen is a rare honor, and in this case we all feel that the rarity was well done.

One of the great problems in a democracy is that some of the people who help select the people's choice like to try to exercise a shopper's prerogative and demand a lifetime guarantee. Even though we all expect a superb performance from our new office-holder(s), we can't help remembering the old adage that first the man holds the office and then, if he isn't careful, the office holds the man. We like to think there will be no holding our new office-holder(s), and that today we are seeing the start of better things to come.

Al Jolson, the greatest performer of his time, used to say to the audience when they cheered him, "You ain't seen nothing yet. " The grammar may leave something to be desired, but the message is crystal-clear, and I believe it furnishes a fitting theme for this inaugural occasion. With the kind of good wishes that accompany this taking of office, with the kind of person on whom the mantle of responsibility now rests, and with the kind of need, challenge, and opportunity that loom before us today, it is fair to say that "You ain't seen nothing yet."

And now, the time has come to install our new officer(s). The days of running are over, and the time has come to stand for us and for the just cause.

INDEPENDENCE DAY

(See also July 4th in Volume 3)

If Independence Day did not exist, a holiday on or about the fourth of July would probably have been invented. It is the natural start of the vacation season—the leading edge of summer, the traditional halfway point of the major league baseball season.

But the Fourth of July, Independence Day, is something more than just another holiday. It is the birthday of a great idea—not merely the idea of independence, not merely the idea of the rights of humankind, but also the birthday of a profoundly idealistic and profoundly influential charter of liberty.

The revolution signaled by the adoption of the Declaration of Independence in Philadelphia on July 4, 1776, laid down the principles which have been the foundation-stones of human progress ever since—the truths which the Continental Congress declared to be self-evident, although, somehow, most of the world had failed to take notice of them. The Declaration established, and the world steadily followed the statement, that all men are created equal and that they are endowed with such inalienable rights as life, liberty and the pursuit of happiness. Also, that government derives its just powers from the consent of the governed.

Ask yourself—more than two centuries after the men of the Continental Congress pledged their lives, their fortunes, and their sacred honor—in how many parts of the world today the very utterance of the words of the Declaration of Independence would still be regarded as sedition or revolution. Then, on the other hand, consider the explosion of recognition for the rights of man which followed, all over the world, in the wake of the Declaration of Independence.

The Declaration of Independence did not merely signal the birth of American freedom and American self-government. It marked the birth of freedom as an international idea. It was the inspiration for democratic movements on other continents. It raised the torch of liberty and kindled an undying flame.

Back in 1857, Abraham Lincoln, in a truly prophetic observation, noted that the mention in the Declaration of Independence that "all men are created equal" was—and I quote—"a stumbling block to all those who in after times might seek to turn a free people back into the hateful paths of despotism."

It is sometimes suggested that the world now needs a Declaration of Interdependence. But a careful reading of what was presented to the Founding Fathers by Thomas Jefferson, John Adams, Benjamin Franklin, Roger Sherman and Robert Livingston, in 1776, contains all the ideas a peaceful, just and democratic world needs to live by.

A quotation from the preamble to the Declaration of Independence makes another point worth noting. It is the phrase which mentions "a decent respect for the opinions of mankind . . ." No nation, any more than any man, is an island. We were the first nation to be concerned about a decent respect for the opinions of mankind. Indeed, even more than 200 years later, we seem to be the people most anxious to reach out. Even when we have waged war, we have ended up working to heal the wounds inflicted upon our erstwhile enemies. A decent respect for the opinions of humankind—just one more example of the almost universal application of the document whose birthday we celebrate today.

INDUCTION OF NEW MEMBERS

One of the traditions of human society, going back as far as the early tribes, is the rite of passage—that's rite, R I T E, which in this case is the opposite of R I G H T. The rite of passage is the ceremony of admitting new members to an already established group. And, as you know, every already established group likes to regard itself as the best judge of whom it wants to add. So it is particularly pleasurable to add all of you to the most wanted list, and to welcome you as new members of this notable group.

We have come a long way, of course, since the first youth was sent out into the jungle to prove that he belonged with the men instead of the boys. We have also come a long way from the tradition of the Heidelberg dueling scars or college hazing. We have come a long way toward recognizing that it is much nicer for all concerned to welcome people than to devise trial by ordeal, or to think up hazardous initiation stunts.

There is always a certain conflict with regard to new members. Some of the older members feel very strongly that the organization—any organization—can always use new blood. Sometimes other members, however, seem to be truly out for blood, determined to keep a good thing to themselves. In this case, I am happy to say that the prevailing wisdom is simply that a good thing is worth sharing.

It is said that an organization can be judged by its members and an individual can be judged by his organizations. What this adds up to is simply the fact that now we are all in this together.

A familiar phenomenon in connection with many ceremonies is the fact that the ceremony itself sometimes seems to overshadow the significance of the event. That's why I counsel you to regard today's event simply as the opening of a door, not the summit achievement of your lifetime. You have, of course, every right to feel gratified that you are going through this new doorway. All who have already entered before you know, as you will soon also come to know, that this is the beginning of further opportunities, not the climax.

They tell the story of the young man who was very anxious to become a member of a very exclusive key club. He sought out everyone he knew who might be a member. He heard that they favored people with low golf scores, so he took lessons to improve his game. He did everything he could to wangle an invitation to join, and finally he got his membership and his key. He came to the club, opened the door, went in and sat down. And as he looked around, he suddenly realized that after all his effort, he was now a member of a club in whose activities he wasn't really interested; all he had wanted was to know that he could get in. I hope that none of you here today are or will be similarly afflicted. We welcome you as active members, colleagues, and friends.

Incidentally, there are more than 14,000 regional or national associations in the United States, plus many times that number of local groups. There is still a lot of the feeling of togetherness left in the land. Congratulations and best wishes for a long and happy association. Welcome!

Introduction

Once upon a time, there was a magnificent public speaker who was asked to introduce the guest of honor and principal orator at an important public dinner. Gazing out at the distinguished audience, which came to a respectful silence as the introducer cleared his throat, he launched into a magnificent discourse describing the sterling qualities of the guest of honor beginning in early childhood. The introducer spoke and spoke and spoke and suddenly realized that he had used more time than the guest of honor had been allotted for the speech of the evening. Trying to recover, the introducer said to the guest of honor, "You'll have to forgive me, because I see I have used up most of your time. I hope you will understand that I was simply carried away." The guest of honor looked at him and said, "You should be."

I do not want to get carried away today, because I am looking forward, as you are, to hearing from the person it is my privilege to introduce. The easy way out, of course, would be to say simply that our honored guest here today needs no introduction. But if he/she needs no introduction, why am I here? Let us say, rather, that our guest deserves to be introduced in terms that convey the interest and appreciation we feel for the opportunity to have so notable a guest among us.

There are several standard methods of introduction. There is the "one who" style, in which you don't mention the name of the person you are introducing until the end, as if the identification is the climax of a mystery. But our guest today is too well known for me to play that kind of game. Then there is the "Who's Who" school of introduction, the dull recital of a canned biography, which always sounds as if it were snipped from a directory. I will not lead you down the road in that direction either. Let me rather confine myself to a few salient facts about our guest and about this occasion as well.

As you can readily understand from the facts I have mentioned, we are most fortunate to have _____ here to speak to this gathering. We are also fortunate that I have come to the end of my allotted time, and I now close by introducing this audience to our honored speaker (name of speaker). As the peanut butter said to the two pieces of bread in the peanut butter sandwich, I have brought you together, and now you are on your own.

INVOCATION

We thank Divine Providence for having given us the opportunity to meet together here today, and we ask most humbly for the blessing of our gathering. It is written that "While the earth remaineth, seedtime and harvest, and cold and heat, and summer and winter, and day and night shall not cease." And while the earth remaineth, so shall the children of earth be grateful for the guidance of the Lord.

Brighten our eyes with greater understanding, enrich our hearts with compassion and with courage, receive our gratitude for the feasts of fellowship and the fellowship of breaking bread together.

For the knowledge that there is hope, for the hope that there is more knowledge yet ahead, for the gifts of the Lord's devising that we enjoy today, and for the vision of tomorrow, we offer a thankful prayer.

As the ancient psalmist David said thousands of years ago, "Lead me to the rock that is higher than I." "Thy word is a lamp into my feet and a light unto my path."

So is it still today. And so today, as in ancient days, we thank Thee, oh Lord, for all thy blessings, and let us say Amen.

(Lighter Material)

In recognition of the hour, this invocation will be brief, though not quite as brief as what I call the drive-through grace, which is simply: "Good food, good meat, Good God, let's eat." Let me say rather, "Oh Lord, bless our gathering and our going forth; let us see the light without being blinded by it."

When Cardinal Cushing was delivering the invocation at the inauguration of President Kennedy, a mishap in the vicinity of the podium caused smoke to rise. One of the correspondents seated nearby turned to a colleague and said, "When the Cardinal is hot he's really hot."

Martin Luther said, "The fewer words, the better prayer." We invoke thy blessing, oh Lord, on this day and in this place, for what we now prepare to face. And lest we seem to plead again, we humbly all now say Amen.

The story is told of the long-winded man of the cloth who, when invited to deliver an invocation, spoke so long that they had to cut the rest of the program short. When one participant complained about the shortened program, a colleague differed. "I thought the invocation was more successful than most," he said. "Any time the average speaking program is shortened, it's a blessing."

Or, to put it another way, a brief invocation is a real blessing.

JUBILEE

There are two sources for the idea of a jubilee. One is the Latin word jubilar, which literally means to make sounds of joy. The other source is the ancient Hebrew word "yobel," which refers to the trumpet that was sounded to call upon the people of Israel to celebrate every fiftieth year, in the words of the Book of Leviticus, Chapter 24, when "it shall be a jubilee unto you." In the jubilee year, it was ordained, and again I quote the Book of Leviticus in the Bible, "Proclaim liberty throughout the land unto all the inhabitants thereof." That, as you may know, is the inscription on the American Liberty Bell. The year of jubilee was very real in meaning at another time in American history, too. In the period of our Civil War, there was a popular song about "the year of Kingdom coming, the year of Jubilo." Jubilo, more properly jubilee, recalled the fact that in the Biblical year of celebration the slaves were to be freed and joy was to be the happy lot of all.

That is always the purpose of a jubilee—joy for all concerned, a time for celebrating, an occasion for looking back with satisfaction and with pride. For what we are celebrating here is not merely the passage of time; not merely the very special birthday that a jubilee represents. We are celebrating a notable accomplishment. We live in times when it sometimes seems that merely surviving is an accomplishment, but what we celebrate here is far more positive. It is recognition of an example of enduring worthiness. And like the Biblical year of jubilee, it isn't a private matter. It is a happiness which many people share.

But there are all kinds of jubilees these days. If you look in the World Almanac, under the heading of anniversaries, you will find that after 25 years a married couple celebrates their silver wedding anniversary; and a king, after 25 years on the throne, has a silver jubilee. The fiftieth anniversary is a golden jubilee year, and as the life of mortals is measured, a diamond jubilee after 75 years is about as far as we go with most individuals. But for nations, for institutions, for ideas, time offers fewer limitations—and if diamonds are for a 75th anniversary, we will simply have to find yet more precious stones or metals to denote the added years.

Go beyond the immediate occasion for this jubilee and ask yourself what we are celebrating. Ask yourself how much went into the building of what we are celebrating here today. Ask yourself what made it work. And join me in saluting those who made this jubilee possible.

So let us, in the spirit of the Latin jubilar, make sounds of joy. Let us, in the tradition of the celebration of the Biblical jubilee, be grateful to have been privileged to be brought together at this time and for this happy occasion. And let us say to all who have been part of the events which made this occasion possible, congratulations.

KEYNOTE ADDRESS

Most of us can remember being led in song at an elementary-school assembly by a teacher who came out and either blew a pitch-pipe or hit a key on the piano to give us the starting tone. I feel somewhat like that teacher here today—not quite certain how close my key note will be to yours, hopeful I have not pitched my sounding-off too high or too low.

We all recall the story of the commander who stood off to the side as his troops rushed forward. "What are you doing back here?" he was asked. He replied, "I am waiting to see which way they go, so I can lead them." The function of a keynoter is to see in advance which way his or her audience is going, so he or she can get there ahead of them or lay out the path; but it is also sometimes the function of a keynoter to conduct him- or herself as a scouting party to explore alternative paths.

One thing, however, is always in order. That is the duty to present, as clearly, concisely and cogently as I can, a statement of the facts as they exist today, the conditions that underlie this meeting, the common concerns and objectives that bring us together.

Above all, we must remember what has brought us together. We must be aware of the challenge, the need, the opportunity we have before us. We can make harmonious music—if we heed each other's voices—or we can produce a cacophony and a dissonance that end up making us not part of the solution, but rather part of the problem.

As the sages have said, all human effort can be reduced to three questions: Where are we, how did we get here and what can we do about it? Let me deal with those basic questions. First, where are we?

Now, as to how we got to this point, I remind you of the familiar Rashomon syndrome. Five people may all have undergone the same experience to get to the same place, but you'd never know it to hear each one tell it. Or, for another example, there is the familiar story of the blind men examining an elephant by touching it. Result: one blind man felt the trunk and said an elephant was like a snake. Another blind man felt a leg and said an elephant was like a tree trunk. A third blind man felt the elephant's tusk and said there was no question about it; an elephant was like a long thin rock. How did we get here? We each have our own ideas on the subject. We each had our own experience along the way. We meet here to have the mutual benefit of all that experience, all that differing perspective.

And, of course, we meet here also to decide what we can do about what brought us together. First we consider the choices available to us, and then we make our choice. Let me list what I believe our options are.

Life has been described as one door after another. I hope that by our meeting here today, we will choose to open the right doors, to walk the right paths and to come ultimately to the right position. For myself, I can only try in this keynote speech to find the right key.

Labor Day

Voltaire once said that "work saves us from three evils: boredom, dissipation and want." Today we have a better cure for boredom. It is the great Labor Day holiday, a time to rest from our labors by working hard to have a good time. Labor Day began as a parade on September 5, 1882 in New York City. It became a national celebration in 1894. It became much more than a parade before long—a patriotic celebration, a picnic, a big day at the airport and the bus station. Most important, it is everybody's end of summer celebration, everybody's salute to the work ethic .

There has been some extraordinary eloquence heard on this day, and also a considerable range of sentiments. President Franklin D. Roosevelt said,

"Labor Day symbolizes our determination to achieve an economic freedom for the average man which will give his political freedom reality." Fiorello LaGuardia, the Mayor of New York, called Labor Day "America's Day" and said, "It is typically American because American labor, whenever it gathers, does so with love for its flag and country and loyalty to its government." And John L. Lewis, on the eve of the Labor Day weekend in 1937, as his C.I.O. faced bitter times, proclaimed that "Labor, like Israel, has many sorrows." President Theodore Roosevelt, in 1903, found Labor Day the occasion to observe that "No man needs sympathy because he has to work. ... Far and away the best prize that life offers is the chance to work hard at work worth doing."

Peter J. McGuire, who was a leader in the Knights of Labor back in 1882, proposed Labor Day as the occasion for a parade to be followed by a picnic, a holiday described as being "representative of the industrial spirit, the great vital force of the nation." He chose a date more or less halfway between Independence Day and Thanksgiving Day, and who is to say his choice was not a perfect one? For many, Labor Day became the dividing line between vacation time and back to work season. For all, it has been the signal to get back to business, to start the new entertainment season, get ready for the new year and so forth. It has been suggested that Labor Day should make a better time for new resolutions than New Year's Day, but that's one tradition that not even the Labor Day weekend has been able to challenge.

There have been suggestions that, in view of the way we celebrate Labor Day, the holiday should be followed, rather than preceded, by a day off. But we might reflect on the fact that in the 1880s, when Labor Day began, child labor was lawful, the 12-hour day and the six-day working week were commonplace. In fact, the idea of a labor union was considered by many people to be revolutionary. What labor has achieved in this country deserves all the celebration it can get.

The United States and U.S. Labor have indeed come a long, long way together. And, it is safe to say, they still have a long way to go. But Labor Day is not just Labor's Day. It is a celebration of an all-American accomplishment and an all-American concept. In most other countries, labor's day is intertwined with the political overtone of May Day. Here, the dignity of labor is not a matter of partisan politics. It is a matter of civic pride and public recognition—and a good time is had by all.

LINCOLN'S BIRTHDAY

Even if February 12th were not Lincoln's birthday, it would be a notable day in history for America and for the world. But the memory of Abraham Lincoln makes the day even more meaningful.

On the 100th birthday of Abraham Lincoln, Henry Cabot Lodge said, and I quote, "That nation has not lived in vain which has given the world Washington and Lincoln, the best great men and the greatest good men whom history can show." We can say, too, that nation has not lived in vain which on this same day of the year saw the birth of so many people who have played an important role in the history of America; Thaddeus Kosciusko, the Polish patriot who fought in the American Revolutionary War; General Omar N. Bradley, the famous GI's general of World War II; labor leader John L. Lewis—all share Lincoln's birthday.

One of the problems of the speaker who is called upon to talk on Lincoln's birthday is that it is so challenging to try to wax eloquent about a man commonly regarded as perhaps the most eloquent American who ever lived. Long before the nation celebrated Lincoln's birthday, he himself made a speech on February 12, 1861—the day he observed his 52nd birthday—which expressed many of the sentiments that caused him to be so greatly venerated in later times. Speaking in Cincinnati, he said; "I hold that while man exists, it is his duty to improve not only his own condition, but to assist in ameliorating mankind . . . It is not my nature, when I see a people borne down by the weight of their shackles—the oppression of tyranny—to make their life more bitter by heaping upon them greater burdens; but rather would I do all in my power to raise the yoke than to add anything that would tend to crush them."

Lincoln was the first of our martyred Presidents. After him there came Garfield, McKinley and Kennedy. It is no disrespect to their honored memories, however, to say that the tall man the people called "Father Abraham" towers in the annals of our land.

It is no coincidence that his presidency and his words have transcended party lines up to present day. It is almost tradition that each candidate for the highest office in the land alludes, at one time or another, to Abraham Lincoln as one of his role models.

Why is this so? Why is it that, so long after his own time, Abraham Lincoln is, as his Secretary of War, Edwin M. Stanton, said of him, a man who "belongs to the ages?" I think the poet and biographer Carl Sandburg captured the secret when he said, on Lincoln's 150th birthday in 1959, that "the well assured and most enduring memorial to Lincoln is invisibly there, today, tomorrow and for a long time yet to come in the hearts of lovers of liberty, men and women who understand that wherever there is freedom there have been those who fought, toiled and sacrificed for it."

When Lincoln delivered his great address at Gettysburg he said, "The world will little note nor long remember what we say here." He was wrong. The world has greatly noted and continues to remember the man of the people who so eloquently reminded us of the battles that were fought so the "government of the people, by the people and for the people shall not perish from the earth."

Lincoln was a rail splitter once, a hair splitter never. He said "the ballot is stronger than the bullet." And so, too, is the memory of a great man, whom not even an assassin's bullet could diminish in the long view of history.

Long service

It has been said that of all the arts of man the most difficult is that of survival. Those who do more than merely survive, those who distinguish themselves not only by the duration but by the quality of their service, are to be doubly saluted. Today we salute a notable combination of seniority and service.

One of the strange contradictions of modern attitudes is that we no longer seem to venerate age, but we have great respect for endurance. It is a contradiction in our thinking because nobody these days grows older without a great deal of endurance. Staying power, like experience, cannot be taught. You develop it—and it develops you. And it is not contagious. You do not pass it on like a condition of the human anatomy. You help create it in others by a good example. That is the method of teaching which, in the real sense, has been the backbone of humanity through countless generations. Today we honor someone with staying power, with experience and with a long and distinguished record of being a good example to colleagues, contemporaries, disciples and even to competitors.

In recent times we have lived in an increasingly mobile world. A new employment ethic is developing in which one tries to get ahead by moving from company to company. The idea of making a long career with one organization is a rebellion against the norm. There is no pressure of conformity, so staying power and commitment are rare and valued qualities, indeed. I must say to our guest of honor here today that we are honoring one who, by a distinguished record of long service, has done honor over the course of years to this organization by ignoring the blandishments of other organizations and by stalwart adherence to the principle that the grass is not always greener on the other side.

There are all sorts of recognition for long service—the stripes on a uniform sleeve, the special lapel pin or the timepiece that commemorates the years by keeping track of the hours—but it has always seemed to me that the truest recognition is that which comes from the hearts of friends and fellow workers. It is the admiration and respect which come to the person who has been mentor to so many, and who, through thick and thin, has never wavered.

One thing that is particularly important to note is that this is not a retirement occasion. We are not saluting the end of a career, but rather the contributions to this date of one who is still contributing, competing, doing. It is fine to have applause at the end of a performance, when all the applaudee can do is bow and thank you. How much better, however, to have that gratifying reaction of approval while the performance is still going on! And the performance of our guest of honor is most assuredly still going on.

They say that you can judge people by the company they keep; I think it is just as true that you can judge a company by the people it keeps. The company that has kept our guest of honor for these many years is entitled, I believe, to a round of applause for the company it keeps.

Above all, we owe to our guest of honor a great debt of gratitude for showing us that the right person doing the right job in the right way stays among the very young in heart.

MEMBERSHIP MEETING

It is a pleasure to welcome you to this meeting. The most important thing at a meeting of a membership organization is that the privileges of membership be exercised by as many members as possible. The voice of this group is most effective when it is the voice of many. In the new dictatorships that arose after the Second World War, many who couldn't raise their voices chose to flee. This was described as voting with their feet. I am happy that so many of you have chosen to vote in person here today.

The democratic meeting is an ancient and honorable tradition in America. We have lived for hundreds of years under the principle that ours is a participatory society, that we have a right to ask questions and to offer answers, to speak for or to speak against, to listen and think and pick sides and stand up or sit down for what we believe in. We can even let it be known that we're going to exercise our option to abstain. What we don't have, of course, is the right, after refusing to participate, to object to the actions of the other people who chose to be present and accounted for. So your presence here gives each of you an expanded franchise to sound off later, as well as in the course of our meeting.

In a poem written for the fiftieth anniversary of his college class, Henry Wadsworth Longfellow talked of "The joy of meeting not unmixed with pain." The playwright Nicholas Rowe, sometime earlier, said, "The joys of meeting pay the pangs of absence." I congratulate you all on being spared the pangs of absence on this occasion.

We all know that it is easier to have a meeting of members than to have a meeting of minds, and we also know that the members have to meet first to get the meeting of the minds. As we proceed with the business of this gathering, let us go about it with the conviction that what brings us together is more important than where we differ, that consensus is better than "nonsensus" and that we can do a lot more together than any of us can do alone. Now let's get down to business.

The first step for any formal meeting is to make sure everybody knows the rules of the game. I do not plan to bore you at this point with a long recital of *Robert's Rules of Order*, or a lecture on parliamentary procedure. Our approach is very simple. We operate on the principle that membership means participation, the right to be heard, and the obligation to let other members be heard as well. Therefore, your cooperation and attention will both be appreciated.

MEMORIAL CEREMONY

"Memory," said Cicero, "is the treasury and guardian of all things." "Praising what is lost," said Shakespeare, "makes the remembrance dear." We meet here today in that spirit. We are gathered to treasure and praise one who has been lost to us, and to share the memories which we hold so dear.

Different peoples have different ways to memorialize and remember those who have preceded us to the ultimate reward. Some build monuments of stone or statuary; some erect shrines; some keep the shrines in their hearts. In ancient times the Pharaohs built their own memorials, which today seems a strange labor to devote one's life to. Pyramids and tombs, for all their awesome grandeur, are totally impersonal. But every human being leaves another memorial of his or her own building. It is the impact of one life on those whose lives were interconnected with it, through the myriad of ties which bind us to those we love, respect, and hold for all time in our hearts.

The function of this gathering is to renew the memory of the impact on our lives of (one) (those) whose journey through life preceded ours. We are reminded here of what that journey left behind.

What distinguishes humans from the beasts of the field is not the construction of monuments nor the composition of epitaphs, but rather the privilege of memory, and the honor of sharing it with one another. Memorials can be found in many places and at many times, but they remain principally in our hearts.

In some ways a memorial service is a transfer—a transfer of the impression and impact of a human being from what used to be a physical presence to a remembrance, a part of our own inner being. Each of us is a storehouse of memories, from which we draw examples, inspirations, lessons in living. As today we remember _____, each of us draws from that remembrance an idea that lives. The virtues and the contributions that we remember have a personal meaning in our own lives.

We have not come together here today, however, just to reinforce our individual memories of one so well worth remembering. We came also for the very real purpose of trying to show those nearest and dearest to (him) (her) that their deep sense of loss is shared. We hope that in some way, by showing our own grief and loss and fond remembrance, we can help further the sense of a life well lived, a time on earth well spent, and a heritage of lasting meaning.

Traditionally, the occasion of a bereavement, or the anniversary of a bereavement, is a time when friends gather with the bereaved to say, "You are not alone in this loss; you are not alone in remembering; you are not alone in holding onto the memory of a good human being and in recollecting the ways in which he made his mark." As we come together and share that process of remembering, the remembrance becomes clearer, stronger, better for us all.

The epitaph of Christopher Wren in St. Paul's in London, the cathedral he designed, reads, in translation from the Latin, "If you would see his monument, look around." Let me paraphrase that here today. If you would see the real monument to the human being we memorialize today, look around. It is in your faces and your hearts.

MEMORIAL DAY

Paying tribute to fallen heroes is, unfortunately, an ancient tradition, because, as long as there have been communities, humankind has gone off to battle and soldiers have fallen in the fight. In our own country, we fought four or five wars before the idea of a Memorial Day became a reality.

For the first time, in 1868, a national memorial occasion was observed. It began when the Grand Army of the Republic, the organization of veterans of the Union Army, adopted on a nationwide scale what Southern women had been observing as a local Spring ceremony—remembering the Civil War dead by placing flowers on the graves of their fallen soldiers. The Grand Army of the Republic asked its members to do the same on May 30, 1868, wherever its fallen comrades lay interred. General James A. Garfield, who was later to become one of our martyred Presidents, spoke at this first Memorial Day observance on the hallowed ground of Arlington National Cemetery. The cemetery had been established only four years earlier; its graves were those of the recent dead, the casualties of a recent war. General Garfield said, "We do not know one promise these men made, one pledge they gave, one word they spoke; but we do know they summed up and perfected, by one supreme act, the highest virtues of men and citizens. For love of country they accepted death, and thus resolved all doubts, and made immortal their patriotism and virtue."

Today, those who laid the flowers on those fresh graves of the Civil War are themselves long passed. And we have seen other generations caught in the savagery of too many other wars. What began as the memorial to the fallen heroes of one war is now our day to honor the memory of the casualties of all our wars.

This is not a time for statistics, but there is one figure that deserves to be remembered. More than half a million Americans have died in battle since the beginning of the Civil War in 1861, and more than half of those dead were killed since 1940. That may be why the observance of Memorial Day has become so major an American occasion.

In the beginning, it was more popularly known as Decoration Day, because it was observed by decorating soldiers' graves with flowers or flags. That tradition of leaving a symbol of our remembrance is still a strong one; but our emphasis today is and must be mainly on remembering the nature of the supreme sacrifice so many made in the service of our country. And the function of a Memorial Day speaker now, as in generations past, must not be merely to remind his audience of past sacrifices. Rather, the occasion is to be used to inspire us to appreciate what we have in times of peace and how willing our predecessors were to risk their lives to protect this heritage.

General John A. Logan, the Commander of the Grand Army of the Republic, sounded the first call for the observance of Memorial Day in 1868. His words on that day are as eloquent and as meaningful today, perhaps even more so: "Let no ravages of time testify to coming generations that we have forgotten as a people the cost of a free and undivided Republic." And the words of Lincoln, spoken at another but related occasion, express our feelings today: "That we here highly resolve that these dead shall not have died in vain." We can do them no greater honor than to keep alive that which they gave their lives to preserve; love of country, duty, honor and defense of the right as it is given to us to see the right.

MODERATOR

Somebody once described the role of the moderator as being the one to say "Let's get ready to rumble." On the other hand, when the rumble does begin, it is the job of the moderator to keep things civil and cool. There is a difference between an argument and a fight. An argument has points and counterpoints, all carefully considered by both sides, with the shared goal of reaching a common ground. A fight, while infinitely more appealing to the darker side of humanity, accomplishes nothing. As the monitor of the middle, so to speak, I shall try to state the subjects and questions of the evening as concisely as possible, so as to elicit the full measure of the wisdom and the zeal of our distinguished participants.

I recall the story of the moderator who kept droning on and on, reciting the conditions, rules and regulations under which the discussion was to proceed. At long last he turned to the first panelist and said, "I'm sure you understand why I wanted to be so thorough and precise. It is very important to understand the ground rules." And the panelist replied, "I've never been so thoroughly grounded in my life, when I had hoped to be flying high." I hope that our speakers tonight will fly high with no fear of grounding.

Essentially, the role of the moderator is precisely what appears in the dictionary definition: to serve as the presiding officer, which means to be your timekeeper, clock-watcher, referee, bailiff and master of ceremonies; also the traffic cop, as far as questions from the floor are concerned. Please hold your questions until you are recognized.

With regard to questions from the floor, I would ask that they be precisely that—questions, not speeches. A wise counselor once told me you can make more points more clearly with questions than with declaratory sentences—and the burden of proof remains with the questionee. I will, however, step in if it seems that the question is too loaded, such as "Have you stopped robbing banks?"

We are here, let us remember, to generate light rather than heat. Such heat as may develop will, I trust, illuminate the subject rather than fry it to a crisp. And I would remind all participants that we have a lot of things to discuss tonight, so we should all bear in mind the observation made by Edgar Allan Poe. "In one case out of a hundred," he said, "a point is excessively discussed because it is obscure; in the ninety-nine remaining it is obscure because it is excessively discussed."

Let us now proceed to consider what has brought us together on this occasion. I invite your careful attention to our distinguished speakers as we consider the subject of

_____.

MOTHER'S DAY

The Reverend Henry Ward Beecher said that "The mother's heart is the child's schoolroom." Mother's Day was dreamed up by a loving daughter, Miss Anna M. Jarvis of Philadelphia. The Encyclopaedia Britannica insists that Mother's Day traces back to mother worship in the pagan world, and cites the rites that were conducted to Rhea, the Great Mother of the Gods, also sometimes known as Cybele, long before the Christian era. But, with all due respect for the ancient Greeks, it is a fact that Anna Jarvis, back in 1907, thought it might be nice to have a special service in church for sons and daughters to honor their mothers. She thought it would dramatize the occasion if every son or daughter wore a white carnation to church on that special Spring day.

Since then, I fear, a great deal more attention has been paid to the merchandise of Mother's Day than to the simplicity of the basic idea. It has become a merchandiser's holiday; there is no limit to the flora and fauna, rolling stock and common stock that, we are assured, is the gift to tell mom you love her. But the simple fact is that generally the best gift of all is the love itself, particularly since you cannot possibly give back to her as much as she has given you since before you were even able to recognize it.

What is a mother? Let me tell you a story. It is about the mother of an eight-year-old boy. They were staying at a fashionable resort and every day the youngster couldn't wait to go swimming in the lake. One day he went in the water and disregarded the warning ropes and swam way out into the lake. His mother couldn't swim, but she sat watching him and suddenly screamed. "He's in trouble," she cried to the lifeguard. The lifeguard looked out and called to the boy, "You're out too far; come on in." But the boy didn't seem to hear. Then his head couldn't be seen, and the lifeguard went plunging into the water. It took him a long time to come back, and before he found the boy he had to go under water a few times looking for him. The boy was lifeless when they came to shore, and the lifeguard, even though he worked many minutes, couldn't revive him. The mother refused to let the lifeguard stop and finally the boy stirred, spat up some water, opened his eyes and came back to life, to be grabbed to his mother's bosom. The lifeguard waited a moment and then said gently to the boy, "I hope that'll teach you not to go out in the deep water." The mother looked at the lifeguard and said, not "Thank you for saving his life" but rather, "He also had a hat."

The moral is that, as far as a mother is concerned, nobody does enough for her child, on any occasion any day of the year. So it is only fair that on this one day of the year, we return the love tenfold.

NEW YEAR'S PARTY

New Year's is a time of good tidings and good cheer. A New Year's party celebrates the end of one year and the beginning of another. If the old year was a great one, you can give it a rousing send-off. If it was bad, you can thank your stars that it's over. If you have high hopes that the new year will be better, you can give it a warm welcome. And if you're a pessimist, I suppose you should enjoy yourself now while you can.

January is named after the Roman god Janus, who had two faces. He could look forward and backward at the same time. And while two faces aren't normally a social asset, the desire to simultaneously take comfort from the past and hope for the future is a human trait. So, isn't it nice to know that on one particular day you, too, can look in two directions at once?

Of course, we have a few other new-year occasions. The new school year and the new U.S. fiscal year happen in the fall. But only summer-weary parents celebrate the coming school year. And for most of us, a new fiscal year isn't exactly a moving occasion. When all is said and done, there's nothing quite like January. The year changes numbers, elected officials take up their new jobs, and we all resolve, once again, to do better.

Everybody strives on this day to make some good resolutions and to keep them. Rather than committing myself to specifics, I prefer to follow Alfred Lord Tennyson's sentiments: "Ring out the old, ring in the new, / Ring, happy bells, across the snow; / The year is going, let him go; / Ring out the false, ring in the true."

It's historically a time for turning over a new leaf. And that goes for matters of state as well. Looking back, on New Year's Day the 1808 U.S. Congress prohibited African slave importation. In 1863 President Lincoln issued the Emancipation Proclamation which officially freed them. On New Year's Day in 1898 Brooklyn finally merged with Manhattan and the rest of the boroughs that make up the City of New York—and if you think that wasn't a new leaf, then in the words of one New Yorker, you've got another thing coming.

Since 1902, this is also known as Rose Bowl Day. It's when California rose growers get to see the fruits of their labor paraded through the downtown Pasadena streets. And football "widows" annually mark the last month of the dreaded sports season. But enough about sports.

You can blame the Scottish for choosing January first as the beginning of the new year. They called it Ne'er Day. And as we look forward to a happy New Year for all, let us also remember the words of the Scottish poet Bobby Burns and "take a cup of kindness yet for auld lang syne."

Opening

(See also Cornerstone Laying, Groundbreaking)

Anybody who is asked to say a few words at the opening of a new attraction faces an immediate challenge. That challenge is to sum up in comparatively few words the attractiveness or significance of what you are about to see and hear—then get out of the way fast to let you judge for yourselves. The challenge lies in the fact that it is very hard to decide how much to say and how much to leave, at least momentarily, to your imaginations.

There is a familiar exercise in psychology that points the way. If you set up a table on the street to sell sunglasses, it is very likely that, in the rush of pedestrian traffic, few if any will stop to look at your wares. But if one or two do stop to inspect your exhibit, the chances are that others will then crowd around it. We all want to get a chance to see something of interest. That, ladies and gentlemen, is why we are here today.

One of the most difficult things in these times of feverish communication is to keep a secret. Every time there is an ambitious endeavor in the world there is a stream of advance reports, most of them usually tinged with but not overladen with accuracy. Even on that rare occasion when nobody knows anything at all in advance, there is an advance diagnosis. One whisperer says, "I haven't heard much about it at all; it must be pretty bad," and another says "They are keeping it quiet because it is a real blockbuster." The fact of the matter is that all this, whether seemingly flattering or destructive for the particular project, fades into insignificance when, at long last, the new entry appears for itself. The preliminaries are now over and the main event is about to start.

A hard-boiled publicist has been known to say, give me three weeks, four searchlights and five famous people in the audience and I will give you a grand opening for a can of sardines. Indeed, part of the fun of an opening is the hoopla, the excitement, the rubbernecking even by the notables who, being human, like to see which other notables are present. I would be refusing to face facts if I did not admit that your presence here is indeed part of the show.

Someone viewing a play by Shakespeare, seeing a sculpture by Michelangelo or hearing a sonata by Beethoven all alone may be transfixed, but how much more so when the experience is to be shared with people by your side.

So here today we are assembled for a collective experience—one which we are all looking forward to, and which will proceed as soon as I get out of the way. Let me then give you the essential advance billing and credits for what you are about to enjoy for yourselves.

And now, ladies and gentlemen, the curtain rises.

Political Campaign

(See also Candidacy Announcement)

Politics is a matter of opinion. One is moved to take a political position either through ambition for public office or firm conviction or both. In any case, the decision of the voters is an expression of opinion, and a political campaign is an effort to persuade public opinion.

"Politics," as President Kennedy observed, at a dinner of the National Football Foundation back in 1961, "is an astonishing profession. It has enabled me," he said, "to go from an obscure member of the junior varsity at Harvard to being an honorary member of the Football Hall of Fame."

The campaign I want to discuss with you here today is not an attempt to promote a candidacy for office or for any Hall of Fame so much as to persuade the electorate. I am here to seek your support for specific governmental action on specific public issues, which, I hope to convince you, require your clear and prompt mandate. I am here particularly to do what I can to lock in the seesaw voters—the ones who never seem to see the issues, and drift toward the first candidate they saw. It's been said that a democracy of uneducated voters is anarchy. If that is truly the case, then I'm here to do battle against the rising tide of anarchy.

Otto von Bismarck, who was known as the Iron Chancellor of Germany, said that politics was the art of the possible, and Ambrose Bierce, the cynic, defined politics as "the conduct of public affairs for private advantage." That, indeed, is what it will be if the electorate does not stand up to be counted for specific positions on specific issues. I am not going to talk to you about compromise proposals which are merely the art of the possible. I am not going to talk to you about proposals to conduct public affairs for private advantage. I am here to talk about positions and actions which—I hope to convince you—are in the best interest of all the good people of this (community, state, nation.)

We do not, as individuals, as professionals or business people or families, all have absolutely the same interests. But we all have the same stake in healthy, prospering, civilized and peaceful existence. We are all dedicated, or should be, to those simple goals—life, liberty and the pursuit of happiness. The campaign about which I speak today is not unique in claiming it is in the spirit of those goals. Every political campaign makes that claim. But a great many campaigns, in an effort to be all things to all people, straddle the issues and ask you to vote for compromise positions. I prefer to state what I believe to be right, as God gives me and you the power to see the right. I ask your support for that which is needed, not merely for that which is the minimum, the compromise, the so-called "possible."

Does this mean I am advocating extremism, fanaticism, all-or-nothingism? No, emphatically no. It means I believe that a political campaign which begins by compromising, by giving ground on matters of principle, is a disservice to the electorate. I believe voters are entitled to clear confrontation of the issues, to forthright proposals which, in their wisdom, they can accept or reject. In that spirit, let us proceed.

Promotion

It is always a pleasure to announce good news, and the occasion for my remarks here today is good news for our organization. I am happy to report to you that _____ is our new (title of position).

On this sort of occasion it is customary to say that we did not take this step lightly. I must tell you that we did indeed take it lightly, if by lightly you mean with pleasure. We regard _____ as being the right person in the right spot at the right time, and I am saying this right out in public as bluntly as I have said it privately.

Anyone assuming a new task deserves to be given the confidence and support of all of his or her colleagues, regardless of whether they report to him, she reports to them, or they all are on the same level of responsibility. In this case, I must tell you that if we had not had confidence in (him) (her) before the fact, we would not have made the appointment. It was, in that respect, an easy decision. The appointment was both earned and deserved.

Part of the strength of this organization, or of any organization, lies in its upward mobility, its capacity for bringing new leadership up from inside. Elbert Hubbard wrote that "Some men succeed by what they know; some by what they do; and a few by what they are." Knowledge, energy and identity: _____ has all three. It is a pleasure to welcome him to his new post for his knowledge, for his accomplishments thus far and for himself as a person.

A very successful business executive once observed that she had encountered two kinds of good people in her move up the ladder. She called them shakers and caretakers. The shakers, she explained, were people who were always looking for a better way or a greater level of accomplishment at their jobs; the caretakers were more concerned with not stirring up the waters or disturbing a satisfactory operation. Another successful person made a different distinction. He said some people just want to be fat cats and others have fire in their bellies. What both of these executives were saying comes down to this: It isn't enough to keep things running smoothly, though that is often hard enough; the people who get things done are the people who always want to get things done better. That is what we look for, and that is what I think we have in _____. She has the experience and background to know the history of the new assignment. She has not been asked to repeat that history but rather to write her own chapter. I will be disappointed if she does not give us a few surprises—all good ones, I am sure. Progress, after all, is a succession of surprises.

But there is nothing that should be surprising about his promotion to his new post. He has earned it. On behalf of all his colleagues, it is a pleasure to ask you to join me in wishing him every success.

RECRUITMENT

The familiar story of recruitment is that of the Army sergeant who lined up his company and said, "I need three volunteers," pointed his finger at three hapless privates and roared, "You, you and you!" If only I had that power here today!

I am here to recruit you. I will tell you what I believe are the temptations, the advantages and the attractions that may motivate you to join up. I cannot pretend to be nonpartisan in this presentation because, after all, I myself have been recruited on the basis of being convinced of the temptations, the advantages and the attractions that I am about to explain to you.

Let me start by saying to you what I hope is clearly understood. I came here to talk to you because you are what we are looking for—you in particular. Only beggars can't be choosers. We are choosers, with a vengeance. We are out looking for people who have both the qualifications and the motivation to join us. First we choose you, then we hope that you will choose us.

This isn't simply a case of "come on in, the water's fine" and "the more the merrier." If it were that kind of deal, my job would be a lot easier, or maybe even nonexistent. But we truly have only a limited number of opportunities and we want to fill them with the best possible people. Let me tell you a little more about us and the way we operate, and I think you will understand why meetings like this are so important to us.

We know we are up against some pretty strong competition in coming to you. There are many good organizations which, like ours, are constantly engaged in trying to bring in the best people. Those of you who are outstanding may have some very difficult decisions to make—just as we do in considering admissions to our ranks.

I want to thank you for the opportunity to present our case, and, as the fiddle said to the bass viol, "Maybe if we pull a few strings we can make beautiful music together."

RESPONSES

(To an Introduction)

Thank you very much. I am reminded of the story of a speaker who, at the conclusion of his splendiferous oration, was congratulated by the gentleman who had introduced him. In turn, he congratulated the introducer for the eloquence of the introduction—to which the introducer replied, "It really was nothing. I had a much simpler subject." As the simple subject of the introduction just concluded, I thank you for your kind words and gracious reception.

In television there is a function called the warm-up, when a very skilled speaker or entertainer comes out to get the audience into the mood for the entertainment that is to come. You did such a good warm-up just now that I found myself waiting with great anticipation for the act that was to follow—until I remembered that I am that act. So I had better get right to it.

I cannot listen to an introduction as gracious and flattering as yours without thinking of the story of the distinguished English statesman who was to be the speaker of the evening. The man who was to introduce him whispered a question to him before the program began, saying, "Shall we let them enjoy themselves out there a little longer or shall I introduce you now?" I thank you today for being somewhat more gracious.

(To a Presentation)

Thank you very much. There are times when the words and the spirit that accompany a presentation are the greatest gifts of all. I am more than doubly honored here today—for the spirit, the words and the item you have chosen to convey to me are all so meaningful that they will have a very special place in my memories. The most precious thing in the world, for anyone, is the esteem of one's friends. Today you have made me very rich, and I thank you.

It has been said that it is more blessed to give than to receive. If so, then you today must be greatly blessed indeed, for you have given me so much. What you have done is extremely gratifying to me, and greatly appreciated. Thank you very, very much.

I used to go to a camp that operated on the principle that every child had to win at least one medal before the season was over. When all else failed, the camp would present what was officially described as an "improvement medal." And, of course, the recipient of an "improvement medal" was expected to march up proudly to receive the award along with the gold medalist for track, the winner of the best camper cup and so forth. I can only say to you, in accepting this wonderful presentation, that I do not regard it as an "improvement medal," or a consolation prize.

(To a Toast)

You have had a tremendous effect on me. Indeed, I may go so far as to say you have driven me to drink. And now, if you're ready to park, I'm ready to drink. "Cheers!"

Some people will find any excuse for a drink. And I am one of those people who likes the dish you have just served me, toast well buttered-up. Thank you very much.

Retirement

(By the Retiree)

I guess you spend a good part of your working career looking forward to the day when you can look back on it. And as you approach retirement you keep looking back, wondering what's gaining on you. But most of all, you look around and you see the wonderful friends you've had, and the way your work has grown and prospered.

But there is no point in retiring unless you look forward also; and so today I'd like to tell you what I am looking forward to.

I start by agreeing with Oliver Wendell Holmes, who wrote that "It is very grand to 'die in harness,' but it is pleasant to have the tight straps unbuckled and the heavy collar lifted from the neck and shoulders." I hesitate to say this to so many people who are still in harness, but it is pleasant somehow to contemplate other people running for the money while you are already nestled in green pastures. The trouble always is, there is never enough of the long green in the pastures. But that's what keeps us on our toes, isn't it?

These days there is a great enthusiasm for early retirement. As a matter of fact, we seem to have some people who retire before they even start work. I want you to know, however, that it took a lot of work to get me here today. And once you get in the habit of working, it's hard to take the cure. So I expect to go on working even if I only work at taking things easy.

When I started work we didn't have all these modern technologies. I was well along in my career before society discovered the easiest way to do the work of 50 men—hire 50 women.

I feel somewhat like the man who was tarred and feathered and ridden out of town on a rail. They asked him how he liked it and he said, "If it wasn't for the honor of the thing, I'd just as soon walk." There is, at least to my way of thinking, a lot of honor in the thing that's happening here today, and to say I am honored and touched by your presence here is putting it mildly. But frankly, I will miss you all so much that I have very mixed emotions. I could speak for more time than you've got, just reminiscing with so many of you, one by one. It's been a pleasure working with you, and it will be a pleasure remembering that pleasure.

It is very difficult to say goodbye when you know it is really goodbye, not just au revoir or auf Wiedersehen. So let me just say that when I walk out of here I'll keep remembering when—I'll think of you and think of this, until we meet again. Thank you very much.

(By Master of Ceremonies)

In the immortal words of that sage of the ballpark, Yogi Berra, I want to thank our guest of honor for making this occasion necessary. It is always difficult to define the nature of a retirement party, because whether you are celebrating the fact that we are finally getting rid of an ancient mariner or coming to tell our guest how sorry we are to see him go, the fact is that we are all here because of our guest's magnificent staying power.

(Name of guest), has given years to this company, and now he is going to get them back. He is going to have the time to do what he wants to do, and I dare say there are a few people here who envy him that privilege. But it was earned the hard way, over the course of a long time.

I would like to remind our guest of honor of a few simple precepts that deserve to be called to his attention at this turning point in his life. Remember that you are not losing your friends, just your expense account. Remember that the years in your life are less important than the life in your years. And above all remember the wise words of Henry Wadsworth Longfellow, namely, "Age is opportunity no less/Than Youth itself, though in another dress."

So we have some advice to give you as you enter this new age of opportunity. First, whatever you do, enjoy yourself. Second, don't write us off your list. You may be leaving the active payroll, but you are not leaving our thoughts. Third, remember that no matter how well the company does hereafter, it's because of the way you helped the company heretofore. And of course, if the company doesn't do as well hereafter, it may prove that a certain human asset is hard to replace.

But let us not dwell on the Company's prospects, and turn rather to your own. It is our earnest hope that in your time here, you have learned a little and are now prepared to leave the bosom of your workaday family for the big outside world. In your time here, we have learned a lot from you.

And as you go forth I cite for you the immortal words first uttered by Jerome K. Jerome many years ago: "I like work: it fascinates me. I can sit and look at it for hours." Or is that what you've been doing all along?

We have a few parting shots—excuse me, I mean parting gifts—to present to you now. I can only say that we are giving you a great deal less than you are taking from us with your departure. We wish you success and happiness now and always.

R EUNION

When the lower animals have a reunion, they all lie down together. When the reunion involves human beings, lying is an occupational hazard. You don't think so? Ask yourself how many times you have said to someone you hardly recognized, "Gee, you haven't changed a bit."

The real test of whether a reunion is worthwhile is not how you look, but how the meeting makes you feel. I know that this reunion makes me feel happy—happy not merely to see old friends, but also to bring those friendships up to date, and to discover new things I never knew before about people I did know before.

Let's face it. Part of any reunion is sort of an informal exercise in comparison shopping. How did I do in the intervening years compared to so-and-so? Does so-and-so's life seem better than mine, or happier? How many of us have done what we set out to do? Who has turned out entirely different from what we expected? For the answers to these and many other questions: circulate, friends, circulate and fraternize. That's the only way to find out.

As a matter of fact, there is a very real dividend that comes out of a reunion such as this. We all have a common frame of reference. We all started with that common frame of reference and from that start we have all gone our separate ways. So, for each of us, today offers a perspective on that old subject, how am I doing. Not a competitive perspective, I hasten to add, but rather an overall assessment of whether life has treated us all kindly, or differently.

Coming together again renews ties with surprising speed. One is tempted to imagine how different things might have been had we gone through the intervening years together. But now we have a new and double bond. To the original one, we now add the medal of survivorship. We have returned.

The times have changed quite a bit since we all first met. If you don't think so, let me read these excerpts from an old (yearbook), (class newspaper). They will remind you all of some old memories.

I found something interesting when I did some research for this occasion. I went to the quotation books to find some bright epigram or clever saying about reunions. I couldn't find any. In the key word index to Bartlett's Familiar Quotations, the word reunion doesn't even appear, nor in the Oxford Dictionary of Quotations—at least not in the second edition. I guess the answer is that, while a great many people have enjoyed reunions, not very many have said anything worth preserving on the subject. As you can see, I am following in that glorious tradition.

There was at least one distinguished man of letters, however, who tried to provide some words. Henry Wadsworth Longfellow wrote a poem for the fiftieth reunion of the Class of 1825 of Bowdoin College, and he read it to his classmates in 1875. It was entitled "Morituri Salutamus," which, as you may know, means "we who are about to die salute you," the cry of the gladiators in the old Roman arenas. He wrote: "Whatever time or space may intervene, / I will not be a stranger in this scene. / Here every doubt, all indecision, ends; / Hail, my companions, comrades, classmates, friends!" You don't have to be as old as Longfellow was to appreciate the unique feeling of being back with the people who knew you when it all began.

ST. PATRICK'S DAY

This is one day of the year when we truly see the greening of America. It commemorates the patron saint of the Emerald Isle, the missionary who is supposed to have driven the snakes out of Ireland. In his honor, I hesitate to calculate the number of potions prescribed for snake bite that have been imbibed over the course of what has sometimes been referred to as time immemorial. And I wonder if anyone has paused to see if we have any reptiles in present company.

The writer Myra Waldo once noted that, while other people speak in black and white, the Irish speak in Technicolor. I am here to say that, while there are some other people who celebrate in black and white, the Irish celebrate in gorgeous living color. We live in a land where some of those most prominent in the wearing of the green have been born to the purple, in the pink of condition—and have even been known to break into song out of the blue.

It is easy and customary for a St. Patrick's Day speaker to discourse on the accomplishments, the charm and the special circumstances of the Irish—the Irish in America, the Irish in Ireland. Today I would rather discourse about what, for want of a better term, I must describe as the Irish in all of us, regardless of our surnames or our antecedents. What exactly is the Irish in all of us? Let me tell you. The ability to hold your head up high no matter how oppressed—there's a lot of Irish in that. The willingness, even the eagerness to fight for what we believe to be right—there's a lot of Irish in that. The ability to charm and to defy and to take pride in your lineage—there's a lot of Irish in all of that.

It is also characteristic of any occasion involving the Irish that there is joyous laughter and good humor in great supply. The Irish firmly believe that they have a very special approach to life. They tell a story of a public-school classroom with a characteristically mixed group of students. The teacher asked one student, "If you were not of Italian descent, what would you like to be?" and the student answered, "Maybe French." Another student was asked, "If you were not of German descent, what would you like to be?" and he answered "I think I'd like to be an Arab prince." Then the teacher asked a third student, "If you were not of Irish descent, what would you be?" and the student answered, "If I were not Irish I'd be ashamed of myself." I sense no wave of shame here today.

It is indeed a privilege to be Irish, although today practically the whole world is Irish by ancestry or adoption. The wearing of the green is number one on today's hit parade and the shamrock is luckier today than its cousin, the four-leaf clover.

We Americans take pride in what America has given to the world. How then should an Irishman, whose homeland is so small, feel about what Ireland has given to the world—the songs, the literature, the leaders, the patriots, the fighting men, the builders. St. Patrick left a great heritage to Ireland and the Irish in turn have given a great heritage to the world. Today, we remember and salute both the people and the heritage. Today there isn't a little bit of Ireland everywhere. There's a whole lot of Ireland everywhere, and I am happy to join with you in celebration of that God-given legacy.

S ELF-INTRODUCTION

It is my function here today, first of all to introduce your speaker. That is to say, to introduce myself. My name is _____ and I am here for the purpose of _____.

I hasten to introduce myself because I imagine that everybody shares the same need—to know the person who is speaking to them. You've probably all had the experience of one of those strange telephone conversations where the phone is picked up and the caller starts by saying, "Hello—who am I speaking to?" and the party at the other end says, "Who's calling?" and both sides spar around a bit verbally because we are all a little reluctant to identify ourselves until we know who is on the line. But now that we have gotten that introduction out of the way, let me proceed to the business of the day.

It is always difficult to introduce oneself from the rostrum. It is much easier to introduce someone else. When you say something complimentary about someone else, it is regarded as a nice, friendly gesture and very probably true. When you start telling things about yourself, to establish your credentials so to speak, it is rather awkward. I hope you will forgive that awkwardness and permit me, very briefly, to indicate my relationship to the matter that has brought us together.

There is one advantage to having a speaker introduce him- or herself, of course. He or she gets to the point quickly. At least that is the hope of the person introducing the speaker today. So let me get right to the point.

SELLING

Let me start by telling you that I am here to sell you something. I say that to you at the outset because, in point of fact, nothing really sells itself. It has to be demonstrated, described, or otherwise impressed upon your consciousness. A good salesman's job is not to sell you a bad product. If he sells you a bad product, he isn't a good salesman at all; he's a skilled salesman, and they don't necessarily go hand-in-hand.

I am here to sell you something I believe in. I believe in it because I have seen it work and I know what it can do. I think I know what it can do for you. It does have a price tag. One way or another, anything worthwhile has a price tag—not always in the coin of the realm, but never something for nothing. Part of my job here today is to convince you that what I have is worth the price. You have the last word, of course. I can only tell you what it's worth in general terms. What it's worth to you is your own decision. My job is to help you make an informed decision.

I ask you to consider the claims of every product carefully—including what I am selling. In that context, remember the story of the famous singer who endorsed a cigarette by saying it had never given him hoarseness or throat discomfort?. Someone who knew him said, "It was ridiculous for you to endorse that cigarette. You don't smoke." "That's true," said the singer, "but read the ad carefully. I said the cigarette had never made me hoarse or irritated my throat. I never said I smoked the cigarette." You will find no such tricky usage of words in my approach to you here today. What you see and what you hear is what you get.

I want you to consider what I am trying to sell you neither as a pessimist nor as an optimist. The pessimist looks at the bottle and says it is half empty. The optimist looks at the same bottle and says it's half full. But then there is the opportunist. That's the person who tries to figure out exactly what half a bottle is worth. That's the person who buys low while the others are just realizing they should be paying attention. They end up buying it from him. Today, don't render judgment as an optimist; don't render judgment as a pessimist. Be an opportunist. What I have to offer is a real opportunity, a real bargain. And here it is.

In the days of the old medicine man/pitch man shows, they would have some free entertainment to collect a crowd before the silver-tongued spieler let his imagination run riot describing the virtues of his particular brand of snake oil. The pitches are apt to be somewhat subtler these days, but there is still plenty of huile de reptile around. One thing worth remembering, however, is that the snake oil salesman operates as a sort of hit-and-run artist. My appearance here today is not a hit-and-run operation, and my product is anything but snake oil. My own good name and reputation are invested in what I am here to sell. It is on that basis that I am offering my wares.

STATEMENT OF POSITION

In a world of ambiguity and equivocation, we tend to describe people's attitudes on the issues of the day in terms of physical position. We say this person is a fence sitter, not committed to either side; or that person is sitting on his hands, meaning he applauds neither side; or is bogged down in the mud, meaning negative campaigning has turned him away from both sides; or he is sitting it out or lying low. I am here today, however, to stand up in plain view with what I hope is a clear, forthright statement of position. I want you to know exactly where I stand.

When George Romney was the Governor of Michigan, he had a news conference back in 1965 at which he said, "I'm as conservative as the Constitution, as liberal as Lincoln, and as progressive as Theodore Roosevelt." Today I propose to be neither conservative nor liberal nor progressive nor classifiable under any overall rubric. I will speak of specific issues and how they should, in my view, be dealt with. If you want, thereafter, to decide whether a particular label fits, whether it be conservative, liberal, radical, reactionary, crackpot, visionary or any other catch-all category, you are welcome to your own judgment. My own feeling is that the time has come to discuss substantive solutions to real questions of policy and of conscience, and the substance is more important than any label.

There is a strong conviction among us, as a peace-loving people, that differences in a democratic society are easily resolved if the various sides are willing to meet halfway, as the saying goes. I should like to stress that the positions I will enunciate here are not bargaining points. I do not have hidden lines of concession. I am not playing poker at this point or trying to bluff. I am not exaggerating or taking the extreme position to leave myself room for compromise. What I am doing is trying to tell you, as simply as I can, where I stand, what I advocate, and what I believe.

Bernard M. Baruch once was quoted as advising people to "Vote for the man who promises least; he'll be the least disappointing." I have another piece of advice along the same line. Vote for positions, not promises. A promise that isn't backed by a carefully enunciated and reasoned position is like Samuel Goldwyn's famous remark about a verbal contract. A verbal contract, Goldwyn said, isn't worth the paper it's written on. I offer premises rather than promises; firm beliefs rather than expediency and, I hope, clarity rather than fuzziness.

In stating my position here today, I begin by asking each of you to do what I think must come first. Establish the goal, the end result, you are seeking. Then figure out the best way of achieving that result. So, as I tell you of my goals, think of whether they agree with yours. If we are not going in the same direction, how we choose to travel there is pointless. I hope you agree with my goals; then we can proceed to examine the specific positions designed to make those goals possible.

Testimonial

It has been said that a man is judged by the company he keeps. A person is also judged by the company that keeps him or her. But the best judgment of all is the judgment of one's peers. The company that has been assembled here does honor, by its presence, and by its deliberate purpose, to a person of distinction, a person who has few peers but many admirers and much for which to be admired

John F. Kennedy once said, "A nation reveals itself not only by the men it produces, but also by the men it honors, the men it remembers." Were President Kennedy alive today, I am sure that he would have changed the word "men" to the word "people," but otherwise there is no change in the basic thesis, namely that we reveal ourselves in the people we choose to honor and in determining what achievements, positions or sacrifices to single out for such distinction. And so sometimes we honor people not only for what they have brought out in themselves but also for what they have brought out in others. Today we are here as a testimonial to our honored guest and friend. A testimonial is, literally, the bearing of witness. We are here to bear witness to the contributions of our guest of honor.

We have a tendency to honor people for doing the seemingly impossible. We have gathered to honor one who has successfully bitten off more than the rest of us could or would chew. Some will say we are honoring accomplishment and others will say that the essential element we are saluting is sheer bravery above and beyond the call of duty. But in fact, we are not honoring abstract ideas; we are here to express our respect, appreciation and faith in an outstanding individual.

At the outset, I should like to apologize to our guest of honor for what is about to happen. We are going to talk about him to his face; and we may even find ourselves saying some of the things that have been said about him behind his back. In fact, I am sure we will be saying some of those same things, because they are very nice things. Let me give you a few samples.

There are many people who do good deeds. But there are differences in the way the deeds are done. There is, for example, the story of the man who passed a most attractive-looking restaurant, walked in, ordered a steak and found the food so marvelous that he returned the next night, found a cozy table in the back and ordered steak again; but this time it was so small and scrawny that he called the waiter. "How come," he asked, "I had such a big juicy steak here last night and tonight you brought me such a small scrawny one?" "Simple," said the waiter; "last night you were sitting in the front window." Some people do good deeds when they are certain to be showcased in the front window. Our guest of honor does good deeds out of the spotlight as well as in front of it. And what you see of his good works is only the front window of his tremendous accomplishments.

It is a pleasure now to ask one who has stood up for so many worthy purposes to stand up now for himself and be recognized.

Toastmaster

I am your toastmaster. That is to say I am here to bridge the gap between the food and the feature attractions. My function is somewhat like that of the person who does the warm-up at a television studio. It is a role based on several established facts. The first is that a full stomach takes some blood away from the brain and therefore there has to be some time to digest the food before you are given anything else to digest. The second is that any important presentation comes with an overture.

The first wish of any toastmaster is a simple one. He prays beforehand that a funny thing will happen to him on the way over. Failing that, he recalls the story of the man who was asked to introduce Senator Spooner of Wisconsin. The man said, "I have been asked to introduce the Honorable Senator Spooner, who will make a speech. I have done so; now he will do so." But our program today requires a bit of mood and a bit of stage setting, and that would not be the way to introduce it.

The late Ed Sullivan was a toastmaster in a class alone. In fact, that was probably how he got into show business—as an introducer. He was a working newspaperman who knew entertainers and could inveigle them into taking part in benefits. It was sometimes said that they liked being introduced by the man who became known as the Great Stone Face because he made them all look good. But of course he did a great deal more than introduce the acts. He set the stage, he bridged between, he timed the acts. There's a famous story about that last—about the occasion when he told a lion tamer a moment before a broadcast that the lion act would have to be cut to three minutes. "That's fine with me," said the trainer, "but who's going to tell the lion?" I am happy to announce that we don't have that problem here today.

(Closing)

I feel like a cheerleader who came too late. Nothing I can say can match the eloquence or the warmth of that applause or the effectiveness of what was being applauded. On behalf of those on the dais, our thanks for the kindness of your reception. On behalf of the audience, our thanks for the excellence of the presentation. We stand adjourned.

Veterans Day

(See also Armistice Day, Memorial Day)

Today we pause to remember those who were called upon to put their lives on the line for their country. We honor those who died in the service of the nation. Let us remember not only those who died, but those who lived; for while the giving of one's life is, as Abraham Lincoln said, "the last full measure of devotion," those who came home from the wars also deserve not merely the grateful thanks but also the salute of their country.

Those who have known war, up close, do not forget it. They have forged a fellowship while facing the fire. They have had more occasion than the rest of us to ask themselves what is worth fighting for, to wonder what are the real values that must be defended. In the history of the United States and of other nations as well—the most remarkable thing about veterans in general is that they come home as motivated in peace as they were in war. Calvin Coolidge once said that "The nation which forgets its defenders will be itself forgotten."

Many a veteran will tell you that, second only to the fear of death, the most difficult aspect of wartime service in the armed forces is the boredom. It is not merely a state of suspended animation; it is the feeling of being in limbo far away from home, the dread of receiving bad news and being unable to do anything about it, the weight of loneliness in the midst of other lonely people. That is part of the alienation of war. And for Americans, used to the freedom of civilian life, military discipline, however it has changed over the years, is still a far more rigid structure than the give and take of peace at home. Yet many veterans of every war have come home and brought new vigor to their interrupted lives. They have not withdrawn; they have not constituted themselves a separate class. They have continued to give of themselves as good citizens. Today we salute them.

As women have served in greater numbers in the armed forces, the percentage of female veterans has grown. In the twentieth century, we have had all too many occasions to create new veterans. We have had all too many occasions to ask our young people—for it is mainly the young who are called upon—to risk that "last full measure of devotion." Perhaps the greatest honor we can pay our veterans, living and dead, is best expressed in another quotation from that most eloquent of American presidents, Abraham Lincoln: "It is for us, the living . . . to be dedicated here to the unfinished work that they have thus far so nobly advanced . . . that we here highly resolve that these dead shall not have died in vain; that this nation, under God, shall have a new birth of freedom, and that government of the people, by the people, for the people shall not perish from the earth."

Lincoln spoke those words on November 19, 1863. For some reason, November is a particular month of remembrance, the time when we give thanks as a people, when we commemorate the end of the first World War, when we go to the polls to exercise the rights in defense of which so many veterans have worn the uniform, carried the flag, fought the good fight. But behind every veteran in the front lines there stood an anxious, gallant and sacrificing family at home. The veteran has never been a separate entity here, perhaps because so many of us are veterans. In paying tribute to our veterans, we are in fact paying tribute to the great heritage that we all share.

WASHINGTON'S BIRTHDAY

It is fitting, in a peculiar way, that the date of observance of George Washington's birthday has varied so through the years. At first, the celebration was on February 11, because when Washington was born, in 1732, we were still using the old calendar. Not until the new calendar was in general use did he himself adjust the date to February 22. It remained at February 22 for not quite two centuries and then, in order to give us a three-day holiday, was moved to a permanent Monday in February. All along, many Americans have felt that the date was less important than the spirit. Indeed, Washington is memorialized in so many ways in the hearts and heritage of his countrymen that setting aside a single day in his honor is almost a contradiction in terms.

If you stop to look back at his role in the creation of the United States of America you can see not one but several historic decisions, made by Washington, that shaped the nation for all time. Perhaps the most dramatic was the one symbolized by Valley Forge—the decision to continue to lead what must have seemed to most a totally hopeless struggle against the British for independence. It was a decision particularly sacrificial for George Washington, patrician planter and pillar of the Virginia establishment, a man with more than most to lose should the Revolution fail and leave him branded traitor to the crown. As we remember what Washington accomplished, we should also remember what he risked.

One of Washington's great decisions came after Cornwallis surrendered and before the Continental Army disbanded. A group of his officers had a plan to get rid of the Continental Congress and make Washington the king of the new nation. He squelched that quickly and thoroughly, and, when the peace treaty was signed, he went back home to lead the life of a quiet civilian. He was then past 50; he had served his nation long and well. But when he was asked to come back as the unanimous choice to be our first President, he again gave of himself, and he set the new country on a firm course.

Not many people remember that George Washington was asked to serve a third term. He could have been President for life; he rejected that proposition as firmly as the idea of being King; a century and a half later, a Constitutional Amendment wrote into law the two-term limitation on Presidential tenure which Washington had insisted upon. He was not merely first in war, first in peace and first in the hearts of his countrymen. He was, first and last, a selfless patriot and a man of principle, and a creator and defender of modern democracy.

One of his successors had this to say of him, though hardly aware at the time that he would follow in Washington's footsteps: "Washington is the mightiest in moral reformation. On that name no eulogy is expected. It cannot be. To add brightness to the sun or glory to the name of Washington alike is impossible. Let none attempt it. In solemn awe pronounce the name, and in its naked deathless splendor leave it shining on." Those somewhat fulsome words were spoken on the 110th birthday of George Washington by a young Illinois lawyer named Abraham Lincoln.

He was not considered an eloquent man, this George Washington, but few documents in our history have spoken more eloquently of the principles of our nation than his acknowledgment of the language and spirit of his correspondence with the Hebrew Congregation of Newport, Rhode Island, in 1790. "For happily," he wrote, confirming some of the words of the Congregation's message to him, "the Government of the United States, which gives to bigotry no sanction, to persecution no assistance, requires only that those who live under its protection should demean themselves as good citizens, in giving it, on all occasions, their effectual support."

"Every post is honorable in which a man can serve his country," George Washington wrote in 1775, and he lived by that unswerving principle. His example proved more effective, however, than those particular words; for he said them to a man named Benedict Arnold. And in that contrast we can see still further the greatness of George Washington.

W EDDING

We are here to welcome two new recruits into an old institution. They are now citizens of the state of matrimony. The wedding is the swearing-in ceremony, at which the bride and groom have a large supporting cast. The rest is up to them.

To a starry-eyed young couple, love is a wonderful miracle. The wedding seems equally miraculous to all the fond relatives who still think of the newlyweds as junior members of the family. But just think of all the hard work that went into what has just happened here. The simple chore of deciding whom to invite, for example. The task of tracking down at least one long-lost relative—because it is always the long-lost one who brings that special element of reunion to a gathering. Sometimes I think the bride and groom don't really know what they are letting the rest of us in for.

I know that it is usually the function of the person who performs the marriage ceremony to deliver a discourse to the newlyweds on what lies ahead. But there are some important facts that always seem to be left out in those ceremonial messages, so I would like, on behalf of this experienced group of veterans of the marriage game, to set the stage for today's featured couple. To begin with, you are starting off with a number of serious problems. These problems are called wedding gifts. There never was a set of wedding gifts yet which didn't include things you wouldn't let into your house, items whose nature you can't even figure out and stuff in boxes from fancy stores that, when you bring them back to said fancy stores, turn out to have been purchased elsewhere. You are going to have to make some very difficult decisions. You are going to have to keep things you don't want, and even display them on appropriate occasions, to avoid blood feuds with the people who gave them to you. You are going to have to lie like Trojans in some of your thank-you notes. And that's only the beginning.

The state of matrimony, like the state of the nation, requires a certain modicum of what are best described as unofficial sacraments. One such is the sweating out of how to address your in-laws. If you don't know whom to call Uncle or just plain Joe, or if you can't bring yourself to call your spouse's mother "Mom," just take consolation in the fact that Uncle Joe and Mom aren't sure either.

There are a number of romantic myths that have been seducing people since the dawn of time. I think this is an appropriate occasion to state, emphatically, that two cannot live as cheaply as one; two's company but three is not always a crowd; absence does not necessarily make the heart grow fonder; one man's mate is another man's poison; a good marriage, like a good brandy, is apt to grow better with age; if courtship isn't a part of marriage, then court is apt to be.

The time has come to toast two fine people as they embark on their life together. So here's to the bride and here's to the groom and here's to marriage in full bloom; here's to a long and happy life for a brand new, grand new husband and wife!

Wedding Anniversary

The almanacs regularly carry a list of anniversaries. The first wedding anniversary is the paper anniversary, followed in successive years by cotton, leather, linen or silk, wood, iron, wool or copper (strange alternatives for the seventh anniversary), bronze and pottery or china. A tenth anniversary is tin or aluminum, the eleventh is steel and so on. I find it interesting that between the eleventh anniversary and the 25th or silver anniversary, there are none that conduct electricity.

The electricity in the marriage we are remembering here today has never failed, and the current has been strong and steady. From the silver 25th anniversary on, we symbolize the passing years of marriage with ever more precious themes—pearl, coral, jade, ruby, sapphire and then the golden 50th, the emerald 55th, the diamond 60th and the super diamond 75th. Few of us indeed ever reach that pinnacle of married life; but each step along the way is itself an occasion to be saluted and to be cherished.

Marriage is often described as a partnership; but it is a partnership which dissolves over the course of time into a sense of unity and mutuality unlike anything else known to humanity. It is not merely the passage of time. In our own days, we have recognized that it is at least as easy for a marriage to break up as to survive. So when we congratulate a couple on their wedding anniversary, we are hailing something far more happy and far more significant than mere survival. We are recognizing a very positive and very triumphant achievement.

One reason the celebration of a wedding anniversary by friends or relatives is so joyous an occasion is that it shows the rest of us that lasting happiness is indeed attainable, and that it does indeed become the good fortune of some very nice people. I guess we all also cherish the hope that it is contagious.

A marriage is like an individual. It starts off very young, then grows into maturity, and gains in wisdom and understanding. If it is a healthy marriage, it gets better with age. This marriage certainly has. If you could sell the secret, you would have no lack of buyers.

George Bernard Shaw said that "marriage is popular because it combines the maximum of temptation with the maximum of opportunity." To this I must add that marriage is also popular because, as our guests here today so happily demonstrate, it can work so well.

In the traditional wedding service the participants are asked whether they "take" each other as lawful wedded wife and husband. I submit that the taking is far less important than the giving. We are here today to give our congratulations and our affectionate greeting to a fine couple. But they have given, and continue to give, each other the real happiness. For this above all we honor them today.

WELCOME

There is a Scottish saying that "welcome's the best dish in the kitchen." It is certainly the warmest, at this moment, as we take advantage most happily of the opportunity to greet you. You are indeed most welcome here and now.

We are honored by your presence among us. It gives us the occasion to show you, face to face, the friendship and the appreciation felt for you here. We pride ourselves on being an open and friendly community. That is an easy reputation to maintain when the visitor is one who, like you, has already established a basis for the cordiality and the hospitality of this greeting.

You need no key to the city; all doors are open to you, all hands outstretched in welcoming greeting, all hearts the happier that you have come to be our guest.

Sam Levenson tells the story of how his mother coped with the problem of the family larder when a guest showed up at the dinner table. She would take some of the children aside and tell them that when the main course was served they should say, "Please don't give me much, because I'm not really hungry." That way there would be enough to go around. But what happened was that when the dessert was served and the children reached for it, mama would say "If you weren't hungry for the main course, you don't need dessert." I am delighted to assure our guest that no such situation applies here. Rather, your coming means a very special gala time for all of us. It is a red-letter day and we have the stuff to prove it.

We have killed the fatted calf, put the icing on the cake, polished the windows and put the welcome sign on brightly. Our house is your house.

You are "well come." I mean to say, it is well that you have come. We have been looking forward to your visit. And I am sure we will long remember it. I hope that we can make it worth your remembering as well.

INDEX

A

Abie's Irish Rose, 602
Academy Awards, 595, 596
Academy of Motion Picture Arts and
  Sciences, 584, 585, 595, 596
Acceptance speeches, 818-19
Accounting, 6-7
Achievement, 7-9
Acknowledgment of honor speeches, 819-20
Act of the Holy Alliance, 729
Acts of the Apostles, 2:17, 89
Act of Supremacy, 774
Adams, Abigail Smith, 779-80
Adams, Ansel, 508, 509
Adams, Henry, 96
Adams, John, 98, 129, 193, 202
Adams, John Quincy, 53, 627-28, 657
Adams, Samuel, 730
Addams, Jane, 229, 712
Addison, Joseph, 41, 135, 148, 262
Adolescence, 9-11
Adrian IV, Pope, 808
Adrian VI, Pope, 460
Adventures of Huckleberry Finn (Twain), 506,
  507
Advertising, 11-13
Aeschylus, 200
Aesop, 289
African National Congress, 488, 489
Age, 13-15
Agriculture, 15-17
Airborn warfare, 600
Air Force, 723
Air Force Song, 35, 36
Airline service, 628
Airmail service, 595
Airplane, 800-801
Air pollution control, 490
Akers, Elizabeth Chase, 55, 272
Akins, Zoe, 254
Alamo, 572
Alamo Day, 525, 526
Alaska discovery, 695
Alaska national park system, 787-88
Alaska purchase, 551
Alaska statehood, 454, 747

Albee, Edward, 184
Alcan Highway, 622
Alexander II, Czar of Russia, 532, 534
Alexander VI, Pope, 584
Alexander the Great, 623
Alibis, 17-18
Ali, Muhammed, 44, 503
Allen, Bryan, 622, 623
Allen, Ethan, 461
Alliluyeva, Svetlana, 525, 526
Althaus, William J., 263
Aluminum manufacturing, 512, 513
Alumni, 18-19
Ambition, 20-21
America, 22-24
American Bandstand, 682
American Federation of Labor (AFL), 482,
  792-93
American flag, 803-4
American Gothic, 501
American Indian Movement, 516, 517, 588
American Minerva, The, 793, 794
American National Red Cross, 600
American in Paris, An, 798
American Society for the Prevention of
  Cruelty to Animals (ASPCA), 561, 562
America's Cup, 697
Amos, 3:3, 196
Amundsen, Roald, 593, 798
Ananiashvili, Nina, 31
Ancestry, 24-26
Ancient Order of Hibernians, 584
Andersen, Hans Christian, 553
Anderson, Marion, 737, 738
Andretti, Mario, 518, 519
Angora, 548, 549
Ankara, 548, 549
Antarctica, 635, 636, 774, 775
Anthony, Susan B., 503, 504
Antiseptic medicine founder, 556
Apartheid, 767-68
Apollo 9, 522, 523
Apollo 11, 661, 662, 689
Apollo 15, 677
Apollo 18, 662, 663
Appendectomy, 455

DEC - 0 2000